THE NORTON BOOK OF
TRAVEL

THE NORTON BOOK OF TRAVEL

Edited by PAUL FUSSELL

W·W·NORTON & COMPANY·NEW YORK·LONDON

Copyright © 1987 By Paul Fussell
All rights reserved.
Published simultaneously in Canada by Penguin Books Canada Ltd., 2801 John Street, Markham, Ontario L3R 1B4
Printed in the United States of America.

The text of this book is composed in Avanta (Electra), with display type set in Bernhard Modern. Composition and Manufacturing by The Haddon Craftsmen, Inc. Book design by Antonina Krass

First Edition

Library of Congress Cataloging-in-Publication Data
The Norton book of travel.
Includes index.
1. Voyages and travels—Literary collections.
I. Fussell, Paul, 1924–   .
PN6071.T7N67   1987   910.4   87-7879

ISBN 0-393-02481-4

W. W. Norton & Company, Inc., 500 Fifth Avenue, New York, N. Y. 10110
W. W. Norton & Company Ltd., 37 Great Russell Street, London WC1B 3NU
1 2 3 4 5 6 7 8 9 0

CONTENTS

II THE EIGHTEENTH CENTURY
AND THE GRAND TOUR · 127

III THE HEYDAY · 269

IV   TOURISTIC TENDENCIES · 649

V   POST-TOURISM · 753

Acknowledgments

I am grateful to the Cooper-Hewitt Museum and the Smithsonian Institution for permission to re-appropriate some material I contributed to their publication *Bon Voyage: Designs for Travel* (1986). And for various kinds of help amiably given I want to thank Margreta DeGrazia, Gary Dyer, Benjamin Goluboff, Daphne Motzkin, Robert Regan, Ralph Rosen, John Scanlan, and Marcy Strock. Kay Whittle's assistance has been invaluable. But my great debt is to Harriette Behringer, who has sustained me in all ways.

P. F.

INTRODUCTION

On Travel and Travel Writing

Why is travel so exciting? Partly because it triggers the thrill of escape, from the constriction of the daily, the job, the boss, the parents. "A great part of the pleasure of travel," says Freud, "lies in the fulfillment of . . . early wishes to escape the family and especially the father." There is thus about travel almost the *frisson* of the unlawful. The escape is also from the traveler's domestic identity, and among strangers a new sense of selfhood can be tried on, like a costume. The anthropologist Claude Lévi-Strauss notes that a traveler takes a journey not just in space and time (most travel being to places more ancient than the traveler's home) but "in the social hierarchy as well"; and he has noticed repeatedly that upon arriving in a new place, he has suddenly become rich (travelers to Mexico, China, or India will know the feeling). The traveler's escape, at least since the Industrial Age, has also been from the ugliness and racket of Western cities, and from factories, parking lots, boring turnpikes, and roadside squalor. Every travel poster constitutes an implicit satire on the modern scene, testifying to the universal longing to escape. The most "advanced" societies prove the most loathsome, and as Nancy Mitford has said, "North Americans very naturally want to get away from North America."

But if travel offers the thrill of quasi-felonious escape, it also conveys the pleasure of learning new things, and as Aristotle observed over 2,300 years ago, not only philosophers but people in general like learning things, even if the learning comes disguised as "entertainment." It is as learners that explorers, tourists, and genuine travelers, otherwise so different in motives and behavior, come together. Explorers learn the contours of undiscovered shorelines and mountains, tourists learn exchange rates and where to go in Paris for the best hamburgers, and travelers learn——well, what they learn can be inferred in detail from the selec-

tions in this book, especially the selections in the middle. Travelers learn
not just foreign customs and curious cuisines and unfamiliar beliefs and
novel forms of government. They learn, if they are lucky, humility.
Experiencing on their senses a world different from their own, they
realize their provincialism and recognize their ignorance. "Traveling
makes one modest," says Flaubert. "You see what a tiny place you
occupy in the world." Travel at its truest is thus an ironic experience,
and the best travelers—and travel-writers—seem to be those able to hold
two or three inconsistent ideas in their minds at the same time, or able
to regard themselves as at once serious persons and clowns.

But the irony of traveling can sometimes end in melancholy. Flaubert
observes how sad it is to experience a foreign place that is wonderful and
to know that you will never return to it. All the pathos and irony of
leaving one's youth behind is thus implicit in every joyous moment of
travel: one knows that the first joy can never be recovered, and the wise
traveler learns not to repeat successes but tries new places all the time.
The *mélancolies du voyage*—Flaubert's term—are as much a part of
travel (but never, significantly, of tourism) as its more obvious delights.
When the ship carrying the young Evelyn Waugh was returning to
England at the end of his first serious trip to the Mediterranean, he did
something he found hard to understand. He was at a farewell party
enjoying himself mightily, but "after a time," he remembers in his first
travel book *Labels* (1930),

> I went out from the brightly lighted cabin on to the dark boat-deck.
> . . . I was carrying my champagne glass in my hand, and for no good reason
> that I can now think of, I threw it out over the side, watched it hover for
> a moment in the air as it lost momentum and was caught by the wind, then
> saw it flutter and tumble into the swirl of water. This gesture . . . has
> become oddly important to me. . . .

In addition, travel sharpens the senses. Abroad, one feels, sees, and
hears things in an abnormal way. Thus D. H. Lawrence, one cold
morning in Sardinia, all by himself, finds the simple experience of
standing alone on a strange road "wonderful":

> Wonderful to go out on a frozen road. . . . Wonderful the bluish, cold
> air, and things standing up in cold distance. . . . I am so glad, on this lonely
> naked road, I don't know what to do with myself. . . .

Lord Byron likewise, who held that "the great object of life is . . . to
feel that we exist," discovered that feeling in three things: gambling,

battle, and travel, all of them "intemperate but keenly felt pursuits
. . . whose principal attraction is the agitation inseparable from their
accomplishment." And the deeply romantic emotion of travel has been
felt by Paul Bowles, always searching for a "magic place" which would
yield its secrets and grant him "wisdom and ecstasy"—and even, he says,
death. Which is to realize that travel—the word derives from *travail*—as
a form of heightened experience is like normal experience in not being
entirely joyous. Homesickness is one of the traveler's ailments, and so
is loneliness. Fear—of strangers, of being embarrassed, of threats to
personal safety—is the traveler's usual, if often unadmitted, companion.
The sensitive traveler will also feel a degree of guilt at his alienation from
ordinary people, at the unearned good fortune that has given him freedom while others labor at their unexciting daily obligations. If a little
shame doesn't mingle with the traveler's pleasure, there is probably
going to be insufficient ironic resonance in his perceptions.

Just as tourism is not travel, the guidebook is not the travel book. The
guidebook is to be carried along and to be consulted frequently for
practical information. How many *rials* are you allowed to bring in? How
expensive is that nice-looking hotel over there? The travel book, on the
other hand, is seldom consulted during a trip. Rather, it is read either
before or after, and at home, and perhaps most often by a reader who
will never take the journey at all. Guidebooks belong to the world of
journalism, and they date; travel books belong to literature, and they last.
Guidebooks are not autobiographical but travel books are, and if the
personality they reveal is too commonplace and un-eccentric, they will
not be very readable. Norman Douglas, both a notable eccentric and a
notable traveler, knows what he's talking about when he says that

> the reader of a good travel book is entitled not only to an exterior voyage,
> to descriptions of scenery and so forth, but to an interior, a sentimental
> or temperamental voyage, which takes place side by side with that outer
> one; . . . the ideal book of this kind offers us, indeed, a triple opportunity
> of exploration—abroad, into the author's brain, and into our own. The
> writer should therefore possess a brain worth exploring; some philosophy
> of life . . . and the courage to proclaim it and put it to the test; he must
> be naïf and profound, both child and sage.

And the ideal travel writer is consumed not just with a will to know. He
is also moved by a powerful will to teach. Inside every good travel writer
there is a pedagogue—often a highly moral pedagogue—struggling to
get out.

But the pedagogic impulse is not sufficient to make a great travel writer. Neither are acute senses, powerful curiosity, physical and intellectual stamina, and a lively historical, political, and social imagination. A commitment to language and to literary artifice must also be there, and the impulse to write must equal the impulse to travel. T. E. Lawrence once asked Charles Doughty why he'd gone on the laborious journey he wrote about in *Arabia Deserta* (1888). Doughty replied that he had traveled in order "to redeem the English language from the slough into which it had fallen since the time of Spenser." In the heyday of travel writing, in the nineteenth century, excesses even crept in. Then, so many people were making books out of moving around and noticing things and then writing about them that William Makepeace Thackeray devised the term "the letterpress landscape" to suggest the way a given sight might look to a lettered observer. Which was the object of interest, the scene itself or its description in scores of travel books? Was the landscape the attraction, or the language used to memorialize it?

The autobiographical narrative at the heart of a travel book will use many of the devices of fiction, which is why a travel diary, whose sequential entries are innocent of what's coming next, is less interesting than a full-fledged travel book, which can create suspense and generate irony by devices of concealment and foreshadowing. The ancient geographer Strabo was convinced that anyone telling about his travels must be a liar, and in a sense he was right, for if a traveler doesn't visit his narrative with the spirit and techniques of fiction, no one will want to hear it. Even if a travel account does not, like the works of Sir John Mandeville and Marco Polo, trade largely in wonders, it will still resemble the literary form of the *romance* by containing more than a mere *novel*'s share of anomalies and scandals and surprises and incredibilities. Travel romances differ from the more overtly fictional ones not in delivering fewer wonders but in being careful to locate their wonders within an actual, verifiable, and often famous topography.

Successful travel writing mediates between two poles: the individual physical things it describes, on the one hand, and the larger theme that it is "about," on the other. That is, the particular and the universal. A travel book will make the reader aware of a lot of *things*—ships, planes, trains, donkeys, sore feet, hotels, bizarre customs and odd people, unfamiliar weather, curious architecture, risky food. At the same time, a travel book will reach in the opposite direction and deal with these data so as to suggest that they are not wholly inert and discrete but are elements of a much larger meaning, a meaning metaphysical, political, psychological, artistic, or religious—but always, somehow, ethical. Stendhal seems to be hinting at something similar when he observes that "It is not enough for a landscape to be interesting in itself. Eventually there must be a moral and historic interest." (A reason, perhaps, why the National Parks are less interesting to the real traveler than, say, the D-Day beaches of Normandy.) The travel book is about two things at once. As the critic Samuel Hynes points out, it is "a dual-plane work with a strong realistic surface, which is yet a parable." And the parable most often takes the form of a metaphor of understanding, and understanding by a process of intellectual kinesis, of the mind in motion.

I am aware that everyone's favorite travel piece is not included in this book, and I am sorry. There is so much good travel writing that a library couldn't contain it all, and this is merely one book of selections. Separating out the best requires draconic standards. I have tried to choose people who are not just admirable travelers, sensitive, indefatigable, and if possible, ironic and even funny when appropriate, but admirable writers as well, equally interested in traveling and making lively sentences out of it. And I hope no one will take the amount of space accorded each writer as an indication of his or her value. Some writers write short, some long, and it is this fact, together with the exigencies of natural divisions, that has determined the length of the selections.

PART I
THE BEGINNINGS

Anyone inquiring into "travel" in the ancient world is embarrassed from the start with problems of definition. There is plenty of movement from place to place, but is there really travel in the later sense? If travel can be defined as an activity which generates travel books, in antiquity there is little, or perhaps strictly speaking, none at all. The works of Herodotus, Strabo, and Pausanias focus, like guidebooks, on what is to be seen and not, like travel books, on the hazards and joys, the ironies and delights, of seeing it. As it developed much later, travel writing depends on conventions of self-consciousness and inward scrutinizing not common much before the Renaissance and not highly developed until people in the later eighteenth century became obsessed with "personality." Until then, it is perhaps best to speak not of travel but of pre-travel.

To constitute real travel, movement from one place to another should manifest some impulse of non-utilitarian pleasure. We recognize the implicit sense of the modern conversational question, "Are you traveling for business or pleasure?" and we sense that to answer "Neither" would be an evasion, and rather rude as well. One way to ascertain whether travel or something else is taking place is to apply the Paul Theroux test. Walking all around the British coast in 1982, he knew he was engaged in *travel* in the pure sense because, as he says, "I was looking hard . . . and because I had no other business there."

But if in antiquity that impulse does not seem very common, a lot of people are moving about on utilitarian errands. Because there was no postal service, on the roads and on ships would be couriers, charged with conveying official documents or private letters and packets. Diplomats and civil servants would be moving from place to place, staying the night at government hostels. Of course many traders and merchants would be in motion all over the Mediterranean and the Near and even the Far East, proceeding on "business trips" with their goods (in sacks or bales) carried by ship or camel caravan. The infirm would be moving about on their way to and from healing spas or miraculous shrines known for cures. Those suffering from tuberculosis might be heeding the advice of the Roman medical authority Aulus Cornelius Celsus, who held that for this disease "a long sea voyage and change of air are efficacious" and recommended especially the voyage from Rome to Alexandria. Pilgrims and religious enthusiasts would be setting off for festivals and games, and professors and students, in the absence of fixed universities and sites for learning, would be moving about in search of each other.

Those on foot would make 20 or 25 miles a day, those riding donkeys or (a late development) horses would go faster, like those fortunate enough to use carts or wagons, uncomfortable though they were with their iron tires and absence of springs. Some of these had curved cloth roofs, like the covered wagons of the American West. Because of the paucity of bridges and fords, rivers were crossed largely by ferries, and that often necessitated the dismantling of wagons to fit them into small boats. The really lucky moved by litter, carried by six or eight men and often attended by a horde of servants—outriders, cooks, buffoons, musicians, and armed bully-boys. By water, such would go in their own many-oared galleys, while the low would move by "freighter," there being no "passenger" ships until the nineteenth century. And until the railway was invented some twenty centuries later, ships and rafts were the best way to transport heavy goods.

Regardless of the method, movement involved great uncertainty and often became what today would count as "adventure." For one thing, there were no "schedules" for the departure of ships. They sailed when they were ready, or when the wind and tide were right, and we hear of would-be passengers waiting in port towns for weeks, living bored to death in sordid inns and waiting for the shouts suddenly telling them they had a half-hour to get themselves and their stuff on board. Travel by sea was so hazardous that elaborate sacrifices and prayers attended boarding and departure. There were not merely storms to be feared but pirates and corsairs, which were not really stamped out in the Mediterranean and Aegean until the nineteenth century. Because there was no paper money or travelers checks or letters of credit, you carried gold—for a long trip, lots of it—and pirates were hungry also for women to use and to sell or hold for ransom. If your ship seemed in imminent danger of sinking, you might fasten some of your gold around your neck to persuade those finding your body to give it a decent burial.

There were similar hazards on land. Early on, of course, demons, monsters, devils, and trolls, and later, the areas outside city walls constituting a virtual no-man's-land, highway robbers, highjackers, extortionists, and pilferers, requiring governments to establish guard-posts along frequently used roads. Whether on water or land, darkness was a special menace. There were few lighthouses or beacons at sea, and in cities and towns almost no public illumination and not even street signs.

If you were smart, you moved about on land only in the daytime, and at night you harbored in the house of friends of friends (hospitality being a sacred duty) or, if you were unknown, in an inn. The rich carried their comforts with them, traveling with tents, bedsteads, table linen, cutlery, and food and wine. The inns ordinary people had to use were a byword for filth and fraud and lechery. Many were little more than whorehouses with bugs, and most were run by depraved women barely distinguishable from madams.

But if there was little traveling in the later sense, there was something resembling tourism and sightseeing. The Seven Wonders of the ancient world were wonders because people came to see them, and as early as 1600 B.C. visitors to the Egyptian monuments were scratching graffiti on them. (By the time of pharoahs like Akhenaton and Rameses, the pyramids and the sphinx were already a thousand years old.) Herodotus writes about Egypt as if supplying a definite tourists' need, for as he observes, "There is no country that possesses so many wonders." The Valley of the Kings, where already the very ancient pharoahs were lodged in their splendid underground tombs, was especially popular as a sight, and many graffiti there testify to the "amazement" of sightseers. "I, Palladius of Hermopolis . . . saw and was amazed"—a typical scratching. One visitor, excited almost beyond words, wrote: "Unique, unique, unique!"

People also went long distances to visit famous spas and shrines, oracles and temples. The site of the oracle at Delphi was a favorite, with its many buildings, relics, and *ex voto* memorials, and on the road leading up to it you could drink from the Castalian spring, useful for improving your prose style as well as inspiring you to poetry. Olympia attracted the devout; Epidaurus, sacred to Aesculapius, god of healing, the sick. The acropolises of Athens and Corinth were popular, and their temples, like most, functioned as art galleries and museums as well as sacred places. It was certainly worth going some distance to behold such relics as Alexander's breastplate and spear, for example, or Helen's bracelets, Orpheus's actual lyre, the ship of Aeneas, or the cradle of Romulus and Remus. Worth the voyage also were the graves of the famous—Oedipus and Orestes, or Xenophon, Pindar, and Virgil. Troy was one of the most exciting attractions, and it swarmed with guides and touts ready to show the tombs of Achilles and Patroclus, the lyre of Paris, and a suit of Homeric armor. And like later tourists, sightseers brought back souvenirs: magic waters, statuettes constituting miniatures of famous statues (like modern tourists returning from Italy with a little marble *Moses* or *David*), and portable representations in silver of significant temples and shrines.

"Scenery," on the other hand, was not a tourist attraction. It is notable that the Seven Wonders were all man-made, with not a Grand Canyon or Carlsbad Cavern among them. People might climb Mt. Etna to enjoy a *frisson* at that version of an entrance to the Underworld, but that was about the limit of the interest in "nature."

Sacred sites attracted pilgrims in antiquity, but it was not until the Christian era that group pilgrimage—to Jerusalem, largely, but also to St. James of Compostella, in Spain, and to Rome—became the thing. After A.D. 313, when Constantine proclaimed Christianity the official religion of the Roman Empire, the roads leading to Christian sites were busy with tourists anxious for spiritual credit—and, like Chaucer's later Canterbury pilgrims—companionship, fun, and perhaps a memorable dirty joke or two. If Egypt had her wonders, for the Christian those in the Holy Land surpassed them by far. You could see large pieces of the True Cross, as well as a number of important caves—Elijah's, the dwellings of Moses and Jesus, the tomb of the Resurrection, and items like the wooden bench at Nazareth where the boy Jesus sat to do His schoolwork and the rock at Jerusalem still stained with blood from His crucifixion. And of course the crown of thorns and the Roman soldier's lance that had pierced His side. Christians were conducted even to the Burning Bush (now merely green again) and the actual pillar of salt that had once been Lot's wife.

Going to see these things was not at all easy, but the suffering you endured on the road had distinct redemptive value. To travel one famous route from Bordeaux to Jerusalem took 170 days, and the usual robbers and pirates were there to threaten Christian pilgrims—and after the institution of Islam in the seventh century, there were angry Moslems as well. (While Christians swarmed to Jerusalem, others were converging on Mecca.) Few travel books of value emerged from these pilgrimages, but a number of pious memoirs did, together with many guidebooks and "roadbooks" telling you where to stay, how much to pay, and how to avoid trouble. On the road you tried to avoid the nastiness and temptations of inns and to stay at hospices, some connected to monasteries. Along the way you might buy "fast food" from victuallers standing invitingly at their roadside tents. They could identify you as a pilgrim because you wore a broad hat and had sewn onto your jacket or cloak a lot of cockleshells, emblem of St. James, the patron of pilgrims.

In addition to pilgrims on the medieval roads, the bureaucracy of the church, now operating parallel with the civil governments, produced its hordes of officials moving far and wide on business. Bishops especially liked pretexts for leaving their sees, and they were seen so often in motion far from home, with their costly exhibitionistic retinues, that in the fourth century one ecumenical council rebuked them for extravagance and told them to stay home.

If there was ample wonder in the ancient and medieval worlds, there was little skepticism of received truths (like the one holding that the earth was flat), which meant that exploration and discovery had to wait until the early Renaissance. (The word *curiosity* dates only from the end of the sixteenth century.) Until then, as Richard S. Lambert has said, "The civilized world had its limits, and beyond those no traveler in his right mind ventured to go." Some thought Marco Polo not at all in his right mind, and to some Elizabethans he seemed an example of a type that fascinated them, the combined traveler and magician, who was also, of course, skilled as a liar as well. A more modern view of Polo is E. M. Forster's. To Forster, Polo is an explorer but not a traveler: "He could manage men and conciliate them and outwit them, but they never fascinated him."

The explorations of the early Renaissance significantly herald the Reformation. The explorers proceed westward from Europe, in a direction opposite from the route to the Holy Land. But the discovers of the New World are not really "travelers" either, for they are moved less by curiosity than by the love of violent adventure, by mercantile acquisitiveness and the erotics of gold, and by the simple lust for power, often cloaked by a due religious fervor. Similarly, the religious refugees of Andrew Marvell's "Bermudas" are scarcely to be viewed as travelers, for they are certainly not traveling for pleasure and are less acting than acted upon.

The time for real travel is not yet, but the end of the age of exploration does mark "that crucial moment in modern thought," as Claude Lévi-Strauss has said, "when . . . a human community which had believed itself to be complete and in its final form suddenly learned . . . that it was not alone, that it was part of a greater whole, and that, in order to achieve self-knowledge, it must first of all contemplate its unrecognizable image in this mirror."

HERODOTUS
c.480–c.425 B.C.

*Sometimes called the first travel writer, as well as the father of history,
Herodotus produced in his* History of the Persian Wars *the earliest
Greek prose work of distinction. He was born in Halicarnassus (now the
site of the Turkish town of Bodrum), in his day a city-state under Persian
control. He left Halicarnassus as a young man, perhaps as an exile, and
began a lifelong career of exploring and observing the ancient world. He
traveled (by ship largely) to Greece and her islands; to North Africa,
Sicily, and Southern Italy; to the Black Sea and the area known now as
Turkey; and the Persian Empire, embracing Syria, Palestine, Babylon,
and Egypt. Now and then he appeared in Athens and is said to have
given a reading of parts of his* History *there. Near the end of his life
he became a citizen of the Greek colony of Thurii, in Italy. He died
there.*

*He is interested in virtually everything, but he is especially curious
about matters of comparative religion, as well as physical geography and
the oddities of unfamiliar fauna. He likes to verify. Careful to distinguish
what he has actually experienced from what he has been told, he can
be considered the originator of what is now recognized as "research."
As a peripatetic commentator, Herodotus, says Lionel Casson, "set not
only the pattern but a standard." He is "the tourist's perfect companion:
. . . articulate, well-informed, a skilled raconteur," including in what he
tells "a fair share of the unusual with a dash of the exotic," and performing the whole operation "with infinite zest."*

*This translation is George Rawlinson's, as amended by Francis R. B.
Godolphin.*

From History of the Persian Wars
(C.440 B.C.)

Concerning Egypt itself I shall extend my remarks to a great length, because there is no country that possesses so many wonders, nor any that has such a number of works which defy description. Not only is the climate different from that of the rest of the world, and the rivers unlike any other rivers, but the people also, in most of their manners and customs, exactly reverse the common practice of mankind. The women attend the markets and trade, while the men sit at home at the loom; and here, while the rest of the world works the woof up the warp, the Egyptians work it down; the women likewise carry burdens upon their shoulders, while the men carry them upon their heads. Women stand up to urinate, men sit down. They eat their food out of doors in the streets, but relieve themselves in their houses, giving as a reason that what is unseemly, but necessary, ought to be done in secret, but what has nothing unseemly about it, should be done openly. A woman cannot serve the priestly office, either for god or goddess, but men are priests to both; sons need not support their parents unless they choose, but daughters must, whether they choose or no.

In other countries the priests have long hair, in Egypt their heads are shaven; elsewhere it is customary, in mourning, for near relations to cut their hair close; the Egyptians, who wear no hair at any other time, when they lose a relative, let their beards and the hair of their heads grow long. All other men pass their lives separate from animals, the Egyptians have animals always living with them; others make barley and wheat their food, it is a disgrace to do so in Egypt, where the grain they live on is spelt, which some call zea. Dough they knead with their feet, but they mix mud, and even take up dung with their hands. They are the only people in the world—they at least, and such as have learnt the practice from them—who use circumcision. Their men wear two garments apiece, their women but one. They put on the rings and fasten the ropes to sails inside, others put them outside. When they write or calculate, instead of going, like the Greeks, from left to right, they move their hand from right to left; and they insist, notwithstanding, that it is they who go to the right, and the Greeks who go to the left. They have two quite different kinds of writing, one of which is called sacred, the other common.

They are religious to excess, far beyond any other race of men, and use the following ceremonies: They drink out of brazen cups, which they scour every day: there is no exception to this practice. They wear linen garments, which they are specially careful to have always fresh washed. They practise circumcision for the sake of cleanliness, considering it better to be cleanly than comely. The priests shave their whole body every other day, that no lice or other impure thing may adhere to them when they are engaged in the service of the gods. Their dress is entirely of linen, and their shoes of the papyrus plant: it is not lawful for them to wear either dress or shoes of any other material. They bathe twice every day in cold water, and twice each night. Besides which they observe, so to speak, thousands of ceremonies. They enjoy, however, not a few advantages. They consume none of their own property, and are at no expense for anything; but every day bread is baked for them of the sacred corn, and a plentiful supply of beef and of goose's flesh is assigned to each, and also a portion of wine made from the grape. Fish they are not allowed to eat; and beans, which none of the Egyptians ever sow, or eat, if they come up of their own accord, either raw or boiled, the priests will not even endure to look on, since they consider it an unclean kind of pulse. Instead of a single priest, each god has the attendance of a college, at the head of which is a chief priest; when one of these dies, his son is appointed in his room.

Male kine are reckoned to belong to Epaphus, and are therefore tested in the following manner: One of the priests appointed for the purpose searches to see if there is a single black hair on the whole body, since in that case the beast is unclean. He examines him all over, standing on his legs, and again laid upon his back; after which he takes the tongue out of his mouth, to see if it be clean in respect of the prescribed marks (what they are I will mention elsewhere); he also inspects the hairs of the tail, to observe if they grow naturally. If the animal is pronounced clean in all these various points, the priest marks him by twisting a piece of papyrus round his horns, and attaching thereto some sealing-clay, which he then stamps with his own signet-ring. After this the beast is led away; and it is forbidden, under the penalty of death, to sacrifice an animal which has not been marked in this way.

The following is their manner of sacrifice: They lead the victim, marked with their signet, to the altar where they are about to offer it, and setting the wood alight, pour a libation of wine upon the altar in front of the victim, and at the same time invoke the god. Then they slay the animal, and cutting off his head, proceed to flay the body. Next they take the head, and heaping imprecations on it, if there is a market-place and a body of Greek traders in the city, they carry it there and sell it instantly; if, however, there are no Greeks among them, they throw the head into the river. The imprecation is to this effect: They pray that if any evil is impending either over those who sacrifice, or over universal Egypt, it may be made to fall upon that head. These practices, the imprecations upon the heads, and the libations of wine, prevail all over Egypt, and extend to victims of all sorts; and hence the Egyptians will never eat the head of any animal.

The disembowelling and burning are however different in different sacrifices. I will mention the mode in use with respect to the goddess whom they regard as the greatest, and honour with the chiefest festival. When they have flayed their steer they pray, and when their prayer is ended they take the paunch of the animal out entire, leaving the intestines and the fat inside the body; they then cut off the legs, the end of the loins, the shoulders, and the neck; and having so done, they fill the body of the steer with clean bread, honey, raisins, figs, frankincense, myrrh, and other aromatics. Thus filled, they burn the body, pouring over it great quantities of oil. Before offering the sacrifice they fast, and while the bodies of the victims are being consumed they beat themselves. Afterwards, when they have concluded this part of the ceremony, they have the other parts of the victim served up to them for a repast.

The male kine, therefore, if clean, and the male calves, are used for sacrifice by the Egyptians universally; but the female they are not allowed to sacrifice, since they are sacred to Isis. The statue of this goddess has the form of a woman but with horns like a cow, resembling thus the Greek representations of Io; and the Egyptians, one and all, venerate cows much more highly than any other animal. This is the reason why no native of Egypt, whether man or woman, will give a Greek a kiss, or use the knife of a Greek, or his spit, or his cauldron, or taste the flesh of an ox, known to be pure, if it has been cut with a Greek knife. When kine die, the following is the manner of their sepulture: The females are thrown into the river; the males are buried in the suburbs of the towns, with one or both of their horns appearing above the surface of the ground to mark the place. When the bodies are decayed, a boat comes, at an appointed time, from the island called Prosopitis, which is a portion of the Delta, sixty miles in circumference, and calls at the several cities in turn to collect the bones of the oxen. Prosopitis is a district containing several cities; the name of that from which the boats come is Atarbechis. Aphrodite has a temple there of much sanctity. Great numbers of men go forth from this city and proceed to the other towns, where they dig up the bones, which they take away with them and bury together in one place. The same practice prevails with respect to the interment of all other cattle—the law so determining; they do not slaughter any of them.

Such Egyptians as possess a temple of the Theban Zeus, or live in the Thebaic nome, offer no sheep in sacrifice, but only goats; for the Egyptians do not all worship the same gods, excepting Isis and Osiris, the latter of whom they say is the Grecian Dionysus. Those, on the contrary, who possess a temple dedicated to Mendes, or belong to the Mendesian nome, abstain from offering goats, and sacrifice sheep instead. The Thebans and such as imitate them in their practice, give the following account of the origin of the custom, "Heracles," they say, "wished of all things to see Zeus, but Zeus did not choose to be seen of him. At length, when Heracles persisted, Zeus hit on a device—to flay a ram, and, cutting off his head, hold the head before him, and cover himself with the fleece. In this guise he showed himself to Heracles." Therefore the Egyptians give their statues of Zeus the face of a ram; and from them the practice has passed to the Ammonians, who are a joint colony of Egyptians and Ethiopians, speaking a language between the two; hence also, in my opinion, the latter people took their name of Ammonians, since the Egyptian name for Zeus is Amun. Such then is the reason why the Thebans do not sacrifice rams, but consider them sacred animals. Upon one day in the year, however, at the festival of Zeus, they slay a single ram, and stripping off the fleece, cover with it the statue of that god, as he once covered himself, and then bring up to the statue of Zeus an image of Heracles. When this has been done, the whole assembly beat their breasts in mourning for the ram, and afterwards bury him in a holy sepulchre.

The account which I received of this Heracles makes him one of the twelve gods. Of the other Heracles, with whom the Greeks are familiar, I could hear nothing in any part of Egypt. That the Greeks, however (those I mean who gave the son of Amphitryon that name), took the name from the Egyptians, and not the Egyptians from the Greeks, is I think clearly proved, among other arguments, by the fact that both the parents of Heracles, Amphitryon as well as Alcmena, were of Egyptian origin. Again, the Egyptians disclaim all knowledge of the names of Poseidon and the Dioscuri, and do not include them in the number of their gods; but had they adopted the name of any god from the Greeks, these would have been the likeliest to obtain notice, since the Egyptians, as I am well convinced, practised navigation at that time, and the Greeks also were some of them mariners, so that they would have been more likely to know the names of these gods than that of Heracles. But the Egyptian Heracles is one of their ancient gods. 17,000 years before the reign of Amasis, the twelve gods were, they affirm, produced from the eight: and of these twelve, Heracles is one.

In the wish to get the best information that I could on these matters,

I made a voyage to Tyre in Phoenicia, hearing there was a temple of Heracles at that place, very highly venerated. I visited the temple, and found it richly adorned with a number of offerings, among which were two pillars, one of pure gold, the other of emerald, shining with great brilliancy at night. In a conversation which I held with the priests, I inquired how long their temple had been built, and found by their answer that they too differed from the Greeks. They said that the temple was built at the same time that the city was founded, and that the foundation of the city took place 2,300 years ago. In Tyre I remarked another temple where the same god was worshipped as the Thasian Heracles. So I went on to Thasos, where I found a temple of Heracles which had been built by the Phoenicians who colonised that island when they sailed in search of Europa. Even this was five generations earlier than the time when Heracles, son of Amphitryon, was born in Greece. These researches show plainly that there is an ancient god Heracles; and my own opinion is, that those Greeks act most wisely who build and maintain two temples of Heracles, in the one of which the Heracles worshipped is known by the name of Olympian, and has sacrifice offered to him as an immortal, while in the other the honours paid are such as are due to a hero.

The Greeks tell many tales without due investigation, and among them the following silly fable respecting Heracles. "Heracles," they say, "went once to Egypt, and there the inhabitants took him, and putting a chaplet on his head, led him out in solemn procession, intending to offer him a sacrifice to Zeus. For a while he submitted quietly; but when they led him up to the altar, and began the ceremonies, he put forth his strength and slew them all." Now to me it seems that such a story proves the Greeks to be utterly ignorant of the character and customs of the people. The Egyptians do not think it allowable even to sacrifice cattle, excepting sheep, and the male kine and calves, provided they be pure, and also geese. How then can it be believed that they would sacrifice men? And again, how would it have been possible for Heracles alone, and, as they confess, a mere mortal, to destroy so many thousands? In saying thus much concerning these matters, may I incur no displeasure either of god or hero!

I mentioned above that some of the Egyptians abstain from sacrificing goats, either male or female. The reason is the following: these Egyptians, who are the Mendesians, consider Pan to be one of the eight gods who existed before the twelve, and Pan is represented in Egypt by the painters and the sculptors, just as he is in Greece, with the face and legs of a goat. They do not, however, believe this to be his shape, or consider him in any respect unlike the other gods; but they represent him thus for a reason which I prefer not to relate. The Mendesians hold all goats in veneration, but the male more than the female, giving the goatherds of the males especial honour. One is venerated more highly than all the rest, and when he dies there is a great mourning throughout all the Mendesian nome. In Egyptian, the goat and Pan are both called Mendes. In my own lifetime a monstrous thing took place in this nome when a woman had intercourse with a goat in public so that it became a matter of common knowledge.

The pig is regarded among them as an unclean animal, so much so that if a man in passing accidentally touch a pig, he instantly hurries to the river, and plunges in with all his clothes on. Hence too the swine-herds, notwithstanding that they are of pure Egyptian blood, are forbidden to enter into any of the temples, which are open to all other Egyptians; and further, no one will give his daughter in marriage to a swineherd, or take a wife from among them, so that the swineherds are forced to intermarry among themselves. They do not offer swine in sacrifice to any of their gods, excepting Dionysus and the Moon, whom they honour in this way at the same time, sacrificing pigs to both of them at the same full moon, and afterwards eating of the flesh. There is a reason alleged by them for their detestation of swine at all other seasons, and their use of them at this festival, with which I am well acquainted, but which I do not think it proper to mention. The following is the mode in which they sacrifice the swine to the Moon: as soon as the victim is slain, the tip of the tail, the spleen, and the caul are put together, and having been covered with all the fat that has been found in the animal's belly, are straightway burnt. The remainder of the flesh is eaten on the same day that the sacrifice is offered, which is the day of the full moon: at any other time they would not so much as taste it. The poorer sort, who cannot afford live pigs, form pigs of dough, which they bake and offer in sacrifice.

To Dionysus, on the eve of his feast, every Egyptian sacrifices a hog before the door of his house, which is then given back to the swineherd by whom it was furnished, and by him carried away. In other respects the festival is celebrated almost exactly as Dionysiac festivals are in Greece, excepting that the Egyptians have no choral dances. They also use instead of phalli another invention, consisting of images eighteen inches high, pulled by strings, which the women carry round to the villages. These images have male members of about the same size also operated by strings. A piper goes in front, and the women follow, singing hymns in honour of Dionysus. They give a religious reason for the peculiarities of the image.

Melampus, the son of Amytheon, cannot (I think) have been ignorant

of this ceremony—nay, he must, I should conceive, have been well
acquainted with it. He it was who introduced into Greece the name of
Dionysus, the ceremonial of his worship, and the procession of the
phallus. He did not, however, so completely apprehend the whole doctrine as to be able to communicate it entirely, but various sages since
his time have carried out his teaching to greater perfection. Still it is
certain that Melampus introduced the phallus, and that the Greeks
learnt from him the ceremonies which they now practise. I therefore
maintain that Melampus, who was a wise man, and had acquired the art
of divination, having become acquainted with the worship of Dionysus
through knowledge derived from Egypt, introduced it into Greece, with
a few slight changes, at the same time that he brought in various other
practices. For I can by no means allow that it is by mere coincidence
that the ceremonies of Dionysus in Greece are so nearly the same as the
Egyptian—they would then have been more Greek in their character,
and less recent in their origin. Much less can I admit that the Egyptians
borrowed these customs, or any other, from the Greeks. My belief is that
Melampus got his knowledge of them from Cadmus the Tyrian, and the
followers whom he brought from Phoenicia into the country which is
now called Boeotia.

Almost all the names of the gods came into Greece from Egypt. My
inquiries prove that they were all derived from a foreign source, and my
opinion is that Egypt furnished the greater number. For with the exception of Poseidon and the Dioscuri, whom I mentioned above, and Hera,
Hestia, Themis, the Graces, and the Nereids, the other gods have been
known from time immemorial in Egypt. This I assert on the authority
of the Egyptians themselves. The gods, with whose names they profess
themselves unacquainted, the Greeks received, I believe, from the
Pelasgi, except Poseidon. Of him they got their knowledge from the
Libyans, by whom he has been always honoured, and who were anciently
the only people that had a god of the name. The Egyptians differ from
the Greeks also in paying no divine honours to heroes.

Besides these which have been here mentioned, there are many other
practices whereof I shall speak hereafter, which the Greeks have borrowed from Egypt. The erection of the phallus, however, which they
observe in their statues of Hermes, they did not derive from the Egyptians, but from the Pelasgi; from them the Athenians first adopted it,
and afterwards it passed from the Athenians to the other Greeks. For
just at the time when the Athenians were entering into the Hellenic
body, the Pelasgi came to live with them in their country, whence it was
that the latter came first to be regarded as Greeks. Whoever has been

initiated into the mysteries of the Cabeiri will understand what I mean. The Samothracians received these mysteries from the Pelasgi, who, before they went to live in Attica, were dwellers in Samothrace, and imparted their religious ceremonies to the inhabitants. The Athenians, then, who were the first of all the Greeks to make their statues of Hermes with phallus erect, learnt the practice from the Pelasgians; and by this people a religious account of the matter is given, which is explained in the Samothracian mysteries.

In early times the Pelasgi, as I know by information which I got at Dodona, offered sacrifices of all kinds, and prayed to the gods, but had no distinct names or appellations for them, since they had never heard of any. They called them gods, because they had disposed and arranged all things in such a beautiful order. After a long lapse of time the names of the gods came to Greece from Egypt, and the Pelasgi learnt them, only as yet they knew nothing of Dionysus, of whom they first heard at a much later date. Not long after the arrival of the names they sent to consult the oracle at Dodona about them. This is the most ancient oracle in Greece, and at that time there was no other. To their question, "Whether they should adopt the names that had been imported from the foreigners?" the oracle replied by recommending their use. Thenceforth in their sacrifices the Pelasgi made use of the names of the gods, and from them the names passed afterwards to the Greeks.

Whence the gods severally sprang, whether or no they had all existed from eternity, what forms they bore—these are questions of which the Greeks knew nothing until the other day, so to speak. For Homer and Hesiod were the first to compose genealogies and give the gods their epithets, to allot them their several offices and occupations, and describe their forms; and they lived but 400 years before my time, as I believe. As for the poets, who are thought by some to be earlier than these, they are, in my judgment, decidedly later writers. In these matters I have the authority of the priestesses of Dodona for the former portion of my statements; what I have said of Homer and Hesiod is my own opinion.

The following tale is commonly told in Egypt concerning the oracle of Dodona in Greece, and that of Ammon in Libya. My informants on the point were the priests of Zeus at Thebes. They said that two of the sacred women were once carried off from Thebes by the Phoenicians, and that the story went that one of them was sold into Libya and the other into Greece, and these women were the first founders of the oracles in the two countries. On my inquiring how they came to know so exactly what became of the women, they answered that diligent search had been made after them at the time, but that it had not been found possible to discover where they were; afterwards, however, they received the information which they had given me.

This was what I heard from the priests at Thebes; at Dodona, however, the women who deliver the oracles relate the matter as follows: "Two black doves flew away from Egyptian Thebes, and while one directed its flight to Libya, the other came to them. She alighted on an oak, and sitting there began to speak with a human voice, and told them that on the spot where she was, there should thenceforth be an oracle of Zeus. They understood the announcement to be from heaven, so they set to work at once and erected the shrine. The dove which flew to Libya bade the Libyans to establish there the oracle of Ammon." This likewise is an oracle of Zeus. The persons from whom I received these particulars were three priestesses of the Dodonaeans, the eldest Promeneia, the next Timarete, and the youngest Nicandra—what they said was confirmed by the other Dodonaeans who dwell around the temple.

My own opinion of these matters is as follows: I think that, if it be true that the Phoenicians carried off the holy women, and sold them for slaves, the one into Libya and the other into Greece, or Pelasgia (as it was then called), this last must have been sold to the Thesprotians. Afterwards, while undergoing servitude in those parts, she built under a real oak a temple to Zeus, her thoughts in her new abode reverting—as it was likely they would do, if she had been an attendant in a temple of Zeus at Thebes—to that particular god. Then, having acquired a knowledge of the Greek tongue, she set up an oracle. She also mentioned that her sister had been sold for a slave into Libya by the same persons as herself.

The Dodonaeans called the women doves because they were foreigners, and seemed to them to make a noise like birds. After a while the dove spoke with a human voice, because the woman, whose foreign talk had previously sounded to them like the chattering of a bird, acquired the power of speaking what they could understand. For how can it be conceived possible that a dove should really speak with the voice of a man? Lastly, by calling the dove black the Dodonaeans indicated that the woman was an Egyptian. And certainly the character of the oracles at Thebes and Dodona is very similar. Besides this form of divination, the Greeks learnt also divination by means of victims from the Egyptians.

The Egyptians were also the first to introduce solemn assemblies, processions, and litanies to the gods; of all which the Greeks were taught the use by them. It seems to me a sufficient proof of this, that in Egypt these practices have been established from remote antiquity, while in Greece they are only recently known.

The Egyptians do not hold a single solemn assembly, but several in the course of the year. Of these the chief, which is better attended than any other, is held at the city of Bubastis in honour of Artemis. The next in importance is that which takes place at Busiris, a city situated in the very middle of the Delta; it is in honour of Isis, who is called in the Greek tongue Demeter. There is a third great festival in Sais to Athena, a fourth in Heliopolis to the Sun, a fifth in Buto to Leto, and a sixth in Papremis to Ares.

The following are the proceedings on occasion of the assembly at Bubastis: Men and women come sailing all together, vast numbers in each boat, many of the women with castanets, which they strike, while some of the men pipe during the whole time of the voyage; the remainder of the voyagers, male and female, sing the while, and make a clapping with their hands. When they arrive opposite any of the towns upon the banks of the stream, they approach the shore, and, while some of the women continue to play and sing, others call aloud to the females of the place and load them with abuse, while a certain number dance, and some standing up expose themselves. After proceeding in this way all along the river-course, they reach Bubastis, where they celebrate the feast with abundant sacrifices. More grapewine is consumed at this festival than in all the rest of the year besides. The number of those who attend, counting only the men and women and omitting the children, amounts, according to the native reports, to 700,000.

The ceremonies at the feast of Isis in the city of Busiris have been already spoken of. It is there that the whole multitude, both of men and women, many thousands in number, beat themselves at the close of the sacrifice, in honour of a god, whose name a religious scruple forbids me to mention. The Carian dwellers in Egypt proceed on this occasion to still greater lengths, even cutting their faces with their knives, whereby they let it be seen that they are not Egyptians but foreigners.

At Sais, when the assembly takes place for the sacrifices, there is one night on which the inhabitants all burn a multitude of lights in the open air round their houses. They use lamps, which are flat saucers filled with a mixture of oil and salt, on the top of which the wick floats. These burn the whole night, and give to the festival the name of the Feast of Lamps. The Egyptians who are absent from the festival observe the night of the sacrifice, no less than the rest, by a general lighting of lamps; so that the illumination is not confined to the city of Sais but extends over the whole of Egypt. And there is a religious reason assigned for the special honour paid to this night, as well as for the illumination which accompanies it.

At Heliopolis and Buto the assemblies are merely for the purpose of sacrifice; but at Papremis, besides the sacrifices and other rites which are performed there as elsewhere, the following custom is observed. When the sun is getting low, a few only of the priests continue occupied about the image of the god, while the greater number, armed with wooden clubs, take their station at the portal of the temple. Opposite to them is drawn up a body of men, in number above a thousand, armed, like the others, with clubs, consisting of persons engaged in the performance of their vows. The image of the god, which is kept in a small wooden shrine covered with plates of gold, is conveyed from the temple into a second sacred building the day before the festival begins. The few priests still in attendance upon the image place it, together with the shrine containing it, on a four-wheeled cart, and begin to drag it along; the others, stationed at the gateway of the temple, oppose its admission. Then the votaries come forward to espouse the quarrel of the god, and set upon the opponents, who are sure to offer resistance. A sharp fight with clubs ensues, in which heads are commonly broken on both sides. Many, I am convinced, die of the wounds that they receive, though the Egyptians insist that no one is ever killed.

The natives give the subjoined account of this festival. They say that the mother of the god Ares once dwelt in the temple. Brought up at a distance from his parent, when he grew to man's estate he conceived a wish for intercourse with her. Accordingly he came, but the attendants, who had never seen him before, refused him entrance, and succeeded in keeping him out. So he went to another city and collected a body of men, with whose aid he handled the attendants very roughly, and forced his way in to his mother. Hence they say arose the custom of a fight with sticks in honour of Ares at this festival.

The Egyptians first made it a point of religion to have no intercourse with women in the sacred places, and not to enter them without washing, after such intercourse. Almost all other nations, except the Greeks and the Egyptians, act differently, regarding man as in this matter under no other law than the brutes. Many animals, they say, and various kinds of birds may be seen to couple in the temples and the sacred precincts, which would certainly not happen if the gods were displeased at it. Such are the arguments by which they defend their practice, but I nevertheless can by no means approve of it. In these points the Egyptians are specially careful, as they are indeed in everything which concerns their sacred edifices.

STRABO
c.64 B.C.–c.A.D. 24

Strabo, author of the most comprehensive ancient work of topographical description, came from the city of Amasia in the territory of Pontus, bordering the Black Sea near Armenia. (It is now part of Turkey.) He received a Stoic education from well-known teachers of grammar and rhetoric in Nysa and Rome. Little more is known of his life.

He wrote his masterpiece, Geographica, *in Greek, working from A.D. 17 to 23. Consisting of 17 books, it describes Asia, North Africa, and much of Europe, over which Strabo had traveled himself. Although like all ancient travelers he tends to see things in relation to the authoritative way predecessors have written about them, he is generally skeptical of travelers' tales and sensational accounts of local wonders. His reputation in his own time and for many years afterward was high. Plutarch, in his* Life of Sulla, *considers him not just a geographical describer but a historian, and for centuries the* Geographica *was used as a textbook in medieval schools.*

These selections have been translated by H. C. Hamilton and W. Falconer.

From GEOGRAPHICA
(C. A.D. 23)

In the interior of the island [Sicily] a few inhabitants possess Enna, in which there is a temple of Ceres; it is situated on a hill, and surrounded by spacious table-lands well adapted for tillage. The fugitive slaves, who placed themselves under the leading of Eunas, and sustained in this city a long siege, scarcely being reduced by the Romans, occasioned much damage to the city. The Catanæi, Tanromenitæ, and many others, suffered, much in like manner. Eryx, a very lofty mountain, is also inhabited. It possesses a temple of Venus, which is very much esteemed; in former times it was well filled with women sacred to the goddess, whom the inhabitants of Sicily, and also many others, offered in accomplishment of their vows; but now, both is the neighbourhood much thinner of inhabitants, and the temple not near so well supplied with priestesses and female attendants. There is also an establishment of this goddess at Rome called the temple of Venus Erycina, just before the Colline Gate; in addition to the temple it has a portico well worthy of notice. The other settlement and most of the interior have been left to the shepherds for pasturage; for we do not know that Himera is yet inhabited, or Gela, or Callipolis, or Selinus, or Eubœa, or many other places; of these the Zanclæi of Mylæ founded Himera, the people of Naxos, Callipolis, the Megaræans of Sicily, Selinus, and the Leontini Eubœa. Many too of the cities of the aboriginal inhabitants have been destroyed, as Camici, the kingdom of Cocalus, at whose house Minos is reported to have been treacherously cut off. The Romans therefore, considering the deserted condition of the country, and having got possession both of the hills and the most part of the plains, have given them over to horse-breeders, herdsmen, and shepherds, by whom the island has frequently been brought into great perils. First of all the shepherds, taking to pillage here and there in different places, and afterwards assembling in numbers and forcibly taking settlements; for instance, as those under the command of Eunus seized upon Enna. And quite recently, during the time that we were at Rome, a certain Selurus, called the son of Ætna, was sent up to that city. He had been the captain of a band of robbers, and had for a long time infested the country round Ætna, committing frequent depredations. We saw him torn to pieces by wild beasts in the forum after a contest of gladiators: he had been set upon a platform fashioned to represent Mount Ætna, which being suddenly unfastened and falling, he was precipitated amongst certain cages of wild beasts, which had also been slightly constructed under the platform for the occasion.

The fertility of the country is so generally extolled by every one, as nothing inferior to Italy, that there is a question as to what we should say of it. Indeed, for wheat, honey, saffron, and some other commodities, it even surpasses that country. In addition to this, its proximity renders the island like a part of Italy itself, so that it supplies the Roman market with produce both commodiously and without trouble. Indeed they call it the granary of Rome, for all the produce of the island is carried thither, except a few things required for home consumption. It consists not only of the fruits of the earth, but of cattle, skins, wool, and the like. Posidonius says that Syracuse and Eryx are situated on the sea like two citadels, and that Enna in the midst, between Syracuse and Eryx, commands the surrounding plains. The whole territory of the Leontini, which was possessed by the people of Naxos settled in Sicily, suffered much, for they always shared in the misfortunes of Syracuse, but not always in its prosperity.

Near to Centoripa is the town we have a little before mentioned, Ætna, which serves as a place for travellers about to ascend Mount Ætna, to halt and refresh themselves for the expedition. For here commences the region in which is situated the summit of the mountain. The districts above are barren and covered with ashes, which are surmounted by the snows in winter: all below it however is filled with woods and plantations of all kinds. It seems that the summits of the mountain take many changes by the ravages of the fire, which sometimes is brought together into one crater, and at another is divided; at one time again it heaves forth streams of lava, and at another flames and thick smoke: at other times again ejecting red-hot masses of fire-stone. In such violent commotions as these the subterranean passages must necessarily undergo a corresponding change, and at times the orifices on the surface around be considerably increased. Some who have very recently ascended the mountain, reported to us that they found at the top an even plain of about 20 stadia in circumference, enclosed by an overhanging ridge of ashes about the height of a wall, so that those who are desirous of proceeding further are obliged to leap down into the plain. They noticed in the midst of it a mound; it was ash-coloured, as was likewise the plain in appearance. Above the mound a column of cloud reared itself in a perpendicular line to the height of 200 stadia, and remained motionless (there being no air stirring at the time); it resembled smoke. Two of the party resolutely attempted to proceed further across this plain, but, finding the sand very hot and sinking very deep in it, they turned back, without however being able to make any more particular observations, as to what we have described, than those who beheld from a greater distance. They were, however, of opinion, from the observations they were able to make, that much exaggeration pervades the accounts we have of the volcano, and especially the tale about Empedocles, that he leaped into the crater, and left as a vestige of his folly one of the brazen sandals which he wore, it being found outside at a short distance from the lip of the crater, with the appearance of having been cast up by the violence of the flame; for neither is the place approachable nor even visible, nor yet was it likely that anything could be cast thither, on account of the contrary current of the vapours and other matters cast up from the lower parts of the mountain, and also on account of the overpowering excess of heat, which would most likely meet any one long before approaching the mouth of the crater; and if eventually anything should be cast down, it would be totally decomposed before it were cast up again, what manner of form soever it might have had at first. And again, although it is not unreasonable to suppose that the force of the vapour and fire is occasionally slackened for want of a continual supply of fuel, still we are not to conclude that it is ever possible for a man to approach it in the presence of so great an opposing power. Ætna more especially commands the shore along the Strait and Catana, but it also overlooks the sea that washes Tyrrhenia and the Lipari Islands. By night a glowing light appears on its summit, but in the day-time it is enveloped with smoke and thick darkness.

*   *   *

The Albanians pursue rather a shepherd life, and resemble more the nomadic tribes, except that they are not savages, and hence they are little disposed to war. They inhabit the country between the Iberians and the Caspian Sea, approaching close to the sea on the east, and on the west border upon the Iberians.

Of the remaining sides the northern is protected by the Caucasian mountains, for these overhang the plains, and are called, particularly those near the sea, Ceraunian mountains. The southern side is formed by Armenia, which extends along it. A large portion of it consists of plains, and a large portion also of mountains, as Cambysene, where the Armenians approach close both to the Iberians and the Albanians.

The Cyrus, which flows through Albania, and the other rivers which swell the stream of the Cyrus, improve the qualities of the land, but remove the sea to a distance. For the mud, accumulating in great quantity, fills up the channel in such a manner that the small adjacent islands are annexed to the continent, irregular marshes are formed, and difficult to be avoided; the reverberation also of the tide increases the irregular formation of the marshes. The mouth of the river is said to be divided into twelve branches, some of which afford no passage through them, others are so shallow as to leave no shelter for vessels. The shore for an extent of more than 60 stadia is inundated by the sea, and by the rivers; all that part of it is inaccessible; the mud reaches even as far as 500 stadia, and forms a bank along the coast. The Araxes discharges its waters not far off, coming with an impetuous stream from Armenia, but the mud which this river impels forward, making the channel pervious, is replaced by the Cyrus.

Perhaps such a race of people have no need of the sea, for they do not make a proper use even of the land, which produces every kind of fruit, even the most delicate, and every kind of plant and evergreen. It is not cultivated with the least care; but all that is excellent grows without sowing, and without ploughing, according to the accounts of persons who have accompanied armies there, and describe the inhabitants as leading a Cyclopean mode of life. In many places the ground, which has been sowed once, produces two or three crops, the first of which is even fifty-fold, and that without a fallow, nor is the ground turned with an iron instrument, but with a plough made entirely of wood. The whole plain is better watered than Babylon or Ægypt, by rivers and streams, so that it always presents the appearance of herbage, and it affords excellent pasture. The air here is better than in those countries. The vines remain always without digging round them, and are pruned every five years. The young trees bear fruit even the second year, but the full grown yield so much that a large quantity of it is left on the branches. The cattle, both tame and wild, thrive well in this country.

The men are distinguished for beauty of person and for size. They are simple in their dealings and not fraudulent, for they do not in general use coined money; nor are they acquainted with any number above a hundred, and transact their exchanges by loads. They are careless with regard to the other circumstances of life. They are ignorant of weights and measures as far as exactness is concerned; they are improvident with respect to war, government, and agriculture. They fight however on foot and on horseback, both in light and in heavy armour, like the Armenians.

They can send into the field a larger army than the Iberians, for they can equip 60,000 infantry and 22,000 horsemen; with such a force they offered resistance to Pompey. The Nomades also co-operate with them against foreigners, as they do with the Iberians on similar occasions. When there is no war they frequently attack these people and prevent them from cultivating the ground. They use javelins and bows, and wear breastplates, shields, and coverings for the head, made of the hides of wild animals, like the Iberians.

To the country of the Albanians belongs Caspiana, and has its name from the Caspian tribe, from whom the sea also has its appellation; the Caspian tribe is now extinct.

The entrance from Iberia into Albania is through the Cambysene, a country without water, and rocky, to the river Alazonius. The people themselves and their dogs are excessively fond of the chase, pursuing it with equal eagerness and skill.

Their kings differ from one another; at present one king governs all the tribes. Formerly each tribe was governed by a king, who spoke the peculiar language of each. They speak six and twenty languages from the want of mutual intercourse and communication with one another.

The country produces some venomous reptiles, as scorpions and tarantulas. These tarantulas cause death in some instances by laughter, in others by grief and a longing to return home.

The gods they worship are the Sun, Jupiter, and the Moon, but the Moon above the rest. She has a temple near Iberia. The priest is a person who, next to the king, receives the highest honours. He has the government of the sacred land, which is extensive and populous, and authority over the sacred attendants, many of whom are divinely inspired, and prophesy. Whoever of these persons, being violently possessed, wanders alone in the woods, is seized by the priest, who, having bound him with sacred fetters, maintains him sumptuously during that year. Afterwards he is brought forth at the sacrifice performed in honour of the goddess, and is anointed with fragrant ointment and sacrificed together with other victims. The sacrifice is performed in the following manner. A person, having in his hand a sacred lance, with which it is the custom to sacrifice human victims, advances out of the crowd and pierces the heart through the side, which he does from experience in this office. When the man has fallen, certain prognostications are indicated by the manner of the fall, and these are publicly declared. The body is carried away to a certain spot, and then they all trample upon it, performing this action as a mode of purification of themselves.

The Albanians pay the greatest respect to old age, which is not confined to their parents, but is extended to old persons in general. It is regarded as impious to show any concern for the dead, or to mention their names. Their money is buried with them, hence they live in poverty, having no patrimony.

So much concerning the Albanians. It is said that when Jason, accompanied by Armenus the Thessalian, undertook the voyage to the Colchi, they advanced as far as the Caspian Sea, and traversed Iberia, Albania, a great part of Armenia, and Media, as the Jasoneia and many other monuments testify. Armenus, they say, was a native of Armenium, one of the cities on the lake Bœbeis, between Pheræ and Parisa, and that his companions settled in Acilisene, and the Suspiritis, and occupied the country as far as Calachene and Adiabene, and that he gave his own name to Armenia.

The Amazons are said to live among the mountains above Albania. Theophanes, who accompanied Pompey in his wars, and was in the country of the Albanians, says that Gelæ and Legæ, Scythian tribes, live between the Amazons and the Albanians, and that the river Mermadalis takes its course in the country lying in the middle between these people and the Amazons. But other writers, and among these Metrodorus of Scepsis, and Hypsicrates, who were themselves acquainted with these places, say that the Amazons bordered upon the Gargarenses on the north, at the foot of the Caucasian mountains, which are called Ceraunia.

When at home they are occupied in performing with their own hands the work of ploughing, planting, pasturing cattle, and particularly in training horses. The strongest among them spend much of their time in hunting on horseback, and practise warlike exercises. All of them from infancy have the right breast seared, in order that they may use the arm with ease for all manner of purposes, and particularly for throwing the javelin. They employ the bow also, and sagaris, (a kind of sword,) and wear a buckler. They make helmets, and coverings for the body, and girdles, of the skins of wild animals. They pass two months of the spring on a neighbouring mountain, which is the boundary between them and the Gargarenses. The latter also ascend the mountain according to some ancient custom for the purpose of performing common sacrifices, and of having intercourse with the women with a view to offspring, in secret and in darkness, the man with the first woman he meets. When the women are pregnant they are sent away. The female children that may be born are retained by the Amazons themselves, but the males are taken to the Gargarenses to be brought up. The children are distributed among families, in which the master treats them as his own, it being impossible to ascertain the contrary.

The Mermodas, descending like a torrent from the mountains through the country of the Amazons, the Siracene, and the intervening desert, discharges itself into the Mæotis.

It is said that the Gargarenses ascended together with the Amazons from Themiscyra to these places, that they then separated, and with the assistance of some Thracians and Eubïans, who had wandered as far as this country, made war against the Amazons, and at length, upon its termination, entered into a compact on the conditions above mentioned, namely, that there should be a companionship only with respect to offspring, and that they should live each independent of the other.

There is a peculiarity in the history of the Amazons. In other histories the fabulous and the historical parts are kept distinct. For what is ancient, false, and marvellous is called fable. But history has truth for its object, whether it be old or new, and it either rejects or rarely admits the marvellous. But, with regard to the Amazons, the same facts are related both by modern and by ancient writers; they are marvellous and exceed belief. For who can believe that an army of women, or a city, or a nation, could ever subsist without men? and not only subsist, but make inroads upon the territory of other people, and obtain possession not only of the places near them, and advance even as far as the present Ionia, but even despatch an expedition across the sea to Attica? This is as much as to say that the men of those days were women, and the women men. But even now the same things are told of the Amazons, and the peculiarity of their history is increased by the credit which is given to ancient, in preference to modern, accounts.

They are said to have founded cities, and to have given their names to them, as Ephesus, Smyrna, Cyme, Myrina, besides leaving sepulchres and other memorials. Themiscyra, the plains about the Thermodon, and the mountains lying above, are mentioned by all writers as once belonging to the Amazons, whence, they say, they were driven out. Where they are at present few writers undertake to point out, nor do they advance proofs or probability for what they state; as in the case of Thalestria, queen of the Amazons, with whom Alexander is said to have had intercourse in Hyrcania with the hope of having offspring. Writers are not agreed on this point, and among many who have paid the greatest regard to truth none mention the circumstance, nor do writers of the highest credit mention anything of the kind, nor do those who record it relate the same facts. Cleitarchus says that Thalestria set out from the Caspian Gates and Thermodon to meet Alexander. Now from the Caspian Gates to Thermodon are more than 6000 stadia.

Stories circulated for the purpose of exalting the fame of eminent persons are not received with equal favour by all; the object of the inventors was flattery rather than truth; they transferred, for example, the Caucasus to the mountains of India, and to the eastern sea, which approaches close to them, from the mountains situated above Colchis, and the Euxine Sea. These are the mountains to which the Greeks give the name of Caucasus, and are distant more than 30,000 stadia from India. Here they lay the scene of Prometheus and his chains, for these were the farthest places towards the east with which the people of those times were acquainted. The expeditions of Bacchus and of Hercules against the Indi indicate a mythological story of later date, for Hercules is said to have released Prometheus a thousand years after he was first chained to the rock. It was more glorious too for Alexander to subjugate Asia as far as the mountains of India, than to the recess only of the Euxine Sea and the Caucasus. The celebrity, and the name of the mountain, together with the persuasion that Jason and his companions had accomplished the most distant of all expeditions when they had arrived in the neighbourhood of the Caucasus, and the tradition that Prometheus had been chained on Caucasus at the extremity of the earth, induced writers to suppose that they should gratify the king by transferring the name of the mountain to India.

The highest points of the actual Caucasus are the most southerly, and lie near Albania, Iberia, the Colchi, and Heniochi. They are inhabited by the people whom I have mentioned as assembling at Dioscurias. They resort thither chiefly for the purpose of procuring salt. Of these tribes some occupy the heights; others live in wooded valleys, and subsist chiefly on the flesh of wild animals, wild fruits, and milk. The heights are impassable in winter; in summer they are ascended by fastening on the feet shoes as wide as drums, made of raw hide, and furnished with spikes on account of the snow and ice. The natives in descending with their loads slide down seated upon skins, which is the practice in Media, Atropatia, and at Mount Masius in Armenia, but there they fasten circular disks of wood with spikes to the soles of their feet. Such then is the nature of the heights of Caucasus.

On descending to the country lying at the foot of these heights the climate is more northerly, but milder, for the land below the heights joins the plains of the Siraces. There are some tribes of Troglodytæ who inhabit caves on account of the cold. There is plenty of grain to be had in the country.

Next to the Troglodytæ are Chamæcœtæ, and a tribe called Polyphagi (the voracious), and the villages of the Eisadici, who are able to cultivate the ground because they are not altogether exposed to the north.

Immediately afterwards follow shepherd tribes, situated between the Mæotis and the Caspian Sea, Nabiani, Pangani, the tribes also of the Siraces and Aorsi.

The Aorsi and Siraces seem to be a fugitive people from parts situated above. The Aorsi lie more to the north.

Abeacus, king of the Siraces, when Pharnases occupied the Bosporus, equipped 20,000 horse, and Spadines, king of the Aorsi 200,000, and the Upper Aorsi even a larger body, for they were masters of a greater extent of territory, and nearly the largest part of the coast of the Caspian Sea was under their power. They were thus enabled to transport on camels the merchandise of India and Babylonia, receiving it from Armenians and Medes. They wore gold also in their dress in consequence of their wealth.

The Aorsi live on the banks of the Tanaïs, and the Siraces on those of Achardeus, which rises in Caucasus, and discharges itself into the Mæotis.

PAUSANIAS
Second Century A.D.

*"The Baedeker of the Ancient World" Pausanias has been called, but
even less is known about him than about the other ancient topographical
writers. It has been conjectured that he was born in the Greek city of
Magnesia, and his evident fondness for Aesculapius, the god of healing,
suggests that perhaps he was trained as a physician. He spent fourteen
years on his Guide to Greece, a work in ten books aimed at Roman
tourists to Greece, which not too long before had become a part of
greater Rome and was now the place to visit.*

*Pausanias actually saw the things he describes, but his interest is less
in mere exotic objects than in their religious meaning. In his performance, the examiner of foreign things becomes a historian of myth and
a collector of popular narrative about events with religious significance.
"They say" is one of his favorite introductory phrases as he surveys the
monuments and respectfully describes the beliefs of numerous local
cults. For Pausanias, as for most of the ancients, sculptures and paintings
are less works of art than emblems of what they depict: they have value
because of the heroic religious narrative they call to mind. Nor does he
make the modern distinction between the "real" and the fabulous. "On
this road," he observes, "Oedipus murdered his father."*

*These selections, translated by Peter Levi, describe the Acropolis at
Athens and the precinct of Delphi sacred to Apollo and his oracle.*

From GUIDE TO GREECE
(c. 170)

The AKROPOLIS has one way in; it offers no other. The whole akropolis
is sheer and strong-walled. The formal entrance has a roof of white
marble, which down to my own times is still incomparable for the size
and beauty of the stone. I am unable to say for certain whether the

statues of the horsemen are the sons of Xenophon or simply created to look handsome. On the right of the formal entrance is the SHRINE OF WINGLESS VICTORY. You can see the sea from here and they say this is where Aigeus leapt to his death. The ship carrying the children to Crete started out with black sails, and Theseus, who was sailing to prove his courage against the Minotaur, promised his father he would use white sails for the voyage home provided he had overcome the monster; but in the loss of Ariadne he forgot this promise, so when Aigeus saw the ship coming in under black sails the old man thought his son was dead, and threw himself down and was killed. He has a hero-shrine at Athens. On the left of the formal entrance is a building with paintings in it. In those that the course of time has not effaced, Odysseus is in Lemnos stealing the bow from Philoktetes, and Diomedes is carrying off Athene from Troy. Here in the paintings Orestes is cutting down Aigisthos and Pylades is killing the sons of Nauplios as they come to Aigisthos's aid; Polyxena is about to be slaughtered near the funeral mound of Achilles. Homer did well to leave out this horribly cruel action; and in my view he did well to have Skyros taken by Achilles, quite unlike what they say about Achilles in Skyros living among the young girls, the story painted by Polygnotos. He also painted Odysseus at the river meeting the girls who were washing clothes with Nausikaa, in just the way Homer describes it. Among the other paintings is Alkibiades; there are symbols in the painting of his victory in the horse-race at Nemea. Perseus is on his way to Seriphos, bringing Medusa's head to Polydektes. I am not eager to deal with Medusa while writing about Attica. Among these paintings, if you pass over the boy carrying water-jars and the wrestler Timainetos painted, you come to Mousaios. I have read a poem in which Mousaios was able to fly, by the gift of the North-east wind: I think Onomakritos wrote it; nothing of Mousaios exists for certain except the *Hymn to Demeter* for the Lykomidai.

By the actual entrance to the akropolis, they say the Hermes of the porch and the Graces were made by that Sokrates who as the Pythian priestess testified was the wisest of all human beings: a thing she said not even to Anacharsis though he wanted her to, and came to Delphi for the purpose. One of the Greek legends is that there were seven Wise Men. They say Periander and the tyrant of Lesbos were two of them, though Peisistratos and his son Hippias were more the friends of humanity than Periander, and had more military wisdom and more practical political wisdom, that is until the death of Hipparchos, when Hippias let loose his temper particularly on a woman called Lioness. This is a story that has not got into history until now, but most Athenians believe it. When Hipparchos died, Hippias kept this woman under torture until he had killed her, because he knew she was Aristogeiton's mistress and could not believe she was innocent in the plot. Because of this, when the dictatorship of Peisistratos's family was finished, the Athenians put up a bronze lioness for the woman's memorial with a statue of Aphrodite beside it which they say is the dedication of Kallias and the work of Kalamis.

Near by is a bronze statue of Diitrephes shot with arrows. Among the things he did that the Athenians tell you about was this: the Thracian mercenaries were too late arriving when Demosthenes sailed for Syracuse, so when they turned up Diitrephes led them back home. He landed in Chalkidian Euripos, where the inland Boiotian city of Mykalessos was, marched on it from the sea-coast, and took it. The Thracians massacred not only the men and boys who could fight at Mykalessos, but women and children as well. I can prove this: the Boiotian cities destroyed by Thebes were inhabited in my time, as the people had run away as the cities fell; if the barbarians had not slaughtered everyone in the attack on Mykalessos, the survivors would have taken back their city afterwards in the same way. I was very much puzzled to see the portrait of Diitrephes full of arrows; no Greek region uses them except for Crete. We know the Opuntian Lokrians were already regimental spearmen in the Persian wars, although Homer has them marching on Troy with bows and slings. Even among the Malians archery has not survived; I think they knew nothing about it until Philoktetes, and gave it up soon afterwards. I do not propose to catalogue the less interesting figures; but near Diitrephes there are statues of gods, one of Health, the daughter of Asklepios they say, and one of Athene of Health. There is a little rock, big enough for a small man to sit on; when Dionysos came to this country, they say Silenos rested on it. They call satyrs of advanced age *silenoi.* I was particularly keen to establish who the satyrs are, and I talked to a great number of people about it. A Carian called Euphemos said he was sailing to Italy and was driven off course, right out into the open sea which is still empty. He told me there were a lot of desert islands, and islands where savages lived; the sailors were unwilling to put in to these islands, as they knew something about the natives from having called there before, but now they were forced to put in again. The sailors call them the Satyr islands. The natives are very noisy and have tails on their behinds as long as horses. As soon as they noticed the ship, they ran down at it without saying a word and grabbed at the women. In the end the sailors were so frightened they threw out a barbarian woman onto the island, and she was raped by the satyrs not only in the usual place but all over her body.

There are some other things I saw in the akropolis of Athens, the bronze boy with the sprinkler by Myron's son Lykios, and Myron's "Perseus after murdering Medusa." There is also a sanctuary of Brauronian Artemis, with its statue by Praxiteles. The goddess gets her name from the country place Brauron, where her ancient wooden cult-statue still is: they call her the Artemis of Tauris. Then there is a bronze Wooden Horse. Anyone who does not suppose Phrygians are utterly stupid will have realized that what Epeios built was an engineer's device for breaking down the wall. They say of that horse that the best of the Greeks were inside it, and this one is made in the same way. Menestheus and Teukros are stooping down from it, and the sons of Theseus as well. As for the statues behind the horse, the portrait of Epicharinos running in armour is by Kritios, and Oinobios is a person who did a great kindness to Thukydides. Oinobios carried the vote recalling Thukydides from exile; he was treacherously murdered on his way home: his memorial is not far from the Melitian gates. Others have written about Hermolykos the all-in wrestler and about Phormion, so I shall leave them out, though I have this much new to write about Phormion. He was like any upper-class Athenian and came from a glorious enough family, but it happened Phormion was in debt; so he retired to the country town of Paiania and when Athens chose him as admiral he refused to sail, because being in debt he was incapable of thinking about his troops until he was out of it. Athens wanted Phormion in command at all costs, so they paid off every debt he owed.

Here there is an Athene striking Marsyas the Silenos for picking up the flutes that she wanted thrown away. Opposite the things I have been talking about is the legendary battle of Theseus with the Minotaur, whether it was man or monster as the established story claims; even in our time women have produced much more amazing monsters than this one. Here is Phrixos carried away to Kolchoi by the ram: he sacrifices the ram to some god, perhaps the one called Laphystios at Orchomenos, cuts up the thighs in the Greek traditional way, and watches them burn. There are a series of other images including Herakles, strangling the serpents as the legend says; Athene rises from the head of Zeus; there is a bull dedicated on some occasion by the Council of the Areopagos: if you wanted you could make a lot of guesses why or when. As I said before the Athenians are more devout about religion than anyone else; they were the first to name Athene the Workwoman.

* * *

For those who prefer things artfully made to antiquities, there are things to see like Kleoitas's helmeted man, who has silver finger-nails. There is also a statue of Earth begging Zeus to rain on her, either because the Athenians needed rain or because there was a drought all over Greece.

Konon's son Timotheos and Konon himself are here too. Alkamenes dedicated Prokne and Itys; Prokne has decided to murder her son. Athene reveals the olive-tree and Poseidon the sea-wave. Here is Leochares' statue of Zeus, here is Zeus of the City, whose traditional sacrifice I shall describe, but I shall not give its legendary origin. They put barley mixed with wheat on the altar of Zeus of the City and leave it unguarded. The steer they have ready for sacrifice visits the altar and touches the grains. They call one of the priests the steer-killer; he drops the axe and runs away. That is the ritual. Then, as if they did not know who had committed this act, they bring up the axe for trial. They do it in the way I describe. As you go into the temple called the PARTHENON, everything on the pediment has to do with the birth of Athene; the far side shows Poseidon quarrelling with Athene over the country. The statue is made of ivory and gold. She has a sphinx on the middle of her helmet, and griffins worked on either side of it. I shall give the legend of the sphinx when we get to Boiotia. Aristeas of Prokonnesos says in his poem that these griffins fight for gold with the Arimaspians, away beyond the north of Thrace, and the gold they guard grows out of the earth; the Arimaspians are born one-eyed, but the griffins are wild monsters like lions with wings and the beak of an eagle. This is enough about griffins. The statue of Athene stands upright in an ankle-length tunic with the head of Medusa carved in ivory on her breast. She has a Victory about eight feet high, and a spear in her hand and a shield at her feet, and a snake beside the shield; this snake might be Erichthonios. The plinth of the statue is carved with the birth of Pandora. Hesiod and others say Pandora was the first woman ever born, and the female sex did not exist before her birth. I remember the only imperial portrait I saw here was of Hadrian, and by the entrance there was one of Iphikrates who achieved many amazing things.

Opposite the temple is a bronze Apollo that they say Pheidias made. They call it the Locust god because locusts were infesting the earth and the god promised to drive them out of the country. They know he did expel them but no one says how. I myself know three occasions when locusts have been wiped out from Mount Sipylos, though not in the same way; one lot were blown away by a violent wind, the second were caught by a violent heat after the god had sent rain, and the third perished in a sudden frost.

*   *   *

There is a way up by Daulis to the heights of Parnassos, longer than the path from Delphi but not so difficult. But turn back from Daulis onto the straight Delphi road, and proceed along it; there is a building on the left of the road called the PHOKIKON where the Phokians assemble from all their cities. The building is a great size; inside it the pillars stand in order of height, ascending in steps to the opposite wall. The Phokian delegates sit on these steps. At the far end there are no pillars and no steps, but statues of Zeus and Athene and Hera. Zeus is enthroned with the goddesses on either side, Athene on the left and Hera on the right.

Further along the road you come to the SPLIT as they call it; on this road Oedipus murdered his father. All Greece must remember the sufferings of Oedipus. When he was born they pierced his ankles and abandoned him in the Plataian country on Mount Kithairon; Corinth nursed him in the country by the isthmus; Phokis and the Split road were polluted by his patricide; Thebes is infamous for the legend of his marriage and the wickedness of Eteokles. The Split road and the crime he committed there were the beginning of Oedipus's curses; the memorial of Laios and his servant is on the midmost of three roads, under a mound of uncut stones. They say it was Damesistratos the king of Plataia who found them lying dead, and who buried them.

The highroad from here to Delphi gets more precipitous and becomes difficult even for an active man. There are a lot of different stories about DELPHI, and even more about Apollo's oracle. They say that in the most ancient times the oracle belonged to Earth, and Daphnis was its prophetess whom Earth appointed; she was one of the nymphs on the mountain. The Greeks have a poem called *Eumolpia*, which they attribute to Mousaios son of Antiophemos, that says Poseidon and Earth shared the oracle: Earth prophesied herself, and Poseidon's servant for the prophecies was Pyrkon. The verse runs like this:

> Then the voice of the Earth spoke her wise words,
> And the servant of the glorious, Earth-shaking god,
> Pyrkon spoke with her.

Some time later they say Earth gave her share to Themis, and Apollo got Themis's share as a gift, but he gave Poseidon the island of Poros off Troizen in exchange for this oracle. I have heard it said that some shepherds out with their herds first stumbled on this oracle and became possessed by the vapour, and prophesied by the power of Apollo. But the greatest and most universal glory belongs to Phemonoe: that she was the god's first prophetess and the first to sing the hexameter. But a woman of the district called Boio wrote a hymn for Delphi saying Olen and the remote Northerners came and founded the oracle of the god, and it was Olen who first prophesied and first sang the hexameter. Boio wrote this:

> Where Pagasos and godlike Aguieus
> sons of the remotest North founded
> this famous oracle. . . .

She goes through other remote Northerners, and at the close of the hymn she names Olen:

> and Olen, Phoibos' first interpreter,
> first singing carpenter of ancient verse.

No record goes back to any other man, only to prophetic women. They say that the most ancient shrine of Apollo was built of sweet bay, with branches brought from the bay-grove at Tempe. This shrine must have been in the form of a hut.

                            *   *   *

As you come into the city is a series of TEMPLES. The first was in ruins, the next empty of statues and offerings, the third had a few portraits of Roman kings, the fourth is called the TEMPLE OF FORESIGHT. The statue in the front is a dedication from Marseilles, bigger than the statue inside. Marseilles is a colony of Ionian Phokaia founded by a detachment of Phokaian refugees from Harpagos the Persian. They beat the Carthaginians in a sea-battle and obtained the territory they have now. They became extremely prosperous; their dedication is in bronze. But as for the golden shield given to Athene of Foresight by Kroisos of Lydia, the Delphians said Philomelos had stolen it. By the sanctuary of Foresight is the sacred enclosure of the divine hero Phylakos. The Delphians have a legend that Phylakos fought for them in the Persian invasion. They say a wild thicket once grew in the open among the training-grounds, and when Odysseus visited Autolykos and went hunting with his sons, this was where he was wounded over the knee by the boar. If you turn left from the training-ground and go down not more than half a mile, I think, you come to a river called the Pleistos, which flows to the sea at Kirra, the port of Delphi. If you go up from the training-grounds to the sanctuary, on the right of that road is the delicious water of KASTALIA. They say it was named after a local woman whose husband was Kastalios. But Panyassis in the verses he composed about Herakles says Kastalia was a daughter of Acheloos. He says of Herakles:

> swift-footed he crossed
> snowy Parnassos to the everlasting water
> of Kastalia, daughter of Acheloos.

I have heard another account, that the water was a present to Kastalia from the river Kephisos; and this is what Alkaios says in his prelude to Apollo. It receives strong confirmation from the Lilaians who drop the sweet-cakes of their district and other traditional offerings into the spring of the Kephisos on certain special days, and maintain they come up again at Kastalia.

The city of Delphi is a steep slope from top to bottom, and the sacred PRECINCT OF APOLLO is no different from the rest of it. This is huge in size and stands at the very top of the city, cut through by a network of alleyways. I shall record those of the dedications that seemed to me most memorable. I do not think it is worth worrying about athletes or obscure musicians, and I have already dealt in my account of Elis with those athletes who left any kind of glory behind them. But Phaÿlos of Kroton has a statue at Delphi; he never won in the Olympic games, though he won twice here in the pentathlon, and a third time in the foot-race. He fought in the seabattle against Persia, providing his own ship and manning it with men from Kroton who were living in Greece. That was his story. As you go into the enclosure there is a BRONZE BULL by Theopropos of Aigina, dedicated by the people of Corfu. The legend is that a bull in Corfu had abandoned the pasture and deserted the other cattle, and went bellowing down by the sea: the same thing happened every day, so that the herdsman came down to the shore and saw a fantastic number of tunny-fish. He showed these fish to the people in the city, and, as they had fearful trouble trying to catch them with no result, they sent to enquire at Delphi: so they slaughtered the bull to Poseidon, and immediately after the sacrifice they caught the fish, and the dedications at Olympia and at Delphi are a tithe of the catch.

* * *

The bronze horses and captive women from Tarentum come from the spoils of the Messapians, their barbarous neighbours; they were made by Ageladas of Argos. Tarentum was a Spartan colony founded by Phalanthos. Phalanthos was on his way to colonize when an oracle came from Delphi: when he felt rain from a clear sky he would get his country and his city. For the present he neither worked out this prophecy on his own nor took it to an interpreter, but steered his fleet for Italy. He was able to beat the savages but not to take a city or subdue territory, and then he remembered the oracle, supposing the god had offered him impossible conditions, since it never rained out of a clear, open sky. He was deeply depressed, and his wife, who had followed him from home, had his head on her lap and was picking off his lice and weeping for love to see all her husband's plans coming to nothing. Her tears dropped generously, and drenched Phalanthos's head, and he understood the oracle, because his wife's name was Aithra [Clear Sky] so the very next night he took Tarentum, the greatest and most prosperous of the barbarous cities of the coast. They say that the hero Taras was a son of Poseidon by a nymph of the district, and the city and the river were named after him: city and river both having the same name.

*   *   *

In the front of the temple at Delphi aids to human life have been inscribed, composed by the Wise Men, as the Greeks call them. The Wise Men were Thales of Miletos and Bias of Priene from Ionia, Pittakos of Mitylene (an Aiolian from Lesbos), Kleoboulos of Lindos (an Asiatic Dorian), Solon of Athens, and Chilon of Sparta. Plato gives Myson of Chenai as the seventh, instead of Periander son of Kypselos. Chenai was a village on Mount Oite. The Wise Men visited Delphi and dedicated to Apollo the KNOW THYSELF and the NOTHING TOO MUCH which have become proverbs. That is what those men wrote here; and you can inspect a bronze portrait of Homer on a pillar, and read the oracle they say was given to him:

> Happy, unfortunate, since you are both,
> you seek your father's country, yet your mother's country
> exists: your father's does not exist.
> The isle of Ios is your mother's fatherland
> and shall take you dead. Watch for the children's riddle.

The people of Ios point out Homer's tomb in the island, and Klymene's in a different part of it: they say she was Homer's mother. But the Cypriots who also lay claim to Homer say that a woman of Cyprus called Themisto was his mother, and that Euklous foretold the birth of Homer in these verses:

> In sea-eaten Cyprus will be a great singer:
> Themisto will bear him in the fields, a godlike woman,
> glorious far from the riches of Salamis:
> he will leave Cyprus sea-drenched, wave-lifted:
> alone and first to chant the troubles of wide Greece:
> he shall not die or grow old for everlasting ages.

I have heard this and read these oracles, but I am writing no discussion of my own about them or about the country or the date of Homer.

In the temple an altar has been built to Poseidon, as in the most ancient period the oracle belonged half to Poseidon. Two statues of Fates stand there; instead of the third Fate, Zeus of the Fates and

Apollo of the Fates stand with them. You can see a hearth here as well, at which the priest of Apollo killed Neoptolemos son of Achilles; I have told the story of Neoptolemos's death somewhere else. Dedicated not far from the hearth is the throne of Pindar. The throne is made of iron, and they say whenever he came to Delphi Pindar used to sit on it and sing the songs he wrote to Apollo. Few penetrate the innermost part of the temple; another STATUE OF APOLLO stands there, made of gold.

If you come out of the temple and turn left, you come to a holy precinct where the grave of Neoptolemos is; every year the Delphians burn offerings to him. Going on upwards from this memorial you come to a stone, not very large; they pour oil on it every day and at every festival they offer unspun wool. There is an opinion that this stone was given to Kronos instead of his child, and that Kronos vomited it up again.

Going back towards the temple after inspecting the stone you come to the SPRING called KASSOTIS; it has a small wall round it and the way up to the spring is through the wall. They say the water of this Kassotis dives under the earth and makes women prophetic in the god's holy places. They say it was one of the nymphs on Parnassos who gave her name to the spring-head.

Above Kassotis is a building with paintings by Polygnotos; it was dedicated by the Knidians, and the Delphians call it the CLUB-HOUSE because this is where they used to meet in ancient times both for old tales and for serious conversations. Homer shows in Melantho's invective against Odysseus that there were many places like it all over Greece:

> You are not willing to sleep inside a forge
> or a club-house, but come making speeches. . . .

As you go into the building all the right of the painting is the fall of Troy and the Greeks sailing away. Menelaos's men are getting ready for the voyage; there is a painting of the ship, with a mixture of men and boys among the sailors, and the ship's steersman Phrontis standing amidships holding two poles. Homer makes Nestor talk to Telemachos particularly about Phrontis; he was Onetor's son and Menelaos's ship's steersman, very famous for his skill at the job; he met his destiny just as he was sailing past Sounion in Attica. Until then Menelaos sailed with Nestor, but he was left behind to build Phrontis a memorial and pay him the dues of the dead. Anyway, Phrontis is in Polygnotos's painting, and below him is someone called Ithaimenes carrying clothes and Echoiax is going down the gangway carrying a bronze water-jar. Polites and Strophios and Alphios are taking down Menelaos's tent not far from the ship. Amphialos is taking down another tent, with a child sitting by his feet. The child has no inscription, and Phrontis is the only man with a beard. His was the only name Polygnotos got from the *Odyssey;* I suppose he made up the other people's names himself.

MARCO POLO
1254–1324

This archetypal adventurer and resider abroad came from a rich merchant family in Venice. As a seventeen-year-old he set off with his father and uncle on a diplomatic mission from Pope Gregory X to Kublai Khan, Emperor of the Tartars. Across Persia they went, and Afghanistan, and the Gobi Desert, proceeding at a leisurely pace. Three and a half years after leaving Venice, they arrived at the highly civilized court of Kublai Khan, in the city later known as Peking. The emperor took to Marco, finding him a bright and useful young man. He quickly learned the local languages, and the emperor employed him in a number of traveling administrative jobs. All in all, the Polos remained in China for twenty years.

Three years after returning to Venice, Marco, serving as an officer aboard a Venetian warship, was captured by the Genoese, and during the year he spent as a prisoner of war, to alleviate the boredom he dictated an account of his experiences to a fellow prisoner, using notebooks he had filled while in Cathay. In Polo's day the concept travel book was virtually synonymous with pack of lies, and when Polo was dying, friends urged him for the sake of his soul to retract his descriptions of some of the more incredible things he said he had seen in the East. But he refused, saying, "I have not told half of what I saw." It is now clear that what he told was the simple truth: there actually was a country called Zipangu (Japan); white bears and reindeer did exist, and so did mines of diamonds and rivers of jade, temples with gold roofs and men with black skin.

This text of the Travels *derives from William Marsden's 1818 translation of one of the manuscripts in French. Corrections have been introduced by Manuel Komroff.*

From TRAVELS (C. 1299)

OF INDIA. OF THE MANNERS AND CUSTOMS OF ITS INHABITANTS. OF
MANY REMARKABLE AND EXTRAORDINARY THINGS TO BE OBSERVED
THERE. OF THE KIND OF VESSELS EMPLOYED IN NAVIGATION

Having treated, in the preceding parts of our work, of various provinces
and regions, we shall now take leave of them, and proceed to the account
of India.

We shall commence with a description of the ships employed by the
merchants, which are built of fir-timber. They have a single deck, and
below this the space is divided into about sixty small cabins, fewer, or
more, according to the size of the vessels, each of them affording accommodation for one merchant. They are provided with a good helm. They
have four masts, with as many sails, and some of them have two masts,
which can be set up and lowered again, as may be found necessary. Some
ships of the larger class have as many as thirteen bulk-heads or divisions
in the hold, formed of thick planks mortised into each other. The object
of these is to guard against accidents which may occasion the vessel to
spring a leak, such as striking on a rock or receiving a stroke from a
whale, a circumstance that not unfrequently occurs; for, when sailing at
night, the motion through the waves causes a white foam that attracts
the notice of the hungry animal. Expecting food, it rushes violently to
the spot, strikes the ship, and often staves in some part of the bottom.
The water, running in at the place where the injury has been sustained,
makes its way to the well, which is always kept clear. The crew, upon
discovering the situation of the leak, immediately remove the goods
from the division affected by the water, which, in consequence of the
boards being so well fitted, cannot pass from one division to another.
They then repair the damage, and return the goods to their place in the
hold.

The ships are all double-planked; that is, they have a course of sheath-
ing-boards laid over the planking in every part. These are caulked with
oakum both inside and without, and are fastened with iron nails. They
are not coated with pitch, as the country does not produce that substance, but the bottoms are smeared over with the following preparation.
The people take quick-lime and hemp, which latter they cut small, and
with these, when pounded together, they mix oil procured from a certain
tree, making of the whole a kind of unguent, which retains its viscous
properties more firmly, and is a better material than pitch.

Ships of the largest size require a crew of three hundred men; others, two hundred; and some, one hundred and fifty only, according to their greater or less bulk. They carry from five to six thousand baskets, or mat bags, of pepper.

In former times they were of greater size than they are at present; but the violence of the sea having in many places broken up the islands, and especially in some of the principal ports, there is a want of depth of water for vessels of such draught. They are on that account built of a smaller size.

The vessels are likewise moved with oars or sweeps, each of which requires four men to work it. Those of the larger class are accompanied by two or three large barks, capable of containing about one thousand baskets of pepper, and are manned with sixty, eighty, or one hundred sailors. These small craft are often employed to tow the larger, when working their oars, or even under sail, provided the wind be on the quarter, but not when right aft, because, in that case, the sails of the larger vessel must becalm those of the smaller. The ships also carry with them as many as ten small boats, for the purpose of carrying out anchors, for fishing, and a variety of other services. They are slung over the sides, and lowered into the water when there is occasion to use them. The barks are in like manner provided with their small boats.

When a ship, having been on a voyage for a year or more, stands in need of repair, the practice is to give her a course of sheathing over the original boarding, forming a third course, which is caulked and paid in the same manner as the others. When she needs further repairs this is repeated, even to the number of six layers, after which she is condemned as unserviceable and not seaworthy.

Having thus described the shipping, we shall proceed to the account of India; but in the first instance we shall speak of certain islands in the part of the ocean where we are at present, and shall commence with the island named Zipangu.

* * *

OF THE NATURE OF THE MANY IDOLS WORSHIPPED IN ZIPANGU, AND
OF THE PEOPLE BEING ADDICTED TO EATING HUMAN FLESH

In this island of Zipangu and the others in its vicinity, their idols are fashioned in a variety of shapes, some of them having the heads of oxen, some of swine, of dogs, goats, and many other animals. Some exhibit the appearance of a single head with two faces; others of three heads, one of them in its proper place, and one upon each shoulder. Some have four arms, others ten, and some an hundred, those which have the greatest number being regarded as the most powerful, and therefore entitled to the most particular worship.

When they are asked by Christians wherefore they give to their deities these diversified forms, they answer that their fathers did so before them. "Those who preceded us," they say, "left them such, and such shall we transmit them to our posterity."

The various ceremonies practiced before these idols are so wicked and diabolical that it would be nothing less than an abomination to give an account of them in this book. The reader should, however, be informed that the idolatrous inhabitants of these islands, when they seize the person of an enemy who has not the means of effecting his ransom for money, invite to their house all their relations and friends. Putting their prisoner to death they cook and eat the body, in a convivial manner, asserting that human flesh surpasses every other in the excellence of its flavour.

It is to be understood that the sea in which the island of Zipangu is situated is called the Sea of Chin, and so extensive is this eastern sea that according to the report of experienced pilots and mariners who frequent it, and to whom the truth must be known, it contains no fewer than seven thousand four hundred and forty islands, mostly inhabited. It is said that of the trees which grow in them, there are none that do not yield a fragrant smell. They produce many spices and drugs, particularly lignum-aloes and pepper, in great abundance, both white and black.

It is impossible to estimate the value of the gold and other articles found in the islands; but their distance from the continent is so great, and the navigation attended with so much trouble and inconvenience, that the vessels engaged in the trade, from the ports of Zai-tun and Kin-sai, do not reap large profits, for they are obliged to consume a whole year in their voyage, sailing in the winter and returning in the summer.

In these regions only two winds prevail, one of them during the winter, and the other during the summer season, so that they must avail themselves of the one for the outward and of the other for the homeward-bound voyage. These countries are far remote from the continent of India. In terming this sea the Sea of Chin, we must understand it, nevertheless, to be a part of the ocean; for as we speak of the English Sea, or of the Egean Sea, so do the eastern people of the Sea of Chin and of the Indian Sea. We shall here cease to treat further of these countries and islands, as well on account of their lying so far out of the way, as of my not having visited them personally, and of their not being under the dominion of the Great Khan. We return now to Zai-tun.

Departing from the port of Zai-tun, and steering a westerly course, but inclining to the south, for fifteen hundred miles, you pass the gulf named Keinan, which extends to the distance of two months' navigation, along its northern shore, where it bounds the southern part of the province of Manji, and from thence to where it approaches the countries of Ania, Toloman, and many others already mentioned. Within this gulf there are a multitude of islands, for the most part well inhabited. About the coasts much gold-dust is collected from the sea, at those places where the rivers discharge themselves. Copper also and many other articles are found there, and with these a trade is carried on, the one island supplying what another does not produce. They traffic also with the people of the continent, exchanging their gold and copper for such necessaries as they may require. In the most of these islands grain is raised in abundance. This gulf is so extensive and the inhabitants so numerous, that it appears like another world.

OF THE ISLAND OF JAVA MINOR

Upon leaving the island of Pentan, and steering in the direction of south-east for about one hundred miles, you reach the island of Java the Lesser. Small, however, as it may be termed by comparison, it is not less than two thousand miles in circuit.

In this island there are eight kingdoms, governed by so many kings, and each kingdom has its own proper language, distinct from those of all the others. The people are idolaters. It contains abundance of riches, and all sorts of spices, sappan-wood for dyeing, and various other kinds of drugs, which, on account of the length of the voyage and the danger of the navigation, are not imported into our country, but which find their way to the provinces of Manji and Cathay.

We shall now treat separately of what relates to the inhabitants of each of these kingdoms; but in the first place it is proper to observe that the island lies so far to the southward as to render the north star invisible. Six of the eight kingdoms were visited by Marco Polo; and these he will describe, omitting the other two, which he had not an opportunity of seeing.

We shall begin with the kingdom of Felech, which is one of the eight. Its inhabitants are for the most part idolaters, but many of those who dwell in the seaport towns have been converted to the religion of Mahomet, by the Saracen merchants who constantly frequent them. Those who inhabit the mountains live in a beastly manner. They eat human flesh, and indiscriminately all other sorts of flesh, clean and unclean. Their worship is directed to a variety of objects, for each individual adores throughout the day the first thing that presents itself to his sight when he rises in the morning.

Upon leaving the last-mentioned kingdom, you enter that of Basman, which is independent of the others, and has its peculiar language. The people profess obedience to the Great Khan, but pay him no tribute, and their distance is so great that his troops cannot be sent to these parts. The whole island, indeed, is nominally subject to him, and when ships pass that way the opportunity is taken of sending him rare and curious articles, and especially a particular sort of falcon.

In the country are many wild elephants and rhinoceroses, which latter are much inferior in size to the elephant, but their feet are similar. Their hide resembles that of the buffalo. In the middle of the forehead they have a single horn; but with this weapon they do not injure those whom they attack, employing only for this purpose their tongue, which is armed with long, sharp spines. Their head is like that of a wild boar, and they carry it low towards the ground. They take delight in muddy pools, and are filthy in their habits. They are not of that description of animals which suffer themselves to be taken by maidens, as our people suppose, but are quite of a contrary nature. There are found in this district monkeys of various sorts, and vultures as black as crows, which are of a large size, and pursue the quarry in a good style.

It should be known that what is reported respecting the dried bodies of diminutive human creatures, or pigmies, brought from India, is an idle tale, such men being manufactured in this island in the following manner. The country produces a species of monkey, of a tolerable size, and having a countenance resembling that of a man. Those persons who make it their business to catch them, shave off the hair, leaving it only about the chin, and those other parts where it naturally grows on the human body. They then dry and preserve them with camphor and other drugs; and having prepared them in such a mode that they have exactly the appearance of little men, they put them into wooden boxes, and sell them to trading people, who carry them to all parts of the world. But this is merely an imposition. Neither in India, nor in any other country, however wild, have pigmies been found of a form so diminutive as these exhibit.

OF THE ISLAND OF ZENZIBAR

Beyond the island of Madagascar lies that of Zenzibar, which is reported to be in circuit two thousand miles. The inhabitants worship idols, have their own peculiar language, and do not pay tribute to any foreign power. They are large in stature, but their height is not proportioned to the bulk of their bodies. Were it otherwise, they would appear gigantic. They are, however, strongly made, and one of them is capable of carrying what would be a load for four of our people. At the same time, he would require as much food as five. They are black, and go naked, covering only the private parts of the body with a cloth. Their hair is so crisp, that even when dipped in water it can with difficulty be drawn out. They have large mouths, their noses turn up towards the forehead, their ears are long, and their eyes so large and frightful, that they have the aspect of demons. The women are equally ill-favoured, having wide mouths, thick noses, and large eyes. Their hands, and also their heads, are large and out of proportion.

There are in this island the most ill-favoured women in the world. Their large mouths and thick noses, and ill-favoured breasts are four times as large as those of other women. They feed on flesh, milk, rice, and dates. They have no grape vines, but make a sort of wine from rice and sugar, with the addition of some spicy drugs, very pleasant to the taste, and having the intoxicating quality of the other.

In this island elephants are found in vast numbers, and their teeth form an important article of trade.

In this country is found also the giraffe, which is a handsome beast. The body is well-proportioned, the fore-legs long and high, the hind-legs short, the neck very long, the head small, and in its manners it is gentle. Its prevailing colour is light, with circular reddish spots. Its neck, including the head, is three paces.

The sheep of the country are different from ours, being all white excepting their heads, which are black; and this also is the colour of the dogs. The animals in general have a different appearance from ours.

Many trading ships visit the place, which barter the goods they bring for elephants' teeth and ambergris, of which much is found on the coasts of the island, in consequence of the sea abounding with whales.

The chiefs of the island are sometimes engaged in warfare with each other, and their people display much bravery in battle and contempt of death. They have no horses, but fight upon elephants and camels. Upon the backs of the former they place castles, capable of containing from fifteen to twenty men, armed with swords, lances, and stones, with which weapons they fight. Previously to the combat they give draughts of wine to their elephants, supposing that it renders them more spirited and more furious in the assault.

CONCLUSION

And now ye have heard all that I can tell you about the Tartars and the Saracens and their customs, and likewise about the other countries of the world as far as my travels and knowledge extend. Only we have said nothing whatever about the Greater Sea and the provinces that lie round it, although we know it thoroughly. But it seems to me a needless task to speak about places which are visited by people every day. For there are so many who sail all about the sea constantly.

Of the manner in which we took our departure from the Court of the Great Khan you have heard at the beginning of the book, in that chapter where we told you of the difficulty that Messer Maffeo and Messer Nicolo and Messer Marco had about getting the Great Khan's leave to go; and in the same chapter is related the lucky chance that led to our departure. And you may be sure that but for that chance, we should never have got away in spite of all our trouble, and never have got back to our country again.

I believe it was God's pleasure that we should get back in order that people might learn about the things that the world contains.

Thanks be to God! Amen! Amen!

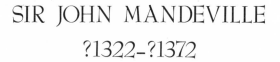

SIR JOHN MANDEVILLE
?1322–?1372

No one knows for sure who this person was. Some have suspected that his kinship is not with any actual traveler but with Baron Münchhausen or even Lemuel Gulliver. If he did exist, did he really travel, or was his longest journey, as some have thought, to the nearest library?

Despite much uncertainty, scholars seem to agree that, although he wrote in French, this author was British and came perhaps from St. Alban's. Whoever he was, by the decade 1356–1366 his book was circulating in manuscript, and soon it was widely translated and known all over Europe, where it became an important source of knowledge about the world. Columbus used it, together with the travels of Marco Polo, in planning his voyages.

One literary form discernible in Mandeville's book is the manual for pilgrims to the Holy Land. But geographically the book ranges much farther than that, and it contains gripping fabulous materials useless to pilgrims. Two topics seem to fascinate the author especially: one is people eating their fellow human beings, and the other is the magical

properties of precious stones, depicted as having the power to copulate and engender further stones as offspring. The tradition that a travel book should reveal wonders curious enough to raise the eyebrows of the reader stems largely from the work of "Mandeville," whoever he was.
The text has been translated by C. W. R. D. Moseley.

From TRAVELS
(c. 1356–57)

OF THE PILGRIMAGES IN JERUSALEM,
AND OF THE HOLY PLACES THEREABOUT

To speak of Jerusalem: you must understand that it stands well set among the hills. There is neither river nor well, but water comes thither by conduit from Hebron. And I must tell you that this city was first called Jebus, down to the time of Melchisedek, and then it was called Salem to the time of King David. And he put these two names together and called it Jebusalem; and then came Solomon and called it Jerusalem, and it is still so called. And round about Jerusalem is the kingdom of Syria; beside is the land of Palestine, and Ascalon. But Jerusalem is in the land of Judea; and it is called Judea because Judas Maccabeus was King of that land. And to the east it marches with the kingdom of Arabia, on the south with Egypt, on the west it is bordered by the Great Sea, and on the north by the kingdom of Syria and the Sea of Cyprus. There used to be a patriarch in Jerusalem, and archbishops and bishops in the country round. Round Jerusalem are these cities: Hebron seven miles away, Beersheba eight miles, Jericho six miles, Ascalon eighteen miles, Jaffa twenty-seven, Rames three miles, and Bethlehem two miles distant. And two miles from Bethlehem to the south is the church of Saint Markaritot, who was once abbot there, for whom the monks made great mourning when he died. There is still a painting which portrays the great grief and mourning they made for him, and it is a piteous thing to look on.

This land of Jerusalem has been in many different peoples' hands—Jews, Cananez, Assirienes, men of Persia, Medaynes; Macedonians, Greeks, Romans, Christians, Saracens, Barbarenes, Turks and many other nations. For Christ desires not that it should long remain in the hands of traitors or sinners, Christian or otherwise. And now unbelievers have held that land seven score years and more—but by the grace of God they shall not keep it for long.

You must understand that when men arrive in Jerusalem they make their first pilgrimage to the church where is the Sepulchre of Our Lord, which was once outside the city on the north; but it is now enclosed within the town wall. There is a very fine church, circular in plan, well-roofed with lead. On its west side is a fine strong tower for the bells. In the middle of that church is a tabernacle, like a little house, built in a semicircle, decorated very handsomely and richly with gold and silver and azure and other colours. On the right side of it is the Sepulchre of Our Lord. This tabernacle is eight feet long, five wide, and eleven high. Not long ago the Sepulchre was quite open, so that men could kiss it and touch it. But because some men who went there used to try to break bits of the stone off to take away with them, the Sultan had a wall built round the Tomb so that nobody could touch it except on the left side. The tabernacle has no windows, but inside there are many lamps burning. Among the other lights there is one which is always burning before the Sepulchre, and every Good Friday it goes out by itself, and on Easter Day it lights again by itself at that very hour when Our Lord rose from the dead to life. Also inside that church, on the right side, is the hill of Calvary, where Our Lord was crucified. The Cross was set in a mortice in the rock, which is white, streaked with red, in colour. Upon the rock blood dropped from the wounds of Our Lord when He suffered on the Cross. It is now called Golgotha; people go up steps to it. And in that mortice Adam's head was found after Noah's flood, as a token that the sins of Adam should be redeemed in that place. And higher on that rock Abraham made sacrifice to Our Lord. There is an altar there, and before it lie Godfray de Boloon and Baudewyne his brother, and other Christian Kings of Jerusalem. Where Our Lord was crucified is a Greek inscription, which reads: *Otheos basileon ysmon presemas ergaste sothias oys*—some books say, *Otheos basileon ymon proseonas ergasa sothias emesotis gis*—which means in Latin *Hic deus, rex noster, ante sacrida operatus est salutem in medio terre,* which is to say, "Here God our King before all worlds has wrought salvation in the midst of the earth." Upon the rock where the Cross was set is written thus: *Gros guist rasis thou pesteos thoy thesmoysi,* or *Oyos iustiys basis thou pesteos thoy themosi,* which means in Latin, *Quod vides, est fundamentum totius fidei mundi huius,* which means, "This that you see is the foundation of all the faith in the world." You must understand that when Our Lord died he was thirty-three years and three months of age. But the prophecy of David said that He would be forty years old when he died, where he says this: *Quadraginta annis proximus fui generacioni huic,* which means, "Forty years was I neighbour to this kindred." By this it might seem that Holy Writ was not true; but indeed it is true enough, for in the old times men counted their years as of ten months, of which the month of March was the first and December last. But Julius Caesar, who was Emperor of Rome, had the two months of January and February inserted, and decided the year of twelve months, that is to say of 365 days (excepting leap years) according to the proper course of the sun. And therefore, if we work on ten months to the year, He died in the fortieth year; but according to our years of twelve months he was thirty-three years and three months old. Close by the Mount of Calvary, on the right side, is an altar where lies the pillar to which Our Lord was bound while He was scourged. Four feet away are four stones, which continually drop water; some men say those stones mourn for Our Lord's death. Near to this altar, in a place forty-two steps underground, Saint Helena found the Cross of Our Lord Jesus Christ, under a rock where the Jews had hidden it. Two other crosses were also found, on which the two thieves who hung on either side of Christ were crucified. Saint Helena did not know for certain which was the cross Christ was killed on; so she took each one in turn and laid it on a dead man, and as soon as the True Cross was laid on the dead body, the corpse rose from death to life. By there in the walls is the place where the four nails which Christ was nailed with through foot and hand were hidden; He had two nails in His hands and two in His feet. The Emperor Constantine had one of these nails made into a bit for his bridle, which he used whenever he went into battle; through its virtue he overcame his enemies and conquered many different kingdoms—that is to say, Asia Minor, Turkey, Armenia the Lesser and the Greater, Syria, Jerusalem, Arabia, Persia, Mesopotamia, the kingdom of Aleppo and of Egypt Upper and Lower, and many other lands way off into Ethiopia and India the Lesser, which was then for the most part Christian. At that time there were many good holy men and holy hermits in those countries, of whom the book *Vitae Patrum* [Lives of the Fathers] speaks. And now for the most part those lands are in the hands of pagans and Saracens. But, when God wills, just as those lands were lost through the sins of Christian men, even so shall they be won again by Christians, with the help of God. In the middle of the choir of this church is a circle, in which Joseph of Arimathea laid the body of Our Lord when he had taken Him off the Cross; and men say that that circle is at the mid-point of the world. In that place Joseph washed Our Lord's wounds. Also in the church of the Sepulchre, on the north side, is a place where Our Lord was imprisoned—for he was imprisoned in many places. There is yet a piece of the chain with which He was bound. It was there He first appeared to Mary Magdalene when He rose from death to life, and she thought He was a gardener. In the church of the Sepulchre there used to be canons of the order of Saint Austyne, and they had a prior; but their lord was the Patriarch. Outside the door of the church, on the right, as you go up twenty-eight steps, Our Lord spoke to His mother, as He hung on the Cross, thus: *Mulier, ecce, filius tuus,* that is to say, "Woman, behold thy son"—He was referring to Saint John who stood there on one side. And to him He said, "Behold thy mother." And up these steps went Our Lord with the Cross on His back to the place where He was crucified. Below these steps is a chapel, where priests hold services, but according to their rite, not ours. They always make the sacrament at the altar of bread, saying the *Pater Noster* and the words of the sacrament and little more; for they do not know the additions of the popes, which our priests are accustomed to use at Mass. Nevertheless they sing their Mass with great devotion. Near there is the place where Our Lord rested when He was weary with carrying the Cross. You ought to know that the city is weakest by the church of the Sepulchre, because of the great plain between the city and the church on the east. Eastward, outside the walls, is the Vale of Iosaphat, which comes right up to the walls. Outside the walls, overlooking that vale, is the church of Saint Stephen, where he was stoned to death. Beside there is the gate which is called *Porta Aurea* [Golden Gate] which may not be opened. Our Lord Jesus came riding in at that gate on an ass on Palm Sunday; and the gate opened before him when he came to the Temple. The hoof-prints of the ass are still to be seen in three places on the paving-stones. Two hundred paces in front of the church of Saint Stephen is a great Hospice of Saint John, where the Hospitallers had their first foundation. Going east from the hospice is a very fine church which is called Notre Dame la Grande. A little way away is another church, Notre Dame des Latins. There stood Mary Magdalene and Mary Cleophas, sorrowing for Our Lord when He was killed, and tearing their hair. In the Hospice of Saint John just mentioned is a great house set aside for sick people, and in it there are six score and four stone pillars supporting it.

*   *   *

The direct route from Trebizond to Greater Armenia is to a city called Artiron, which used to be a fine, rich city; but the Turks have destroyed it. In the neighbourhood little wine is grown or any other fruits, for the land is high and cold; but there are many rivers and good springs which come underground from the Euphrates, which is a day's journey from that city. This River Euphrates comes under the earth from the direction of India and comes up again in the land of Allazar. Men go through Greater Armenia to the Sea of Persia. From the city of Erzerum you can go to a mountain called Sabissebella or Sabissacolle. Near it is another hill called Ararat (the Jews call it Thano) where

Noah's ship rested after the Flood. It is still there, and can be seen from far off in clear weather. That mountain is seven miles high. Some men say they have been there and put their fingers into the hole where the Devil came out when Noah said *Benedicite;* but they are not telling the truth. No man can climb that hill because of the snow, which is always there, winter and summer. And never a man went there since Noah's time except for one monk, who, through the grace of God, went there and brought back a timber of the ship, which is still in an abbey at the foot of the mountain. This monk greatly desired to climb that hill, and so one day he set about it. By the time he had climbed a third of the way up, he was so weary that he could not go further, and he rested there and fell asleep. When he awoke he found himself once more back at the foot of the hill. Then he beseeched God to allow him to go up; and an angel came to him and told him go up. He did so, and brought the plank down. Since then no man went there, and so those who say they have been are lying.

*   *   *

Next to Chaldea is the land of Amazoun, which we call the Maiden Land or the Land of Women; no man lives there, only women. This is not because, as some say, no man can live there, but because the women will not allow men to rule the kingdom. There was once a king in that land called Colopheus, and there were once men living there as they do elsewhere. It so happened that this king went to war with the King of Scythia, and was slain with all his great men in battle with his enemy. And when the Queen and the other ladies of that land heard the news that the King and the lords were slain, they marshalled themselves with one accord and armed themselves well. They took a great army of women and slaughtered all the men left among them. And since that time they will never let a man live with them more than seven days, nor will they allow a boy child to be brought up among them. But when they want to have the company of man, they go to that side of their country where their lovers live, stay with them eight or nine days and then go home again. If any of them bears a child and it is a son, they keep it until it can speak and walk and eat by itself and then they send it to the father—or they kill it. If they have a girl child, they cut off one of her breasts and cauterize it; in the case of a woman of great estate, the left one, so that she can carry her shield better, and, in one of low degree, they cut off the right, so that it will not hinder them shooting—for they know very well the skill of archery. There is always a queen to rule that land, and they all obey her. This queen is always chosen by election, for they choose the woman who is the best fighter. These women are noble and wise warriors; and therefore kings of neighbouring realms hire them to help them in their wars. This land of the Amazons is an island, surrounded by water, except at two points where there are two ways in. Beyond the water live their lovers to whom they go when it pleases them to have bodily pleasure with them. Next to the land of the Amazons is a country called Termegutte, a fair and pleasant country; because of the great beauty and richness of this land King Alexander wanted to build there his first city of Alexandria. For in that land he built twelve Alexandrias, of which this was the first; but it is now called Celsite.

On the other side of Chaldea, to the south, is the land of Ethiopia, which is a great country, reaching as far as Egypt. Ethiopia is divided into two main parts, that is, the southern and the eastern parts. The southern is called Mauritayne, and the people of this part are blacker than those in the eastern part. In this part there is a well which during the day is so cold that no man can drink from it, and at night too hot to put a hand in. Beyond Mauretania, going by sea to the south, is a vast country, but it is uninhabitable because of the terrible heat of the sun. In Ethiopia all the rivers are so turbid and so salt because of the excessive heat of the sun that no one dare use them. The people of that country very easily get drunk; they have little appetite for their food, and commonly have diarrhoea. They live only a short time. In that land, too, there are people of different shapes. There are some who have only one foot, and yet they run so fast on that one foot that it is a marvel to see them. That foot is so big that it will cover and shade all the body from the sun. In Ethiopia are young children whose hair is white, and as they grow old, their hair gets black. In this land of Ethiopia is the city of Saba, of which one of the Three Kings who gave gifts to Our Lord was King.

From Ethiopia you go to India through many different countries. You should know that India is divided into three parts, that is to say, India the Greater, which is a mountainous and hot land; India the Lesser, to the south, a temperate land; and the third part, to the north, so cold that, because of the great cold and continual frost, water congeals into crystal. On the rocks of crystal good diamonds grow, which are of the colour of crystal; but they are dimmer than crystal and as brown as oil. They are so hard that no metal can polish or split them. Other diamonds are found in Arabia, which are not so good, and softer. Some are found in Cyprus, which are still softer; and so they can be polished more easily. Also they are found in Macedonia; but those of India are the best. And some are often found in a mass, in the mines where men find gold, and those are as hard as those of India. And just as good diamonds are found in India on the rocks of crystal, men find good hard diamonds on the rocks of adamant in the sea, and on the mountains too—about as big as hazel nuts. They naturally grow in cube shapes. They grow together, male and female, and are fed with the dew of Heaven. And according to their nature they engender and conceive small children, and so they constantly grow and multiply. I have many times tested and seen that if a man takes with them a little of the rock they grew on, provided they are taken up by the roots and watered with the dew of May, each year they grow visibly, so that the small ones become bigger. A man should carry a diamond on his left side; then it is of more virtue than when on the right, for the natural bent of its growth is to the north, which is the left side of the world and the left side of a man when he turns to face the east.

And if you wish to know the virtues of the diamond, I will tell you them according to Ysidre. . . and Bertilmew. . . . The diamond gives to the man who carries it boldness (if it is freely given to him) and keeps his limbs healthy. It gives him grace to overcome his enemies, if his cause is righteous, in both war and law. It keeps him in his right mind. It protects him from quarrels, fights, debauchery, and from evil dreams and fantasies, and from wicked spirits. And if any man who meddles in sorcery or enchantments wants to hurt one who carries a diamond, he will not worry him. No wild or poisonous animal will hurt one who carries it. You ought to understand that the diamond must be freely given as a present, not coveted or bought, and then it is of greater power and makes a man more stalwart against his enemies. It heals the man who is lunatic; and if poison should be brought to the place where the diamond is, the stone immediately grows moist and begins to sweat, and men can easily polish it. But some craftsmen out of deceitfulness will not polish the stone, in order that it should be believed that the stone cannot be polished. In India too diamonds can be found of a violet colour, and somewhat brown, which are very good and very precious. But some do not like them as well as these others I have spoken of. Nevertheless they seem to me as good and as precious as the others; for truly, I have often seen them tested. They have others too which are as white as crystal, but they are dimmer and cloudy; still, they are very good and of great virtue. And they are nearly all quadrangular and pointed; but there are some that of their own nature are three cornered and some six.

* * *

OF THE FOUL CUSTOMS FOLLOWED IN THE ISLE OF LAMORY;
AND HOW THE EARTH AND SEA ARE OF ROUND SHAPE,
PROVED BY MEANS OF THE STAR ANTARCTIC

From this country men go through the Great Sea Ocean by way of many isles and different countries, which would be tedious to relate. At last, after fifty-two days' journey, men come to a large country called Lamory. In that land it is extremely hot; the custom there is for men and women to go completely naked and they are not ashamed to show themselves as God made them. They scorn other folk who go clothed; for they say that God made Adam and Eve naked, and men ought not to be ashamed of what God has made, for nothing natural is ugly. They say also that men who wear clothes are of another world, or else believe not in God who made all the world. In that land there is no marriage between man and woman; all the women of that land are common to every man. They say that if they were to do otherwise they would sin greatly, because God said to Adam and Eve, *Crescite et multiplicamini et replete terram*, that is to say, "Increase and multiply and fill the earth." And therefore no man says, "This is my wife," nor any woman, "This is my husband." When women are delivered of a child, they give it to whom they want of the men who have slept with them. And in the same way the land is common property. So one year a man has one house, another year another; each man takes what pleases him, now here, now there. For all things are common, as I said, corn and other goods too; nothing is locked up, and every man is as rich as another. But they have an evil custom among them, for they will eat human flesh more gladly than any other. Nevertheless the land is abundant enough in meat and fish and corn, and also gold and silver and other goods. Merchants bring children there to sell, and the people of the country buy them. Those that are plump they eat; those that are not plump they feed up and fatten, and then kill and eat them. And they say it is the best and sweetest flesh in the world.

* * *

From here one goes to another isle, called Tracota, where the people are like animals lacking reason. They live in caves, for they do not have the intelligence to build houses; and when they see a stranger passing through the country, they run and hide in their caves. They eat snakes, and do not speak, but hiss to one another like adders. They care nothing for gold, silver, or other worldly goods, only for one precious stone which has sixty colours. It is called traconite after the country. They love this stone very much indeed, even though they do not know its properties; they desire it simply for its beauty.

Thence one travels by sea to another land, called Natumeran. It is a large and fair island, whose circuit is nearly a thousand miles. Men and women of that isle have heads like dogs, and they are called Cynocephales. These people, despite their shape, are fully reasonable and intelligent. They worship an ox as their god. Each one of them carries an ox made of gold or silver on his brow, as a token that they love their god well. They go quite naked except for a little cloth round their privy parts. They are big in stature and good warriors; they carry a large shield, which covers all their body, and a long spear in their hand, and dressed in this way they go boldly against their enemies. If they capture any man in battle, they eat him. The King of that land is a great and mighty lord, rich, and very devout according to his creed. He has round his neck a cord of silk on which are three hundred precious stones like our rosary of amber. And just as we say our *Pater Noster* and *Aue Maria* by telling our beads, just so the King says each day on his beads three hundred prayers to his god, before he eats. He wears a splendid ruby round his neck, which is nearly a foot long and five fingers broad. They give him this ruby when they make him King, to carry in his hand, and so he rides round the city and they all make obeisance to him. After that he always wears it round his neck, for if he did not he would be King no longer. The Great Khan of Cathay has much coveted that ruby, but he could never win it in war or by any other means. This King is a very righteous man and just according to his law, for he punishes everyone who does another man wrong in his realm. Therefore men can travel safely and securely through his land, and no one is so bold as to annoy them, rob them, or take any kind of goods from them.

From here one goes to another isle called Silha. The circumference of it is eight hundred miles. A great part of this country is waste and wilderness, and uninhabited; therefore there are great numbers of dragons, crocodiles and other kinds of reptiles, so that men cannot live there. The crocodile is a kind of snake, brown on top of the back, with four feet and short legs and two great eyes. The body is so long and so big that where it has travelled across the sand it is as if a great tree has been dragged there. In that wilderness there are also many other kinds of wild beast, especially elephants. And in that isle there is a high mountain, and on the very top of it is a great loch full of water. Men of that land say that Adam and Eve wept for a hundred years on that hill after they were expelled from Paradise, and that that water collected from their tears. In the bottom of that lake precious stones are found, and round it grow reeds in great profusion, among which there are crocodiles and other snakes living; in the lake there are horse eels of marvellous size. Once a year the King of that isle gives all the poor people leave to go into the lake and gather precious stones, out of charity and for love of Adam and Eve's God; each year enough of those precious stones are found. When these poor folk go into the lake to gather the stones, they anoint themselves all over with the juice of the fruit called lemons, and do not fear the crocodiles nor the other poisonous reptiles. The water of this lake empties down the side of the mountain. And by that river pearls and precious stones are found. Men say in that land that snakes and other venomous animals do no harm to strangers or pilgrims who pass through; they hurt only the natives and those who live there. There are also wild geese with two heads and white wolves with bodies as big as oxen, and many other kinds of animals. And understand that the sea which surrounds this island and other isles nearby seems so high above the land that it looks to men who see it as if it hung in the air on the point of falling and covering the earth; and that is a marvellous thing, as the prophet says, *Mirabiles elaciones maris*, that is, "Wonderful are the risings of the sea."

HOW MEN KNOW THROUGH THE IDOL IF SICK MEN WILL DIE OR NOT;

OF THE PEOPLE OF DIFFERENT SHAPES, AND VERY UGLY;

AND OF THE MONKS WHO GIVE THEIR ALMS

TO BABOONS, MONKEYS AND MARMOSETS

From this isle men go south by sea to another which is called Dundeya, a big island. There live here a people of evil customs, for fathers eat their sons and sons their fathers, husbands their wives and wives their husbands. For if it chance that a man's father is sick, the son goes to the priest of their religion and asks him to inquire of their god—who is an idol—whether his father will live or die of that sickness. And the devil within that idol may answer that he will not die at that time, and indicates some medicines to heal him with; then the son returns to his father and does as instructed until he is well again. But if it says he will die, the priest and the son and the wife of the sick man come to him and throw a cloth over his mouth and stop him breathing, and kill him. When he is dead they take his body and cut it in little pieces, and summon all his friends, and all the musicians they can get, and make a solemn feast and eat the dead man's body. And when they have eaten all the flesh, they collect all the bones together and bury them according to their custom with great solemnity and loud singing. And thus each friend does to another; and if it so happen that a man who is a relation of the dead man keeps away from the feast and comes not to the funeral, all the family will accuse him of a serious fault, and he will never after be counted among their friends. They say that they eat the flesh of their friend so that worms should not eat him in the earth, and to release him from the great pain that his soul would suffer if worms gnawed him in the earth. They also say, when they find his flesh lean through long illness, that it would be a great sin to allow him to live longer or suffer pain without a cause. If they find his flesh fat, they say they have done well to have killed him so quickly and sent him to Paradise, not allowing him to be tormented too long in this world. The King of that land is a great and mighty lord, and has under his rule fifty-four large islands; in each of them is a crowned king, all obedient to him.

There are many different kinds of people in these isles. In one, there is a race of great stature, like giants, foul and horrible to look at; they have one eye only, in the middle of their foreheads. They eat raw flesh and raw fish. In another part, there are ugly folk without heads, who have eyes in each shoulder; their mouths are round, like a horseshoe, in the middle of their chest. In yet another part there are headless men whose eyes and mouths are on their backs. And there are in another place folk with flat faces, without noses or eyes; but they have two small holes instead of eyes, and a flat lipless mouth. In another isle there are ugly fellows whose upper lip is so big that when they sleep in the sun they cover all their faces with it. In another there are people of small stature, like dwarfs, a little bigger than pygmies. They have no mouth, but instead a little hole, and so when they must eat they suck their food through a reed or pipe. They have no tongues, and hiss and make signs as monks do, to each other, and each of them understands what the other means. In another isle there are people whose ears are so big that they hang down to their knees. In another, people have feet like horses, and run so swiftly on them that they overtake wild beasts and kill them for their food. In another isle there are people who walk on their hands and their feet like four-footed beasts; they are hairy and climb up trees as readily as apes. There is another isle where the people are hermaphrodite, having the parts of each sex, and each has a breast on one side. When they use the male member, they beget children; and when they use the female, they bear children. There is another isle where the folk move on their knees marvellously, and it seems as if at each step they would fall; on each foot they have eight toes. There is still another isle where the people have only one foot which is so broad that it will cover all the body and shade it from the sun. They will run so fast on this one foot that it is a marvel to see them. There is also another isle where the people live just on the smell of a kind of apple; and if they lost that smell, they would die forthwith. Many other kinds of folk there are in other isles about there, which are too numerous to relate.

* * *

And I, John Mandeville, knight, left my country and crossed the sea in the year of Our Lord Jesus Christ 1332; I have travelled through many lands, countries and isles, and have been on many honourable journeys, and many honourable deeds of arms with worthy men, although I am unworthy; I am now come to rest, a man worn out by age and travel and the feebleness of my body, and certain other causes which force me to rest. I have compiled this book and written it, as it came into my mind, in the year of Our Lord Jesus Christ 1366, that is to say in the thirty-fourth year after I left this land and took my way to those parts.

CHRISTOPHER COLUMBUS
?1446–1506

Columbus was born probably at Genoa, and at the age of fourteen he began going to sea as a merchant mariner. Soon he made Lisbon his home port, married, and undertook the study of ships' logs, maps, and travel accounts, including Marco Polo's. Conceiving the earth to be a sphere and concluding that he could reach Asia by sailing west as well as east, he asked King John II of Portugal for money and ships to support an exploratory voyage. Unsuccessful there, he turned to Ferdinand and Isabella of Spain, and after repeated solicitations and arguments, succeeded in persuading them to back his hunch.

On August 3, 1492, his three ships, carrying 88 men in all, set out from Palos, Spain, and after a little more than two months arrived at the Bahamas—Asia, Columbus thought. After exploring Cuba, Hispaniola, and other islands, he returned triumphant to the Spanish court, which lavished many honors upon him. A year later he went back, this time with 17 ships and 1,500 men, and located Domenica and Jamaica. On a third voyage five years later he discovered Trinidad and the coast of South America, and on a fourth voyage, in 1502, he found the Isthmus of Panama. But finally his triumph turned to disaster as he was held responsible, back in Spain, for the greed and mismanagement of the colonists he had installed in the New World, and he died poor, gouty, and neglected.

In 1493 he wrote a letter to the Spanish court, reporting on his first voyage. Frank E. Robbins has translated a Latin text of that letter. Columbus calls Cuba Juana in honor of the infant prince Don Juan.

To Lord Gabriel Sanchez,
Treasurer of the Spanish Court

[*March 14, 1493*]

As I know that it will please you that I have carried to completion the duty which I assumed, I decided to write you this letter to advise you of every single event and discovery of this voyage of ours. On the thirty-third day after I left [the Canaries] I reached the Indian Sea; there I found very many islands, inhabited by numberless people, of all of which I took possession without opposition in the name of our most fortunate king by making formal proclamation and raising standards; and to the first of them I gave the name of San Salvador, the blessed Savior, through dependence on whose aid we reached both this and the others. The Indians however call it Guanahani. I gave each one of the others too a new name; to wit, one Santa Maria de la Concepción, another Fernandina, another Isabella, another Juana, and I ordered similar names to be used for the rest.

When we first put in at the island which I have just said was named Juana, I proceeded along its shore westward a little way, and found it so large (for no end to it appeared) that I believed it to be no island but the continental province of Cathay; without seeing, however, any towns or cities situated in its coastal parts except a few villages and rustic farms, with whose inhabitants I could not talk because they took to flight as soon as they saw us.

I went on further, thinking that I would find a city or some farmhouses. Finally, seeing that nothing new turned up, though we had gone far enough, and that this course was carrying us off to the north (a thing which I myself wanted to avoid, for winter prevailed on those lands, and it was my hope to hasten to the south) and since the winds too were favorable to our desires, I concluded that no other means of accomplishment offered, and thus reversing my course I returned to a certain harbor which I had marked and from that point sent ashore two men of our number to find out whether there was a king in that province, or any cities. These men proceeded afoot for three days and found countless people and inhabited places, but all small and without any government; and therefore they returned.

In the meantime I had already learned from some Indians whom I had taken aboard at this same place that this province was in fact an island; and so I went on toward the east, always skirting close to its shores, for 322 miles, where is the extremity of the island. From this point I observed another island to eastward, 54 miles from this island Juana, which I immediately called Hispana. I withdrew to it, and set my course along its northern coast, as I had at Juana, to the east for 564 miles.

The before-mentioned island Juana and the other islands of the region, too, are as fertile as they can be. This one is surrounded by harbors, numerous, very safe and broad, and not to be compared with any others that I have seen anywhere; many large, wholesome rivers flow through this land; and there are also many very lofty mountains in it. All these islands are most beautiful and distinguished by various forms; one can travel through them, and they are full of trees of the greatest variety, which brush at the stars; and I believe they never lose their foliage. At any rate, I found them as green and beautiful as they usually are in the month of May in Spain; some of them were in bloom, some loaded with fruit, some flourished in one state, others in the other, each according to its kind; the nightingale was singing and there were countless other birds of many kinds in the month of November when I myself was making my way through them. There are furthermore, in the before-mentioned island Juana, seven or eight kinds of palm trees, which easily surpass ours in height and beauty, as do all the other trees, grasses, and fruits. There are also remarkable pines, vast fields and meadows, many kinds of birds, many kinds of honey, and many kinds of metals, except iron.

There are moreover in that island which I said above was called Hispaniola fine, high mountains, broad stretches of country, forests, and extremely fruitful fields excellently adapted for sowing, grazing, and building dwelling houses. The convenience and superiority of the harbors in this island and its wealth in rivers, joined with wholesomeness for man, is such as to surpass belief unless one has seen them. The trees, coverage, and fruits of this island are very different from those of Juana. Besides, this Hispaniola is rich in various kinds of spice and in gold and in mines, and its inhabitants (and those of all the others which I saw, and of which I have knowledge) of either sex always go as naked as when they were born, except some women who cover their private parts with a leaf or a branch of some sort, or with a skirt of cotton which they themselves prepare for the purpose.

They all of them lack, as I said above, iron of whatever kind, as well as arms, for these are unknown to them; nor are they fitted for weapons, not because of any bodily deformity, for they are well built, but in that they are timid and fearful. However, instead of arms they carry reeds baked in the sun, in the roots of which they fasten a sort of spearhead made of dry wood and sharpened to a point. And they do not dare to use these at close quarters; for it often happened that when I had sent two or three of my men to certain farmhouses to talk with their inhabitants a closely packed body of Indians would come out and when they saw our men approach they would quickly take flight, children deserted by father and vice versa; and that too not that any hurt or injury had been brought upon a single one of them; on the contrary, whenever I approached any of them and whenever I could talk with any of them I was generous in giving them whatever I had, cloth and very many other things, without any return being made to me; but they are naturally fearful and timid.

However when they see that they are safe and all fear has been dispelled they are exceedingly straightforward and trustworthy and most liberal with all that they have; none of them denies to the asker anything that he possesses; on the contrary they themselves invite us to ask for it. They exhibit great affection to all and always give much for little, content with very little or nothing in return. However I forbade such insignificant and valueless things to be given to them, as pieces of platters, dishes, and glass, or again nails and lace points; though if they could acquire such it seemed to them that they possessed the most beautiful trinkets in the world. For it happened that one sailor got in return for one lace point a weight of gold equivalent to three golden solidi, and similarly others in exchange for other things of slighter value; especially in exchange for brand-new blancas, certain gold coins, to secure which they would give whatever the seller asks, for example, an ounce and a half or two ounces of gold, or thirty or forty pounds of cotton by weight, which they themselves had spun; likewise they bought pieces of hoops, pots, pitchers, and jars for cotton and gold, like dumb beasts. I forbade this, because it was clearly unjust, and gave them free many pretty and acceptable objects that I had brought with me, in order more easily to win them over to me, and that they might become Christians, and be inclined to love our King and Queen and Prince and all the peoples of Spain, and to make them diligent to seek out and accumulate and exchange with us the articles in which they abound and which we greatly need.

They know nothing of idolatry; on the contrary they confidently believe that all might, all power, all good things, in fact, are in the heavens; they thought that I too had descended thence with these ships and sailors, and in that opinion I was received everywhere after they had rid themselves of fear. Nor are they slow or ignorant; on the contrary, they are of the highest and keenest wit; and the men who navigate that sea give an admirable account of each detail; but they have never seen men wearing clothes, or ships of this sort. As soon as I came to that sea I forcibly seized some Indians from the first island, so that they might learn from us and similarly teach us the things of which they had knowledge in those parts; and it came out just as I had hoped; for we quickly taught them, and then they us, by gestures and signs; finally they understood by means of words, and it paid us well to have them. The ones who now go with me persist in the belief that I leaped down out of the skies, although they have associated with us for a long time and are still doing so today; and they were the first to announce that fact wherever we landed, some of them calling out loudly to the others, "Come, come, and you will see the men from heaven." And so women as well as men, children and grown people, youths and old men, laying aside the fear they had conceived shortly before, vied with each other in coming to look at us, the great crowd of them clogging the road, some bringing food, others drink, with the greatest manifestation of affection and unbelievable good will.

Each island possesses many canoes of solid wood, and though they are narrow, nevertheless in length and shape they are like our double-banked galleys, but faster. They are steered with oars alone. Some of these are large, some small, some of medium size; a considerable number however are larger than the galley which is rowed by eighteen benches. With these they cross to all the islands, which are innumerable, and with them they ply their trade, and commerce is carried out between them. I saw some of these galleys or canoes which carried seventy or eighty oarsmen.

In all the islands there is no difference in the appearance of the people, nor in their habits or language; on the contrary, they all understand each other, which circumstance is most useful to that end which I think our most serene sovereigns especially desire, namely, their conversion to the holy faith of Christ, to which indeed as far as I could see they are readily submissive and inclined.

I have told how I sailed along the island of Juana on a straight course from west to east 322 miles; from this voyage and the length of the course I can say that this Juana is larger than England and Scotland together; for beyond the aforesaid 322 miles, in the western part, there are two more provinces which I did not visit, one of which the Indians call Anan, whose inhabitants are born with tails. These provinces extend to a length of 180 miles, as I have found out from these Indians whom I am bringing with me, who are well acquainted with all these islands.

The circumference of Hispaniola, indeed, is more than all Spain from Catalonia to Fuenterrabia. And this is easily proved by this fact, that the one of its four sides which I myself traversed on a straight course from west to east measures 540 miles. We should seek possession of this island and once gained it is not to be thrown away; for although, as I said, I formally took possession of all the others in the name of our invincible King and their sovereignty is entirely committed to that said King, nevertheless in this island I took possession in a special way of a certain large village in a more favorable situation, suitable for all sorts of gain and trade, to which I gave the name Navidad del Señor; and I gave orders to erect a fort there at once. This should by now be built, and in it I left behind the men who seemed necessary with all kinds of arms and suitable food for more than a year, furthermore, one caravel, and for the construction of others men skilled in this art as well as in others; and, besides, an unbelievable goodwill and friendship on the part of the king of that island toward the men. For all those peoples are so gentle and kind that the aforesaid king took pride in my being called his brother. Even if they should change their minds and want to injure the men who stayed in the fort they cannot, since they have no arms, go naked, and are extremely timid; and so if our men only hold the said fort they can hold the whole island, with no hazard on the part of the people to threaten them as long as they do not depart from the laws and government which I gave them.

In all those islands, as I understood it, each man is content with only one wife, except the princes or kings, who may have twenty. The women seem to do more work than the men. I could not clearly make out whether they have private property, for I noted that what an individual had he shared with others, especially food, meats, and the like. I did not find any monsters among them, as many expected, but men of great dignity and kindliness. Nor are they black, like the Negroes; they have long, straight hair; they do not live where the heat of the sun's rays shines forth; for the strength of the sun is very great here, since apparently it is only twenty-six degrees from the equator. On the mountain peaks extreme cold reigns, but this the Indians mitigate both by being used to the region and by the aid of very hot foods upon which they dine often and luxuriously.

And so I did not see any monsters, nor do I have knowledge of them anywhere with the exception of a certain island called Charis, which is the second as you sail from Spain toward India and which a tribe inhabits that is held by its neighbors to be extremely savage. These feed on human flesh. The aforesaid have many kinds of galleys in which they cross to all the Indian islands, rob, and steal all they can. They differ in no respect from the others, except that in feminine fashion they wear their hair long; and they use bows and arrows with shafts of reeds fitted as we said at the thicker end with sharpened arrowheads. On that account they are held to be savage, and the other Indians are afflicted with constant fear of them, but I do not rate them any more highly than the rest. These are the ones who cohabit with certain women who are the only inhabitants of the island of Mateunin, which is the first encountered in the passage from Spain toward India. These women, moreover, do not occupy themselves with any of the work that properly belongs to their sex, for they use bows and arrows just as I related of their husbands; they protect themselves with copper plates of which there is an ample supply in their land. They assure me that there is another island larger than the above-mentioned Hispaniola; its inhabitants are hairless, and it abounds in gold more than all the others. I am bringing with me men from this island and the others that I saw who bear testimony to what I have said.

Finally, to compress into a few words the advantage and profit of our journey hence and our speedy return, I make this promise, that supported by only small aid from them I will give our invincible sovereigns as much gold as they need, as much spices, cotton, and the mastic, which is found only in Chios, as much of the wood of the aloe, as many slaves to serve as sailors as their Majesties wish to demand; furthermore, rhubarb and other kinds of spices which I suppose those whom I left in the before-mentioned fort have already discovered and will discover, since indeed I lingered nowhere longer than the winds compelled, except at the village of Navidad while I took care to establish the fort and to make all safe. Though these things are great and unheard of, nevertheless they would have been much greater if the ships had served me as they reasonably should.

Indeed this outcome was manifold and marvelous, and fitting not to my own claims to merit, but rather to the holy Christian faith and the piety and religion of our sovereigns, for what the human mind could not comprehend, that the divine mind has granted to men. For God is accustomed to listen to his servants, and to those who love his commands, even in impossible circumstances, as has happened to us in the present instance, for we have succeeded in that to which hitherto mortal powers have in no wise attained. For if others have written or spoken of these islands, they have all done so by indirection and guesses; no one claims to have seen them, whence it seemed to be almost a fable. Therefore let the King and Queen, the Prince, their happy realms, and all other provinces of Christendom give thanks to the Savior, our Lord Jesus Christ, who has granted us so great a victory and reward; let processions be celebrated; let solemn holy rites be performed; and let the churches be decked with festival branches; let Christ rejoice on earth as He does in heaven when He foresees that so many souls of peoples hitherto lost are to be saved. Let us too rejoice, both for the exaltation of our faith and for the increase in temporal goods in which not only Spain but all Christendom together are to share. As these things were done, so have they been briefly narrated. Farewell.

Lisbon, the day before the Ides of March,

Christopher Columbus
Admiral of the Ocean Fleet

PEDRO VAS DE CAMINHA
Fifteenth Century

The years 1400 to 1600 were the high point of Portuguese exploration and overseas expansion, beginning with Prince Henry the Navigator's embarkation from Sagres and ending with the rise to maritime power of such rivals as England and the Netherlands. Portugal was anxious to extend its trading presence to India, and to that end, in the year 1500, sent out an expedition of 13 ships headed for India via the Cape of Good Hope. Admiral Pedro Álvares Cabral was in command, and other ship captains included Bartolomeu Dias and Nicolau Coelho. For some unknown reason, when in the South Atlantic, the fleet turned westward instead of proceeding to the south and accidentally discovered Brazil, which Cabral at first assumed was a large island. He took possession of it in the name of Portugal.

Accompanying this expedition was a scribe named Pedro Vas de Caminha, of whom little more is known than that he was "a gentleman of good family." He was clearly pious, and a precise, responsible observer. His report to the King, retailing the astonishing news of a wholly unsuspected world populated by curiously benign naked savages, has been translated by Charles David Ley.

To Manuel I, King of Portugal

Pôrto-Seguro, Vera Cruz, May 1, 1500

Sire,

The admiral of this fleet, besides the other captains, will write to Your Majesty telling you the news of the finding of this new territory of Your Majesty's which has just been discovered on this voyage. But I, too, cannot but give my account of this matter to Your Majesty, as well as I can, though I know that my powers of telling and relating it are less than any man's. May it please Your Majesty, however, to let my good faith serve as an excuse for my ignorance, and to rest assured that I shall not set down anything beyond what I have seen and reflected on, either to add beauty or ugliness to the narrative. I shall not give any account of the crew or the ship's course, since that is the pilot's concern, and I should not know how to do so. Therefore, Sire, I begin what I have to tell thus:

And I say that our departure from Belém was, as Your Majesty knows, on Monday, 9th March. On Saturday, the 14th of the same month, between eight and nine o'clock we sailed between the Canary Islands, going in nearest to the Grand Canary. We were becalmed in sight of them the whole day, for some three or four leagues. On Sunday the 22nd of the same month, at about ten o'clock, we came in sight of the Cape Verde Islands, or, to be precise, St. Nicholas's Island, as the pilot, Pero Escobar, declared.

On the following night, the Monday, we discovered at dawn that Vasca de Ataide and his ship had been lost, though there was no strong or contrary wind to account for this. The admiral sought him diligently in all directions, but he did not appear again. So we continued on our way across the ocean until on the Tuesday of Easter week, which was 21st April, we came across some signs of being near land, at some 660 or 670 leagues from the aforesaid island, by the pilot's computation. These signs were a great quantity of those long seaweeds sailors call *botelho*, as well as others to which they give the name of "asses' tails." On the following morning, Wednesday, we came across the birds they call "belly-rippers."

This same day, at the hour of vespers we sighted land, that is to say, first a very high rounded mountain, then other lower ranges of hills to the south of it, and a plain covered with large trees. The admiral named the mountain Easter Mount and the country the Land of the True Cross.

He ordered them to drop the plumb-line, and they measured twenty-five fathoms. At sunset, about six leagues from the shore, we dropped anchor in nineteen fathoms, and it was a good clean anchorage. There we lay all that night. On Thursday morning we set sail and made straight for land, with the smaller ships leading, the water being seventeen, sixteen, fifteen, fourteen, thirteen, twelve, ten and nine fathoms deep, until we were half a league from the shore. Here we all cast anchor opposite a river mouth. It must have been more or less ten o'clock when we reached this anchorage.

From there we caught sight of men walking on the beaches. The small ships which arrived first said that they had seen some seven or eight of them. We let down the longboats and the skiffs. The captains of the other ships came straight to this flagship, where they had speech with the admiral. He sent Nicolau Coelho on shore to examine the river. As soon as the latter began to approach it, men came out on to the beach in groups of twos and threes, so that, when the longboat reached the river mouth, there were eighteen or twenty waiting.

They were dark brown and naked, and had no covering for their private parts, and they carried bows and arrows in their hands. They all came determinedly towards the boat. Nicolau Coelho made a sign to them to put down their bows, and they put them down. But he could not speak to them or make himself understood in any other way because of the waves which were breaking on the shore. He merely threw them a red cap, and a linen bonnet he had on his head, and a black hat. And one of them threw him a hat of large feathers with a small crown of red and grey feathers, like a parrot's. Another gave him a large bough covered with little white beads which looked like seed-pearls. I believe that the admiral is sending these articles to Your Majesty. After this, as it was late, the expedition returned to the ships, without succeeding in having further communication with them, because of the sea.

That night there was such a strong south-easterly wind and squalls that it dragged the ships out of their position, more especially the flagship. On Friday morning at about eight o'clock, by the pilot's advice, the captain ordered the anchors to be weighed and the sails hoisted. We went up the coast to the northwards with the longboats and skiffs tied to our sterns, to see if we could find a sheltered spot to anchor in where we could stay to take in water and wood. Not that these were lacking to us, but so as to be provided with everything now, in good time. At the hour when we set sail about sixty or seventy men had gradually come up and were seated near the river. We sailed on, and the admiral told the small ships to run under the shore and to slacken sails if they found a sufficiently protected spot for the ships.

Thus we sailed along the coast, and, ten leagues from the spot where we had weighed anchor, the aforesaid small ships found a ridge of rock which contained a very good, safe port with a very large entrance. So they went in and struck sails. The bigger ships came up behind them, and, a little while after sundown, they struck sails also, perhaps at a league from the rocks, and anchored in eleven fathoms.

Our pilot, Afonso Lopes, was in one of the small ships, and he received orders from the admiral to go in the skiff to take the soundings inside the port, for he was a lively and capable man for the work. He took up two of the men of the country from a canoe. They were young and well formed and one of them had a bow and six or seven arrows. There were many others on the shore with bows and arrows, but they did not use them. Later, in the evening, he took the two men to the flagship where they were received with great rejoicings and festivities.

They are of a dark brown, rather reddish colour. They have good well-made faces and noses. They go naked, with no sort of covering. They attach no more importance to covering up their private parts or leaving them uncovered than they do to showing their faces. They are very ingenuous in that matter. They both had holes in their lower lips and a bone in them as broad as the knuckles of a hand and as thick as a cotton spindle and sharp at one end like a bodkin. They put these bones in from inside the lip and the part which is placed between the lip and the teeth is made like a rook in chess. They fit them in in such a way that they do not hurt them nor hinder them talking or eating or drinking.

Their hair is straight. They shear their hair, but leave it a certain length, not cutting it to the roots, though they shave it above the ears. One of them had on a kind of wig covered with yellow feathers which ran round from behind the cavity of the skull, from temple to temple, and so to the back of the head; it must have been about a hand's breadth wide, was very close-set and thick, and covered his occiput and his ears. It was fastened, feather by feather, to his hair with a white paste like wax (but it was not wax), so that the wig was very round and full and regular, and did not need to be specially cleaned when the head was washed, only lifted up.

When they came, the admiral was seated on a chair, with a carpet at his feet instead of a dais. He was finely dressed, with a very big golden collar round his neck. Sancho de Toar, Simão de Miranda, Nicolau Coelho, Aires Correia, and the rest of us who were in the ship with him were seated on this carpet. Torches were lit. They entered. However, they made no gesture of courtesy or sign of a wish to speak to the admiral or any one else.

For all that, one of them gazed at the admiral's collar and began to point towards the land and then at the collar as if he wished to tell us that there was gold in the country. And he also looked at a silver candlestick and pointed at the land in the same way, and at the candlestick, as if there was silver there, too. We showed them a grey parrot the admiral had brought with him. They took it in their hands at once and pointed to the land, as if there were others there. We showed them a ram, but they took no notice of it. We showed them a hen, and they were almost afraid of it and did not want to take it in their hands; finally they did, but as if alarmed by it. We gave them things to eat: bread, boiled fish, comfits, sweetmeats, cakes, honey, dried figs. They would hardly eat anything of all this, and, if they tasted it, they spat it out at once. We brought them wine in a cup; they merely sipped it, did not like it at all, and did not want any more of it. We brought them water in a pitcher, and they each took a mouthful, but did not drink it; they just put it in their mouths and spat it out.

One of them saw the white beads of a rosary. He made a sign to be given them and was very pleased with them, and put them round his neck. Then he took them off and put them round his arm, pointing to the land, and again at the beads and at the captain's collar, as if he meant they would give gold for them.

We took it in this sense, because we preferred to. If, however, he was trying to tell us that he would take the beads and the collar as well, we did not choose to understand him, because we were not going to give it to him. Then he returned the beads to the man who had given them to him. Finally they lay on their backs on the carpet to sleep. They did not try to cover up their private parts in any way; these were uncircumcised and had their hairs well shaved and arranged.

The admiral ordered one of his cushions to be put under either of their heads, and the one in the wig took care that this should not be spoiled. They had a cloak spread over them. They consented to this, pulled it over themselves, and slept.

On the Saturday morning the admiral ordered the sails to be hoisted. We approached the entrance, which was very broad, and some six or seven fathoms in depth. All the ships entered it and anchored in five or six fathoms. The anchorage was so good and fine and safe inside that more than two hundred ships and vessels could lie in it. As soon as the ships had taken up their positions and anchored, all the captains came to this flagship. Now the admiral ordered Nicolau Coelho and Bartolomeu Dias to go on shore and take the two men and let them go with their bows and arrows. He also ordered each of them to be given a new shirt, a red bonnet, a rosary of white beads of bone, which they put on their arms, a varvel, and a bell. And he sent with them, to remain there, a banished youth of the household of Dom João Telo, named Afonso Ribeiro, who was to stay with them there and learn about their lives and their customs. I, also, was told to accompany Nicolau Coelho.

So we went towards the shore, as straight as an arrow. Nearly two hundred men came up at once there, all naked, with bows and arrows in their hands. The men we had brought with us made signs to them to retire and to put down their bows. They put them down, but they did not retire very far off. Still, they did put them down, and then those we had brought with us went out to them, and the banished youth as well. Once they had left us, they did not stop. They did not wait one for the other, but rather raced each other. They crossed a very full freshwater river there, wading in up to their thighs. And many others went with them so that they all ran to some groups of palm-trees on the other side of the river, where more again were waiting. There they stopped. The banished man took part in all this, accompanied by a man who had taken him into his care on the exile's leaving the boat and who went with him to the other side. However, they brought him back to us at once; the two we had brought with us came back with him; they were again naked and were not wearing their bonnets.

After this, many more began to arrive. They walked out into the sea towards the boats till they could go no farther. They brought gourds of water to us, and they took some barrels we had with us, filled them with water, and came back with them to the boats. Not that they got so far as absolutely to board the boats, but they came up near to them, and threw these things in, and we caught them. Then they asked us to give them something.

Nicolau Coelho had brought them varvels and bracelets. To some he gave a varvel and to others a bracelet, so that with that fleshing we nearly won them to our service. They gave us some of their bows and arrows in exchange for hats and linen bonnets and for anything we were willing to give them.

The two youths went away and we did not see them again.

Many of the men who were there—practically the greater part of them—had those sticks of bone in their lips. Some of them had their lips pierced and wore wooden pegs in the rifts which looked like the stoppers of wineskins. Others, again, wore three sticks, one in the middle and one at each side. Others were covered with a motley paint, that is to say, half of them was their own colour and half was covered with a black, slightly bluish paint. Others were painted in quarters.

There were three or four girls among them. These were very young and pretty, and had abundant long black hair down their backs. Their private parts were tightly knit, well raised, and half free from hairs; thus we were not at all ashamed to look at them.

It was not possible to speak to these people or understand them. There was such a chattering in uncouth speech that no one could be heard or understood. We made signs to them to go away. They did so, and went across the river. Then three or four of our men left the boats and filled I do not know how many water barrels we had brought with us, and so we returned. When they saw us going they made signs to us to come back. We went back, and they sent us the exile, for they did not wish him to remain there with them. He had had a small basin with him and two or three red bonnets, which were to be given to their lord, if they had one. They did not attempt to take anything from him, but sent him back with it all. However, Bartolomeu Dias told him to return and give them, in our sight, to the man who had first taken him into his care. After which he joined us again and we took him back with us.

The man who had taken him into his care was elderly, and he had feathers stuck all over his body as finery, so that he seemed covered with arrows like Saint Sebastian. Others had head-dresses of yellow feathers, or of red, or of green. One of the girls was all dyed from top to toe with that paint of theirs, and she certainly was so well made and so rounded, and her private parts (of which she made no privacy) so comely that many women in our country would be ashamed, if they saw such perfection, that theirs were not equally perfect. None of the men was circumcised, but all just as we are.

After these events we returned and they went away. In the afternoon the admiral went in his longboat and the other captains in theirs, to take their ease round the bay near the beach. Nobody went on shore, because the admiral did not wish to go, in spite of there being nobody there. He only left the boat, as we all did, on a big island there is in the bay, which runs a long way out at low tide. But the island is surrounded by water on every side, so that none can go there except by boat or swimming. There he and all of us took our ease for a good hour and a half. And some sailors had brought a net, and fished; they killed some small fish, but not many. At last we returned to the ships well after nightfall.

On the morning of Low Sunday the admiral decided to go to hear Mass and a sermon on that island. He commanded all the captains to take their places in the boats and come with him—which they did. He ordered a pavilion to be set up on the island and in it a finely adorned altar. Then he had Mass said in the presence of all of us. It was chanted by Friar Henrique and the responses were chanted by the other fathers and priests, who were all present. In my opinion every one heard the Mass with great joy and devoutness. The admiral stood on the Gospel side with the banner of the Order of the Knights of Christ, with which he had left Belém, uplifted before him.

When the Mass was finished, the priest removed his vestments and mounted a tall chair and we all cast ourselves down on the sands. He preached a solemn and edifying sermon on the Gospel. Finally he spoke of our coming hither and finding this land, as befitting to the Cross of the Knights of Christ in the service of which we were voyaging. This last observation was very timely, and increased our devotion.

At the time at which we were hearing the Mass and the sermon, there were more or less the same number of people on the beach as the day before. They had their bows and arrows and they were taking their ease. First they sat looking at us; but when the Mass was over, and while we were seated listening to the sermon, many of them got up and played on horns or shells and began to leap and dance, for a short while. Some of them got into two or three canoes they had there, which were not like those I had seen; they were merely three beams tied together. Four or five or as many as wished got into them, but they hardly moved off any distance from the land, only as far out as they could have waded.

After the sermon the admiral and all of us made our way towards the boats, with our banner uplifted. We embarked and all made towards the shore so as to pass along by where those people were. By the admiral's orders, Bartolomeu Dias went first in his skiff, to give them back a board from one of their canoes which the sea had borne away from them. We all followed him at a stone's throw. When they saw Bartolomeu Dias's skiff they all came down to the water's brink and walked as far out as they could. He made a sign to them to put down their bows. Many of them went and put them down on the ground immediately, but others did not put them down.

There was one of them there who was always telling the others to keep away. Not that it seemed to me that they had any respect or fear for him. This man who was keeping them away had his bows and arrows with him. He was dyed with red paint on chest, back, hips, thighs, and all down his legs, but his hypochondries, belly, and stomach were of his own colour. The paint was so red that the water did not eat into it nor wash it away. Rather was he redder than before when he left the water. One of our men left Bartolomeu Dias's skiff and went in among them, but they did not interfere with him, much less did they think of hurting him. Indeed, they gave him gourds of water, and made signs to those in the skiff to come on shore. So Bartolomeu Dias turned his course back towards the admiral. We went to our ships to eat, playing trumpets and bagpipes, and not troubling them further. They sat down on the beach again, and remained there for the time being.

The sea runs out a very long way at low tide on the island where we went to hear Mass and a sermon, and leaves a large expanse of sand and pebbles uncovered. When we were there some men had gone to look for shell-fish, but had not found any. They had, however, found some short thick prawns, one of which was so large and thick, however, that I can say I never saw such a big one. They had also found some cockle and mussel shells but none in a complete state.

Immediately we had eaten, all the captains came to our flagship by the admiral's orders. He took them aside, and I went with them. He asked us all if it seemed advisable to us to send the supply ship to Your Majesty, with the news of the discovery, so that this place might be better explored and known than we could know it, for we should have to continue our journey. Many opinions were given on the matter, but every one, or the majority, agreed in saying that the plan was excellent. On this resolution being taken, the admiral asked if it would then be advisable to take a pair of those men by force so as to send them to Your Majesty, and leave two of the exiles in their places. But they agreed that it was not necessary to take men by force, since those taken anywhere by force usually say of everything that they are asked about that they have it in their country. If we left two of the exiles there, they would give better, very much better information than those men would if we took them; for nobody can understand them, nor would it be a speedy matter for them to learn to speak well enough to be able to tell us nearly so much about that country as the exiles will when Your Majesty sends to them here. Therefore let us not think of taking any one away from here by force, nor of causing scandal. Rather let us conciliate and pacify them and merely leave the two exiles here when we go. All agreed to this, as it seemed the best course.

When we had finished, the admiral said we would go on shore from the boats. Then we could see what the river was like, and also we could take our ease. We all went armed on shore from the boats, taking the banner with us. They were there on the beach at the river mouth, towards which we were going; and before we arrived they had put down all their bows, as we had taught them to do, and signed to us to land. But, as soon as our prows ran aground, they immediately fled on to the other side of the river, which is no broader than a skittle alley. Immediately we had disembarked some of our men crossed the river and went in amongst them. Some of them waited there, others moved away. In any case, the fact of the matter was that both our people and theirs moved about in a single group. They gave away their bows and arrows for hats and linen caps and whatever else we could give them. So many of our men crossed the river and went in amongst them that they sheered off and moved away. Some went inland to where there were others. The admiral made two men carry him on their shoulders across the river and called every one back. There were not more people than usual on the other side. But when they saw the admiral calling up every one around him, those who were there came up with our people. It was not because they recognized him as the Master (indeed, it would seem that they neither understand nor conceive what this means), but because many of our people, had by then crossed over on to that side of the river. They spoke to us there and brought us several bows, and beads like the ones I have spoken of. These they exchanged for anything, so that our men took many bows, arrows, and beads back to the ship.

Then the admiral returned to the original bank of the river. Many at once flocked up to him. There you could see gallants painted red, or black, or in quarters, both on body and legs; they really looked well so. There were five or six women, too, among them. They were young, and their appearance was not bad, naked like that. One of them had a thigh painted with that black paint, from her knee to her hip and her buttocks, and otherwise she was of her natural colour. Another was painted round the backs of her knees and on the palms of her feet; her private parts were all naked and ingenuously uncovered, and there was no immodesty at all in this. There was also a young woman there carrying a child at her breast tied up in a cloth (of what material, I do not know) so that nothing could be seen of it but its little legs. But there was no cloth over the legs and the rest of its mother.

Next the admiral went along up the river which ran beside the shore. He waited there for an old man who came up carrying a canoe paddle. He went on speaking to us as long as the admiral was there. However, nobody ever understood him, nor did he us, in spite of all we asked him about gold; for we wished to know if there was any in that land. The old man's lip was so deeply pierced that a thick thumb could have been put into the hole. He wore a valueless green stone in the cleft, which closed it on the outside. The admiral ordered it to be taken out. The man said the devil knows what, and tried to put it in the admiral's mouth. We laughed a little and jested about that, but the admiral was displeased and left him. One of our men gave him an old hat for the stone; not that it was worth anything, but just as something to show. Afterwards the admiral had it, I·believe, to send to Your Majesty with the other things.

We went along to see the river, the water of which was good and plentiful. There are a few not very high palms along it with very good dates in them. We gathered and ate many. Then the admiral turned back to the river mouth where we had disembarked.

On the other bank of the river a number of them were dancing and making merry, opposite each other, but without touching hands—which they did very well. Diogo Dias, who was an exciseman in Sacavém before, an amusing pleasure-loving fellow, went over on to the other bank of the river, taking with him one of our bagpipe players with his bagpipe. He began dancing with them, taking them by the hand. They laughed and were pleased and danced very well with him to the sound of the bagpipe. After dancing he showed them many kinds of light turns on the ground, and a somersault; they laughed, it surprised them and pleased them. Yet, though he held their attention and diverted them in that way, they soon took fright as wild things from the hills do, and went away inland.

So the admiral and all of us crossed the river and went along the beach whilst the boats went along in near the land. We reached a big freshwater lake which is near the beach. All that coast is marshy inland and there is water in many places there. After we had crossed the river, seven or eight of them went in among the sailors returning to the boats. They took a shark Bartolomeu Dias had killed off with them—took it up, and threw it down on the beach.

As may be seen, whenever up to now they seemed partly tamed, in the passing of them from one hand to the other they fled away like birds from a net. One does not dare raise one's voice to them for fear they may sheer off even more. And yet we do everything that they wish, in order to tame them.

The admiral gave a red cap to the old man he had spoken to. But he, despite the talk he had had with the admiral and the cap he had been given, made away as soon as the admiral had taken leave and begun to cross the river; he would not come to the other side of the river. The other two whom the admiral had had in the ships and to whom he had given what has already been related never appeared again. I deduce from these facts that they are a savage, ignorant people, and for that very reason they are so timid. For all which, they are healthy and very clean. So that I am even surer that they are like the wild birds or animals whose feathers and hair the air makes finer than when they are domesticated, and whose bodies are as clean, as plump, and as beautiful as they could possibly be. Which all makes me suppose that these people lodge in no houses or dwellings. The air in which they are nurtured makes them what they are. We, at any rate, did not see any houses of theirs nor anything resembling such.

The admiral ordered the exile, Afonso Ribeiro, to go with them again. He went, and was there for some time, but returned in the evening, for they made him come. They would not allow him to stay there, though they gave him bows and arrows, and took nothing that was his. Actually, he said, one of them had taken some yellow beads he was wearing, and run off with them; but he had complained, and the others had pursued the thief, taken them from him, and given them back to the owner again. After which they had told him to go. He said that all he had seen amongst them were some little grottoes of green boughs and large fern leaves like those in the province of Entre Douro e Minho. So, just before nightfall, we returned to our ships to sleep.

On the Monday, after eating, we all went on shore to take in water. Many of them came up, but not so many as the other times. And they brought very few bows with them. They kept at some distance from us at first, but later, and little by little, some intermingled with us, rejoicing to see us and embracing us. They gave us bows for sheets of paper, or for an old cap, or anything else. Though there were others who sheered away at once. Things turned out so well that a good twenty or thirty of our people went with them to a place where there was a large band of them including girls and women. They brought away from there many bows and headpieces of feathers, some green and others yellow, of which I believe the admiral will send you specimens.

Those who went with them say that they were glad to have them there. We saw them closer to and more at our leisure that day because we had nearly all intermingled. Some were painted in quarters with those paints, others by halves, and others all over, like a tapestry. They all had their lips pierced; some had bones in them, though many had not. Some wore spiky green seedshells off some tree, which were coloured like chestnut shells, though they were much smaller. These were full of little red berries which, on being squeezed, squirted out a very red juice with which they dyed themselves. The more they wet themselves after being dyed with this red, the redder they become. They were all shaven to above the ears; likewise their eyelids and eyelashes were shaven. All their foreheads are painted with black paint from temple to temple. This gives the impression of their wearing a ribbon round them two inches wide.

The admiral ordered the exile, Afonso Ribeiro, and the two other exiles to mix in amongst them. And he told Diogo Dias, of Sacavém, to do the same, since he was a merry fellow and knew how to amuse them. He told the exiles to stay there that night. So they all went in amongst those people.

As they afterwards related, they went a good league and a half to a hamlet of nine or ten houses. They said those houses were each as big as this flagship. They were made of wooden planks sideways on, had roofs of straw, and were fairly high. Each enclosed a single space with no partitions, but a number of posts. High up from post to post ran nets, in which they slept. Down below they lit fires to warm themselves. Each house had two little doors, one at one end and one at the other. Our men said that thirty or forty people were lodged in each house, and they saw them there. They gave our men such food as they had, consisting of plenty of *inhame* [yams] and other seeds there are in the country which they eat. It was getting late, however, and they soon made all our men turn back, for they would not let any of them stay. They even wanted to come with them, our men said. Our men exchanged some varvels and other small things of little value which they had brought with them for some very large and beautiful red parrots and two small green ones, some caps of green feathers, and a cloth of many colours, also of feathers, a rather beautiful kind of material, as Your Majesty will see when you receive all these things, for the admiral says he is sending them to you. So our men came back, and we returned to our ships.

After our meal on the Tuesday we went on shore to fetch water and wood and to wash our clothes. There were sixty or seventy on the beach without bows or anything else when we arrived. As soon as we landed they came up to us straight away and did not try to escape. Also many others came up later, a good two hundred, and all without bows. They came in amongst us so readily that some of them helped us to carry out the wood and put it in the boats. They vied with our men in doing this, and it gave them great pleasure. Whilst we were gathering wood, two carpenters formed a large cross out of a piece which had been cut for the purpose the day before. Many of them came and stood around the carpenters. I believe they did so more to see the iron tool it was being made with than to see the cross. For they have nothing made of iron and cut their wood and sticks with stones fashioned like wedges which they fit into a stick between two laths which they tie up very tightly to make them secure. (The men who had been to their houses told us this, because they had seen it there.) They were by now so intimate with us that they almost hindered us in what we had to do.

The admiral sent the two exiles and Diogo Dias back to the village they had visited (or to others, if they should obtain knowledge of any others), telling them not to come back to the ship to sleep in any case, even if they were sent away. So they went off.

Whilst we were cutting timber in the wood, some parrots flew through the trees. Some were green, others grey, some big, others little. It seems to me, after this, that there must be many of them in this land, even though there cannot have been more than nine or ten of those I saw, if so many. We did not see any other birds on that occasion, except some rock pigeons which seemed to me considerably bigger than those in Portugal. Many say they saw doves, but I did not see them. However, as the trees are very tall and thick and of an infinite variety, I do not doubt but that there are many birds in this jungle. Near nightfall we returned to the ships with our wood.

I believe, Sire, that I have as yet given Your Majesty no account of how their bows and arrows are made. The bows are long and black, and the arrows are long also. Their heads are of sharpened cane, as Your Majesty will see from some which I believe the admiral will send you.

We did not go on land on the Wednesday, because the admiral spent the whole day in the supply ship having it cleared and as much as each could take of what was in it carried off to the other ships. But they came down on to the beach in great numbers as we saw from the ships. There must have been about three hundred of them according to Sancho de Toar, who went there. Diogo Dias and the exile, Afonso Ribeiro, whom the admiral had ordered the day before to sleep there under any circumstances, had come back after nightfall, because they did not want them to remain there. They brought green parrots with them and some black birds, almost like magpies, but different in that they had white beaks and short tails. When Sancho de Toar made for the ship again, some of them wanted to come with him. But he only allowed two youths to do so who were healthy and vigorous. He ordered them to be well cleaned and cared for that night. They ate all the portion they were given and he gave orders, as he said, for them to be provided with a bed with sheets. They slept and took their ease that night. Nothing else worth relating happened on that day.

On Thursday, the last day of April, we ate early, almost in the early morning, and then went on shore for more wood and water. Just as the admiral was thinking of leaving this ship, Sancho de Toar came up with his two guests. As he had not yet eaten, a table-cloth was put down for him and food came for him. So he ate. The guests each had a chair to themselves. They ate very heartily of everything that was given to them, especially cold boiled ham and rice. They were not given wine, because Sancho de Toar said they did not care for it.

After the meal we all got into the boat, and they did, too. A cabin boy gave one of them a large, very curly boar's tusk. He put it into his lip straight away upon taking it, and, since it would not stay fixed there, they gave him a little red wax. So he arranged the back part to stay firm and put the tusk into his lip so that the curve came out upwards. He was as pleased with it as if he had been given a wonderful jewel. As soon as we went on shore, he made off with it at once. And he did not appear there again.

When we left the boat there must have been eight or ten of them on the beach. In a little while more began to come. It seems to me that four hundred or four hundred and fifty must have come on that day. Some of them brought bows and arrows, but they gave them all away in exchange for caps or anything else they were given. They ate what we gave them and some of them drank wine, though others would not. But I should think that if they were made accustomed to it they would drink it very willingly. They were so healthy and well made and gallant in their paint that it was a pleasure to see them. They brought us as much wood as they could with the best will in the world and carried it out to the boats. By now they were tamer and more assured amongst us than we were amongst them.

The admiral went with us through the trees a little way till we came to a broad river of abundant waters from which we took in water. This, to our minds, was the same as the one which came down to the beach. We rested a little there and drank and took our ease on its banks amongst the trees. The number, size, and thickness of these trees and the variety of their foliage beggars calculation. There were many palm-trees there from which we gathered several fine dates.

The admiral had said when we had left the boat, that it would be best if we went straight to the cross which was leaning against a tree near the river ready to be set up on the next day, Friday; we ought then all to kneel and kiss it so that they could see the respect we had for it. We did so and signed to the ten or twelve who were there to do the same, and they at once all went and kissed it.

They seem to be such innocent people that, if we could understand their speech and they ours, they would immediately become Christians, seeing that, by all appearances, they do not understand about any faith. Therefore if the exiles who are to remain here learn their speech and understand them, I do not doubt but that they will follow that blessed path Your Majesty is desirous they should and become Christians and believe in our holy religion. May it please God to bring them to a knowledge of it, for truly these people are good and have a fine simplicity. Any stamp we wish may be easily printed on them, for the Lord has given them good bodies and good faces, like good men. I believe it was not without cause that He brought us here. Therefore Your Majesty who so greatly wishes to spread the Holy Catholic faith may look for their salvation. Pray God it may be accomplished with few difficulties.

They do not plough or breed cattle. There are no oxen here, nor goats, sheep, fowls, nor any other animal accustomed to live with man. They only eat this *inhame*, which is very plentiful here, and those seeds and

fruits that the earth and the trees give of themselves. Nevertheless, they
are of a finer, sturdier, and sleeker condition than we are for all the wheat
and vegetables we eat.

While they were there that day they danced and footed it continuously with our people to the sound of one of our tambourines, as if they
were more our friends than we theirs. If we signed to them asking them
if they wanted to come to our ships they at once came forward ready
to come. So that, if we had invited them all, they would all have come.
We did not, however, take more than four or five with us that night.
The admiral took two, Simão de Miranda, one whom he took as a page,
and Aires Gomes another, also as a page. One of those whom the admiral
took was one of the guests who had been brought him when we first
arrived here; on this day he came dressed in his shirt and his brother with
him. That night they were very handsomely treated, not only in the way
of food, but also to a bed with mattress and sheets, the better to tame
them.

To-day, Friday, 1st May, in the morning, we went on shore with our
banner. We made our way up the river and disembarked on the southern
bank at a place where it seemed best to us to set up the cross so that
it might be seen to the best advantage. There the admiral marked the
place for a pit to be made to plant the cross in. Whilst they were digging
this, he and all of us went for the cross, down the river to where it was.
We brought it from there as in a procession, with the friars and priests
singing in front of us. There were a quantity of people about, some
seventy or eighty. When they saw us coming, some of them went to help
us to support the cross. We passed over the river along by the beach.
We then went to set up the cross where it was to be at some two
bow-shots from the river. When we went to do this a good hundred and
fifty of those people and more came up. The cross was then planted, with
Your Majesty's arms and motto on it, which had before been fastened
to it, and they set up an altar by its side. Friar Henrique said Mass there,
and the singing and officiating was done by the others who have been
already mentioned. About fifty or sixty of the people of the place were
at the Mass all on their knees as we were. When the Gospel came and
we all stood with uplifted hands, they arose with us, lifted their hands,
and stayed like that till it was ended. After which they again sat, as we
did. When God's Body was elevated and we knelt, they all knelt and
lifted their hands as we did and were so silent that I assure Your Majesty
it much increased our devotion.

They stayed with us thus until the Communion was over. After the
Communion, the friars and priests communicated, as did the admiral

and some of us. Since the sun was very strong some of them arose whilst we were communicating, but others stayed to the end. Amongst those who stayed was a man of fifty or fifty-five years old—or rather he came up amongst those already there and also called others to come. He went in amongst them and spoke to them pointing to the altar and afterwards at Heaven, as if he were speaking to a good purpose. We took it so.

When Mass was over, the priest removed his vestments, and mounted on a chair near the altar in his surplice. He preached to us on the Gospel and about the Apostles whose day it was. At the end of the sermon he referred to the aim of your most holy and virtuous quest, which caused much devoutness.

The men who stayed all through the sermon looked at him as we did. The one I have spoken of called others to come. Some came and some went. At the end of the sermon Nicolau Coelho brought a number of tin crucifixes which had remained over from his former journey. It was thought well that those people should each have one hung round their necks. Friar Henrique stood beside the cross for this purpose. There he hung a crucifix round each of their necks, first making him kiss it and raise his hands. Many came for this. All who came, some forty or fifty, had crucifixes hung round their necks.

At last, a good hour after midday, we went to the ships to eat. The admiral took with him the man who had pointed out the altar and Heaven to the others; he also took a brother of his. The admiral did him much honour and gave him a Moorish shirt and his brother a shirt like the others had had.

My opinion and every one's opinion is that these people lack nothing to become completely Christian except understanding us; for they accepted as we do all they saw us do, which makes us consider that they have no idolatry or worship. I believe that if Your Majesty could send someone who could stay awhile here with them, they would all be persuaded and converted as Your Majesty desires. Therefore, if any one is coming out here, let him not omit to bring a clergyman to baptize them. For, by that time, they will have knowledge of our religion through the two exiles who are remaining with them, who also communicated to-day.

Only one woman came with those who were with us to-day. She was young and stayed throughout the Mass. We gave her a cloth to cover herself with and put it around her. But she did not pull it down to cover herself when she sat down. Thus, Sire, the innocence of Adam himself was not greater than these people's, as concerns the shame of the body. Your Majesty will judge if people who live in such innocence could be converted or no if they were taught the things that belong to their salvation.

Our last action was to go and kiss the cross in their presence. We then took our leave and went to eat.

I think, Sire, that two cabin-boys will also stay with the exiles we are leaving here, for they escaped to land in the skiff to-night and have not returned again. We think, I say, that they will stay, because, if God be willing, we are taking our departure from here in the morning.

It appears to me, Sire, that the coast of this country must be a good twenty or twenty-five leagues in length from the most southerly point we saw to the most northerly point we can see from this port. In some parts there are great banks along by the shore, some of which are red and some white; inland it is all flat and very full of large woods. All the coastal country from one point to the other is very flat and very beautiful. As to the jungle, it seemed very large to us seen from the sea; for, look as we would, we could see nothing but land and woods, and the land seemed very extensive. Till now we have been unable to learn if there is gold or silver or any other kind of metal or iron there; we have seen none. However, the air of the country is very healthful, fresh, and as temperate as that of Entre Douro e Minho; we have found the two climates alike at this season. There is a great plenty, an infinitude of waters. The country is so well-favoured that if it were rightly cultivated it would yield everything, because of its waters.

For all that, the best fruit that could be gathered hence would be, it seems to me, the salvation of these people. That should be the chief seed for Your Majesty to scatter here. It would be enough reason, even if this was only a rest-house on the voyage to Calicut. How much more so will it be if there is a will to accomplish and perform in this land what Your Majesty so greatly desires, which is the spreading of our holy religion.

Thus I have given Your Majesty an account of what I have seen in this land. If at some length, Your Majesty will pardon me, since my desire to tell you all made me relate it with such minuteness. And since, Sire, Your Majesty may be sure of my very faithful service in my present duties as in whatever may do you service, I beg of you as a signal favour that you send for Jorge de Ossório, my son-in-law, from the island of São Tomé—I should take this as great kindness from you.

I kiss Your Majesty's hands.

From this Pôrto-Seguro, in Your Majesty's island of Vera Cruz, to-day, Friday, 1st May 1500.

PEDRO VAZ DE CAMINHA.

EUGENIO DE SALAZAR
born c.1530

*Little is known about Salazar except that he was a judge with a distin-
guished career in the Spanish colonial lawcourts of Tenerife, Hispaniola,
Guatemala, and Mexico. His literary remains consist of some allegorical
poems and a number of entertaining "literary" letters replete with
untranslatable puns. This one, written to a friend in Spain, describes
Salazar's voyage with his wife, Doña Catalina, and family, from Tenerife
to Santo Domingo, where he was to take up a new judicial assignment.*

*The vessel Salazar traveled in was small, old, and commanded by a
relatively inexperienced captain. The crew numbered thirty. Salazar's
tribulations were probably a bit worse than average for a crossing like
this, but not a great deal worse.*

The letter has been translated by John H. Parry.

To the Licentiate Miranda de Ron

[*1573*]

Qui navigant mare, enarrant pericula ejus. Those who go to sea may
speak of the perils of the deep; and since I have just had to make a sea
voyage, for my sins, I write to tell you about my maritime sufferings;
though I must admit that they included (thank God) no pirates or
shipwrecks.

I was in the island of Tenerife when my new appointment came
through, and I had to make my own arrangements for getting to Hispaniola. I inquired about sailings, and eventually booked passage, at
great expense, in a ship called the *Nuestra Señora de los Remedios*—
better by name than by nature, as it turned out. Her master assured me
that she was a roomy ship, a good sailer, seaworthy, sound in frames and
members, well rigged and well manned. Accordingly, on the day we were
to sail and at the hour of embarkation, Doña Catalina and I, with all

our household, presented ourselves on the bank of the Styx. Charon, with his skiff, met us there, ferried us out to the ship, and left us on board. We were given, as a great privilege, a tiny cabin, about two feet by three by three; and packed in there, the movement of the sea upset our heads and stomachs so horribly that we all turned white as ghosts and began to bring up our very souls. In plain words, we were seasick; we vomited, we gagged, we shot out of our mouths everything which had gone in during the last two days; we endured by turns cold depressing phlegm, bitter burning choler, thick and heavy melancholy. There we lay, without seeing the sun or the moon; we never opened our eyes, or changed our clothes, or moved, until the third day. Then, lying in the darkness, I was startled by a voice nearby which cried out, "Blessed be the light of day, and the Holy True Cross, and the Lord of Truth, and the Holy Trinity; blessed be the day and the Lord who makes it; blessed be the day and the Lord who sends it"; and then the voice recited the prayers, Our Father and Hail Mary; and then said, "Amen. God give us good weather and a prosperous voyage; may the ship make a good passage, Sir Captain, and master, and all our good company, amen; so let us make, let us make a good voyage; God give your worships good day, gentlemen aft and forward." I was somewhat reassured when I heard this, and said to my wife, "Madam, though I fear we may be in the Devil's house, I still hear talk of God. I will get up and go out, and see what is happening—whether we are moving, or being carried away." So I dressed as well as I could, and crawled out of the whale's belly or closet in which we lay. I discovered that we were riding on what some people call a wooden horse, or a timber nag, or a flying pig; though to me it looked more like a town, a city even. It was certainly not the city of God that the sainted Augustine talked about; I saw no churches, nor courts of justice: nobody says mass there, nor do the inhabitants live by the laws of reason. It is a long narrow city, sharp and pointed at one end, wider at the other, like the pier of a bridge; it has its streets, open spaces and dwellings; it is encircled by its walls—that is to say, its planking; at one end it has its forecastle, with more than ten thousand knights in barracks, and at the other its citadel, so strong and firmly built that a puff of wind could tear it from its foundations and tip it into the sea. It has its batteries, and a gunner to command them; it has chain-wales, foresail, fore topsail, main course, topsail and top-gallant, bonnet and second bonnet. It has a capstan, the bane of the sailors because of the labor of turning it, and of the passengers because of the noise it makes; one or two fountains, called pumps, the water from which is unfit for tongue and palate to taste, or nostrils to smell, or even eyes to see, for it comes out bubbling like Hell and stinking like the Devil. The dwellings are so closed-in, dark, and evil-smelling that they seem more like burial vaults or charnelhouses. The entrances to these dwellings are openings in the deck, which they call companionways or hatches, and anyone who goes through them can say goodbye to the order, the comfort and the pleasant smells of dwellings on the earth; since, indeed, these lodgings seem to be the caves of Hell (even if they are not so in fact) it is only natural that those who enter them should do so through holes in the ground, as if they were being buried. There is such a complicated network of ropes and rigging on every side that the men inside it are like hens or capons being carried to market in grass or netting coops.

There are trees in the city, not fragrant with gums and aromatic spices, but greased with fish-oil and stinking tallow. There are running rivers, not of sweet, clear, flowing water, but of turbid filth; full not of grains of gold like the Cibao or the Tagus, but of grains of very singular pearl—enormous lice, so big that sometimes they are seasick and vomit bits of apprentice.

The ground of this city is such, that when it rains the soil is hard, but when the sun is hot the mud becomes soft and your feet stick to the ground so that you can hardly lift them. For game in the neighborhood, there are fine flights of cockroaches—they call them *curianas* here—and very good rat-hunting, the rats so fierce that when they are cornered they turn on the hunters like wild boars. The lamp and the *aguja* [compass needle] of the city are kept at night in the binnacle, which is a chest very like the commodes which some gentlemen keep in their bedrooms. The city is dark and gloomy, black without and pitch-black within; black ground and walls, dark inhabitants, swarthy officers. In sum, from bowsprit to bonaventure, from stem to stern, from hawse-holes to tiller-port, from the port chains to the starboard topgallant yardarms, from one side to the other, there is nothing for which a good word can be said; except indeed that, like women, it is a necessary evil.

There is in the city a whole community of people, all with their duties and dignities in strict (if not angelic) hierarchy. The wind is the real owner and master; the navigator governs as his deputy. The captain is responsible for defense; and though this captain is no Roldán, the ship is full of *roldanas* and has dashing *bigotes*—*bigotas* [pulleys; bowwaves (or mustaches)] even. The master has charge of the general work of the ship; the bo'su'n, of stowing and breaking out the cargo. The able seamen work the ship; the ordinary seamen help the able seamen; and the boys wait on the able seamen and the ordinary seamen, sweep and scrub, chant the prayers, and keep watch. The bo'su'n's mate is no Franciscan; he has charge of the ship's boat, sees to the water supply, and looks out for ways of cheating the passengers. The steward is responsible for the food. The caulker is the engineer who fortifies the city and secures the posterns through which the enemy might enter. The city has a surgeon-barber, to scrape the sailors' heads and bleed them when they need it. In general, the citizens of this city have as much faith, charity and friendship as sharks encountering in the sea.

I watched the navigator, the wind's lieutenant, seated in all his dignity upon his wooden throne; there he sits, an imitation Neptune, claiming to rule the sea and its waves. From time to time the sea unseats him with an unexpected lurch, so that he has to hold on to the pommel of his saddle to avoid a ducking in salt water. From there he rules and governs; "since Lanzarote out of Brittany came," no knight has been more faithfully served. Certainly I have never seen a gang of rogues obey more promptly, or earn their wages better, than these sailors; for when he shouts, "up forrard there," they come tumbling aft in a moment, like conjured demons, all their eyes on him and mouths open, awaiting his command. He gives the helmsman his orders—"Port your helm—steady as you go—bear up, don't let her yaw—steer sou'-sou'-west—watch out for that whipstaff or you'll break the hinge—keep her full and by." In the same way he orders the other seamen, "Hoist the t'gallant—lower the fore-topsail—hoist the foresail—haul the tack aboard—harden in the spritsail a little—set the main course—bend on the bonnet—pass the points through the eyelets, quick—take in the mizen—furl it on the yard in the gaskets—man the jeers—grease the halliard block—belay the halliard round the cleat—haul in the topsail sheets—two hands out on the yard arms—check away the halliards—ease to the lifts—grease the parral-trucks and ribs—rig the parrals, pass them round the mast—cast off the gaskets—hold onto that tack—gather aft the main sheet—turn up round the bitts—haul out the tack to windward—haul taut the bowline—haul up that buntline—clew up—haul away on that brace—turn up—make fast those backstays—well the clewlines—set up the stays—slip that toggle through and free the line—man the pump—make sure the collar is secure—work the brake till she sucks—clear the well—clear out the scuppers." When the master gives his orders it is astonishing to see the diligence and speed of the sailors in carrying them out. In a moment some will be up on the main crosstrees; some running up the ratlines holding on to the shrouds; some riding on the yards; some on the lower mastheads clinging to the caps, or swarming up the topmasts and hanging from the trucks; some on deck, hauling and gathering aft the sheets; some climbing and swinging about in the rigging like monkeys in the trees, or like the souls of those who fell from Heaven and stayed suspended in the air.

And when they hoist the sails—to hear the sailors singing as they work! for they hoist to the time of the chanty, like an ox-team straining in time to the leader's bell.

*   *   *

As the leader chants [a] couplet, all the others reply in chorus "oh—oh" and haul away at the jeers to hoist the sail.

I was fascinated to watch the city and the activities of its people, and intrigued to hear the marine (or malign) language, which I could follow no better than heathen gibberish; and I doubt whether Your Honor, for all his cleverness, has understood all the words and phrases I have written. If any have escaped you, look them up in Antonio's word-book; and if you don't find them, ask the sailors in the town of Illescas to translate, for this jargon is much used there; but don't ask me. I have only learnt the sounds of the words and cries of this complicated language, without understanding the meanings, and I chatter them like a cageful of parrots. It is enough for me to have made in forty days as much progress as the student from Lueches, who studied Latin four years at the University of Alcalá de Henares; when he presented himself to be ordained with the first tonsure, the Archbishop of Toledo asked him, "What does *Dominus vobiscum* mean?" and he in reply construed as follows: "*Do*, I give, *minus*, less, *vobiscum*, to fools." "That is my way too," said the Archbishop, "Go back to your books, and when you have learnt a little elementary grammar, we will give you the crown you ask," and he sent him away with his head still unshaven. But it is not surprising that I should know a little of this jargon; I have worked hard at it, and use it constantly in my ordinary speech. If I want something to drink I say "Let go the mainsheet"; if something to eat, "Set the spritsail." If I need a napkin I say "Open up the sail locker." When I go to the galley I say "The pots are boiling nicely"; when it is time for a meal, I call out "Set the mizen"; when a sailor lifts his elbow more than usual I say "Now she sucks"; and when somebody breaks wind—as often happens—I cry "Down aft, there!" So the use of this argot has become a habit which I cannot now break.

I would pass the time listening to the master giving his orders and watching the sailors carrying them out, until the sun was high in the sky; and then I would see the ship's boys emerge from the half-deck with a bundle of what they called table cloths; but alas, not white or handsomely embroidered. They spread out these damp and dirty lengths of canvas in the waist of the ship, and on them piled little mounds of broken biscuit, as white and clean as the cloths, so that the general effect was that of a cultivated field covered with little heaps of manure. They would then place on the "table" three or four big wooden platters full of beefbones without their marrow, with bits of parboiled sinew clinging to them. They call the platters *saleres*, and so have no need of saltcellars. When the meal is laid out, one of the boys sings out, "Table, table, Sir Captain and master and all the company, the table is set, the food is ready; the water is drawn for his honor the captain, the master and all our good company. Long live the King of Castile by land and by sea! Down with his enemies, cut off their heads! The man who won't say 'amen' shall have nothing to drink. All hands to dinner! If you don't come you won't eat." In a twinkling, out come pouring all the ship's company saying "amen," and sit on the deck round the "table," the bo'sun at the head and the gunner on his right, some crosslegged, some with legs stretched out, others squatting or reclining, or in any posture they choose; and without pausing for grace these knights of the round table whip out their knives or daggers—all sorts of weapons, made for killing pigs or skinning sheep or cutting purses—and fall upon those poor bones, stripping off nerves and muscles as if they had been practicing anatomy at Guadalupe or Valencia all their lives; and before you can say a *credo*, they leave them as clean and smooth as ivory. On Fridays and vigils they have beans cooked in salt water, on fast days salt cod. One of the boys takes round the mess-kettle and ladles out the drink ration— a little wine, poor thin stuff, not improved by the baptism it receives. And so, dining as best they can, without ceremony or order, they get up from the table still hungry.

The captain, the master, the navigator and the ship's notary dine at the same time, but at their own mess; and the passengers also eat at the same time, including myself and my family, for in this city you have to cook and eat when your neighbors do, otherwise you find no fire in the galley, and no sympathy. I have a squeamish stomach, and I found these arrangements very trying; but I had no choice but to eat when the others were hungry, or else to dine by myself on cold scraps, and sup in darkness. The galley—"pot island" as they call it—is a great scene of bustle and activity at meal times, and it is amazing how many hooks and kettles are crowded on to it; there are so many messes to be supplied, so many diners and so many different dinners. They all talk about food. One will say, "Oh for a bunch of Guadalajara grapes!"; another, "What would I give for a dish of Illescas berries?"; somebody else, "I should prefer some turnips from Somo de Sierra"; or again, "For me, a lettuce and an artichoke head from Medina del Campo"; and so they all belch out their longings for things they can't get. The worst longing is for something to drink; you are in the middle of the sea, surrounded by water, but they dole out the water for drinking by ounces, like apothecaries, and all the time you are dying of thirst from eating dried beef and food pickled in brine; for My Lady Sea won't keep or tolerate meat or fish unless they have tasted her salt. Even so, most of what you eat is half-rotten and stinking, like the disgusting fu-fu that the *bozal* [African] negroes eat. Even the water, when you can get it, is so foul that you have to close your eyes and hold your nose before you can swallow it. So we eat and drink in this delectable city. And if the food and drink are so exquisite, what of the social life? It is like an ant-heap; or, perhaps, a melting-pot. Men and women, young and old, clean and dirty, are all mixed up together, packed tight, cheek by jowl. The people around you will belch, or vomit, or break wind, or empty their bowels, while you are having your breakfast. You can't complain or accuse your neighbors of bad manners, because it is all allowed by the laws of the city. Whenever you stand on the open deck, a sea is sure to come aboard to visit and kiss your feet; it fills your boots with water, and when they dry they are caked with salt, so that the leather cracks and burns in the sun. If you want to walk the deck for exercise, you have to get two sailors to take your arms, like a village bride; if you don't, you will end up with your feet in the air and your head in the scuppers. If you want to relieve yourself—leave it to Vargas! You have to hang out over the sea like a cat-burglar clinging to a wall. You have to placate the sun and its twelve signs, the moon and the other planets, commend yourself to all of them, and take a firm grip of the wooden horse's mane; for if you let go, he will throw you and you will never ride him again. The perilous perch and the splashing of the sea are both discouraging to your purpose, and your only hope is to dose yourself with purgatives.

There is always music in the city: the sighing of the wind and the roaring of the sea as the waves strike the ship.

If there are women on board (and no city is without them) what a caterwauling they make with every lurch of the ship! "Mother of God, put me back on shore!" but the shore is a thousand miles away. If it rains in torrents, there are, it is true, roofs and doorways for the people to shelter; if the sun beats down, enough to melt the masts, there are shady places where you can escape it, and food and drink (of sorts) to refresh you. But if you are becalmed in the midst of the sea, the victuals running out and no water left to drink, then indeed you have need of comfort; the ship rolling night and day; your seasickness, which you thought you had left behind, returning; your head swimming; then there is no recourse but prayer, till the wind gets up again. When the sails are filled, and drawing well, they are a beautiful sight; but when the wind draws ahead, and the canvas slats against the masts, and the ship can make no headway, then life in her becomes a misery. If the navigator is inexperienced, and does not know when to look out for the land, or how to avoid reefs and shoals, you may seem one minute to be sailing in open water, and the next be fast aground, filling with water and about to drown. If the ship is a sluggish sailer, as ours was, she will hardly move with the wind before the beam. The other ships in company must constantly haul their luff, lie to and wait for her, or else take her in tow. But when she has a fair wind on the beam she will forge ahead, heeling well over to the wind; and we are all seasick once again.

Everything in the city is dark by day and pitch-black by night; but in the first watch of the night, after supper (which is announced in the same way as dinner), the city is reminded of God by the voice of the boy who sets the lamp in the binnacle. He cries, "Amen, and God give us good-night, Sir Captain, master and all the company." After that, two boys come on deck and say prayers, *Pater Noster, Ave Maria* and *Salve Regina.* Then they take their places to watch the hour-glass, and chant, "Blessed was the hour when God was born, Saint Mary who bore him and Saint John who baptized him. The watch is set, the glass is running. We shall make a good passage, if God wills." When the sand has run through the glass, the boy on watch sings out, "That which is past was good, better is that which is to come. One glass is gone, the second is running; more will run, if God wills; keep a good count, for a prosperous voyage; up forward there, attention and keep a good watch." The look-outs in the bows reply with a shout, or rather a grunt, to show that they are awake. This is done for each glass, that is, every half-hour, until morning. At midnight the boy calls the men who are to keep the middle watch. He shouts "Turn out, turn out, the watch; turn out, turn out, hurry along, the navigator's watch; time is up, show a leg, turn out, turn out." The rest of us sit up till then; but after midnight we can no longer keep our eyes open, and we all go off to the accommodation allotted to us. I creep into my little hutch with my family, and we doze fitfully, to the sound of the waves pounding the ship. All night we rock about as if we were sleeping in hammocks; for anyone who travels in a ship, even if he is a hundred years old, must go back to his cradle, and sometimes he is rocked so thoroughly that the cradle overturns and he ends up in a heap with cradles and seachests on top of him.

We sailed on alone for the first six days; for the eight other ships which left Santa Cruz harbor in Tenerife in our company all disobeyed the instructions which the judge of the *Contratación de Indias* sent us, and each went off on his own during the first night. What pleasure can a man have on board a solitary ship at sea? No land in sight, nothing but lowering sky and heaving water; he travels in a blue-green world, the ground dark and deep and far below, without seeming to move, without seeing even the wake of another ship, always surrounded by the same

horizon, the same at night as in the morning, the same today as yesterday, no change, no incident. What interest can such a journey hold?
How can he escape the boredom and misery of such a journey and such
a lodging?

It is pleasant to travel on land, well mounted and with money in your
purse. You ride for a while on the flat, then climb a hill and go down
into the valley on the other side; you ford a running river and cross a
pasture full of cattle; you raise your eyes and watch the birds flying above
you; you meet all kinds of people by the way and ask the news of the
places they have come from. You overtake two Franciscan friars, staves
in their hands, skirts tucked into their girdles, riding the donkeys of the
seraphic tradition, and they give you "Good-day and thanks be to God."
Then, here comes a Jeronymite father on a good trotting mule, his feet
in wooden stirrups, a bottle of wine and a piece of good ham in his
saddle-bag. There will be a pleasant encounter with some fresh village
wench going to town scented with pennyroyal and marjoram, and you
call out to her, "Would you like company, my dear?" Or you may meet
a traveling whore wrapped up in a cloak, her little red shoes peeping
below the hem, riding a hired mule, her pimp walking beside her. A
peasant will sell you a fine hare to make a fricassée; or you may buy a
brace of partridge from a hunter. You see in the distance the town where
you intend to sleep or stop for a meal, and already feel rested and
refreshed by the sight. If today you stay in some village where the food
is scanty and bad, tomorrow you may be in a hospitable and well-
provided city. One day you will dine at an inn kept by some knife-scarred
ruffian, brought up to banditry and become a trooper of the *Santa
Hermandad;* he will sell you cat for hare, billy-goat for mutton, old horse
for beef and watered vinegar for wine; yet the same day you may sup
with a host who gives you bread for bread and wine for wine. If, where
you lodge tonight, your hostess is old, dirty, quarrelsome, querulous and
mean, tomorrow you will do better and find a younger one, clean,
cheerful, gracious, liberal, pious and attractive; and you will forget the
bad lodging of the previous day. But at sea there is no hope that the road,
or the host, or the lodging will improve; everything grows steadily worse;
the ship labors more and more and the food gets scantier and nastier
every day.

On the first Saturday out, we were still alone; and on that day, at the
usual time for prayers, we held a solemn service in the city, a *Salve* and
sung litany with full choir. They put up an altar with images and lighted
candles. First of all the master asked, "Are we all here?" and the
company responded "God be with us." Then the master: "Let us say
the *Salve*, and pray for a good passage; we will say the *Salve*, and our

passage will be prosperous." So we begin the *Salve;* we all sing together, we all give tongue—no fancy harmonies, but all eight keys at once. Sailors are great dividers; just as they divide each wind into its eight points, so they break the eight notes of the scale into thirty-two, diverse and perverse, resonant and dissonant. Our *Salve* was a storm, a hurricane of music. If God and his Holy Mother, and the saints to whom we prayed, attended to our singing voices and not to our hearts and spirits, it would have done us no good to beg for mercies with such raucous bawling. After the *Salve* and the litany the master, who acts as priest, continues: "Let us say together the creed in honor of the holy apostles, and ask them to intercede with Our Lord Jesus Christ, to give us a safe passage"; and all who believe the creed recite it. Then one of the boys, who acts as acolyte: "Let us say the Hail Mary for ship and company"; the other boys respond, "May our prayer be received," and we all recite the *Ave.* At the end the boys all stand and say, "Amen, God give us good-night, etc."; and so ends the celebration for the day. This takes place every Saturday.

The next day, Sunday, in the morning, we sighted our vice-commodore, and she saluted us (for we were the flagship of the convoy); and we sailed contentedly in company for the next fifteen days. Then one morning the look-out at the masthead called out "Sail ho!" This caused great excitement, for to merchantmen, sailing as we were without escorting warships, any stranger is an object of suspicion; even the smallest may turn out to be a pirate. "Two sail!" cried the look-out, and doubled our alarm; "three sail"; and by this time we were convinced that we had to deal with corsairs. You may imagine how I felt, with my wife and children all on board. The gunner began to give the orders to clear away for action; the ports were opened for the falcons and culverins; the guns were loaded and run out, and small arms were mustered. Women began to shriek, "Why did we come here, miserable wretches? What-ever possessed us, to go to sea?" Those who had money or jewels ran to hide them in the dark corners of the frames and futtock-timbers. We all stood by with our weapons at the best points of vantage we could find—for the ship had no nettings—all ready to defend ourselves; and we could see the same preparations on board the vice-commodore. The three ships drew closer, on a course to intercept. One was a very big ship, and caused much ironical speculation among the sailors. Some said she must be the Florentine galleon; "More likely the *Bucentaur,*" said others; "She's the English *Minion*"—"No, she looks like the *Cacafogo* out of Portugal." Although there were three of them, they approached us at first as cautiously as we them; but when they came near enough for recognition, they saw who we were, and we recognized them as friends. They were, in fact, three of the missing ships of our own convoy; and all our fears vanished in the pleasure of reunion. Even so, the sea played us another trick. The big ship closed us to speak, and as she bore down on us her helmsman misjudged his distance, and put us all in fear of our lives. His beakhead collided with our poop and holed us on the quarter so that the water poured in. Our city might have been taken by the forces of the sea within the hour; but our people ran to work and soon repaired the damage. It was an alarming experience for Doña Catalina, whose cabin was in that part of the ship. When the volleys of abuse had died down (though not the pounding of hearts) our fears were washed away with the salt water, and we greeted one another with relief and joy. The three stragglers promised to keep in sight of the flagship in future. We hoisted our flag at the mainmast head, mounted a crossbow on the poop, and lit our stern lantern at night. The other ships, when they closed us to salute, took care to come up under our lee; and all our subsequent operations were carried out in good order. The form of greeting each morning is a call on the bosun's whistle and a shout, "Good passage to you!"—bellowed loud enough to frighten anyone out of their wits; to hear this "Good voyage" unexpectedly one day would be enough to give one a bad voyage for a year of days.

We ran with a stiff northeast wind for the next four days; and the navigator and the sailors began to sniff the land, like asses scenting fresh grass. It is like watching a play, at this time, to see the navigator taking his Pole Star sights; to see him level his cross-staff, adjust the transom, align it on the star, and produce an answer to the nearest three or four thousand leagues. He repeats the performance with the midday sun; takes his astrolabe, squints up at the sun, tries to catch the rays in the pinhole sight, and fiddles about endlessly with the instrument; looks up his almanac; and finally makes his own guess at the sun's altitude. Sometimes he overestimates by a thousand degrees or so; sometimes he puts his figure so low that it would take a thousand years to complete the voyage. They always went to great pains to prevent the passengers knowing the observed position and the distance the ship had made good. I found this secretiveness very irritating, until I discovered the reason for it; that they never really knew the answer themselves, or understood the process. They were very sensible, as I had to admit, in keeping the details of this crazy guesswork to themselves. Their readings of altitudes are rough approximations, give or take a degree or so; yet on the scale of their instruments the difference of a pin's head can produce an error of five hundred miles in the observed position. It is yet another demonstration of the inscrutable omnipotence of God, that the vital and intricate art of navigation should be left to the dull wits and ham fists of these tarpaulin louts. You hear them discussing it among themselves: "How many degrees does Your Honor make it?" and one says "Sixteen," another "Barely twenty," and yet a third, "Thirteen and a half." Then somebody will ask, "How far does Your Honor reckon we are from land?"; one answers, "I make it forty leagues," another, "A hundred and fifty," and the third says, "This morning I reckoned ninety-two." It may be three or it may be three hundred; they never agree, either with one another or with the truth.

In the middle of all these vain conflicting arguments among masters, navigators, and sailors who claimed to be graduates in the art, on the twenty-sixth day out, God be praised, we sighted land; and how much lovelier the land appears from the sea than the sea from the land! We saw Deseada—appropriately named—and Antigua, and set our course between them, leaving Deseada to the east. We ploughed on; Santa Cruz hove in sight to windward, and we passed it at a distance; we reached San Juan del Puerto Rico and coasted along the shore some way, keeping a careful watch on Cape Bermejo, which is a notorious haunt of pirates. We recognized Mona and the Monitos—easy to identify, even at a distance—looked for Santa Catalina but failed to see it; and eventually came in sight of Saona, the land of the blessed saint, and blessed sight to us. All this time we were repeatedly soaked by downpours of rain; but we made light of them, and thought ourselves lucky to have been spared hurricanes.

In the general rejoicing at the sight of our destination, the navigator—the wind's lieutenant and deputy, who held the reins of the wooden horse—grew a little careless, and allowed the ship to fall away to leeward of the harbor, so that we had to beat with short boards in order to regain lost ground; with the result that it was already dark when we arrived off the mouth of the Santo Domingo River. We had to feel our way in, sounding as we went, and find a sheltered place to anchor for the night. We should certainly have looked very foolish if we had allowed ourselves to drift into danger, and perhaps founder, so close to the shore. We let go two anchors and a good length of cable and (thanks be to God) rode safely through the night. I did not allow any of my people ashore, because the authorities had not yet been warned of my arrival. It was the most disagreeable night of the whole voyage, for the ship pitched abominably, and our stomachs rebelled as they had done on the first day out. But I will weary you no more with the perils and miseries of the sea; except to ask you to imagine, if life can be so uncomfortable with fair winds and a relatively calm sea, what it must be like to experience contrary winds, encounters with pirates, mountainous seas and howling gales. Let men stay on firm ground and leave the sea to the fishes, say I.

Next day at dawn our city came to life, with much opening of trunks and shaking out of clean shirts and fine clothes. All the people dressed in their best, especially the ladies, who came out on deck so pink and white, so neat, so crimped, curled and adorned, that they looked like the granddaughters of the women we had seen each day at sea.

The master went ashore, and I sent my servant with a message of greeting to the president of the court. Boats began to put out to the ship; and since there was a head wind and the ship had to be warped up the river, my family and I went ashore directly in a launch which they sent for us. So we reached the longed-for land, and the city of Santo Domingo. We were kindly welcomed; and after a few days' rest I took my seat on the Bench, and here I stay for as long as God wills, without any desire to cross the sea again. I hope soon to hear that you also have the appointment which you deserve. Doña Catalina and the children send their respects and best wishes.

BERNAL DIAZ DEL CASTILLO
c.1492–c.1581

This free-lance soldier and historian was born in the town of Medina del Campo, 75 miles northwest of Madrid. His father was a reputable local magistrate who managed to give his son a decent education. But there was little money, and at the age of 22 the youth set out for the New World to seek his fortune—quite literally, for rumors of gold in unbeliev-able abundance were circulating around Europe.

After adventures with various bands of explorers in Panama, Cuba, and Florida, in 1517 and 1518 Diaz took part in several very dangerous forays into Mexico, where many of his fellows were killed by the natives. Having not yet laid his hands on much gold, and indeed suffering from severe poverty, in 1519 he joined in Cuba a promising expedition com-manded by Hernando Cortés aiming deep into Mexico and focusing singlemindedly on gold.

This expedition, consisting of 508 soldiers, 100 sailors, and 16 horses, encountered strenuous hardships and bloody opposition, and during the two years required by "the conquest of Mexico" Diaz was badly

*wounded several times by Indian arrows. Finally humbling the Aztec
king Montezuma and extorting his fealty to Spain, Cortés carried away
as much gold as possible but gave his soldiers much less than they had
thought their due. The ravages he and his men committed in Mexico
have become legendary but are not less believable for that reason.*

*This selection from Diaz's account of the campaign, preserved in
manuscript but not published until 1632, is translated by A. P.
Maudsley.*

From THE TRUE HISTORY OF THE CONQUEST OF NEW SPAIN (1632)

CHAPTER XXIV

On Holy Thursday, in the year 1519, we arrived with all the fleet at the
Port of San Juan de Ulúa, and as the Pilot Alaminos knew the place well
from having come there with Juan de Grijalva he at once ordered the
vessels to drop anchor where they would be safe from the northerly gales.
The flagship hoisted her royal standards and pennants, and within half
an hour of anchoring, two large canoes came out to us, full of Mexican
Indians. Seeing the big ship with the standards flying they knew that
it was there they must go to speak with the captain; so they went direct
to the flagship and going on board asked who was the Tatuan which in
their language means the chief. Doña Marina who understood the
language well, pointed him out. Then the Indians paid many marks of
respect to Cortés, according to their usage, and bade him welcome, and
said that their lord, a servant of the great Montezuma, had sent them
to ask what kind of men we were, and of what we were in search, and
added that if we were in need of anything for ourselves or the ships, that
we should tell them and they would supply it. Our Cortés thanked them
through the two interpreters, Aguilar and Doña Marina, and ordered
food and wine to be given them and some blue beads, and after they
had drunk he told them that we came to see them and to trade with
them and that our arrival in their country should cause them no uneasiness but be looked on by them as fortunate. The messengers returned
on shore well content, and the next day, which was Good Friday, we
disembarked with the horses and guns, on some sand hills which rise to
a considerable height, for there was no level land, nothing but sand

dunes; and the artilleryman Mesa placed the guns in position to the best of his judgment. Then we set up an altar where mass was said and we made huts and shelters for Cortés and the captains, and three hundred of the soldiers brought wood and made huts for themselves and we placed the horses where they would be safe and in this way was Good Friday passed.

The next day, Saturday, Easter Eve, many Indians arrived sent by a chief who was a governor under Montezuma, named Pitalpitoque (whom we afterwards called Ovandillo), and they brought axes and dressed wood for the huts of the Captain Cortés and the other ranchos near to it, and covered them with large cloths on account of the strength of the sun, for the heat was very great—and they brought fowls, and maize cakes and plums, which were then in season, and I think that they brought some gold jewels, and they presented all these things to Cortés; and said that the next day a governor would come and would bring more food. Cortés thanked them heartily and ordered them to be given certain articles in exchange with which they went away well content. The next day, Easter Sunday, the governor whom they spoke of arrived. His name was Tendile, a man of affairs, and he brought with him Pitalpitoque who was also a man of importance amongst the natives and there followed them many Indians with presents of fowls and vegetables. Tendile ordered these people to stand aside on a hillock and with much humility he made three obeisances to Cortés according to their custom, and then to all the soldiers who were standing around. Cortés bade them welcome through our interpreters and embraced them and asked them to wait, as he wished presently to speak to them. Meanwhile he ordered an altar to be made as well as it could be done in the time, and Fray Bartolomé de Olmedo, who was a fine singer, chanted Mass, and Padre Juan Diaz assisted, and the two governors and the other chiefs who were with them looked on. When Mass was over, Cortés and some of our captains and the two Indian Officers of the great Montezuma dined together. When the tables had been cleared away—Cortés went aside with the two Caciques and our two interpreters and explained to them that we were Christians and vassals of the greatest lord on earth who had many great princes as his vassals and servants, and that it was at his orders that we had come to this country, because for many years he had heard rumours about the country and the great prince who ruled it. That he wished to be friends with this prince and to tell him many things in the name of the Emperor which things, when he knew and understood them, would please him greatly. Moreover, he wished to trade with their prince and his Indians in good friendship, and he wanted to know where this prince would wish that they should meet so that they might confer together. Tendile replied somewhat proudly, and said:—"You have only just now arrived and you already ask to speak with our prince; accept now this present which we give you in his name, and afterwards you will tell me what you think fitting." With that he took out a *petaca*—which is a sort of chest, many articles of gold beautifully and richly worked and ordered ten loads of white cloth made of cotton and feathers to be brought, wonderful things to see, besides quantities of food. Cortés received it all with smiles in a gracious manner and gave in return, beads of twisted glass and other small beads from Spain, and he begged them to send to their towns to ask the people to come and trade with us as he had brought many beads to exchange for gold, and they replied that they would do as he asked. Cortés then ordered his servants to bring an arm-chair, richly carved and inlaid and some *margaritas*, stones with many intricate designs in them, and a string of twisted glass beads packed in cotton scented with musk and a crimson cap with a golden medal engraved with a figure of St. George on horseback, lance in hand, slaying the dragon, and he told Tendile that he should send the chair to his prince Montezuma, so that he could be seated in it when he, Cortés, came to see and speak with him, and that he should place the cap on his head, and that the stones and all the other things were presents from our lord the King, as a sign of his friendship, for he was aware that Montezuma was a great prince, and Cortés asked that a day and a place might be named where he could go to see Montezuma. Tendile received the present and said that his lord Montezuma was such a great prince that it would please him to know our great King, and that he would carry the present to him at once and bring back a reply.

It appears that Tendile brought with him some clever painters such as they had in Mexico and ordered them to make pictures true to nature of the face and body of Cortés and all his captains, and of the soldiers, ships, sails and horses, and of Doña Marina and Aguilar, even of the two greyhounds, and the cannon and cannon balls, and all of the army we had brought with us, and he carried the pictures to his master. Cortés ordered our gunners to load the lombards with a great charge of powder so that they should make a great noise when they were fired off, and he told Pedro de Alvarado that he and all the horsemen should get ready so that these servants of Montezuma might see them gallop and told them to attach little bells to the horses' breastplates. Cortés also mounted his horse and said: "It would be well if we could gallop on these sand dunes but they will observe that even when on foot we get stuck in the sand—let us go out to the beach when the tide is low and gallop two and two"—and to Pedro de Alvarado whose sorrel coloured mare was a great galloper, and very handy, he gave charge of all the horsemen.

All this was carried out in the presence of the two ambassadors, and so that they should see the cannon fired, Cortés made as though he wished again to speak to them and a number of other chieftains, and the lombards were fired off, and as it was quite still at that moment, the stones went flying through the forest resounding with a great din, and the two governors and all the other Indians were frightened by things so new to them, and ordered the painters to record them so that Montezuma might see. It happened that one of the soldiers had a helmet half gilt but somewhat rusty, and this Tendile noticed, for he was the more forward of the two ambassadors, and said that he wished to see it as it was like one that they possessed which had been left to them by their ancestors of the race from which they had sprung, and that it had been placed on the head of their god—Huichilobos, and that their prince Montezuma would like to see this helmet. So it was given to him, and Cortes said to them that as he wished to know whether the gold of this country was the same as that we find in our rivers, they could return the helmet filled with grains of gold so that he could send it to our great Emperor. After this, Tendile bade farewell to Cortés and to all of us and after many expressions of regard from Cortés he took leave of him and said he would return with a reply without delay. After Tendile had departed we found out that besides being an Indian employed in matters of great importance, Tendile was the most active of the servants whom his master, Montezuma, had in his employ, and he went with all haste and narrated everything to his prince, and showed him the pictures which had been painted and the present which Cortés had sent. When the great Montezuma gazed on it he was struck with admiration and received it on his part with satisfaction. When he examined the helmet and that which was on his Huichilobos, he felt convinced that we belonged to the race which, as his forefathers had foretold, would come to rule over that land.

CHAPTER LXIV

The Great Montezuma was about forty years old, of good height and well proportioned, slender and spare of flesh, not very swarthy, but of the natural colour and shade of an Indian. He did not wear his hair long, but so as just to cover his ears, his scanty black beard was well shaped and thin. His face was somewhat long, but cheerful, and he had good eyes and showed in his appearance and manner both tenderness and, when necessary, gravity. He was very neat and clean and bathed once every day in the afternoon. He had many women as mistresses, daughters of Chieftains, and he had two great Cacicas as his legitimate wives.

He was free from unnatural offences. The clothes that he wore one day, he did not put on again until four days later. He had over two hundred chieftains in his guard, in other rooms close to his own, not that all were meant to converse with him, but only one or another, and when they went to speak to him they were obliged to take off their rich mantles and put on others of little worth, but they had to be clean, and they had to enter barefoot with their eyes lowered to the ground, and not to look up in his face. And they made him three obeisances, and said: "Lord, my Lord, my Great Lord," before they came up to him, and then they made their report and with a few words he dismissed them, and on taking leave they did not turn their backs, but kept their faces towards him with their eyes to the ground, and they did not turn their backs until they left the room. I noticed another thing, that when other great chiefs came from distant lands about disputes or business, when they reached the apartments of the Great Montezuma, they had to come barefoot and with poor mantles, and they might not enter directly into the Palace, but had to loiter about a little on one side of the Palace door, for to enter hurriedly was considered to be disrespectful.

For each meal, over thirty different dishes were prepared by his cooks according to their ways and usage, and they placed small pottery braziers beneath the dishes so that they should not get cold. They prepared more than three hundred plates of the food that Montezuma was going to eat, and more than a thousand for the guard. When he was going to eat, Montezuma would sometimes go out with his chiefs and stewards, and they would point out to him which dish was best, and of what birds and other things it was composed, and as they advised him, so he would eat, but it was not often that he would go out to see the food, and then merely as a pastime.

I have heard it said that they were wont to cook for him the flesh of young boys, but as he had such a variety of dishes, made of so many things, we could not succeed in seeing if they were of human flesh or of other things, for they daily cooked fowls, turkeys, pheasants, native partridges, quail, tame and wild ducks, venison, wild boar, reed birds, pigeons, hares and rabbits, and many sorts of birds and other things which are bred in this country, and they are so numerous that I cannot finish naming them in a hurry; so we had no insight into it, but I know for certain that after our Captain censured the sacrifice of human beings, and the eating of their flesh, he ordered that such food should not be prepared for him thenceforth.

Let us cease speaking of this and return to the way things were served to him at meal times. It was in this way: if it was cold they made up a large fire of live coals of a firewood made from the bark of trees which did not give off any smoke, and the scent of the bark from which the fire was made was very fragrant, and so that it should not give off more heat than he required, they placed in front of it a sort of screen adorned with figures of idols worked in gold. He was seated on a low stool, soft and richly worked, and the table, which was also low, was made in the same style as the seats, and on it they placed the table cloths of white cloth and some rather long napkins of the same material. Four very beautiful cleanly women brought water for his hands in a sort of deep basin which they call *xicales*, and they held others like plates below to catch the water, and they brought him towels. And two other women brought him tortilla bread, and as soon as he began to eat they placed before him a sort of wooden screen painted over with gold, so that no one should watch him eating. Then the four women stood aside, and four great chieftains who were old men came and stood beside them, and with these Montezuma now and then conversed, and asked them questions, and as a great favour he would give to each of these elders a dish of what to him tasted best. They say that these elders were his near relations, and were his counsellors and judges of law suits, and the dishes and food which Montezuma gave them they ate standing up with much reverence and without looking at his face. He was served on Cholula earthenware either red or black. While he was at his meal the men of his guard who were in the rooms near to that of Montezuma, never dreamed of making any noise or speaking aloud. They brought him fruit of all the different kinds that the land produced, but he ate very little of it. From time to time they brought him, in cup-shaped vessels of pure gold, a certain drink made from cacao, and the women served this drink to him with great reverence.

Sometimes at meal-times there were present some very ugly hump-backs, very small of stature and their bodies almost broken in half, who are their jesters, and other Indians, who must have been buffoons, who told him witty sayings, and others who sang and danced, for Montezuma was fond of pleasure and song, and to these he ordered to be given what was left of the food and the jugs of cacao. Then the same four women removed the table cloths, and with much ceremony they brought water for his hands. And Montezuma talked with those four old chieftains about things that interested him, and they took leave of him with the great reverence in which they held him, and he remained to repose.

As soon as the Great Montezuma had dined, all the men of the Guard had their meal and as many more of the other house servants, and it seems to me that they brought out over a thousand dishes of the food of which I have spoken, and then over two thousand jugs of cacao all frothed up, as they make it in Mexico, and a limitless quantity of fruit, so that with his women and female servants and bread makers and cacao makers his expenses must have been very great.

Let us cease talking about the expenses and the food for his household and let us speak of the Stewards and the Treasurers and the stores and pantries and of those who had charge of the houses where the maize was stored. I say that there would be so much to write about, each thing by itself, that I should not know where to begin, but we stood astonished at the excellent arrangements and the great abundance of provisions that he had in all, but I must add what I had forgotten, for it is as well to go back and relate it, and that is, that while Montezuma was at table eating, as I have described, there were waiting on him two other graceful women to bring him tortillas, kneaded with eggs and other sustaining ingredients, and these tortillas were very white, and they were brought on plates covered with clean napkins, and they also brought him another kind of bread, like long balls kneaded with other kinds of sustaining food, and *pan pachol*, for so they call it in this country, which is a sort of wafer. There were also placed on the table three tubes much painted and gilded, which held *liquidambar* mixed with certain herbs which they call *tabaco*, and when he had finished eating, after they had danced before him and sung and the table was removed, he inhaled the smoke from one of those tubes, but he took very little of it and with that he fell asleep.

I remember that at that time his steward was a great Cacique to whom we gave the name of Tápia, and he kept the accounts of all the revenue that was brought to Montezuma, in his books which were made of paper which they call *amal*, and he had a great house full of these books. Now we must leave the books and the accounts for it is outside our story, and say how Montezuma had two houses full of every sort of arms, many of them richly adorned with gold and precious stones. There were shields great and small, and a sort of broad-swords, and others like two-handed swords set with stone knives which cut much better than our swords, and lances longer than ours are, with a fathom of blade with many knives set in it, which even when they are driven into a buckler or shield do not come out, in fact they cut like razors so that they can shave their heads with them. There were very good bows and arrows and double-pointed lances and others with one point, as well as their throwing sticks, and many slings and round stones shaped by hand, and some sort of artful shields which are so made that they can be rolled up, so as not to be in the way when they are not fighting, and when they are needed for fighting they let them fall down, and they cover the body from top to toe. There was also much quilted cotton armour, richly ornamented on the outside with many coloured feathers, used as devices and distin-

guishing marks, and there were casques or helmets made of wood and
bone, also highly decorated with feathers on the outside, and there were
other arms of other makes which, so as to avoid prolixity, I will not
describe, and there were artisans who were skilled in such things and
worked at them, and stewards who had charge of the arms.

Let us leave this and proceed to the Aviary, and I am forced to abstain
from enumerating every kind of bird that was there and its peculiarity,
for there was everything from the Royal Eagle and other smaller eagles,
and many other birds of great size, down to tiny birds of many-coloured
plumage, also the birds from which they take the rich plumage which
they use in their green feather work. The birds which have these feathers
are about the size of the magpies in Spain, they are called in this country
Quezales, and there are other birds which have feathers of five colours—
green, red, white, yellow and blue; I don't remember what they are
called; then there were parrots of many different colours, and there are
so many of them that I forget their names, not to mention the beautifully marked ducks and other larger ones like them. From all these birds
they plucked the feathers when the time was right to do so, and the
feathers grew again. All the birds that I have spoken about breed in these
houses, and in the setting season certain Indian men and women who
look after the birds, place the eggs under them and clean the nests and
feed them, so that each kind of bird has its proper food. In this house
that I have spoken of there is a great tank of fresh water and in it there
are other sorts of birds with long stilted legs, with body, wings and tail
all red; I don't know their names, but in the Island of Cuba they are
called *Ypiris*, and there are others something like them, and there are
also in that tank many other kinds of birds which always live in the
water.

Let us leave this and go on to another great house, where they keep
many idols, and they say that they are their fierce gods, and with them
many kinds of carnivorous beasts of prey, tigers and two kinds of lions,
and animals something like wolves and foxes, and other smaller carnivorous animals, and all these carnivores they feed with flesh, and the
greater number of them breed in the house. They give them as food deer
and fowls, dogs and other things which they are used to hunt, and I have
heard it said that they feed them on the bodies of the Indians who have
been sacrificed. It is in this way: you have already heard me say that
when they sacrifice a wretched Indian they saw open the chest with
stone knives and hasten to tear out the palpitating heart and blood, and
offer it to their idols, in whose name the sacrifice is made. Then they
cut off the thighs, arms and head and eat the former at feasts and
banquets, and the head they hang up on some beams, and the body of

the man sacrificed is not eaten but given to these fierce animals. They also have in that cursed house many vipers and poisonous snakes which carry on their tails things that sound like bells. These are the worst vipers of all, and they keep them in jars and great pottery vessels with many feathers, and there they lay their eggs and rear their young, and they give them to eat the bodies of the Indians who have been sacrificed, and the flesh of dogs which they are in the habit of breeding.

Let me speak now of the infernal noise when the lions and tigers roared and the jackals and the foxes howled and the serpents hissed, it was horrible to listen to and it seemed like a hell. Let us go on and speak of the skilled workmen Montezuma employed all of whom attended to the work of his houses, I say that he had as many as he wished for. We must not forget the gardens of flowers and sweet-scented trees, and the many kinds that there were of them, and the arrangement of them and the walks, and the ponds and tanks of fresh water where the water entered at one end and flowed out of the other; and the baths which he had there, and the variety of small birds that nested in the branches, and the medicinal and useful herbs that were in the gardens. It was a wonder to see, and to take care of it there were many gardeners. Everything was made in masonry and well cemented, baths and walks and closets, and apartments like summer houses where they danced and sang. There was as much to be seen in these gardens as there was everywhere else, and we could not tire of witnessing his great power. Thus as a consequence of so many crafts being practised among them, a large number of skilled Indians were employed.

ANDREW MARVELL
1621–1678

Although he spent four years traveling on the Continent, mastering French, Italian, Spanish, and Dutch while there, Marvell can hardly be designated a traveler, for his interests were always more theological-political and philosophic than social or geographical.

He was the son of a clergyman in Yorkshire and was educated at the University of Cambridge. During the English Civil Wars he leaned

toward Cromwell's cause and sympathized with Dissenters who exiled
themselves, to the Bermudas and elsewhere, to escape "prelate's rage."
Always fond of pastoral imagining, he here supplies a boatload of reli-
gious refugees with a compensatory "eternal spring" in the New World.
Although not published until posthumously in 1681, "Bermudas" was
written in the 1650's.

BERMUDAS
(1681)

> Where the remote Bermudas ride,
> In th' ocean's bosom unespied,
> From a small boat that rowed along,
> The listening winds received this song:
> "What should we do but sing His praise,
> That led us through the watery maze
> Unto an isle so long unknown,
> And yet far kinder than our own?
> Where He the huge sea monsters wracks,
> That lift the deep upon their backs;
> He lands us on a grassy stage,
> Safe from the storms, and prelate's rage.
> He gave us this eternal spring
> Which here enamels everything,
> And sends the fowls to us in care,
> On daily visits through the air;
> He hangs in shades the orange bright,
> Like golden lamps in a green night,
> And does in the pomegranates close
> Jewels more rich than Ormus shows;
> He makes the figs our mouths to meet,
> And throws the melons at our feet;
> But apples plants of such a price,
> No tree could ever bear them twice;
> With cedars, chosen by His hand,
> From Lebanon, He stores the land;
> And makes the hollow seas, that roar,
> Proclaim the ambergris on shore;
> He cast (of which we rather boast)

The Gospel's pearl upon our coast,
And in these rocks for us did frame
A temple, where to sound His name.
O! let our voice His praise exalt,
Till it arrive at heaven's vault,
Which, thence (perhaps) rebounding, may
Echo beyond the Mexique Bay."
    Thus sung they in the English boat,
An holy and a cheerful note;
And all the way, to guide their chime,
With falling oars they kept the time.

PART II
THE EIGHTEENTH CENTURY
AND THE GRAND TOUR

T heir roads were appalling and their inns were nasty and they had neither passenger liners nor railway trains. But people in the eighteenth century often seem more travel-minded than those at other times when actual travel was more inviting. If you read novels then you traveled vicariously with the numerous characters discovering their destinies on the road. The age is full of traveling heroes enmeshed in journey-plots, like Fielding's Joseph Andrews and Tom Jones, Smollett's Roderick Random and Humphry Clinker and Matthew Bramble, and countless other avatars of the Continental picaro. Furthermore, almost every author of consequence produced one overt travel book, from Defoe and Addison to Fielding and Smollett, Johnson, Boswell, and Sterne. Not to mention numerous essayistic and philosophic performances evoking the mode of the travel book, like Swift's *Gulliver's Travels*, Voltaire's *Candide*, Johnson's *Rasselas*, and Oliver Goldsmith's *Citizen of the World*.

Perhaps the curious awareness of travel in the eighteenth century was due in part to the unquestioned acceptance of the psychological theory of John Locke, as set forth in his influential *Essay Concerning Human Understanding* (1690). No one doubted Locke's argument that knowledge comes entirely through the external senses, and from the mind's later contemplation of materials laid up in the memory as a result of sense experience. This meant that external conditions become crucial and that what one knows results entirely from the impingement on one's receptors of physical stimuli. Thus you could "exhaust" one environment by taking in all it had to offer, necessitating a change of scene. Travel, therefore, became something like an obligation for the person conscientious about developing the mind and accumulating knowledge. A typical eighteenth-century sensibility, consequently, is that of the sturdy commonsense observer, skeptical of internal promptings or vague, noncommunicable emanations but loyal to a constantly changing panorama of external data, wandering about foreign parts and reporting his findings about human nature (or hers, Lady Mary Wortley Montagu being exemplary) for the benefit of stay-at-homes. *Observation* becomes virtually a duty, and *extensive* observation as well. As Johnson says at the beginning of *The Vanity of Human Wishes,*

> Let Observation, with extensive view,
> Survey mankind from China to Peru,

and only then venture generalizations about life.

Curiosity about the actual social and political behavior of people externally observed was what now propelled the traveler. The medical student Oliver Goldsmith did Europe on the cheap, wandering about for a year and supporting himself by gambling, playing the flute, and "borrowing." Afterwards he made some money from a poem about European national characteristics titled *The Traveller.* But the well-off did it differently. If you had money and wanted to acquire some culture (or if your father wanted you to), you would be likely to spend some time on a Grand Tour of the Continent. The Grand Tour was a convention of the high-middle and upper classes; it flourished between the time of the Restoration, in 1660, and the arrival of mass rail travel around 1825. By the second and third quarters of the eighteenth century the Grand Tour was well established. In 1772 one observer wrote: "Where one Englishman travelled in the reigns of the first two Georges [i.e., 1714 to 1760], ten now go on a grand tour. Indeed, to such a pitch is the spirit of travelling come in the kingdom, that there is scarce a citizen of large fortune but takes a flying view of France, Italy, and Germany in a summer's excursion." But most Grand Tours lasted longer than a summer: a year was about average, and some, like Lord Chesterfield's son, were sent touring abroad for as long as five years to acquire, as Chesterfield never tired of saying, "the Graces." Most Grand Tourists were young men, just extruded from one of the universities, and most were accompanied by a tutor or governor, probably a minister of the Church of England, which every university teacher had to be.

Setting out from London, the typical Grand Tourist would cross the Channel between Dover and Calais. On the French side he would (like Laurence Sterne) bargain for a coach which he would sell upon leaving the Continent. He would then head for Paris and Versailles and Fontainbleau, attracted by court, salon, gallery, cuisine, and women (heavy surveillance work here for the tutor). It was in Paris that the traveler might undertake "lessons"—in French conversation (including gestures), dancing, fencing, and riding, with perhaps drawing thrown in. From Paris he would proceed to Geneva and experience Switzerland for a while. Thence, crossing one scary mountain pass or another, to northern Italy, where the traveler might spend months in Florence studying

Renaissance sculpture and painting before moving on to Venice to do the same. From there, one went on to Rome for the great neo-classical experience among the ruins. A visit to Naples (music appreciation) might follow. Naples was an attraction also because of the newly ex-cavated archeological sites of Herculaneum and Pompeii, as well as the thrills offered by the ascent of the smoking Vesuvius. After all this, back you would go through the Alps again, stopping this time perhaps at Innsbruck and taking in life in the local German duchies before visiting Berlin and Potsdam. The studious might be drawn to the universities at Munich or Heidelberg for a while. Then slowly back to England by way of Holland and Flanders, with more gallery-going and art apprecia-tion.

In addition to providing a sort of peripatetic liberal education, the Grand Tour resembled later consumer tourism in offering an opportu-nity for buying things not available at home and testifying, when dis-played later, to the purchaser's culture and sophistication. The conscientious Grand Tourist returned with crates of pictures and art books, sculptures, medals, and other objects of *virtu*, which found their places in his display cabinets, drawing room, and gardens. The Grand Tour so automatically connoted aristocratic wealth, freedom, and taste that even today the concept retains much snob-appeal. Witness the presence in virtually every mass-travel company's summer offerings of a group tour labeled the "Grand Tour." One, advertised on slick paper in full color, reproduces the eighteenth-century route (London–Dover–Calais–Switzerland–Florence–Venice–Rome–Germany–Paris) but compresses the whole thing to 18 days. (A version extended to 21 days earns the designation "The Golden Grand.") The clichés are the same as those visited on the original Grand Tour (Doges' Palace, Michelan-gelo's *David*, the Forum and Colosseum, the Leaning Tower, etc.), and indeed even in the eighteenth century voices were raised against the Grand Tour's lack of adventurousness. "The tour of Europe is a paltry thing," one critic noted; it is, he said, "a tame, uniform, unvaried prospect." Better to travel in less-frequented places, like America, Africa, or Asia. And it is true that the Grand Tour very seldom encour-aged original inquiry or fresh perceptions. It rather invited all the stan-dard preconceptions about national characteristics, confirming the traveler's prejudices and teaching little except the generalizations set forth by books like Jean Gailhard's *Compleat Gentleman* (1678): "French courteous. Spanish lordly. Italian amorous. German clownish."

But if the Grand Tour was largely a possession of the privileged, it would be a mistake to imagine that it was very comfortable. Much of it was hard work, like abandoning your coach while crossing the Alps and having it broken down and carried by mules while you, wrapped in furs, made your way over snow and ice on foot or, if you were lucky, in a chair carried by blasphemous porters. Dr. Charles Burney, the British historian of music, was proceeding through Germany in 1772. One evening at seven he set out by wagon from a town in the Saarland, planning to arrive in Berlin by midnight. It was cold and rainy, and

> before nine o'clock it rained violently, and became so dark that the postillion lost his way and descended from his place in the front of the wagon in order to feel for it with his hands. But being unable to distinguish any track of a carriage, he mounted again, and in driving on at a venture got into a bog on a bleak and barren heath, where we were stuck fast, and obliged to remain from eleven o'clock at night till near six the next morning. . . . It never ceased raining and blowing the whole night. The cold was intense, and nothing could be more forlorn than my condition.

Grand, we can infer, is most accurately interpreted as *costly* or *extensive*. Hardly *luxurious*.

LADY MARY WORTLEY MONTAGU
1689–1762

In 1712 the studious and sprightly Mary Pierrepont married the dull Edward Wortley Montagu, Member of Parliament. He was made ambassador to Turkey four years later, and from 1716 to 1718 Lady Mary sent home hundreds of letters, most addressed to her sister, describing the Turkish scene and focusing especially on the condition of women in Islam. She threw herself enthusiastically into the task of understanding the Turks, and to this end even learned Turkish. When she returned to England in 1718, she gradually persuaded British physicians to adopt the Turkish practice of inoculating against smallpox, hitherto the curse of the age.

While she was absent in Turkey, her old friend Alexander Pope— already fond of her as a fellow wit and satirist—wrote her some amorous letters. The quarrel which developed between them thus seemed the more strange, and by 1727 they were bitter enemies, although Pope kept her portrait always on his wall. His quotable abuse has conveyed to posterity an excessively dark image of her. She loved being abroad, and after traveling in France and Italy, in 1738 she settled in the Italian Lake country in the town of Lovere—"It is the Tunbridge of this part of the world"—where she spent her time reading novels shipped to her from England and writing pointed, gossipy letters back. As she lay dying her last words are said to have been: "It's been very interesting. Yes, it's all been very interesting."

To The Lady—.

Adrianople, April 1, [1717]

I am now got into a new world, where everything I see appears to me a change of scene; and I write to your ladyship with some content of mind, hoping at least that you will find the charm of novelty in my letters, and no longer reproach me, that I tell you nothing extraordinary.

I won't trouble you with a relation of our tedious journey; but I must not omit what I saw remarkable at Sophia, one of the most beautiful towns in the Turkish empire, and famous for its hot baths, that are resorted to both for diversion and health. I stopped here one day on purpose to see them. Designing to go *incognita*, I hired a Turkish coach. These voitures are not at all like ours, but much more convenient for the country, the heat being so great that glasses would be very troublesome. They are made a good deal in the manner of the Dutch coaches, having wooden lattices painted and gilded; the inside being painted with baskets and nosegays of flowers, intermixed commonly with little poetical mottoes. They are covered all over with scarlet cloth, lined with silk, and very often richly embroidered and fringed. This covering entirely hides the persons in them, but may be thrown back at pleasure, and the ladies peep through the lattices. They hold four people very conveniently, seated on cushions, but not raised.

In one of these covered waggons, I went to the bagnio about ten o'clock. It was already full of women. It is built of stone, in the shape of a dome, with no windows but in the roof, which gives light enough. There were five of these domes joined together, the outmost being less than the rest, and serving only as a hall, where the portress stood at the door. Ladies of quality generally give this woman the value of a crown or ten shillings; and I did not forget that ceremony. The next room is a very large one paved with marble, and all round it, raised, two sofas of marble, one above another. There were four fountains of cold water in this room, falling first into marble basins, and then running on the floor in little channels made for that purpose, which carried the streams into the next room, something less than this, with the same sort of marble sofas, but so hot with steams of sulphur proceeding from the baths joining to it, it was impossible to stay there with one's clothes on. The two other domes were the hot baths, one of which had cocks of cold water turning into it, to temper it to what degree of warmth the bathers have a mind to.

I was in my travelling habit, which is a riding dress, and certainly appeared very extraordinary to them. Yet there was not one of them that shewed the least surprise or impertinent curiosity, but received me with all the obliging civility possible. I know no European court where the ladies would have behaved themselves in so polite a manner to a stranger. I believe in the whole there were two hundred women, and yet none of those disdainful smiles, or satiric whispers, that never fail in our assemblies when anybody appears that is not dressed exactly in the fashion. They repeated over and over to me, "Uzelle, pék uzelle," which is nothing but Charming, very charming.—The first sofas were covered with cushions and rich carpets, on which sat the ladies; and on the second, their slaves behind them, but without any distinction of rank by their dress, all being in the state of nature, that is, in plain English, stark naked, without any beauty or defect concealed. Yet there was not the least wanton smile or immodest gesture amongst them. They walked and moved with the same majestic grace which Milton describes of our general mother. There were many amongst them as exactly proportioned as ever any goddess was drawn by the pencil of Guido or Titian, —and most of their skins shiningly white, only adorned by their beautiful hair divided into many tresses, hanging on their shoulders, braided either with pearl or ribbon, perfectly representing the figures of the Graces.

I was here convinced of the truth of a reflection I had often made, that if it was the fashion to go naked, the face would be hardly observed. I perceived that the ladies with the finest skins and most delicate shapes had the greatest share of my admiration, though their faces were sometimes less beautiful than those of their companions. To tell you the truth, I had wickedness enough to wish secretly that Mr. Jervas could have been there invisible. I fancy it would have very much improved his art, to see so many fine women naked, in different postures, some in conversation, some working, others drinking coffee or sherbet, and many negligently lying on their cushions, while their slaves (generally pretty girls of seventeen or eighteen) were employed in braiding their hair in several pretty fancies. In short, it is the women's coffee-house, where all the news of the town is told, scandal invented, &c.—They generally take this diversion once a week, and stay there at least four or five hours, without getting cold by immediate coming out of the hot bath into the cold room, which was very surprising to me. The lady that seemed the most considerable among them, entreated me to sit by her, and would fain have undressed me for the bath. I excused myself with some difficulty. They being all so earnest in persuading me, I was at last forced to open my shirt, and shew them my stays; which satisfied them very well, for, I saw, they believed I was so locked up in that machine, that it was not in my own power to open it, which contrivance they attributed to my husband.—I was charmed with their civility and beauty, and should have been very glad to pass more time with them; but Mr. W—resolving to pursue his journey the next morning early, I was in haste to see the ruins of Justinian's church, which did not afford me so agreeable a prospect as I had left, being little more than a heap of stones.

Adieu, madam: I am sure I have now entertained you with an account of such a sight as you never saw in your life, and what no book of travels could inform you of. 'Tis no less than death for a man to be found in one of these places.

To the Countess of Mar.

Adrianople, April 1, [1717].

I wish to God, dear sister, that you were as regular in letting me have the pleasure of knowing what passes on your side of the globe, as I am careful in endeavouring to amuse you by the account of all I see that I think you care to hear of. You content yourself with telling me over and over that the town is very dull: it may possibly be dull to you, when every day does not present you with something new; but for me that am in arrear at least two months' news, all that seems very stale with you would be fresh and sweet here. Pray let me into more particulars, and I will try to awaken your gratitude, by giving you a full and true relation of the novelties of this place, none of which would surprise you more than a sight of my person, as I am now in my Turkish habit, though I believe you would be of my opinion, that 'tis admirably becoming.—I intend to send you my picture; in the mean time accept of it here.

The first piece of my dress is a pair of drawers, very full, that reach to my shoes, and conceal the legs more modestly than your petticoats. They are of a thin rose-coloured damask, brocaded with silver flowers, my shoes are of white kid leather, embroidered with gold. Over this hangs my smock, of a fine white silk gauze, edged with embroidery. This smock has wide sleeves, hanging half way down the arm, and is closed at the neck with a diamond button; but the shape and colour of the bosom very well to be distinguished through it. The *antery* is a waistcoat, made close to the shape, of white and gold damask, with very long sleeves falling back, and fringed with deep gold fringe, and should have diamond or pearl buttons. My *caftan*, of the same stuff with my drawers, is a robe exactly fitted to my shape, and reaching to my feet, with very long strait falling sleeves. Over this is the girdle, of about four fingers broad, which all that can af'ord have entirely of diamonds or other precious stones; those who will not be at that expense, have it of exquisite embroidery on satin; but it must be fastened before with a clasp of diamonds. The *curdee* is a loose robe they throw off or put on according to the weather, being of a rich brocade (mine is green and gold), either lined with ermine or sables; the sleeves reach very little below the shoulders. The head-dress is composed of a cap, called *talpock*, which is in winter of fine velvet embroidered with pearls or diamonds, and in summer of a light shining silver stuff. This is fixed on one side of the head, hanging a little way down with a gold tassel, and bound on, either with a circle of diamonds (as I have seen several) or a rich embroidered handkerchief. On the other side of the head, the hair is laid flat; and here the ladies are at liberty to shew their fancies; some putting flowers, others a plume of heron's feathers, and, in short, what they please; but the most general fashion is a large *bouquet* of jewels, made like natural flowers; that is, the buds of pearl; the roses, of different coloured rubies; the jessamines, of diamonds; the jonquils, of topazes, &c., so well set and enamelled, 'tis hard to imagine anything of that kind so beautiful. The hair hangs at its full length behind, divided into tresses braided with pearl or ribbon, which is always in great quantity.

I never saw in my life so many fine heads of hair. I have counted a hundred and ten of the tresses of one lady's all natural; but it must be owned, that every beauty is more common here than with us. 'Tis surprising to see a young woman that is not very handsome. They have naturally the most beautiful complexion in the world, and generally large black eyes. I can assure you with great truth, that the court of England (though I believe it the fairest in Christendom) cannot shew so many beauties as are under our protection here. They generally shape their eyebrows; and the Greeks and Turks have a custom of putting round their eyes (on the inside) a black tincture, that, at a distance, or by candle-light, adds very much to the blackness of them. I fancy many of our ladies would be overjoyed to know this secret; but 'tis too visible by day. They dye their nails a rose-colour. I own, I cannot enough accustom myself to this fashion to find any beauty in it.

As to their mortality or good conduct, I can say, like Harlequin, that 'tis just as it is with you; and the Turkish ladies don't commit one sin the less for not being Christians. Now I am a little acquainted with their ways, I cannot forbear admiring either the exemplary discretion or extreme stupidity of all the writers that have given accounts of them. 'Tis very easy to see they have more liberty than we have. No woman, of what rank soever, being permitted to go into the streets without two muslins; one that covers her face all but her eyes, and another that hides the whole dress of her head, and hangs half way down her back, and their shapes are wholly concealed by a thing they call a *ferigee*, which no woman of any sort appears without; this has strait sleeves, that reach to their finger-ends, and it laps all round them, not unlike a riding-hood. In winter 'tis of cloth, and in summer plain stuff or silk. You may guess how effectually this disguises them, so that there is no distinguishing the great lady from her slave. 'Tis impossible for the most jealous husband to know his wife when he meets her; and no man dare either touch or follow a woman in the street.

This perpetual masquerade gives them entire liberty of following their inclinations without danger of discovery. The most usual method of intrigue is, to send an appointment to the lover to meet the lady at a Jew's shop, which are as notoriously convenient as our Indian-houses; and yet, even those who don't make use of them, do not scruple to go to buy pennyworths, and tumble over rich goods, which are chiefly to be found amongst that sort of people. The great ladies seldom let their gallants know who they are; and it is so difficult to find it out, that they can very seldom guess at her name they have corresponded with above half a year together. You may easily imagine the number of faithful wives very small in a country where they have nothing to fear from a lover's indiscretion, since we see so many that have the courage to expose themselves to that in this world, and all the threatened punishment of the next, which is never preached to the Turkish damsels. Neither have they much to apprehend from the resentment of their husbands; those ladies that are rich having all their money in their own hands, which they take with them upon a divorce, with an addition which he is obliged to give them.

Upon the whole, I look upon the Turkish women as the only free people in the empire: the very Divan pays a respect to them; and the Grand Signior himself, when a pasha is executed, never violates the privileges of the *harém* (or women's apartment), which remains un-searched and entire to the widow. They are queens of their slaves, whom the husband has no permission so much as to look upon, except it be an old woman or two that his lady chooses. 'Tis true their law permits them four wives; but there is no instance of a man of quality that makes use of this liberty, or of a woman of rank that would suffer it. When a husband happens to be inconstant (as those things will happen), he keeps his mistress in a house apart, and visits her as privately as he can, just as it is with you. Amongst all the great men here, I only know the *tefterdar* (*i.e.* treasurer), that keeps a number of she slaves for his own use (that is, on his own side of the house; for a slave once given to serve a lady is entirely at her disposal), and he is spoken of as a libertine, or what we should call a rake, and his wife won't see him, though she continues to live in his house.

Thus, you see, dear sister, the manners of mankind do not differ so widely as our voyage writers would make us believe. Perhaps it would be more entertaining to add a few surprising customs of my own invention; but nothing seems to me so agreeable as truth, and I believe nothing

so acceptable to you. I conclude with repeating the great truth of my being,
Dear sister, &c.

TO MRS. THISTLETHWAYTE.

Adrianople, April 1, [*1717*].

I can now tell dear Mrs. T. that I am safely arrived at the end of my very long journey. I will not tire you with the account of the many fatigues I have suffered. You would see something of what I see here; and a letter out of Turkey that has nothing extraordinary in it, would be as great a disappointment as my visitors will receive at London if I return thither without any rarities to shew them.

What shall I tell you of?—You never saw camels in your life; and, perhaps, the description of them will appear new to you: I can assure you the first sight of them was very much so to me; and, though I have seen hundreds of pictures of those animals, I never saw any that was resembling enough to give a true idea of them. I am going to make a bold observation, and possibly a false one, because nobody has ever made it before me; but I do take them to be of the stag kind; their legs, bodies and necks, are exactly shaped like them, and their colour very near the same. 'Tis true, they are much larger, being a great deal higher than a horse; and so swift, that, after the defeat of Peterwaradin, they far outran the swiftest horses, and brought the first news of the loss of the battle to Belgrade. They are never thoroughly tamed; the drivers take care to tie them one to another with strong ropes, fifty in string, led by an ass, on which the driver rides. I have seen three hundred in one caravan. They carry the third part more than any horse; but 'tis a particular art to load them, because of the hunch on their back. They seem to me very ugly creatures; their heads being ill-formed and disproportionated to their bodies. They carry all the burthens; and the beasts destined to the plough are buffaloes, an animal you are also unacquainted with. They are larger and more clumsy than an ox; they have short, black horns close to their heads, which grow turning backwards. They say this horn looks very beautiful when 'tis well polished. They are all black, with very short hair on their hides, and extremely little white eyes, that make them look like devils. The country people dye their tails, and the hair of their forehead, red, by way of ornament.

Horses are not put here to any laborious work, nor are they at all fit for it. They are beautiful and full of spirit, but generally little, and not so strong as the breed of colder countries; very gentle, with all their vivacity, swift and surefooted. I have a little white favourite that I would not part with on any terms; he prances under me with so much fire, you would think that I had a great deal of courage to dare to mount him; yet, I'll assure you, I never rid a horse in my life so much at my command. My side-saddle is the first was ever seen in this part of the world, and gazed at with as much wonder as the ship of Columbus was in America. Here are some birds held in a sort of religious reverence, and, for that reason, multiply prodigiously: turtles, on the account of their innocence; and storks, because they are supposed to make every winter the pilgrimage to Mecca. To say truth, they are the happiest subjects under the Turkish government, and are so sensible of their privileges, they walk the streets without fear, and generally build in the low parts of houses. Happy are those that are so distinquished. The vulgar Turks are perfectly persuaded that they will not be that year either attacked by fire or pestilence. I have the happiness of one of their sacred nests just under my chamber window.

Now I am talking of my chamber, I remember the description of the houses here would be as new to you as any of the birds or beasts. I suppose you have read in most of our accounts of Turkey that their houses are the most miserable pieces of building in the world. I can speak very learnedly on that subject, having been in so many of them; and I assure you 'tis no such thing. We are now lodging in a palace belonging to the Grand Signior. I really think the manner of building here very agreeable, and proper for the country. 'Tis true they are not at all solicitous to beautify the outsides of their houses, and they are generally built of wood, which I own is the cause of many inconveniences; but this is not to be charged on the ill-taste of the people, but the oppression of the government. Every house upon the death of its master is at the Grand Signior's disposal; and, therefore, no man cares to make a great expense, which he is not sure his family will be the better for. All their design is to build a house commodious, and that will last their lives; and they are very indifferent if it falls down the year after.

Every house, great and small, is divided into two distinct parts, which only join together by a narrow passage. The first house has a large court before it, and open galleries all round it, which is to me a thing very agreeable. This gallery leads to all the chambers, which are commonly large, and with two rows of windows, the first being of painted glass: they seldom build above two stories, each of which has such galleries. The stairs are broad, and not often above thirty steps. This is the house belonging to the lord, and the adjoining one is called the *harém*, that

is, the ladies' apartment (for the name of *seraglio* is peculiar to the
Grand Signior); it has also a gallery running round it towards the garden,
to which all the windows are turned, and the same number of chambers
as the other, but more gay and splendid, both in painting and furniture.
The second row of windows is very low, with grates like those of convents; the rooms are all spread with Persian carpets, and raised at one
end of them (my chamber is raised at both ends) about two feet. This
is the sofa, and is laid with a richer sort of carpet, and all round it a sort
of couch, raised half a foot, covered with rich silk according to the fancy
or magnificence of the owner. Mine is of scarlet cloth, with a gold fringe;
round this are placed, standing against the wall, two rows of cushions,
the first very large, and the next little ones; and here the Turks display
their greatest magnificence. They are generally brocade, or embroidery
of gold wire upon white satin;—nothing can look more gay and splendid.
These seats are so convenient and easy, I shall never endure chairs as
long as I live. The rooms are low, which I think no fault, and the ceiling
is always of wood, generally inlaid or painted and gilded. They use
no-hangings, the rooms being all wainscoted with cedar set off with silver
nails or painted with flowers, which open in many places with folding-
doors, and serve for cabinets, I think, more conveniently than ours.
Between the windows are little arches to set pots of perfume, or baskets
of flowers. But what pleases me best is the fashion of having marble
fountains in the lower part of the room, which throw up several spouts
of water, giving at the same time an agreeable coolness, and a pleasant
dashing sound, falling from one basin to another. Some of these fountains are very magnificent. Each house has a bagnio, which is generally
two or three little rooms, leaded on the top, paved with marble, with
basins, cocks of water, and all conveniences for either hot or cold baths.

You will perhaps be surprised at an account so different from what
you have been entertained with by the common voyage-writers, who are
very fond of speaking of what they don't know. It must be under a very
particular character, or on some extraordinary occasion, when a Christian is permitted into the house of a man of quality; and their *haréms*
are always forbidden ground. Thus they can only speak of the outside,
which makes no great appearance; and the women's apartments are all
built backward, removed from sight, and have no other prospect than
the gardens, which are enclosed with very high walls. There are none
of our parterres in them; but they are planted with high trees, which give
an agreeable shade, and, to my fancy, a pleasing view. In the midst of
the garden is the *chiosk*, that is, a large room, commonly beautified with
a fine fountain in the midst of it. It is raised nine or ten steps, and
inclosed with gilded lattices, round which vines, jessamines, and honey-

suckles twining, make a sort of green wall. Large trees are planted round this place, which is the scene of their greatest pleasures, and where the ladies spend most of their hours, employed by their music or embroidery. In the public gardens there are public *chiosks*, where the people go that are not so well accommodated at home, and drink their coffee, sherbet, &c. Neither are they ignorant of a more durable manner of building: their mosques are all of freestone, and the public *hanns*, or inns, extremely magnificent, many of them taking up a large square, built round with shops under stone arches, where poor artificers are lodged *gratis*. They have always a mosque joining to them, and the body of the *hann* is a most noble hall, capable of holding three or four hundred persons, the court extremely spacious, and cloisters round it, that give it the air of our colleges. I own I think these foundations a more reasonable piece of charity than the founding of convents.

I think I have now told you a great deal for once. If you don't like my choice of subjects, tell me what you would have me write upon; there is nobody more desirous to entertain you than, dear Mrs. T.,

Yours, &c.

To the Abbé Conti.

Adrianople, May 17, [*1717*].

I am going to leave Adrianople, and I would not do it without giving some account of all that is curious in it, which I have taken a great deal of pains to see.

I will not trouble you with wise dissertations, whether or not this is the same city that was anciently called Orestesit or Oreste, which you know better than I do. It is now called from the Emperor Adrian, and was the first European seat of the Turkish empire, and has been the favourite residence of many sultans. Mahomet the Fourth, and Mustapha, the brother of the reigning emperor, were so fond of it that they wholly abandoned Constantinople: which humour so far exasperated the janissaries, it was a considerable motive to the rebellions which deposed them. Yet this man seems to love to keep his court here. I can give no reason for this partiality. 'Tis true the situation is fine, and the country all round very beautiful; but the air is extremely bad, and the seraglio itself is not free from the ill effect of it. The town is said to be eight miles in compass; I suppose they reckon in the gardens. There are some good houses in it, I mean large ones; for the architecture of their palaces never makes any great show. It is now very full of people; but they are most of them such as follow the court, or camp; and when they are removed, I am told 'tis no populous city. The river Maritza (anciently the Hebrus), on which it is situated is dried up every summer, which contributes very much to make it unwholesome. It is now a very pleasant stream. There are two noble bridges built over it.

I had the curiosity to go to see the Exchange in my Turkish dress, which is disguise sufficient. Yet I own I was not very easy when I saw it crowded with janissaries; but they dare not be rude to a woman, and made way for me with as much respect as if I had been in my own figure. It is half a mile in length, the roof arched, and kept extremely neat. It holds three hundred and sixty-five shops, furnished with all sorts of rich goods, exposed to sale in the same manner as at the New Exchange in London; but the pavement kept much neater; and the shops all so clean, they seemed just new painted. Idle people of all sorts walk here for their diversion, or amuse themselves with drinking coffee, or sherbet, which is cried about as oranges and sweetmeats are in our play-houses.

I observed most of the rich tradesmen were Jews. That people are in incredible power in this country. They have many privileges above all the natural Turks themselves, and have formed a very considerable commonwealth here, being judged by their own laws, and have drawn the whole trade of the empire into their own hands, partly by the firm union among themselves, and prevailing on the idle temper and want of industry of the Turks. Every pasha has his Jew, who is his *homme d'affaires* [agent]; he is let into all his secrets, and does all his business. No bargain is made, no bribe received, no merchandise disposed of, but what passes through their hands. They are the physicians, the stewards, and the interpreters of all the great men.

You may judge how advantageous this is to a people who never fail to make use of the smallest advantages. They have found the secret of making themselves so necessary, they are certain of the protection of the court, whatever ministry is in power. Even the English, French, and Italian merchants, who are sensible of their artifices, are, however, forced to trust their affairs to their negotiation, nothing of trade being managed without them, and the meanest among them is too important to be disobliged, since the whole body take care of his interests with as much vigour as they would those of the most considerable of their members. There are many of them vastly rich, but take care to make little public show of it; though they live in their houses in the utmost luxury and magnificence.—This copious subject has drawn me from my description of the exchange, founded by Ali Pasha, whose name it bears. Near it is the *tchartshi*, a street of a mile in length, full of shops of all kinds of fine merchandise, but excessive dear, nothing being made here. It is covered over the top with boards, to keep out the rain, that merchants may meet conveniently in all weathers. The *bessiten* near it, is another exchange, built upon pillars, where all sorts of horse-furniture is sold: glittering everywhere with gold, rich embroidery, and jewels, it makes a very agreeable show.

From this place I went, in my Turkish coach, to the camp, which is to move in a few days to the frontiers. The Sultan is already gone to his tents, and all his court; the appearance of them is, indeed, very magnificent. Those of the great men are rather like palaces than tents, taking up a great compass of ground, and being divided into a vast number of apartments. They are all of green, and the *pashas of three tails* have those ensigns of their power placed in a very conspicuous manner before their tents, which are adorned on the top with gilded balls, more or less according to their different ranks. The ladies go in their coaches to see this camp, as eagerly as ours did to that of Hyde-park; but it is easy to observe that the soldiers do not begin the campaign with any great cheerfulness. The war is a general grievance upon the people, but particularly hard upon the tradesmen, now that the Grand Signior is resolved to lead his army in person. Every company of them is obliged, upon this occasion, to make a present according to their ability.

I took the pains of rising at six in the morning to see that ceremony, which did not, however, begin till eight. The Grand Signior was at the seraglio window, to see the procession, which passed through all the principal streets. It was preceded by an *effendi,* mounted on a camel, richly furnished, reading aloud the Alcoran, finely bound, laid upon a cushion. He was surrounded by a parcel of boys, in white, singing some verses of it, followed by a man dressed in green bough, representing a clean husbandman sowing seed. After him several reapers, with garlands and ears of corn, as Ceres is pictured, with scythes in their hands, seeming to mow. Then a little machine drawn by oxen, in which was a windmill, and boys employed in grinding corn, followed by another machine, drawn by buffaloes, carrying an oven, and two more boys, one employed in kneading the bread, and another in drawing it out of the oven. These boys threw little cakes on both sides among the crowd, and were followed by the whole company of bakers, marching on foot, two and two, in their best clothes, with cakes, loaves, pasties, and pies of all sorts, on their heads, and after them two buffoons, or jack-puddings, with their faces and clothes smeared with meal, who diverted the mob with their antic gestures. In the same manner followed all the companies of trade in the empire; the nobler sort, such as jewellers, mercers, &c.,

finely mounted, and many of the pageants that represented their trades perfectly magnificent; among which the furrier's made one of the best figures, being a very large machine, set round with the skins of ermines, foxes, &c., so well stuffed, the animals seemed to be alive, followed by music and dancers. I believe they were, upon the whole, at least twenty thousand men, all ready to follow his highness if he commanded them. The rear was closed by the volunteers, who came to beg the honour of dying in his service. This part of the show seemed to me so barbarous, that I removed from the window upon the first appearance of it. They were all naked to the middle. Some had their arms pierced through with arrows, left sticking in them. Others had them sticking in their heads, the blood trickling down their faces, and some slashed their arms with sharp knives, making the blood spout out upon those that stood near; and this is looked upon as an expression of their zeal for glory. I am told that some make use of it to advance their love; and, when they are near the window where their mistress stands, (all the women in town being veiled to see this spectacle,) they stick another arrow for her sake, who gives some sign of approbation and encouragement to this gallantry. The whole show lasted for near eight hours, to my great sorrow, who was heartily tired, though I was in the house of the widow of the capitain-pasha (admiral), who refreshed me with coffee, sweetmeats, sherbet, &c., with all possible civility.

I went, two days after, to see the mosque of Sultan Selim I., which is a building very well worth the curiosity of a traveller. I was dressed in my Turkish habit, and admitted without scruple: though I believe they guessed who I was, by the extreme officiousness of the door-keeper to shew me every part of it. It is situated very advantageously in the midst of the city, and in the highest part, making a very noble show. The first court has four gates, and the innermost three. They are both of them surrounded with cloisters, with marble pillars of the Ionic order, finely polished, and of very lively colours; the whole pavement being white marble, the roof of the cloisters being divided into several cupolas or domes, leaded, with gilt balls on the top. In the midst of each court are fine fountains of white marble; before the great gate of the mosque, a portico, with green marble pillars. It has five gates, the body of the mosque being one prodigious dome.

I understand so little of architecture, I dare not pretend to speak of the proportions. It seemed to me very regular; this I am sure of, it is vastly high, and I thought it the noblest building I ever saw. It had two rows of marble galleries on pillars, with marble balusters; the pavement marble, covered with Persian carpets and, in my opinion, it is a great addition to its beauty, that it is not divided into pews, and incumbered with forms and benches like our churches; nor the pillars (which are most of them red and white marble) disfigured by the little tawdry images and pictures, that give the Roman Catholic churches the air of toy-shops. The walls seemed to me inlaid with such very lively colours, in small flowers, I could not imagine what stones had been made use of. But going nearer, I saw they were crusted with japan china, which has a very beautiful effect. In the midst hung a vast lamp of silver, gilt; besides which, I do verily believe, there were at least two thousand of a lesser size. This must look very glorious when they are all lighted; but that being at night, no women are suffered to enter. Under the large lamp is a great pulpit of carved wood, gilt; and just by it, a fountain to wash, which you know is an essential part of their devotion. In one corner is a little gallery, inclosed with gilded lattices, for the Grand Signior. At the upper end, a large niche, very like an altar, raised two steps, covered with gold brocade, and, standing before it, two silver gilt candlesticks, the height of a man, and in them white wax candles, as thick as a man's waist. The outside of the mosque is adorned with four towers, vastly high, gilt on the top, from whence the *imaums* call the people to prayers. I had the curiosity to go up one of them, which is contrived so artfully, as to give surprise to all that see it. There is but one door, which leads to three different staircases, going to the three different stories of the tower, in such a manner, that three priests may ascend, rounding, without ever meeting each other; a contrivance very much admired.

Behind the mosque, is an exchange full of shops, where poor artificers are lodged *gratis*. I saw several dervises at their prayers here. They are dressed in a plain piece of woollen, with their arms bare, and a woollen cap on their heads, like a high-crowned hat without brims. I went to see some other mosques, built much after the same manner, but not comparable in point of magnificence to this I have described, which is infinitely beyond any church in Germany or England; I won't talk of other countries I have not seen. The seraglio does not seem a very magnificent palace. But the gardens are very large, plentifully supplied with water, and full of trees; which is all I know of them, having never been in them.

I tell you nothing of the order of Mr. W——'s entry, and his audience. Those things are always the same, and have been so often described, I won't trouble you with the repetition. The young prince, about eleven years old, sits near his father when he gives audience: he is a handsome boy; but, probably will not immediately succeed the Sultan, there being two sons of Sultan Mustapha (his eldest brother) remaining; the eldest about twenty years old, on whom the hopes of the people are fixed. This reign has been bloody and avaricious. I am apt to believe, they are very impatient to see the end of it.

I am, Sir, your, &c.

I will write to you again from Constantinople.

To the Countess of Bristol.

[*10 April, 1718.*]

At length I have heard for the first time from my dear Lady——. I am persuaded you have had the goodness to write before, but I have had the ill fortune to lose your letters. Since my last, I have staid quietly at Constantinople, a city that I ought in conscience to give your ladyship a right notion of, since I know you can have none but what is partial and mistaken from the writings of travellers. 'Tis certain there are many people that pass years here in Pera, without having ever seen it, and yet they all pretend to describe it.

Pera, Tophana, and Galata, wholly inhabited by Frank Christians (and which, together, make the appearance of a very fine town), are divided from it by the sea, which is not above half so broad as the broadest part of the Thames; but the Christian men are loth to hazard the adventures they sometimes meet with amongst the *levents* or sea-men (worse monsters than our watermen), and the women must cover their faces to go there, which they have a perfect aversion to do. 'Tis true they wear veils in Pera, but they are such as only serve to shew their beauty to more advantage, and which would not be permitted in Constantinople. These reasons deter almost every creature from seeing it; and the French embassadress will return to France (I believe) without ever having been there.

You'll wonder, madam, to hear me add, that I have been there very often. The *asmáck*, or Turkish veil, is become not only very easy, but agreeable to me; and, if it was not, I would be content to endure some inconveniency to content a passion so powerful with me as curiosity. And, indeed, the pleasure of going in a barge to Chelsea is not comparable to that of rowing upon the canal of the sea here, where, for twenty miles together, down the Bosphorus, the most beautiful variety of prospects present themselves. The Asian side is covered with fruit trees, villages, and the most delightful landscapes in nature; on the European, stands Constantinople situate on seven hills. The unequal heights make it seem as large again as it is (though one of the largest cities in the world), shewing an agreeable mixture of gardens, pine and cypress-trees, palaces, mosques, and public buildings, raised one above another, with as much beauty and appearance of symmetry as your ladyship ever saw in a cabinet adorned by the most skilful hands, jars shewing themselves above jars, mixed with canisters, babies, and candlesticks. This is a very odd comparison; but it gives me an exact image of the thing.

I have taken care to see as much of the seraglio as is to be seen. It is on a point of land running into the sea; a palace of prodigious extent, but very irregular. The gardens take in a large compass of ground, full of high cypress-trees, which is all I know of them: the buildings all of white stone, leaded on top, with gilded turrets and spires, which look very magnificent; and, indeed, I believe, there is no Christian king's palace half so large. There are six large courts in it, all built round, and set with trees, having galleries of stone; one of these for the guard, another for the slaves, another for the officers of the kitchen, another for the stables, the fifth for the divan, the sixth for the apartment destined for audiences. On the ladies' side there are at least as many more, with distinct courts belonging to their eunuchs and attendants, their kitchens, &c.

The next remarkable structure is that of St. Sophia, which is very difficult to see. I was forced to send three times to the *caimaican* (the governor of the town), and he assembled the chief *effendis*, or heads of the law, and enquired of the *mufti* whether it was lawful to permit it. They passed some days in this important debate; but I insisting on my request, permission was granted. I can't be informed why the Turks are more delicate on the subject of this mosque than any of the others, where what Christian pleases may enter without scruple. I fancy they imagine that, having been once consecrated, people, on pretence of curiosity, might profane it with prayers, particularly to those saints who are still very visible in Mosaic work, and no other way defaced but by the decays of time; for it is absolutely false, what is so universally asserted, that the Turks defaced all the images that they found in the city. The dome of St. Sophia is said to be one hundred and thirteen feet diameter, built upon arches, sustained by vast pillars of marble, the pavement and staircase marble. There are two rows of galleries, supported with pillars of parti-coloured marble, and the whole roof Mosaic work, part of which decays very fast, and drops down. They presented me a handful of it; the composition seems to me a sort of glass, or that paste with which they make counterfeit jewels. They show here the tomb of the Emperor Constantine, for which they have a great veneration.

This is a dull imperfect description of this celebrated building; but I understand architecture so little that I am afraid of talking nonsense in endeavouring to speak of it particularly. Perhaps I am in the wrong, but some Turkish mosques please me better. That of Sultan Solyman is an exact square, with four fine towers in the angles; in the midst a noble cupola, supported with beautiful marble pillars; two lesser at the ends, supported in the same manner; the pavement and gallery round the mosque of marble; under the great cupola is a fountain, adorned with such fine coloured pillars I can hardly think them natural marble; on one side is the pulpit, of white marble, and on the other, the little gallery for the Grand Signior. A fine staircase leads to it, and it is built up with gilded lattices. At the upper end is a sort of altar, where the name of God is written; and before it stand two candlesticks as high as a man, with wax candles as thick as three flambeaux. The pavement is spread with fine carpets, and the mosque illuminated with a vast number of lamps. The court leading to it is very spacious, with galleries of marble, with green columns, covered with twenty-eight leaded cupolas on two sides, and a fine fountain of three basins in the midst of it.

This description may serve for all the mosques in Constantinople. The model is exactly the same, and they only differ in largeness and richness of materials. That of the Valide is the largest of all, built entirely of marble, the most prodigious, and, I think, the most beautiful structure I ever saw, be it spoken to the honour of our sex, for it was founded by the mother of Mahomet IV. Between friends, St. Paul's church would make a pitiful figure near it, as any of our squares would do near the *atlerdan*, or place of horses (*at* signifying a horse in Turkish). This was the *hippodrome* in the reign of the Greek emperors. In the midst of it is a brazen column, of three serpents twisted together, with their mouths gaping. 'Tis impossible to learn why so odd a pillar was erected; the Greeks can tell nothing but fabulous legends when they are asked the meaning of it, and there is no sign of it having ever had any inscription. At the upper end is an obelisk of porphyry, probably brought from Egypt, the hieroglyphics all very entire, which I look upon as mere ancient puns. It is placed on four little brazen pillars, upon a pedestal of square free-stone, full of figures in bas-relief on two sides; one square representing a battle, another an assembly.

* * *

All the figures have their heads on; and I cannot forbear reflecting again on the impudence of authors, who all say they have not: but I dare swear the greatest part of them never saw them; but took the report from the Greeks, who resist, with incredible fortitude, the conviction of their own eyes, whenever they have invented lies to the dishonour of their enemies. Were you to ask them, there is nothing worth seeing in Constantinople but Sancta Sophia, though there are several larger mosques. That of Sultan Achmet has this particularity, that it has gates of brass. In all these mosques there are little chapels, where are the tombs of the founders and their families, with vast candles burning before them.

The exchanges are all noble buildings, full of fine alleys, the greatest part supported with pillars, and kept wonderfully neat. Every trade has their distinct alley, the merchandize disposed in the same order as in the New Exchange at London. The *besistén*, or jewellers' quarter, shews so much riches, such a vast quantity of diamonds, and all kinds of precious stones, that they dazzle the sight. The embroiderers' is also very glittering, and people walk here as much for diversion as business. The markets are most of them handsome squares, and admirably well provided, perhaps better than in any other part of the world.

I know you'll expect I should say something particular of the slaves; and you will imagine me half a Turk when I don't speak of it with the same horror other Christians have done before me. But I cannot forbear applauding the humanity of the Turks to these creatures; they are never ill-used, and their slavery is, in my opinion, no worse than servitude all over the world. 'Tis true they have no wages; but they give them yearly clothes to a higher value than our salaries to any ordinary servant. But you'll object, men buy women with an eye to evil. In my opinion, they are bought and sold as publicly and more infamously in all our Christian great cities.

I must add to the description of Constantinople that the historical pillar is no more; it dropped down about two years before I came. I have seen no other footsteps of antiquity except the aqueducts, which are so vast, that I am apt to believe they are yet more ancient than the Greek empire, though the Turks have clapped in some stones with Turkish inscriptions, to give their nation the honour of so great a work; but the deceit is easily discovered.

The other public buildings are the hánns and monasteries; the first very large and numerous; the second few in number, and not at all magnificent. I had the curiosity to visit one of them, and observe the devotions of the dervises, which are as whimsical as any in Rome. These fellows have permission to marry, but are confined to an odd habit, which is only a piece of coarse white cloth wrapped about them, with their legs and arms naked. Their order has few other rules, except that of performing their fantastic rites every Tuesday and Friday, which is in this manner: They meet together in a large hall, where they all stand with their eyes fixed on the ground, and their arms across, while the *imaum*, or preacher, reads part of the Alcoran from a pulpit placed in the midst; and when he has done, eight or ten of them make a melancholy concert with their pipes, which are no unmusical instruments. Then he reads again, and makes a short exposition on what he has read; after which they sing and play till their superior (the only one of them dressed in green) rises and begins a sort of solemn dance. They all stand about him in a regular figure; and while some play, the others tie their robe (which is very wide) fast round their waists, and begin to turn round with an amazing swiftness, and yet with great regard to the music, moving slower or faster as the tune is played. This lasts about an hour, without any of them shewing the least appearance of giddiness; which is not to be wondered at, when it is considered they are all used to it from infancy; most of them being devoted to this way of life from their birth, and sons of dervises. There turned amongst them some little dervises of six or seven years old, who seemed no more disordered by that exercise than the others. At the end of the ceremony they shout out, "There is no other god but God, and Mahomet is his prophet"; after which they kiss the superior's hand and retire. The whole is performed with the most solemn gravity. Nothing can be more austere than the form of these people; they never raise their eyes, and seem devoted to contemplation. And as ridiculous as this is in description, there is something touching in the air of submission and mortification they assume.

This letter is of a horrible length; but you may burn it when you have read enough, &c. &c.

JONATHAN SWIFT
1667–1745

Less the crazy misanthrope of legend than a conservative Christian divine with an antic sense of humor, Swift has earned a place as the greatest of satirists, pre-eminently because of Gulliver's Travels, *his send-up of both the often fanciful travel books of his own day and the permanent vices and follies of human beings.*

Born in Dublin, Swift attended Trinity College there, and after disappointment in politics, took holy orders and finally became dean of St. Patrick's Cathedral, Dublin. (His early satire on "corruptions in religion and learning," A Tale of a Tub, *is said to have shocked Queen Anne and persuaded her that Swift was too frivolous to deserve what his intelligence clearly merited, a bishopric.) His own travels were largely limited to trips between Dublin and London, where he delighted to trade wit with his friends Alexander Pope, John Gay, and Dr. John Arbuthnot. With satires like* A Modest Proposal *(1729), where he suggested with grave irony that Irish poverty cried out for a simple solution—infanticide and cannibalism—and journalistic hoaxes like the* Drapier's Letters *(1724), designed to frustrate English manipulation of the Irish coinage, he won a reputation as an immensely popular Irish patriot.*

But as a writer his triumph is the character of the naive but sturdy traveler Lemuel Gulliver, always curious, always anxious to learn, always faithfully recording for stay-at-homes the wonderful anomalies he meets on his four voyages. It seems remarkable that Gulliver was invented by a writer who never traveled out of the British Isles and who simply made it all up. Swift was delighted to tell Pope of an Irish bishop who thought Gulliver's Travels *"full of improbable lies" and asserted that "for his part, he hardly believed a word of it."*

From Travels Into Several Remote
Nations of the World
(1726)

PART III:

A VOYAGE TO LAPUTA, BALNIBARBI, GLUBBDUBDRIB,
LUGGNAGG, AND JAPAN

CHAPTER I

* * *

I sailed to another island, and thence to a third and fourth, sometimes using my sail, and sometimes my paddles. But not to trouble the reader with a particular account of my distresses, let it suffice that on the fifth day I arrived at the last island in my sight, which lay south-south-east to the former.

This island was at a greater distance than I expected, and I did not reach it in less than five hours. I encompassed it almost round before I could find a convenient place to land in, which was a small creek about three times the wideness of my canoe. I found the island to be all rocky, only a little intermingled with tufts of grass and sweet smelling herbs. I took out my small provisions, and after having refreshed myself, I secured the remainder in a cave, whereof there were great numbers. I gathered plenty of eggs upon the rocks, and got a quantity of dry sea-weed and parched grass, which I designed to kindle the next day, and roast my eggs as well as I could. (For I had about me my flint, steel, match, and burning-glass.) I lay all night in the cave where I had lodged my provisions. My bed was the same dry grass and sea-weed which I intended for fuel. I slept very little, for the disquiets of my mind prevailed over my weariness, and kept me awake. I considered how impossible it was to preserve my life in so desolate a place, and how miserable my end must be. Yet I found myself so listless and desponding that I had not the heart to rise, and before I could get spirits enough to creep out of my cave the day was far advanced. I walked a while among the rocks; the sky was perfectly clear, and the sun so hot that I was forced to turn my face from it: when all on a sudden it became obscured, as I thought, in a manner very different from what happens by the interposition of a cloud. I turned back, and perceived a vast opaque body between me and the sun, moving forwards towards the island: it seemed to be about two miles high, and hid the sun six or seven minutes, but I did not observe the air to be much colder, or the sky more darkened, than if I had stood under the shade of a mountain. As it approached nearer over the place where I was, it appeared to be a firm substance, the bottom flat, smooth, and shining very bright from the reflection of the sea below. I stood upon a height about two hundred yards from the shore, and saw this vast body descending almost to a parallel with me, at less than an English mile distance. I took out my pocket-perspective, and could plainly discover numbers of people moving up and down the sides of it, which appeared to be sloping, but what those people were doing, I was not able to distinguish.

The natural love of life gave me some inward motions of joy, and I was ready to entertain a hope that this adventure might some way or other help to deliver me from the desolate place and condition I was in. But at the same time the reader can hardly conceive my astonishment, to behold an island in the air, inhabited by men, who were able (as it should seem) to raise or sink, or put it into a progressive motion, as they pleased. But not being at that time in a disposition to philosophise upon this phenomenon, I rather chose to observe what course the island would take, because it seemed for a while to stand still. Yet soon after it advanced nearer, and I could see the sides of it, encompassed with several gradations of galleries, and stairs at certain intervals, to descend from one to the other. In the lowest gallery I beheld some people fishing with long angling rods, and others looking on. I waved my cap (for my hat was long since worn out) and my handkerchief towards the island; and upon its nearer approach, I called and shouted with the utmost strength of my voice; and then looking circumspectly, I beheld a crowd gather to that side which was most in my view. I found by their pointing towards me and to each other, that they plainly discovered me, although they made no return to my shouting. But I could see four or five men running in great haste up the stairs to the top of the island, who then disappeared. I happened rightly to conjecture, that these were sent for orders to some person in authority upon this occasion.

The number of people increased, and in less than half an hour the island was moved and raised in such a manner, that the lowest gallery appeared in a parallel of less than an hundred yards distance from the height where I stood. I then put myself into the most supplicating postures, and spoke in the humblest accent, but received no answer. Those who stood nearest over against me seemed to be persons of distinction, as I supposed by their habit. They conferred earnestly with each other, looking often upon me. At length one of them called out in a clear, polite, smooth dialect, not unlike in sound to the Italian; and therefore I returned an answer in that language, hoping at least that the cadence might be more agreeable to his ears. Although neither of us understood the other, yet my meaning was easily known, for the people saw the distress I was in.

They made signs for me to come down from the rock, and go towards the shore, which I accordingly did; and the flying island being raised to a convenient height, the verge directly over me, a chain was let down from the lowest gallery, with a seat fastened to the bottom, to which I fixed myself, and was drawn up by pulleys.

CHAPTER II *The humours and dispositions of the Laputians described. An account of their learning. Of the King and his Court. The Author's reception there. The inhabitants subject to fear and disquietudes. An account of the women.*

At my alighting I was surrounded by a crowd of people, but those who stood nearest seemed to be of better quality. They beheld me with all the marks and circumstances of wonder; neither indeed was I much in their debt, having never till then seen a race of mortals so singular in their shapes, habits, and countenances. Their heads were all reclined either to the right or the left; one of their eyes turned inward, and the other directly up to the zenith. Their outward garments were adorned with the figures of suns, moons, and stars, interwoven with those of fiddles, flutes, harps, trumpets, guitars, harpsichords, and many other instruments of music, unknown to us in Europe. I observed here and there many in the habit of servants, with a blown bladder fastened like a flail to the end of a short stick, which they carried in their hands. In each bladder was a small quantity of dried pease, or little pebbles (as I was afterwards informed). With these bladders they now and then flapped the mouths and ears of those who stood near them, of which practice I could not then conceive the meaning; it seems the minds of these people are so taken up with intense speculations, that they neither can speak, nor attend to the discourses of others, without being roused by some external taction upon the organs of speech and hearing; for which reason those persons who are able to afford it always keep a flapper (the original is *climenole*) in their family, as one of their domestics, nor ever walk abroad or make visits without him. And the business of this officer is, when two or more persons are in company, gently to strike with his bladder the mouth of him who is to speak, and the right ear of him or them to whom the speaker addresseth himself. This flapper is likewise employed diligently to attend his master in his walks, and upon occasion to give him a soft flap on his eyes, because he is always so wrapped up in cogitation, that he is in manifest danger of falling down every precipice, and bouncing his head against every post, and in the streets, of justling others, or being justled himself into the kennel.

It was necessary to give the reader this information, without which he would be at the same loss with me, to understand the proceedings of these people, as they conducted me up the stairs, to the top of the island, and from thence to the royal palace. While we were ascending, they forgot several times what they were about, and left me to myself, till their memories were again roused by their flappers; for they appeared altogether unmoved by the sight of my foreign habit and countenance, and by the shouts of the vulgar, whose thoughts and minds were more disengaged.

At last we entered the palace, and proceeded into the chamber of presence, where I saw the King seated on his throne, attended on each side by persons of prime quality. Before the throne was a large table filled with globes and spheres, and mathematical instruments of all kinds. His Majesty took not the least notice of us, although our entrance was not without sufficient noise, by the concourse of all persons belonging to the court. But he was then deep in a problem, and we attended at least an hour, before he could solve it. There stood by him on each side a young page, with flaps in their hands, and when they saw he was at leisure, one of them gently struck his mouth, and the other his right ear; at which he started like one awakened on the sudden, and looking towards me and the company I was in, recollected the occasion of our coming, whereof he had been informed before. He spoke some words, whereupon immediately a young man with a flap came up to my side, and flapped me gently on the right ear; but I made signs, as well as I could, that I had no occasion for such an instrument; which, as I afterwards found, gave his Majesty and the whole court a very mean opinion of my understanding. The King, as far as I could conjecture, asked me several questions, and I addressed myself to him in all the languages I had. When it was found that I could neither understand nor be understood, I was conducted by the King's order to an apartment in his palace (this prince being distinguished above all his predecessors for his hospitality to strangers), where two servants were appointed to attend me. My dinner was brought, and four persons of quality, whom I remembered to have seen very near the King's person, did me the honour to dine with me. We had two courses of three dishes each. In the first course there was a shoulder of mutton, cut into an equilateral triangle, a piece of beef into a rhomboides, and a pudding into a cycloid. The second course was two ducks, trussed up into the form of fiddles; sausages and puddings resembling flutes and hautboys, and a breast of veal in the shape of a harp. The servants cut our bread into cones, cylinders, parallelograms, and several other mathematical figures.

While we were at dinner, I made bold to ask the names of several things in their language; and those noble persons, by the assistance of their flappers, delighted to give me answers, hoping to raise my admiration of their great abilities, if I could be brought to converse with them. I was soon able to call for bread and drink, or whatever else I wanted.

After dinner my company withdrew, and a person was sent to me by the King's order, attended by a flapper. He brought with him pen, ink, and paper, and three or four books, giving me to understand by signs, that he was sent to teach me the language. We sat together four hours, in which time I wrote down a great number of words in columns, with the translations over against them. I likewise made a shift to learn several short sentences. For my tutor would order one of my servants to fetch something, to turn about, to make a bow, to sit, or stand, or walk, and the like. Then I took down the sentence in writing. He showed me also in one of his books the figures of the sun, moon, and stars, the zodiac, the tropics, and polar circles, together with the denominations of many figures of planes and solids. He gave me the names and descriptions of all the musical instruments, and the general terms of art in playing on each of them. After he had left me, I placed all my words with their interpretations in alphabetical order. And thus in a few days, by the help of a very faithful memory, I got some insight into their language.

The word, which I interpret the *Flying* or *Floating Island*, is in the original *Laputa*, whereof I could never learn the true etymology. *Lap* in the old obsolete language signifieth *high*, and *untuh*, a *governor*, from which they say by corruption was derived *Laputa*, from *Lapuntuh*. But I do not approve of this derivation, which seems to be a little strained. I ventured to offer to the learned among them a conjecture of my own, that *Laputa* was *quasi lap outed; lap* signifying properly the dancing of the sunbeams in the sea, and *outed*, a wing, which however I shall not obtrude, but submit to the judicious reader.

Those to whom the King had entrusted me, observing how ill I was clad, ordered a tailor to come next morning, and take my measure for a suit of clothes. This operator did his office after a different manner from those of his trade in Europe. He first took my altitude by a quadrant, and then with a rule and compasses described the dimensions and outlines of my whole body, all which he entered upon paper, and in six days brought my clothes very ill made, and quite out of shape, by happening to mistake a figure in the calculation. But my comfort was, that I observed such accidents very frequent, and little regarded.

During my confinement for want of clothes, and by an indisposition that held me some days longer, I much enlarged my dictionary; and when I went next to court, was able to understand many things the King spoke, and to return him some kind of answers. His Majesty had given orders that the island should move north-east and by east, to the vertical point over Lagado, the metropolis of the whole kingdom below upon the firm earth. It was about ninety leagues distant, and our voyage lasted four days and an half. I was not in the least sensible of the progressive motion made in the air by the island. On the second morning about eleven o'clock, the King himself in person, attended by his nobility, courtiers, and officers, having prepared all their musical instruments, played on them for three hours without intermission, so that I was quite stunned with the noise; neither could I possibly guess the meaning, till my tutor informed me. He said that the people of their island had their ears adapted to hear the music of the spheres, which always played at certain periods, and the court was now prepared to bear their part in whatever instrument they most excelled.

In our journey towards Lagado, the capital city, his Majesty ordered that the island should stop over certain towns and villages, from whence he might receive the petitions of his subjects. And to this purpose several packthreads were let down with small weights at the bottom. On these packthreads the people strung their petitions, which mounted up directly like the scraps of paper fastened by school-boys at the end of the string that holds their kite. Sometimes we received wine and victuals from below, which were drawn up by pulleys.

The knowledge I had in mathematics gave me great assistance in acquiring their phraseology, which depended much upon that science and music; and in the latter I was not unskilled. Their ideas are perpetually conversant in lines and figures. If they would, for example, praise the beauty of a woman, or any other animal, they describe it by rhombs, circles, parallelograms, ellipses, and other geometrical terms, or by words of art drawn from music, needless here to repeat. I observed in the King's kitchen all sorts of mathematical and musical instruments, after the figures of which they cut up the joints that were served to his Majesty's table.

Their houses are very ill built, the walls bevil, without one right angle in any apartment, and this defect ariseth from the contempt they bear to practical geometry, which they despise as vulgar and mechanic, those instructions they give being too refined for the intellectuals of their workmen, which occasions perpetual mistakes. And although they are dexterous enough upon a piece of paper in the management of the rule, the pencil, and the divider, yet in the common actions and behaviour of life, I have not seen a more clumsy, awkward, and unhandy people, nor so slow and perplexed in their conceptions upon all other subjects, except those of mathematics and music. They are very bad reasoners, and vehemently given to opposition, unless when they happen to be of the right opinion, which is seldom their case. Imagination, fancy, and invention, they are wholly strangers to, nor have any words in their language by which those ideas can be expressed; the whole compass of their thoughts and mind being shut up within the two forementioned sciences.

Most of them, and especially those who deal in the astronomical part, have great faith in judicial astrology, although they are ashamed to own it publicly. But what I chiefly admired, and thought altogether unaccountable, was the strong disposition I observed in them towards news and politics, perpetually enquiring into public affairs, giving their judgments in matters of state, and passionately disputing every inch of a party opinion. I have indeed observed the same disposition among most of the mathematicians I have known in Europe, although I could never discover the least analogy between the two sciences; unless those people suppose, that because the smallest circle hath as many degrees as the largest, therefore the regulation and management of the world require no more abilities than the handling and turning of a globe. But I rather take this quality to spring from a very common infirmity of human nature, inclining us to be more curious and conceited in matters where we have least concern, and for which we are least adapted either by study or nature.

These people are under continual disquietudes, never enjoying a minute's peace of mind; and their disturbances proceed from causes which very little affect the rest of mortals. Their apprehensions arise from several changes they dread in the celestial bodies. For instance, that the earth, by the continual approaches of the sun towards it, must in course of time be absorbed or swallowed up. That the face of the sun will by degrees be encrusted with its own effluvia, and give no more light to the world. That the earth very narrowly escaped a brush from the tail of the last comet, which would have infallibly reduced it to ashes; and that the next, which they have calculated for one and thirty years hence, will probably destroy us. For if in its perihelion it should approach within a certain degree of the sun (as by their calculations they have reason to dread) it will conceive a degree of heat ten thousand times more intense than that of red-hot glowing iron; and in its absence from the sun, carry a blazing tail ten hundred thousand and fourteen miles long; through which if the earth should pass at the distance of one hundred thousand miles from the nucleus or main body of the comet, it must in its passage be set on fire, and reduced to ashes. That the sun daily spending its rays without any nutriment to supply them, will at last be wholly consumed and annihilated; which must be attended with the destruction of this earth, and of all the planets that receive their light from it.

They are so perpetually alarmed with the apprehensions of these and the like impending dangers, that they can neither sleep quietly in their beds, nor have any relish for the common pleasures or amusements of life. When they meet an acqaintance in the morning, the first question is about the sun's health, how he looked at his setting and rising, and what hopes they have to avoid the stroke of the approaching comet. This conversation they are apt to run into with the same temper that boys discover, in delighting to hear terrible stories of sprites and hobgoblins, which they greedily listen to, and dare not go to bed for fear.

The women of the island have abundance of vivacity: they contemn their husbands, and are exceedingly fond of strangers, whereof there is always a considerable number from the continent below, attending at court, either upon affairs of the several towns and corporations, or their own particular occasions, but are much despised, because they want the same endowments. Among these the ladies choose their gallants: but the vexation is, that they act with too much ease and security, for the husband is always so rapt in speculation, that the mistress and lover may proceed to the greatest familiarities before his face, if he be but provided with paper and implements, and without his flapper at his side.

The wives and daughters lament their confinement to the island, although I think it the most delicious spot of ground in the world; and although they live here in the greatest plenty and magnificence, and are allowed to do whatever they please, they long to see the world, and take the diversions of the metropolis, which they are not allowed to do without a particular license from the King; and this is not easy to be obtained, because the people of quality have found by frequent experience how hard it is to persuade their women to return from below. I was told that a great court lady, who had several children, is married to the prime minister, the richest subject in the kingdom, a very graceful person, extremely fond of her, and lives in the finest palace of the island, went down to Lagado, on the pretence of health, there hid herself for several months, till the King sent a warrant to search for her, and she was found in an obscure eating-house all in rags, having pawned her clothes to maintain an old deformed footman, who beat her every day, and in whose company she was taken much against her will. And although her husband received her with all possible kindness, and without the least reproach, she soon after contrived to steal down again with all her jewels, to the same gallant, and hath not been heard of since.

This may perhaps pass with the reader rather for an European or English story, than for one of a country so remote. But he may please to consider, that the caprices of womankind are not limited by any climate or nation, and that they are much more uniform than can be easily imagined.

In about a month's time I had made a tolerable proficiency in their language, and was able to answer most of the King's questions, when I had the honour to attend him. His Majesty discovered not the least curiosity to enquire into the laws, government, history, religion, or manners of the countries where I had been, but confined his questions to the state of mathematics, and received the account I gave him with great contempt and indifference, though often roused by his flapper on each side.

* * *

CHAPTER IV   *The Author leaves Laputa; is conveyed to Balnibarbi, arrives at the metropolis. A description of the metropolis, and the country adjoining. The Author hospitably received by a great lord. His conversation with that lord.*

Although I cannot say that I was ill treated in this island, yet I must confess I thought myself too much neglected, not without some degree of contempt. For neither prince nor people appeared to be curious in any part of knowledge, except mathematics and music, wherein I was far their inferior, and upon that account very little regarded.

On the other side, after having seen all the curiosities of the island, I was very desirous to leave it, being heartily weary of those people. They were indeed excellent in two sciences for which I have great esteem, and wherein I am not unversed; but at the same time so abstracted and involved in speculation, that I never met with such disagreeable companions. I conversed only with women, tradesmen, flappers, and court-pages, during two months of my abode there, by which at last I rendered myself extremely contemptible; yet these were the only people from whom I could ever receive a reasonable answer.

I had obtained by hard study a good degree of knowledge in their language; I was weary of being confined to an island where I received so little countenance, and resolved to leave it with the first opportunity.

There was a great lord at court, nearly related to the King, and for that reason alone used with respect. He was universally reckoned the most ignorant and stupid person among them. He had performed many eminent services for the crown, had great natural and acquired parts, adorned with integrity and honour, but so ill an ear for music, that his detractors reported he had been often known to beat time in the wrong place; neither could his tutors without extreme difficulty teach him to demonstrate the most easy proposition in the mathematics. He was pleased to show me many marks of favour, often did me the honour of a visit, desired to be informed in the affairs of Europe, the laws and customs, the manners and learning of the several countries where I had travelled. He listened to me with great attention, and made very wise observations on all I spoke. He had two flappers attending him for state, but never made use of them except at court, and in visits of ceremony, and would always command them to withdraw when we were alone together.

I entreated this illustrious person to intercede in my behalf with his Majesty for leave to depart, which he accordingly did, as he was pleased to tell me, with regret: for indeed he had made me several offers very advantageous, which however I refused with expressions of the highest acknowledgment.

On the 16th day of February I took leave of his Majesty and the court. The King made me a present to the value of about two hundred pounds English, and my protector his kinsman as much more, together with a letter of recommendation to a friend of his in Lagado, the metropolis. The island being then hovering over a mountain about two miles from it, I was let down from the lowest gallery, in the same manner as I had been taken up.

The continent, as far as it is subject to the monarch of the Flying Island, passes under the general name of *Balnibarbi,* and the metropolis, as I said before, is called *Lagado.* I felt some little satisfaction in finding myself on firm ground. I walked to the city without any concern, being clad like one of the natives, and sufficiently instructed to converse with them. I soon found out the person's house to whom I was recommended, presented my letter from his friend the grandee in the island, and was received with much kindness. This great lord, whose name was Munodi, ordered me an apartment in his own house, where I continued during my stay, and was entertained in a most hospitable manner.

The next morning after my arrival, he took me in his chariot to see the town, which is about half the bigness of London, but the houses very strangely built, and most of them out of repair. The people in the streets walked fast, looked wild, their eyes fixed, and were generally in rags. We passed through one of the town gates, and went about three miles into the country, where I saw many labourers working with several sorts of tools in the ground, but was not able to conjecture what they were about; neither did I observe any expectation either of corn or grass, although the soil appeared to be excellent. I could not forbear admiring at these odd appearances both in town and country, and I made bold to desire my conductor, that he would be pleased to explain to me what could be meant by so many busy heads, hands, and faces, both in the streets and the fields, because I did not discover any good effects they produced; but on the contrary, I never knew a soil so unhappily cultivated, houses so ill contrived and so ruinous, or a people whose countenances and habit expressed so much misery and want.

This Lord Munodi was a person of the first rank, and had been some years Governor of Lagado, but by a cabal of ministers was discharged for insufficiency. However, the King treated him with tenderness, as a well-meaning man, but of a low contemptible understanding.

When I gave that free censure of the country and its inhabitants, he made no further answer than by telling me that I had not been long enough among them to form a judgment, and that the different nations of the world had different customs, with other common topics to the same purpose. But when we returned to his palace, he asked me how I liked the building, what absurdities I observed, and what quarrel I had with the dress or looks of his domestics. This he might safely do, because every thing about him was magnificent, regular, and polite. I answered that his Excellency's prudence, quality, and fortune, had exempted him from those defects which folly and beggary had produced in others. He said if I would go with him to his country-house, about twenty miles distant, where his estate lay, there would be more leisure for this kind of conversation. I told his Excellency that I was entirely at his disposal, and accordingly we set out next morning.

During our journey he made me observe the several methods used by farmers in managing their lands, which to me were wholly unaccountable; for except in some very few places I could not discover one ear of corn or blade of grass. But in three hours travelling the scene was wholly altered; we came into a most beautiful country; farmers' houses at small distances, neatly built; the fields enclosed, containing vineyards, corn-grounds, and meadows. Neither do I remember to have seen a more delightful prospect. His Excellency observed my countenance to clear up; he told me with a sigh that there his estate began, and would continue the same till we should come to his house. That his country-men ridiculed and despised him for managing his affairs no better, and for setting so ill an example to the kingdom, which however was followed by very few, such as were old, and wilful, and weak like himself.

We came at length to the house, which was indeed a noble structure, built according to the best rules of ancient architecture. The fountains, gardens, walks, avenues, and groves were all disposed with exact judgment and taste. I gave due praises to every thing I saw, where of his Excellency took not the least notice till after supper, when, there being no third companion, he told me with a very melancholy air that he doubted he must throw down his houses in town and country, to rebuild them after the present mode, destroy all his plantations, and cast others into such a form as modern usage required, and give the same directions to all his tenants, unless he would submit to incur the censure of pride, singularity, affectation, ignorance, caprice, and perhaps increase his Majesty's displeasure.

That the admiration I appeared to be under would cease or diminish when he had informed me of some particulars, which probably I never heard of at court, the people there being too much taken up in their own speculations, to have regard to what passed here below.

The sum of his discourse was to this effect. That about forty years ago certain persons went up to Laputa, either upon business or diversion and after five months continuance came back with a very little smattering in mathematics but full of volatile spirits acquired in that airy region. That these persons upon their return began to dislike the management of every thing below and fell into schemes of putting all arts sciences languages and mechanics upon a new foot. To this end they procured a royal patent for erecting an Academy of Projectors in Lagado and the humour prevailed so strongly among the people that there is not a town of any consequence in the kingdom without such an academy. In these colleges the professors contrive new rules and methods of agriculture and building and new instruments and tools for all trades and manufactures whereby, as they undertake, one man shall do the work of ten; a palace may be built in a week, of materials so durable as to last for ever without repairing. All the fruits of the earth shall come to maturity at whatever season we think fit to choose, and increase an hundred fold more than they do at present, with innumerable other happy proposals. The only inconvenience is, that none of these projects are yet brought to perfection, and in the mean time, the whole country lies miserably waste, the houses in ruins, and the people without food or clothes. By all which, instead of being discouraged, they are fifty times more violently bent upon prosecuting their schemes, driven equally on by hope and despair; that as for himself, being not of an enterprising spirit, he was content to go on in the old forms, to live in the houses his ancestors had built, and act as they did in every part of life without innovation. That some few other persons of quality and gentry had done the same, but were looked on with an eye of contempt and ill-will, as enemies to art, ignorant, and ill commonwealth's-men, preferring their own ease and sloth before the general improvement of their country.

His Lordship added that he would not by any further particulars prevent the pleasure I should certainly take in viewing the grand Academy, whither he was resolved I should go. He only desired me to observe a ruined building upon the side of a mountain about three miles distant, of which he gave me this account. That he had a very convenient mill within half a mile of his house, turned by a current from a large river, and sufficient for his own family as well as a great number of his tenants. That about seven years ago a club of those projectors came to him with proposals to destroy this mill, and build another on the side of that mountain, on the long ridge where of a long canal must be cut for a repository of water, to be conveyed up by pipes and engines to supply the mill; because the wind and air upon a height agitated the water, and thereby made it fitter for motion; and because the water descending down a declivity would turn the mill with half the current of a river whose course is more upon a level. He said, that being then not very well with the court, and pressed by many of his friends, he complied with the proposal; and after employing an hundred men for two years, the work miscarried, the projectors went off, laying the blame entirely upon him, railing at him ever since, and putting others upon the same experiment, with equal assurance of success, as well as equal disappointment.

In a few days we came back tó town, and his Excellency, considering the bad character he had in the Academy, would not go with me himself, but recommended me to a friend of his to bear me company thither. My lord was pleased to represent me as a great admirer of projects, and a person of much curiosity and easy belief; which indeed was not without truth, for I had myself been a sort of projector in my younger days.

CHAPTER V   *The Author permitted to see the Grand Academy of Lagado. The Academy largely described. The Arts wherein the professors employ themselves.*

This Academy is not an entire single building, but a continuation of several houses on both sides of a street, which growing waste was purchased and applied to that use.

I was received very kindly by the Warden, and went for many days to the Academy. Every room hath in it one or more projectors, and I believe I could not be in fewer than five hundred rooms.

The first man I saw was of a meagre aspect, with sooty hands and face, his hair and beard long, ragged and singed in several places. His clothes, shirt, and skin were all of the same colour. He had been eight years upon a project for extracting sun-beams out of cucumbers, which were to be put into vials hermetically sealed, and let out to warm the air in raw inclement summers. He told me he did not doubt in eight years more he should be able to supply the Governor's gardens with sunshine at a reasonable rate; but he complained that his stock was low, and entreated me to give him something as an encouragement to ingenuity, especially since this had been a very dear season for cucumbers. I made him a small present, for my lord had furnished me with money on purpose, because he knew their practice of begging from all who go to see them.

I went into another chamber, but was ready to hasten back, being almost overcome with a horrible stink. My conductor pressed me forward, conjuring me in a whisper to give no offence, which would be highly resented, and therefore I durst not so much as stop my nose. The projector of this cell was the most ancient student of the Academy; his face and beard were of a pale yellow; his hands and clothes daubed over with filth. When I was presented to him, he gave me a close embrace (a compliment I could well have excused). His employment from his first coming into the Academy, was an operation to reduce human excrement to its original food, by separating the several parts, removing the tincture which it receives from the gall, making the odour exhale, and scumming off the saliva. He had a weekly allowance from the society, of a vessel filled with human ordure, about the bigness of a Bristol barrel.

I saw another at work to calcine ice into gunpowder, who likewise showed me a treatise he had written concerning the malleability of fire, which he intended to publish.

There was a most ingenious architect who had contrived a new method for building houses, by beginning at the roof, and working downwards to the foundation, which he justified to me by the like practice of those two prudent insects, the bee and the spider.

There was a man born blind, who had several apprentices in his own condition: their employment was to mix colours for painters, which their master taught them to distinguish by feeling and smelling. It was indeed my misfortune to find them at that time not very perfect in their lessons, and the professor himself happened to be generally mistaken: this artist is much encouraged and esteemed by the whole fraternity.

In another apartment I was highly pleased with a projector, who had found a device of ploughing the ground with hogs, to save the charges of ploughs, cattle, and labour. The method is this: in an acre of ground you bury, at six inches distance and eight deep, a quantity of acorns, dates, chestnuts, and other mast or vegetables whereof these animals are fondest; then you drive six hundred or more of them into the field, where in a few days they will root up the whole ground in search of their food, and make it fit for sowing, at the same time manuring it with their dung. It is true, upon experiment they found the charge and trouble very great, and they had little or no crop. However, it is not doubted that this invention may be capable of great improvement.

I went into another room, where the walls and ceiling were all hung round with cobwebs, except a narrow passage for the artist to go in and out. At my entrance he called aloud to me not to disturb his webs. He lamented the fatal mistake the world had been so long in of using silk-worms, while we had such plenty of domestic insects, who infinitely excelled the former, because they understood how to weave as well as spin. And he proposed farther that by employing spiders the charge of dyeing silks should be wholly saved, whereof I was fully convinced when he showed me a vast number of flies most beautifully colored, wherewith he fed his spiders, assuring us that the webs would take a tincture from them; and as he had them of all hues, he hoped to fit everybody's fancy, as soon as he could find proper food for the flies, of certain gums, oils, and other glutinous matter to give a strength and consistence to the threads.

There was an astronomer who had undertaken to place a sun-dial upon the great weathercock on the town-house, by adjusting the annual and diurnal motions of the earth and sun, so as to answer and coincide with all accidental turnings by the wind.

I was complaining of a small fit of the colic, upon which my conductor led me into a room, where a great physician resided, who was famous for curing that disease by contrary operations from the same instrument.

He had a large pair of bellows with a long slender muzzle of ivory. This he conveyed eight inches up the anus, and drawing in the wind, he affirmed he could make the guts as lank as a dried bladder. But when the disease was more stubborn and violent, he let in the muzzle while the bellows were full of wind, which he discharged into the body of the patient, then withdrew the instrument to replenish it, clapping his thumb strongly against the orifice of the fundament; and this being repeated three or four times, the adventitious wind would rush out, bringing the noxious along with it (like water put into a pump), and the patient recover. I saw him try both experiments upon a dog, but could not discern any effect from the former. After the latter, the animal was ready to burst, and made so violent a discharge, as was very offensive to me and my companions. The dog died on the spot, and we left the doctor endeavouring to recover him by the same operation.

I visited many other apartments, but shall not trouble my reader with all the curiosities I observed, being studious of brevity.

I had hitherto seen only one side of the Academy, the other being appropriated to the advancers of speculative learning, of whom I shall say something when I have mentioned one illustrious person more, who is called among them *the universal artist.* He told us he had been thirty years employing his thoughts for the improvement of human life. He had two large rooms full of wonderful curiosities, and fifty men at work. Some were condensing air into a dry tangible substance, by extracting the nitre, and letting the aqueous or fluid particles percolate; others softening marble for pillows and pin-cushions; others petrifying the hoofs of a living horse to preserve them from foundering. The artist himself was at that time busy upon two great designs; the first, to sow land with chaff, wherein he affirmed the true seminal virtue to be contained, as he demonstrated by several experiments which I was not skilful enough to comprehend. The other was, by a certain composition of gums, minerals, and vegetables outwardly applied, to prevent the growth of wool upon two young lambs; and he hoped in a reasonable time to propagate the breed of naked sheep all over the kingdom.

We crossed a walk to the other part of the Academy, where, as I have already said, the projectors in speculative learning resided.

The first professor I saw was in a very large room, with forty pupils about him. After salutation, observing me to look earnestly upon a frame, which took up the greatest part of both the length and breadth of the room, he said perhaps I might wonder to see him employed in a project for improving speculative knowledge by practical and mechanical operations. But the world would soon be sensible of its usefulness, and he flattered himself that a more noble exalted thought never sprang in any other man's head. Every one knew how laborious the usual method is of attaining to arts and sciences; whereas by his contrivance the most ignorant person at a reasonable charge, and with a little bodily labour, may write books in philosophy, poetry, politics, law, mathematics, and theology, without the least assistance from genius or study. He then led me to the frame, about the sides whereof all his pupils stood in ranks. It was twenty foot square, placed in the middle of the room. The superficies were composed of several bits of wood, about the bigness of a die, but some larger than others. They were all linked together by slender wires. These bits of wood were covered on every square with paper pasted on them, and on these papers were written all the words of their language, in their several moods, tenses, and declensions, but without any order. The professor then desired me to observe, for he was going to set his engine at work. The pupils at his command took each of them hold of an iron handle, whereof there were forty fixed round the edges of the frame, and giving them a sudden turn, the whole disposition of the words was entirely changed. He then commanded six and thirty of the lads to read the several lines softly as they appeared upon the frame; and where they found three or four words together that might make part of a sentence, they dictated to the four remaining boys who were scribes. This work was repeated three or four times, and at every turn the engine was so contrived that the words shifted into new places, as the square bits of wood moved upside down.

Six hours a day the young students were employed in this labour, and the professor showed me several volumes in large folio already collected, of broken sentences, which he intended to piece together, and out of those rich materials to give the world a complete body of all arts and sciences; which however might be still improved, and much expedited, if the public would raise a fund for making and employing five hundred such frames in Lagado, and oblige the managers to contribute in common their several collections.

He assured me, that this invention had employed all his thoughts from his youth, that he had emptied the whole vocabulary into his frame, and made the strictest computation of the general proportion there is in books between the numbers of particles, nouns, and verbs, and other parts of speech.

I made my humblest acknowledgment to this illustrious person for his great communicativeness, and promised if ever I had the good fortune to return to my native country, that I would do him justice, as the sole inventor of this wonderful machine; the form and contrivance of which

I desired leave to delineate upon paper. I told him, although it were the custom of our learned in Europe to steal inventions from each other, who had thereby at least this advantage, that it became a controversy which was the right owner, yet I would take such caution, that he should have the honour entire without a rival.

We next went to the school of languages, where three professors sat in consultation upon improving that of their own country.

The first project was to shorten discourse by cutting polysyllables into one, and leaving out verbs and participles, because in reality all things imaginable are but nouns.

The other project was a scheme for entirely abolishing all words whatsoever; and this was urged as a great advantage in point of health as well as brevity. For it is plain that every word we speak is in some degree a diminution of our lungs by corrosion, and consequently contributes to the shortening of our lives. An expedient was therefore offered, that since words are only names for *things*, it would be more convenient for all men to carry about them such things as were necessary to express the particular business they are to discourse on. And this invention would certainly have taken place, to the great ease as well as health of the subject, if the women, in conjunction with the vulgar and illiterate, had not threatened to raise a rebellion, unless they might be allowed the liberty to speak with their tongues, after the manner of their ancestors; such constant irreconcilable enemies to science are the common people. However, many of the most learned and wise adhere to the new scheme of expressing themselves by things, which hath only this inconvenience attending it, that if a man's business be very great, and of various kinds, he must be obliged in proportion to carry a greater bundle of things upon his back, unless he can afford one or two strong servants to attend him. I have often beheld two of those sages almost sinking under the weight of their packs, like pedlars among us; who, when they met in the streets, would lay down their loads, open their sacks, and hold conversation for an hour together; then put up their implements, help each other to resume their burthens, and take their leave.

But for short conversations a man may carry implements in his pockets and under his arms, enough to supply him, and in his house he cannot be at a loss. Therefore the room where company meet who practise this art, is full of all things ready at hand, requisite to furnish matter for this kind of artificial converse.

Another great advantage proposed by this invention was that it would serve as an universal language to be understood in all civilised nations, whose goods and utensils are generally of the same kind, or nearly resembling, so that their uses might easily be comprehended. And thus ambassadors would be qualified to treat with foreign princes or ministers of state, to whose tongues they were utter strangers.

I was at the mathematical school, where the master taught his pupils after a method scarce imaginable to us in Europe. The proposition and demonstration were fairly written on a thin wafer, with ink composed of a cephalic tincture. This the student was to swallow upon a fasting stomach, and for three days following eat nothing but bread and water. As the wafer digested, the tincture mounted to his brain, bearing the proposition along with it. But the success hath not hitherto been answerable, partly by some error in the *quantum* or composition, and partly by the perverseness of lads, to whom this bolus is so nauseous, that they generally steal aside, and discharge it upwards before it can operate; neither have they been yet persuaded to use so long an abstinence as the prescription requires.

CHAPTER VI   *A further account of the Academy. The Author*
proposes some improvements, which are honourably received.

In the school of political projectors I was but ill entertained, the professors appearing in my judgement wholly out of their senses, which is a scene that never fails to make me melancholy. These unhappy people were proposing schemes for persuading monarchs to choose favourites upon the score of their wisdom, capacity, and virtue; of teaching ministers to consult the public good; of rewarding merit, great abilities, eminent services; of instructing princes to know their true interest by placing it on the same foundation with that of their people; of choosing for employments persons qualified to exercise them; with many other wild impossible chimæras, that never entered before into the heart of man to conceive, and confirmed in me the old observation, that there is nothing so extravagant and irrational which some philosophers have not maintained for truth.

But however I shall so far do justice to this part of the Academy, as to acknowledge that all of them were not so visionary. There was a most ingenious doctor who seemed to be perfectly versed in the whole nature and system of government. This illustrious person had very usefully employed his studies in finding out effectual remedies for all diseases and corruptions, to which the several kinds of public administration are subject by the vices or infirmities of those who govern, as well as by the licentiousness of those who are to obey. For instance, whereas all writers and reasoners have agreed, that there is a strict universal resemblance between the natural and the political body; can there be any thing more evident, than that the health of both must be preserved, and the diseases cured by the same prescriptions? It is allowed that senates and great councils are often troubled with redundant, ebullient, and other peccant humours, with many diseases of the head, and more of the heart; with strong convulsions, with grievous contractions of the nerves and sinews in both hands, but especially the right; with spleen, flatus, vertigoes, and deliriums; with scrofulous tumours full of foetid virulent matter; with sour frothy ructations, with canine appetites and crudeness of digestion, besides many others needless to mention. This doctor therefore proposed, that upon the meeting of a senate, certain physicians should attend at the three first days of their sitting, and at the close of each day's debate, feel the pulses of every senator; after which, having maturely considered, and consulted upon the nature of the several maladies, and the methods of cure, they should on the fourth day return to the senate house, attended by their apothecaries stored with proper medicines; and before the members sat, administer to each of them lenitives, aperitives, abstersives, corrosives, restringents, palliatives, laxatives, cephalalgics, icterics, apophlegmatics, acoustics, as their several cases required; and according as these medicines should operate, repeat, alter, or omit them at the next meeting.

This project could not be of any great expense to the public, and would, in my poor opinion, be of much use for the dispatch of business in those countries where senates have any share in the legislative power; beget unanimity, shorten debates, open a few mouths which are now closed, and close many more which are now open; curb the petulancy of the young, and correct the positiveness of the old; rouse the stupid, and damp the pert.

Again, because it is a general complaint, that the favourites of princes are troubled with short and weak memories, the same doctor proposed, that whoever attended a first minister, after having told his business with the utmost brevity and in the plainest words, should at his departure give the said minister a tweak by the nose, or a kick in the belly, or tread on his corns, or lug him thrice by both ears, or run a pin into his breech, or pinch his arm black and blue, to prevent forgetfulness; and at every levee day repeat the same operation, till the business were done or absolutely refused.

He likewise directed, that every senator in the great council of a nation, after he had delivered his opinion, and argued in the defence of it, should be obliged to give his vote directly contrary; because if that were done, the result would infallibly terminate in the good of the public.

When parties in a state are violent, he offered a wonderful contrivance to reconcile them. The method is this. You take a hundred leaders of each party, you dispose them into couples of such whose heads are nearest of a size; then let two nice operators saw off the occiput of each couple at the same time, in such a manner that the brain may be equally divided. Let the occiputs thus cut off be interchanged, applying each to the head of his opposite party-man. It seems indeed to be a work that requireth some exactness, but the professor assured us that if it were dexterously performed the cure would be infallible. For he argued thus: that the two half brains being left to debate the matter between themselves within the space of one skull, would soon come to a good understanding, and produce that moderation, as well as regularity of thinking, so much to be wished for in the heads of those who imagine they come into the world only to watch and govern its motion: and as to the difference of brains in quantity or quality among those who are directors in faction, the doctor assured us from his own knowledge that it was a perfect trifle.

I heard a very warm debate between two professors, about the most commodious and effectual ways and means of raising money without grieving the subject. The first affirmed the justest method would be to lay a certain tax upon vices and folly, and the sum fixed upon every man to be rated after the fairest manner by a jury of his neighbours. The second was of an opinion directly contrary, to tax those qualities of body and mind for which men chiefly value themselves, the rate to be more or less according to the degrees of excelling, the decision whereof should be left entirely to their own breast. The highest tax was upon men who are the greatest favourites of the other sex, and the assessments according to the number and natures of the favours they have received; for which they are allowed to be their own vouchers. Wit, valour, and politeness were likewise proposed to be largely taxed, and collected in the same manner, by every person's giving his own word for the quantum of what he possessed. But as to honour, justice, wisdom, and learning, they should not be taxed at all, because they are qualifications of so singular a kind, that no man will either allow them in his neighbour, or value them in himself.

The women were proposed to be taxed according to their beauty and skill in dressing, wherein they had the same privilege with the men, to be determined by their own judgment. But constancy, chastity, good sense, and good nature were not rated, because they would not bear the charge of collecting.

To keep senators in the interest of the crown, it was proposed that the members should raffle for employments, every man first taking an oath, and giving security that he would vote for the court, whether he won or no; after which the losers had in their turn the liberty of raffling upon the next vacancy. Thus hope and expectation would be kept alive, none would complain of broken promises, but impute their disappointments wholly to fortune, whose shoulders are broader and stronger than those of a ministry.

Another professor showed me a large paper of instructions for discovering plots and conspiracies against the government. He advised great statesmen to examine into the diet of all suspected persons; their times of eating; upon which side they lay in bed; with which hand they wiped their posteriors; to take a strict view of their excrements, and, from the colour, the odour, the taste, the consistence, the crudeness or maturity of digestion, form a judgment of their thoughts and designs. Because men are never so serious, thoughtful, and intent, as when they are at stool, which he found by frequent experiment; for in such conjunctures, when he used merely as a trial to consider which was the best way of murdering the king, his ordure would have a tincture of green, but quite different when he thought only of raising an insurrection or burning the metropolis.

The whole discourse was written with great acuteness, containing many observations both curious and useful for politicans, but as I conceived not altogether complete. This I ventured to tell the author, and offered if he pleased to supply him with some additions. He received my proposition with more compliance than is usual among writers, especially those of the projecting species, professing he would be glad to receive farther information.

I told him that in the kingdom of Tribnia, by the natives called Langden, where I had sojourned some time in my travels, the bulk of the people consist in a manner wholly of discoverers, witnesses, informers, accusers, prosecutors, evidences, swearers, together with their several subservient and subaltern instruments, all under the colours and conduct of ministers of state and their deputies. The plots in that kingdom are usually the workmanship of those persons who desire to raise their own characters of profound politicians, to restore new vigour to a crazy administration, to stifle or divert general discontents, to fill their pockets with forfeitures, and raise or sink the opinion of public credit, as either shall best answer their private advantage. It is first agreed and settled among them, what suspected persons shall be accused of a plot; then, effectual care is taken to secure all their letters and papers, and put the criminals in chains. These papers are delivered to a set of artists, very dexterous in finding out the mysterious meanings of words, syllables, and letters. For instance, they can discover a close-stool to signify a privy council; a flock of geese, a senate; a lame dog, an invader; a codshead, a —; the plague, a standing army; a buzzard, a prime minister; the gout, a high priest; a gibbet, a secretary of state; a chamber-pot, a committee of grandees; a sieve, a court lady; a broom, a revolution; a mouse-trap, an employment; a bottomless pit, the treasury; a sink, the court; a cap and bells, a favourite; a broken reed, a court of justice; an empty tun, a general; a running sore, the administration.

When this method fails, they have two others more effectual, which the learned among them call acrostics and anagrams. First they can decipher all initial letters into political meanings. Thus, *N.* shall signify a plot; *B.* a regiment of horse; *L.* a fleet at sea; or secondly by transposing the letters of the alphabet in any suspected paper, they can discover the deepest designs of a discontented party. So for example if I should say in a letter to a friend, *Our brother* Tom *has just got the piles*, a skilful decipherer would discover that the same letters which compose that sentence may be analysed into the following words: *Resist, a plot is brought home; The tour*. And this is the anagrammatic method.

The professor made me great acknowledgments for communicating these observations, and promised to make honourable mention of me in his treatise.

I saw nothing in this country that could invite me to a longer continuance, and began to think of returning home to England.

*   *   *

ALEXANDER POPE
1688–1744

Deformed and in constant ill health, Pope never traveled abroad except in his imagination, which was both lively and profound. He knew by both precept and learned inference that

By travel, generous souls enlarge the mind.

That sentiment he puts into the mouth of his version of the King of Brobdingnag, the leader of the virtuous giants Gulliver encounters on his Second Voyage.

As the foremost satiric poet in English and as an acute observer of the corruption of once-noble institutions, Pope couldn't help noticing the farce the Grand Tour had become by the 1740s, and in The Dunciad *he ridiculed this conventional way of acquainting a young man with the glories of the Continent. In the selection below, the youth's tutor-guide presents his finished handiwork to the Goddess of Dullness (i.e., Stupidity). She blesses the student, learned now only in dress, drink, cuisine, operas, and bawdyhouses. He has had to hurry home, it proves, because he has sneaked away from a duel and impregnated a nun, who is after him. Indeed, if he is not soon elected to Parliament, where he will be immune to arrest for debt, he will be quite ruined.*

THE WORDS OF THE KING OF BROBDINGNAG, AS HE HELD CAPTAIN GULLIVER BETWEEN HIS FINGER AND THUMB FOR THE INSPECTION OF THE SAGES AND LEARNED MEN OF THE COURT (C. 1727)

In miniature see nature's power appear;
Which wings the Sun-born Insects of the Air,
Which frames the harvest-bug, too small for sight,
And forms the bones and muscles of the mite!
Here view him stretch'd. The microscope explains
That the blood, circling, flows in human veins;
See, in the tube he pants, and sprawling lies,
Stretches his little hands, and rolls his eyes!

Smit with his country's Love, I've heard him prate
Of laws and manners in his pigmy state.
By travel, generous souls enlarge the mind,
Which home-bred prepossession had confin'd;
Yet will he boast of many regions known,
But still, with partial love, extol his own.
He talks of senates, and of courtly tribes,
Admires their ardour, but forgets their bribes;
Of hireling lawyers tells the just decrees,
Applauds their eloquence, but sinks their fees.

Yet who his country's partial love can blame?
'Tis sure some virtue to conceal its shame.

The world's the native city of the wise;
He sees his Britain with a mother's eyes;
Softens defects, and heightens all its charms,
Calls it the seat of empire, arts and arms!
Fond of his hillock isle, his narrow mind
Thinks worth, wit, learning, to that spot confin'd;
Thus ants, who for a grain employ their cares,
Think all the business of the earth is theirs.
Thus honeycombs seem palaces to bees;
And mites imagine all the world a cheese.

When pride in such contemptuous beings lies,
In beetles, Britons, bugs and butterflies,
Shall we, like reptiles, glory in conceit?
Humility's the virtue of the Great.

From THE DUNCIAD
(1742)

In flowed at once a gay embroidered race,
And tittering pushed the pedants off the place:
Some would have spoken, but the voice was drowned
By the French horn, or by the opening hound.
The first came forwards with as easy mien
As if he saw St. James's and the Queen.
When thus the attendant orator begun,
"Receive, great Empress! thy accomplished son:
Thine from the birth, and sacred from the rod,
A dauntless infant! never scared with God.
The sire saw, one by one, his virtues wake:
The mother begged the blessing of a rake.
Thou gav'st that ripeness, which so soon began,
And ceased so soon, he ne'er was boy nor man.
Through school and college, thy kind cloud o'ercast,
Safe and unseen the young Aeneas passed.
Thence bursting glorious, all at once let down,

Stunned with his giddy larum half the town.
Intrepid then, o'er seas and lands he flew:
Europe he saw, and Europe saw him too.
There all thy gifts and graces we display,
Thou, only thou, directing all our way!
To where the Seine, obsequious as she runs,
Pours at great Bourbon's feet her silken sons;
Or Tiber, now no longer Roman, rolls,
Vain of Italian arts, Italian souls:
To happy convents, bosomed deep in vines,
Where slumber abbots, purple as their wines:
To isles of fragrance, lily-silvered vales,
Diffusing languor in the panting gales:
To lands of singing, or of dancing slaves,
Love-whispering woods, and lute-resounding waves.
But chief her shrine where naked Venus keeps,
And cupids ride the lion of the deeps;
Where, eased of fleets, the Adriatic main
Wafts the smooth eunuch and enamored swain.
Led by my hand, he sauntered Europe round,
And gathered every vice on Christian ground;
Saw every court, heard every king declare
His royal sense of operas or the fair;
The stews and palace equally explored,
Intrigued with glory, and with spirit whored;
Tried all hors d'oeuvres, all liqueurs defined,
Judicious drank, and greatly-daring dined;
Dropped the dull lumber of the Latin store,
Spoiled his own language, and acquired no more;
All classic learning lost on classic ground;
And last turned *air*, the echo of a sound!
See now, half-cured, and perfectly well-bred,
With nothing but a solo in his head;
As much estate, and principle, and wit,
As Jansen, Fleetwood, Cibber shall think fit;
Stolen from a duel, followed by a nun,
And, if a borough choose him not, undone;
See, to my country happy I restore
This glorious youth, and add one Venus more.
Her too receive (for her my soul adores)
So may the sons of sons of sons of whores,
Prop thine, O Empress! like each neighbour throne,

And make a long posterity thy own."
Pleased, she accepts the hero, and the dame
Wraps in her veil, and frees from sense of shame.

JAMES BOSWELL
1740–1795

This sensitive, alcoholic, and promiscuous Scottish lawyer produced one of the greatest of biographies, The Life of Samuel Johnson, *but the full extent of his writings was not entirely realized until the twentieth century, when his private papers, long thought destroyed, were discovered practically intact. The most important of these is the journal he kept from the age of eighteen. This records his quarrels with his father, his legal studies in Edinburgh and Glasgow, his heady residence in London and his attempt to get a commission in the Guards there, his meeting and growing friendship with Johnson, his frantic sexual obsessions and gratifications, and his travels.*

In 1764, bored by further legal studies at Utrecht, in Holland, he set off on his Grand Tour, which took him to the German courts, Switzerland, Italy, and France. He contrived "interviews" with both Voltaire and Rousseau and stopped off at the island of Corsica, where an interesting revolutionary leader, Pasquali di Paoli, was asserting the independence of Corsica from the Genoese. Boswell stayed long enough to collect materials for his immensely popular book An Account of Corsica, The Journal of a Tour to that Island. *This brought him a most welcome celebrity as "Corsica Boswell": "I am really the Great Man now," he noted. His trip to the Hebridean Islands with the illustrious Johnson in 1773 resulted in another travel book,* A Journal of a Tour to the Hebrides with Samuel Johnson, LL.D., *published only in 1785, after Johnson's death.*

The first passage below, describing Boswell's encounter with the sights of Rome, he wrote in French. It has been translated by Frederick A. Pottle and Frank Brady.

From JOURNAL
(1765)

MONDAY 25 MARCH. Mr. Morison, a Scottish antiquary, began to show me the most remarkable sights of Rome. We went out in the morning, as we intended to do every day. We saw the Pope go by in procession through one of the principal streets on his way to the Minerva. It was thus I saw for the first time a dignitary who was so important in former times, and who still remains a prince of extraordinary power. We saw the ceremony at the Minerva, where his Holiness was carried on a magnificent chair decorated with a figure of the Holy Ghost. He made the round of the church and gave his blessing to the whole congregation, who knelt before his Holiness. Then he took his place on a sort of throne, where, after he had performed certain sacred rites of which I understood nothing, people kissed his slipper. After this there was a procession of Roman girls who had received dowries from a public foundation, some to be married and others to become nuns. They marched in separate groups, the nuns coming last and wearing crowns. Only a few of them were pretty, and most of the pretty ones were nuns. It was a curious enough function.

Then we went to the Capitoline hill. We climbed on the roof of the modern Senate, from which Mr. Morison pointed out ancient Rome on its seven hills. He showed me a little map of it, and read me a clear summary of the growth of this famous city to its present extent.

TUESDAY 26 MARCH. We viewed the celebrated Forum. I experienced sublime and melancholy emotions as I thought of all the great affairs which had taken place there, and saw the place now all in ruins, with the wretched huts of carpenters and other artisans occupying the site of that rostrum from which Cicero had flung forth his stunning eloquence. I saw there the remains of the magnificent portico that once adorned the Forum, whose three remaining columns give us a superb idea of what it was. We entered the famous Colosseum, which certainly presents a vast and sublime idea of the grandeur of the ancient Romans. It is hard to tell whether the astonishing massiveness or the exquisite taste of this superb building should be more admired. A hermit has a little apartment inside. We passed through his hermitage to climb to where the seats and corridors of the theatre once were; Mr. Morison gave me a clear picture of all this. It was shocking to discover several portions of this theatre full of dung. It is rented to people who use it in this fashion.

WEDNESDAY 27 MARCH. We went out in the afternoon. We climbed the Palatine hill, where the magnificent Palace of the emperors stood. Since it has suffered many changes, we must believe that the ruins we now see date from the time of Domitian. We saw a superb hall from which one can judge the grandeur of this imperial mansion, and we went down to see the baths, where one can yet see on the ceiling fragments of stucco-work painted and gilded in a very elegant manner. We walked to where the house of Cicero had stood. A statue there resembles him a great deal. Struck by these famous places, I was seized with enthusiasm. I began to speak Latin. Mr. Morison replied. He laughed a bit at the beginning. But we made a resolution to speak Latin continually during this course of antiquities. We have persisted, and every day we speak with greater facility, so that we have harangued on Roman antiquities in the language of the Romans themselves.

THURSDAY 28 MARCH. We climbed to the Palace again, where the cypresses seem to mourn for the ruin of the grandeur of the Roman emperors. The view from here is magnificent. We went to the Capitoline hill. We saw a fragment of the temple of Jupiter Tonans, which was architecturally very handsome. We saw in a church the famous Tullia prison, of which Sallust gives so hideous a picture and where Paul and Silas were imprisoned. Catholics say Peter and Paul. They show a stone against which the head of the Prince of the Apostles was dashed. The mark remains very distinct. We saw the hole down which criminals were thrown, the stone to which the two apostles were chained, a well which sprang up by miracle to furnish them with water to baptize the [jailer]. The water has a taste like milk. It's only a little [impregnated with] sulphur.

SATURDAY 30 MARCH. We saw the Baths of Diocletian, whose plan was explained to me by my antiquary. In the Carthusian church we saw also a fresco by Pompeo Batoni depicting Simon Magus carried in the air by demons to show that he could perform miracles as well as Peter. The Saint worships God, and points with his finger to the place where Simon Magus will fall. A group watches this event. The composition of this painting is excellent. But Peter appears too uneasy, as if he were afraid that his prayers would not be effective. The colouring is false and unnatural, as if Peter had not only caused Simon to fall but had discoloured the flesh of all those around him. In Santa Maria Maggiore we saw some fine columns of oriental marble. I must not forget to add in passing that we saw a strange fellow sitting in the sun reading Tasso to a group of others in rags like himself.

* * *

It is true that Siena does not have great variety and may appear a little tedious to an active mind. The nobility is very ignorant, or if they have knowledge, they make very little use of it in conversation. I have often wondered how it is possible for human beings to live from day to day without cultivating the mind, without progressing in knowledge, without any increase in intellectual enjoyment. The philosophical systems which assert man to be an animal who is continuously improving are contradicted by this city.

The Emperor's death has been a great source of conversation for our ladies and gentlemen. The mourning which will have to be worn has been conceived of in a thousand different fashions, and the lively, fantastical imagination of the Italians has shown itself all in its splendour.

I am naturally of a timid disposition, and my education has increased this timidity. Philosophy has cured this weakness somewhat, but occasionally it recurs and makes me feel ridiculous and miserable as before. The circulation of the blood is certainly what makes a man lively or sluggish, and yesterday my blood was circulating very badly. I sat then by Signora Girolama and looked at some ladies whom I saw for the first time, and I had an absurd but real anxiety. I could not escape this feeling, and I suffered like a man who has never been in company.

I am now in a beautiful town in Tuscany. I am well thought of by all the nobility. I enjoy the honest friendship of some pleasant ladies. I am studying the beautiful Italian language and making good progress. I am also studying music with an excellent teacher; I play my flute and sing with real enjoyment. I am enjoying good health. The weather is clear and agreeable. I can do everything I wish. I am in a situation which I imagined in my most delicious moments. And yet I cannot say I am happy. I am surprised at this. I don't know what to think. I don't know what to look for. Undoubtedly, in this world no man can be completely happy. Oh, no—sad thought! Abbé Crocchi, my esteemed instructor, advises me to consider this lack of happiness as a strong proof of the immortality of the soul, and of a better life in another world.

*   *   *

From THE JOURNAL OF A
TOUR TO CORSICA
(1768)

Having resolved to pass some years abroad for my instruction and entertainment, I conceived a design of visiting the island of Corsica. I wished for something more than just the common course of what is called the tour of Europe; and Corsica occurred to me as a place which nobody else had seen, and where I should find what was to be seen nowhere else, a people actually fighting for liberty and forming themselves from a poor, inconsiderable, oppressed nation into a flourishing and independent state.

When I got into Switzerland, I went to see M. Rousseau. He was then living in romantic retirement, from whence, perhaps, it had been better for him never to have descended. While he was at a distance, his singular eloquence filled our minds with high ideas of the wild philosopher. When he came into the walks of men, we know alas! how much these ideas suffered.

He entertained me very courteously, for I was recommended to him by my honoured friend the Earl Marischal, with whom I had the happiness of travelling through a part of Germany. I had heard that M. Rousseau had some correspondence with the Corsicans, and had been desired to assist them in forming their laws. I told him my scheme of going to visit them after I had completed my tour of Italy, and I insisted that he should give me a letter of introduction. He immediately agreed to do so whenever I should acquaint him of my time of going thither, for he saw that my enthusiasm for the brave islanders was as warm as his own.

I accordingly wrote to him from Rome, in April 1765, that I had fixed the month of September for my Corsican expedition, and therefore begged of him to send me the letter of introduction, which if he refused I should certainly go without it and probably be hanged as a spy. So let him answer for the consequences.

* * *

The charms of sweet Siena detained me longer than they should have done. I required the hardy air of Corsica to brace me after the delights of Tuscany.

I recollect with astonishment how little the real state of Corsica was known, even by those who had good access to know it. An officer of rank in the British navy, who had been in several ports of the island, told me that I run the risk of my life in going among these barbarians; for that his surgeon's mate went ashore to take the diversion of shooting and every moment was alarmed by some of the natives who started from the bushes with loaded guns and, if he had not been protected by Corsican guides, would have certainly blown out his brains.

Nay at Leghorn, which is within a day's sailing of Corsica and has a constant intercourse with it, I found people who dissuaded me from going thither because it might be dangerous.

I was, however, under no apprehension in going to Corsica. Count

Rivarola, the Sardinian Consul, who is himself a Corsican, assuring me that the island was then in a very civilized state; and besides that in the rudest times no Corsican would ever attack a stranger. The Count was so good as to give me most obliging letters to many people in the island. I had now been in several foreign countries. I had found that I was able to accommodate myself to my fellow creatures of different languages and sentiments. I did not fear that it would be a difficult task for me to make myself easy with the plain and generous Corsicans.

The only danger I saw was that I might be taken by some of the Barbary corsairs, and have a trial of slavery among the Turks at Algiers. I spoke of it to Commodore Harrison, who commanded the British squadron in the Mediterranean and was then lying with his ship, the *Centurion*, in the bay of Leghorn. He assured me that if the Turks did take me they should not keep me long, but in order to prevent it he was so good as to grant me a very ample and particular passport; and as it could be of no use if I did not meet the corsairs, he said very pleasantly when he gave it me, "I hope, Sir, it shall be of no use to you."

Before I left Leghorn, I could observe that my tour was looked upon by the Italian politicians in a very serious light, as if truly I had a commission from my Court to negotiate a treaty with the Corsicans. The more I disclaimed any such thing the more they persevered in affirming it, and I was considered as a very close young man. I therefore just allowed them to make a minister of me till time should undeceive them.

I sailed from Leghorn in a Tuscan vessel which was going over to Capo Corso for wine. I preferred this to a vessel going to Bastia, because as I did not know how the French General was affected towards the Corsicans I was afraid that he might not permit me to go forward to Paoli. I therefore resolved to land on the territories of the nation, and after I had been with the illustrious chief to pay my respects to the French if I should find it safe.

Though from Leghorn to Corsica is usually but one day's sailing, there was so dead a calm that it took us two days. The first day was the most tedious. However, there were two or three Corsicans aboard, and one of them played on the *cetra* [zither], which amused me a good deal. At sunset all the people in the ship sung the Ave Maria with great devotion and some melody. It was pleasing to enter into the spirit of their religion, and hear them offering up their evening orisons.

The second day we became better acquainted, and more lively and cheerful. The worthy Corsicans thought it was proper to give a moral lesson to a young traveller just come from Italy. They told me that in their country I should be treated with the greatest hospitality, but if I attempted to debauch any of their women I might expect instant death.

I employed myself several hours in rowing, which gave me great spirits. I relished fully my approach to the island, which had acquired an unusual grandeur in my imagination. As long as I can remember anything I have heard of "the malcontents of Corsica, with Paoli at their head." It was a curious thought that I was just going to see them.

About seven o'clock at night we landed safely in the harbour of Centuri. I learnt that Signor Giacomini of this place, to whom I was recommended by Count Rivarola, was just dead. He had made a handsome fortune in the East Indies; and having had a remarkable warmth in the cause of liberty during his whole life he showed it in the strongest manner in his last will. He bequeathed a considerable sum of money and some pieces of ordnance to the nation. He also left it in charge to his heir to live in Corsica, and be firm in the patriotic interest; and if ever the island should again be reduced under the power of the Genoese, he ordered him to retire with all his effects to Leghorn. Upon these conditions only could his heir enjoy his estate.

I was directed to the house of Signor Giacomini's cousin, Signor Antonio Antonetti at Morsiglia, about a mile up the country. The prospect of the mountains covered with vines and olives was extremely agreeable, and the odour of the myrtle and other aromatic shrubs and flowers that grew all around me was very refreshing. As I walked along, I often saw Corsican peasants come suddenly out from the covert; and as they were all armed, I saw how the frightened imagination of the surgeon's mate had raised up so many assassins. Even the man who carried my baggage was armed and, had I been timorous, might have alarmed me. But he and I were very good company to each other. As it grew dusky, I repeated to myself these lines from a fine passage in Ariosto:

> E pur per selve oscure e calli obliqui
> Insieme van senza sospetto aversi.
>
> [Together through dark woods and winding ways
> They walk, nor on their hearts suspicion preys.]

I delivered Signor Antonetti the letter for his deceased cousin. He read it, and received me with unaffected cordiality, making an apology for my frugal entertainment but assuring me of a hearty welcome. His true kindly hospitality was also shown in taking care of my servant, an honest Swiss who loved to eat and drink well.

I had formed a strange notion that I should see everything in Corsica totally different from what I had seen in any other country. I was therefore much surprised to find Signor Antonetti's house quite an Italian one, with very good furniture, prints, and copies of some of the famous pictures. In particular, I was struck to find here a small copy from Raphael of St. Michael and the Dragon. There was no necessity for its being well done. To see the thing at all was what surprised me.

Signor Antonetti gave me an excellent light repast and a very good bed. He spoke with great strength of the patriotic cause, and with great veneration of the General. I was quite easy, and liked much the opening of my Corsican tour.

The next day, being Sunday, it rained very hard; and I must observe that the Corsicans with all their resolution are afraid of bad weather to a degree of effeminacy. I got indeed a droll but a just enough account of this from one of them: "Sir," said he, "if you were as poor as a Corsican and had but one coat, so as that after being wet you could not put on dry clothes, you would be afraid too." Signor Antonetti would not allow me to set out while it rained, for, said he, "If a man finds himself abroad, there is no help for it. But to go deliberately out is too much."

When the day grew a little better, I accompanied Signor Antonetti and his family to hear mass in the parish church, a very pretty little building about half a quarter of a mile off.

Signor Antonetti's parish priest was to preach to us, at which I was much pleased, being very curious to hear a Corsican sermon. Our priest did very well. His text was in the Psalms: "Descendunt ad infernum viventes." ["They go down alive into the pit."] After endeavouring to move our passions with a description of the horrors of hell, he told us, "Saint Catherine of Siena wished to be laid on the mouth of this dreadful pit that she might stop it up, so as no more unhappy souls should fall into it. I confess, my brethren, I have not the zeal of holy Saint Catherine. But I do what I can; I warn you how to avoid it." He then gave us some good practical advice, and concluded.

The weather being now cleared up, I took leave of the worthy gentleman to whom I had been a guest. He gave me a letter to Signor Damiano Tomasi, Padre del Commune at Pino, the next village. I got a man with an ass to carry my baggage. But such a road I never saw. It was absolutely scrambling along the face of a rock overhanging the sea, upon a path sometimes not above a foot broad. I thought the ass rather retarded me, so I prevailed with the man to take my portmanteau and other things on his back.

Had I formed my opinion of Corsica from what I saw this morning,

I might have been in as bad humour with it as Seneca was, whose reflections in prose are not inferior to his epigrams: "What can be found so bare, what so rugged all around as this rock? what more barren of provisions? what more rude as to its inhabitants? what in the very situation of the place more horrible? what in climate more intemperate? Yet there are more foreigners than natives here. So far then is a change of place from being disagreeable, that even this place hath brought some people away from their country."

At Pino I was surprised to find myself met by some brisk young fellows dressed like English sailors and speaking English tolerably well. They had been often with cargoes of wine at Leghorn, where they had picked up what they knew of our language, and taken clothes in part of payment for some of their merchandise.

I was cordially entertained at Signor Tomasi's. Throughout all Corsica, except in garrison towns, there is hardly an inn. I met with a single one about eight miles from Corte. Before I was accustomed to the Corsican hospitality, I sometimes forgot myself, and imagining I was in a public house called for what I wanted with the tone which one uses in calling to the waiters at a tavern. I did so at Pino, asking for a variety of things at once; when Signora Tomasi perceiving my mistake looked in my face and smiled, saying with much calmness and good nature, "One thing after another, Sir."

In writing this Journal, I shall not tire my readers with relating the occurrences of each particular day. It will be much more agreeable to them to have a free and continued account of what I saw or heard most worthy of observation.

For some time I had very curious travelling, mostly on foot, and attended by a couple of stout women who carried my baggage upon their heads. Every time that I prepared to set out from a village, I could not help laughing to see the good people eager to have my equipage in order and roaring out, "The women, the women."

I had full leisure and the best opportunities to observe everything in my progress through the island. I was lodged sometimes in private houses, sometimes in convents, being always well recommended from place to place. The first convent in which I lay was at Canari. It appeared a little odd at first. But I soon learnt to repair to my dormitory as naturally as if I had been a friar for seven years.

The convents were small, decent buildings, suited to the sober ideas of their pious inhabitants. The religious who devoutly endeavour to "walk with God" are often treated with raillery by those whom pleasure or business prevents from thinking of future and more exalted objects. A little experience of the serenity and peace of mind to be found in convents would be of use to temper the fire of men of the world. At Patrimonio I found the seat of a provincial magistracy. The chief judge was there, and entertained me very well. Upon my arrival, the captain of the guard came out and demanded who I was. I replied "English." He looked at me seriously, and then said in a tone between regret and upbraiding, "The English—they were once our friends, but they are so no more." I felt for my country, and was abashed before this honest soldier.

At Oletta I visited Count Nicholas Rivarola, brother to my friend at Leghorn. He received me with great kindness, and did everything in his power to make me easy. I found here a Corsican who thought better of the British than the captain of the guard at Patrimonio. He talked of our bombarding San Fiorenzo in favour of the patriots, and willingly gave me his horse for the afternoon, which he said he would not have done to a man of any other nation.

When I came to Murato, I had the pleasure of being made acquainted with Signor Barbaggi, who is married to the niece of Paoli. I found him to be a sensible, intelligent, well-bred man. The mint of Corsica was in his house. I got specimens of their different kinds of money in silver and copper, and was told that they hoped in a year or two to strike some gold coins. Signor Barbaggi's house was repairing, so I was lodged in the convent. But in the morning returned to breakfast and had chocolate, and at dinner we had no less than twelve well-dressed dishes, served on Dresden china, with a dessert, different sorts of wine, and a liqueur, all the produce of Corsica. Signor Barbaggi was frequently repeating to me that the Corsicans inhabited a rude, uncultivated country and that they lived like Spartans. I begged leave to ask him in what country he could show me greater luxury than I had seen in his house; and I said I should certainly tell wherever I went what tables the Corsicans kept, notwithstanding their pretensions to poverty and temperance. A good deal of pleasantry passed upon this. His lady was a genteel woman, and appeared to be agreeable though very reserved.

From Murato to Corte, I travelled through a wild, mountainous, rocky country, diversified with some large valleys. I got little beasts for me and my servant, sometimes horses but oftener mules or asses. We had no bridles but cords fixed round their necks, with which we managed them as well as we could.

At Corte I waited upon the Supreme Council, to one of whom, Signor Boccheciampe, I had a letter from Signor Barbaggi. I was very politely received, and was conducted to the Franciscan convent where I got the apartment of Paoli, who was then some days' journey beyond the mountains, holding a court of sindacato [circuit] at a village called Sollacarò.

As the General resided for some time in this convent, the fathers made a better appearance than any I saw in the island. I was principally attended by the Prior, a resolute divine who had formerly been in the army, and by Padre Giulio, a man of much address who still favours me with his correspondence.

These fathers have a good vineyard and an excellent garden. They have between thirty and forty beehives in long wooden cases or trunks of trees, with a covering of the bark of the cork tree. When they want honey they burn a little juniper-wood, the smoke of which makes the bees retire. They then take an iron instrument with a sharp-edged crook at one end of it and bring out the greatest part of the honey-comb, leaving only a little for the bees, who work the case full again. By taking the honey in this way they never kill a bee. They seemed much at their ease, living in peace and plenty. I often joked with them on the text which is applied to their order: "Nihil habentes et omnia possidentes." ["Having nothing, and yet possessing all things."]

I went to the choir with them. The service was conducted with propriety, and Padre Giulio played on the organ. On the great altar of their church is a tabernacle carved in wood by a religious. It is a piece of exquisite workmanship. A Genoese gentleman offered to give them one in silver for it, but they would not make the exchange.

These fathers have no library worth mentioning, but their convent is large and well built. I looked about with great attention to see if I could find any inscriptions, but the only one I found was upon a certain useful edifice:

> Sine necessitate huc non intrate,
> Quia necessaria sumus.
>
> [Enter here only if necessary,
> this being the Necessary House.]

A studied, rhyming Latin conceit marked upon such a place was truly ludicrous.

I chose to stop a while at Corte to repose myself after my fatigues, and to see everything about the capital of Corsica. The morning after my arrival here, three French deserters desired to speak with me. The foolish fellows had taken it into their heads that I was come to raise recruits for Scotland, and so they begged to have the honour of going along with me; I suppose with intention to have the honour of running off from me as they had done from their own regiments.

I received many civilities at Corte from Signor Boccheciampe and from Signor Massesi, the Great Chancellor, whose son Signor Luigi, a young gentleman of much vivacity and natural politeness, was so good as to attend me constantly as my conductor. I used to call him my governor. I liked him much, for as he had never been out of the island his ideas were entirely Corsican.

Such of the members of the Supreme Council as were in residence during my stay at Corte I found to be solid and sagacious, men of penetration and ability well calculated to assist the General in forming his political plans and in turning to the best advantage the violence and enterprise of the people.

The University was not then sitting, so I could only see the rooms, which were shown me by the Abbé Valentini, Procurator of the University. The professors were all absent except one Capuchin father whom I visited at his convent. It is a tolerable building with a pretty large collection of books. There is in the church here a tabernacle carved in wood, in the manner of that at the Franciscans', but much inferior to it.

I went up to the Castle of Corte. The Commandant very civilly showed me every part of it. As I wished to see all things in Corsica, I desired to see even the unhappy criminals. There were then three in the Castle: a man for the murder of his wife, a married lady who had hired one of her servants to strangle a woman of whom she was jealous, and the servant who had actually perpetrated this barbarous action. They were brought out from their cells that I might talk with them. The murderer of his wife had a stupid, hardened appearance, and told me he did it at the instigation of the devil. The servant was a poor despicable wretch. He had at first accused his mistress but was afterwards prevailed with to deny his accusation, upon which he was put to the torture by having lighted matches held between his fingers. This made him return to what he had formerly said, so as to be a strong evidence against his mistress. His hands were so miserably scorched that he was a piteous object. I asked him why he had committed such a crime; he said, "Because I was without understanding." The lady seemed of a bold and resolute spirit. She spoke to me with great firmness and denied her guilt, saying with a contemptuous smile as she pointed to her servant, "They can force that creature to say what they please."

The hangman of Corsica was a great curiosity. Being held in the utmost detestation, he durst not live like another inhabitant of the island. He was obliged to take refuge in the Castle, and there he was kept in a little corner turret, where he had just room for a miserable bed and a little bit of fire to dress such victals for himself as were sufficient to keep him alive; for nobody would have any intercourse with him, but all turned their backs upon him. I went up and looked at him. And a more dirty, rueful spectacle I never beheld. He seemed sensible of his situation and held down his head like an abhorred outcast.

It was a long time before they could get a hangman in Corsica, so that the punishment of the gallows was hardly known, all their criminals being shot. At last this creature whom I saw, who is a Sicilian, came with a message to Paoli. The General, who has a wonderful talent for physiognomy, on seeing the man said immediately to some of the people about him, "Behold our hangman." He gave orders to ask the man if he would accept of the office, and his answer was, "My grandfather was a hangman, my father was a hangman. I have been a hangman myself and am willing to continue so." He was therefore immediately put into office, and the ignominious death dispensed by his hands hath had more effect than twenty executions by firearms.

It is remarkable that no Corsican would upon any account consent to be a hangman. Not the greatest criminals, who might have had their lives upon that condition. Even the wretch who for a paltry hire had strangled a woman would rather submit to death than do the same action as the executioner of the law.

When I had seen everything about Corte, I prepared for my journey over the mountains, that I might be with Paoli. The night before I set out I recollected that I had forgotten to get a passport, which in the present situation of Corsica is still a necessary precaution. After supper, therefore, the Prior walked with me to Corte to the house of the Great Chancellor, who ordered the passport to be made out immediately, and, while his secretary was writing it, entertained me by reading to me some of the minutes of the General Consulta. When the passport was finished and ready to have the seal put to it, I was much pleased with a beautiful, simple incident. The Chancellor desired a little boy who was playing in the room by us to run to his mother and bring the great seal of the kingdom. I thought myself sitting in the house of a Cincinnatus.

Next morning I set out in very good order, having excellent mules and active, clever Corsican guides. My worthy fathers of the convent, who treated me in the kindest manner while I was their guest, would also give me some provisions for my journey, so they put up a gourd of their best wine and some delicious pomegranates. My Corsican guides appeared so hearty that I often got down and walked along with them, doing just what I saw them do. When we grew hungry, we threw stones among the thick branches of the chestnut trees which overshadowed us, and in that manner we brought down a shower of chestnuts with which we filled our pockets, and went on eating them with great relish; and when this made us thirsty, we lay down by the side of the first brook, put our mouths to the stream and drank sufficiently. It was just being for a little while one of the "prisca gens mortalium, [primitive race of men]," who ran about in the woods eating acorns and drinking water.

While I stopped to refresh my mules at a little village, the inhabitants came crowding about me as an ambassador going to their General. When they were informed of my country, a strong, black fellow among them said, "English! they are barbarians; they don't believe in the great God." I told him, "Excuse me, Sir. We do believe in God, and in Jesus Christ too." "Um," said he, "and in the Pope?" "No." "And why?" This was a puzzling question in these circumstances, for there was a great audience to the controversy. I thought I would try a method of my own, and very gravely replied, "Because we are too far off." A very new argument against the universal infallibility of the Pope. It took, however, for my opponent mused a while, and then said, "Too far off! Why, Sicily is as far off as England. Yet in Sicily they believe in the Pope." "Oh," said I, "we are ten times farther off than Sicily." "Aha!" said he, and seemed quite satisfied. In this manner I got off very well. I question whether any of the learned reasonings of our Protestant divines would have had so good an effect.

My journey over the mountains was very entertaining. I passed some immense ridges and vast woods. I was in great health and spirits, and fully able to enter into the ideas of the brave, rude men whom I found in all quarters.

At Bastelica, where there is a stately spirited race of people, I had a large company to attend me in the convent. I liked to see their natural frankness and ease, for why should men be afraid of their own species? They just came in, making an easy bow, placed themselves round the room where I was sitting, rested themselves on their muskets, and immediately entered into conversation with me. They talked very feelingly of the miseries that their country had endured, and complained that they were still but in a state of poverty. I happened at that time to have an unusual flow of spirits, and as one who finds himself amongst utter strangers in a distant country has no timidity, I harangued the men of Bastelica with great fluency. I expatiated on the bravery of the Corsicans by which they had purchased liberty, the most valuable of all possessions, and rendered themselves glorious over all Europe. Their poverty, I told them, might be remedied by a proper cultivation of their island and by engaging a little in commerce. But I bid them remember that they were much happier in their present state than in a state of refinement and vice, and that therefore they should beware of luxury.

What I said had the good fortune to touch them, and several of them repeated the same sentiments much better than I could do. They all expressed their strong attachment to Paoli, and called out in one voice that they were all at his command. I could with pleasure have passed a long time here.

At Ornano I saw the ruins of the seat where the great Sampiero had his residence. They were a pretty droll society of monks in the convent at Ornano. When I told them that I was an Englishman, "Ay, ay," said one of them, "as was well observed by a reverend bishop, when talking of your pretended reformation, 'Angli olim angeli nunc diaboli.' ['The English. once angels, now devils.']" I looked upon this as an honest effusion of spiritual zeal. The fathers took good care of me in temporals.

When I at last came within sight of Sollacarò, where Paoli was, I could not help being under considerable anxiety. My ideas of him had been greatly heightened by the conversations I had held with all sorts of people in the island, they having represented him to me as something above humanity. I had the strongest desire to see so exalted a character, but I feared that I should be unable to give a proper account why I had presumed to trouble him with a visit, and that I should sink to nothing before him. I almost wished yet to go back without seeing him. These workings of sensibility employed my mind till I rode through the village and came up to the house where he was lodged.

Leaving my servant with my guides, I passed through the guards and was met by some of the General's people, who conducted me into an antechamber where were several gentlemen in waiting. Signor Boccheciampe had notified my arrival, and I was shown into Paoli's room. I found him alone, and was struck with his appearance. He is tall, strong, and well made; of a fair complexion, a sensible, free, and open countenance, and a manly and noble carriage. He was then in his fortieth year. He was dressed in green and gold. He used to wear the common Corsican habit, but on the arrival of the French he thought a little external elegance might be of use to make the government appear in a more respectable light.

He asked me what were my commands for him. I presented him a letter from Count Rivarola, and when he had read it I showed him my letter from Rousseau. He was polite but very reserved. I had stood in the presence of many a prince, but I never had such a trial as in the presence of Paoli. I have already said that he is a great physiognomist. In consequence of his being in continual danger from treachery and assassination, he has formed a habit of studiously observing every new face. For ten minutes we walked backwards and forwards through the room hardly saying a word, while he looked at me with a steadfast, keen, and penetrating eye, as if he searched my very soul.

This interview was for a while very severe upon me. I was much relieved when his reserve wore off and he began to speak more. I then ventured to address him with this compliment to the Corsicans: "Sir, I am upon my travels, and have lately visited Rome. I am come from seeing the ruins of one brave and free people; I now see the rise of another."

He received my compliment very graciously, but observed that the Corsicans had no chance of being like the Romans, a great conquering nation who should extend its empire over half the globe. Their situation, and the modern political systems, rendered this impossible. "But," said he, "Corsica may be a very happy country."

He expressed a high admiration of M. Rousseau, whom Signor Buttafoco had invited to Corsica to aid the nation in forming its laws. It seems M. de Voltaire had reported, in his rallying manner, that the invitation was merely a trick which he had put upon Rousseau. Paoli told me that when he understood this, he himself wrote to Rousseau enforcing the invitation.

*   *   *

Some of the nobles who attended him came into the room, and in a little we were told that dinner was served up. The General did me the honour to place me next him. He had a table of fifteen or sixteen covers, having always a good many of the principal men of the island with him. He had an Italian cook who had been long in France, but he chose to have a few plain substantial dishes, avoiding every kind of luxury and drinking no foreign wine.

I felt myself under some constraint in such a circle of heroes. The General talked a great deal on history and on literature. I soon perceived that he was a fine classical scholar, that his mind was enriched with a variety of knowledge, and that his conversation at meals was instructive and entertaining. Before dinner he had spoken French. He now spoke Italian, in which he is very eloquent.

We retired to another room to drink coffee. My timidity wore off. I no longer anxiously thought of myself; my whole attention was employed in listening to the illustrious commander of a nation.

He recommended me to the care of the Abbé Rostini, who had lived many years in France. Signor Colonna, the lord of the manor here, being from home, his house was assigned for me to live in. I was left by myself till near supper time when I returned to the General, whose conversation improved upon me as did the society of those about him, with whom I gradually formed an acquaintance.

Every day I felt myself happier. Particular marks of attention were shown me as a subject of Great Britain, the report of which went over to Italy and confirmed the conjectures that I was really an envoy. In the morning I had my chocolate served up upon a silver salver adorned with the arms of Corsica. I dined and supped constantly with the General. I was visited by all the nobility, and whenever I chose to make a little tour I was attended by a party of guards. I begged of the General not to treat me with so much ceremony, but he insisted upon it.

One day when I rode out, I was mounted on Paoli's own horse with rich furniture of crimson velvet, with broad gold lace, and had my guards marching along with me. I allowed myself to indulge a momentary pride in this parade, as I was curious to experience what could really be the pleasure of state and distinction with which mankind are so strangely intoxicated. When I returned to the Continent after all this greatness, I used to joke with my acquaintance and tell them that I could not bear to live with them, for they did not treat me with a proper respect.

My time passed here in the most agreeable manner. I enjoyed a sort of luxury of noble sentiment. Paoli became more affable with me. I made myself known to him. I forgot the great distance between us, and had every day some hours of private conversation with him.

From my first setting out on this tour, I wrote down every night what I had observed during the day, throwing together a great deal that I might afterwards make a selection at leisure.

Of these particulars, the most valuable to my readers, as well as to myself, must surely be the memoirs and remarkable sayings of Paoli, which I am proud to record.

Talking of the Corsican war, "Sir," said he, "if the event prove happy, we shall be called great defenders of liberty. If the event shall prove unhappy, we shall be called unfortunate rebels."

The French objected to him that the Corsican nation had no regular troops. "We would not have them," said Paoli. "We should then have the bravery of this and the other regiment. At present every single man is as a regiment himself. Should the Corsicans be formed into regular troops, we should lose that personal bravery which has produced such actions among us as in another country would have rendered famous even a marshal."

I asked him how he could possibly have a soul so superior to interest. "It is not superior," said he; "my interest is to gain a name. I know well that he who does good to his country will gain that, and I expect it. Yet could I render this people happy, I would be content to be forgotten. I have an unspeakable pride. The approbation of my own heart is enough."

He said he would have great pleasure in seeing the world and enjoying the society of the learned and the accomplished in every country. I asked him how with these dispositions he could bear to be confined to an island yet in a rude uncivilized state, and instead of participating Attic evenings, "noctes coenaeque Deum [the nights and banquets of the gods]," be in a continual course of care and of danger. He replied in one line of Virgil: "Vincet amor patriae laudumque immensa cupido [The love of country will prevail, and the irresistible desire for praise]" This, uttered with the fine open Italian pronunciation, and the graceful dignity of his manner, was very noble. I wished to have a statue of him taken at that moment.

I asked him if he understood English. He immediately began and spoke it, which he did tolerably well. When at Naples, he had known several Irish gentlemen who were officers in that service. Having a great facility in acquiring languages, he learnt English from them. But as he had been now ten years without ever speaking it, he spoke very slow. One could see that he was possessed of the words, but for want of what I may call mechanical practice he had a difficulty in expressing himself.

I was diverted with his English library. It consisted of some broken volumes of the *Spectator* and *Tatler*, Pope's *Essay on Man*, *Gulliver's Travels*, a *History of France* in old English, and Barclay's *Apology for the Quakers*. I promised to send him some English books.

He convinced me how well he understood our language, for I took the liberty to show him a memorial which I had drawn up on the advantages to Great Britain from an alliance with Corsica, and he translated this memorial into Italian with the greatest facility. He has since given me more proofs of his knowledge of our tongue by his answers to the letters which I have had the honour to write to him in English, and in particular by a very judicious and ingenious criticism on some of Swift's works.

He was well acquainted with the history of Britain. He had read many of the Parliamentary debates, and had even seen a number of *The North Briton*. He showed a considerable knowledge of this country, and often introduced anecdotes and drew comparisons and allusions from Britain.

He said his great object was to form the Corsicans in such a manner that they might have a firm constitution, and might be able to subsist without him. "Our state," said he, "is young, and still requires the leading strings. I am desirous that the Corsicans should be taught to walk of themselves. Therefore when they come to me to ask whom they should choose for their Padre del Commune or other magistrate, I tell them, 'You know better than I do the able and honest men among your neighbours. Consider the consequence of your choice, not only to yourselves in particular but to the island in general.' In this manner I accustom them to feel their own importance as members of the state."

After representing the severe and melancholy state of oppression under which Corsica had so long groaned, he said, "We are now to our

country like the prophet Elisha stretched over the dead child of the
Shunammite, eye to eye, nose to nose, mouth to mouth. It begins to
recover warmth and to revive. I hope it shall yet regain full health and
vigour."

I said that things would make a rapid progress, and that we should
soon see all the arts and sciences flourish in Corsica. "Patience, Sir," said
he. "If you saw a man who had fought a hard battle, who was much
wounded, who was beaten to the ground, and who with difficulty could
lift himself up, it would not be reasonable to ask him to get his hair well
dressed and to put on embroidered clothes. Corsica has fought a hard
battle, has been much wounded, has been beaten to the ground, and
with difficulty can lift herself up: The arts and sciences are like dress and
ornament. You cannot expect them from us for some time. But come
back twenty or thirty years hence, and we'll show you arts and sciences,
and concerts and assemblies, and fine ladies, and we'll make you fall in
love among us, Sir."

He smiled a good deal when I told him that I was much surprised to
find him so amiable, accomplished, and polite; for although I knew I was
to see a great man, I expected to find a rude character, an Attila King
of the Goths, or a Luitprand King of the Lombards.

I observed that although he had often a placid smile upon his countenance, he hardly ever laughed. Whether loud laughter in general society
be a sign of weakness or rusticity I cannot say; but I have remarked that
real great men, and men of finished behaviour, seldom fall into it.

The variety, and I may say versatility, of the mind of this great man
is amazing. One day when I came to pay my respects to him before
dinner, I found him in much agitation, with a circle of his nobles around
him and a Corsican standing before him like a criminal before his judge.
Paoli immediately turned to me, "I am glad you are come, Sir. You
Protestants talk much against our doctrine of transubstantiation. Behold
here the miracle of transubstantiation, a Corsican transubstantiated into
a Genoese. That unworthy man who now stands before me is a Corsican,
who has been long a lieutenant under the Genoese in Capo Corso.
Andrew Doria and all their greatest heroes could not be more violent
for the Republic than he has been, and all against his country." Then
turning to the man, "Sir," said he, "Corsica makes it a rule to pardon
the most unworthy of her children when they surrender themselves,
even when they are forced to do so as is your case. You have now
escaped. But take care. I shall have a strict eye upon you, and if ever
you make the least attempt to return to your traitorous practices, you
know I can be avenged of you." He spoke this with the fierceness of a
lion, and from the awful darkness of his brow one could see that his

thoughts of vengeance were terrible. Yet when it was over he all at once resumed his usual appearance, called out "Come along," went to dinner, and was as cheerful and gay as if nothing had happened.

His notions of morality are high and refined, such as become the father of a nation. Were he a libertine his influence would soon vanish, for men will never trust the important concerns of society to one they know will do what is hurtful to society for his own pleasures. He told me that his father had brought him up with great strictness, and that he had very seldom deviated from the paths of virtue. That this was not from a defect of feeling and passion, but that his mind being filled with important objects, his passions were employed in more noble pursuits than those of licentious pleasure. I saw from Paoli's example the great art of preserving young men of spirit from the contagion of vice, in which there is often a species of sentiment, ingenuity, and enterprise nearly allied to virtuous qualities. Show a young man that there is more real spirit in virtue than in vice, and you have a surer hold of him during his years of impetuosity and passion than by convincing his judgment of all the rectitude of ethics.

One day at dinner he gave us the principal arguments for the being and attributes of God. To hear these arguments repeated with graceful energy by the illustrious Paoli in the midst of his heroic nobles was admirable. I never felt my mind more elevated.

I took occasion to mention the King of Prussia's infidel writings, and in particular his *Epistle to Marshal Keith*. Paoli, who often talks with admiration of the greatness of that monarch, instead of uttering any direct censure of what he saw to be wrong in so distinguished a hero, paused a little, and then said with a grave and most expressive look, "It is fine consolation for an old general when dying, 'In a little while you shall be no more.' "

He observed that the Epicurean philosophy had produced but one exalted character, whereas Stoicism had been the seminary of great men. What he now said put me in mind of these noble lines of Lucan:

> . . . Hi mores, haec duri inmota Catonis
> Secta fuit, servare modum finemque tenere,
> Naturamque sequi patriaeque inpendere vitam,
> Nec sibi sed toti genitum se credere mundo.

> [These were the stricter manners of the man,
> And this the stubborn course in which they ran:
> The Golden Mean unchanging to pursue,
> Constant to keep the purposed end in view.

Religiously to follow Nature's laws,
And die with pleasure in his country's cause.
To think he was not for himself designed
But born to be of use to all mankind.]

When he was asked if he would quit the island of which he had under-taken the protection, supposing a foreign power should create him a marshal and make him governor of a province, he replied, "I hope they will believe I am more honest, or more ambitious; for," said he, "to accept of the highest offices under a foreign power would be to serve."

"To have been a colonel, a general, or a marshal," said he, "would have been sufficient for my table, for my taste in dress, for the beauty whom my rank would have entitled me to attend. But it would not have been sufficient for this spirit, for this imagination"—putting his hand upon his bosom.

He reasoned one day in the midst of his nobles whether the comman-der of a nation should be married or not. "If he is married," said he, "there is a risk that he may be distracted by private affairs and swayed too much by a concern for his family. If he is unmarried, there is a risk that not having the tender attachments of a wife and children, he may sacrifice all to his own ambition." When I said he ought to marry and have a son to succeed him; "Sir," said he, "what security can I have that my son will think and act as I do? What sort of a son had Cicero, and what had Marcus Aurelius?"

He said to me one day when we were alone, "I never will marry, I have not the conjugal virtues. Nothing would tempt me to marry but a woman who should bring me an immense dowry, with which I might assist my country."

But he spoke much in praise of marriage, as an institution which the experience of ages had found to be the best calculated for the happiness of individuals and for the good of society. Had he been a private gentle-man, he probably would have married, and I am sure would have made as good a husband and father as he does a supreme magistrate and a general. But his arduous and critical situation would not allow him to enjoy domestic felicity. He is wedded to his country, and the Corsicans are his children.

He often talked to me of marriage, told me licentious pleasures were delusive and transient, that I should never be truly happy till I was married, and that he hoped to have a letter from me soon after my return home, acquainting him that I had followed his advice and was convinced from experience that he was in the right. With such an engaging condescension did this great man behave to me. If I could but paint his manner, all my readers would be charmed with him.

He has a mind fitted for philosophical speculations as well as for affairs of state. One evening at supper he entertained us for some time with some curious reveries and conjectures as to the nature of the intelligence of beasts, with regard to which he observed human knowledge was as yet very imperfect. He in particular seemed fond of inquiring into the language of the brute creation. He observed that beasts fully communicate their ideas to each other, and that some of them, such as dogs, can form several articulate sounds. In different ages there have been people who pretended to understand the language of birds and beasts. "Perhaps," said Paoli, "in a thousand years we may know this as well as we know things which appeared much more difficult to be known." I have often since this conversation indulged myself in such reveries. If it were not liable to ridicule, I would say that an acquaintance with the language of beasts would be a most agreeable acquisition to man, as it would enlarge the circle of his social intercourse.

* * *

TOBIAS SMOLLETT
1721–1771

The splenetic Dr. Smollett, constantly swindled by innkeepers and let down by the over-publicized sights, could stand as the patron saint of such costive post-touristic travelers of the late twentieth century as V. S. Naipaul and Paul Theroux.

He was born in Scotland and educated as a surgeon, a profession he practiced in the bloody and rowdy British navy, at war with Spain in the 1740s. His experiences there he recalled in his novel Roderick Random *(1748). He spent much of the middle of his life hack-writing for magazines in London, but by 1763 his lung trouble had grown so bad that he sought relief by traveling abroad for two years. He returned to England and to writing, bringing out in 1771, just before his death, his best novel,* The Expedition of Humphry Clinker.

His Travels through France and Italy *(1766) consists of 41 "letters"* to a fictional friend at home. Armed with Thomas Nugent's popular guidebook, The Grand Tour *(1749)*, and accompanied by his wife, two young ladies, and a portable library of *150* volumes, Smollett energetically roamed the Continent and encountered an unremitting series of rascally postillions, greedy porters, and dishonest couriers and guides. "All the inns of France are execrable," he concluded, and there were even worse things: "If a Frenchman is admitted into your family . . .," he wrote, "the first return he makes for your civilities is to make love to your wife, if she is handsome; if not, to your sister, or daughter, or niece." If Continental readers were appalled by his travel book, most British readers were delighted. But Laurence Sterne was not, and in his Sentimental Journey through France and Italy *(1768)* he set out to redress the numerous outrages against delicacy, tolerance, and sensibility committed by Smollett, or, as he called him, "the learned Smelfungus."

From TRAVELS THROUGH FRANCE AND ITALY
(1766)

LETTER I.

Boulogne sur Mer, June 23, 1763.

Dear Sir,

You laid your commands upon me at parting, to communicate from time to time the observations I should make in the course of my travels, and it was an injunction I received with pleasure. In gratifying your curiosity, I shall find some amusement to beguile the tedious hours, which, without some such employment, would be rendered insupportable by distemper and disquiet.

You knew, and pitied my situation, traduced by malice, persecuted by faction, abandoned by false patrons, and overwhelmed by the sense of a domestic calamity, which it was not in the power of fortune to repair.

You know with what eagerness I fled from my country as a scene of illiberal dispute and incredible infatuation, where a few worthless incendiaries had, by dint of perfidious calumnies and atrocious abuse, kindled up a flame which threatened all the horrors of civil dissension.

I packed up my little family in a hired coach, and attended by my trusty servant, who had lived with me a dozen of years, and now refused to leave me, took the road to Dover, in my way to the South of France, where I hoped the mildness of the climate would prove favourable to the weak state of my lungs.

You advised me to have recourse again to the Bath waters, from the use of which I had received great benefit the preceding winter: but I had many inducements to leave England. My wife earnestly begged I would convey her from a country where every object served to nourish her grief: I was in hopes that a succession of new scenes would engage her attention, and gradually call off her mind from a series of painful reflections; and I imagined the change of air, and a journey of near a thousand miles, would have a happy effect upon my own constitution. But, as the summer was already advanced, and the heat too excessive for travelling in warm climates, I proposed staying at Boulogne till the beginning of autumn, and in the meantime to bathe in the sea, with a view to strengthen and prepare my body for the fatigues of such a long journey.

A man who travels with a family of five persons, must lay his account with a number of mortifications; and some of these I have already happily overcome. Though I was well acquainted with the road to Dover, and made allowances accordingly, I could not help being chagrined at the bad accommodation and impudent imposition to which I was exposed. These I found the more disagreeable, as we were detained a day extraordinary on the road, in consequence of my wife's being indisposed.

I need not tell you this is the worst road in England, with respect to the conveniencies of travelling, and must certainly impress foreigners with an unfavourable opinion of the nation in general. The chambers are in general cold and comfortless, the beds paultry, the cookery execrable, the wine poison, the attendance bad, the publicans insolent, and the bills extortion; there is not a drop of tolerable malt liquor to be had from London to Dover.

Every landlord and every waiter harangued upon the knavery of a publican in Canterbury, who had charged the French ambassador forty pounds for a supper that was not worth forty shillings. They talked much of honesty and conscience; but when they produced their own bills, they appeared to be all of the same family and complexion. If it was a reproach upon the English nation that an innkeeper should pillage strangers at that rate; it is a greater scandal that the same fellow should be able to keep his house still open. I own, I think it would be for the honour of the kingdom to reform the abuses of this road; and in particular to improve the avenue to London by the way of Kent-Street, which is a most disgraceful entrance to such an opulent city. A foreigner, in passing through this beggarly and ruinous suburb, conceives such an idea of misery and meanness as all the wealth and magnificence of London and Westminster are afterwards unable to destroy. A friend of mine, who brought a Parisian from Dover in his own post-chaise, contrived to enter Southwark after it was dark, that his friend might not perceive the nakedness of this quarter. The stranger was much pleased with the great number of shops full of merchandize, lighted up to the best advantage. He was astonished at the display of riches in Lombard-Street and Cheapside. The badness of the pavement made him find the streets twice as long as they were. They alighted in Upper Brook-Street by Grosvenor-Square; and when his conductor told him they were then about the middle of London, the Frenchman declared, with marks of infinite surprize, that London was very near as long as Paris.

On my arrival at Dover I paid off my coachman, who went away with a heavy heart. He wanted much to cross the sea, and endeavoured to persuade me to carry the coach and horses to the other side. If I had been resolved to set out immediately for the South, perhaps I should have taken his advice. If I had retained him at the rate of twenty guineas per month, which was the price he demanded, and begun my journey without hesitation, I should travel more agreeably than I can expect to do in the carriages of this country; and the difference of the expence would be a mere trifle. I would advise every man who travels through France to bring his own vehicle along with him, or at least to purchase one at Calais or Boulogne, where second-hand berlins and chaises may be generally had at reasonable rates. I have been offered a very good berlin for thirty guineas: but before I make the purchase, I must be better informed touching the different methods of travelling in this country.

Dover is commonly termed a den of thieves; and I am afraid it is not altogether without reason it has acquired this appellation. The people are said to live by piracy in time of war; and by smuggling and fleecing strangers in time of peace: but I will do them the justice to say, they make no distinction between foreigners and natives. Without all doubt a man cannot be much worse lodged and worse treated in any part of Europe; nor will he in any other place meet with more flagrant instances of fraud, imposition, and brutality. One would imagine they had formed a general conspiracy against all those who either go to, or return from the Continent. About five years ago, in my passage from Flushing to Dover, the master of the packet-boat brought to all of a sudden off the South Foreland, although the wind was as favourable as it could blow. He was immediately boarded by a custom-house boat, the officer of which appeared to be his friend. He then gave the passengers to understand that as it was low water, the ship could not go into the harbour; but that the boat would carry them ashore with their baggage.

The custom-house officer demanded a guinea for this service, and the bargain was made. Before we quitted the ship, we were obliged to gratify the cabin-boy for his attendance, and to give drink-money to the sailors. The boat was run aground on the open beach; but we could not get ashore without the assistance of three or four fellows, who insisted upon being paid for their trouble. Every parcel and bundle, as it was landed, was snatched up by a separate porter: one ran away with a hat-box, another with a wig-box, a third with a couple of shirts tied up in a handkerchief, and two were employed in carrying a small portmanteau that did not weigh forty pounds. All our things were hurried to the custom-house to be searched, and the searcher was paid for disordering our cloaths: from thence they were removed to the inn, where the porters demanded half a crown each for their labour. It was in vain to expostulate; they surrounded the house like a pack of hungry hounds, and raised such a clamour that we were fain to comply. After we had undergone all this imposition, we were visited by the master of the packet, who, having taken our fares, and wished us joy of our happy arrival in England, expressed his hope that we would remember the poor master, whose wages were very small, and who chiefly depended upon the generosity of the passengers. I own I was shocked at his meanness, and could not help telling him so. I told him I could not conceive what title he had to any such gratification: he had sixteen passengers, who paid a guinea each, on the supposition that every person should have a bed; but there were no more than eight beds in the cabin, and each of these was occupied before I came on board; so that if we had been detained at sea a whole week by contrary winds and bad weather, one half of the passengers must have slept upon the boards, howsoever their health might have suffered from this want of accommodation. Notwithstanding this check, he was so very abject and importunate, that we gave him a crown apiece, and he retired.

The first thing I did when I arrived at Dover this last time was to send for the master of a packet-boat, and agree with him to carry us to Boulogne at once, by which means I saved the expence of travelling by land from Calais to this last place, a journey of four-and-twenty miles. The hire of a vessel from Dover to Boulogne is precisely the same as from Dover to Calais, five guineas; but this skipper demanded eight, and, as I did not know the fare, I agreed to give him six. We embarked between six and seven in the evening, and found ourselves in a most wretched hovel, on board what is called a Folkstone cutter. The cabin was so small that a dog could hardly turn in it, and the beds put me in mind of the holes described in some catacombs, in which the bodies of the dead were deposited, being thrust in with the feet foremost; there was no getting into them but end-ways, and indeed they seemed so dirty, that nothing but extreme necessity could have obliged me to use them. We sat up all night in a most uncomfortable situation, tossed about by the sea, cold, and cramped and weary, and languishing for want of sleep. At three in the morning the master came down, and told us we were just off the harbour of Boulogne; but the wind blowing off shore, he could not possibly enter, and therefore advised us to go ashore in the boat. I went upon deck to view the coast, when he pointed to the place where he said Boulogne stood, declaring at the same time we were within a short mile of the harbour's mouth. The morning was cold and raw, and I knew myself extremely subject to catch cold; nevertheless we were all so impatient to be ashore, that I resolved to take his advice. The boat was already hoisted out, and we went on board of it, after I had paid the captain and gratified his crew. We had scarce parted from the ship, when we perceived a boat coming towards us from the shore; and the master gave us to understand it was coming to carry us into the harbour. When I objected to the trouble of shifting from one boat to another in the open sea, which (by the bye) was a little rough; he said it was a privilege which the watermen of Boulogne had, to carry all passengers ashore, and that this privilege he durst not venture to infringe. This was no time nor place to remonstrate. The French boat came alongside half filled with water, and we were handed from the one to the other. We were then obliged to lie upon our oars, till the captain's boat went on board and returned from the ship with a packet of letters. We were afterwards rowed a long league, in a rough sea, against wind and tide, before we reached the harbour, where we landed, benumbed with cold, and the women excessively sick: from our landing-place we were obliged to walk very near a mile to the inn where we purposed to lodge, attended by six or seven men and women, bare-legged, carrying our baggage. This boat cost me a guinea, besides paying exorbitantly the people who carried our things; so that the inhabitants of Dover and of Boulogne seem to be of the same kidney, and indeed they understand one another perfectly well. It was our honest captain who made the signal for the shore-boat before I went upon deck; by which means he not only gratified his friends, the watermen of Boulogne, but also saved about fifteen shillings portage, which he must have paid had he gone into the harbour; and thus he found himself at liberty to return to Dover, which he reached in four hours. I mention these circumstances as a warning to other passengers. When a man hires a packet-boat from Dover to Calais or Boulogne, let him remember that the stated price is five guineas; and let him insist upon being carried into the harbour in the ship, without paying the least regard to the representations of the master, who is generally a little dirty knave. When he tells you it is low water, or the wind is in your teeth, you may say you will stay on board till it is high water, or till the wind comes favourable. If he sees you are resolute, he will find means to bring his ship into the harbour, or at least to convince you, without a possibility of your being deceived, that it is not in his power. After all, the fellow himself was a loser by his finesse; if he had gone into the harbour, he would have had another fare immediately back to Dover, for there was a Scotch gentleman at the inn waiting for such an opportunity.

Knowing my own weak constitution, I took it for granted this morning's adventure would cost me a fit of illness; and what added to my chagrin, when we arrived at the inn, all the beds were occupied; so that we were obliged to sit in a cold kitchen above two hours, until some of the lodgers should get up. This was such a bad specimen of French accommodation, that my wife could not help regretting even the inns of Rochester, Sittingbourn, and Canterbury: bad as they are, they certainly have the advantage, when compared with the execrable auberges of this country, where one finds nothing but dirt and imposition. One would imagine the French were still at war with the English, for they pillage them without mercy.

Among the strangers at this inn where we lodged there was a gentleman of the faculty, just returned from Italy. Understanding that I intended to winter in the South of France, on account of a pulmonic disorder, he strongly recommended the climate of Nice in Provence, which, indeed, I had often heard extolled; and I am almost resolved to go thither, not only for the sake of the air, but also for its situation on the Mediterranean, where I can have the benefit of bathing; and from whence there is a short cut by sea to Italy, should I find it necessary to try the air of Naples.

After having been ill accommodated three days at our inn, we have at last found commodious lodgings, by means of Mrs. B—, a very agreeable French lady, to whom we were recommended by her husband, who is my countryman and at present resident in London. For three guineas a month we have the greatest part of a house tolerably furnished; four bed-chambers on the first floor, a large parlour below, a kitchen, and the use of a cellar.

These, I own, are frivolous incidents, scarce worth committing to paper; but they may serve to introduce observations of more consequence; and in the meantime I know nothing will be indifferent to you, that concerns

Your humble servant.

LETTER V.

Boulogne, September 12, 1763.

Dear Sir,

My stay in this place now draws towards a period. 'Till within these few days I have continued bathing, with some advantage to my health, though the season has been cold and wet, and disagreeable. There was a fine prospect of a plentiful harvest in this neighbourhood. I used to have great pleasure in driving between the fields of wheat, oats, and barley; but the crop has been entirely ruined by the rain, and nothing is now to be seen on the ground but the tarnished straw, and the rotten spoils of the husbandman's labour. The ground scarce affords subsistence to a few flocks of meagre sheep, that crop the stubble and the intervening grass; each flock under the protection of its shepherd, with his crook and dogs, who lies every night in the midst of the fold, in a little thatched travelling lodge, mounted on a wheel-carriage. Here he passes the night, in order to defend his flock from the wolves, which are sometimes, especially in winter, very bold and desperate.

Two days ago we made an excursion with Mrs. B— and Capt. L— to the village of Samers, on the Paris road, about three leagues from Boulogne. Here is a venerable abbey of Benedictines, well endowed, with large agreeable gardens prettily laid out. The monks are well lodged and well entertained. Though restricted from flesh meals by the rules of their order, they are allowed to eat wild duck and teal, as a species of fish; and when they long for a good *bouillon,* or a partridge, or pullet, they have nothing to do but to say they are out of order. In that case the appetite of the patient is indulged in his own apartment. Their church is elegantly contrived, but kept in a very dirty condition. The greatest curiosity I saw in this place was an English boy, about eight or nine years old, from Dover, whom his father had sent hither to learn the French language. In less than eight weeks, he was become captain of the boys of the place, spoke French perfectly well, and had almost forgot his mother tongue. But to return to the people of Boulogne.

The burghers here, as in other places, consist of merchants, shop-keepers, and artisans. Some of the merchants have got fortunes by fitting out privateers during the war. A great many single ships were taken from the English, notwithstanding the good look-out of our cruisers, who were so alert, that the privateers from this coast were often taken in four hours after they sailed from the French harbour; and there is hardly a captain of an *armateur* [privateer] in Boulogne, who has not been prisoner in England five or six times in the course of the war. They were fitted out

at a very small expence, and used to run over in the night to the coast
of England, where they hovered as English fishing smacks, until they
kidnapped some coaster, with which they made the best of their way
across the Channel. If they fell in with a British cruizer, they surrend-
ered without resistance: the captain was soon exchanged, and the loss
of the proprietor was not great: if they brought their prize safe into
harbour, the advantage was considerable. In time of peace the merchants of Boulogne deal in wine, brandies, and oil, imported from the
South, and export fish, with the manufactures of France, to Portugal,
and other countries; but the trade is not great. Here are two or three
considerable houses of wine-merchants from Britain, who deal in Bourdeaux wine, with which they supply London and other parts of England,
Scotland, and Ireland. The fishery of mackarel and herring is so considerable on this coast that it is said to yield annually eight or nine hundred
thousand livres, about thirty-five thousand pounds sterling.

The shop-keepers here drive a considerable traffic with the English
smugglers, whose cutters are almost the only vessels one sees in the
harbour of Boulogne, if we except about a dozen of those flat-bottomed
boats, which raised such alarms in England, in the course of the war.
Indeed they seem to be good for nothing else, and perhaps they were
built for this purpose only. The smugglers from the coast of Kent and
Sussex pay English gold for great quantities of French brandy, tea,
coffee, and small wine, which they run from this country. They likewise
buy glass trinkets, toys, and coloured prints, which sell in England, for
no other reason, but that they come from France, as they may be had
as cheap and much better finished, of our own manufacture. They
likewise take off ribbons, laces, linen, and cambrics; though this branch
of trade is chiefly in the hands of traders that come from London, and
make their purchases at Dunkirk, where they pay no duties. It is certainly worth while for any traveller to lay in a stock of linen either at
Dunkirk or Boulogne; the difference of the price at these two places is
not great. Even here I have made a provision of shirts for one half of
the money they would have cost in London. Undoubtedly the practice
of smuggling is very detrimental to the fair trader, and carries considerable sums of money out of the kingdom, to enrich our rivals and enemies.
The customhouse officers are very watchful, and make a great number
of seizures: nevertheless, the smugglers find their account in continuing
this contraband commerce; and are said to indemnify themselves, if they
save one cargo out of three. After all, the best way to prevent smuggling
is to lower the duties upon the commodities which are thus introduced.
I have been told that the revenue upon tea has encreased ever since the
duty upon it was diminished. By the bye, the tea smuggled on the coast

of Sussex is most execrable stuff. While I stayed at Hastings, for the conveniency of bathing, I must have changed my breakfast if I had not luckily brought tea with me from London: yet we have as good tea at Boulogne for nine livres a pound, as that which sells at fourteen shillings at London.

The bourgeois of this place seem to live at their ease, probably in consequence of their trade with the English. Their houses consist of the ground-floor, one story above, and garrets. In those which are well furnished you see pier-glasses and marble slabs; but the chairs are either paultry things, made with straw bottoms, which cost about a shilling apiece, or old-fashioned, high-backed seats of needlework, stuffed, very clumsy and incommodious. The tables are square fir boards that stand on edge in a corner, except when they are used, and then they are set upon cross legs that open and shut occasionally. The king of France dines off a board of this kind. Here is plenty of table-linen however. The poorest tradesman in Boulogne has a napkin on every cover, and silver forks with four prongs, which are used with the right hand, there being very little occasion for knives; for the meat is boiled or roasted to rags. The French beds are so high that sometimes one is obliged to mount them by the help of steps; and this is also the case in Flanders. They very seldom use feather-beds; but they lie upon a *paillasse*, or bag of straw, over which are laid two, and sometimes three mattrasses. Their testers are high and old-fashioned, and their curtains generally of thin bays, red, or green, laced with taudry yellow, in imitation of gold. In some houses, however, one meets with furniture of stamped linen; but there is no such thing as a carpet to be seen, and the floors are in a very dirty condition. They have not even the implements of cleanliness in this country. Every chamber is furnished with an *armoire*, or clothes-press, and a chest of drawers, of very clumsy workmanship. Every thing shews a deficiency in the mechanic arts. There is not a door, nor a window, that shuts close. The hinges, locks, and latches, are of iron, coarsely made and ill contrived. The very chimnies are built so open that they admit both rain and sun, and all of them smoke intolerably. If there is no cleanliness among these people, much less shall we find delicacy, which is the cleanliness of the mind. Indeed they are utter strangers to what we call common decency; and I could give you some high-flavoured instances, at which even a native of Edinburgh would stop his, nose. There are certain mortifying views of human nature, which undoubtedly ought to be concealed as much as possible, in order to prevent giving offence: and nothing can be more absurd than to plead the difference of custom in different countries, in defence of those usages which cannot fail giving disgust to the organs and senses of all mankind. Will custom exempt from the imputation of gross indecency a French lady who shifts her frowsy smock in presence of a male visitant, and talks to him of her *lavement,* her *medicine,* and her *bidet!* An Italian *signora* makes no scruple of telling you she is such a day to begin a course of physic for the *pox.* The celebrated reformer of the Italian comedy introduces a child befouling itself on the stage, OE, NO TI SENTI? BISOGNA DESFAS-SARLO, *(fa cenno che sentesi mal odore)* [Hey, can't you smell? The baby's diaper needs changing. Surely you smell something bad!]. I have known a lady handed to the house of office by her admirer, who stood at the door and entertained her with *bons mots* all the time she was within. But I should be glad to know whether it is possible for a fine lady to speak and act in this manner without exciting ideas to her own disadvantage in the mind of every man who has any imagination left and enjoys the entire use of his senses, howsoever she may be authorised by the customs of her country? There is nothing so vile or repugnant to nature but you may plead prescription for it, in the customs of some nation or other. A Parisian likes mortified flesh: a native of Legiboli will not taste his fish till it is quite putrefied: the civilized inhabitants of Kamschatka get drunk with the urine of their guests, whom they have already intoxicated: the Nova Zemblans make merry on train-oil: the Groenlanders eat in the same dish with their dogs: the Caffres, at the Cape of Good Hope, piss upon those whom they delight to honour, and feast upon a sheep's intestines with their contents, as the greatest dainty that can be presented. A true-bred Frenchman dips his fingers, im-browned with snuff, into his plate filled with ragout: between every three mouthfuls, he produces his snuff-box, and takes a fresh pinch, with the most graceful gesticulations; then he displays his handkerchief, which may be termed the *flag of abomination,* and, in the use of both, scatters his favours among those who have the happiness to sit near him. It must be owned, however, that a Frenchman will not drink out of a tankard, in which, perhaps, a dozen of filthy mouths have slabbered, as is the custom in England. Here every individual has his own goblet, which stands before him, and he helps himself occasionally with wine, or water, or both, which likewise stand upon the table. But I know no custom more beastly than that of using water-glasses, in which polite company spirt, and squirt, and spew the filthy scourings of their gums, under the eyes of each other. I knew a lover cured of his passion by seeing this nasty cascade discharged from the mouth of his mistress. I don't doubt but I shall live to see the day when the hospitable custom of the ancient Egyptians will be revived; then a conveniency will be placed behind every chair in company, with a proper provision of waste paper, that individuals may make themselves easy without parting company. I insist upon it, that this practice would not be more indelicate than that which is now in use. What then, you will say, must a man sit with his chops and fingers up to the ears and knuckles in grease? No; let those who cannot eat without defiling themselves step into another room, provided with basins and towels: but I think it would be better to institute schools where youth may learn to eat their victuals, without daubing themselves, or giving offence to the eyes of one another.

The bourgeois of Boulogne have commonly soup and bouillé [soiled meat] at noon, and a roast, with a salad, for supper; and at all their meals there is a dessert of fruit. This indeed is the practice all over France. On meagre days they eat fish, omelettes, fried beans, fricassees of eggs and onions, and burnt cream. The tea which they drink in the afternoon is rather boiled than infused; it is sweetened all together with coarse sugar, and drank with an equal quantity of boiled milk.

We had the honour to be entertained the other day by our landlord, Mr. B—, who spared no cost on this banquet, exhibited for the glory of France. He had invited a new-married couple, together with the husband's mother, and the lady's father, who was one of the noblesse of Montreuil, his name Mons. L—y. There were likewise some merchants of the town, and Mons. B—'s uncle, a facetious little man, who had served in the English navy, and was as big and as round as a hogshead; we were likewise favoured with the company of father K—, a native of Ireland, who is *vicaire,* or curate of the parish; and among the guests was Mons. L—y's son, a pretty boy, about thirteen or fourteen years of age. The *repas* served up in three services, or courses, with *entrées* and *hors d'œuvres,* exclusive of the fruit, consisted of above twenty dishes, extremely well dressed by the *rotisseur,* who is the best cook I ever knew, in France, or elsewhere; but the *plats* were not presented with much order. Our young ladies did not seem to be much used to do the honours of the table. The most extraordinary circumstance that I observed on this occasion was, that all the French who were present ate of every dish that appeared; and I am told, that if there had been an hundred articles more, they would have had a trial of each. This is what they call doing justice to the founder. Mons. L—y was placed at the head of the table; and indeed he was the oracle and orator of the company; tall, thin, and weather-beaten, not unlike the picture of Don Quixote after he had lost his teeth. He had been *garde du corps,* or life-guardsman at Versailles; and by virtue of this office he was perfectly well acquainted with the persons of the king and the dauphin, with the characters of the ministers and grandees, and, in a word, with all the secrets of state, on which he held forth with equal solemnity and elocution. He exclaimed against the jesuits, and the farmers of the revenue, who, he said, had ruined France. Then, addressing himself to me, asked, if the English did not every day drink to the health of *madame la marquise?* I did not at first comprehend his meaning; but answered in general, that the English were not deficient in complaisance for the ladies. "Ah! (cried he) she is the best friend they have in the world. If it had not been for her, they would not have such reason to boast of the advantages of the war." I told him the only conquest which the French had made in the war was achieved by one of her generals: I meant the taking of Mahon. But I did not choose to prosecute the discourse, remembering that in the year 1749, I had like to have had an affair with a Frenchman at Ghent, who affirmed that all the battles gained by the great duke of Marlborough were purposely lost by the French generals, in order to bring the schemes of madame de Maintenon into disgrace. This is no bad resource for the national vanity of these people: though, in general, they are really persuaded that theirs is the richest, the bravest, the happiest, and the most powerful nation under the sun; and therefore, without some such cause, they must be invincible. By the bye, the common people here still frighten their wayward children with the name of *Marlborough.* Mr. B—'s son, who was nursed at a peasant's house, happening one day, after he was brought home, to be in disgrace with his father, who threatened to correct him, the child ran for protection to his mother, crying, *"faites sortir ce vilain Malbroug,"* "turn out that rogue Malbrough." It is amazing to hear a sensible Frenchman assert that the revenues of France amount to four hundred millions of livres, about twenty millions sterling, clear of all incumbrances, when in fact their clear revenue is not much above ten. Without all doubt they have reason to inveigh against the *fermiers généraux* [tax collectors], who oppress the people in raising the taxes, not above two thirds of which are brought into the king's coffers: the rest enriches themselves, and enables them to bribe high for the protection of the great, which is the only support they have against the remonstrances of the states and parliaments, and the suggestions of common sense; which will ever demonstrate this to be, of all others, the most pernicious method of supplying the necessities of government.

Mons. L—y seasoned the severity of his political apothegms with intermediate sallies of mirth and gallantry. He ogled the venerable gentlewoman his *commère* [gossip], who sat by him. He looked, sighed, and languished, sung tender songs, and kissed the old lady's hand with all the ardour of a youthful admirer. I unfortunately congratulated him on having such a pretty young gentleman to his son. He answered, sighing, that the boy had talents, but did not put them to a proper use—"long before I attained his age (said he) I had finished my rhetoric." Captain B——, who had eaten himself black in the face, and, with the napkin under his chin, was no bad representation of Sancho Panza in the suds, with the dishclout about his neck, when the duke's scullions insisted upon shaving him; this sea-wit, turning to the boy, with a waggish leer, "I suppose (said he) you don't understand the figure of *amplification* so well as Monsieur your father." At that instant, one of the nieces, who knew her uncle to be very ticklish, touched him under the short ribs, on which the little man attempted to spring up, but lost the centre of gravity. He overturned his own plate in the lap of the person that sat next to him, and falling obliquely upon his own chair, both tumbled down upon the floor together, to the great discomposure of the whole company; for the poor man would have been actually strangled, had not his nephew loosed his stock with great expedition. Matters being once more adjusted, and the captain condoled on his disaster, Mons. L——y took it in his head to read his son a lecture upon filial obedience. This was mingled with some sharp reproof, which the boy took so ill that he retired. The old lady observed that he had been too severe: her daughter-in-law, who was very pretty, said her brother had given him too much reason; hinting, at the same time, that he was addicted to some terrible vices; upon which several individuals repeated the interjection, ah! ah! "Yes (said Mons. L——y, with a rueful aspect) the boy has a pernicious turn for gaming: in one afternoon he lost, at billiards, such a sum as gives me horror to think of it." "Fifty sols in one afternoon," (cried the sister). "Fifty sols! (exclaimed the mother-in-law, with marks of astonishment) that's too much—that's too much!—he's to blame—he's to blame! but youth, you know Mons. L——y—ah! vive la jeunesse!" "et l'amour!" cried the father, wiping his eyes, squeezing her hand, and looking tenderly upon her. Mr. B—— took this opportunity to bring in the young gentleman, who was admitted into favour, and received a second exhortation. Thus harmony was restored, and the entertainment concluded with fruit, coffee, and *liqueurs.*

When a bourgeois of Boulogne takes the air, he goes in a one-horse chaise, which is here called *cabriolet,* and hires it for half-a-crown a day. There are also travelling chaises, which hold four persons, two seated with their faces to the horses, and two behind their backs; but those vehicles are all very ill made, and extremely inconvenient. The way of riding most used in this place is on assback. You will see every day, in the skirts of the town, a great number of females thus mounted, with the feet on either side occasionally, according as the wind blows, so that sometimes the right and sometimes the left hand guides the beast: but in other parts of France, as well as in Italy, the ladies sit on horseback with their legs astride, and are provided with drawers for that purpose.

When I said the French people were kept in good humour by the fopperies of their religion, I did not mean that there were no gloomy spirits among them. There will be fanatics in religion, while there are people of a saturnine disposition, and melancholy turn of mind. The character of a *devotee*, which is hardly known in England, is very common here. You see them walking to and from church at all hours, in their hoods and long camblet cloaks, with a slow pace, demure aspect, and downcast eye. Those who are poor become very troublesome to the monks, with their scruples and cases of conscience: you may see them on their knees, at the confessional, every hour in the day. The rich *devotee* has her favourite confessor, whom she consults and regales in private, at her own house; and this spiritual director generally governs the whole family. For my part, I never knew a fanatic that was not an hypocrite at bottom. Their pretensions to superior sanctity, and an absolute conquest over all the passions, which human reason was never yet able to subdue, introduce a habit of dissimulation, which, like all other habits, is confirmed by use, till at length they become adepts in the art and science of hypocrisy. Enthusiasm and hypocrisy are by no means incompatible. The wildest fanatics I ever knew, were real sensualists in their way of living, and cunning cheats in their dealings with mankind.

Among the lower class of people at Boulogne, those who take the lead are the seafaring men, who live in one quarter, divided into classes, and registered for the service of the king. They are hardy and raw-boned, exercise the trade of fishermen and boatmen, and propagate like rabbits. They have put themselves under the protection of a miraculous image of the Virgin Mary, which is kept in one of their churches, and every year carried in procession. According to the legend, this image was carried off, with other pillage, by the English, when they took Boulogne, in the reign of Henry VIII. The lady, rather than reside in England, where she found a great many heretics, trusted herself alone in an open boat, and crossed the sea to the road of Boulogne, where she was seen waiting for a pilot. Accordingly a boat put off to her assistance, and brought her safe into the harbour: since which time she has continued to patronize the watermen of Boulogne. At present she is very black and very ugly, besides being cruelly mutilated in different parts of her body, which I suppose have been amputated, and converted into tobacco-stoppers; but once a year she is dressed in very rich attire, and carried in procession, with a silver boat, provided at the expence of the sailors. That vanity which characterises the French extends even to the canaille [riff-raff]. The lowest creature among them is sure to have her ear-rings and golden cross hanging about her neck. Indeed this last is an implement of superstition as well as of dress, without which no female appears. The common people here, as in all countries where they live poorly and dirtily, are hard-featured, and of very brown, or rather tawny complexions. As they seldom eat meat, their juices are destitute of that animal oil which gives a plumpness and smoothness to the skin, and defends those fine capillaries from the injuries of the weather, which would otherwise coalesce, or be shrunk up, so as to impede the circulation on the external surface of the body. As for the dirt, it undoubtedly blocks up the pores of the skin, and disorders the perspiration; consequently must contribute to the scurvy, itch, and other cutaneous distempers.

In the quarter of the *matelots* [sailors] at Boulogne, there is a number of poor Canadians, who were removed from the island of St. John, in the gulf of St. Laurence, when it was reduced by the English. These people are maintained at the expence of the king, who allows them soldier's pay, that is five sols, or two-pence halfpenny a day; or rather three sols and ammunition bread. How the soldiers contrive to subsist upon this wretched allowance I cannot comprehend: but, it must be owned that those invalids who do duty at Boulogne betray no marks of want. They are hale and stout, neatly and decently cloathed, and on the whole look better than the pensioners of Chelsea.

About three weeks ago I was favoured with a visit by one Mr. M—, an English gentleman, who seems far gone in a consumption. He passed the last winter at Nismes in Languedoc, and found himself much better in the beginning of summer, when he embarked at Cette, and returned by sea to England. He soon relapsed, however, and (as he imagines) in consequence of a cold caught at sea. He told me his intention was to try the South again, and even to go as far as Italy. I advised him to make trial of the air of Nice, where I myself proposed to reside. He seemed to relish my advice, and proceeded towards Paris in his own carriage.

I shall to-morrow ship my great chests on board of a ship bound to Bourdeaux; they are directed, and recommended to the care of a merchant of that place, who will forward them by Thoulouse, and the canal of Languedoc, to his correspondent at Cette, which is the sea-port of Montpellier. The charge of their conveyance to Bourdeaux does not exceed one guinea. They consist of two very large chests and a trunk, about a thousand pounds weight; and the expence of transporting them from Bourdeaux to Cette will not exceed thirty livres. They are already sealed with lead at the custom-house, that they may be exempted from further visitation. This is a precaution which every traveller takes, both by sea and land: he must likewise provide himself with a *passe-avant* [customs certificate] at the bureau, otherwise he may be stopped, and rummaged at every town through which he passes. I have hired a berline and four horses to Paris, for fourteen loui'dores; two of which the *voiturier* [driver] is obliged to pay for a permission from the farmers of the poste; for every thing is farmed in this country; and if you hire a carriage, as I have done, you must pay twelve livres, or half a guinea, for every person that travels in it. The common coach between Calais and Paris is such a vehicle as no man would use who has any regard to his own ease and convenience; and it travels at the pace of an English waggon.

In ten days I shall set out on my journey; and I shall leave Boulogne with regret. I have been happy in the acquaintance of Mrs. B—, and a few British families in the place; and it was my good fortune to meet here with two honest gentlemen, whom I had formerly known in Paris, as well as with some of my countrymen, officers in the service of France. My next will be from Paris. Remember me to our friends at A—'s. I am a little heavy-hearted at the prospect of removing to such a distance from you. It is a moot point whether I shall ever return. My health is very precarious.

Adieu.

LETTER XXIX.

Nice, February 20, 1765.

Dear Sir,

Having seen all the curiosities of Florence, and hired a good travelling coach for seven weeks, at the price of seven zequines, something less than three guineas and a half, we set out post for Rome, by the way of Sienna, where we lay the first night. The country through which we passed is mountainous but agreeable. Of Sienna I can say nothing from my own observation, but that we were indifferently lodged in a house that stunk like a privy, and fared wretchedly at supper. The city is large and well built: the inhabitants pique themselves upon their politeness, and the purity of their dialect. Certain it is, some strangers reside in this place on purpose to learn the best pronunciation of the Italian tongue. The Mosaic pavement of their duomo, or cathedral, has been much admired; as well as the history of Æneas Sylvius, afterwards pope Pius II. painted on the walls of the library, partly by Pietro Perugino, and partly by his pupil Raphael D'Urbino.

Next day, at Buon Convento, where the emperor Henry VII. was poisoned by a friar with the sacramental wafer, I refused to give money to the hostler, who in revenge put two young unbroke stone-horses in the traces next to the coach, which became so unruly, that before we had gone a quarter of a mile, they and the postilion were rolling in the dust. In this situation they made such efforts to disengage themselves, and kicked with such violence, that I imagined the carriage and all our trunks would have been beaten in pieces. We leaped out of the coach, however, without sustaining any personal damage, except the fright; nor was any hurt done to the vehicle. But the horses were terribly bruised, and almost strangled, before they could be disengaged. Exasperated at the villany of the hostler, I resolved to make a complaint to the *uffiziale* or magistrate of the place. I found him wrapped in an old, greasy, ragged great-coat, sitting in a wretched apartment, without either glass, paper, or boards in the windows; and there was no sort of furniture but a couple of broken chairs and a miserable truckle-bed. He looked pale, and meagre, and had more the air of a half-starved prisoner than of a magistrate. Having heard my complaint, he came forth into a kind of outward room or bellfrey, and rung a great bell with his own hand. In consequence of this signal, the post-master came up stairs, and I suppose he was the first man in the place, for the *uffiziale* stood before him cap-in-hand, and with great marks of humble respect repeated the complaint I had made. This man assured me, with an air of conscious importance, that he himself had ordered the hostler to supply me with those very horses, which were the best in his stable; and that the misfortune which happened was owing to the misconduct of the fore-postilion, who did not keep the fore horses to a proper speed proportioned to the mettle of the other two. As he took the affair upon himself, and I perceived had an ascendancy over the magistrate, I contented myself with saying I was certain the two horses had been put to the coach on purpose, either to hurt or frighten us; and that since I could not have justice here I would make a formal complaint to the British minister at Florence. In passing through the street to the coach, which was by this time furnished with fresh horses, I met the hostler, and would have caned him heartily; but perceiving my intention, he took to his heels and vanished. Of all the people I have ever seen, the hostlers, postilions, and other fellows hanging about the post-houses in Italy are the most greedy, impertinent, and provoking. Happy are those travelers who have phlegm enough to disregard their insolence and importunity: for this is not so disagreeable as their revenge is dangerous. An English gentleman at Florence told me that one of those fellows, whom he had struck for his impertinence, flew at him with a long knife, and he could hardly keep him at sword's point. All of them wear such knives, and are very apt to use them on the slightest provocation. But their open attacks are not so formidable as their premediated schemes of revenge; in the

prosecution of which the Italians are equally treacherous and cruel.
This night we passed at a place called Radicofani, a village and fort,
situated on the top of a very high mountain. The inn stands still lower
than the town. It was built at the expence of the last grand-duke of
Tuscany; is very large, very cold, and uncomfortable. One would imagine
it was contrived for coolness, though situated so high, that even in the
midst of summer, a traveller would be glad to have a fire in his chamber.
But few or none of them have fire-places, and there is not a bed with
curtains or tester in the house. All the adjacent country is naked and
barren. On the third day we entered the pope's territories, some parts
of which are delightful. Having passed Aqua-Pendente, a beggarly town,
situated on the top of a rock, from whence there is a romantic cascade
of water which gives it the name, we travelled along the side of the Lake
Bolsena, a beautiful piece of water about thirty miles in circuit, with two
islands in the middle, the banks covered with noble plantations of oak
and cypress. The town of Bolsena standing near the ruins of the antient
Volsinium, which was the birth-place of Sejanus, is a paltry village; and
Montefiascone, famous for its wine, is a poor decayed town in this
neighbourhood, situated on the side of a hill, which, according to the
author of the Grand Tour, the only directory I had along with me, is
supposed to be the Soracte of the ancients. If we may believe Horace,
Soracte was visible from Rome: for, in his ninth ode, addressed to
Thaliarchus, he says,

> *Vides, ut alta stet nive candidum*
> *Soracte—*
>
> [You see how deeply wreath'd with snow,
> *Soracte* lifts his hoary head,]

but, in order to see Montefiascone, his eye-sight must have penetrated
through the Mons Cyminus, at the foot of which stands the city of
Viterbo. Pliny tells us, that Soracte was not far from Rome, *haud procul*
ab urbe Roma; but Montefiascone is fifty miles from this city. And
Desprez, in his notes upon Horace, says it is now called Monte S. Oreste.
Addison tells us he passed by it in the Campania. I could not without
indignation reflect upon the bigotry of Mathilda, who gave this fine
country to the see of Rome, under the dominion of which no country
was ever known to prosper.

About half way between Montefiascone and Viterbo, one of our
fore-wheels flew off, together with a large splinter of the axle-tree; and
if one of the postilions had not by great accident been a remarkably

ingenious fellow, we should have been put to the greatest inconvenience, as there was no town, or even house, within several miles. I mention this circumstance, by way of warning to other travellers, that they may provide themselves with a hammer and nails, a spare iron-pin or two, a large knife, and bladder of grease, to be used occasionally in case of such misfortune.

The mountain of Viterbo is covered with beautiful plantations and villas belonging to the Roman nobility, who come hither to make the *villegiatura* [vacation] in summer. Of the city of Viterbo I shall say nothing, but that it is the capital of that country which Mathilda gave to the Roman see. The place is well built, adorned with public fountains, and a great number of churches and convents; yet far from being populous, the whole number of inhabitants not exceeding fifteen thousand. The post-house is one of the worst inns I ever entered.

After having passed this mountain, the Cyminus of the ancients, we skirted part of the lake, which is now called de Vico, and whose banks afford the most agreeable rural prospects of hill and vale, wood, glade and water, shade and sunshine. A few other very inconsiderable places we passed, and descended into the Campania of Rome, which is almost a desert. The view of this country, in its present situation, cannot but produce emotions of pity and indignation in the mind of every person who retains any idea of its ancient cultivation and fertility. It is nothing but a naked withered down, desolate and dreary, almost without enclosure, cornfield, hedge, tree, shrub, house, hut, or habitation; exhibiting here and there the ruins of an ancient castellum, tomb, or temple, and in some places the remains of a Roman via. I had heard much of these ancient pavements, and was greatly disappointed when I saw them. The Via Cassia or Cymina is paved with broad, solid, flint-stones, which must have greatly incommoded the feet of horses that travelled upon it, as well as endangered the lives of the riders from the slipperiness of the pavement: besides, it is so narrow that two modern carriages could not pass one another upon it, without the most imminent hazard of being overturned. I am still of opinion that we excel the ancient Romans in understanding the conveniencies of life.

The Grand Tour says that within four miles of Rome you see a tomb on the road-side, said to be that of Nero, with sculpture in basso relievo at both ends. I did see such a thing more like a common grave-stone, than the tomb of an emperor. But we are informed by Suetonius that the dead body of Nero, who slew himself at the villa of his freedman, was by the care of his two nurses and his concubine Atta removed to the sepulchre of the Gens Domitia, immediately within the Porta del Popolo, on your left hand as you enter Rome, precisely on the spot where now stands the church of S. Maria del Popolo. His tomb was even distinguished by an epitaph, which has been preserved by Gruterus. Giacomo Alberici tells us very gravely in his History of the Church that a great number of devils, who guarded the bones of this wicked emperor, took possession, in the shape of black ravens, of a walnut-tree, which grew upon the spot; from whence they insulted every passenger, until pope Paschal II, in consequence of a solemn fast and a revelation, went thither in procession with his court and cardinals, cut down the tree, burned it to ashes, which, with the bones of Nero, were thrown into the Tyber: then he consecrated an altar on the place, where afterwards the church was built. You may guess what I felt at first sight of the city of Rome, which, notwithstanding all the calamities it has undergone, still maintains an august and imperial appearance. It stands on the farther side of the Tyber, which we crossed at the Ponte Molle, formerly called Pons Milvius, about two miles from the gate by which we entered. This bridge was built by Æmilius Censor, whose name it originally bore. It was the road by which so many heroes returned with conquest to their country; by which so many kings were led captive to Rome; and by which the ambassadors of so many kingdoms and states approached the seat of empire, to deprecate the wrath, to solicit the friendship, or sue for the protection of the Roman people. It is likewise famous for the defeat and death of Maxentius, who was here overcome by Constantine the Great. The space between the bridge and Porta del Popolo, on the right hand, which is now taken up with gardens and villas, was part of the antient Campus Martius, where the comitiæ [assemblies] were held; and where the Roman people inured themselves to all manner of exercises: it was adorned with porticos, temples, theatres, baths, circi, basilicæ, obelisks, columns, statues, and groves. Authors differ in their opinions about the extent of it; but as they all agree that it contained the Pantheon, the Circus Agonis, now the Piazza Navona, the Bustum and Mausoleum Augusti, great part of the modern city must be built upon the antient Campus Martius. The highway that leads from the bridge to the city, is part of the Via Flaminia, which extended as far as Rimini; and is well paved, like a modern street. Nothing of the antient bridge remains but the piles; nor is there any thing in the structure of this, or of the other five Roman bridges over the Tyber, that deserves attention. I have not seen any bridge in France or Italy comparable to that of Westminster, either in beauty, magnificence, or solidity; and when the bridge at Blackfriars is finished, it will be such a monument of architecture as all the world cannot parallel. As for the Tyber, it is, in comparison with the Thames, no more than an inconsiderable stream, foul, deep, and rapid. It is navigable by small boats, barks, and lighters;

and, for the conveniency of loading and unloading them, there is a handsome quay by the new custom-house, at the Porto di Ripetta, provided with stairs of each side, and adorned with an elegant fountain, that yields abundance of excellent water.

We are told that the bed of this river has been considerably raised by the rubbish of old Rome, and this is the reason usually given for its being so apt to overflow its banks. A citizen of Rome told me that a friend of his, lately digging to lay the foundation of a new house in the lower part of the city, near the bank of the river, discovered the pavement of an ancient street, at the depth of thirty-nine feet from the present surface of the earth. He therefore concluded that modern Rome is near forty feet higher in this place, than the site of the ancient city, and that the bed of the river is raised in proportion; but this is altogether incredible. Had the bed of the Tyber been anciently forty feet lower at Rome, than it is at present, there must have been a fall or cataract in it immediately above this tract, as it is not pretended that the bed of it is raised in any part above the city; otherwise such an elevation would have obstructed its course, and then it would have overflowed the whole Campania. There is nothing extraordinary in its present overflowings: they frequently happened of old, and did great mischief to the ancient city. Appian, Dio, and other historians describe an inundation of the Tyber immediately after the death of Julius Cæsar, which inundation was occasioned by the sudden melting of a great quantity of snow upon the Appenines. This calamity is recorded by Horace in his ode to Augustus.

> *Vidimus flavum Tiberim retortis*
> *Littore Etrusco violenter undis,*
> *Ire dejectum monumenta regis,*
>   *Templaque Vestæ:*
> *Iliæ dum se nimium querenti,*
> *Jactat ultorem; vagus et sinistrâ*
> *Labitur ripâ, Jove non probante*
>   *Uxorius Amnis.*

["We saw, push'd backward to his native Source,
The yellow Tiber roll his rapid Course,
With impious Ruin threatning Vesta's Fane,
And awful Monument's of Numa's Reign;
With Grief and Rage while Ilia's Bosom glows,
Boastful, for her Revenge, his Waters rose,
But now, th' uxorious River glides away,
So Jove commands, smooth-winding to the Sea."]

Livy expressly says, *"ita abundavit Tiberis, ut Ludi Apollinares, circo inundato, extra portam Collinam ad ædem Erycinae Veneris parati sint"*—"There was such an inundation of the *Tyber* that, the *Circus* being overflowed, the *Ludi Apollinares* were exhibited without the gate *Collina*, hard by the temple of *Venus Erycina.*" To this custom of transferring the *Ludi Apollinares* to another place when the Tyber had overflowed the *Circus Maximus*, Ovid alludes in his Fasti.

> *Altera gramineo spectabis equiria campo*
> *Quem Tiberis curvis in latus urget aquis.*
> *Qui tamen ejecta is forte tenebitur unda,*
> *Cælius accipiet pulverulentus equos.*

> [Another race thy view shall entertain,
> Where bending Tyber skirts the grassy plain;
> Or, should his vagrant stream that plain o'erflow,
> The *Cælian* hill the dusty course will shew.]

The Porta del Popolo (formerly, Flaminia), by which we entered Rome, is an elegant piece of architecture, adorned with marble columns and statues, executed after the design of Buonaroti. Within side you find yourself in a noble piazza, from whence three of the principal streets of Rome are detached. It is adorned with the famous Ægyptian obelisk, brought hither from the Circus Maximus, and set up by the architect Dominico Fontana in the pontificate of Sixtus V. Here is likewise a beautiful fountain designed by the same artist; and at the beginning of the two principal streets are two very elegant churches fronting each other. Such an august entrance cannot fail to impress the stranger with a sublime idea of this venerable city.

Having given our names at the gate, we repaired to the dogana, or custom-house, where our trunks and carriage were searched; and here we were surrounded by a number of servitori de piazza [guides], offering their services with the most disagreeable importunity. Though I told them several times I had no occasion for any, three of them took possession of the coach, one mounting before and two of them behind; and thus we proceeded to the Piazza d'Espagna, where the person lived to whose house I was directed. Strangers that come to Rome seldom put up at public inns, but go directly to lodging houses, of which there is great plenty in this quarter. The Piazza d'Espagna is open, airy, and pleasantly situated in a high part of the city immediately under the Colla Pinciana, and adorned with two fine fountains. Here most of the English reside: the apartments are generally commodious and well furnished;

and the lodgers are well supplied with provisions and all necessaries of life. But, if I studied economy, I would choose another part of the town than the Piazza d'Espagna, which is, besides, at a great distance from the antiquities. For a decent first floor and two bed-chambers on the second, I payed no more than a scudo (five shillings) per day. Our table was plentifully furnished by the landlord for two and thirty pauls, being equal to sixteen shillings. I hired a town-coach at the rate of fourteen pauls, or seven shillings a day; and a servitore di piazza for three pauls, or eighteen-pence. The coachman has also an allowance of two pauls a day. The provisions at Rome are reasonable and good; the vitella mongana [suckling calf] however, which is the most delicate veal I ever tasted, is very dear, being sold for two pauls, or a shilling, the pound. Here are the rich wines of Montepulciano, Montefiascone, and Monte di Dragone; but what we commonly drink at meals is that of Orvieto, a small white wine, of an agreeable flavour. Strangers are generally advised to employ an antiquarian to instruct them in all the curiosities of Rome; and this is a necessary expence, when a person wants to become a connoisseur in painting, statuary, and architecture. For my own part I had no such ambition. I longed to view the remains of antiquity by which this metropolis is distinguished; and to contemplate the originals of many pictures and statues, which I had admired in prints and descriptions. I therefore chose a servant, who was recommended to me as a sober intelligent fellow, acquainted with these matters: at the same time I furnished myself with maps and plans of ancient and modern Rome, together with the little manual called *Itinerario istruttivo per ritrovare con facilita tutte le magnificenze di Roma e di alcune citta', e castelli suburbani* [Guide to Locating All the Sights of Rome, as well as Some Nearby Castles and Towns]. But I found still more satisfaction in perusing the book in three volumes entitled *Roma antica, e moderna*, which contains a description of everything remarkable in and about the city, illustrated with a great number of copper-plates, and many curious historical annotations. This directory cost me a zequine; but a hundred zequines will not purchase all the books and prints which have been published at Rome on these subjects. Of these the most celebrated are the plates of Piranesi, who is not only an ingenious architect and en-graver, but also a learned antiquarian; though he is apt to run riot in his conjectures; and with regard to the arts of ancient Rome, has broached some doctrines which he will find it very difficult to maintain. Our young gentlemen who go to Rome will do well to be upon their guard against a set of sharpers (some of them of our own country) who deal in pictures and antiques, and very often impose upon the uninformed stranger by selling him trash, as the productions of the most celebrated artists. The

English are more than any other foreigners exposed to this imposition. They are supposed to have more money to throw away; and therefore a greater number of snares are laid for them. This opinion of their superior wealth they take a pride in confirming, by launching out into all manner of unnecessary expence: but, what is still more dangerous, the moment they set foot in Italy, they are seized with the ambition of becoming connoisseurs in painting, music, statuary, and architecture; and the adventurers of this country do not fail to flatter this weakness for their own advantage. I have seen in different parts of Italy a number of raw boys, whom Britain seemed to have poured forth on purpose to bring her national character into contempt: ignorant, petulant, rash, and profligate, without any knowledge or experience of their own, without any director to improve their understanding, or superintend their conduct. One engages in play with an infamous gamester, and is stripped perhaps in the very first party: another is poxed and pillaged by an antiquated cantatrice ["opera singer"]: a third is bubbled by a knavish antiquarian; and a fourth is laid under contribution by a dealer in pictures. Some turn fiddlers, and pretend to compose: but all of them talk familiarly of the arts, and return finished connoisseurs and coxcombs to their own country. The most remarkable phænomenon of this kind, which I have seen, is a boy of seventy-two, now actually travelling through Italy, for improvement, under the auspices of another boy of twenty-two. When you arrive at Rome, you receive cards from all your country-folks in that city: they expect to have the visit returned next day, when they give orders not to be at home; and you never speak to one another in the sequel. This is a refinement in hospitality and politeness, which the English have invented by the strength of their own genius, without any assistance either from France, Italy, or Lapland. No Englishman above the degree of a painter or cicerone frequents any coffee-house at Rome; and as there are no public diversions, except in carnival-time, the only chance you have for seeing your compatriots is either in visiting the curiosities, or at a conversazione. The Italians are very scrupulous in admitting foreigners, except those who are introduced as people of quality: but if there happens to be any English lady of fashion at Rome, she generally keeps an assembly, to which the British subjects resort. In my next, I shall communicate, without ceremony or affectation, what further remarks I have made at Rome, without any pretence, however, to the character of a connoisseur, which, without all doubt, would sit very awkwardly upon,

Dear Sir,

Your Friend and Servant.

LAURENCE STERNE
1713–1768

This whimsical clergyman, author of Tristram Shandy, *the best-known as well as the longest of joke "novels," was born in Clonmel, Ireland, the son of an army officer stationed there. He was educated at Jesus College, Cambridge, and subsequently held clerical livings in Yorkshire, where his parishioners sometimes found his behavior very antic and unseemly and where he devoted himself mainly to hunting, painting, music, and wayward but far-ranging reading.* Tristram Shandy *appeared in nine volumes over an eight-year period and made Sterne famous and the rage of London. But his worsening tuberculosis impelled him to seek a cure in France and Italy, and he spent almost four years living and traveling there in the early 1760's.*

The fruit of these travels was a book (published posthumously) designed to counterbalance by "sentiment" and generosity earlier accounts of Continental usages Sterne felt to be coarse and unfeeling, if not offensively splenetic, notably Travels through France and Italy *by Dr. Tobias Smollett (here designated "Smelfungus") and* Letters from Italy, *by Dr. Samuel Sharp, aka "Mundungus." Too many travel writers, Sterne thought, merely described such externals of a place as they were pointed toward by any common guidebook. Or if they looked inward and dilated on their own reactions, too often they condemned local sights and customs for their strangeness instead of relishing them for that very reason. His object, on the other hand, was to produce a book registering his own original, delicate, and complicated responses to the foreign, a book which might "teach us to love the world and our fellow creatures."*

From A SENTIMENTAL JOURNEY THROUGH FRANCE AND ITALY (1768)

THE DESOBLIGEANT

CALAIS

When a man is discontented with himself, it has one advantage, however, that it puts him into an excellent frame of mind for making a bargain. Now there being no travelling through France and Italy without a chaise—and nature generally prompting us to the thing we are fittest for, I walked out into the coach yard to buy or hire something of that kind to my purpose: an old Desobligeant* in the furthest corner of the court hit my fancy at first sight, so I instantly got into it, and finding it in tolerable harmony with my feelings, I ordered the waiter to call Monsieur Dessein the master of the hotel—but Monsieur Dessein being gone to vespers, and not caring to face the Franciscan whom I saw on the opposite side of the court, in conference with a lady just arrived, at the inn—I drew the taffeta curtain betwixt us, and being determined to write my journey, I took out my pen and ink, and wrote the preface to it in the *Desobligeant.*

PREFACE

IN THE DESOBLIGEANT

It must have been observed by many a peripatetic philosopher that nature has set up by her own unquestionable authority certain boundaries and fences to circumscribe the discontent of man: she has effected her purpose in the quietest and easiest manner by laying him under almost insuperable obligations to work out his ease, and to sustain his sufferings at home. It is there only that she has provided him with the most suitable objects to partake of his happiness, and bear a part of that burden which, in all countries and ages, has ever been too heavy for one pair of shoulders. 'Tis true we are endued with an imperfect power of spreading our happiness sometimes beyond *her* limits, but 'tis so ordered, that from the want of languages, connections, and dependencies,

---

*A chaise, so called in France, from its holding but one person.

and from the difference in education, customs and habits, we lie under so many impediments in communicating our sensations out of our own sphere, as often amount to a total impossibility.

It will always follow from hence, that the balance of sentimental commerce is always against the expatriated adventurer: he must buy what he has little occasion for at their own price—his conversation will seldom be taken in exchange for theirs without a large discount—and this, by the by, eternally driving him into the hands of more equitable brokers for such conversation as he can find, it requires no great spirit of divination to guess at his party—

This brings me to my point; and naturally leads me (if the seesaw of this *Desobligeant* will but let me get on) into the efficient as well as the final causes of travelling—

Your idle people that leave their native country and go abroad for some reason or reasons which may be derived from one of these general causes—

> Infirmity of body,
> Imbecility of mind, or
> Inevitable necessity.

The first two include all those who travel by land or by water, labouring with pride, curiosity, vanity or spleen, subdivided and combined *in infinitum.*

The third class includes the whole army of peregrine martyrs; more especially those travellers who set out upon their travels with the benefit of the clergy, either as delinquents travelling under the direction of governors recommended by the magistrate—or young gentlemen transported by the cruelty of parents and guardians, and travelling under the direction of governors recommended by Oxford, Aberdeen, and Glasgow.

There is a fourth class, but their number is so small that they would not deserve a distinction, was it not necessary in a work of this nature to observe the greatest precision and nicety, to avoid a confusion of character. And these men I speak of are such as cross the seas and sojourn in a land of strangers with a view of saving money for various reasons and upon various pretences: but as they might also save themselves and others a great deal of unnecessary trouble by saving their money at home—and as their reasons for travelling are the least complex of any other species of emigrants, I shall distinguish these gentlemen by the name of

Simple Travellers.

Thus the whole circle of travellers may be reduced to the following *Heads.*

> Idle Travellers,
> Inquisitive Travellers,
> Lying Travellers,
> Proud Travellers,
> Vain Travellers,
> Splenetic Travellers.

Then follow the Travellers of Necessity.

> The delinquent and felonious Traveller,
> The unfortunate and innocent Traveller,
> The simple Traveller,

And last of all (if you please) The Sentimental Traveller (meaning thereby myself) who have travelled, and of which I am now sitting down to give an account—as much out of *Necessity,* and the *besoin de* Voyager [needs of the traveller], as any one in the class.

I am well aware, at the same time, as both my travels and observations will be altogether of a different cast from any of my fore-runners; that I might have insisted upon a whole niche entirely to myself—but I should break in upon the confines of the *Vain* Traveller, in wishing to draw attention towards me, till I have some better grounds for it, than the mere *Novelty of my Vehicle.*

It is sufficient for my reader, if he has been a traveller himself, that with study and reflection hereupon he may be able to determine his own place and rank in the catalogue—it will be one step towards knowing himself; as it is great odds, but he retains some tincture and resemblance, of what he imbibed or carried out, to the present hour.

The man who first transplanted the grape of Burgundy to the Cape of Good Hope (observe he was a Dutchman) never dreamt of drinking the same wine at the Cape, that the same grape produced upon the French mountains—he was too phlegmatic for that—but undoubtedly he expected to drink some sort of vinous liquor; but whether good, bad, or indifferent—he knew enough of this world to know that it did not depend upon his choice, but that what is generally called *chance* was to decide his success: however, he hoped for the best; and in these hopes, by an intemperate confidence in the fortitude of his head, and the depth of his discretion, *Mynheer* might possibly overset both in his new vineyard; and by discovering his nakedness, become a laughing-stock to his people.

Even so it fares with the poor Traveller, sailing and posting through the politer kingdoms of the globe in pursuit of knowledge and improvements.

Knowledge and improvements are to be got by sailing and posting for that purpose; but whether useful knowledge and real improvements, is all a lottery—and even where the adventurer is successful, the acquired stock must be used with caution and sobriety to turn to any profit—but as the chances run prodigiously the other way both as to the acquisition and application, I am of opinion, that a man would act as wisely if he could prevail upon himself to live contented without foreign knowledge or foreign improvements, especially if he lives in a country that has no absolute want of either—and indeed, much grief of heart has it oft and many a time cost me, when I have observed how many a foul step the inquisitive Traveller has measured to see sights and look into discoveries; all which, as Sancho Panza said to Don Quixote, they might have seen dry-shod at home. It is an age so full of light, that there is scarce a country or corner of Europe whose beams are not crossed and interchanged with others—Knowledge in most of its branches, and in most affairs, is like music in an Italian street, whereof those may partake, who pay nothing—But there is no nation under heaven—and God is my record (before whose tribunal I must one day come and give an account of this work)—that I do not speak it vauntingly—But there is no nation under heaven abounding with more variety of learning—where the sciences may be more fitly wooed or more surely won than here—where art is encouraged, and will so soon rise high—where Nature (take her all together) has so little to answer for—and, to close all, where there is more wit and variety of character to feed the mind with—Where then, my dear countrymen, are you going—

—We are only looking at this chaise, said they—Your most obedient servant, said I, skipping out of it, and pulling off my hat—We were wondering, said one of them, who, I found, was an *inquisitive traveller*—what could occasion its motion.—'Twas the agitation, said I coolly, of writing a preface—I never heard, said the other, who was a *simple traveller,* of a preface wrote in a *Desobligeant.*—It would have been better, said I, in a *Vis a Vis* [carriage holding two people sitting face to face].

—*As an Englishman does not travel to see Englishmen,* I retired to my room.

CALAIS

I perceived that something darkened the passage more than myself, as I stepped along it to my room; it was effectually Mons. Dessein, the master of the hotel, who had just returned from vespers, and, with his hat under his arm, was most complaisantly following me, to put me in mind of my wants. I had wrote myself pretty well out of conceit with the *Desobligeant;* and Mons. Dessein speaking of it with a shrug, as if it would no way suit me, it immediately struck my fancy that it belonged to some *innocent traveller,* who, on his return home, had left it to Mons. Dessein's honour to make the most of. Four months had elapsed since it had finished its career of Europe in the corner of Mons. Dessein's coachyard; and having sallied out from thence but a vamped-up business at the first, though it had been twice taken to pieces on Mount Sennis, it had not profited much by its adventures—but by none so little as the standing so many months unpitied in the corner of Mons. Dessein's coachyard. Much indeed was not to be said for it—but something might—and when a few words will rescue misery out of her distress, I hate the man who can be a churl of them.

—Now was I the master of this hotel, said I, laying the point of my forefinger on Mons. Dessein's breast, I would inevitably make a point of getting rid of this unfortunate *Desobligeant*—it stands swinging reproaches at you every time you pass by it—

Mon Dieu! [Egad!] said Mons. Dessein—I have no interest—Except the interest, said I, which men of a certain turn of mind take, Mons. Dessein, in their own sensations—I'm persuaded, to a man who feels for others as well as for himself, every rainy night, disguise it as you will, must cast a damp upon your spirits—You suffer, Mons. Dessein, as much as the machine—

I have always observed, when there is as much *sour* as *sweet* in a compliment, that an Englishman is eternally at a loss within himself, whether to take it, or let it alone: a Frenchman never is: Mon. Dessein made me a bow.

C'est bien vrai [True enough], said he—But in this case I should only exchange one disquietude for another, and with loss: figure to yourself, my dear Sir, that in giving you a chaise which would fall to pieces before you had got half way to Paris—figure to yourself how much I should suffer, in giving an ill impression of myself to a man of honour, and lying at the mercy, as I must do, *d'un homme d'esprit* [of a man of sense].

The dose was made up exactly after my own prescription; so I could not help taking it—and returning Mons. Dessein his bow, without more casuistry we walked together towards his Remise [coach house] to take a view of his magazine of chaises.

IN THE STREET

CALAIS

It must needs be a hostile kind of a world, when the buyer (if it be but of a sorry post-chaise) cannot go forth with the seller thereof into the street to terminate the difference betwixt them, but he instantly falls into the same frame of mind and views his conventionist with the same sort of eye, as if he was going along with him to Hyde-park corner to fight a duel. For my own part, being but a poor swordsman, and no way a match for Monsieur *Dessein,* I felt the rotation of all the movements within me, to which the situation is incident—I looked at Monsieur *Dessein* through and through—eyed him as he walked along in profile— then, *en face* [face to face]—thought he looked like a Jew—then a Turk—disliked his wig—cursed him by my gods—wished him at the devil—

—And is all this to be lighted up in the heart for a beggarly account of three or four louis d'ors, which is the most I can be over-reached in?—Base passion! said I, turning myself about, as a man naturally does upon a sudden reverse of sentiment—base, ungentle passion! thy hand is against every man, and every man's hand against thee—heaven forbid! said she, raising her hand up to her forehead, for I had turned full in front upon the lady whom I had seen in conference with the monk—she had followed us unperceived—Heaven forbid indeed! said I, offering her my own—she had a black pair of silk gloves open only at the thumb and two fore-fingers, so accepted it without reserve—and I led her up to the door of the Remise.

Monsieur *Dessein* had *diabled* [wished to the devil] the key above fifty times before he found out he had come with a wrong one in his hand: we were as impatient as himself to have it opened; and so attentive to the obstacle, that I continued holding her hand almost without knowing it; so that Monsieur *Dessein* left us together with her hand in mine, and with our faces turned towards the door of the Remise, and said he would be back in five minutes.

Now a colloquy of five minutes, in such a situation, is worth one of as many ages, with your faces turned towards the street: in the latter case, 'tis drawn from the objects and occurrences without—when your eyes are fixed upon a dead blank—you draw purely from yourselves. A silence of a single moment upon Monsieur *Dessein's* leaving us, had been fatal to the situation—she had infallibly turned about—so I begun the conversation instantly.—

—But what were the temptations (as I write not to apologize for the weaknesses of my heart in this tour,—but to give an account of them)— shall be described with the same simplicity, with which I felt them.

THE REMISE DOOR

CALAIS

When I told the reader that I did not care to get out of the *Desobligeant*, because I saw the monk in close conference with a lady just arrived at the inn—I told him the truth; but I did not tell him the whole truth; for I was full as much restrained by the appearance and figure of the lady he was talking to. Suspicion crossed my brain, and said, he was telling her what had passed: something jarred upon it within me—I wished him at his convent.

When the heart flies out before the understanding, it saves the judgment a world of pains—I was certain she was of a better order of beings—however, I thought no more of her, but went on and wrote my preface.

The impression returned upon my encounter with her in the street; a guarded frankness with which she gave me her hand, shewed, I thought, her good education and her good sense; and as I led her on, I felt a pleasurable ductility about her, which spread a calmness over all my spirits—

—Good God! how a man might lead such a creature as this round the world with him!—

I had not yet seen her face—'twas not material; for the drawing was instantly set about, and long before we had got to the door of the Remise, *Fancy* had finished the whole head, and pleased herself as much with its fitting her goddess, as if she had dived into the TIBER for it—but thou art a seduced, and a seducing slut; and albeit thou cheatest us seven times a day with thy pictures and images, yet with so many charms dost thou do it, and thou deckest out thy pictures in the shapes of so many angels of light, 'tis a shame to break with thee.

When we had got to the door of the Remise, she withdrew her hand from across her forehead, and let me see the original—it was a face of about six and twenty—of a clear transparent brown, simply set off without rouge or powder—it was not critically handsome, but there was that in it, which in the frame of mind I was in, which attached me much more to it—it was interesting; I fancied it wore the characters of a widowed look, and in that state of its declension, which had passed the two first paroxysms of sorrow, and was quietly beginning to reconcile itself to its loss—but a thousand other distresses might have traced the same lines; I wished to know what they had been—and was ready to enquire (had the same *bon ton* of conversation permitted, as in the days of Esdras)—*"What aileth thee? and why art thou disquieted? and why is thy understanding troubled?"*—In a word, I felt benevolence for her; and resolved some way or other to throw in my mite of courtesy—if not of service.

Such were my temptations—and in this disposition to give way to them, was I left alone with the lady with her hand in mine, and with our faces both turned closer to the door of the Remise than what was absolutely necessary.

THE REMISE DOOR

CALAIS

This certainly, fair lady! said I, raising her hand up a little lightly as I begun, must be one of Fortune's whimsical doings: to take two utter strangers by their hands—of different sexes, and perhaps from different corners of the globe, and in one moment place them together in such a cordial situation, as Friendship herself could scarce have achieved for them, had she projected it for a month—

—And your reflection upon it, shews how much, Monsieur, she has embarassed you by the adventure.—

When the situation is, what we would wish, nothing is so ill-timed as to hint at the circumstances which make it so: you thank Fortune, continued she—you had reason—the heart knew it, and was satisfied; and who but an English philosopher would have sent notices of it to the brain to reverse the judgment?

In saying this, she disengaged her hand with a look which I thought a sufficient commentary upon the text.

It is a miserable picture which I am going to give of the weakness of my heart, by owning that it suffered a pain, which worthier occasions could not have inflicted.—I was mortified with the loss of her hand, and the manner in which I lost it carried neither oil nor wine to the wound: I never felt the pain of a sheepish inferiority so miserably in my life.

The triumphs of a true feminine heart are short upon these discomfitures. In a very few seconds she laid her hand upon the cuff of my coat, in order to finish her reply; so some way or other, God knows how, I regained my situation.

—She had nothing to add.

I forthwith began to model a different conversation for the lady, thinking from the spirit as well as moral of this, that I had been mistaken in her character; but upon turning her face towards me, the spirit which had animated the reply was fled—the muscles relaxed, and I beheld the same unprotected look of distress which first won me to her interest— melancholy! to see such sprightliness the prey of sorrow.—I pitied her from my soul; and though it may seem ridiculous enough to a torpid heart,—I could have taken her into my arms, and cherished her, though it was in the open street, without blushing.

The pulsations of the arteries along my fingers pressing across hers told her what was passing within me: she looked down—a silence of some moments followed.

I fear, in this interval, I must have made some slight efforts towards a closer compression of her hand, from a subtle sensation I felt in the palm of my own—not as if she was going to withdraw hers—but as if she thought about it—and I had infallibly lost it a second time, had not instinct more than reason directed me to the last resource in these dangers—to hold it loosely, and in a manner as if I was every moment going to release it of myself; so she let it continue, till Monsieur *Dessein* returned with the key; and in the mean time I set myself to consider how I should undo the ill impressions which the poor monk's story, in case he had told it her, must have planted in her breast against me.

THE SNUFF-BOX

CALAIS

The good old monk was within six paces of us, as the idea of him crossed my mind; and was advancing towards us a little out of the line, as if uncertain whether he should break in upon us or no.—He stopped, however, as soon as he came up to us, with a world of frankness; and having a horn snuff-box in his hand, he presented it open to me—You shall taste mine—said I, pulling out my box (which was a small tortoise one) and putting it into his hand—'Tis most excellent, said the monk; Then do me the favour, I replied, to accept of the box and all, and when you take a pinch out of it, sometimes recollect it was the peace offering of a man who once used you unkindly, but not from his heart.

The poor monk blushed as red as scarlet. *Mon Dieu!* said he, pressing his hands together—you never used me unkindly.—I should think, said the lady, he is not likely. I blushed in my turn; but from what movements, I leave to the few who feel to analyse—Excuse me, Madame, replied I—I treated him most unkindly; and from no provocations—'Tis impossible, said the lady.—My God! cried the monk, with a warmth of asseveration which seemed not to belong to him—the fault was in me, and in the indiscretion of my zeal—the lady opposed it, and I joined with her in maintaining it was impossible, that a spirit so regulated as his, could give offence to any.

I knew not that contention could be rendered so sweet and pleasurable a thing to the nerves as I then felt it.—We remained silent, without any sensation of that foolish pain which takes place when in such a circle you look for ten minutes in one another's faces without saying a word. Whilst this lasted, the monk rubbed his horn box upon the sleeve of his tunic; and as soon as it had acquired a little air of brightness by the friction—he made a low bow, and said, 'twas too late to say whether it was the weakness or goodness of our tempers which had involved us in this contest—but be it as it would—he begged we might exchange boxes—in saying this, he presented his to me with one hand, as he took mine from me in the other; and having kissed it—with a stream of good nature in his eyes he put it into his bosom—and took his leave.

I guard this box, as I would the instrumental parts of my religion, to help my mind on to something better: in truth, I seldom go abroad without it; and oft and many a time have I called up by it the courteous spirit of its owner to regulate my own, in the justlings of the world; they had found full employment for his, as I learnt from his story, till about the forty-fifth year of his age, when upon some military services ill requited, and meeting at the same time with a disappointment in the tenderest of passions, he abandoned the sword and the sex together and took sanctuary, not so much in his convent as in himself.

I feel a damp upon my spirits, as I am going to add, that in my last return through Calais, upon inquiring after Father Lorenzo, I heard he had been dead near three months, and was buried, not in his convent, but, according to his desire, in a little cemetery belonging to it, about two leagues off: I had a strong desire to see where they had laid him—when, upon pulling out his little horn box, as I sat by his grave, and plucking up a nettle or two at the head of it, which had no business to grow there, they all struck together so forcibly upon my affections, that I burst into a flood of tears—but I am as weak as a woman; and I beg the world not to smile, but pity me.

THE REMISE DOOR

CALAIS

I had never quitted the lady's hand all this time; and had held it so long, that it would have been indecent to have let it go, without first pressing it to my lips: the blood and spirits, which had suffered a revulsion from her, crowded back to her as I did it.

Now the two travellers who had spoke to me in the coach-yard, happening at that crisis to be passing by, and observing our communications, naturally took it into their heads that we must be *man and wife* at least; so stopping as soon as they came up to the door of the Remise, the one of them, who was the inquisitive traveller, asked us, if we set out for Paris the next morning?—I could only answer for myself, I said; and the lady added, she was for Amiens.—We dined there yesterday, said the simple traveller—You go directly through the town, added the other, in your road to Paris. I was going to return a thousand thanks for the intelligence, *that Amiens was in the road to Paris;* but, upon pulling out my poor monk's little horn box to take a pinch of snuff—I made them a quiet bow, and wishing them a good passage to Dover—they left us alone—

—Now where would be the harm, said I to myself, if I was to beg of this distressed lady to accept of half of my chaise?—and what mighty mischief could ensue?

Every dirty passion and bad propensity in my nature took the alarm as I stated the proposition—It will oblige you to have a third horse, said AVARICE, which will put twenty livres out of your pocket.—You know not who she is, said CAUTION—or what scrapes the affair may draw you into, whispered COWARDICE—

Depend upon it, Yorick! said DISCRETION, 'twill be said you went off with a mistress, and came by assignation to Calais for that purpose—

—You can never after, cried HYPOCRISY aloud, shew your face in the world—or rise, quoth MEANNESS, in the church—or be anything in it, said PRIDE, but a lousy prebendary.

—But 'tis a civil thing, said I—and as I generally act from the first impulse, and therefore seldom listen to these cabals, which serve no purpose that I know of but to encompass the heart with adamant—I turned instantly about to the lady—

—But she had glided off unperceived, as the cause was pleading, and had made ten or a dozen paces down the street, by the time I had made

the determination; so I set off after her with a long stride, to make her
the proposal with the best address I was master of; but observing she
walked with her cheek half resting upon the palm of her hand—with
the slow, short-measured step of thoughtfulness, and with her eyes, as
she went step by step, fixed upon the ground, it struck me, she was trying
the same cause herself.—God help her! said I, she has some mother-in-
law, or tartufish aunt, or nonsensical old woman, to consult upon the
occasion, as well as myself: so not caring to interrupt the processe, and
deeming it more gallant to take her at discretion than by surprise, I faced
about, and took a short turn or two before the door of the Remise, whilst
she walked musing on one side.

IN THE STREET

CALAIS

Having, on first sight of the lady, settled the affair in my fancy, "that
she was of the better order of beings"—and then laid it down as a second
axiom, as indisputable as the first, that she was a widow, and wore a
character of distress—I went no further; I got ground enough for the
situation which pleased me—and had she remained close beside my
elbow till midnight, I should have held true to my system, and considered her only under that general idea.

She had scarce got twenty paces distant from me, ere something
within me called out for a more particular inquiry—it brought on the
idea of a further separation—I might possibly never see her more—the
heart is for saving what it can; and I wanted the traces thro' which my
wishes might find their way to her, in case I should never rejoin her
myself: in a word, I wished to know her name—her family's—her condition; and as I knew the place to which she was going, I wanted to know
from whence she came: but there was no coming at all this intelligence:
a hundred little delicacies stood in the way. I formed a score different
plans—There was no such thing as a man's asking her directly—the
thing was impossible.

A little French *debonaire* captain, who came dancing down the street,
shewed me, it was the easiest thing in the world; for popping in betwixt
us, just as the lady was returning back to the door of the Remise, he
introduced himself to my acquaintance, and before he had well got
announced, begged I would do him the honour to present him to the
lady—I had not been presented myself—so turning about to her, he did
it just as well by asking her, if she had come from Paris?—No: she was

going that route, she said.—*Vous n'etez pas de Londre?* [Aren't you from London?]—She was not, she replied.—Then Madame must have come thro' Flanders.—*Apparamment vous etez Flammande?* [Apparently you are Flemish?] said the French captain.—The lady answered, she was.—*Peutêtre, de Lisle?* [Perhaps from Lisle?] added he—She said, she was not of Lisle.—Nor Arras?—nor Cambray?—nor Ghent?—nor Brussels? She answered, she was of Brussels.

He had had the honour, he said, to be at the bombardment of it last war—that it was finely situated, *pour cela* [for that]—and full of noblesse when the Imperialists were driven out by the French (the lady made a slight curtsy)—so giving her an account of the affair, and of the share he had had in it—he begged the honour to know her name—so made his bow.

—*Et Madame a son Mari?* [Does madame have a husband?]—said he, looking back when he had made two steps—and without staying for an answer—danced down the street.

Had I served seven years apprenticeship to good breeding, I could not have done as much.

THE REMISE

CALAIS

As the little French captain left us, Mons. Dessein came up with the key of the Remise in his hand, and forthwith let us into his magazine of chaises.

The first object which caught my eye, as Mons. Dessein opened the door of the Remise, was another old tattered *Desobligeant:* and notwithstanding it was the exact picture of that which had hit my fancy so much in the coach-yard but an hour before—the very sight of it stirred up a disagreeable sensation within me now; and I thought 'twas a churlish beast into whose heart the idea could first enter, to construct such a machine; nor had I much more charity for the man who could think of using it.

I observed the lady was as little taken with it as myself: so Mons. Dessein led us on to a couple of chaises which stood abreast, telling us as he recommended them, that they had been purchased by my Lord A. and B. to go the *grand tour,* but had gone no further than Paris, so were in all respects as good as new—They were too good—so I passed on to a third, which stood behind, and forthwith began to chaffer for the price—But 'twill scarce hold two, said I, opening the door and getting in—Have the goodness, Madam, said Mons. Dessein, offering his arm, to step in—The lady hesitated half a second, and stepped in; and the waiter that moment beckoning to speak to Mons. Dessein, he shut the door of the chaise upon us, and left us.

THE REMISE

CALAIS

C'est bien comique, 'tis very droll, said the lady smiling, from the reflection that this was the second time we had been left together by a parcel of nonsensical contingencies—*c'est bien comique*, said she—

—There wants nothing, said I, to make it so, but the comic use which the gallantry of a Frenchman would put it to—to make love the first moment, and an offer of his person the second.

'Tis their *fort* [talent]: replied the lady.

It is supposed so at least—and how it has come to pass, continued I, I know not; but they have certainly got the credit of understanding more of love, and making it better than any other nation upon earth: but for my own part I think them errant bunglers, and in truth the worst set of marksmen that ever tried Cupid's patience.

—To think of making love by *sentiments!*

I should as soon think of making a genteel suit of clothes out of remnants:—and to do it—pop—at first sight by declaration—is submitting the offer and themselves with it, to be sifted, with all their *pours* and *contres* [pros and cons], by an unheated mind.

The lady attended as if she expected I should go on.

Consider then, madam, continued I, laying my hand upon hers—

That grave people hate Love for the name's sake—

That selfish people hate it for their own—

Hypocrites for heaven's—

And that all of us both old and young, being ten times worse frightened than hurt by the very *report*—What a want of knowledge in this branch of commerce a man betrays, whoever lets the word come out of his lips, till an hour or two at least after the time that his silence upon it becomes tormenting. A course of small, quiet attentions, not so pointed as to alarm—nor so vague as to be misunderstood,—with now and then a look of kindness, and little or nothing said upon it—leaves Nature for your mistress, and she fashions it to her mind.—

Then I solemnly declare, said the lady, blushing—you have been making love to me all this while.

THE REMISE

CALAIS

Monsieur Dessein came back to let us out of the chaise, and acquaint the lady, the Count de L— her brother was just arrived at the hotel. Though I had infinite good will for the lady, I cannot say that I rejoiced in my heart at the event—and could not help telling her so—for it is fatal to a proposal, Madam, said I, that I was going to make you—

—You need not tell me what the proposal was, said she, laying her hand upon both mine, as she interrupted me.—A man, my good Sir, has seldom an offer of kindness to make to a woman, but she has a presentiment of it some moments before—

Nature arms her with it, said I, for immediate preservation—But I think, said she, looking in my face, I had no evil to apprehend—and to deal frankly with you, had determined to accept it.—If I had—(she stopped a moment)—I believe your good will would have drawn a story from me, which would have made pity the only dangerous thing in the journey.

In saying this, she suffered me to kiss her hand twice, and with a look of sensibility mixed with a concern she got out of the chaise—and bid adieu.

IN THE STREET

CALAIS

I never finished a twelve-guinea bargain so expeditiously in my life: my time seemed heavy upon the loss of the lady, and knowing every moment of it would be as two, till I put myself into motion—I ordered post horses directly, and walked towards the hotel.

Lord! said I, hearing the town clock strike four, and recollecting that I had been little more than a single hour in Calais—

—What a large volume of adventures may be grasped within this little span of life by him who interests his heart in everything and who, having eyes to see what time and chance are perpetually holding out to him as he journeyeth on his way, misses nothing he can *fairly* lay his hands on.—

—If this won't turn out something—another will—no matter—'tis an assay upon human nature—I get my labour for my pains—'tis enough—

the pleasure of the experiment has kept my senses and the best part of my blood awake, and laid the gross to sleep.

I pity the man who can travel from *Dan* to *Beersheba,* and cry, 'Tis all barren—and so it is; and so is all the world to him who will not cultivate the fruits it offers. I declare, said I, clapping my hands cheerily together, that was I in a desert, I would find out wherewith in it to call forth my affections—If I could not do better, I would fasten them upon some sweet myrtle, or seek some melancholy cypress to connect myself to—I would court their shade, and greet them kindly for their protection—I would cut my name upon them, and swear they were the loveliest trees throughout the desert: if their leaves withered, I would teach myself to mourn, and when they rejoiced, I would rejoice along with them.

The learned SMELFUNGUS travelled from Boulogne to Paris—from Paris to Rome—and so on—but he set out with the spleen and jaundice, and every object he passed by was discoloured or distorted—He wrote an account of them, but 'twas nothing but the account of his miserable feelings.

I met Smelfungus in the grand portico of the Pantheon—he was just coming out of it—*'Tis nothing but a huge cock-pit,* said he—I wish you had said nothing worse of the Venus of Medicis, replied I—for in passing through Florence, I had heard he had fallen foul upon the goddess, and used her worse than a common strumpet, without the least provocation in nature.

I popped upon Smelfungus again at Turin, in his return home; and a sad tale of sorrowful adventures had he to tell, "wherein he spoke of moving accidents by flood and field, and of the cannibals which each other eat: the Anthropophagi"—he had been flayed alive, and bedeviled, and used worse than St. Bartholomew, at every stage he had come at—

—I'll tell it, cried Smelfungus, to the world. You had better tell it, said I, to your physician.

Mundungus, with an immense fortune, made the whole tour; going on from Rome to Naples—from Naples to Venice—from Venice to Vienna—to Dresden, to Berlin, without one generous connection or pleasurable anecdote to tell of; but he had travelled straight on looking neither to his right hand or his left, lest Love or Pity should seduce him out of his road.

Peace be to them! if it is to be found; but heaven itself, was it possible to get there with such tempers, would want objects to give it—every gentle spirit would come flying upon the wings of Love to hail their arrival—Nothing would the souls of Smelfungus and Mundungus hear of, but fresh anthems of joy, fresh raptures of love, and fresh congratulations of their common felicity—I heartily pity them: they have brought up no faculties for this work; and was the happiest mansion in heaven to be allotted to Smelfungus and Mundungus, they would be so far from being happy, that the souls of Smelfungus and Mundungus would do penance there to all eternity.

SAMUEL JOHNSON
1709–1784

The renowned author of The Rambler, A Dictionary of the English Language, Rasselas, *and* The Lives of the Poets *is so intimately associated with London ("When a man is tired of London," he once asserted, "he is tired of life") that it is hard to imagine him away from it. Yet he did travel a great deal, if out of Great Britain only once, when he visited Paris with his friends the Thrales. His main journey was to the Scottish Highlands and the Hebridean Islands with James Boswell, a trip that resulted in travel books for both of them.*

Johnson wanted his to be different from the common travel accounts of his time, which he thought superficial and useless, testimony only to their authors' lack of curiosity. Indeed, he wrote, "Few books disappoint their readers more than the narrations of travelers." The reason is simple: "The greater part of travelers tell nothing because their method of traveling supplies them with nothing to be told. He that enters a town at night and surveys it in the morning, and then hastens away to another place, and guesses at the manners of the inhabitants by the entertainment which his inn afforded him, may please himself," says Johnson, but he cannot please others. And even worse, he cannot instruct others, for "Every writer of travels should consider that, like all other authors, he undertakes either to instruct or please, or to mingle pleasure with instruction." Some may think Johnson instructs rather too much, but there is certainly pleasure likewise to be had from his quick wit and ready humanity.

From A Journey to the Western Islands of Scotland

(1775)

I had desired to visit the Hebrides, or Western Islands of Scotland, so long, that I scarcely remember how the wish was originally excited; and was in the autumn of the year 1773 induced to undertake the journey, by finding in Mr. Boswell a companion whose acuteness would help my inquiry, and whose gaiety of conversation and civility of manners are sufficient to counteract the inconveniencies of travel, in countries less hospitable than we have passed.

* * *

INVERNESS

Inverness was the last place which had a regular communication by high roads with the southern counties. All the ways beyond it have, I believe, been made by the soldiers in this century. At Inverness therefore Cromwell, when he subdued Scotland, stationed a garrison, as at the boundary of the Highlands. The soldiers seem to have incorporated afterwards with the inhabitants, and to have peopled the place with an English race; for the language of this town has been long considered as peculiarly elegant.

Here is a castle called the castle of Macbeth, the walls of which are yet standing. It was no very capacious edifice, but stands upon a rock so high and steep, that I think it was once not accessible, but by the help of ladders, or a bridge. Over against it, on another hill, was a fort built by Cromwell, now totally demolished; for no faction of Scotland loved the name of Cromwell, or had any desire to continue his memory.

* * *

We were now to bid farewell to the luxury of travelling and to enter a country upon which perhaps no wheel has ever rolled. We could indeed have used our post-chaise one day longer, along the military road to Fort Augustus, but we could have hired no horses beyond Inverness, and we were not so sparing of ourselves as to lead them, merely that we might have one day longer the indulgence of a carriage.

At Inverness therefore we procured three horses for ourselves and a servant, and one more for our baggage, which was no very heavy load. We found in the course of our journey the convenience of having disencumbered ourselves, by laying aside whatever we could spare; for it is not to be imagined without experience, how in climbing crags, and treading bogs, and winding through narrow and obstructed passages, a little bulk will hinder, and a little weight will burden; or how often a man that has pleased himself at home with his own resolution, will, in the hour of darkness and fatigue, be content to leave behind him every thing but himself.

LOUGH NESS

We took two Highlanders to run beside us, partly to show us the way, and partly to take back from the sea-side the horses, of which they were the owners. One of them was a man of great liveliness and activity, of whom his companion said that he would tire any horse in Inverness. Both of them were civil and ready-handed. Civility seems part of the national character of Highlanders. Every chieftain is a monarch, and politeness, the natural product of royal government, is diffused from the laird through the whole clan. But they are not commonly dexterous: their narrowness of life confines them to a few operations, and they are accustomed to endure little wants more than to remove them.

We mounted our steeds on the thirtieth of August, and directed our guides to conduct us to Fort Augustus. It is built at the head of Lough Ness, of which Inverness stands at the outlet. The way between them has been cut by the soldiers, and the greater part of it runs along a rock, levelled with great labour and exactness, near the water-side.

Most of this day's journey was very pleasant. The day, though bright, was not hot; and the appearance of the country, if I had not seen the Peak, would have been wholly new. We went upon a surface so hard and level, that we had little care to hold the bridle, and were therefore at full leisure for contemplation. On the left were high and steep rocks shaded with birch, the hardy native of the North, and covered with fern or heath. On the right the limpid waters of Lough Ness were beating their bank, and waving their surface by a gentle agitation. Beyond them were rocks sometimes covered with verdure, and sometimes towering in horrid nakedness. Now and then we espied a little corn-field, which served to impress more strongly the general barrenness.

Lough Ness is about twenty-four miles long, and from one mile to two miles broad. It is remarkable that Boethius, in his description of Scotland, gives it twelve miles of breadth. When historians or geographers exhibit false accounts of places far distant, they may be forgiven, because they can tell but what they are told; and that their accounts exceed the truth may be justly supposed, because most men exaggerate to others, if not to themselves: but Boethius lived at no great distance; if he never saw the lake, he must have been very incurious, and if he had seen it, his veracity yielded to very slight temptations.

Lough Ness, though not twelve miles broad, is a very remarkable diffusion of water without islands. It fills a large hollow between two ridges of high rocks, being supplied partly by the torrents which fall into it on either side, and partly, as is supposed, by springs at the bottom. Its water is remarkably clear and pleasant, and is imagined by the natives to be medicinal. We were told that it is in some places a hundred and forty fathom deep, a profundity scarcely credible, and which probably those that relate it have never sounded. Its fish are salmon, trout, and pike.

It was said at Fort Augustus that Lough Ness is open in the hardest winters, though a lake not far from it is covered with ice. In discussing these exceptions from the course of nature, the first question is, whether the fact be justly stated. That which is strange is delightful, and a pleasing error is not willingly detected. Accuracy of narration is not very common, and there are few so rigidly philosophical as not to represent as perpetual what is only frequent, or as constant what is really casual. If it be true that Lough Ness never freezes, it is either sheltered by its high banks from the cold blasts, and exposed only to those winds which have more power to agitate than congeal; or it is kept in perpetual motion by the rush of streams from the rocks that inclose it. Its profundity though it should be such as is represented can have little part in this exemption; for though deep wells are not frozen, because their water is secluded from the external air, yet where a wide surface is exposed to the full influence of a freezing atmosphere, I know not why the depth should keep it open. Natural philosophy is now one of the favourite studies of the Scottish nation, and Lough Ness well deserves to be diligently examined.

The road on which we travelled, and which was itself a source of entertainment, is made along the rock, in the direction of the lough, sometimes by breaking off protuberances, and sometimes by cutting the great mass of stone to a considerable depth. The fragments are piled in a loose wall on either side, with apertures left at very short spaces, to give a passage to the wintry currents. Part of it is bordered with low trees, from which our guides gathered nuts, and would have had the appearance of an English lane, except that an English lane is almost always dirty. It has been made with great labour, but has this advantage, that it cannot, without equal labour, be broken up.

Within our sight there were goats feeding or playing. The mountains have red deer, but they came not within view; and if what is said of their vigilance and subtlety be true, they have some claim to that palm of wisdom, which the eastern philosopher, whom Alexander interrogated, gave to those beasts which live furthest from men.

Near the way, by the water side, we espied a cottage. This was the first Highland hut that I had seen; and as our business was with life and manners, we were willing to visit it. To enter a habitation without leave seems to be not considered here as rudeness or intrusion. The old laws of hospitality still give this licence to a stranger.

A hut is constructed with loose stones, ranged for the most part with some tendency to circularity. It must be placed where the wind cannot act upon it with violence, because it has no cement; and where the water will run easily away, because it has no floor but the naked ground. The wall, which is commonly about six feet high, declines from the perpendicular a little inward. Such rafters as can be procured are then raised for a roof, and covered with heath, which makes a strong and warm thatch, kept from flying off by ropes of twisted heath, of which the ends, reaching from the center of the thatch to the top of the wall, are held firm by the weight of a large stone. No light is admitted but at the entrance, and through a hole in the thatch, which gives vent to the smoke. This hole is not directly over the fire, lest the rain should extinguish it; and the smoke therefore naturally fills the place before it escapes. Such is the general structure of the houses in which one of the nations of this opulent and powerful island has been hitherto content to live. Huts however are not more uniform than palaces; and this which we were inspecting was very far from one of the meanest, for it was divided into several apartments; and its inhabitants possessed such property as a pastoral poet might exalt into riches.

When we entered, we found an old woman boiling goatsflesh in a kettle. She spoke little English, but we had interpreters at hand; and she was willing enough to display her whole system of economy. She has five children, of which none are yet gone from her. The eldest, a boy of thirteen, and her husband, who is eighty years old, were at work in the wood. Her two next sons were gone to Inverness to buy "meal," by which oatmeal is always meant. Meal she considered as expensive food, and told us that in spring, when the goats gave milk, the children could live without it. She is mistress of sixty goats, and I saw many kids in an enclosure at the end of her house. She had also some poultry. By the lake we saw a potato garden, and a small spot of ground on which stood four shucks, containing each twelve sheaves of barley. She has all this from the labour of their own hands, and for what is necessary to be bought, her kids and her chickens are sent to market.

With the true pastoral hospitality, she asked us to sit down and drink whisky. She is religious, and though the kirk is four miles off, probably eight English miles, she goes thither every Sunday. We gave her a shilling, and she begged snuff; for snuff is the luxury of a Highland cottage.

Soon afterwards we came to the General's Hut, so called because it was the temporary abode of Wade, while he superintended the works upon the road. It is now a house of entertainment for passengers, and we found it not ill stocked with provisions.

*   *   *

FORT AUGUSTUS

In the morning we viewed the fort, which is much less than that of St. George, and is said to be commanded by the neighbouring hills. It was not long ago taken by the Highlanders. But its situation seems well chosen for pleasure, if not for strength; it stands at the head of the lake, and, by a sloop of sixty tons, is supplied from Inverness with great convenience.

We were now to cross the Highlands towards the western coast, and to content ourselves with such accommodations as a way so little frequented could afford. The journey was not formidable, for it was but of two days, very unequally divided, because the only house where we could be entertained was not further off than a third of the way. We soon came to a high hill, which we mounted by a military road, cut in traverses, so that as we went upon a higher stage, we saw the baggage following us below in a contrary direction. To make this way, the rock has been hewn to a level with labour that might have broken the perseverance of a Roman legion.

The country is totally denuded of its wood, but the stumps both of oaks and firs, which are still found, show that it has been once a forest of large timber. I do not remember that we saw any animals, but we were told that, in the mountains, there are stags, roebucks, goats and rabbits.

We did not perceive that this tract was possessed by human beings, except that once we saw a corn field, in which a lady was walking with some gentlemen. Their house was certainly at no great distance, but so situated that we could not descry it.

Passing on through the dreariness of solitude, we found a party of soldiers from the fort, working on the road, under the superintendence of a serjeant. We told them how kindly we had been treated at the garrison, and as we were enjoying the benefit of their labours, begged leave to show our gratitude by a small present.

ANOCH

Early in the afternoon we came to Anoch, a village in Glenmollison of three huts, one of which is distinguished by a chimney. Here we were to dine and lodge, and were conducted through the first room, that had the chimney, into another lighted by a small glass window. The landlord attended us with great civility, and told us what he could give us to eat and drink. I found some books on a shelf, among which were a volume or more of Prideaux's *Connection.*

This I mentioned as something unexpected, and perceived that I did not please him: I praised the propriety of his language, and was answered that I need not wonder, for he had learned it by grammar.

By subsequent opportunities of observation, I found that my host's diction had nothing peculiar. Those Highlanders that can speak English commonly speak it well, with few of the words, and little of the tone by which a Scotchman is distinguished. Their language seems to have been learned in the army or the navy, or by some communication with those who could give them good examples of accent and pronunciation. By their Lowland neighbours they would not willingly be taught; for they have long considered them as a mean and degenerate race. These prejudices are wearing fast away; but so much of them still remains, that when I asked a very learned minister in the islands which they considered as their most savage clans: "Those," said he, "that live next the Lowlands."

As we came hither early in the day, we had time sufficient to survey the place. The house was built like other huts of loose stones, but the part in which we dined and slept was lined with turf and wattled with twigs, which kept the earth from falling. Near it was a garden of turnips and a field of potatoes. It stands in a glen, or valley, pleasantly watered by a winding river. But this country, however it may delight the gazer or amuse the naturalist, is of no great advantage to its owners. Our landlord told us of a gentleman who possesses lands eighteen Scotch miles in length, and three in breadth; a space containing at least a hundred square English miles. He has raised his rents, to the danger of depopulating his farms, and he sells his timber, and by exerting every art of augmentation, has obtained an yearly revenue of four hundred pounds, which for a hundred square miles is three halfpence an acre.

Some time after dinner we were surprised by the entrance of a young woman, not inelegant either in mien or dress, who asked us whether we would have tea. We found that she was the daughter of our host, and desired her to make it. Her conversation, like her appearance, was gentle and pleasing. We knew that the girls of the Highlands are all gentle-women, and treated her with great respect, which she received as customary and due, and was neither elated by it, nor confused, but repaid my civilities without embarassment, and told me how much I honoured her country by coming to survey it.

She had been at Inverness to gain the common female qualifications, and had, like her father, the English pronunciation. I presented her with a book which I happened to have about me, and should not be pleased to think that she forgets me.

In the evening the soldiers, whom we had passed on the road, came to spend at our inn the little money that we had given them. They had the true military impatience of coin in their pockets, and had marched at least six miles to find the first place where liquor could be bought. Having never been before in a place so wild and unfrequented, I was glad of their arrival, because I knew that we had made them friends, and to gain still more of their good will, we went to them, where they were carousing in the barn, and added something to our former gift. All that we gave was not much, but it detained them in the barn, either merry or quarrelling, the whole night, and in the morning they went back to their work, with great indignation at the bad qualities of whisky.

We had gained so much the favour of our host that, when we left his house in the morning, he walked by us a great way, and entertained us with conversation both on his own condition, and that of the country. His life seemed to be merely pastoral, except that he differed from some of the ancient Nomads in having a settled dwelling. His wealth consists of one hundred sheep, as many goats, twelve milk-cows, and twenty-eight beeves ready for the drover.

From him we first heard of the general dissatisfaction which is now driving the Highlanders into the other hemisphere; and when I asked him whether they would stay at home if they were well treated, he answered with indignation that no man willingly left his native country. Of the farm, which he himself occupied, the rent had, in twenty-five years, been advanced from five to twenty pounds, which he found himself so little able to pay, that he would be glad to try his fortune in some other place. Yet he owned the reasonableness of raising the Highland rents in a certain degree, and declared himself willing to pay ten pounds for the ground which he had formerly had for five.

Our host having amused us for a time, resigned us to our guides. The journey of this day was long, not that the distance was great, but that the way was difficult. We were now in the bosom of the Highlands, with full leisure to contemplate the appearance and properties of mountainous regions, such as have been, in many countries, the last shelters of national distress, and are everywhere the scenes of adventures, stratagems, surprises and escapes.

Mountainous countries are not passed but with difficulty, not merely from the labour of climbing; for to climb is not always necessary: but because that which is not mountain is commonly bog, through which the way must be picked with caution. Where there are hills, there is much rain, and the torrents pouring down into the intermediate spaces seldom find so ready an outlet, as not to stagnate, till they have broken the texture of the ground.

Of the hills, which our journey offered to the view on either side, we did not take the height, nor did we see any that astonished us with their loftiness. Towards the summit of one, there was a white spot, which I should have called a naked rock, but the guides, who had better eyes, and were acquainted with the phenomena of the country, declared it to be snow. It had already lasted to the end of August, and was likely to maintain its contest with the sun till it should be reinforced by winter.

The height of mountains philosophically considered is properly computed from the surface of the next sea; but as it affects the eye or imagination of the passenger, as it makes either a spectacle or an obstruction, it must be reckoned from the place where the rise begins to make a considerable angle with the plain. In extensive continents the land may, by gradual elevation, attain great height, without any other appearance than that of a plane gently inclined, and if a hill placed upon such raised ground be described as having its altitude equal to the whole space above the sea, the representation will be fallacious.

These mountains may be properly enough measured from the inland base; for it is not much above the sea. As we advanced at evening towards the western coast, I did not observe the declivity to be greater than is necessary for the discharge of the inland waters.

We passed many rivers and rivulets, which commonly ran with a clear shallow stream over a hard pebbly bottom. These channels, which seem so much wider than the water that they convey would naturally require, are formed by the violence of wintry floods, produced by the accumulation of innumerable streams that fall in rainy weather from the hills, and bursting away with resistless impetuosity, make themselves a passage proportionate to their mass.

Such capricious and temporary waters cannot be expected to produce many fish. The rapidity of the wintry deluge sweeps them away, and the scantiness of the summer stream would hardly sustain them above the ground. This is the reason why in fording the northern rivers, no fishes are seen, as in England, wandering in the water.

Of the hills many may be called with Homer's Ida "abundant in springs," but few can deserve the epithet which he bestows upon Pelion by "waving their leaves." They exhibit very little variety; being almost wholly covered with dark heath, and even that seems to be checked in its growth. What is not heath is nakedness, a little diversified by now and then a stream rushing down the steep. An eye accustomed to flowery pastures and waving harvests is astonished and repelled by this wide extent of hopeless sterility. The appearance is that of matter incapable of form or usefulness, dismissed by nature from her care and disinherited of her favours, left in its original elemental state, or quickened only with one sullen power of useless vegetation.

It will very readily occur that this uniformity of barrenness can afford very little amusement to the traveller; that it is easy to sit at home and conceive rocks and heath, and waterfalls; and that these journeys are useless labours, which neither impregnate the imagination, nor enlarge the understanding. It is true that of far the greater part of things, we must content ourselves with such knowledge as description may exhibit, or analogy supply; but it is true likewise, that these ideas are always incomplete, and that at least, till we have compared them with realities, we do not know them to be just. As we see more, we become possessed of more certainties, and consequently gain more principles of reasoning, and found a wider basis of analogy.

Regions mountainous and wild, thinly inhabited, and little cultivated, make a great part of the earth, and he that has never seen them, must live unacquainted with much of the face of nature, and with one of the great scenes of human existence.

As the day advanced towards noon, we entered a narrow valley not very flowery, but sufficiently verdant. Our guides told us that the horses could not travel all day without rest or meat, and entreated us to stop here, because no grass would be found in any other place. The request was reasonable and the argument cogent. We therefore willingly dismounted and diverted ourselves as the place gave us opportunity.

I sat down on a bank, such as a writer of romance might have delighted to feign. I had indeed no trees to whisper over my head, but a clear rivulet streamed at my feet. The day was calm, the air soft, and all was rudeness, silence, and solitude. Before me, and on either side, were high hills, which by hindering the eye from ranging, forced the mind to find entertainment for itself. Whether I spent the hour well I know not; for here I first conceived the thought of this narration.

We were in this place at ease and by choice, and had no evils to suffer or to fear; yet the imaginations excited by the view of an unknown and untravelled wilderness are not such as arise in the artificial solitude of parks and gardens, a flattering notion of self-sufficiency, a placid indulgence of voluntary delusions, a secure expansion of the fancy, or a cool concentration of the mental powers. The phantoms which haunt a desert are want, and misery, and danger; the evils of dereliction rush upon the thoughts; man is made unwillingly acquainted with his own weakness, and meditation shows him only how little he can sustain, and how little he can perform. There were no traces of inhabitants, except perhaps a rude pile of clods called a summer hut, in which a herdsman had rested in the favourable seasons. Whoever had been in the place where I then sat, unprovided with provisions and ignorant of the country, might, at least before the roads were made, have wandered among the rocks till he had perished with hardship, before he could have found either food or shelter. Yet what are these hillocks to the ridges of Taurus, or these spots of wildness to the deserts of America?

It was not long before we were invited to mount, and continued our journey along the side of a lough, kept full by many streams, which with more or less rapidity and noise, crossed the road from the hills on the other hand. These currents, in their diminished state, after several dry months, afford, to one who has always lived in level countries, an unusual and delightful spectacle; but in the rainy season, such as every winter may be expected to bring, must precipitate an impetuous and tremendous flood. I suppose the way by which we went, is at that time impassable.

GLENSHEALS

The lough at last ended in a river broad and shallow like the rest, but that it may be passed when it is deeper, there is a bridge over it. Beyond it is a valley called Glensheals, inhabited by the clan of Macrae. Here we found a village called Auknasheals, consisting of many huts, perhaps twenty, built all of "dry-stone," that is, stones piled up without mortar.

We had, by the direction of the officers at Fort Augustus, taken bread for ourselves, and tobacco for those Highlanders who might show us any kindness. We were now at a place where we could obtain milk, but must have wanted bread if we had not brought it. The people of this valley did not appear to know any English, and our guides now became doubly necessary as interpreters. A woman whose hut was distinguished by greater spaciousness and better architecture brought out some pails of milk. The villagers gathered about us in considerable numbers, I believe without any evil intention, but with a very savage wildness of aspect and manner. When our meal was over, Mr. Boswell sliced the bread, and divided it amongst them, as he supposed them never to have tasted a wheaten loaf before. He then gave them little pieces of twisted tobacco, and among the children we distributed a small handful of half-pence, which they received with great eagerness. Yet I have been since told that the people of that valley are not indigent; and when we mentioned them afterwards as needy and pitiable, a Highland lady let us know that we might spare our commiseration; for the dame whose milk we drank had probably more than a dozen milk-cows. She seemed unwilling to take any price, but being pressed to make a demand, at last named a shilling. Honesty is not greater where elegance is less. One of the by-standers, as we were told afterwards, advised her to ask more, but she said a shilling was enough. We gave her half a crown, and I hope got some credit by our behaviour; for the company said, if our interpreters did not flatter us, that they had not seen such a day since the old laird of Macleod passed through their country.

The Macraes, as we heard afterwards in the Hebrides, were originally an indigent and subordinate clan, and having no farms nor stock, were in great numbers servants to the Maclellans, who, in the war of Charles the First, took arms at the call of the heroic Montrose, and were, in one of his battles, almost all destroyed. The women that were left at home, being thus deprived of their husbands, like the Scythian ladies of old, married their servants, and the Macraes became a considerable race.

THE HIGHLANDS

As we continued our journey, we were at leisure to extend our speculations, and to investigate the reason of those peculiarities by which such rugged regions as these before us are generally distinguished.

Mountainous countries commonly contain the original, at least the oldest race of inhabitants, for they are not easily conquered, because they must be entered by narrow ways, exposed to every power of mischief from those that occupy the heights; and every new ridge is a new fortress, where the defendants have again the same advantages. If the assailants either force the strait, or storm the summit, they gain only so much ground; their enemies are fled to take possession of the next rock, and the pursuers stand at gaze, knowing neither where the ways of escape wind among the steeps, nor where the bog has firmness to sustain them: besides that, mountaineers have an agility in climbing and descending distinct from strength or courage, and attainable only by use. If the war be not soon concluded, the invaders are dislodged by hunger; for in those anxious and toilsome marches, provisions cannot easily be carried, and are never to be found. The wealth of mountains is cattle, which, while the men stand in the passes, the women drive away. Such lands at last cannot repay the expence of conquest, and therefore perhaps have not been so often invaded by the mere ambition of dominion; as by resentment of robberies and insults, or the desire of enjoying in security the more fruitful provinces.

As mountains are long before they are conquered, they are likewise long before they are civilized. Men are softened by intercourse mutually profitable, and instructed by comparing their own notions with those of others. Thus Caesar found the maritime parts of Britain made less barbarous by their commerce with the Gauls. Into a barren and rough tract no stranger is brought either by the hope of gain or of pleasure. The inhabitants having neither commodities for sale, nor money for purchase, seldom visit more polished places, or if they do visit them, seldom return.

It sometimes happens that by conquest, intermixture, or gradual refinement, the cultivated parts of a country change their language. The mountaineers then become a distinct nation, cut off by dissimilitude of speech from conversation with their neighbours. Thus in Biscay, the original Cantabrian, and in Dalecarlia, the old Swedish still subsists. Thus Wales and the Highlands speak the tongue of the first inhabitants of Britain, while the other parts have received first the Saxon, and in some degree afterwards the French, and then formed a third language between them.

That the primitive manners are continued where the primitive language is spoken, no nation will desire me to suppose, for the manners of mountaineers are commonly savage, but they are rather produced by their situation than derived from their ancestors.

Such seems to be the disposition of man that whatever makes a distinction produces rivalry. England, before other causes of enmity were found, was disturbed for some centuries by the contests of the northern and southern counties; so that at Oxford, the peace of study could for a long time be preserved only by chusing annually one of the Proctors from each side of the Trent. A tract intersected by many ridges of mountains naturally divides its inhabitants into petty nations, which are made by a thousand causes enemies to each other. Each will exalt its own chiefs, each will boast the valour of its men, or the beauty of its women, and every claim of superiority irritates competition; injuries will sometimes be done, and be more injuriously defended; retaliation will sometimes be attempted, and the debt exacted with too much interest.

In the Highlands it was a law that if a robber was sheltered from justice, any man of the same clan might be taken in his place. This was a kind of irregular justice, which, though necessary in savage times, could hardly fail to end in a feud, and a feud once kindled among an idle people with no variety of pursuits to divert their thoughts, burnt on for ages either sullenly glowing in secret mischief, or openly blazing into publick violence. Of the effects of this violent judicature, there are not wanting memorials. The cave is now to be seen to which one of the Campbells, who had injured the Macdonalds, retired with a body of his own clan. The Macdonalds required the offender, and being refused, made a fire at the mouth of the cave, by which he and his adherents were suffocated together.

Mountaineers are warlike because by their feuds and competitions they consider themselves as surrounded with enemies, and are always prepared to repel incursions, or to make them. Like the Greeks in their unpolished state, described by Thucydides, the Highlanders, till lately, went always armed, and carried their weapons to visits, and to church.

Mountaineers are thievish, because they are poor, and having neither manufactures nor commerce, can grow richer only by robbery. They regularly plunder their neighbours, for their neighbours are commonly their enemies; and having lost that reverence for property by which the order of civil life is preserved, soon consider all as enemies, whom they do not reckon as friends, and think themselves licensed to invade whatever they are not obliged to protect.

By a strict administration of the laws, since the laws have been introduced into the Highlands, this disposition to thievery is very much repressed. Thirty years ago no herd had ever been conducted through the mountains, without paying tribute in the night, to some of the clans; but cattle are now driven, and passengers travel without danger, fear, or molestation.

Among a warlike people, the quality of highest esteem is personal courage, and with the ostentatious display of courage are closely connected promptitude of offence and quickness of resentment. The Highlanders, before they were disarmed, were so addicted to quarrels that the boys used to follow any public procession or ceremony, however festive, or however solemn, in expectation of the battle which was sure to happen before the company dispersed.

Mountainous regions are sometimes so remote from the seat of government, and so difficult of access, that they are very little under the influence of the sovereign, or within the reach of national justice. Law is nothing without power; and the sentence of a distant court could not be easily executed, nor perhaps very safely promulgated, among men ignorantly proud and habitually violent, unconnected with the general system, and accustomed to reverence only their own lords. It has therefore been necessary to erect many particular jurisdictions, and commit the punishment of crimes and the decision of right to the proprietors of the country who could enforce their own decrees. It immediately appears that such judges will be often ignorant, and often partial; but in the immaturity of political establishments no better expedient could be found. As government advances towards perfection, provincial judicature is perhaps in every empire gradually abolished.

Those who had thus the dispensation of law, were by consequence themselves lawless. Their vassals had no shelter from outrages and oppressions; but were condemned to endure, without resistance, the caprices of wantonness, and the rage of cruelty.

In the Highlands, some great lords had an hereditary jurisdiction over counties; and some chieftains over their own lands; till the final conquest of the Highlands afforded an opportunity of crushing all the local courts, and of extending the general benefits of equal law to the low and the high, in the deepest recesses and obscurest corners.

While the chiefs had this resemblance of royalty, they had little inclination to appeal, on any question, to superior judicatures. A claim of lands between two powerful lairds was decided like a contest for dominion between sovereign powers. They drew their forces into the field, and right attended on the strongest. This was, in ruder times, the common practice, which the kings of Scotland could seldom control.

Even so lately as in the last years of King William, a battle was fought at Mull Roy, on a plain a few miles to the south of Inverness, between the clans of Mackintosh and Macdonald of Keppoch. Col. Macdonald, the head of a small clan, refused to pay the dues demanded from him by Mackintosh, as his superior lord. They disdained the interposition of judges and laws, and calling each his followers to maintain the dignity of the clan, fought a formal battle, in which several considerable men fell on the side of Mackintosh, without a complete victory to either. This is said to have been the last open war made between the clans by their own authority.

The Highland lords made treaties, and formed alliances, of which some traces may still be found, and some consequences still remain as lasting evidences of petty regality. The terms of one of these confederacies were, that each should support the other in the right, or in the wrong, except against the king.

The inhabitants of mountains form distinct races, and are careful to preserve their genealogies. Men in a small district necessarily mingle blood by intermarriages, and combine at last into one family, with a common interest in the honour and disgrace of every individual. Then begins that union of affections, and co-operation of endeavours, that constitute a clan. They who consider themselves as ennobled by their family, will think highly of their progenitors, and they who through successive generations live always together in the same place, will preserve local stories and hereditary prejudices. Thus every Highlander can talk of his ancestors, and recount the outrages which they suffered from the wicked inhabitants of the next valley.

Such are the effects of habitation among mountains, and such were the qualities of the Highlanders, while their rocks secluded them from the rest of mankind, and kept them an unaltered and discriminated race. They are now losing their distinction, and hastening to mingle with the general community.

GLENELG

We left Auknasheals and the Macraes in the afternoon, and in the evening came to Ratiken, a high hill on which a road is cut, but so steep and narrow that it is very difficult. There is now a design of making another way round the bottom. Upon one of the precipices, my horse, weary with the steepness of the rise, staggered a little, and I called in haste to the Highlander to hold him. This was the only moment of my journey in which I thought myself endangered.

Having surmounted the hill at last, we were told that at Glenelg, on the sea-side, we should come to a house of lime and slate and glass. This image of magnificence raised our expectation. At last we came to our inn weary and peevish, and began to inquire for meat and beds.

Of the provisions the negative catalogue was very copious. Here was no meat, no milk, no bread, no eggs, no wine. We did not express much satisfaction. Here however we were to stay. Whisky we might have, and I believe at last they caught a fowl and killed it. We had some bread, and with that we prepared ourselves to be contented, when we had a very eminent proof of Highland hospitality. Along some miles of the way, in the evening, a gentleman's servant had kept us company on foot with very little notice on our part. He left us near Glenelg, and we thought on him no more till he came to us again, in about two hours, with a present from his master of rum and sugar. The man had mentioned his company, and the gentleman, whose name, I think, is Gordon, well knowing the penury of the place, had this attention to two men, whose names perhaps he had not heard, by whom his kindness was not likely to be ever repaid, and who could be recommended to him only by their necessities.

We were now to examine our lodging. Out of one of the beds, on which we were to repose, started up, at our entrance, a man black as a Cyclops from the forge. Other circumstances of no elegant recital concurred to disgust us. We had been frighted by a lady at Edinburgh, with discouraging representations of Highland lodgings. Sleep, however, was necessary. Our Highlanders had at last found some hay, with which the inn could not supply them. I directed them to bring a bundle into the room, and slept upon it in my riding coat. Mr. Boswell, being more delicate, laid himself sheets with hay over and under him, and lay in linen like a gentleman.

To John Perkins

July 28, 1782

Dear Sir,

I am much pleased that you are going a very long journey, which may by proper conduct restore your health and prolong your life.

Observe these rules:

1. Turn all care out of your head as soon as you mount the chaise.

2. Do not think about frugality: your health is worth more than it can cost.

3. Do not continue any day's journey to fatigue.

4. Take now and then a day's rest.

5. Get a smart seasickness if you can.

6. Cast away all anxiety, and keep your mind easy.

This last direction is the principal; with an unquiet mind neither exercise, nor diet, nor physic can be of much use.

I wish you, dear Sir, a prosperous journey, and a happy recovery, for I am

Dear Sir, Your most affectionate
humble servant,
Sam: Johnson

KARL PHILIPP MORITZ
1757 – 1793

Born in Hamelin, near Hanover, the son of an oboist, Moritz was educated at the Hanover Gymnasium but spent much of his young manhood as a member of a Sturm-und-Drang *stage company in Gotha before returning to respectability and pursuing theological studies at Erfurt and Wittenberg. He was finally ordained and became a teacher of philosophy and languages in Berlin.*

He was a copious writer, and the range of his work suggests his intellectual curiosity and restlessness. In addition to his Journeys of a German in England, *he brought out* An Inquiry into German Prosody *in 1786, and followed that with two autobiographical novels, learned works on aesthetics and psychology, and* Travels of a German in Italy. *(One of his friends was another Italy-lover, Goethe.) In 1789 he was appointed professor of archeology at the Academy of Art in Berlin.*

His first book, his account of a walking tour over England in 1782, constitutes a series of letters to his friend Friedrich Gedike, a noted Prussian educator and, like Moritz, a confirmed hiker. Persuaded that you see a place only when you walk it, Moritz can be considered one of the major hikers of history. In England he was quite willing to risk seeming a vagabond or sturdy beggar—and thus a menace on the roads, likely to be arrested or abused—by not using a horse, let alone a coach, items every decent eighteenth-century traveler was expected to employ. Moritz's reward for his eccentricity was frequently to be refused accommodation at inns, but because of his oddity he did get in touch with the texture of the country and as he says, "the customs of the people."

This selection has been translated by Reginald Nettel.

From Journeys of a German in England in 1782 (1783)

Oxford, June 25th

By what a fate is the wanderer beset in this land of horses and carriages! And what adventures!

Still, I only want to tell my tale properly from the beginning.

For an old hen I ate at supper, for a bedroom given to me grudgingly and in which I was pestered by a besotted oaf, and for two cups of tea at breakfast, I had to pay in Windsor nine shillings—and the old hen alone came to six shillings!

When I was about to leave, the waiter who had served me so unwillingly and with such ill temper stood at the foot of the stairs and said: "Remember the waiter."

I gave him three halfpence, to which he returned a hearty "God damn you, sir."

At the door stood the surly maid who said: "Remember the chambermaid."

"I'll remember your civility," I said, and gave her nothing.

At this she vented her anger in a loud, coarse laugh. So I left Windsor followed by a flood of curses and derision.

How happy was I now to have the towers of Windsor behind me! It is not good for a wanderer to be near the palace of a king; so I sat down in the shadow of a hedge and read my Milton, whom I could trust to commend me to the true aristocracy of Nature.

I took my way again through Slough and continued by Salthill and Maidenhead. Right at the very end of Salthill village—if indeed it can be called that—a wigmaker had a booth in which he was shaving and hairdressing. I had to pay him a shilling to shave me and put my hair a bit more in order. His booth was opposite to a very elegant house and garden.

Between Salthill and Maidenhead the first of my adventures on this journey came my way.

As yet I had met hardly a single pedestrian, though coaches rolled past me continuously; for the Oxford road is very busy. I met also many people on horseback, which is here the usual mode of travel.

The road lay through a deep gulley between high trees, so I could not see far ahead, when a man in a brown coat, with a round hat and a stick in his hand a good deal stouter than mine, came towards me. From the first he struck me as suspicious, but he passed me by. But before I was aware of it he suddenly turned and demanded a halfpenny—only a halfpenny—to buy beer, because his belly was empty.

I felt in my pocket but found that I had no coppers, nor even a single sixpence, but I had plenty of shillings.

I excused myself for having no small change, whereupon he said: "God bless my soul!" and clenched his fist on his stick so deliberately that I at once put my hand in my pocket again and gave him a shilling.

At that moment a coach came by.

He thanked me very politely and went away.

Had that coach arrived a moment sooner I should not so easily have given him a shilling I could ill spare. I do not want to assert that this man was a footpad, but he had every appearance of one.

I entered Maidenhead over the bridge of the same name, which is twenty-five miles from London. The English milestones are a great convenience for travellers; they have often seemed to relieve me of half the distance because I am always anxious to know how far I have come and if I am on the right road. The distance from London is always given on these milestones together with the distance to the next town, and at crossroads there is always a signpost, so it is almost impossible to lose your way. My journey was practically carefree.

From Maidenhead Bridge is a delightful view of a hill standing up from the bank of the Thames and crowned with two most splendid residences situated amid parks and meadows. The first is called Taplow and belongs to the Earl of Inchiquin. A little farther on lies Cliveden which also belongs to him. These mansions are set off charmingly by the surrounding fields and the thick woods.

It is not far from this bridge to Maidenhead, where there is another delightful country seat on the left as you enter the town, belonging to Pennyston Powney, Esq.

This information I have gained for the most part from my English Guide-book, which is almost continually in my hand and contains practically everything of note, mile by mile. I check the truth of the information with those with whom I stay, and they wonder how I, a foreigner, am so familiar with their district.

Maidenhead itself is a place of little note. I asked them to make me a mulled ale and had to pay ninepence for it. They evidently didn't take me for a man of much consequence, for I heard one say as I passed: "A lusty comrade!", and the tone of it did not sound very creditable.

At the end of the village a shoemaker had his shop, just as had the barber at Salthill.

I went from here to Henley, eleven miles from Maidenhead and thirty-six from London.

When I had gone six English miles fairly quickly and was still five from Henley, I came to a piece of rising ground where stood a milestone. There I sat down to enjoy one of the most ravishing views. I certainly advise anyone who comes to this spot to make a point of seeing it.

Close in front of me was a gentle hill, patterned with cornfields fenced with hedges and encircled above by a wood. Behind it in the distance there rose up from the opposite side of the Thames one green hill after another embellished with woodlands, meadows, hedges and villages. At their feet the river slid in delightful curves through a rich green valley studded with villages and elegant houses.

The banks of the Thames are fascinating everywhere, but especially so after a little separation, when you suddenly catch sight of it again with all its rich adjoining lands.

In the valley below the flocks were grazing and the sound of bells came up to me on the hill.

What makes such an English spot so magically beautiful is the blending of everything into a composition that ensures a peaceful prospect. There is no spot on which the eye does not long lovingly to rest. After what I have already seen of the English countryside, what is merely average here would be regarded as a paradise in other lands.

With my heart inspired by this rewarding scene I went on up and down hill at a sharp pace for the remaining five miles to Henley. I arrived there at four in the afternoon.

Just short of Henley, on the left, standing on a hill rising up from the near bank of the river, is a country house within a park, the residence of General Conway. I walked a little way along the opposite bank of the Thames from where the park lay, before I went into Henley itself, and lay down in some tall grass. Being somewhat tired I went to sleep. When I awoke I found that the last rays of the setting sun were shining straight into my face.

Refreshed by this sweet slumber I went on again into the town. But my experience suggested it was too grand a place for me to stay in, and that I should do better to put up at a roadside inn of the kind the Vicar of Wakefield called "the usual retreat of Indigence and Frugality."

Only, the worst of it was that nobody wanted to take me into a refuge such as that. I met two farmers on the way; I asked the first of them if I should find hospitality for the night in a house which I saw in the distance by the wayside. "I dare say you may," was his reply. But when

I came to it the answer was, "We have got no beds, and you can't stay here tonight!"

It was the same at the next house I called at on the road. So I had to make up my mind to go on for another five miles to Nettlebed. There I arrived late in the evening; in fact it was already dark.

Everything was going swimmingly in this little village. Some soldiers on leave were making music after their own fashion. The very first house on the left on entering the village proved to be an inn with a crossbeam extending across the road to the house opposite and from which an astonishingly large signboard hung displaying the name of the proprietor.

"May I stay here the night?" was my first question as I came up to the house.

"Yes, you may," was the answer. It was spoken coldly but under the circumstances it cheered me greatly.

They showed me into the kitchen and put me to eat at a table with soldiers and domestic servants. Thus I found myself for the first time in the sort of kitchen which figures so often in the novels of Fielding, and in which so many adventures usually take place.

The open fireplace where the cooking was done was separated from the rest of the kitchen by a wooden partition. Thus screened, the rest of the room served as a combined living and eating-room. All round its walls were shelves for pewter dishes and plates, while from the ceiling hung an abundance of provisions such as loaves of sugar, sausages, sides of bacon, and so on.

While I was eating, a post-chaise drove up to the inn, and immediately the whole household started into motion to receive the distinguished guests they heard approaching. But the gentlemen got out for only a moment, called for nothing more than a couple of pots of beer and then drove on again. But if you come in a post-chaise you are treated with all possible respect!

Although this was but a small village and they knew me to be a guest of no distinction, they nevertheless put me in a carpeted bedroom with a good bed.

The following morning I put on the clean linen I was carrying with me and came downstairs. This time they did not show me into the kitchen as on the previous evening, but into the parlour on the ground floor, and called me "sir." On the previous evening it had been "master," by which term only the farmers and common people are addressed.

It was Sunday and everyone in the house had put on his best clothes. I found myself extraordinarily drawn to this pleasant village and resolved to stay and attend divine service that morning. To this end I borrowed a prayer-book from my host, Mr. Illing. (This was his name! It struck me the more because it is such a common name in Germany.) I turned over the leaves during breakfast and read several parts of the English liturgy. My attention was taken by the fact that every word was set down for the priest for his conformity. If he were visiting a sick man, for example, he had to say "Peace dwell in this house," etc.

That such a book is called a prayer-book and not a hymn-book is because the English service is usually not sung but prayed. Nevertheless the Psalms translated into English verse are included in this prayer-book.

That which my host lent me was truly a family possession containing the date of his wedding and the birthdays and baptismal days of all his children. It had all the more value consequently in my eyes.

Divine service was due to begin at half-past nine. Right opposite our house the boys of the village were lined up all bright and beautiful, very nice and clean, and their hair (cut round in a fringe after the English fashion) combed. The white collars of their shirts were turned back at both sides and their breasts were open to the air. It seemed they were gathered here at the entrance of the village to await the parson.

I went out of the village for a short walk towards where I saw some men coming from another village to attend divine service in ours.

At last the parson arrived on horseback. The boys took off their hats and bowed low to him. He had a somewhat elderly appearance, with his own hair dressed very much as if in natural curls.

The bell rang and I went into the church with the general public, my prayer-book under my arm. The clerk or verger showed me into a seat in front of the pulpit very politely.

The furnishing of the church was quite simple. Right above the altar were displayed the Ten Commandments in large letters on two tablets. And indeed there can be no better way of impressing the essential qualities of the faith on a waiting congregation than this.

Under the pulpit was a reading-desk where the preacher stood before the sermon and read out a very long liturgy to which the parish clerk responded each time, the congregation joining in softly. When, for example, the preacher said: "God have mercy upon us," the clerk and congregation answered: "and forgive us our sins." Or the preacher read a prayer and the whole congregation said "Amen" to it.

This is very difficult for the preacher, since he must not only address the people while preaching his sermon but continually do so during the service. The responding of the people, however, has something about it very restful and ceremonially appropriate.

Two soldiers sitting by me, who had recently come from London and considered themselves to be keen wits, did not pray aloud.

After the ritual had gone on for some time I noticed some shuffling in the choir. The clerk was very busy and they all seemed to be getting ready for some special ceremony. I noticed also several musical instruments of various sorts as the preacher stopped his reading and the clerk announced from the choir: "Let us praise God by singing the forty-seventh Psalm. "Awake, our hearts, awake with joy.' "

How peaceful and heart-uplifting it was to hear vocal and instrumental music in this little country church, not made by hired musicians but joyfully offered by the happy dwellers in the place in praise of their God. This kind of music now began to alternate several times with the ritual prayers, and the tunes of the metrical psalms were so lively and joyful—and yet so wholly sincere—that I gave my heart unrestrainedly to devotion and was often touched to tears.

The preacher now stood up and gave a short address on the text: "Not all who say 'Lord! Lord!' shall enter into the Kingdom of Heaven." He dealt with the subject in common terms and his presentation was sturdy. He spoke of the need to do God's will, but there was nothing out of the usual run in his matter. The sermon lasted less than half-an-hour.

Apart from all this the preacher was unsociable; he seemed haughty when he acknowledged the greetings of the country people, doing so with a superior nod.

I stayed until the service was all over and then went out of the church with the congregation. I then examined the gravestones in the churchyard and their inscriptions, which, because of their restraint, were simpler and in better taste than ours.

Some, to be sure, were frank enough—even comical. One on the gravestone of a blacksmith I have set down in writing so that you can't prove it is not so:

> My Sledge and Anvil lie declined,
> My bellows too have lost their Wind;
> My Fire's extinct, my Forge decayed,
> And in the Dust my Vice is laid;
> My Coals are spent, my Iron's gone,
> My Nails are drove: my Work is done.

Many inscriptions I found ending with the following rhyme:

> Physicians were in vain;
> God knew the best
> And laid his Dust to rest.

In the church itself I saw the marble epitaph to a son of the famous Dr. Wallis with the following simple, peaceful inscription:

> That Learning and Good Sense which rendered HIM
> fit for any Publick Station Induc'd Him to choose a
> Private Life.

All the farmers I saw here were dressed in good cloth and good taste. (Not as ours are, in coarse smocks.) In appearance they are to be distinguished from townsmen less by their dress than by their natural dignity.

A few soldiers trying to show off joined me as I was looking at the church. They seemed thoroughly ashamed—saying it was a most contemptible church. At this I took the liberty to tell them that no church was contemptible if it held well-behaved and sensible people.

I remained in Nettlebed over midday. In the afternoon there was no divine service but the villagers again made music together. They sang several psalms while others listened to them. All this was done in so seemly a manner that it might have been a kind of service too. I stayed until it was over, as one enchanted by this village. Three times I started to leave it to continue my walk, and each time I was drawn back to it, on the verge of resolving to stay there a week or longer.

Yet the thought that I had only a few weeks to spare before my return to Germany, and that I still wanted to see Derbyshire, drove me finally forth. I looked back often at the little church tower and the tranquil cottages where I had been so much at home; and I looked back with a heavy heart.

It was nearly three o'clock in the afternoon as I went away from Nettlebed. Oxford was eighteen miles away, so I decided not to go right there but to stay the night some five or six miles short of Oxford and reach the city in good time on the following morning.

My journey from Nettlebed was as an uninterrupted stroll through a great garden. Often I turned from the road and read some Milton. When I was come without mishap about eight miles from Nettlebed and was not far from Dorchester, and had the Thames on my left, I saw at some distance beyond it a long hill with what appeared to be the mast of a ship standing up from behind it. This led me to suppose that another river ran on the other side of the hill.

This promised me a view which I would not willingly pass by the way. I turned off the road to the left, crossed a bridge over the Thames and then went up the hill towards the mast. When I got to the top, however, I found that the whole thing was an optical illusion. Before me lay nothing but a great plain and the mast was stuck in the ground to entice the curious from the road.

So I descended the hill again. At its foot was a house with many people looking out of the window and apparently laughing at me, but this affected me very little and I went on my way. The journey to the mast had not grieved me but I was rather tired from the climb.

Not far from there—near to Dorchester—I had yet another richly rewarding scene. The country became so beautiful that I had no wish to go farther, but lay down on the green turf and feasted my eyes on the view as if enchanted. The moon had already risen and stood at the full; the sun's last rays were darting through the hedges; and as if these were not enough there came a sleepy fragrance from the meadows and the song of the birds. The hills by the Thames revealed their many shades of green—bright green, pale green, dark green—with the tufted tops of trees here and there among them. I nearly fainted under the spell of all these ravishing delights.

Dorchester, where I arrived rather late, is only a small village but it has a large and imposing church. As I went by, this place also seemed too grand for me; the ladies stood in front of their houses with their hair trimmed.

WILLIAM BLAKE
1757–1827

Except for a three-year period at Felpham, in Sussex, Blake spent his entire life in London and traveled only in his mind, which was sufficient.

AH SUN-FLOWER
(1794)

Ah Sun-flower! weary of time,
Who countest the steps of the sun,

Seeking after that sweet golden clime
Where the traveler's journey is done;

Where the youth pined away with desire,
And the pale virgin shrouded in snow,
Arise from their graves and aspire
Where my Sun-flower wishes to go.

Part III — The Heyday

T he heyday of travel and travel writing—the nineteenth and early twentieth centuries—is coincident with the gradual democratization of the West—and doubtless a result. The whole period can be called the Bourgeois Age, and its outlines are visible as early as the late seventeenth century. Some of its signals are the beginnings of parliamentary government; a growing boldness of intellectual and religious skepticism; a rapidly complicating technology and an incipient industrialism; a heightened egalitarianism, including gestures toward wide public education; and the ascendancy of an ambitious middle class bent on self-improvement. These forces helped transform the Grand Tour of the eighteenth century into the citizens' travel of the nineteenth century and finally into the mass tourism of the twentieth.

The instrument of the Grand Tour, the coach, was conspicuously a non- or even an anti-plebeian vehicle, heavy, tall, exclusive, private, and costly. Its function as a mechanism of social domination was noted by John Ruskin, who spoke of its "general stateliness of effect" serving for "the abashing of plebeian beholders." (The same effect is aimed at by the modern "limousine.") When Byron left England in 1816, he did so in a custom-built coach costing 500 pounds—in a day when a hundred pounds was a decent annual income. His coach sported a bed, a plate- and cutlery-chest, and a library. But even private and elegant as it was designed to be, by modern standards coach travel (as Charles Burney could testify) was physically and socially miserable. On the heaviest models, for example, the brakes were so little to be trusted that on steep grades drag-chains had to be deployed out the rear. In the 1760s Edward Gibbon specified the qualifications needed by a traveler: "He should be endowed with an active, indefatigable vigor of mind and body, which can . . . support, with a careless smile, every hardship of the road, the weather, or the inn." And the impediments to felicity were appalling: "Bad roads and indifferent inns," Gibbon notes, and worse, "the continual converse one is obliged to have with the vilest part of mankind—innkeepers, post-masters, and custom house officers." And even that wasn't the worst of it. In Italy south of Naples, in Spain, Portugal, the Balkans, Greece, and the Near East, brigands and highwaymen were to be met with. Travelers had to be not only armed but crack pistol shots, and their coaches were often equipped with cunning false floors and similar hiding places for valuables.

The Napoleonic Wars meant that for some years European travel was restricted or impossible. It revived with a vengeance after the peace, as it does after all wars, and as usual, with a startling advance in technology—this time, the steam engine. (After the Great War, it would be the propeller plane, newly pressed into bourgeois travel service. After the World War II, it would be the jet engine.) When rail travel began, in the second quarter of the nineteenth century, a "train" consisted of a number of coach bodies mounted on flanged iron wheels and hooked together, an eloquent emblem of the overnight democratization of the coach. The origin of railway cars as demeaned coaches is kept alive by the custom, honored today even by Amtrak, of calling a passenger car a "coach." By the 1860s and 1870s sleeping cars had arrived to add unheard-of comfort to traveling, and by the 1880s trains no longer had to stop at station restaurants for meals. They now had dining cars, and even third-class passengers enjoyed ostentatious "luxury" in napery, service, and cuisine. What had happened to travel in two generations was a comfort revolution. Traveling could now gratify fantasies of social-class ascent, and the hotels to which the trains carried travelers assisted the fantasy work by naming themselves the Majestic, the Grand, the Excelsior, or the Palace.

It was the railway that opened opportunities for mass tourism and gave its originator, Thomas Cook, the bright idea of conveying travelers in groups with reduced fares and no anxieties about arrangements. Considering the ultimate association of tourism with such pleasures of the flesh as nudity, rich diet, and copious drinks, it is ironic that tourism began as an adjunct of the temperance movement. Cook was a thirty-three-year-old Baptist temperance zealot, and his first tour, in 1841, carried 570 teetotalers by rail from Leicester to a temperance rally eleven miles away. Soon he was arranging group tours (dry) to the rugged scenery of the Scottish Highlands, and by 1864 he was doing the Continent, strenuously: one of his tours to Paris enrolled 1,500 people. If the tourists loved it, some observers were horrified. The novelist Charles Lever recorded his reaction to one of Cook's early announcements:

> When I first read the scheme in a newspaper advertisement, I caught at the hope that the speculation would break down. I imagined that the characteristic independence of Englishmen would revolt against a plan that reduces the traveler to the level of his trunk and obliterates every trace and trait of the individual. I was all wrong.

He was indeed, and Cook's brand of guided tours flourished as the bourgeois classes produced an ever-expanding cohort of aspirants to foreign culture. Contempt for tourism flourished too, until finally Kingsley Martin stigmatized it as "a disease of the mind, [whose] germ is the idea that one may learn that which is valuable, or in any way acquire virtue, by the process of being shown things."

Regardless, a group of sixty satisfied Cook's tourists crossed the Atlantic in 1865 to be shown the battlefields of the American Civil War, a venture which a half-century of improvements in ocean travel had finally made feasible. Fifty years earlier transatlantic crossings had been thoroughly miserable affairs—cramped, sick-making, smelly, with terrible food and unremitting discomfort, and often fear. The passage frequently took well over a month. But by the 1860s the *Great Eastern* was making the crossing in 12 days, and with almost unbelievable amenity. This iron vessel, almost 700 feet long, had six masts but was propelled mainly by two immense paddle wheels, run by coal-generated steam. Its 3,000 passengers unwittingly set the style for all subsequent sea voyagers by playing deck games, loping around the ample decks for exercise, enjoying the gas lighting and the hot baths, attending the nightly musical entertainments in the Grand Saloon, and consuming excellent food, with plenty of champagne.

Anyone whose experience of long-distance travel is limited to conveyance by jet will wonder that travel could ever have been comfortable and dignified, not to say elegant. In addition, it was once an experience humane and social as well as technological, and there is profound truth as well as pleasant light comedy in a bit of dialogue by Noël Coward:

> "How was your flight?"
> "Well, aeronautically it was a great success. Socially, it left quite a bit to be desired."

It was the Bourgeois Age that defined the classic modern idea of travel as an excitement and a treat and that established the literary genre of the "travel book." For the first time in history travel was convenient, and ships and trains took you where you wanted to go. At the same time, mass tourism, with its homogenizing simplifications and conveniences, had not yet displaced genuine, individual, eccentric travel. That still had about it an element of adventure and surprise and a quality of the *ad hoc.* The Bourgeois Age was also the great moment for travel books. There was still a large class of general readers whose curiosity had been stirred by a limited but very solid education historically and geographically oriented, and these readers knew the pleasures of learning for themselves by means of books. After all, reading, together with stage shows and churchgoing, was about the only form of entertainment. Public libraries were being founded everywhere and a sophisticated publishing and book-distribution industry arose to keep them supplied. Even the guidebooks of the Bourgeois Age will strike the contemporary user of Fodor and Fielding and Frommer as extraordinarily civilized. Baedeker, for example, assumes an audience with a historical imagination and notable aesthetic experience and curiosity. Many guidebooks, now disused and quite obsolete, were indistinguishable from works of actual scholarship, like the 34 volumes of the Medieval Town Series (Ravenna, Canterbury, Rouen, Bruges, Prague, etc.). A great many travelers, many more than now, would have felt insulted to be addressed in the style of late-twentieth-century guidebooks as mere shoppers and consumers.

Not that the bourgeois traveler was unremittingly high-minded. A lot of his attention had to go toward looking after his things, for he was much more heavily laden than later travelers. He had to carry items either not provided by inns or hotels, or necessitated by flagrant threats to his possessions or person. Mariana Starke's book *Information and Directions for Travelers on the Continent,* published in 1824, advises British readers never to travel without the following, among many other items: Sheets, pillows, and blankets—these were sometimes supplied by the more up-to-date sort of inns, but their state of cleanliness was likely to appall the genteel. The same with towels, tablecloths, and napkins: the traveler had to carry his own. Also a traveling lock for the room door, a mosquito net, and a medicine chest, with thermometer. Lamps and candles would doubtless be insufficient for reading: you should bring your own lantern, and don't forget matches. Pens, ink, and paper, of course. Inn cutlery would probably be filthy and the knives dull as well: you must bring your own knives, forks, and spoons, and your carving set for roasts and fowl. The inclusion of your own teapot goes almost without saying. And the Continent not being the British Isles, you must also, according to Ms. Starke, carry "pistols" (note plural), as well as "Essential Oil of Lavender," ten drops of which, "distributed about a bed, will drive away either bugs or fleas." And all this in addition to one's extensive wardrobe. Clearly many trunks would be required for even the briefest venture abroad.

Writing at about the same time, the physician Dr. William Kitchener, in his book *Traveler's Oracle,* advises that all these items be packed, and more: not just pistols, but a swordstick; a tinder-box for fire-making, and a saw and screwdriver; an umbrella, of course; and drawing instruments in their own case, together with sketchbook, pen, and ink. The serious traveler is not to neglect bringing a compass, barometer, and thermometer, nor omit opera glasses and telescope. A portable medicine chest is indispensable, and in it Dr. Kitchener hopes to find all the standard medicaments, together with a supply of "Dr. Kitchener's Peristaltic Persuader." If you were headed for any place within the Ottoman Empire, you would need to bring along your own bedstead, together with mattresses and bedding, lest you spend nights on wet mud floors fully accessible to vermin. One enterprising luggage manufacturer in the late nineteenth century came up with a combination trunk and bed, an apparently normal trunk from which, when opened, sprang a bed complete with mattress.

Even if you took a short rail journey within your own country, you would carry things long disused, like canes. Most gentlemen equipped themselves with them, both as a sign, like the latter-day necktie, of secure social status and as a handy non-lethal weapon against insolent porters, mad dogs, and the like. (A century earlier the Grand Tourist might have used a sword for this purpose.) On the luggage racks of nineteenth-century trains you might find bird cages, portable footrests, rugs, portable bathtubs (rubber), bedrolls, water bottles, and of course food baskets. Porters were indispensable then because you carried so much. With the development of modern travel and tourism, with the expectation that, say, towels will be supplied wherever you stay, the institution of porters has virtually withered away.

What you took along traveling depended, naturally, on the sort of person you were. If you were artistic, you carried not only sketching equipment—the early equivalent of the Kodak—but perhaps also a "Claude Glass." This was an optical device favored by those educated to enjoy the Sublime in scenery. Named after Claude Lorrain (1600–1682), the French landscape painter whose works were thought the most sublime, that is, awe-inspiring, the Claude Glass was a darkened mirror, flat on one side, convex on the other, which gave off a reflection of a scene emphasizing its painterly aspects. When these proved sufficiently sublime—or even picturesque, a less exciting but still sought-after characteristic of scenery—the wielder of the Claude Glass could sketch the view to take home.

It was this vogue of the Sublime that helped make Switzerland a prime travelers' goal for a century. As early as 1739 the poet Thomas Gray was rhapsodizing about the Alps in terms suggesting their future as a magical resource of highminded tourism. As Gray wrote his friend Richard West, "Not a precipice, not a torrent, not a cliff but is pregnant with religion and poetry. There are certain scenes that would awe an atheist into belief, without the help of other argument." In addition to serving as world headquarters of the Sublime, Switzerland was also popular both because it seemed to propose a model of enlightened non-monarchical government and because its hotels and restaurants were soon setting a standard for cleanliness, efficiency, and honesty. (César Ritz, whose name became synonymous with excellence in hotels, was a Swiss.)

Thomas Cook early discovered the appeal of Switzerland to clients who wanted to taste the ennobling with a minimum of discomfort, and by the 1860s he was sending tour groups of hundreds there. Mountain scenery, both terrifyingly sublime and soothingly picturesque, remained popular throughout the nineteenth century, attracting tourists not just to the Alps and the Rhine Valley but even upstate New York. Mountain "views" were the ones most commonly starred as meriting special attention in Baedeker's guidebooks. Italy was not far behind Switzerland as a nineteenth-century attraction, especially its more mountainous parts like the settings of Lakes Como and Garda. Conveyed there by clean, punctual, and trustworthy railways, you could take long walks, wait for dinner, and observe from a distance those awful people from Cincinnati. And you could write postcards depicting hotels, lake steamers, and cheerful non-insurrectionary peasants, or long letters describing the trip and the scenes. These you would write in the public Writing Rooms, with which every decent hotel, in those days of written language, was equipped. (Game rooms or discos, they are now.) What with the appeal of Florence and Venice to the artistically sophisticated, Italy became so popular among the Victorians that, as one observer noted, there "almost every other person one sees is a foreigner." Next in popularity probably came Spain, despite its more primitive accommodations. The romantic charms of Sevilla and Granada were the reason. Uncomfortable also for travelers but popular nevertheless, perhaps because of the asceticism it imposed, was the Holy Land. A nice package could be worked out—and Cook did work it out—combining a tour of the Holy Land with an excursion to Egypt, where Cook had the franchise on the whole fleet of 15 Nile steamboats.

But bourgeois travel aimed at other sorts of self-improvement than the cultural. Sea bathing had begun to be thought salubrious as early as 1730, and soon the British beaches of Margate and Scarborough were attracting swarms of holidaymakers. The Prince Regent's Brighton was next, and soon it was discovered that the French Riviera was the place to go not just in winter (it was one of Queen Victoria's favorite retreats) but in summer as well. This meant that hot sunshine was no longer considered bad for you, and by the end of the nineteenth century what can be called the new heliophily was helping establish on beaches all up and down the Mediterranean the décor and atmosphere of international tourist hedonism.

Some travel targets became popular for more mystical reasons. Rome and Lourdes and Fatima attracted Christians replaying the rites of medieval pilgrimage, just as Moslems took the Hadj to Mecca and Jews aspired to see Jerusalem. Shakespeare's Stratford became virtually a place of pilgrimage in its own right after the Shakespeare Jubilee of 1769, which can be considered one of the earliest publicity stunts designed to entice tourists. Popular since the days of Herodotus for its wonders, Egypt became an especially attractive spot to visit after the publicity attending the discovery of Tutankhamen's tomb in 1922. About the same time, for Americans, at least, Canada became for some years the place to go: you could not only hunt and fish there. You could get a drink. The same reason helps account for the popularity of Europe (as well as Bermuda) for American travelers from 1920 to 1933. In the 1960s Greece seemed the place everyone wanted to go. One reason was the impact of the film *Never on Sunday.* Also in the 1960s the vogue of "Eastern religions" promoted Nepal, as well as India, as places to go—and to be seen.

Discovering early in the twentieth century the vast sums earnable through tourist exploitation, countries hastened to establish national tourist offices to publicize the local attractions and get their share of the pie. Italy was first, in 1919, followed by Holland, Belgium, the Scandinavian countries, Czechoslovakia, Germany, and Japan. Many ingenious schemes were contrived. In 1936, for example, Yugoslav Railways offered newlywed couples "starting their journey within fourteen days after their wedding . . . a reduction of fifty per cent on the normal fare up till one month after the wedding." The modern tourist trade has found its customers wonderfully susceptible to hints and leads and guidance, and just as *Never on Sunday* performed miracles for the cause of Greek travel—contrast the way travel to neighboring Turkey languished for want of an equivalent film advertising its *louche* delights—so the television series *The Love Boat* has powerfully reinforced the impulse of middle-class Americans to go on a cruise. Indeed, to survey the serial popularity of the various places which have attracted travelers from the beginning of the Bourgeois Age to the present would be to sketch a virtual cultural and psychological history of the modern world. It would also be to appreciate how central to the modern experience are the (usually secret) exotic fantasies and desires—for escape, as well as for the foreign, the novel, the nonindustrial, the archaic, and the luscious-erotic—which travel satisfies and which even travel books go some way toward fulfilling.

GEORGE GORDON, LORD BYRON
1788-1824

This restless, scandalous aristocrat was born with a club foot which, although it caused him deep shame, served at least to set off his dramatic good looks. He attended Harrow School and pursued debauchery at Trinity College, Cambridge, while writing romantic lyric poems, and in 1809 he traveled with his friend John Cam Hobhouse for two years in Portugal, Spain, Albania, Malta, Turkey, and Greece. It was during these travels that he developed his enthusiasm for helping the Greeks free themselves from Turkish domination, and it was these travels that provided material for his immensely popular long poem Childe Harold's Pilgrimage (1812–18). *This emotional performance was carried like a guidebook by generations of tourists visiting Europe, and it taught thousands the correct way to respond to the picturesque and the sublime in scenery and architecture.*

Back in England, for a while Byron seemed headed for a more or less normal career in the House of Lords, where he spoke supporting liberal causes. But his passions were too strong for such a life, and in 1816 he quit England forever, driven out by gossip about his incest with his half-sister, his separation from his wife, his debts, and by boredom. At this point, some thought him simply mad.

First he went to Geneva to live with his fellow authors the Percy Bysshe Shelleys and Claire Clairmont, who became his mistress and bore him a daughter. Then (rather like an early D. H. Lawrence in his impulse to keep moving) he took off for Italy, where in Venice he recreated himself with love affairs. Ravenna called next. There he formed a liaison with the Countess Guiccioli, and subsequently he lived in Pisa, Livorno, and Genoa.

In 1819 he began publishing his facetious long poem Don Juan, *among other things a narrative satire on British prudery and respectability. It was regarded by some critics and by genteel readers as "a filthy*

and impious poem", and "an insult and an outrage." But Goethe liked
it, and so did most people in England. A year before his death he sailed
for Greece to equip a brigade for action against the Turks, but he died
there while trying to persuade numerous antipathetic Greek factions to
join against the common enemy.

To Henry Drury

Falmouth June 25th. 1809

My dear Drury,—We sail tomorrow in the Lisbon packet having been
detained till now by the lack of wind and other necessaries; these being
at last procured, by this time tomorrow evening we shall be embarked
on the vide vorld of vaters vor all the vorld like Robinson Crusoe.———
—The Malta vessel not sailing for some weeks we have determined to
go by way of Lisbon, and as my servants term it to see "that there
Portingale" thence to Cadiz and Gibraltar and so on our old route to
Malta and Constantinople, if so be that Capt. Kidd our gallant or rather
gallows commander understands plain sailing and Mercator, and takes
us on our voyage all according to the Chart.———Will you tell Dr.
Butler that I have taken the treasure of a servant Friese the native of
Prussia Proper into my service from his recommendation.———He has
been all among the worshippers of Fire in Persia and has seen Persepolis
and all that.—Hobhouse has made woundy preparations for a book at
his return, 100 pens two gallons Japan Ink, and several vols best blank
is no bad provision for a discerning Public.—I have laid down my pen,
but have promised to contribute a chapter on the state of morals, and
a further treatise on the same to be entituled "Sodomy simplified or
Paederasty proved to be praiseworthy from ancient authors and modern
practice."—Hobhouse further hopes to indemnify himself in Turkey for
a life of exemplary chastity at home by letting out his "fair bodye" to
the whole Divan.—Pray buy his missellingany as the Printer's Devil calls
it, I suppose 'tis in print by this time. Providence has interposed in our
favour with a fair wind to carry us out of its reach, or he would have hired
a Faquir to translate it into the Turcoman Lingo.———

> "The Cock is crowing
> I must be going
> And can no more"

> *Ghost of Gaffer Thumb*

Adieu believe me yours as in duty bound
BYRON

P.S.—We have been sadly fleabitten at Falmouth.——

LINES TO MR. HODGSON

WRITTEN ON BOARD THE LISBON PACKET

Huzza! Hodgson, we are going,
    Our embargo's off at last;
Favorable breezes blowing
    Bend the canvas o'er the mast.
From aloft the signal's streaming,
    Hark! the farewell gun is fired;
Women screeching, tars blaspheming,
    Tell us that our time's expired.
        Here's a rascal
        Come to task all,
Prying from the custom-house;
        Trunks unpacking
        Cases cracking,
Not a corner for a mouse
'Scapes unsearch'd amid the racket,
Ere we sail on board the packet.

Now our boatmen quit their mooring,
    And all hands must ply the oar;
Baggage from the quay is lowering,
    We're impatient,—push from shore.
"Have a care! that case holds liquor—
    Stop the boat—I'm sick—oh Lord!"
"Sick, ma'am, damme, you'll be sicker,
    Ere you've been an hour on board."
        Thus are screaming
        Men and women,

Gemmen, ladies, servants, Jacks;
    Here entangling,
    All are wrangling,
Stuck together close as wax.—
Such the general noise and racket,
Ere we reach the Lisbon packet.

Now we've reach'd her, lo! the captain,
    Gallant Kidd, commands the crew;
Passengers their berths are clapt in,
    Some to grumble, some to spew.
Hey day! call you that a cabin?
    Why 't is hardly three feet square;
Not enough to stow Queen Mab in—
    Who the deuce can harbour there?"
        "Who, sir? Plenty—
        Nobles twenty
Did at once my vessel fill."—
        "Did they? Jesus,
        How you squeeze us!
Would to God they did so still:
Then I'd 'scape the heat and racket
Of the good ship, Lisbon Packet."

Fletcher! Murray! Bob! Where are you?
    Stretch'd along the deck like logs—
Bear a hand, you jolly tar, you!
    Here's a rope's end for the dogs.
Hobhouse muttering fearful curses,
    As the hatchway down he rolls,
Now his breakfast, now his verses,
    Vomits forth—and damns our souls.
        "Here's a stanza
        On Braganza—
Help!"—"A couplet?"—"No, a cup
        Of warm water—"
        "What's the matter?"
"Zounds! my liver's coming up;
I shall not survive the racket
Of this brutal Lisbon Packet."

Now at length we're off for Turkey,
 Lord knows when we shall come back!
Breezes foul and tempests murky
 May unship us in a crack.
But, since life at most a jest is,
 As philosophers allow,
Still to laugh by far the best is,
 Then laugh on—as I do now.
  Laugh at all things,
  Great and small things,
 Sick or well, at sea or shore;
  While we're quaffing,
  Let's have laughing—
Who the devil cares for more?—
Some good wine! and who would lack it,
Ev'n on board the Lisbon Packet?
 FALMOUTH ROADS, June 30, 1809.

To Mrs. Catherine Gordon Byron

Gibraltar
August 11th. 1809

Dear mother,—I have been so much occupied since my departure from England that till I could address you a little at length, I have forborn writing altogether.—As I have now passed through Portugal & a considerable part of Spain, & have leisure at this place I shall endeavour to give you a short detail of my movements.—We sailed from Falmouth on the 2d. of July, reached Libson after a very favourable passage of four days and a half, and took up our abode for a time in that city.—It has been often described without being worthy of description, for, except the view from the tagus which is beautiful, and some fine churches & convents it contains little but filthy streets & more filthy inhabitants.—To make amends for this the village of Cintra about fifteen miles from the capitol is perhaps in every respect the most delightful in Europe, it contains beauties of every description natural & artificial, palaces and gardens rising in the midst of rocks, cataracts, and precipices, convents on stupendous heights a distant view of the sea and the Tagus, and besides (though that is a secondary consideration) is remarkable as the scene of Sir H D's Convention.—It unites in itself all the wildness of the western highlands with the verdure of the south of France. Near this place about 10 miles to the right is the palace of Mafra, the boast of Portugal, as it might be of any country, in point of magnificence without elegance; there is a convent annexed, the monks who possess large revenues are courteous enough, & understand Latin, so that we had a long conversation, they have a large library & asked if the *English* had *any books* in their country.——I sent my baggage & part of the servants by sea to Gibraltar, and travelled on horseback from Adea Gallega (the first stage from Libson which is only accessible by water) to Seville (one of the most famous cities in Spain where the government called the Junta is now held) the distance to Seville is nearly four hundred miles & to Cadiz about 90 further towards the coast.——I had orders from the government & every possible accommodation on the road, as an English nobleman in an English uniform is a very respectable personage in Spain at present. The horses are remarkably good, and the roads (I assure you upon my honour for you will hardly believe it) very far superior to the best British roads, without the smallest toll or turnpike, you will suppose this when I rode post to Seville in four days, through this parching country in the midst of summer, without fatigue or annoyance.—Seville is a beautiful town, though the streets are narrow they are clean, we lodged in the house of two Spanish unmarried ladies, who possess *six* houses in Seville, and gave me a curious specimen of Spanish manners.—They are women of character, and the eldest a fine woman, the youngest pretty but not so good a figure as Donna Josepha, the freedom of women which is general here astonished me not a little, and in the course of further observation I find that reserve is not the characteristic of the Spanish Belles, who are in general very handsome, with large black eyes, and very fine forms.—The eldest honoured your *unworthy* son with very particular attention, embracing him with great tenderness at parting (I was there but 3 days) after cutting off a lock of his hair, & presenting him with one of her own about three feet in length, which I send, and beg you will retain till my return.—Her last words were "adio tu hermoso! me gusto mucho" "adieu, you pretty fellow you please me much."—She offered a share of her apartment which my *virtue* induced me to decline, she laughed and said I had some English "amante," (lover) and added that she was going to be married to an officer in the Spanish Army.—I left Seville and rode on to Cadiz! through a beautiful country, at Xeres where the Sherry we drink is made I met a great merchant a Mr. Gordon of Scotland, who was extremely polite and favoured me with the inspection of his vaults & cellars, so that I quaffed at the fountain head.—Cadiz, sweet Cadiz! is the most delightful town I ever beheld, very different from our English cities in every

respect except cleanliness (and it is as clean as London) but still beautiful
and full of the finest women in Spain, the Cadiz belles being the
Lancashire witches of their land.—Just as I was introduced and began
to like the Grandees I was forced to leave it for this cursed place, but
before I return to England I will visit it again.—The night before I left
it, I sat in the box at the opera with Admiral Cordova's family, he is the
commander whom Ld. St. Vincent defeated in 1797, and has an aged
wife and a fine daughter.———Signorita Cordova the girl is very pretty
in the Spanish style, in my opinion by no means inferior to the English
in charms, and certainly superior in fascination.—Long black hair, dark
languishing eyes, *clear* olive complexions, and forms more graceful in
motion than can be conceived by an Englishman used to the drowsy
listless air of his countrywomen, added to the most becoming dress &
at the same time the most decent in the world, render a Spanish beauty
irresistible. I beg leave to observe that intrigue here is the business of
life, when a woman marries she throws off all restraint but I believe their
conduct is chaste enough before.—If you make a proposal which in
England would bring a box on the ear from the meekest of virgins, to
a Spanish girl, she thanks you for the honour you intend her, and replies
"wait till I am married, & I shall be too happy."—This is literally &
strictly true.—Miss C & her little brother understood a little French,
and after regretting my ignorance of the Spanish she proposed to become my preceptress in that language; I could only reply by a low bow,
and express my regret that I quitted Cadiz too soon to permit me to
make the progress which would doubtless attend my studies under so
charming a directress; I was standing at the back of the box which
resembles our opera boxes (the theater is large and finely decorated, the
music admirable) in the manner which Englishmen generally adopt for
fear of incommoding the ladies in front, when this fair Spaniard dispos-
sessed an old women (an aunt or a duenna) of her chair, and commanded
me to be seated next herself, at a tolerable distance from her mamma.—
At the close of the performance I withdrew and was lounging with a
party of men in the passage, when "en passant" the lady turned round
and called me, & I had the honour of attending her to the admiral's
mansion.—I have an invitation on my return to Cadiz which I shall
accept, if I repass through the country on my way from Asia.—I have
met Sir John Carr Knight Errant at Seville & Cadiz, he is a pleasant
man.—I like the Spaniards much, you have heard of the battle near
Madrid, & in England they will call it a victory, a pretty victory! two
hundred officers and 5000 men killed all English, and the French in as
great force as ever.—I should have joined the army but we have no time
to lose before we get up the Mediterranean & Archipelago,—I am going

over to Africa tomorrow, it is only six miles from this fortress.—My next stage is Cagliari in Sardinia where I shall be presented to his S majesty, I have a most superb uniform as a court dress, indispensable in travelling.—

August 15th

I could not dine with Castanos yesterday, but this afternoon I had that honour, he is pleasant, & for aught I know to the contrary, clever,—I cannot go to Barbary, the Malta packet sails tomorrow & myself in it, Admiral Purvis with whom I dined at Cadiz gave me a passage in a frigate to Gibraltar, but we have no ship of war destined for Malta at present, the Packets sail fast & have good accommodations, you shall hear from me on our route, Joe Murray delivers this, I have sent him & the boy back, pray shew the lad any kindness as he is my great favourite, I would have taken him on but you *know* boys are not *safe* amongst the Turks.—Say this to his father, who may otherwise think he has behaved ill.—[I hope] This will find you well, believe me yours ever sincerely—

BYRON

TO MRS. CATHERINE GORDON BYRON

Prevesa. Nov. 12th. 1809

My dear Mother,—I have now been some time in Turkey: this place is on the coast but I have traversed the interior of the province of Albania on a visit to the Pacha.—I left Malta in the Spider a brig of war on the 21st. of Septr. & arrived in eight days at Prevesa.—I thence have been about 150 miles as far as Tepaleen his highness's country palace where I staid three days.—The name of the Pacha is Ali, & he is considered a man of the first abilities, he governs the whole of Albania (the ancient Illyricum) Epirus, & part of Macedonia, his Son *Velly* Pacha to whom he has given me letters governs the Morea & he has great influence in Egypt, in short he is one of the most powerful men in the Ottoman empire.—When I reached Yanina the capital after a journey of three days over the mountains through a country of the most picturesque beauty, I found that Ali Pacha was with his army in Illyricum besieging Ibraham Pacha in the castle of Berat.—He had heard that an Englishman of rank was in his dominions & had left orders in Yanina with the Commandant to provide a house & supply me with every kind of necessary, *gratis*, & though I have been allowed to make presents to the slaves &c. I have not been permitted to pay for a single article of household consumption.—I rode out on the viziers horses & saw the palaces of himself & grandsons, they are splendid but too much ornamented with silk & gold.—I then went over the mountains through Zitza a village with a Greek monastery (where I slept on my return) in the most beautiful Situation (always excepting Cintra in Portugal) I ever beheld.—In nine days I reached Tepaleen, our Journey was much prolonged by the torrents that had fallen from the mountains & intersected the roads. I shall never forget the singular scene on entering Tepaleen at five in the afternoon as the Sun was going down, it brought to my recollection (with some change of *dress* however) Scott's description of Branksome Castle in his lay, & the feudal system.—The Albanians in their dresses (the most magnificent in the world, consisting of a long *white kilt,* gold worked cloak, crimson velvet gold laced jacket & waistcoat, silver mounted pistols & daggers,) the Tartars with their high caps, the Turks in their vast pelisses & turbans, the soldiers & black slaves with the horses, the former stretched in groups in an immense open gallery in front of the palace, the latter placed in a kind of cloister below it, two hundred steeds ready caparisoned to move in a moment, couriers entering or passing out with dispatches, the kettle drums beating, boys calling the hour from the minaret of the mosque, altogether, with the singular appearance of the building itself, formed a new & delightful spectacle to a stranger.—I was conducted to a very handsome apartment & my health enquired after by the vizier's secretary "a la mode de Turque."—The next day I was introduced to Ali Pacha, I was dressed in a full suit of Staff uniform with a very magnificent sabre &c.——The Vizier received me in a large room paved with marble, a fountain was playing in the centre, the apartment was surrounded by scarlet Ottomans, he received me *standing,* a wonderful compliment from a Mussulman, & made me sit down on his right hand.—I have a Greek interpreter for general use, but a Physician of Ali's named Seculario who understands Latin acted for me on this occasion.—His first question was why at so early an age I left my country? (the Turks have no idea of travelling for amusement) he then said the English Minister Capt. Leake had told him I was of a great family, & desired his respects to my mother, which I now in the name of Ali Pacha present to you. He said he was certain I was a man of birth because I had small ears, curling hair, & little white hands, and expressed himself pleased with my appearance & garb.—He told me to consider him as a father whilst I was in Turkey, & said he looked on me as his son.—Indeed he treated me like a child, sending me almonds & sugared sherbet, fruit & sweetmeats 20 times a day.—He begged me to visit him often, and at night when he was more at leisure—I then after coffee & pipes retired for the first time. I saw him thrice afterwards.—It is singular that the Turks who have no hereditary dignities & few great families except the Sultan's pay so much respect to birth, for I found my pedigree more regarded than even my title.— His Highness is 60 years old, very fat & not tall, but with a fine face, light blue eyes & a white beard, his manner is very kind & at the same time he possesses that dignity which I find universal amongst the Turks.——He has the appearance of anything but his real character, for he is a remorseless tyrant, guilty of the most horrible cruelties, very brave & so good a general, that they call him the Mahometan Buonaparte.— Napoleon has twice offered to make him King of Epirus, but he prefers the English interest & abhors the French as he himself told me, he is of so much consequence that he is much courted by both, the Albanians being the most warlike subjects of the Sultan, though Ali is only nominally dependent on the Porte. He has been a mighty warrior, but is as barbarous as he is successful, roasting rebels &c. &c.—Bonaparte sent him a snuffbox with his picture; he said the snuffbox was very well, but the picture he could excuse, as he neither liked *it* nor the *original.*—His ideas of judging of a man's birth from ears, hands &c. were curious enough.—To me he was indeed a father, giving me letters, guards, & every possible accommodation.—Our next conversations were of war & travelling, politics & England.—He called my Albanian soldier who attends me, and told him to protect me at all hazards.—His name is Viscillie & like all the Albanians he is brave, rigidly honest, & faithful, but they are cruel though not treacherous, & have several vices, but no meannesses.—They are perhaps the most beautiful race in point of countenance in the world, their women are sometimes handsome also, but they are treated like slaves, *beaten* & in short complete beasts of burthen, they plough, dig & sow, I found them carrying wood & actually repairing the highways, the men are all soldiers, & war & the chase their sole occupations, the women are the labourers, which after all is no great hardship in so delightful a climate, yesterday the 11th. Nov. I bathed in the sea, today It is so hot that I am writing in a shady room of the English Consul's with three doors wide open no fire or even *fireplace* in the house except for culinary purposes. . . . Today I saw the remains of the town of *Actium* near which Anthony lost the world in a small bay where two frigates could hardly manoeuvre, a broken wall is the sole remnant.—On another part of the gulph stand the ruins of Nicopolis built by Augustus in honour of his victory.———Last night I was at a Greek marriage, but this & 1000 things more I have neither time or *space* to describe.—I am going tomorrow with a guard of fifty men to

Patras in the Morea, & thence to Athens where I shall winter.—Two days ago I was nearly lost in a Turkish ship of war owing to the ignorance of the captain & crew though the storm was not violent.—Fletcher yelled after his wife, the Greeks called on all the Saints, the Mussulmen on Alla, the Captain burst into tears & ran below deck telling us to call on God, the sails were split, the mainyard shivered, the wind blowing fresh, the night setting in, & all our chance was to make Corfu which is in possession of the French, or (as Fletcher *pathetically* termed it) "a *watery* grave."—I did what I could to console Fletcher but finding him incorrigible wrapped myself up in my Albanian capote (an immense cloak) & lay down on deck to wait the worst, I have learnt to philosophize on my travels, & if I had not, complaint was useless.—Luckily the wind abated & only drove us on the coast of Suli on the main land where we landed & proceeded by the help of the natives to Prevesa again; but I shall not trust Turkish Sailors in future, though the Pacha had ordered one of his own galleots to take me to Patras, I am therefore going as far as Missolonghi by land & there have only to cross a small gulph to get to Patras.—Fletcher's next epistle will be full of marvels, we were one night lost for *nine* hours in the mountains in a *thunder* storm, & since nearly wrecked, in both cases Fletcher was sorely bewildered, from apprehensions of famine & banditti in the first, & drowning in the second instance.—His eyes were a little hurt by the lightning or crying (I don't know which) but are now recovered.—When you write address to me at Mr. *Strané's* English Consul, Patras, Morea.——— I could tell you I know not how many incidents that I think would amuse you, but they crowd on my mind as much as would swell my paper, & I can neither arrange them in the one, or put them down on the other, except in the greatest confusion & in my usual horrible hand.—I like the Albanians much, they are not all Turks, some tribes are Christians, but their religion makes little difference in their manner or conduct; they are esteemed the best troops in the Turkish service.—I lived on my route two days at once, & three days again in a Barrack at Salora, & never found soldiers so tolerable, though I have been in the garrisons of Gibraltar & Malta & seen Spanish, French, Sicilian & British troops in abundance, I have had nothing stolen, & was always welcome to their provision & milk.—Not a week ago, an Albanian chief (every village has its chief who is called Primate) after helping us out of the Turkish Galley in her distress, feeding us & lodging my suite consisting of Fletcher, a Greek, Two Albanians, a Greek Priest and my companion Mr. Hobhouse, refused any compensation but a written paper stating that I was well received, & when I pressed him to accept a few sequins, "no, he replied, I wish you to love me, not to pay me." These were his words.—It is astonishing how far money goes in this country, while I was in the capital, I had nothing to pay by the vizier's order, but since, though I have generally had sixteen horses & generally 6 or 7 men, the expence has not been *half* as much as staying only 3 weeks in Malta, though Sir A. Ball the governor gave me a house for nothing, & I had only *one servant.*—By the bye I expect Hanson to remit regularly, for I am not about to stay in this province for ever, let him write to me at Mr. Strané's, English Consul, Patras.——The fact is, the fertility of the plains are wonderful, & specie is scarce, which makes this remarkable cheapness.—I am now going to Athens to study modern Greek which differs much from the ancient though radically similar.—I have no desire to return to England, nor shall I unless compelled by absolute want & Hanson's neglect, but I shall not enter Asia for a year or two as I have much to see in Greece & I may perhaps cross into Africa at least the Ægyptian part.—Fletcher like all Englishmen is very much dissatisfied, though a little reconciled to the Turks by a present of 80 piastres from the vizier, which if you consider everything & the value of specie here is nearly worth ten guineas English.—He has suffered nothing but from *cold,* heat, & vermin which those who lie in cottages & cross mountains in a wild country must undergo, & of which I have equally partaken with himself, but he is not valiant, & is afraid of robbers & tempests.—I have no one to be remembered to in England, & wish to hear nothing from it but that you are well, & a letter or two on business from Hanson, whom you may tell to write.——I will write when I can, & beg you to believe me,

yr affect. Son
BYRON

P.S.—I have some very "magnifique" Albanian dresses the only expensive articles in this country they cost 50 guineas each & have so much gold they would cost in England two hundred.—I have been introduced to Hussein Bey, & Mahmout Pacha both little boys grandchildren of Ali at Yanina. They are totally unlike our lads, have painted complexions like rouged dowagers, large black eyes & features perfectly regular. They are the prettiest little animals I ever saw, & are broken into the court ceremonies already, the Turkish salute is a slight inclination of the head with the hand on the breast, intimates always kiss, Mahmout is ten years old & hopes to see me again, we are friends without understanding each other, like many other folks, though from a different cause;—he has given me a letter to his father in the Morea, to whom I have also letters from Ali *Pacha.*—

To Henry Drury

Salsette Frigate. May 3d. 1810
in the Dardanelles off Abydos

My dear Drury,—When I left England nearly a year ago you requested me to write to you.—I will do so.—I have crossed Portugal, traversed the South of Spain, visited Sardinia, Sicily, Malta, and thence passed into Turkey where I am still wandering.—I first landed in Albania the ancient Epirus where we penetrated as far as Mount Tomerit, excellently treated by the Chief Ali Pacha, and after journeying through Illyria, Chaonia, &ctr, crossed the Gulph of Actium with a guard of 50 Albanians and passed the Achelous in our route through Acarnania and Ætolia.—We stopped a short time in the Morea, crossed the gulph of Lepanto and landed at the foot of Parnassus, saw all that Delphi retains and so on to Thebes and Athens at which last we remained ten weeks.—His majesty's ship Pylades brought us to Smyrna but not before we had topographised Attica including of course Marathon, and the Sunian Promontory.—From Smyrna to the Troad which we visited when at anchor for a fortnight off the Tomb of Antilochus, was our next stage, and now we are in the Dardanelles waiting for a wind to proceed to Constantinople.—This morning I *swam* from *Sestos* to *Abydos*, the immediate distance is not above a mile but the current renders it hazardous, so much so, that I doubt whether Leander's conjugal powers must not have been exhausted in his passage to Paradise.—I attempted it a week ago and failed owing to the North wind and the wonderful rapidity of the tide, though I have been from my childhood a strong swimmer, but this morning being calmer I succeeded and crossed the "broad Hellespont" in an hour and ten minutes.——Well, my dear Sir, I have left my home and seen part of Africa & Asia and a tolerable portion of Europe.—I have been with Generals, and Admirals, Princes and Pachas, Governors and Ungovernables, but I have not time or paper to expatiate. I wish to let you know that I live with a friendly remembrance of you and a hope to meet you again, and if I do this as shortly as possible, attribute it to anything but forgetfulness.—Greece ancient and modern you know too well to require description. Albania indeed I have seen more of than any Englishman (but a Mr. Leake) for it is a country rarely visited from the savage character of the natives, though abounding in more natural beauties than the classical regions of Greece, which however are still eminently beautiful, particularly Delphi, and Cape Colonna in Attica.—Yet these are nothing to parts of Illyria, and Epirus, where places without a name, and rivers not laid down in maps, may one day when more known be justly esteemed superior subjects for the pencil, and the pen, than the dry ditch of the Ilissus, and the bogs of Bœotia.— The Troad is a fine field for conjecture and Snipe-shooting, and a good sportsman and an ingenious scholar may exercise their feet and faculties to great advantage upon the spot, or if they prefer riding lose their way (as I did) in a cursed quagmire of the Scamander who wriggles about as if the Dardan virgins still offered their wonted tribute. The only vestige of Troy, or her destroyers, are the barrows supposed to contain the carcases of Achilles, Antilochus, Ajax &c. but Mt. Ida is still in high feather, though the Shepherds are nowadays not much like Ganymede.—But why should I say more of these things? are they not written in the *Boke* of Gell? and has not Hobby got a journal? I keep none as I have renounced scribbling.—I see not much difference between ourselves & the Turks, save that we have foreskins and they none, that they have long dresses and we short, and that we talk much and they little.— In England the vices in fashion are whoring & drinking, in Turkey, Sodomy & smoking, we prefer a girl and a bottle, they a pipe and pathic.—They are sensible people, Ali Pacha told me he was sure I was a man of rank because I had *small ears* and hands and *curling hair.*—By the bye, I speak the Romaic or Modern Greek tolerably, it does not differ from the ancient dialects so much as you would conceive, but the pronunciation is diametrically opposite, of verse except in rhyme they have no idea.—I like the Greeks, who are plausible rascals, with all the Turkish vices without their courage.—However some are brave and all are beautiful, very much resembling the busts of Alcibiades, the women not quite so handsome.—I can swear in Turkish, but except one horrible oath, and *"pimp"* and "bread" and "water" I have got no great vocabulary in that language.—They are extremely polite to strangers of any rank properly protected, and as I have got 2 servants and two soldiers we get on with great eclât. We have been occasionally in danger of thieves & once of shipwreck but always escaped.—At Malta I fell in love with a married woman and challenged an aid du camp of Genl. Oakes (a rude fellow who grinned at something, I never rightly knew what,) but he explained and apologised, and the lady embarked for Cadiz, & so I escaped murder and adultery.—Of Spain I sent some account to our Hodgson, but I have subsequently written to no one save notes to relations and lawyers to keep them out of my premises.—I mean to give up all connection on my return with many of my best friends as I supposed them, and to snarl all my life, but I hope to have one good humoured laugh with you, and to embrace Dwyer and pledge Hodgson, before I commence Cynicism.—Tell Dr. Butler I am now writing with the gold pen he gave me before I left England, which is the reason my scrawl is more unintelligible than usual.—I have been at Athens and seen plenty of those reeds for scribbling, some of which he refused to bestow upon me because topographer Gell had brought them from Attica.——But I will not describe, no, you must be satisfied with simple detail till my return, and then we will unfold the floodgates of Colloquoy.—I am in a 36 gun frigate going up to fetch Bob Adair from Constantinople, who will have the honour to carry this letter.—And so Hobby's *boke* is out, with some sentimental singsong of mine own to fill up, and how does it take? eh! and where the devil is the 2d Edition of my Satire with additions? and my name on the title page? and more lines tagged to the end with a new exordium and what not, hot from my anvil before I cleared the Channel?—The Mediterranean and the Atlantic roll between me and Criticism, and the thunders of the Hyberborean Review are deafened by the roar of the Hellespont.—Remember me to Claridge if not translated to College, and present to Hodgson assurances of my high consideration.—Now, you will ask, what shall I do next? and I answer I do not know, I may return in a few months, but I have intents and projects after visiting Constantinople, Hobhouse however will probably be back in September.—On the 2d. of July we have left Albion one year, "oblitus meorum, obliviscendus et illis [forgetting my friends and forgotten by them]," I was sick of my own country, and not much prepossessed in favour of any other, but I drag on "my chain" without "lengthening it at each remove".—I am like the jolly miller caring for nobody and not cared for. All countries are much the same in my eyes, I smoke and stare at mountains, and twirl my mustachios very independently, I miss no comforts, and the Musquïtoes that rack the morbid frame of Hobhouse, have luckily for me little effect on mine because I live more temperately.—I omitted Ephesus in my Catalogue, which I visited during my sojourn at Smyrna,—but the temple has almost perished, and St. Paul need not trouble himself to epistolize the present brood of Ephesians who have converted a large church built entirely of marble into a Mosque, and I dont know that the edifice looks the worse for it.—My paper is full and my ink ebbing, Good Afternoon!—If you address to me at Malta, the letter will be forwarded wherever I may be.—Hobhouse greets you, he pines for his poetry, at least some tidings of it.—I almost forgot to tell you that I am dying for love of three Greek Girls at Athens, sisters, two of whom have promised to accompany me to England, I lived in the same house, Teresa, Mariana, and Kattinka, are the names of these divinities all of them under 15.—your ταπεινοτατοσ δουλοσ [most humble servant],

BYRON

JOHN KEATS
1795–1821

*George Chapman, a poet and playwright contemporary with Shakes-
peare and Ben Jonson, began translating the* Iliad *and the* Odyssey *in
1598, and in 1616 published* The Whole Works of Homer, Prince of
Poets.

*For Keats, only the imagery of travel, and finally of ecstatic explora-
tory surprise, is adequate to render the thrill of literary discovery. (He
misremembered the explorer in question: it was Balboa, not Cortez.)*

ON FIRST LOOKING INTO CHAPMAN'S HOMER
(1816)

Much have I travelled in the realms of gold,
And many goodly states and kingdoms seen;
Round many western islands have I been
Which bards in fealty to Apollo hold.
Oft of one wide expanse had I been told
That deep-browed Homer ruled as his demesne:
Yet did I never breathe its pure serene
Till I heard Chapman speak out loud and bold:
Then felt I like some watcher of the skies
When a new planet swims into his ken;
Or like stout Cortez, when with eagle eyes
He stared at the Pacific—and all his men
Looked at each other with a wild surmise—
Silent, upon a peak in Darien.

FRANCES TROLLOPE
1780-1863

Mother of Anthony, the Victorian novelist, Frances Trollope became a profuse writer herself, author of over 40 books, 35 of them novels, the rest travel books and volumes of poetry. Her father was an Anglican minister, her husband an irascible lawyer and gentleman farmer who experienced great difficulty staying out of debt. She and her family lived in Harrow, where she took a lively part in amateur literary and theatrical circles and developed her lifelong scorn for puritanical, Evangelical clergy hostile to the arts.

Intrigued by her friend Fanny Wright's enthusiasm for the principles of the new American republic and rather hoping to install her unpromising son Henry in some career in the New World, at the age of 48 she sailed for America. She stayed three years, two of them in the frontier town of Cincinnati (pop: 20,000), known to the disrespectful as Porkopolis. There she invested in an architecturally exotic "bazaar"—an early kind of shopping mall—which failed. Money was now very short, and in March 1830, she decided to recover by traveling and writing a best-seller about the United States. It appeared in England just in time to fuel the rabid debate there about "democracy" and the extension of the franchise attending the Reform Bill of 1832.

Her book created a sensation in Britain and a scandal in the U.S.A., where it was pirated widely. One American reviewer sought revenge by writing: "There is much in a name. . . . The name of Mrs. Trollope, therefore, may be, at least, the shadow of a thing." But Mark Twain was more fair, writing in Life on the Mississippi: *"She knew her subject well, and she set it forth fairly and squarely without any weak ifs and ands and buts. She deserved gratitude but it is an error to suppose she got it." It was the popularity of* Domestic Manners of the Americans, *published when she was over 50, that set Frances Trollope on her long career as an author.*

From DOMESTIC MANNERS OF THE AMERICANS
(1832)

ABSENCE OF PUBLIC AND PRIVATE AMUSEMENT—CHURCHES
AND CHAPELS—INFLUENCE OF THE CLERGY—A REVIVAL

I never saw any people who appeared to live so much without amusement as the Cincinnatians. Billiards are forbidden by law, so are cards. To sell a pack of cards in Ohio subjects the seller to a penalty of fifty dollars. They have no public balls, excepting, I think, six, during the Christmas holidays. They have no concerts. They have no dinner-parties.

They have a theatre, which is, in fact, the only public amusement of this triste little town; but they seem to care little about it, and either from economy or distaste, it is very poorly attended. Ladies are rarely seen there, and by far the larger proportion of females deem it an offence against religion to witness the representation of a play. It is in the churches and chapels of the town that the ladies are to be seen in full costume: and I am tempted to believe that a stranger from the continent of Europe would be inclined, on first reconnoitring the city, to suppose that the places of worship were the theatres and cafés of the place. No evening in the week but brings throngs of the young and beautiful to the chapels and meeting-houses, all dressed with care, and sometimes with great pretension; it is there that all display is made, and all fashionable distinction sought. The proportion of gentlemen attending these evening meetings is very small, but often, as might be expected, a sprinkling of smart young clerks makes this sedulous display of ribbons and ringlets intelligible and natural. Were it not for the churches, indeed, I think there might be a general bonfire of best bonnets, for I never could discover any other use for them.

The ladies are too actively employed in the interior of their houses to permit much parading in full dress for morning visits. There are no public gardens or lounging shops of fashionable resort, and were it not for public worship, and private tea-drinkings, all the ladies in Cincinnati would be in danger of becoming perfect recluses.

The influence which the ministers of all the innumerable religious sects throughout America have on the females of their respective congregations approaches very nearly to what we read of in Spain, or in other strictly Roman Catholic countries. There are many causes for this peculiar influence. Where equality of rank is affectedly acknowledged by the rich, and clamorously claimed by the poor, distinction and preeminence are allowed to the clergy only. This gives them high importance in the eyes of the ladies. I think, also, that it is from the clergy only that the women of America receive that sort of attention which is so dearly valued by every female heart throughout the world. With the priests of America the women hold that degree of influential importance which, in the countries of Europe, is allowed them throughout all orders and ranks of society, except, perhaps, the very lowest; and in return for this they seem to give their hearts and souls into their keeping. I never saw, or read of, any country where religion had so strong a hold upon the women, or a slighter hold upon the men.

I mean not to assert that I met with no men of sincerely religious feelings, or with no women of no religious feelings at all; but I feel perfectly secure of being correct as to the great majority in the statement I have made.

We had not been many months in Cincinnati when our curiosity was excited by hearing the "revival" talked of by every one we met throughout the town. "The revival will be very full," "We shall be constantly engaged during the revival," were the phrases we constantly heard repeated, and for a long time without in the least comprehending what was meant; but at length I learnt that the un-national church of America required to be roused, at regular intervals, to greater energy and exertion. At these seasons the most enthusiastic of the clergy travel the country, and enter the cities and towns by scores, or by hundreds, as the accommodation of the place may admit, and for a week or fortnight, or, if the population be large, for a month, they preach and pray all day, and often for a considerable portion of the night, in the various churches and chapels of the place. This is called a Revival.

I took considerable pains to obtain information on this subject; but in detailing what I learnt I fear that it is probable I shall be accused of exaggeration; all I can do is cautiously to avoid deserving it. The subject is highly interesting, and it would be a fault of no trifling nature to treat it with levity.

These itinerant clergymen are of all persuasions, I believe, except the Episcopalian, Catholic, Unitarian, and Quaker. I heard of Presbyterians of all varieties; of Baptists of I know not how many divisions; and of Methodists of more denominations than I can remember; whose innumerable shades of varying belief it would require much time to explain and more to comprehend. They enter all the cities, towns, and villages of the Union in succession; I could not learn, with sufficient certainty to repeat, what the interval generally is between their visits. These itinerants are, for the most part, lodged in the houses of their respective followers, and every evening that is not spent in the churches and meeting-houses is devoted to what would be called parties by others, but which they designate as prayer-meetings. Here they eat, drink, pray, sing, hear confessions, and make converts. To these meetings I never got invited, and therefore I have nothing but hearsay evidence to offer, but my information comes from an eye-witness, and one on whom I believe I may depend. If one half of what I heard may be believed, these social prayer-meetings are by no means the least curious, or the least important part of the business.

It is impossible not to smile at the close resemblance to be traced between the feelings of a first-rate Presbyterian or Methodist lady, fortunate enough to have secured a favourite itinerant for her meeting, and those of a first-rate London Blue, equally blessed in the presence of a fashionable poet. There is a strong family likeness among us all the world over.

The best rooms, the best dresses, the choicest refreshments solemnise the meeting. While the party is assembling, the code-star of the hour is occupied in whispering conversations with the guests as they arrive. They are called brothers and sisters, and the greetings are very affectionate. When the room is full, the company, of whom a vast majority are always women, are invited, entreated, and coaxed to confess before their brothers and sisters, all their thoughts, faults, and follies.

These confessions are strange scenes; the more they confess, the more invariably are they encouraged and caressed. When this is over, they all kneel, and the itinerant prays extempore. They then eat and drink; and then they sing hymns, pray, exhort, sing, and pray again, till the excitement reaches a very high pitch indeed. These scenes are going on at some house or other every evening during the revival, nay, at many at the same time, for the churches and meeting-houses cannot give occupation to half the itinerants, though they are all open throughout the day, and till a late hour in the night, and the officiating ministers succeed each other in the occupation of them.

It was at the principal of the Presbyterian churches that I was twice witness to scenes that made me shudder; in describing one, I describe both, and every one; the same thing is constantly repeated.

It was in the middle of summer, but the service we were recommended to attend did not begin till it was dark. The church was well lighted, and crowded almost to suffocation. On entering, we found three priests standing side by side, in a sort of tribune, placed where the altar usually is, handsomely fitted up with crimson curtains, and elevated about as high as our pulpits. We took our places in a pew close to the rail which surrounded it.

The priest who stood in the middle was praying; the prayer was extravagantly vehement, and offensively familiar in expression; when this ended, a hymn was sung, and then another priest took the centre place and preached. The sermon had considerable eloquence, but of a frightful kind. The preacher described, with ghastly minuteness, the last feeble fainting moments of human life, and then the gradual progress of decay after death, which he followed through every process up to the last loathsome stage of decomposition. Suddenly changing his tone, which had been that of sober accurate description, into the shrill voice of horror, he bent forward his head, as if to gaze on some object beneath the pulpit. And as Rebecca made known to Ivanhoe what she saw through the window, so the preacher made known to us what he saw in the pit that seemed to open before him. The device was certainly a happy one for giving effect to his description of hell. No image that fire, flame, brimstone, molten lead, or red hot pincers could supply, with flesh, nerves, and sinews quivering under them, was omitted. The perspiration ran in streams from the face of the preacher; his eyes rolled, his lips were covered with foam, and every feature had the deep expression of horror it would have borne, had he, in truth, been gazing at the scene he described. The acting was excellent. At length he gave a languishing look to his supporters on each side, as if to express his feeble state, and then sat down, and wiped the drops of agony from his brow.

The other two priests arose, and began to sing a hymn. It was some seconds before the congregation could join as usual; every up-turned face looked pale and horror-struck. When the singing ended, another took the centre place, and began in a sort of coaxing affectionate tone, to ask the congregation if what their dear brother had spoken had reached their hearts? Whether they would avoid the hell he had made them see? "Come, then!" he continued, stretching out his arms towards them; "come to us and tell us so, and we will make you see Jesus, the dear gentle Jesus, who shall save you from it. But you must come to him! You must not be ashamed to come to him! This night you shall tell him that you are not ashamed of him; we will make way for you; we will clear the bench for anxious sinners to sit upon. Come, then! come to the anxious bench, and we will show you Jesus! Come! Come! Come!"

Again a hymn was sung, and while it continued, one of the three was employed in clearing one or two long benches that went across the rail, sending the people back to the lower part of the church. The singing ceased, and again the people were invited, and exhorted not to be ashamed of Jesus, but to put themselves upon "the anxious benches," and lay their heads on his bosom. "Once more we will sing," he concluded, "that we may give you time." And again they sung a hymn.

And now in every part of the church a movement was perceptible, slight at first, but by degrees becoming more decided. Young girls arose, and sat down, and rose again; and then the pews opened, and several came tottering out, their hands clasped, their heads hanging on their bosoms, and every limb trembling, and still the hymn went on; but as the poor creatures approached the rail their sobs and groans became audible. They seated themselves on the "anxious benches"; the hymn ceased, and two of the three priests walked down from the tribune, and going, one to the right, and the other to the left, began whispering to the poor tremblers seated there. These whispers were inaudible to us, but the sobs and groans increased to a frightful excess. Young creatures, with features pale and distorted, fell on their knees on the pavement, and soon sunk forward on their faces; the most violent cries and shrieks followed, while from time to time a voice was heard in convulsive accents, exclaiming "O Lord!," "O Lord Jesus!," "Help me, Jesus!" and the like.

Meanwhile the two priests continued to walk among them; they repeatedly mounted on the benches, and trumpet-mouthed proclaimed to the whole congregation "the tidings of salvation", and then from every corner of the building arose in reply, short sharp cries of "Amen!," "Glory!," "Amen!," while the prostrate penitents continued to receive whispered comfortings, and from time to time a mystic caress. More than once I saw a young neck encircled by a reverend arm. Violent hysterics and convulsions seized many of them, and when the tumult was at the highest, the priest who remained above again gave out a hymn as if to drown it.

It was a frightful sight to behold innocent young creatures, in the gay morning of existence, thus seized upon, horror-struck, and rendered feeble and enervated forever. One young girl, apparently not more than fourteen, was supported in the arms of another some years older; her face was pale as death; her eyes wide open and perfectly devoid of meaning; her chin and bosom wet with slaver; she had every appearance of idiot-ism. I saw a priest approach her, he took her delicate hand. "Jesus is with her! Bless the Lord!" he said, and passed on.

Did the men of America value their women as men ought to value their wives and daughters, would such scenes be permitted among them?

It is hardly necessary to say that all who obeyed the call to place themselves on the "anxious benches" were women, and by far the greater number, very young women. The congregation was, in general, extremely well-dressed, and the smartest and most fashionable ladies of the town were there; during the whole revival, the churches and meet-ing-houses were every day crowded with well-dressed people.

It is thus the ladies of Cincinnati amuse themselves: to attend the theatre is forbidden; to play cards is unlawful; but they work hard in their families, and must have some relaxation. For myself, I confess that I think the coarsest comedy ever written would be a less detestable exhibition for the eyes of youth and innocence than such a scene.

SCHOOLS—CLIMATE—WATER-MELONS—FOURTH OF JULY—
STORMS—PIGS—MOVING HOUSES—MR FLINT—
LITERATURE

Cincinnati contains many schools, but of their rank or merit I had very little opportunity of judging; the only one which I visited was kept by Dr Lock, a gentleman who appears to have liberal and enlarged opinions on the subject of female education. Should his system produce practical results proportionably excellent, the ladies of Cincinnati will probably, some years hence, be much improved in their powers of companionship. I attended the annual public exhibition at this school, and perceived, with some surprise, that the higher branches of science were among the studies of the pretty creatures I saw assembled there. One lovely girl of sixteen *took her degree* in mathematics, and another was examined in moral philosophy. They blushed so sweetly, and looked so beautifully puzzled and confounded, that it might have been difficult for an abler judge than I was to decide how far they merited the diplomas they received.

This method of letting young ladies graduate, and granting them diplomas on quitting the establishment, was quite new to me; at least, I do not remember to have heard of anything similar elsewhere. I should fear that the time allowed to the fair graduates of Cincinnati for the acquirement of these various branches of education would seldom be sufficient to permit their reaching the eminence in each which their enlightened instructor anticipates. "A quarter's" mathematics, or "two quarters'" political economy, moral philosophy, algebra and quadratic equations, would seldom, I should think, enable the teacher and the scholar, by their joint efforts, to lay in such a stock of these sciences as would stand the wear and tear of half a score of children, and one help.

Towards the end of May we began to feel that we were in a climate warmer than any we had been accustomed to, and my son suffered severely from the effects of it. A bilious complaint, attended by a frightful degree of fever, seized him, and for some days we feared for his life. The treatment he received was, I have no doubt, judicious, but the quantity of calomel prescribed was enormous. I asked one day how many grains I should prepare, and was told to give half a tea-spoonful. The difference of climate must, I imagine, make a difference in the effect of this drug, or the practice of the old and new world could hardly differ so widely as it does in the use of it. Anstey, speaking of the Bath physicians, says:

> No one e'er viewed
> Any one of the medical gentlemen stewed.

But I can vouch, upon my own experience, that no similar imputation lies against the gentlemen who prescribe large quantities of calomel in America. To give one instance in proof of this, when I was afterwards in Montgomery county, near Washington, a physician attended one of our neighbors, and complained that he was himself unwell. "You must take care of yourself, doctor" said the patient: "I do so," he replied; "I took forty grains of calomel yesterday, and I feel better than I did." Repeated and violent bleeding was also had recourse to, in the case of my son, and in a few days he was able to leave his room, but he was dreadfully emaciated, and it was many weeks before he recovered his strength.

As the heat of the weather increased, we heard of much sickness around us. The city is full of physicians, and they were all to be seen driving about in their cabs at a very alarming rate. One of these gentlemen told us that when a medical man intended settling in a new situation, he always, if he knew his business, walked through the streets at night, before he decided. If he saw the dismal twinkle of the watch-light from many windows, he might be sure that disease was busy, and that the "location" might suit him well. Judging by this criterion, Cincinnati was far from healthy; I began to fear for our health, and determined to leave the city; but for a considerable time I found it impossible to procure a dwelling out of it. There were many boarding-houses in the vicinity, but they were all overflowing with guests. We were advised to avoid, as much as possible, walking out in the heat of the day; but the mornings and evenings were delightful, particularly the former, if taken sufficiently early. For several weeks I was never in bed after four o'clock, and at this hour I almost daily accompanied my "help" to market, where the busy novelty of the scene afforded me much amusement.

Many wagon-loads of enormous water-melons were brought to market every day, and I was sure to see groups of men, women, and children seated on the pavement round the spot where they were sold, sucking in prodigious quantities of this watery fruit. Their manner of devouring them is extremely unpleasant; the huge fruit is cut into half-a-dozen sections, of about a foot long, and then, dripping as it is with water, applied to the mouth, from either side of which pour copious streams of the fluid, while, ever and anon, a mouthful of the hard black seeds are shot out in all directions, to the great annoyance of all within reach. When I first tasted this fruit, I thought it very vile stuff indeed; but before the end of the season we all learned to like it. When taken with claret and sugar, it makes delicious wine and water.

It is the custom for the gentlemen to go to market at Cincinnati; the smartest men in the place, and those of the "highest standing," do not scruple to leave their beds with the sun six days in the week, and, prepared with a mighty basket, to sally forth in search of meat, butter, eggs, and vegetables. I have continually seen them returning, with their weighty basket on one arm and an enormous ham depending from the other.

And now arrived the 4th of July, that greatest of all American festivals. On the 4th of July, 1776, the declaration of their independence was signed, at the State House in Philadelphia.

To me the dreary coldness and want of enthusiasm in American manner is one of their greatest defects, and I therefore hailed the demonstrations of general feeling which this day elicits with real pleasure. On the 4th of July the hearts of the people seem to awaken from a three hundred and sixty-four days' sleep; they appear high-spirited, gay, animated, social, generous, or at least, liberal in expense; and would they but refrain from spitting on that hallowed day, I should say that, on the 4th of July, at least, they appeared to be an amiable people. It is true that the women have but little to do with the pageantry, the splendour, or the gaiety of the day; but, setting this defect aside, it was indeed a glorious sight to behold a jubilee so heartfelt as this; and had they not the bad taste and bad feeling to utter an annual oration, with unvarying abuse of the mother country, to say nothing of the warlike manifesto called the Declaration of Independence, our gracious king himself might look upon the scene and say that it was good; nay, even rejoice, that twelve millions of bustling bodies, at four thousand miles distance from his throne and his altars, should make their own laws, and drink their own tea, after the fashion that pleased them best.

One source of deep interest to us, in this new clime, was the frequent recurrence of thunderstorms. Those who have only listened to thunder in England have but a faint idea of the language which the gods speak when they are angry. Thomson's description, however, will do: it is

hardly possible that words can better paint the spectacle, or more truly
echo to the sound, than his do. The only point he does not reach is the
vast blaze of rose-coloured light that ever and anon sets the landscape
on fire.

It seems hardly fair to quarrel with a place because its staple commod-
ity is not pretty, but I am sure I should have liked Cincinnati much
better if the people had not dealt so very largely in hogs. The immense
quantity of business done in this line would hardly be believed by those
who had not witnessed it. I never saw a newspaper without remarking
such advertisements as the following:
"Wanted, immediately, 4,000 fat hogs."
"For sale, 2,000 barrels of prime pork."
But the annoyance came nearer than this; if I determined upon a walk
up Main Street, the chances were five hundred to one against my
reaching the shady side without brushing by a snout fresh dripping from
the kennel; when we had screwed our courage to the enterprise of
mounting a certain noble-looking sugarloaf hill, that promised pure air
and a fine view, we found the brook we had to cross, at its foot, red with
the stream from a pig slaughter-house; while our noses, instead of meeting "the thyme that loves the green hill's breast," were greeted by odours
that I will not describe, and which I heartily hope my readers cannot
imagine; our feet, that on leaving the city had expected to press the
flowery sod, literally got entangled in pigs' tails and jaw-bones; and thus
the prettiest walk in the neighborhood was interdicted for ever.

One of the sights to stare at in America is that of houses moving from
place to place. We were often amused by watching this exhibition of
mechanical skill in the streets. They make no difficulty of moving dwellings from one part of the town to another. Those I saw travelling were
all of them frame-houses, that is built wholly of wood, except the chimneys; but it is said that brick buildings are sometimes treated in the same
manner. The largest dwelling that I saw in motion was one containing
two stories of four rooms each; forty oxen were yoked to it. The first few
yards brought down the two stacks of chimneys, but it afterwards went
on well. The great difficulties were the first getting it in motion and the
stopping exactly in the right place. This locomotive power was extremely
convenient to Cincinnati, as the constant improvements going on there
made it often desirable to change a wooden dwelling for one of brick;
and whenever this happened, we were sure to see the ex-No. 100 of
Main Street, or the ex-No. 55 of Second Street, creeping quietly out of

town, to take possession of an humble suburban station on the common above it.

The most agreeable acquaintance I made in Cincinnati, and indeed one of the most talented men I ever met, was Mr Flint, the author of several extremely clever volumes, and the editor of the *Western Monthly Review*. His conversational powers are of the highest order; he is the only person I remember to have known with first-rate powers of satire, and even of sarcasm, whose kindness of nature and of manner remained perfectly uninjured. In some of his critical notices there is a strength and keenness second to nothing of the kind I have ever read. He is a warm patriot, and so true-hearted an American that we could not always be of the same opinion on all the subjects we discussed; but whether it were the force and brilliancy of his language, his genuine and manly sincerity of feeling, or his bland and gentleman-like manner that beguiled me, I know not, but certainly he is the only American I ever listened to whose unqualified praise of his country did not appear to me somewhat over-strained and ridiculous.

On one occasion, but not at the house of Mr Flint, I passed an evening in company with a gentleman, said to be a scholar, and a man of reading; he was also what is called a *serious* gentleman, and he appeared to have pleasure in feeling that his claim to distinction was acknowledged in both capacities. There was a very amiable *serious* lady in the company, to whom he seemed to trust for the development of his celestial pretensions, and to me he did the honour of addressing most of his terrestrial superiority. The difference between us was that when he spoke to her, he spoke as to a being who, if not his equal, was at least deserving high distinction; and he gave her smiles, such as Michael might have vouchsafed to Eve. To me he spoke as Paul to the offending Jews; he did not, indeed, shake his raiment at me, but he used his pocket-handkerchief so as to answer the purpose; and if every sentence did not end with "I am clean," pronounced by his lips, his tone, his look, his action, fully supplied the deficiency.

Our poor Lord Byron, as may be supposed, was the bull's-eye against which every dart in his black little quiver was aimed. I had never heard any serious gentleman talk of Lord Byron at full length before, and I listened attentively. It was evident that the noble passages which are graven on the hearts of the genuine lovers of poetry had altogether escaped the serious gentleman's attention; and it was equally evident that he knew by rote all those that they wish the mighty master had never written. I told him so, and I shall not soon forget the look he gave me.

Of other authors his knowledge was very imperfect, but his criticisms very amusing. Of Pope, he said: "He is so entirely gone by, that in *our* country it is considered quite fustian to speak of him."

But I persevered, and named *The Rape of the Lock* as evincing some little talent, and being in a tone that might still hope for admittance in the drawing-room; but, on the mention of this poem, the serious gentleman became almost as strongly agitated as when he talked of *Don Juan;* and I was unfeignedly at a loss to comprehend the nature of his feelings, till he muttered, with an indignant shake of the handkerchief: "The very title!"

At the name of Dryden he smiled, and the smile spoke as plainly as a smile could speak "How the old woman twaddles!"

"We only know Dryden by quotations, madam, and these, indeed, are found only in books that have long since had their day."

"And Shakespeare, sir?"

"Shakspeare, madam, is obscene, and, thank God, we are sufficiently advanced to have found it out! If we must have the abomination of stage plays, let them at least be marked by the refinement of the age in which we live."

This was certainly being *au courant du jour* [up to date].

Of Massinger he knew nothing. Of Ford he had never heard. Gray had had his day. Prior he had never read, but understood he was a very childish writer. Chaucer and Spenser he tied in a couple, and dismissed by saying that he thought it was neither more nor less than affectation to talk of authors who wrote in a tongue no longer intelligible.

This was the most literary conversation I was ever present at in Cincinnati.

In truth, there are many reasons which render a very general diffusion of literature impossible in America. I can scarcely class the universal reading of newspapers as an exception to this remark; if I could, my statement would be exactly the reverse, and I should say that America beat the world in letters. The fact is, that throughout all ranks of society, from the successful merchant, which is the highest, to the domestic serving man, which is the lowest, they are all too actively employed to read, except at such broken moments as may suffice for a peep at a newspaper. It is for this reason, I presume, that every American newspaper is more or less a magazine, wherein the merchant may scan, while he holds out his hand for an invoice, "Stanzas by Mrs. Hemans," or a garbled extract from Moore's *Life of Byron;* the lawyer may study his brief faithfully, and yet contrive to pick up the valuable dictum of some

American critic, that "Bulwer's novels are decidedly superior to Sir Walter Scott's"; nay, even the auctioneer may find time, as he bustles to the tub, or his tribune, to support his pretensions to polite learning, by glancing his quick eye over the columns, and reading that "Miss Mitford's descriptions are indescribable." If you buy a yard of ribbon, the shopkeeper lays down his newspaper, perhaps two or three, to measure it. I have seen a brewer's drayman perched on the shaft of his dray and reading one newspaper, while another was tucked under his arm; and I once went into the cottage of a country shoemaker, of the name of Harris, where I saw a newspaper half full of "original" poetry, directed to Madison F. Harris. To be sure of the fact, I asked the man if his name were Madison. "Yes, madam, Madison Franklin Harris is my name." The last and the lyre divided his time, I fear too equally, for he looked pale and poor.

This, I presume, is what is meant by the general diffusion of knowledge, so boasted of in the United States; such as it is, the diffusion of it is general enough, certainly; but I greatly doubt its being advantageous to the population.

The only reading men I met with were those who made letters their profession; and of these, there were some who would hold a higher rank in the great republic (not of America, but of letters) did they write for persons less given to the study of magazines and newspapers; and they might hold a higher rank still, did they write for the few and not for the many. I was always drawing a parallel, perhaps a childish one, between the external and internal deficiency of polish and of elegance in the native volumes of the country. Their compositions had not that condensation of thought, or that elaborate finish, the which consciousness of writing for the scholar and the man of taste is calculated to give; nor have their dirty blue paper and slovenly types the polished elegance that fits a volume for the hand or the eye of the fastidious epicure in literary enjoyment. The first book I bought in America was *The Chronicles of the Canongate.* On asking the price, I was agreeably surprised to hear a dollar and a half named, being about one sixth of what I used to pay for its fellows in England; but on opening the grim pages, it was long before I could again call them cheap. To be sure, the pleasure of a bright well-printed page ought to be quite lost sight of in the glowing, galloping, bewitching course that the imagination sets out upon with a new Waverley novel; and so it was with me till I felt the want of it; and then I am almost ashamed to confess how often, in turning the thin dusky pages, my poor earth-born spirit paused in its pleasure, to sigh for hot-pressed wire-wove.

WILLIAM WORDSWORTH
1770–1850

Wordsworth was gifted at expressing travel excitement, as in his poetic reponse to the Sublime of the Simplon Pass. But as this sonnet indicates, he could confront travel disappointment as well. And further, make of it a spur to Higher Things.

At Rome
(1840–41)

Is this, ye Gods, the Capitolian Hill?
Yon petty steep in truth the fearful rock,
Tarpeian named of yore, and keeping still
That name, a local phantom proud to mock
The traveler's expectation?—Could our will
Destroy the ideal power within, 'twere done
Through what men see and touch—slaves wandering on,
Impelled by thirst of all but heaven-taught skill.
Full oft, our wish obtained, deeply we sigh;
Yet not unrecompensed are they who learn,
From that depression raised, to mount on high
With stronger wing, more clearly to discern
Eternal things; and, if need be, defy
Change, with a brow not insolent, though stern.

CHARLES DICKENS
1812–1870

The miserable background from which Dickens emerged—his father's imprisonment for debt, his own child labor in a blacking warehouse— illuminates much of his fiction, especially David Copperfield *and* Oliver Twist. *His energy and ambition soon carried him into journalism, and ultimately into authorship, and by the 1850s and 1860s, with* Bleak House, Hard Times, Little Dorrit, A Tale of Two Cities, Great Expectations, *and* Our Mutual Friend, *he became the best-known and most popular British novelist.*

His travels included a trip to America in 1842, which he recorded in American Notes, *a book whose clear-sighted criticism of such American usages as Black slavery and the ubiquitous spitting of tobacco juice occasioned considerable patriotic outrage here. Two years later he toured Italy, producing another travel book,* Pictures from Italy. *But no matter what he observes, his perception is both vigilant and literary, registering itself in frequent, often satiric, personification and ready irony directed commonly at social crimes like cruelty and hypocrisy.*

As George Orwell has noticed, Dickens writes from "the English puritan tradition." And reading Dickens, Orwell imagines he can see his face before him: "It is the face of a man of about forty, with a small beard and a high colour. He is laughing, with a touch of anger in his laughter, but no triumph, no malignity. It is the face of a man who is always fighting against something, but who fights in the open and is not frightened, the face of a man who is generously angry." As such, Dickens can stand as the type of the nineteenth-century reformist traveler, looking on all he sees with compassion and principle, but alert always to possibilities of moral improvement.

From AMERICAN NOTES
(1842)

WASHINGTON. THE LEGISLATURE.

We left Philadelphia by steamboat, at six o'clock one very cold morning, and turned our faces towards Washington.

In the course of this day's journey, as on subsequent occasions, we encountered some Englishmen (small farmers, perhaps, or country publicans at home) who were settled in America, and were travelling on their own affairs. Of all grades and kinds of men that jostle one in the public conveyances of the States, these are often the most intolerable and the most insufferable companions. United to every disagreeable characteristic that the worst kind of American travellers possess, these countrymen of ours display an amount of insolent conceit and cool assumption of superiority quite monstrous to behold. In the coarse familiarity of their approach, and the effrontery of their inquisitiveness (which they are in great haste to assert, as if they panted to revenge themselves upon the decent old restraints of home), they surpass any native specimens that came within my range of observation: and I often grew so patriotic when I saw and heard them that I would cheerfully have submitted to a reasonable fine if I could have given any other country in the whole world, the honour of claiming them for its children.

As Washington may be called the headquarters of tobacco-tinctured saliva, the time is come when I must confess, without any disguise, that the prevalence of those two odious practices of chewing and expectorating began about this time to be anything but agreeable, and soon became most offensive and sickening. In all the public places of America, this filthy custom is recognised. In the courts of law, the judge has his spittoon, the crier his, the witness his, and the prisoner his; while the jurymen and spectators are provided for, as so many men who in the course of nature must desire to spit incessantly. In the hospitals, the students of medicine are requested, by notices upon the wall, to eject their tobacco juice into the boxes provided for that purpose, and not to discolour the stairs. In public buildings, visitors are implored, through the same agency, to squirt the essence of their quids, or "plugs," as I have heard them called by gentlemen learned in this kind of sweetmeat, into the national spittoons, and not about the bases of the marble columns. But in some parts, this custom is inseparably mixed up with every meal and morning call, and with all the transactions of social life. The stranger who follows in the track I took myself will find it in its full bloom and glory, luxuriant in all its alarming recklessness, at Washington. And let him not persuade himself (as I once did, to my shame) that previous tourists have exaggerated its extent. The thing itself is an exaggeration of nastiness which cannot be outdone.

On board this steamboat, there were two young gentlemen, with shirt-collars reversed as usual, and armed with very big walking-sticks; who planted two seats in the middle of the deck, at a distance of some four paces apart; took out their tobacco-boxes; and sat down opposite each other, to chew. In less than a quarter of an hour's time, these hopeful youths had shed about them on the clean boards a copious shower of yellow rain; clearing, by that means, a kind of magic circle, within whose limits no intruders dared to come, and which they never failed to refresh and re-refresh before a spot was dry. This being before breakfast, rather disposed me, I confess, to nausea; but looking attentively at one of the expectorators, I plainly saw that he was young in chewing, and felt inwardly uneasy, himself. A glow of delight came over me at this discovery; and as I marked his face turn paler and paler, and saw the ball of tobacco in his left cheek quiver with his suppressed agony, while yet he spat, and chewed, and spat again, in emulation of his older friend, I could have fallen on his neck and implored him to go on for hours.

We all sat down to a comfortable breakfast in the cabin below, where there was no more hurry or confusion than at such a meal in England, and where there was certainly greater politeness exhibited than at most of our stage-coach banquets. At about nine o'clock we arrived at the railroad station, and went on by the cars. At noon we turned out again, to cross a wide river in another steamboat; landed at a continuation of the railroad on the opposite shore; and went on by other cars; in which, in the course of the next hour or so, we crossed by wooden bridges, each a mile in length, two creeks, called respectively Great and Little Gunpowder. The water in both was blackened with flights of canvas-backed ducks, which are most delicious eating, and abound hereabouts at that season of the year.

These bridges are of wood, have no parapet, and are only just wide enough for the passage of the trains; which, in the event of the smallest accident, would inevitably be plunged into the river. They are startling contrivances, and are most agreeable when passed.

We stopped to dine at Baltimore, and being now in Maryland, were waited on, for the first time, by slaves. The sensation of exacting any service from human creatures who are bought and sold, and being, for the time, a party as it were to their condition, is not an enviable one. The institution exists, perhaps, in its least repulsive and most mitigated form in such a town as this; but it *is* slavery; and though I was, with respect to it, an innocent man, its presence filled me with a sense of shame and self-reproach.

After dinner, we went down to the railroad again, and took our seats in the cars for Washington. Being rather early, those men and boys who happened to have nothing particular to do, and were curious in foreigners, came (according to custom) round the carriage in which I sat; let down all the windows; thrust in their heads and shoulders; hooked themselves on conveniently, by their elbows; and fell to comparing notes on the subject of my personal appearance, with as much indifference as if I were a stuffed figure. I never gained so much uncompromising information with reference to my own nose and eyes, and various impressions wrought by my mouth and chin on different minds, and how my head looks when it is viewed from behind, as on these occasions. Some gentlemen were only satisfied by exercising their sense of touch; and the boys (who are surprisingly precocious in America) were seldom satisfied, even by that, but would return to the charge over and over again. Many a budding president has walked into my room with his cap on his head and his hands in his pockets, and stared at me for two whole hours: occasionally refreshing himself with a tweak of his nose, or a draught from the water-jug; or by walking to the windows and inviting other boys in the street below, to come up and do likewise: crying, "Here he is!" "Come on!" "Bring all your brothers!" with other hospitable entreaties of that nature.

We reached Washington at about half-past six that evening, and had upon the way a beautiful view of the Capitol, which is a fine building of the Corinthian order, placed upon a noble and commanding eminence. Arrived at the hotel, I saw no more of the place that night, being very tired, and glad to get to bed.

Breakfast over next morning, I walk about the streets for an hour or two, and, coming home, throw up the window in the front and back, and look out. Here is Washington, fresh in my mind and under my eye.

Take the worst parts of the City Road and Pentonville, or the straggling outskirts of Paris, where the houses are smallest, preserving all their oddities, but especially the small shops and dwellings, occupied in Pentonville (but not in Washington) by furniture-brokers, keepers of poor eating-houses, and fanciers of birds. Burn the whole down; build it up again in wood and plaster; widen it a little; throw in part of St. John's Wood; put green blinds outside all the private houses, with a red curtain and a white one in every window; plough up all the roads; plant a great deal of coarse turf in every place where it ought *not* to be; erect three handsome buildings in stone and marble, anywhere, but the more entirely out of everybody's way the better; call one the Post Office, one the Patent Office, and one the Treasury; make it scorching hot in the morning, and freezing cold in the afternoon, with an occasional tornado of wind and dust; leave a brick-field without the bricks in all central places where a street may naturally be expected: and that's Washington.

The hotel in which we live is a long row of small houses fronting on the street, and opening at the back upon a common yard, in which hangs a great triangle. Whenever a servant is wanted, somebody beats on this triangle from one stroke up to seven, according to the number of the house in which his presence is required; and as all the servants are always being wanted, and none of them ever come, this enlivening engine is in full performance the whole day through. Clothes are drying in the same yard; female slaves, with cotton handkerchiefs twisted round their heads, are running to and from on the hotel business; black waiters cross and recross with dishes in their hands; two great dogs are playing upon a mound of loose bricks in the centre of the little square; a pig is turning up his stomach to the sun, and grunting "that's comfortable!"; and neither the men, nor the women, nor the dogs, nor the pig, nor any created creature, takes the smallest notice of the triangle, which is tingling madly all the time.

I walk to the front window, and look across the road upon a long, straggling row of houses, one story high, terminating, nearly opposite, but a little to the left, in a melancholy piece of waste ground with frowzy grass, which looks like a small piece of country that has taken to drinking, and has quite lost itself. Standing anyhow and all wrong, upon this open space, like something meteoric that has fallen down from the moon, is an odd, lop-sided, one-eyed kind of wooden building, that looks like a church, with a flag-staff as long as itself sticking out of a steeple something larger than a tea-chest. Under the window is a small stand of coaches, whose slave-drivers are sunning themselves on the steps of our door and talking idly together. The three most obtrusive houses near at hand are the three meanest. On one—a shop, which never has anything in the window, and never has the door open—is painted in large characters, "THE CITY LUNCH." At another, which looks like a backway to somewhere else, but is an independent building in itself, oysters are procurable in every style. At the third, which is a very, very little tailor's shop, pants are fixed to order; or in other words, pantaloons are made to measure. And that is our street in Washington.

It is sometimes called the City of Magnificent Distances, but it might with greater propriety be termed the City of Magnificent Intentions; for it is only on taking a bird's-eye view of it from the top of the Capitol that one can at all comprehend the vast designs of its projector, an aspiring Frenchman. Spacious avenues, that begin in nothing, and lead nowhere; streets, mile-long, that only want houses, roads, and inhabitants; public buildings that need but a public to be complete; and ornaments of great thoroughfares, which only lack great thoroughfares to ornament—are its leading features. One might fancy the season over, and most of the houses gone out of town for ever with their masters. To the admirers of cities it is a Barmecide Feast; a pleasant field for the imagination to rove in; a monument raised to a deceased project, with not even a legible inscription to record its departed greatness.

Such as it is, it is likely to remain. It was originally chosen for the seat of Government, as a means of averting the conflicting jealousies and interests of the different States; and very probably, too, as being remote from mobs: a consideration not to be slighted, even in America. It has no trade or commerce of its own, having little or no population beyond the President and his establishment; the members of the legislature who reside there during the session; the Government clerks and officers employed in the various departments; the keepers of the hotels and boarding-houses; and the tradesmen who supply their tables. It is very unhealthy. Few people would live in Washington, I take it, who were not obliged to reside there; and the tides of emigration and speculation, those rapid and regardless currents, are little likely to flow at any time towards such dull and sluggish water.

The principal features of the Capitol, are, of course, the two houses of Assembly. But there is, besides, in the centre of the building, a fine rotunda, ninety-six feet in diameter, and ninety-six high, whose circular wall is divided into compartments, ornamented by historical pictures. Four of these have for their subjects prominent events in the revolutionary struggle. They were painted by Colonel Trumbull, himself a member of Washington's staff at the time of their occurrence; from which circumstance they derive a peculiar interest of their own. In this same hall Mr. Greenough's large statue of Washington has been lately placed. It has great merits of course, but it struck me as being rather strained and violent for its subject. I could wish, however, to have seen it in a better light than it can ever be viewed in, where it stands.

There is a very pleasant and commodious library in the Capitol; and from a balcony in front, the bird's-eye view, of which I have just spoken, may be had, together with a beautiful prospect of the adjacent country. In one of the ornamented portions of the building, there is a figure of Justice; whereunto the Guide Book says, "the artist at first contemplated giving more of nudity, but he was warned that the public sentiment in this country would not admit of it, and in his caution he has gone, perhaps, into the opposite extreme." Poor Justice! she has been made to wear much stranger garments in America than those she pines in, in the Capitol. Let us hope that she has changed her dress-maker since they were fashioned, and that the public sentiment of the country did not cut out the clothes she hides her lovely figure in, just now.

The House of Representatives is a beautiful and spacious hall, of semicircular shape, supported by handsome pillars. One part of the gallery is appropriated to the ladies, and there they sit in front rows, and come in, and go out, as at a play or concert. The chair is canopied, and raised considerably above the floor of the House; and every member has an easy chair and a writing desk to himself: which is denounced by some people out of doors as a most unfortunate and injudicious arrangement, tending to long sittings and prosaic speeches. It is an elegant chamber to look at, but a singularly bad one for all purposes of hearing. The Senate, which is smaller, is free from this objection, and is exceedingly well adapted to the uses for which it is designed. The sittings, I need hardly add, take place in the day; and the parliamentary forms are modelled on those of the old country.

I was sometimes asked, in my progress through other places, whether I had not been very much impressed by the *heads* of the law-makers at Washington; meaning not their chiefs and leaders, but literally their individual and personal heads, whereon their hair grew, and whereby the phrenological character of each legislator was expressed: and I almost as often struck my questioner dumb with indignant consternation by answering 'No, that I didn't remember being at all overcome.' As I must, at whatever hazard, repeat the avowal here, I will follow it up by relating my impressions on this subject in as few words as possible.

In the first place—it may be from some imperfect development of my organ of veneration—I do not remember having ever fainted away, or having been moved to tears of joyful pride, at sight of any legislative body. I have borne the House of Commons like a man, and have yielded to no weakness but slumber in the House of Lords. I have seen elections for borough and county, and have never been impelled (no matter which party won) to damage my hat by throwing it up into the air in triumph, or to crack my voice by shouting forth any reference to our Glorious Constitution, to the noble purity of our independent voters, or the unimpeachable integrity of our independent members. Having withstood such strong attacks upon my fortitude, it is possible that I may be of a cold and insensible temperament, amounting to iciness, in such matters; and therefore my impressions of the live pillars of the Capitol at Washington must be received with such grains of allowance as this free confession may seem to demand.

Did I see in this public body an assemblage of men, bound together in the sacred names of Liberty and Freedom, and so asserting the chaste dignity of those twin goddesses, in all their discussions, as to exalt at once the Eternal Principles to which their names are given, and their own character and the character of their countrymen, in the admiring eyes of the whole world?

It was but a week, since an aged, grey-haired man, a lasting honour to the land that gave him birth, who has done good service to his country, as his forefathers did, and who will be remembered scores upon scores of years, after the worms bred in its corruption are but so many grains of dust—it was but a week, since this old man had stood for days upon his trial before this very body, charged with having dared to assert the infamy of that traffic, which has for its accursed merchandise men and women, and their unborn children. Yes. And publicly exhibited in the same city all the while; gilded, framed and glazed; hung up for general admiration; shown to strangers not with shame, but pride; its face not turned towards the wall, itself not taken down and burned; is the Unanimous Declaration of the Thirteen United States of America which solemnly declares that All Men are created Equal; and are endowed by their Creator with the Inalienable Rights of Life, Liberty, and the Pursuit of Happiness!

It was not a month since this same body had sat calmly by, and heard a man, one of themselves, with oaths which beggars in their drink reject, threaten to cut another's throat from ear to ear. There he sat, among them; not crushed by the general feeling of the assembly, but as good a man as any.

There was but a week to come, and another of that body, for doing his duty to those who sent him there; for claiming in a Republic the Liberty and Freedom of expressing their sentiments, and making known their prayer; would be tried, found guilty, and have strong censure passed upon him by the rest. His was a grave offence indeed; for years before, he had risen up and said, 'A gang of male and female slaves for sale, warranted to breed like cattle, linked to each other by iron fetters, are passing now along the open street beneath the windows of your Temple of Equality! Look!' But there are many kinds of hunters engaged in the Pursuit of Happiness, and they go variously armed. It is the Inalienable Right of some among them to take the field after *their* Happiness equipped with cat and cart-whip, stocks, and iron collar, and to shout their view halloa! (always in praise of Liberty) to the music of clanking chains and bloody stripes.

Where sat the many legislators of coarse threats; of words and blows such as coalheavers deal upon each other, when they forget their breeding? On every side. Every session had its anecdotes of that kind, and the actors were all there.

Did I recognise in this assembly, a body of men, who, applying themselves in a new world to correct some of the falsehoods and vices of the old, purified the avenues to Public Life, paved the dirty ways to Place and Power, debated and made laws for the Common Good, and had no party but their Country?

I saw in them the wheels that move the meanest perversion of virtuous Political Machinery that the worst tools ever wrought. Despicable trickery at elections; under-handed tamperings with public officers; cowardly attacks upon opponents, with scurrilous newspapers for shields, and hired pens for daggers; shameful trucklings to mercenary knaves, whose claim to be considered, is, that every day and week they sow new crops of ruin with their venal types, which are the dragon's teeth of yore, in everything but sharpness; aidings and abettings of every bad inclination in the popular mind, and artful suppressions of all its good influences: such things as these, and in a word, Dishonest Faction in its most depraved and most unblushing form, stared out from every corner of the crowded hall.

Did I see among them the intelligence and refinement, the true, honest, patriotic heart of America? Here and there were drops of its blood and life, but they scarcely coloured the stream of desperate adventurers which sets that way for profit and for pay. It is the game of these men, and of their profligate organs, to make the strife of politics so fierce and brutal, and so destructive of all self-respect in worthy men, that sensitive and delicate-minded persons shall be kept aloof, and they, and such as they, be left to battle out their selfish views unchecked. And thus this lowest of all scrambling fights goes on, and they who in other countries would, from their intelligence and station, most aspire to make the laws, do here recoil the farthest from that degradation.

That there are, among the representatives of the people in both Houses, and among all parties, some men of high character and great abilities, I need not say. The foremost among those politicians who are known in Europe have been already described, and I see no reason to depart from the rule I have laid down for my guidance, of abstaining from all mention of individuals. It will be sufficient to add, that to the most favourable accounts that have been written of them, I more than fully and most heartily subscribe; and that personal intercourse and free communication have bred within me, not the result predicted in the very doubtful proverb, but increased admiration and respect. They are striking men to look at, hard to deceive, prompt to act, lions in energy,

Crichtons in varied accomplishments, Indians in fire of eye and gesture, Americans in strong and generous impulse; and they as well represent the honour and wisdom of their country at home, as the distinguished gentleman who is now its minister at the British Court sustains its highest character abroad.

I visited both houses nearly every day during my stay in Washington. On my initiatory visit to the House of Representatives, they divided against a decision of the chair; but the chair won. The second time I went, the member who was speaking, being interrupted by a laugh, mimicked it, as one child would in quarrelling with another, and added, "that he would make honourable gentlemen opposite, sing out a little more on the other side of their mouths presently." But interruptions are rare. the speaker being usually heard in silence. There are more quarrels than with us, and more threatenings than gentlemen are accustomed to exchange in any civilised society of which we have record: but farm-yard imitations have not as yet been imported from the Parliament of the United Kingdom. The feature in oratory which appears to be the most practised, and most relished, is the constant repetition of the same idea or shadow of an idea in fresh words; and the inquiry out of doors is not, "What did he say?" but, "How long did he speak?" These, however, are but enlargements of a principle which prevails elsewhere.

The Senate is a dignified and decorous body, and its proceedings are conducted with much gravity and order. Both houses are handsomely carpeted; but the state to which these carpets are reduced by the universal disregard of the spittoon with which every honourable member is accommodated, and the extraordinary improvements on the pattern which are squirted and dabbled upon it in every direction, do not admit of being described. I will merely observe that I strongly recommend all strangers not to look at the floor; and if they happen to drop anything, though it be their purse, not to pick it up with an ungloved hand on any account.

It is somewhat remarkable, too, at first, to say the least, to see so many honourable members with swelled faces; and it is scarcely less remarkable to discover that this appearance is caused by the quantity of tobacco they contrive to stow within the hollow of the cheek. It is strange enough too, to see an honourable gentleman leaning back in his tilted chair with his legs on the desk before him, shaping a convenient 'plug' with his penknife, and when it is quite ready for use, shooting the old one from his mouth, as from a pop-gun, and clapping the new one in its place.

I was surprised to observe that even steady old chewers of great experience are not always good marksmen, which has rather inclined me to doubt that general proficiency with the rifle, of which we have heard so much in England. Several gentlemen called upon me who, in the course of conversation, frequently missed the spittoon at five paces; and one (but he was certainly short-sighted) mistook the closed sash for the open window, at three. On another occasion, when I dined out, and was sitting with two ladies and some gentlemen round a fire before dinner, one of the company fell short of the fireplace, six distinct times. I am disposed to think, however, that this was occasioned by his not aiming at that object; as there was a white marble hearth before the fender, which was more convenient, and may have suited his purpose better.

The Patent Office at Washington furnishes an extraordinary example of American enterprise and ingenuity; for the immense number of models it contains are the accumulated inventions of only five years. the whole of the previous collection having been destroyed by fire. The elegant structure in which they are arranged is one of design rather than execution, for there is but one side erected out of four, though the works are stopped. The Post Office is a very compact and very beautiful building. In one of the departments, among a collection of rare and curious articles, are deposited the presents which have been made from time to time to the American ambassadors at foreign courts by the various potentates to whom they were the accredited agents of the Republic; gifts which by the law they are not permitted to retain. I confess that I looked upon this as a very painful exhibition, and one by no means flattering to the national standard of honesty and honour. That can scarcely be a high state of moral feeling which imagines a gentleman of repute and station likely to be corrupted, in the discharge of his duty, by the present of a snuff-box, or a richly-mounted sword, or an Eastern shawl; and surely the Nation who reposes confidence in her appointed servants is likely to be better served, than she who makes them the subject of such very mean and paltry suspicions.

From PICTURES FROM ITALY
(1846)

GOING THROUGH FRANCE

On a fine Sunday morning in the Midsummer time and weather of eighteen hundred and forty-four, it was, my good friend, when—don't be alarmed; not when two travellers might have been observed slowly making their way over that picturesque and broken ground by which the first chapter of a Middle Aged novel is usually attained—but when an English travelling-carriage of considerable proportions, fresh from the shady halls of the Pantechnicon near Belgrave Square, London, was observed (by a very small French soldier; for I saw him look at it) to issue from the gate of the Hôtel Meurice in the Rue Rivoli at Paris.

I am no more bound to explain why the English family travelling by this carriage, inside and out, should be starting for Italy on a Sunday morning, of all good days in the week, than I am to assign a reason for all the little men in France being soldiers, and all the big men postilions; which is the invariable rule. But, they had some sort of reason for what they did, I have no doubt; and their reason for being there at all, was, as you know, that they were going to live in fair Genoa for a year; and that the head of the family purposed, in that space of time, to stroll about, wherever his restless humour carried him.

And it would have been small comfort to me to have explained to the population of Paris generally, that I was that Head and Chief; and not the radiant embodiment of good humour who sat beside me in the person of a French Courier—best of servants and most beaming of men! Truth to say, he looked a great deal more patriarchal than I, who, in the shadow of his portly presence, dwindled down to no account at all. There was, of course, very little in the aspect of Paris—as we rattled near the dismal Morgue and over the Pont Neuf—to reproach us for Sunday travelling. The wine-shops (every second house) were driving a roaring trade; awnings were spreading, and chairs and tables arranging, outside the cafés, preparatory to the eating of ices, and drinking of cool liquids, later in the day; shoe-blacks were busy on the bridges; shops were open; carts and wagons clattered to and fro; the narrow, up-hill, funnel-like streets across the River were so many dense perspectives of crowd and bustle, parti-coloured nightcaps, tobacco-pipes, blouses, large boots, and shaggy heads of hair; nothing at that hour denoted a day of rest, unless it were the appearance, here and there, of a family pleasure party, crammed into a bulky old lumbering cab; or of some contemplative holiday-maker in the freest and easiest dishabille, leaning out of a low garret window, watching the drying of his newly polished shoes on the little parapet outside (if a gentleman), or the airing of her stockings in the sun (if a lady), with calm anticipation.

Once clear of the never-to-be-forgotten-or-forgiven pavement which surrounds Paris, the first three days of travelling towards Marseilles are quiet and monotonous enough. To Sens. To Avallon. To Chalons. A sketch of one day's proceedings is a sketch of all three; and here it is.

We have four horses, and one postilion, who has a very long whip, and drives his team, something like the Courier of Saint Petersburg in the circle at Astley's or Franconi's: only he sits his own horse instead of standing on him. The immense jack-boots worn by these postilions are sometimes a century or two old; and are so ludicrously disproportionate to the wearer's foot that the spur, which is put where his own heel comes, is generally half way up the leg of the boots. The man often comes out of the stableyard, with his whip in his hand and his shoes on, and brings out, in both hands, one boot at a time, which he plants on the ground by the side of his horse, with great gravity, until everything is ready. When it is—and oh Heaven! the noise they make about it!—he gets into the boots, shoes and all, or is hoisted into them by a couple of friends; adjusts the rope harness, embossed by the labours of innumerable pigeons in the stables; makes all the horses kick and plunge; cracks his whip like a madman; shouts 'En route—Hi!' and away we go. He is sure to have a contest with his horse before we have gone very far; and then he calls him a Thief, and a Brigand, and a Pig, and what not; and beats him about the head as if he were made of wood.

There is little more than one variety in the appearance of the country, for the first two days. From a dreary plain, to an interminable avenue, and from an interminable avenue to a dreary plain again. Plenty of vines there are in the open fields, but of a short low kind, and not trained in festoons, but about straight sticks. Beggars innumerable there are, everywhere; but an extraordinarily scanty population, and fewer children than I ever encountered. I don't believe we saw a hundred children between Paris and Chalons. Queer old towns, draw-bridged and walled: with odd little towers at the angles, like grotesque faces, as if the wall had put a mask on, and were staring down into the moat; other strange little towers, in gardens and fields, and down lanes, and in farmyards: all alone, and always round, with a peaked roof, and never used for any purpose at all; ruinous buildings of all sorts; sometimes an hôtel de ville, sometimes a guard-house, sometimes a dwelling-house, sometimes a château with a rank garden, prolific in dandelion, and watched over by extinguisher-topped turrets, and blink-eyed little casements are the standard objects, repeated over and over again. Sometimes we pass a village inn, with a crumbling wall belonging to it, and a perfect town of out-houses; and painted over the gateway, "Stabling for Sixty Horses," as indeed there might be stabling for sixty score, were there any horses to be stabled there, or anybody resting there, or anything stirring about the place but a dangling bush, indicative of the wine inside: which flutters idly in the wind, in lazy keeping with everything else, and certainly is never in a green old age, though always so old as to be dropping to pieces. And all day long, strange little narrow wagons, in strings of six or eight, bringing cheese from Switzerland, and frequently in charge, the whole line, of one man, or even boy—and he very often asleep in the foremost cart—come jingling past: the horses drowsily ringing the bells upon their harness, and looking as if they thought (no doubt they do) their great blue woolly furniture, of immense weight and thickness, with a pair of grotesque horns growing out of the collar, very much too warm for the Midsummer weather.

Then, there is the Diligence, twice or thrice a day; with the dusty outsides in blue frocks, like butchers; and the insides in white night-caps: and its cabriolet head on the roof, nodding and shaking, like an idiot's head; and its Young-France passengers staring out of window, with beards down to their waists, and blue spectacles awfully shading their warlike eyes, and very big sticks clenched in their National grasp. Also the Malle Poste, with only a couple of passengers, tearing along at a real good dare-devil pace, and out of sight in no time. Steady old Curés come jolting past, now and then, in such ramshackle, rusty, musty, clattering coaches as no Englishman would believe in; and bony women dawdle about in solitary places, holding cows by ropes while they feed, or digging and hoeing or doing field-work of a more laborious kind, or representing real shepherdesses with their flocks—to obtain an adequate idea of which pursuit and its followers, in any country, it is only necessary to take any pastoral poem, or picture, and imagine to yourself whatever is most exquisitely and widely unlike the descriptions therein contained.

You have been travelling along, stupidly enough, as you generally do in the last stage of the day; and the ninety-six bells upon the horses—twenty-four apiece—have been ringing sleepily in your ears for half an hour or so; and it has become a very jog-trot, monotonous, tiresome sort of business; and you have been thinking deeply about the dinner you will have at the next stage; when, down at the end of the long avenue of trees through which you are travelling, the first indication of a town appears, in the shape of some straggling cottages: and the carriage begins to rattle and roll over a horribly uneven pavement. As if the equipage were a great firework, and the mere sight of a smoking cottage chimney had lighted it, instantly it begins to crack and splutter, as if the very devil were in it. Crack, crack, crack, crack. Crack-crack-crack. Crick-crack. Crick-crack. Helo! Hola! Vite! Voleur! Brigand! Hi hi hi! En r-r-r-r-route! Whip, wheels, driver, stones, beggars, children, crack, crack, crack; helo! hola! charité pour l'amour de Dieu! crick-crack-crick-crack; crick, crick, crick; bump, jolt, crack, bump, crick-crack; round the corner, up the narrow street, down the paved hill on the other side; in the gutter; bump, bump; jolt, jog, crick, crick, crick; crack, crack, crack; into the shop-windows on the left-hand side of the street, preliminary to a sweeping turn into the wooden archway on the right; rumble, rumble, rumble;

clatter, clatter, clatter; crick, crick, crick; and here we are in the yard of the Hôtel de l'Ecu d'Or, used up, gone out, smoking, spent, exhausted; but sometimes making a false start unexpectedly, with nothing coming of it—like a firework to the last!

The landlady of the Hôtel de l'Ecu d'Or is here; and the landlord of the Hôtel de l'Ecu d'Or is here; and the femme de chambre of the Hôtel de l'Ecu d'Or is here; and a gentleman in a glazed cap, with a red beard like a bosom friend, who is staying at the Hôtel de l'Ecu d'Or, is here; and Monsieur le Curé is walking up and down in a corner of the yard by himself, with a shovel hat upon his head, and a black gown on his back, and a book in one hand, and an umbrella in the other; and everybody, except Monsieur le Curé, is open-mouthed and open-eyed, for the opening of the carriage-door. The landlord of the Hôtel de l'Ecu d'Or dotes to that extent upon the Courier that he can hardly wait for his coming down from the box, but embraces his very legs and boot-heels as he descends. "My Courier! My brave Courier! My friend! My brother!" The landlady loves him, the femme de chambre blesses him, the garçon worships him. The Courier asks if his letter has been received? It has, it has. Are the rooms prepared? They are, they are. The best rooms for my noble Courier. The rooms of state for my gallant Courier; the whole house is at the service of my best of friends! He keeps his hand upon the carriage-door, and asks some other question to enhance the expectation. He carries a green leathern purse outside his coat, suspended by a belt. The idlers look at it; one touches it. It is full of five-franc pieces. Murmurs of admiration are heard among the boys. The landlord falls upon the Courier's neck, and folds him to his breast. He is so much fatter than he was, he says! He looks so rosy and so well!

The door is opened. Breathless expectation. The lady of the family gets out. Ah sweet lady! Beautiful lady! The sister of the lady of the family gets out. Great Heaven, Ma'amselle is charming! First little boy gets out. Ah, what a beautiful little boy! First little girl gets out. Oh, but this is an enchanting child! Second little girl gets out. The landlady, yielding to the finest impulse of our common nature, catches her up in her arms! Second little boy gets out. Oh, the sweet boy! Oh, the tender little family! The baby is handed out. Angelic baby! The baby has topped everything. All the rapture is expended on the baby! Then the two nurses tumble out; and the enthusiasm swelling into madness, the whole family are swept upstairs as on a cloud; while the idlers press about the carriage, and look into it, and walk round it, and touch it. For it is something to touch a carriage that has held so many people. It is a legacy to leave one's children.

The rooms are on the first floor, except the nursery for the night, which is a great rambling chamber, with four or five beds in it: through a dark passage, up two steps, down four, past a pump, across a balcony, and next door to the stable. The other sleeping apartments are large and lofty; each with two small bedsteads, tastefully hung, like the windows, with red and white drapery. The sitting-room is famous. Dinner is already laid in it for three; and the napkins are folded in cocked-hat fashion. The floors are of red tile. There are no carpets, and not much furniture to speak of; but there is abundance of looking-glass, and there are large vases under glass shades, filled with artificial flowers; and there are plenty of clocks. The whole party are in motion. The brave Courier, in particular, is everywhere: looking after the beds, having wine poured down his throat by his dear brother the landlord, and picking up green cucumbers—always cucumbers; Heaven knows where he gets them— with which he walks about, one in each hand, like truncheons.

Dinner is announced. There is very thin soup; there are very large loaves—one apiece; a fish; four dishes afterwards; some poultry afterwards; a dessert afterwards; and no lack of wine. There is not much in the dishes; but they are very good, and always ready instantly. When it is nearly dark, the brave Courier, having eaten the two cucumbers, sliced up in the contents of a pretty large decanter of oil, and another of vinegar, emerges from his retreat below, and proposes a visit to the Cathedral, whose massive tower frowns down upon the courtyard of the inn. Off we go; and very solemn and grand it is, in the dim light: so dim at last, that the polite, old, lanthorn-jawed Sacristan has a feeble little bit of candle in his hand, to grope among the tombs with—and looks among the grim columns, very like a ghost who is searching for his own.

Underneath the balcony, when we return, the inferior servants of the inn are supping in the open air, at a great table; the dish, a stew of meat and vegetables, smoking hot, and served in the iron caldron it was boiled in. They have a pitcher of thin wine, and are very merry; merrier than the gentleman with the red beard, who is playing billiards in the light room on the left of the yard, where shadows, with cues in their hands, and cigars in their mouths, cross and recross the window constantly. Still the thin Curé walks up and down alone, with his book and umbrella. And there he walks, and there the billiard-balls rattle, long after we are fast asleep.

We are astir at six next morning. It is a delightful day, shaming yesterday's mud upon the carriage, if anything could shame a carriage, in a land where carriages are never cleaned. Everybody is brisk; and as we finish breakfast, the horses come jingling into the yard from the Post-house. Everything taken out of the carriage is put back again. The brave Courier announces that all is ready, after walking into every room, and looking all round it, to be certain that nothing is left behind. Everybody gets in. Everybody connected with the Hôtel de l'Ecu d'Or is again enchanted. The brave Courier runs into the house for a parcel containing cold fowl, sliced ham, bread and biscuits, for lunch; hands it into the coach; and runs back again.

What has he got in his hand now? More cucumbers? No. A long strip of paper. It's the bill.

The brave Courier has two belts on, this morning: one supporting the purse: another, a mighty good sort of leathern bottle, filled to the throat with the best light Bordeaux wine in the house. He never pays the bill till this bottle is full. Then he disputes it.

He disputes it now, violently. He is still the landlord's brother, but by another father or mother. He is not so nearly related to him as he was last night. The landlord scratches his head. The brave Courier points to certain figures in the bill, and intimates that if they remain there, the Hôtel de l'Ecu d'Or is thenceforth and for ever an hôtel de l'Ecu de cuivre. The landlord goes into a little counting-house. The brave Courier follows, forces the bill and a pen into his hand, and talks more rapidly than ever. The landlord takes the pen. The Courier smiles. The landlord makes an alteration. The Courier cuts a joke. The landlord is affectionate, but not weakly so. He bears it like a man. He shakes hands with his brave brother, but he don't hug him. Still, he loves his brother; for he knows that he will be returning that way, one of these fine days, with another family, and he foresees that his heart will yearn towards him again. The brave Courier traverses all round the carriage once, looks at the drag, inspects the wheels, jumps up, gives the word, and away we go!

ALFRED, LORD TENNYSON
1809–1892

Intensely British and un-Continental, as a young man Tennyson did travel on the Continent with his friend Arthur Henry Hallam, whose death in 1833 occasioned Tennyson's famous long poem In Memoriam. *"Ulysses," written the same year but not published until nine years later, likewise can be thought to register Tennyson's need to go on undaunted despite his sorrow. But it can also be taken to reflect the intense wanderlust of the Victorians in general, who like Ulysses, found (encouraged by Thomas Cook, railways, and convenient shipping schedules) that they could not rest from travel. Or at least tourism.*

Ulysses
(1842)

It little profits that, an idle king,
By this still hearth, among these barren crags,
Matched with an agèd wife, I mete and dole
Unequal laws unto a savage race,
That hoard, and sleep, and feed, and know not me.

I cannot rest from travel: I will drink
Life to the lees: all times I have enjoyed
Greatly, have suffered greatly, both with those
That loved me, and alone; on shore, and when
Through scudding drifts the rainy Hyades
Vext the dim sea: I am become a name;
For always roaming with a hungry heart
Much have I seen and known; cities of men
And manners, climates, councils,
Myself not least, but honoured of them all;
And drunk delight of battle with my peers,
Far on the ringing plains of windy Troy.

I am a part of all that I have met;
Yet all experience is an arch wherethrough
Gleams that untravelled world, whose margin fades
For ever and for ever when I move.
How dull it is to pause, to make an end,
To rust unburnished, not to shine in use!
As though to breathe were life. Life piled on life
Were all too little, and of one to me
Little remains: but every hour is saved
From that eternal silence, something more,
A bringer of new things; and vile it were

For some three suns to store and hoard myself,
And this gray spirit yearning in desire
To follow knowledge like a sinking star,
Beyond the utmost bound of human thought.

This is my son, mine own Telemachus,
To whom I leave the sceptre and the isle—
Well-loved of me, discerning to fulfil
This labour, by slow prudence to make mild
A rugged people, and through soft degrees
Subdue them to the useful and the good.
Most blameless is he, centred in the sphere
Of common duties, decent not to fail
In offices of tenderness, and pay
Meet adoration to my household gods,
When I am gone. He works his work, I mine.

There lies the port; the vessel puffs her sail:
There gloom the dark broad seas. My mariners,
Souls that have toiled, and wrought, and thought with me—
That ever with a frolic welcome took
The thunder and the sunshine, and opposed
Free hearts, free foreheads—you and I are old;
Old age hath yet his honour and his toil;
Death closes all: but something ere the end,
Some work of noble note, may yet be done,
Not unbecoming men that strove with Gods.

The lights begin to twinkle from the rocks:
The long day wanes: the slow moon climbs: the deep
Moans round with many voices. Come, my friends,
'Tis not too late to seek a newer world.
Push off, and sitting well in order smite
The sounding furrows; for my purpose holds
To sail beyond the sunset, and the baths
Of all the western stars, until I die.
It may be that the gulfs will wash us down:
It may be we shall touch the Happy Isles,
And see the great Achilles, whom we knew.
Though much is taken, much abides; and though
We are not now that strength which in old days
Moved earth and heaven; that which we are, we are;

One equal temper of heroic hearts,
Made weak by time and fate, but strong in will
To strive, to seek, to find, and not to yield.

ALEXANDER KINGLAKE
1809–1891

This merriest of travelers came from an upper-middle-class family in Taunton, in the west of England, and studied at Eton and Trinity College, Cambridge, where his immersion in the Greek and Roman classics persuaded him to adopt a skeptical, "pagan" attitude towards contemporary society, far gone, it seemed, in Evangelicism and solemnity. He moved to London to study law, but before entering the profession he decided, in the fall of 1834, to amuse himself with a fifteen-month tour of the Near East. That area in his day was managed largely by the Ottoman Empire, and it promised what he wanted to experience—oddity. In this bemused plunge into Islam he was attended by his faithful interpreter Mysseri.

Ten years after his travels—he was now thirty-five years old—he published (anonymously) his wonderfully self-indulgent account of his experiences, which he titled Eothen—*the Greek word means "from the East." The "you" he addresses at home is his Eton friend Eliot Warburton, who was thought to be planning a similar trip and who wanted some hints about how to do it. In* Eothen, *as Jan Morris has said, Kinglake produced "one of the most original, graceful, and creative of all travel books, which has cast a sort of spell over the genre from that day to this." Deriving its eccentric, personal view ultimately from Sterne's* Sentimental Journey, *the book has helped transmit that tone to our own time, where, as Morris observes, it can be noticed in the funny, iconoclastic performances of Robert Byron and Paul Theroux.*

From Eothen: Or, Traces of Travel Brought Home from the East

(1844)

PREFACE

* * *

It is right to forewarn people . . . that [this] book is quite superficial in its character. I have endeavoured to discard from it all valuable matter derived from the works of others, and it appears to me that my efforts in this direction have been attended with great success; I believe I may truly acknowledge that from all details of geographical discovery or antiquarian research—from all display of "sound learning and religious knowledge"—from all historical and scientific illustrations—from all useful statistics—from all political disquisitions—and from all good moral reflections, the volume is thoroughly free.

CAIRO AND THE PLAGUE[1]

Cairo and Plague! During the whole time of my stay the Plague was so master of the city, and stared so plain in every street and every alley, that I can't now affect to dissociate the two ideas.

When, coming from the Desert, I rode through a village lying near to the city on the eastern side, there approached me with busy face and earnest gestures a personage in the Turkish dress; his long flowing beard gave him rather a majestic look, but his briskness of manner and his

---

[1]There is some semblance of bravado in my manner of talking about the Plague. I have been more careful to describe the terrors of other people than my own. The truth is, that during the whole period of my stay at Cairo I remained thoroughly impressed with a sense of my danger. I may almost say that I lived under perpetual apprehension, for even in sleep, as I fancy, there remained with me some faint notion of the peril with which I was encompassed. But Fear does not necessarily damp the spirits; on the contrary, it will often operate as an excitement giving rise to unusual animation; and thus it affected me. If I had not been surrounded at this time by new faces, new scenes, and new sounds, the effect produced upon my mind by one unceasing cause of alarm may have been very different. As it was, the eagerness with which I pursued my rambles among the wonders of Egypt was sharpened and increased by the sting of the fear of death. Thus my account of the matter plainly conveys an impression that I remained at Cairo without losing my cheerfulness and buoyancy of spirits. And this is the truth, but it is also true, as I have freely confessed, that my sense of danger during the whole period was lively and continuous.

visible anxiety to accost me seemed strange in an Oriental. The man in fact was French or of French origin, and his object was to warn me of the Plague, and prevent me from entering the city.

Arrêtez-vous, Monsieur, je vous en prie—arrêtez-vous; il ne faut pas entrer dans la ville; la Peste y règne partout.

Oui, je sais, mais——

Mais, Monsieur, je dis la Peste—la Peste; c'est de LA PESTE qu'il est question.

Oui, je sais, mais—

Mais, Monsieur, je dis encore LA PESTE—LA PESTE. Je vous conjure de ne pas entrer dans la ville—vous seriez dans une ville empestée.

Oui, je sais, mais—

Mais, Monsieur, je dois donc vous avertir tout bonnement que is vous entrez dans la ville, vous serez—enfin vous serez COMPROMIS!

Oui, je sais, mais——

["Stop, Sir, I beg you—stop; you must not enter the city; the plague is raging everywhere."

"Yes, I know, but—"

"But Sir, the plague I say—the plague. The problem is *The Plague.*"

"Yes, I know, but—"

"But Sir, I repeat, The Plague, The Plague. I beg you not to enter the city—you would be in an infected city."

"Yes, I know, but—"

"But Sir, I am informing you plainly that if you enter the city you will be endangered!"

"Yes, I know, but—"]

The Frenchman was at last convinced that it was vain to reason with a mere Englishman who could not understand what it was to be 'compromised'. I thanked him most sincerely for his kindly meant warning. In hot countries it is very unusual indeed for a man to go out in the glare of the sun and give free advice to a stranger.

When I arrived at Cairo I summoned Osman Effendi, who was, as I knew, the owner of several houses, and would be able to provide me with apartments; he had no difficulty in doing this, for there was not one European traveller in Cairo besides myself. Poor Osman! he met me with a sorrowful countenance, for the fear of the Plague sat heavily on his soul; he seemed as if he felt that he was doing wrong in lending me a resting-place, and he betrayed such a listlessness about temporal matters as one might look for in a man who believed that his days were numbered. He caught me, too, soon after my arrival, coming out from the public baths, and from that time forward he was sadly afraid of me, for upon the subject of contagion he held European opinions.

Osman's history is a curious one. He was a Scotchman born, and when very young, being then a drummer-boy, he landed in Egypt with Fraser's force. He was taken prisoner, and according to Mahometan custom, the alternative of Death or the Koran was offered to him; he did not choose Death, and therefore went through the ceremonies necessary for turning him into a good Mahometan. But what amused me most in his history was this—that very soon after having embraced Islam, he was obliged in practice to become curious and discriminating in his new faith—to make war upon Mahometan dissenters, and follow the orthodox standard of the Prophet in fierce campaigns against the Wahabees, the Unitarians of the Mussulman world. The Wahabees were crushed, and Osman, returning home in triumph from his holy wars, began to flourish in the world; he acquired property, and became effendi, or gentleman. At the time of my visit to Cairo he seemed to be much respected by his brother Mahometans, and gave pledge of his sincere alienation from Christianity by keeping a couple of wives. He affected the same sort of reserve in mentioning them as is generally shown by Orientals. He invited me, indeed, to see his Hareem, but he made both his wives bundle out before I was admitted; he felt, as it seemed to me, that neither of them would bear criticism, and I think that this idea, rather than any motive of sincere jealousy, induced him to keep them out of sight. The rooms of the hareem reminded me of an English nursery, rather than of a Mahometan paradise. One is apt to judge of a woman before one sees her by the air of elegance or coarseness with which she surrounds her home: I judged Osman's wives by this test, and condemned them both. But the strangest feature in Osman's character was his inextinguishable nationality. In vain they had brought him over the seas in early boyhood—in vain had he suffered captivity, conversion, circumcision—in vain they had passed him through fire in their Arabian campaigns—they could not cut away or burn out poor Osman's inborn love of all that was Scotch; in vain men called him Effendi—in vain he swept along in eastern robes—in vain the rival wives adorned his hareem; the joy of his heart still plainly lay in this, that he had three shelves of books, and that the books were thoroughbred Scotch—the Edinburgh this, the Edinburgh that, and above all, I recollect he prided himself upon the "Edinburgh Cabinet Library."

The fear of the Plague is its forerunner. It is likely enough that at the time of my seeing poor Osman the deadly taint was beginning to creep through his veins, but it was not till after I had left Cairo that he was visibly stricken. He died.

As soon as I had seen all that interested me in Cairo and its neighbourhood, I wished to make my escape from a city that lay under the terrible curse of the Plague, but Mysseri fell ill in consequence, I believe, of the hardships which he had been suffering in my service; after a while he recovered sufficiently to undertake a journey, but then there was some difficulty in procuring beasts of burden, and it was not till the nineteenth day of my sojourn that I quitted the city.

During all this time the power of the Plague was rapidly increasing. When I first arrived, it was said that the daily number of "accidents" by Plague out of a population of about 200,000 did not exceed four or five hundred, but before I went away the deaths were reckoned at twelve hundred a day. I had no means of knowing whether the numbers (given out, as I believe they were, by officials) were at all correct, but I could not help knowing that from day to day the number of the dead was increasing. My quarters were in one of the chief thoroughfares of the city, and as the funerals in Cairo take place between day-break and noon (a time during which I generally stayed in my rooms), I could form some opinion as to the briskness of the Plague. I don't mean that I got up every morning with the sun. It was not so, but the funerals of most people in decent circumstances at Cairo are attended by singers and howlers, and the performances of these people woke me in the early morning and prevented me from remaining in ignorance of what was going on in the street below.

These funerals were very simply conducted. The bier was a shallow wooden tray carried upon a light and weak wooden frame. The tray had in general no lid, but the body was more or less hidden from view by a shawl or scarf. The whole was borne upon the shoulders of men, and hurried forward at a great pace. Two or three singers generally preceded the bier; the howlers (these are paid for their vocal labours) followed after; and last of all came such of the dead man's friends and relations as could keep up with such a rapid procession; these, especially the women, would get terribly blown, and would straggle back into the rear; many were fairly "beaten off." I never observed any appearance of mourning in the mourners; the pace was too severe for any solemn affectation of grief.

When first I arrived at Cairo the funerals that daily passed under my windows were many, but still there were frequent and long intervals without a single howl. Every day, however (except one, when I fancied that I observed a diminution of funerals), these intervals became less frequent and shorter, and at last, the passing of the howlers from morn to noon was almost incessant. I believe that about one half of the whole people was carried off by this visitation. The Orientals, however, have more quiet fortitude than Europeans under afflictions of this sort, and they never allow the Plague to interfere with their religious usages. I rode one day round the great burial-ground. The tombs are strewed over a great expanse among the vast mountains of rubbish (the accumulations of many centuries) which surround the city. The ground, unlike the Turkish "cities of the dead," which are made so beautiful by their dark cypresses, has nothing to sweeten melancholy—nothing to mitigate the hatefulness of death. Carnivorous beasts and birds possess the place by night, and now in the fair morning it was all alive with fresh comers—alive with dead. Yet at this very time when the Plague was raging so furiously, and on this very ground which resounded so mournfully with the howls of arriving funerals, preparations were going on for the religious festival called the Kourban Bairam. Tents were pitched, and *swings hung for the amusement of children*—a ghastly holiday! but the Mahometans take a pride, and a just pride, in following their ancient customs undisturbed by the shadow of death.

I did not hear whilst I was at Cairo that any prayer for a remission of the Plague had been offered up in the mosques. I believe that, however frightful the ravages of the disease may be, the Mahometans refrain from approaching Heaven with their complaints until the Plague has endured for a long space, and then at last they pray God—not that the Plague may cease, but that it may go to another city!

A good Mussulman seems to take pride in repudiating the European notion that the will of God can be eluded by shunning the touch of a sleeve. When I went to see the Pyramids of Sakkara, I was the guest of a noble old fellow—an Osmanlee (how sweet it was to hear his soft rolling language, after suffering as I had suffered of late from the shrieking tongue of the Arabs!). This man was aware of the European ideas about contagion, and his first care therefore was to assure me that not a single instance of Plague had occurred in his village; he then inquired as to the progress of the Plague at Cairo. I had but a bad account to give. Up to this time my host had carefully refrained from touching me, out of respect to the European theory of contagion, but as soon as it was made plain that he, and not I, would be the person endangered by contact, he gently laid his hand upon my arm in order to make me feel sure that the circumstance of my coming from an infected city did not occasion him the least uneasiness. In that touch there was true hospitality.

Very different is the faith and the practice of the Europeans, or rather I mean of the Europeans settled in the East, and commonly called Levantines. When I came to the end of my journey over the desert I had been so long alone that the prospect of speaking to somebody at Cairo seemed almost a new excitement. I felt a sort of consciousness that I had a little of the wild beast about me, but I was quite in the humour to be charmingly tame and to be quite engaging in my manners, if I should have an opportunity of holding communion with any of the human race whilst at Cairo. I knew no one in the place, and had no letters of introduction, but I carried letters of credit; and it often happens in places remote from England that those "advices" operate as a sort of introduction, and obtain for the bearer (if disposed to receive them) such ordinary civilities as it may be in the power of the banker to offer.

Very soon after my arrival I found out the abode of the Levantine to whom my credentials were addressed. At his door several persons (all Arabs) were hanging about and keeping guard. It was not till after some delay and the interchange of some communications with those in the interior of the citadel that I was admitted. At length, however, I was conducted through the court, and up a flight of stairs, and finally into the apartment where business was transacted. The room was divided by a good substantial fence of iron bars, and behind these defences the banker had his station. The truth was that from fear of the Plague he had adopted the course usually taken by European residents, and had shut himself up "in strict quarantine,"—that is to say, that he had, as he hoped, cut himself off from all communication with infecting substances. The Europeans long resident in the East, without any, or with scarcely any exception, are firmly convinced that the Plague is propagated by contact, and by contact only—that if they can but avoid the touch of an infecting substance, they are safe, and that if they cannot, they die. This belief induces them to adopt the contrivance of putting themselves in that state of siege which they call "Quarantine." It is a part of their faith that metals and hempen rope, and also, I fancy, one or two other substances, will not carry the infection: and they likewise believe that the germ of pestilence lying in an infected substance may be destroyed by submersion in water, or by the action of smoke. They, therefore, guard the doors of their houses with the utmost care against intrusion, and condemn themselves with all the members of their family, including European servants, to a strict imprisonment within the walls of their dwelling. Their native attendants are not allowed to enter at all, but they make the necessary purchases of provisions: these are hauled up through one of the windows by means of a rope, and are afterwards soaked in water.

I knew nothing of these mysteries, and was not therefore prepared for the sort of reception I met with. I advanced to the iron fence, and putting my letter between the bars, politely proffered it to Mr. Banker. Mr. Banker received me with a sad and dejected look, and not "with open arms," or with any arms at all, but with—a pair of tongs! I placed my letter between the iron fingers: these instantly picked it up as it were a viper, and conveyed it away to be scorched and purified by fire and smoke. I was disgusted at this reception, and at the idea that anything of mine could carry infection to the poor wretch who stood on the other side of the bars—pale and trembling, and already meet for Death. I looked with something of the Mahometan's feeling upon these little contrivances for eluding Fate: and in this instance at least they were vain: a little while and the poor money-changer who had strived to guard the days of his life (as though they were coins) with bolts and bars of iron—he was seized by the Plague, and he died.

To people entertaining such opinions as these respecting the fatal effect of contact, the narrow and crowded streets of Cairo were terrible as the easy slope that leads to Avernus. The roaring Ocean and the beetling crags owe something of their sublimity to this—that if they be tempted, they can take the warm life of a man. To the contagionist, filled as he is with the dread of final causes, having no faith in Destiny, nor in the fixed will of God, and with none of the devil-may-care indifference which might stand him instead of creeds—to such one, every rag that shivers in the breeze of a plague-stricken city has this sort of sublimity. If by any terrible ordinance he be forced to venture forth, he sees Death dangling from every sleeve; and as he creeps forward, he poises his shuddering limbs between the imminent jacket that is stabbing at his right elbow, and the murderous pelisse, that threatens to mow him clean down as it sweeps along on his left. But most of all he dreads that which most of all he should love—the touch of a woman's dress; for mothers and wives hurrying forth on kindly errands from the bedsides of the dying go slouching along through the streets more wilfully and less courteously than the men. For a while it may be that the caution of the poor Levantine may enable him to avoid contact, but sooner or later perhaps the dreaded chance arrives: that bundle of linen, with the dark tearful eyes at the top of it that labours along with the voluptuous clumsiness of Grisi—she has touched the poor Levantine with the hem of her sleeve! From that dread moment, his peace is gone; his mind, for ever hanging upon the fatal touch, invites the blow which he fears; he watches for the symptoms of plague so carefully that sooner or later they come in truth. The parched mouth is a sign—his mouth *is* parched; the throbbing brain—his brain *does* throb; the rapid pulse—he touches his own wrist (for he dares not ask counsel of any man, lest he be deserted), he touches his wrist, and feels how his frightened blood goes galloping out of his heart. There is nothing but the fatal swelling that is wanting to make his sad conviction complete; immediately he has an odd feel under the arm—no pain, but a little straining of the skin; he would to

God it were his fancy that were strong enough to give him that sensation: this is the worst of all. It now seems to him that he could be happy and contented with his parched mouth, and his throbbing brain, and his rapid pulse, if only he could know that there were no swelling under the left arm; but dares he try?—in a moment of calmness and deliberation he dares not, but when for a while he has writhed under the torture of suspense, a sudden strength of will drives him to seek and know his fate; he touches the gland, and finds the skin sane and sound, but under the cuticle there lies a small lump like a pistol bullet, that moves as he pushes it. Oh! but is this for all certainty, is this the sentence of death? Feel the gland of the other arm: there is not the same lump exactly, yet something a little like it: have not some people glands naturally enlarged?—would to Heaven he were one! So he does for himself the work of the Plague, and when the Angel of Death thus courted does indeed and in truth come, he has only to finish that which has been so well begun; he passes his fiery hand over the brain of the victim, and lets him rave for a season, but all chance-wise, of people and things once dear, or of people and things indifferent. Once more the poor fellow is back at his home in fair Provence, and sees the sun-dial that stood in his childhood's garden—sees part of his mother, and the long-since-forgotten face of that little dear sister—(he sees her, he says, on a Sunday morning, for all the church bells are ringing;) he looks up and down through the universe and owns it well piled with bales upon bales of cotton and cotton eternal—so much so, that he feels—he knows—he swears he could make that winning hazard, if the billiard table would not slant upwards, and if the cue were a cue worth playing with; but it is not—it's a cue that won't move—his own arm won't move—in short, there's the devil to pay in the brain of the poor Levantine, and, perhaps, the next night but one he becomes the "life and the soul" of some squalling jackal family who fish him out by the foot from his shallow and sandy grave.

Better fate was mine: by some happy perverseness (occasioned perhaps by my disgust at the notion of being received with a pair of tongs) I took it into my pleasant head that all the European notions about contagion were thoroughly unfounded,—that the Plague might be providential, or "epidemic" (as they phrase it), but was not contagious, and that I could not be killed by the touch of a woman's sleeve, nor yet by her blessed breath. I therefore determined that the Plague should not alter my habits and amusements in any one respect. Though I came to this resolve from impulse, I think that I took the course which was in effect the most prudent, for the cheerfulness of spirits which I was thus enabled to retain discouraged the yellow-winged Angel, and prevented

him from taking a shot at me. I, however, so far respected the opinion
of the Europeans that I avoided touching when I could do so without
privation or inconvenience. This endeavour furnished me with a sort of
amusement as I passed through the streets. The usual mode of moving
from place to place in the city of Cairo is upon donkeys; of these great
number are always in readiness with donkey-boys attached. I had two
who constantly (until one of them died of the Plague) waited at my door
upon the chance of being wanted. I found this way of moving about
exceedingly pleasant, and never attempted any other. I had only to
mount my beast, and tell my donkey-boy the point for which I was
bound, and instantly I began to glide on at a capital pace. The streets
of Cairo are not paved in any way, but strewed with a dry sandy soil so
deadening to sound, that the foot-fall of my donkey could scarcely be
heard. There is no trottoir [sidewalk], and as you ride through the streets,
you mingle with the people on foot: those who are in your way upon
being warned by the shouts of the donkey-boy move very slightly aside
so as to leave you a narrow lane for your passage. Through this you move
at a gallop, gliding on delightfully in the very midst of crowds without
being inconvenienced or stopped for a moment; it seems to you that it
is not the donkey, but the donkey-boy who wafts you along with his
shouts through pleasant groups and air that comes thick with the fragrance of burial spice. "Eh! Sheik, Eh! Bint,—reggalek,—shumalek,
&c., &c.,—O old man, O virgin, get out of the way on the right—O
virgin, O old man get out of the way on the left,—this Englishman
comes, he comes, he comes!" The narrow alley which these shouts
cleared for my passage made it possible, though difficult, to go on for
a long way without touching a single person, and my endeavours to avoid
such contact were a sort of game for me in my loneliness. If I got through
a street without being touched, I won; if I was touched, I lost,—lost a
deuce of a stake according to the theory of the Europeans, but that I
deemed to be all nonsense,—I only lost that game, and would certainly
win the next.

There is not much in the way of public buildings to admire at Cairo,
but I saw one handsome mosque, and to this an instructive history is
attached. A Hindostanee merchant, having amassed an immense fortune, settled in Cairo, and soon found that his riches in the then state
of the political world gave him vast power in the city—power, however,
the exercise of which was much restrained by the counteracting influence of other wealthy men. With a view to extinguish every attempt at
rivalry, the Hindostanee merchant built this magnificent mosque at his
own expense; when the work was complete, he invited all the leading
men of the city to join him in prayer within the walls of the newly-built

temple, and he then caused to be massacred all those who were sufficiently influential to cause him any jealousy or uneasiness,—in short, all "the respectable men" of the place; after this he possessed undisputed power in the city, and was greatly revered,—he is revered to this day. It struck me that there was a touching simplicity in the mode which this man so successfully adopted for gaining the confidence and good will of his fellow-citizens. There seems to be some improbability in the story (though not nearly so gross as it might appear to an European ignorant of the East, for witness Mehemet Ali's destruction of the Mamelukes, a closely similar act, and attended with the like brilliant success); but even if the story be false as a mere fact, it is perfectly true as an illustration,—it is a true exposition of the means by which the respect and affection of Orientals may be conciliated.

I ascended one day to the citadel, and gained from its ramparts a superb view of the town. The fanciful and elaborate gilt work of the many minarets gives a light, a florid grace to the city as seen from this height; but before you can look for many seconds at such things, your eyes are drawn westward—drawn westward and over the Nile till they rest upon the massive enormities of the Ghizeh pyramids.

I saw within the fortress many yoke of men all haggard and woebegone, and a kennel of very fine lions well fed and flourishing; I say *yoke* of men, for the poor fellows were working together in bonds; I say a *kennel* of lions, for the beasts were not enclosed in cages, but simply chained up like dogs.

I went round the Bazaars: it seemed to me that pipes and arms were cheaper here than at Constantinople, and I should advise you therefore, if you reach both places, to prefer the market of Cairo. In the open slave-market I saw about fifty girls exposed for sale, but all of them black or "invisible" brown. A slave agent took me to some rooms in the upper story of the building, and also into several obscure houses in the neighbourhood with a view to show me some white women. The owners raised various objections to the display of their ware, and well they might, for I had not the least notion of purchasing: some refused on account of the illegality of selling to unbelievers, and others declared that all transactions of this sort were completely out of the question as long as the Plague was raging. I only succeeded in seeing one white slave who was for sale, but on this treasure the owner affected to set an immense value, and raised my expectations to a high pitch by saying that the girl was Circassian and was "fair as the full moon." There was a good deal of delay, but at last I was led into a long dreary room, and there, after marching timidly forward for a few paces, I descried at the farther end that mass of white linen which indicates an Eastern woman. She was bid to uncover her face, and I presently saw that, though very far from being good looking, according to my notion of beauty, she had not been inaptly described by the man who compared her to the full moon, for her large face was perfectly round, and perfectly white. Though very young, she was nevertheless extremely fat. She gave me the idea of having been got up for sale,—of having been fattened, and whitened by medicines or by some peculiar diet. I was firmly determined not to see any more of her than the face. She was perhaps disgusted at this my virtuous resolve, as well as with my personal appearance,—perhaps she saw my distaste and disappointment; perhaps she wished to gain favour with her owner by showing her attachment to his faith: at all events she halloed out very lustily and very decidedly that "she would not be bought by the Infidel."

Whilst I remained at Cairo, I thought it worth while to see something of the Magicians, because I considered that these men were in some sort the descendants of those who contended so stoutly against the superior power of Aaron. I therefore sent for an old man who was held to be the chief of the Magicians, and desired him to show me the wonders of his art. The old man looked and dressed his character exceedingly well; the vast turban, the flowing beard, and the ample robes were all that one could wish in the way of appearance. The first experiment (a very stale one) which he attempted to perform for me was that of showing the forms and faces of my absent friends, not to me, but to a boy brought in from the streets for the purpose, and said to be chosen at random. A mangale (pan of burning charcoal) was brought into my room, and the Magician bending over it, sprinkled upon the fire some substances consisting, I suppose, of spices or sweetly burning woods; for immediately a fragrant smoke arose that curled around the bending form of the Wizard, the while that he pronounced his first incantations. When these were over, the boy was made to sit down, and a common green shade was bound over his brow; then the Wizard took ink, and, still continuing his incantations, wrote certain mysterious figures upon the boy's palm and directed him to rivet his attention to these marks without looking aside for an instant. Again the incantations proceeded, and after a while the boy, being seemingly a little agitated, was asked whether he saw anything on the palm of his hand. He declared that he saw, and he described it rather minutely, a kind of military procession with royal flags, and warlike banners flying. I was then called upon to name the absent person whose form was to be made visible. I named Keate. You were not at Eton, and I must tell you, therefore, what manner of man it was that I named, though I think you must have some idea of him already, for wherever from utmost Canada to Bundelcund—wherever there was the white-washed wall of an officer's room or of any other apartment in which English gentlemen are forced to kick their heels, there, likely enough (in the days of his reign) the head of Keate would be seen, scratched, or drawn with those various degrees of skill which one observes in the representation of Saints. Anybody without the least notion of drawing could still draw a speaking, nay scolding likeness of Keate. If you had no pencil, you could draw him well enough with a poker, or the leg of a chair, or the smoke of a candle. He was little more (if more at all) than five feet in height, and was not very great in girth, but within this space was concentrated the pluck of ten battalions. He had a really noble voice, and this he could modulate with great skill, but he had also the power of quacking like an angry duck, and he almost always adopted this mode of communication in order to inspire respect. He was a capital scholar, but his ingenuous learning had *not* "softened his manners," and *had* "permitted them to be fierce"—tremendously fierce; he had such a complete command over his temper—I mean, over his *good* temper, that he scarcely ever allowed it to appear: you could not put him out of humour—that is, out of the *ill-*humour which he thought to be fitting for a headmaster. His red, shaggy eyebrows were so prominent, that he habitually used them as arms and hands for the purpose of pointing out any object towards which he wished to direct attention; the rest of his features were equally striking in their way, and were all and all his own. He wore a fancy dress, partly resembling the costume of Napoleon, and partly that of a widow woman. I could not have named anybody more decidedly differing in appearance from the rest of the human race.

"Whom do you name?"—"I name John Keate."—"Now what do you see?" said the Wizard to the boy.—"I see," answered the boy, "I see a fair girl with golden hair, blue eyes, pallid face, rosy lips." *There* was a shot! I shouted out my laughter with profane exultation, and the Wizard, perceiving the grossness of his failure, declared that the boy must have known sin (for none but the innocent can see truth), and accordingly kicked him down stairs.

One or two other boys were tried, but none could "see truth."

Notwithstanding the failure of these experiments, I wished to see what sort of mummery my Magician would practise if I called upon him to show me some performances of a higher order than those already attempted. I therefore made a treaty with him, in virtue of which he was to descend with me into the tombs near the Pyramids, and there evoke the Devil. The negotiation lasted some time, for Dthemetri, as in duty bound, tried to beat down the Wizard as much as he could, and the Wizard on his part manfully stuck up for his price, declaring that to raise the Devil was really no joke, and insinuating that to do so was an awesome crime. I let Dthemetri have his way in the negotiation, but I felt in reality very indifferent about the sum to be paid, and for this reason, namely, that the payment (except a very small present which I might make, or not, as I chose) was to be *contingent on success*. At length the bargain was finished, and it was arranged that, after a few days to be allowed for preparation, the Wizard should raise the Devil for two pounds ten, play or pay—no Devil, no piastres.

The Wizard failed to keep his appointment. I sent to know why the deuce he had not come to raise the Devil. The truth was that my Mahomet had gone to the mountain. The Plague had seized him, and he died.

Although the Plague was now spreading quick and terrible havoc around him, I did not see very plainly any corresponding change in the looks of the streets until the seventh day after my arrival: I then first observed that the city was *silenced*. There were no outward signs of despair nor of violent terror, but many of the voices that had swelled the busy hum of men were already hushed in death, and the survivors, so used to scream and screech in their earnestness whenever they bought or sold, now showed an unwonted indifference about the affairs of this world: it was less worth while for men to haggle and haggle, and crack the sky with noisy bargains, when the Great Commander was there, who could "pay all their debts with the roll of his drum."

At this time I was informed that of 25,000 people at Alexandria, 12,000 had died already; the Destroyer had come rather later to Cairo, but there was nothing of weariness in his strides. The deaths came faster than ever they befell in the Plague of London; but the calmness of Orientals under such visitations, and their habit of using biers for interment instead of burying coffins along with the bodies, rendered it practicable to dispose of the dead in the usual way, without shocking the people by any unaccustomed spectacle of horror. There was no tumbling of bodies into carts, as in the Plague of Florence, and the Plague of London; every man, according to his station, was properly buried, and that in the accustomed way, except that he went to his grave at a pace more than usually rapid.

The funerals pouring through the streets were not the only public evidence of deaths. In Cairo this custom prevails:—at the instant of a man's death (if his property is sufficient to justify the expense) professional howlers are employed. I believe that these persons are brought near to the dying man, when his end appears to be approaching, and the moment that life is gone, they lift up their voices, and send forth a loud wail from the chamber of Death. Thus I knew when my near

neighbours died: sometimes the howls were near; sometimes more distant. Once I was awakened in the night by the wail of death in the next
house, and another time by a like howl from the house opposite; and
there were two or three minutes, I recollect, during which the howl
seemed to be actually *running* along the street.

I happened to be rather teased at this time by a sore throat, and I
thought it would be well to get it cured, if I could, before I again started
on my travels. I therefore inquired for a Frank doctor, and was informed
that the only one then at Cairo was a Bolognese Refugee, a very young
practitioner, and so poor that he had not been able to take flight, as the
other medical men had done. At such a time as this it was out of the
question to *send* for an European physician; a person thus summoned
would be sure to suppose that the patient was ill of the Plague, and
would decline to come. I therefore rode to the young Doctor's residence,
ascended a flight or two of stairs, and knocked at his door. No one came
immediately, but after some little delay the Medico himself opened the
door and admitted me. I, of course, made him understand that I had
come to consult him, but before entering upon my throat grievance, I
accepted a chair, and exchanged a sentence or two of common-place
conversation. Now, the natural common-place of the city at this season
was of a gloomy sort—"Comme va la peste?" (how goes the plague?),
and this was precisely the question I put. A deep sigh, and the words
"Sette cento per giorno, Signor" (seven hundred a day), pronounced in
a tone of the deepest sadness and dejection, were the answer I received.
The day was not oppressively hot, yet I saw that the Doctor was transpir-
ing profusely, and even the outside surface of the thick shawl dressing-
gown in which he had wrapped himself appeared to be moist. He was
a handsome, pleasant-looking young fellow, but the deep melancholy of
his tone did not tempt me to prolong the conversation, and without
farther delay, I requested that my throat might be looked at. The
Medico held my chin in the usual way, and examined my throat; he then
wrote me a prescription, and almost immediately afterwards I bid him
farewell; but as he conducted me towards the door, I observed an
expression of strange and unhappy watchfulness in his rolling eyes. It was
not the next day, but the next day but one, if I rightly remember, that
I sent to request another interview with my Doctor. In due time Dthemetri, my messenger, returned, looking sadly aghast. He had "*met* the
Medico," for so he phrased it, "coming out from his house—in a bier!"

It was, of course, plain that when the poor Bolognese stood looking
down my throat and almost mingling his breath with mine, he was
already stricken of the Plague. I suppose that his violent sweat must have
been owing to some medicine administered by himself in the faint hope

of a cure. The peculiar rolling of his eyes which I had remarked is, I believe, to experienced observers a pretty sure test of the Plague. A Russian acquaintance of mine, speaking from the information of men who had made the Turkish campaigns of 1828 and 1829, told me that by this sign the officers of Sabalkansky's force were able to make out the plague-stricken soldiers with a good deal of certainty.

It so happened that most of the people with whom I had anything to do, during my stay at Cairo, were seized with Plague; and all these died. Since I had been for a long time *en route* before I reached Egypt, and was about to start again for another long journey over the Desert, there were of course many little matters touching my wardrobe and my travelling equipments which required to be attended to whilst I remained in the city. It happened so many times that Dthemetri's orders in respect to these matters were frustrated by the deaths of the tradespeople and others whom he employed, that at last I became quite accustomed to the peculiar manner of the man when he prepared to announce a new death to me. The poor fellow naturally supposed that I should feel some uneasiness at hearing of the "accidents" continually happening to persons employed by me, and he therefore communicated their deaths as though they were the deaths of friends; he would cast down his eyes, and look like a man abashed, and then gently, and with a mournful gesture, allow the words "Morto, Signor," to come through his lips. I don't know how many of such instances occurred, but they were several, and besides these (as I told you before), my banker, my doctor, my landlord, and my magician, all died of the Plague. A lad who acted as a helper in the house I occupied lost a brother and a sister within a few hours. Out of my two established donkey-boys one died. I did not hear of any instance in which a plague-stricken patient had recovered.

Going out one morning, I met unexpectedly the scorching breath of the Khamseen wind, and fearing that I should faint under the infliction, I returned to my rooms. Reflecting, however, that I might have to encounter this wind in the desert, where there would be no possibility of avoiding it, I thought it would be better to brave it once more in the city, and to try whether I could really bear it or not. I, therefore, mounted my ass, and rode to old Cairo and along the gardens by the banks of the Nile. The wind was hot to the touch as though it came from a furnace; it blew strongly, but yet with such perfect steadiness, that the trees bending under its force remained fixed in the same curves without perceptibly waving; the whole sky was obscured by a veil of yellowish gray that shut out the face of the sun. The streets were utterly silent, being indeed almost entirely deserted, and not without cause, for the scorching blast, whilst it fevers the blood, closes up the pores of the skin,

and is terribly distressing therefore to every animal that encounters it.
I returned to my rooms dreadfully ill. My head ached with a burning
pain, and my pulse bounded quick and fitfully, but perhaps (as in the
instance of the poor Levantine whose death I was mentioning) the fear
and excitement I felt in trying my own wrist may have made my blood
flutter the faster.

It is a thoroughly well believed theory that, during the continuance
of the Plague, you can't be ill of any other febrile malady; an unpleasant
privilege that! for ill I was, and ill of fever; and I anxiously wished that
the ailment might turn out to be anything rather than Plague. I had
some right to surmise that my illness might have been merely the effect
of the hot wind; and this notion was encouraged by the elasticity of my
spirits, and by a strong forefeeling that much of my destined life in this
world was yet to come, and yet to be fulfilled. That was my instinctive
belief; but when I carefully weighed the probabilities on the one side,
and on the other, I could not help seeing that the strength of argument
was all against me. There was a strong antecedent likelihood in *favour*
of my being struck by the same blow as the rest of the people who had
been dying around me. Besides, it occurred to me that, after all, the
universal opinion of the Europeans upon a medical question, such as that
of contagion, might probably be correct; and *if it were*, I was so
thoroughly "compromised," especially by the touch and breath of the
dying Medico, that I had no right to expect any other fate than that
which now seemed to have overtaken me. Balancing then as well as I
could all the considerations suggested by hope and fear, I slowly and
reluctantly came to the conclusion that, according to all merely reasonable probability, the Plague had come upon me.

You might suppose that this conviction would have induced me to
write a few farewell lines to those who were dearest, and that having
done that, I should have turned my thoughts towards the world to come.
Such, however, was not the case; I believe that the prospect of death
often brings with it strong anxieties about matters of comparatively
trivial import, and certainly with me the whole energy of the mind was
directed towards the one petty object of concealing my illness until the
latest possible moment—until the delirious stage. I did not believe that
either Mysseri, or Dthemetri, who had served me so faithfully in all
trials, would have deserted me (as most Europeans are wont to do) when
they knew that I was stricken by Plague; but I shrank from the idea of
putting them to this test, and I dreaded the consternation which the
knowledge of my illness would be sure to occasion.

I was very ill indeed at the moment when my dinner was served, and
my soul sickened at the sight of the food, but I had luckily the habit

of dispensing with the attendance of servants during my meal, and as soon as I was left alone, I made a melancholy calculation of the quantity of food I should have eaten if I had been in my usual health, and filled my plates accordingly, and gave myself salt, and so on, as though I were going to dine; I then transferred the viands to a piece of the omnipresent *Times* newspaper, and hid them away in a cupboard, for it was not yet night, and I dared not to throw the food into the street until darkness came. I did not at all relish this process of fictitious dining, but at length the cloth was removed, and I gladly reclined on my divan (I would not lie down), with the *Arabian Nights* in my hand.

I had a feeling that tea would be a capital thing for me, but I would not order it until the usual hour. When at last the time came, I drank deep draughts from the fragrant cup. The effect was almost instantaneous. A plenteous sweat burst through my skin, and watered my clothes through and through. I kept myself thickly covered. The hot tormenting weight which had been loading my brains was slowly heaved away. The fever was extinguished. I felt a new buoyancy of spirits, and an unusual activity of mind. I went into my bed under a load of thick covering, and when the morning came, and I asked myself how I was, I answered, "perfectly well."

I was very anxious to procure, if possible, some medical advice for Mysseri, whose illness prevented my departure. Every one of the European practising doctors, of whom there had been many, had either died or fled; it was said, however, that there was an Englishman in the medical service of the Pasha who quietly remained at his post, but that he never engaged in private practice. I determined to try if I could obtain assistance in this quarter. I did not venture at first, and at such a time as this, to ask him to visit a servant who was prostrate on the bed of sickness; but thinking that I might thus gain an opportunity of persuading him to attend Mysseri, I wrote a note mentioning my own affair of the sore throat, and asking for the benefit of his medical advice; he instantly followed back my messenger, and was at once shown up into my room. I entreated him to stand off, telling him fairly how deeply I was "compromised," and especially by my contact with a person actually ill, and since dead of Plague. The generous fellow, with a good-humoured laugh at the terrors of the contagionists, marched straight up to me, and forcibly seized my hand, and shook it with manly violence. I felt grateful indeed, and swelled with fresh pride of race, because that my countryman could carry himself so nobly. He soon cured Mysseri, as well as me, and all this he did from no other motives than the pleasure of doing a kindness, and the delight of braving a danger.

At length the great difficulty I had had in procuring beasts for my departure was overcome, and now, too, I was to have the new excitement of travelling on dromedaries. With two of these beasts, and three camels, I gladly wound my way from out of the pest-stricken city. As I passed through the streets, I observed a grave elder, stretching forth his arms, and lifting up his voice in a speech which seemed to have some reference to me. Requiring an interpretation, I found that the man had said, "The Pasha seeks camels, and he finds them not—the Englishman says, 'let camels be brought,' and behold—there they are."

I no sooner breathed the free, wholesome air of the desert, than I felt that a great burden which I had been scarcely conscious of bearing was lifted away from my mind. For nearly three weeks I had lived under peril of death; the peril ceased, and not till then did I know how much alarm and anxiety I had really been suffering.

CHARLES DARWIN
1809–1892

Grandson of the eighteenth-century physician, botanist, and poet Erasmus Darwin, Charles was educated first in medicine at the University of Edinburgh and then in divinity at the University of Cambridge. But natural history and geology became his passions, and at the age of twenty-five he sailed aboard HMS Beagle *on a survey voyage along the coast of South America lasting almost five years. He went along as an unpaid naturalist whose job was to collect and interpret specimens of flora and fauna unfamiliar in Europe. This work earned him the title "The Flycatcher" from the crew, with whom he was popular for his modesty and willingness to help out. "At sea, when the weather is calm," he wrote his sister, "I work at marine animals, with which the whole ocean abounds. If there is any sea up I am either sick or contrive to read some voyage or travels." In addition to these and a book of Milton's poems, Darwin carried along the first volume of Sir Charles Lyell's* Principles of Geology, *which held that the scientific study of the earth's physical features led to the conclusion that the Biblical account of Creation was a charming fiction. Darwin's own observations on the transmutation of species tended to confirm this view and to suggest the outlines of his own ultimate theory of evolution articulated in* The Origin of Species *(1859) and* The Descent of Man *(1871). Although attentive to human manners and customs (viewed from a wholly satisfied British perspective), Darwin remains a model of the specifically scientific traveler, always calm, always observant, always accurate. As he says, "A traveler should be a botanist."*

From THE VOYAGE OF THE *BEAGLE*
(1845)

MALDONADO

Monte Video — Maldonado — Excursion to R. Polanco — Lazo and Bolas — Partridges — Absence of Trees — Deer — Capybara, or River Hog — Tucutuco — Molothrus, cuckoo-like habits — Tyrant Flycatcher — Mocking-bird — Carrion Hawks — Tubes formed by Lightning—House struck

July 5th, 1832.—In the morning we got under way, and stood out of the splendid harbour of Rio de Janeiro. In our passage to the Plata, we saw nothing particular, excepting on one day a great shoal of porpoises, many hundreds in number. The whole sea was in places furrowed by them; and a most extraordinary spectacle was presented, as hundreds, proceeding together by jumps, in which their whole bodies were exposed, thus cut the water. When the ship was running nine knots an hour, these animals could cross and recross the bows with the greatest ease, and then dash away right ahead. As soon as we entered the estuary of the Plata, the weather was very unsettled. One dark night we were surrounded by numerous seals and penguins, which made such strange noises, that the officer on watch reported he could hear the cattle bellowing on shore. On a second night we witnessed a splendid scene of natural fireworks; the masthead and yard-arm-ends shone with St. Elmo's light; and the form of the vane could almost be traced, as if it had been rubbed with phosphorus. The sea was so highly luminous, that the tracks of the penguins were marked by a fiery wake, and the darkness of the sky was momentarily illuminated by the most vivid lightning.

When within the mouth of the river, I was interested by observing how slowly the waters of the sea and river mixed. The latter, muddy and discoloured, from its less specific gravity, floated on the surface of the salt water. This was curiously exhibited in the wake of the vessel, where a line of blue water was seen mingling in little eddies, with the adjoining fluid.

July 26th.—We anchored at Monte Video. The *Beagle* was employed in surveying the extreme southern and eastern coasts of America, south of the Plata, during the two succeeding years. To prevent useless repetitions, I will extract those parts of my journal which refer to the same districts, without always attending to the order in which we visited them.

Maldonado is situated on the northern bank of the Plata, and not very far from the mouth of the estuary. It is a most quiet, forlorn, little town; built, as is universally the case in these countries, with the streets running at right angles to each other, and having in the middle a large plaza or square, which, from its size, renders the scantiness of the population more evident. It possesses scarcely any trade; the exports being confined to a few hides and living cattle. The inhabitants are chiefly land owners, together with a few shopkeepers and the necessary tradesmen, such as blacksmiths and carpenters, who do nearly all the business for a circuit of fifty miles round. The town is separated from the river by a band of sand-hillocks, about a mile broad: it is surrounded, on all other sides, by an open slightly-undulating country, covered by one uniform layer of fine green turf, on which countless herds of cattle, sheep, and horses graze. There is very little land cultivated even close to the town. A few hedges, made of cacti and agave, mark out where some wheat or Indian corn has been planted. The features of the country are very similar along the whole northern bank of the Plata. The only difference is, that here the granitic hills are a little bolder. The scenery is very uninteresting; there is scarcely a house, an enclosed piece of ground, or even a tree, to give it an air of cheerfulness. Yet, after being imprisoned for some time in a ship, there is a charm in the unconfined feeling of walking over boundless plains of turf. Moreover, if your view is limited to a small space, many objects possess beauty. Some of the smaller birds are brilliantly coloured; and the bright green sward, browsed short by the cattle, is ornamented by dwarf flowers, among which a plant, looking like the daisy, claimed the place of an old friend. What would a florist say to whole tracts so thickly covered by the Verbena melindres, as, even at a distance, to appear of the most gaudy scarlet?

I stayed ten weeks at Maldonado, in which time a nearly perfect collection of the animals, birds, and reptiles, was procured. Before making any observations respecting them, I will give an account of a little excursion I made as far as the river Polanco, which is about seventy miles distant, in a northerly direction. I may mention, as a proof how cheap everything is in this country, that I paid only two dollars a day, or eight shillings, for two men, together with a troop of about a dozen riding-horses. My companions were well armed with pistols and sabres; a precaution which I thought rather unnecessary; but the first piece of news we heard was, that, the day before, a traveller from Monte Video had been found dead on the road, with his throat cut. This happened close to a cross, the record of a former murder.

On the first night we slept at a retired little country-house; and there I soon found out that I possessed two or three articles, especially a pocket compass, which created unbounded astonishment. In every house I was asked to show the compass, and by its aid, together with a map, to point out the direction of various places. It excited the liveliest admiration that I, a perfect stranger, should know the road (for direction and road are synonymous in this open country) to places where I had never been. At one house a young woman, who was ill in bed, sent to entreat me to come and show her the compass. If their surprise was great, mine was greater, to find such ignorance among people who possessed their thousands of cattle, and "estancias" [ranches] of great extent. It can only be accounted for by the circumstance that this retired part of the country is seldom visited by foreigners. I was asked whether the earth or sun moved; whether it was hotter or colder to the north; where Spain was, and many other such questions. The greater number of the inhabitants had an indistinct idea that England, London, and North America, were different names for the same place; but the better informed well knew that London and North America were separate countries close together, and that England was a large town in London! I carried with me some promethean matches, which I ignited by biting; it was thought so wonderful that a man should strike fire with his teeth, that it was usual to collect the whole family to see it: I was once offered a dollar for a single one. Washing my face in the morning caused much speculation at the village of Las Minas; a superior tradesman closely cross-questioned me about so singular a practice; and likewise why on board we wore our beards; for he had heard from my guide that we did so. He eyed me with much suspicion; perhaps he had heard of ablutions in the Mahomedan religion, and knowing me to be a heretic, probably he came to the conclusion that all heretics were Turks. It is the general custom in this country to ask for a night's lodging at the first convenient house. The astonishment at the compass, and my other feats in jugglery, was to a certain degree advantageous, as with that, and the long stories my guides told of my breaking stones, knowing venomous from harmless snakes, collecting insects, etc., I repaid them for their hospitality. I am writing as if I had been among the inhabitants of central Africa: Banda Oriental would not be flattered by the comparison; but such were my feelings at the time.

The next day we rode to the village of Las Minas. The country was rather more hilly, but otherwise continued the same; an inhabitant of the Pampas no doubt would have considered it as truly Alpine. The country is so thinly inhabited, that during the whole day we scarcely met a single person. Las Minas is much smaller even than Maldonado. It is seated on a little plain, and is surrounded by low rocky mountains. It is of the usual symmetrical form; and with its whitewashed church standing in the centre, had rather a pretty appearance. The outskirting houses rose out of the plain like isolated beings, without the accompaniment of gardens or courtyards. This is generally the case in the country, and all the houses have, in consequence, an uncomfortable aspect. At night we stopped at a pulperia, or drinking-shop. During the evening a great number of Gauchos came in to drink spirits and smoke cigars: their appearance is very striking; they are generally tall and handsome; but with a proud and dissolute expression of countenance. They frequently wear their moustaches, and long black hair curling down their backs. With their brightly-coloured garments, great spurs clanking about their heels, and knives stuck as daggers (and often so used) at their waists, they look a very different race of men from what might be expected from their name of Gauchos, or simple countrymen. Their politeness is excessive; they never drink their spirits without expecting you to taste it; but whilst making their exceedingly graceful bow, they seem quite as ready, if occasion offered, to cut your throat.

On the third day we pursued rather an irregular course, as I was employed in examining some beds of marble. On the fine plains of turf we saw many ostriches (Struthio rhea). Some of the flocks contained as many as twenty or thirty birds. These, when standing on any little eminence, and seen against the clear sky, presented a very noble appearance. I never met with such tame ostriches in any other part of the country: it was easy to gallop up within a short distance of them; but then, expanding their wings, they made all sail right before the wind, and soon left the horse astern.

At night we came to the house of Don Juan Fuentes, a rich landed proprietor, but not personally known to either of my companions. On approaching the house of a stranger, it is usual to follow several little points of etiquette: riding up slowly to the door, the salutation of Ave Maria is given, and until somebody comes out and asks you to alight, it is not customary even to get off your horse: the formal answer of the owner is, "sin pecado concebida"—that is, conceived without sin. Having entered the house, some general conversation is kept up for a few minutes, till permission is asked to pass the night there. This is granted as a matter of course. The stranger then takes his meals with the family, and a room is assigned him, where with the horsecloths belonging to his recado (or saddle of the Pampas) he makes his bed. It is curious how similar circumstances produce such similar results in manners. At the Cape of Good Hope the same hospitality, and very nearly the same points of etiquette, are universally observed. The difference, however, between the character of the Spaniard and that of the Dutch boor is shown, by the former never asking his guest a single question beyond the strictest rules of politeness, whilst the honest Dutchman demands where he has been, where he is going, what is his business, and even how many brothers, sisters, or children he may happen to have.

Shortly after our arrival at Don Juan's, one of the large herds of cattle was driven in towards the house, and three beasts were picked out to be slaughtered for the supply of the establishment. These half-wild cattle are very active; and knowing full well the fatal lasso, they led the horses a long and laborious chase. After witnessing the rude wealth displayed in the number of cattle, men, and horses, Don Juan's miserable house was quite curious. The floor consisted of hardened mud, and the windows were without glass; the sitting-room boasted only of a few of the roughest chairs and stools, with a couple of tables. The supper, although several strangers were present, consisted of two huge piles, one of roast beef, the other of boiled, with some pieces of pumpkin: besides this latter there was no other vegetable, and not even a morsel of bread. For drinking, a large earthenware jug of water served the whole party. Yet this man was the owner of several square miles of land, of which nearly every acre would produce corn, and, with a little trouble, all the common vegetables. The evening was spent in smoking, with a little impromptu singing, accompanied by the guitar. The signoritas all sat together in one corner of the room, and did not sup with the men.

So many works have been written about these countries, that it is almost superfluous to describe either the lasso or the bolas. The lasso consists of a very strong, but thin, well-plaited rope, made of raw hide. One end is attached to the broad surcingle, which fastens together the complicated gear of the recado, or saddle used in the Pampas; the other is terminated by a small ring of iron or brass, by which a noose can be formed. The Gaucho, when he is going to use the lasso, keeps a small coil in his bridle-hand, and in the other holds the running noose, which is made very large, generally having a diameter of about eight feet. This he whirls round his head, and by the dexterous movement of his wrist keeps the noose open; then, throwing it, he causes it to fall on any particular spot he chooses. The lasso, when not used, is tied up in a small coil to the after part of the recado. The bolas, or balls, are of two kinds: the simplest, which is chiefly used for catching ostriches, consists of two round stones, covered with leather, and united by a thin plaited thong, about eight feet long. The other kind differs only in having three balls united by the thongs to a common centre. The Gaucho holds the smallest of the three in his hand, and whirls the other two round and round his head; then, taking aim, sends them like chain shot revolving through the air. The balls no sooner strike any object, than, winding round it, they cross each other, and become firmly hitched. The size and weight of the balls varies, according to the purpose for which they are made: when of stone, although not larger than an apple, they are sent with such force as sometimes to break the leg even of a horse. I have seen the balls made of wood, and as large as a turnip, for the sake of catching these animals without injuring them. The balls are sometimes made of iron, and these can be hurled to the greatest distance. The main difficulty in using either lasso or bolas is to ride so well as to be able at full speed, and while suddenly turning about, to whirl them so steadily round the head, as to take aim: on foot any person would soon learn the art. One day, as I was amusing myself by galloping and whirling the balls round my head, by accident the free one struck a bush; and its revolving motion being thus destroyed, it immediately fell to the ground, and like magic caught one hind leg of my horse; the other ball was then jerked out of my hand, and the horse fairly secured. Luckily he was an old practised animal, and knew what it meant; otherwise he would probably have kicked till he had thrown himself down. The Gauchos roared with laughter; they cried out that they had seen every sort of animal caught, but had never before seen a man caught by himself.

* * *

BUENOS AYRES TO ST. FÉ

Excursion to St. Fé — Thistle Beds — Habits of the Bizcacha — Little Owl — Saline Streams — Level Plains — Mastodon — St. Fé — Change in Landscape — Geology — Tooth of extinct Horse — Relation of the Fossil and recent Quadrupeds of North and South America — Effects of a great Drought — Parana — Habits of the Jaguar — Scissor-beak — Kingfisher, Parrot, and Scissor-tail— Revolution — Buenos Ayres — State of Government

September 27th—In the evening I set out on an excursion to St. Fé, which is situated nearly three hundred English miles from Buenos Ayres, on the banks of the Parana. The roads in the neighbourhood of the city, after the rainy weather, were extraordinarily bad. I should never have thought it possible for a bullock wagon to have crawled along: as it was, they scarcely went at the rate of a mile an hour, and a man was kept ahead, to survey the best line for making the attempt. The bullocks were terribly jaded: it is a great mistake to suppose that with improved roads, and an accelerated rate of travelling, the sufferings of the animals increase in the same proportion. We passed a train of wagons and a troop of beasts on their road to Mendoza. The distance is about 580 geographical miles, and the journey is generally performed in fifty days. These wagons are very long, narrow, and thatched with reeds; they have only two wheels, the diameter of which in some cases is as much as ten feet. Each is drawn by six bullocks, which are urged on by a goad at least twenty feet long: this is suspended from within the roof; for the wheel bullocks a smaller one is kept; and for the intermediate pair, a point projects at right angles from the middle of the long one. The whole apparatus looked like some implement of war.

September 28th.—We passed the small town of Luxan, where there is a wooden bridge over the river—a most unusual convenience in this country. We passed also Areco. The plains appeared level, but were not so in fact; for in various places the horizon was distant. The estancias are here wide apart; for there is little good pasture, owing to the land being covered by beds either of an acrid clover, or of the great thistle. The latter, well known from the animated description given by Sir F. Head, were at this time of the year two-thirds grown; in some parts they were as high as the horse's back, but in others they had not yet sprung up, and the ground was bare and dusty as on a turnpike-road. The clumps were of the most brilliant green, and they made a pleasing miniature-likeness of broken forest land. When the thistles are full grown, the great beds are impenetrable, except by a few tracks, as intricate as those in a labyrinth. These are only known to the robbers, who at this season inhabit them, and sally forth at night to rob and cut throats with impunity. Upon asking at a house whether robbers were numerous, I was answered, "The thistles are not up yet;"—the meaning of which reply was not at first very obvious. There is little interest in passing over these tracts, for they are inhabited by few animals or birds, excepting the bizcacha and its friend the little owl.

The bizcacha is well known to form a prominent feature in the zoology of the Pampas. It is found as far south as the Rio Negro, in lat. 41°, but not beyond. It cannot, like the agouti, subsist on the gravelly and desert plains of Patagonia, but prefers a clayey or sandy soil, which produces a different and more abundant vegetation. Near Mendoza, at the foot of the Cordillera, it occurs in close neighbourhood with the allied alpine species. It is a very curious circumstance in its geographical distribution, that it has never been seen, fortunately for the inhabitants of Banda Oriental, to the eastward of the river Uruguay: yet in this province there are plains which appear admirably adapted to its habits. The Uruguay has formed an insuperable obstacle to its migration; although the broader barrier of the Parana has been passed, and the bizcacha is common in Entre Rios, the province between these two great rivers. Near Buenos Ayres these animals are exceedingly common. Their most favourite resort appears to be those parts of the plain which during one half of the year are covered with giant thistles, to the exclusion of other plants. The Gauchos affirm that it lives on roots; which, from the great strength of its gnawing teeth, and the kind of places frequented by it, seems probable. In the evening the bizcachas come out in numbers, and quietly sit at the mouths of their burrows on their haunches. At such times they are very tame, and a man on horseback passing by seems only to present an object for their grave contemplation. They run very awkwardly, and when running out of danger, from their elevated tails and short front legs, much resemble great rats. Their flesh, when cooked, is very white and good, but it is seldom used.

The bizcacha has one very singular habit; namely, dragging every hard object to the mouth of its burrow: around each group of holes many bones of cattle, stones, thistle-stalks, hard lumps of earth, dry dung, &c., are collected into an irregular heap, which frequently amounts to as much as a wheelbarrow would contain. I was credibly informed that a gentleman, when riding on a dark night, dropped his watch; he returned in the morning, and by searching the neighbourhood of every bizcacha hole on the line of road, as he expected, he soon found it. This habit of picking up whatever may be lying on the ground any where near its habitation must cost much trouble. For what purpose it is done, I am quite unable to form even the most remote conjecture: it cannot be for defence, because the rubbish is chiefly placed above the mouth of the burrow, which enters the ground at a very small inclination. No doubt there must exist some good reason; but the inhabitants of the country are quite ignorant of it. The only fact which I know analogous to it is the habit of that extraordinary Australian bird, the Calodera maculata, which makes an elegant vaulted passage of twigs for playing in, and which collects near the spot, land and sea-shells, bones, and the feathers of birds, especially brightly coloured ones. Mr. Gould, who has described these facts, informs me, that the natives, when they lose any hard object, search the playing passages, and he has known a tobacco-pipe thus recovered.

The little owl (Athene cunicularia), which has been so often mentioned, on the plains of Buenos Ayres exclusively inhabits the holes of the bizcacha; but in Banda Oriental it is its own workman. During the open day, but more especially in the evening, these birds may be seen in every direction standing frequently by pairs on the hillock near their burrows. If disturbed they either enter the hole, or, uttering a shrill harsh cry, move with a remarkably undulatory flight to a short distance, and then turning round, steadily gaze at their pursuer. Occasionally in the evening they may be heard hooting. I found in the stomachs of two which I opened the remains of mice, and I one day saw a small snake killed and carried away. It is said that snakes are their common prey during the daytime. I may here mention, as showing on what various kinds of food owls subsist, that a species killed among the islets of the Chonos Archipelago, had its stomach full of good-sized crabs. In India there is a fishing genus of owls, which likewise catches crabs.

In the evening we crossed the Rio Arrecife on a simple raft made of barrels lashed together, and slept at the post-house on the other side. I this day paid horse-hire for thirty-one leagues; and although the sun was glaring hot I was but little fatigued. When Captain Head talks of riding fifty leagues a day, I do not imagine the distance is equal to 150 English miles. At all events, the thirty-one leagues was only 76 miles in a straight line, and in an open country I should think four additional miles for turning would be a sufficient allowance.

29th and 30th.—We continued to ride over plains of the same character. At San Nicolas I first saw the noble river of the Parana. At the foot of the cliff on which the town stands, some large vessels were at anchor. Before arriving at Rozario, we crossed the Saladillo, a stream of fine clear running water, but too saline to drink. Rozario is a large town built on a dead level plain, which forms a cliff about sixty feet high over the Parana. The river here is very broad, with many islands, which are low and wooded, as is also the opposite shore. The view would resemble that of a great lake, if it were not for the linear-shaped islets, which alone give the idea of running water. The cliffs are the most picturesque part; sometimes they are absolutely perpendicular, and of a red colour; at other times in large broken masses, covered with cacti and mimosa-trees. The real grandeur, however, of an immense river like this, is derived from reflecting how important a means of communication and commerce it forms between one nation and another; to what a distance it travels; and from how vast a territory it drains the great body of fresh water which flows past your feet.

For many leagues north and south of San Nicolas and Rozario, the country is really level. Scarcely anything which travellers have written about its extreme flatness can be considered as exaggeration. Yet I could never find a spot where, by slowly turning round, objects were not seen at greater distances in some directions than in others; and this manifestly proves inequality in the plain. At sea, a person's eye being six feet above the surface of the water, his horizon is two miles and four-fifths distant. In like manner, the more level the plain, the more nearly does the horizon approach within these narrow limits; and this, in my opinion, entirely destroys that grandeur which one would have imagined that a vast level plain would have possessed.

October 1st.—We started by moonlight and arrived at the Rio Tercero by sunrise. This river is also called the Saladillo, and it deserves the name, for the water is brackish. I stayed here the greater part of the day, searching for fossil bones. Besides a perfect tooth of the Toxodon, and many scattered bones, I found two immense skeletons near each other, projecting in bold relief from the perpendicular cliff of the Parana. They were, however, so completely decayed, that I could only bring away small fragments of one of the great molar teeth; but these are sufficient to show that the remains belonged to a Mastodon, probably to the same species with that, which formerly must have inhabited the Cordillera in Upper Peru in such great numbers. The men who took me in the canoe, said they had long known of these skeletons, and had often wondered how they had got there: the necessity of a theory being felt, they came to the conclusion that, like the bizcacha, the mastodon was formerly a burrowing animal! In the evening we rode another stage, and crossed the Monge, another brackish stream, bearing the dregs of the washings of the Pampas.

October 2nd.—We passed through Corunda, which, from the luxuriance of its gardens, was one of the prettiest villages I saw. From this point to St. Fé the road is not very safe. The western side of the Parana northward, ceases to be inhabited; and hence the Indians sometimes come down thus far, and waylay travellers. The nature of the country also favours this, for instead of a grassy plain, there is an open woodland, composed of low prickly mimosas. We passed some houses that had been ransacked and since deserted; we saw also a spectacle, which my guides viewed with high satisfaction; it was the skeleton of an Indian with the dried skin hanging on the bones, suspended to the branch of a tree.

In the morning we arrived at St. Fé. I was surprised to observe how great a change of climate a difference of only three degrees of latitude between this place and Buenos Ayres had caused. This was evident from the dress and complexion of the men—from the increased size of the ombu-trees—the number of new cacti and other plants—and especially from the birds. In the course of an hour I remarked half-a-dozen birds, which I had never seen at Buenos Ayres. Considering that there is no natural boundary between the two places, and that the character of the country is nearly similar, the difference was much greater than I should have expected.

October 3rd and 4th.—I was confined for these two days to my bed by a headache. A good-natured old woman, who attended me, wished me to try many odd remedies. A common practice is to bind an orange-leaf or a bit of black plaster to each temple: and a still more general plan is to split a bean into halves, moisten them, and place one on each temple, where they will easily adhere. It is not thought proper ever to remove the beans or plaster, but to allow them to drop off; and sometimes if a man, with patches on his head, is asked, what is the matter? he will answer, "I had a headache the day before yesterday." Many of the remedies used by the people of the country are ludicrously strange, but too disgusting to be mentioned. One of the least nasty is to kill and cut open two puppies and bind them on each side of a broken limb. Little hairless dogs are in great request to sleep at the feet of invalids.

St. Fé is a quiet little town, and is kept clean and in good order. The governor, Lopez, was a common soldier at the time of the revolution; but has now been seventeen years in power. This stability of government is owing to his tyrannical habits; for tyranny seems as yet better adapted to these countries than republicanism. The governor's favourite occupation is hunting Indians: a short time since he slaughtered forty-eight, and sold the children at the rate of three or four pounds apiece.

October 5th.—We crossed the Parana to St. Fé Bajada, a town on the opposite shore. The passage took some hours, as the river here consisted of a labyrinth of small streams, separated by low wooded islands. I had a letter of introduction to an old Catalonian Spaniard, who treated me with the most uncommon hospitality. The Bajada is the capital of Entre Rios. In 1825 the town contained 6000 inhabitants, and the province 30,000; yet, few as the inhabitants are, no province has suffered more from bloody and desperate revolutions. They boast here of representatives, ministers, a standing army, and governors: so it is no wonder that they have their revolutions. At some future day this must be one of the richest countries of La Plata. The soil is varied and productive; and its almost insular form gives it two grand lines of communication by the rivers Parana and Uruguay.

* * *

Our voyage having come to an end, I will take a short retrospect of the advantages and disadvantages, the pains and pleasures, of our circumnavigation of the world. If a person asked my advice, before undertaking a long voyage, my answer would depend upon his possessing a decided taste for some branch of knowledge, which could by this means be advanced. No doubt it is a high satisfaction to behold various countries and the many races of mankind, but the pleasures gained at the time do not counterbalance the evils. It is necessary to look forward to a harvest, however distant that may be, when some fruit will be reaped, some good effected.

Many of the losses which must be experienced are obvious; such as that of the society of every old friend, and of the sight of those places with which every dearest remembrance is so intimately connected. These losses, however, are at the time partly relieved by the exhaustless delight of anticipating the long wished-for day of return. If, as poets say, life is a dream, I am sure in a voyage these are the visions which best serve to pass away the long night. Other losses, although not at first felt, tell heavily after a period: these are the want of room, of seclusion, of rest; the jading feeling of constant hurry; the privation of small luxuries, the loss of domestic society, and even of music and the other pleasures of imagination. When such trifles are mentioned, it is evident that the real grievances, excepting from accidents, of a sea-life are at an end. The short space of sixty years has made an astonishing difference in the facility of distant navigation. Even in the time of Cook, a man who left his fireside for such expeditions underwent severe privations. A yacht now, with every luxury of life, can circumnavigate the globe. Besides the vast improvements in ships and naval resources, the whole western shores of America are thrown open, and Australia has become the capital of a rising continent. How different are the circumstances to a man shipwrecked at the present day in the Pacific, to what they were in the time of Cook! Since his voyage a hemisphere has been added to the civilized world.

If a person suffer much from sea-sickness, let him weigh it heavily in the balance. I speak from experience: it is no trifling evil, cured in a week. If, on the other hand, he take pleasure in naval tactics, he will assuredly have full scope for his taste. But it must be borne in mind how large a proportion of the time, during a long voyage, is spent on the water, as compared with the days in harbour. And what are the boasted glories of the illimitable ocean? A tedious waste, a desert of water, as the Arabian calls it. No doubt there are some delightful scenes. A moonlight night, with the clear heavens and the dark glittering sea, and the white sails filled by the soft air of a gently-blowing trade-wind; a dead calm, with the heaving surface polished like a mirror, and all still except the occasional flapping of the canvas. It is well once to behold a squall with its rising arch and coming fury, or the heavy gale of wind and mountainous waves. I confess, however, my imagination had painted something more grand, more terrific in the full-grown storm. It is an incomparably finer spectacle when beheld on shore, where the waving trees, the wild flight of the birds, the dark shadows and bright lights, the rushing of the torrents, all proclaim the strife of the unloosed elements. At sea the albatross and little petrel fly as if the storm were their proper sphere, the water rises and sinks as if fulfilling its usual task: the ship alone and its inhabitants seem the objects of wrath. On a forlorn and weather-beaten coast, the scene is indeed different, but the feelings partake more of horror than of wild delight.

Let us now look at the brighter side of the past time. The pleasure derived from beholding the scenery and the general aspect of the various countries we have visited has decidedly been the most constant and highest source of enjoyment. It is probable that the picturesque beauty of many parts of Europe exceeds anything which we beheld. But there is a growing pleasure in comparing the character of the scenery in different countries, which to a certain degree is distinct from merely admiring its beauty. It depends chiefly on an acquaintance with the individual parts of each view: I am strongly induced to believe that, as in music, the person who understands every note will, if he also possesses a proper taste, more thoroughly enjoy the whole, so he who examines each part of a fine view, may also thoroughly comprehend the full and combined effect. Hence, a traveller should be a botanist, for in all views plants form the chief embellishment. Group masses of naked rock even in the wildest forms, and they may for a time afford a sublime spectacle, but they will soon grow monotonous. Paint them with bright and varied colours, as in Northern Chile, they will become fantastic; clothe them with vegetation, they must form a decent, if not a beautiful picture.

When I say that the scenery of parts of Europe is probably superior to anything which we beheld, I except, as a class by itself, that of the intertropical zones. The two classes cannot be compared together; but I have already often enlarged on the grandeur of those regions. As the force of impressions generally depends on preconceived ideas, I may add, that mine were taken from the vivid descriptions in the Personal Narrative of Humboldt, which far exceed in merit anything else which I have read. Yet with these high-wrought ideas, my feelings were far from partaking of a tinge of disappointment on my first and final landing on the shores of Brazil.

Among the scenes which are deeply impressed on my mind, none exceed in sublimity the primeval forests undefaced by the hand of man; whether those of Brazil, where the powers of Life are predominant, or those of Tierra del Fuego, where Death and Decay prevail. Both are temples filled with the varied productions of the God of Nature:—no one can stand in these solitudes unmoved, and not feel that there is more in man than the mere breath of his body. In calling up images of the past, I find that the plains of Patagonia frequently cross before my eyes; yet these plains are pronounced by all wretched and useless. They can be described only by negative characters; without habitations, without water, without trees, without mountains, they support merely a few dwarf plants. Why then, and the case is not peculiar to myself, have these arid wastes taken so firm a hold on my memory? Why have not the still more level, the greener and more fertile Pampas, which are serviceable to mankind, produced an equal impression? I can scarcely analyze these feelings: but it must be partly owing to the free scope given to the imagination. The plains of Patagonia are boundless, for they are scarcely passable, and hence unknown: they bear the stamp of having lasted, as they are now, for ages, and there appears no limit to their duration through future time. If, as the ancients supposed, the flat earth was surrounded by an impassable breadth of water, or by deserts heated to an intolerable excess, who would not look at these last boundaries to man's knowledge with deep but ill-defined sensations?

Lastly, of natural scenery, the views from lofty mountains, though certainly in one sense not beautiful, are very memorable. When looking down from the highest crest of the Cordillera, the mind, undisturbed by minute details, was filled with the stupendous dimensions of the surrounding masses.

Of individual objects, perhaps nothing is more certain to create astonishment than the first sight in his native haunt of a barbarian,—of man in his lowest and most savage state. One's mind hurries back over past centuries, and then asks, could our progenitors have been men like these?—men, whose very signs and expressions are less intelligible to us than those of the domesticated animals; men, who do not possess the instinct of those animals, nor yet appear to boast of human reason, or at least of arts consequent on that reason. I do not believe it is possible to describe or paint the difference between savage and civilized man. It is the difference between a wild and tame animal: and part of the interest in beholding a savage, is the same which would lead every one to desire to see the lion in his desert, the tiger tearing his prey in the jungle, or the rhinoceros wandering over the wild plains of Africa.

Among the other most remarkable spectacles which we have beheld, may be ranked the Southern Cross, the cloud of Magellan, and the other constellations of the southern hemisphere—the water-spout—the glacier leading its blue stream of ice, overhanging the sea in a bold precipice—a lagoon-island raised by the reef-building corals—an active volcano—and the overwhelming effects of a violent earthquake. These latter phenomena, perhaps, possess for me a peculiar interest, from their intimate connexion with the geological structure of the world. The earthquake, however, must be to every one a most impressive event: the earth, considered from our earliest childhood as the type of solidity, has oscillated like a thin crust beneath our feet; and in seeing the laboured works of man in a moment overthrown, we feel the insignificance of his boasted power.

It has been said that the love of the chase is an inherent delight in man—a relic of an instinctive passion. If so, I am sure the pleasure of living in the open air, with the sky for a roof and the ground for a table, is part of the same feeling; it is the savage returning to his wild and native habits. I always look back to our boat cruises, and my land journeys, when through unfrequented countries, with an extreme delight, which no scenes of civilization could have created. I do not doubt that every traveller must remember the glowing sense of happiness which he experienced when he first breathed in a foreign clime, where the civilized man had seldom or never trod.

There are several other sources of enjoyment in a long voyage which are of a more reasonable nature. The map of the world ceases to be a blank; it becomes a picture full of the most varied and animated figures. Each part assumes its proper dimensions: continents are not looked at in the light of islands, or islands considered as mere specks, which are, in truth, larger than many kingdoms of Europe. Africa, or North and South America, are well-sounding names, and easily pronounced; but it is not until having sailed for weeks along small portions of their shores, that one is thoroughly convinced what vast spaces on our immense world these names imply.

From seeing the present state, it is impossible not to look forward with high expectations to the future progress of nearly an entire hemisphere. The march of improvement, consequent on the introduction of Christianity throughout the South Sea, probably stands by itself in the records of history. It is the more striking when we remember that only sixty years since, Cook, whose excellent judgment none will dispute, could foresee no prospect of a change. Yet these changes have now been effected by the philanthropic spirit of the British nation.

In the same quarter of the globe Australia is rising, or indeed may be said to have risen, into a grand centre of civilization, which, at some not very remote period, will rule as empress over the southern hemisphere. It is impossible for an Englishman to behold these distant colonies without a high pride and satisfaction. To hoist the British flag, seems to draw with it as a certain consequence, wealth, prosperity, and civilization.

In conclusion, it appears to me that nothing can be more improving to a young naturalist than a journey in distant countries. It both sharpens, and partly allays that want and craving, which, as Sir J. Herschel remarks, a man experiences although every corporeal sense be fully satisfied. The excitement from the novelty of objects, and the chance of success, stimulate him to increased activity. Moreover, as a number of isolated facts soon become uninteresting, the habit of comparison leads to generalization. On the other hand, as the traveller stays but a short time in each place, his descriptions must generally consist of mere sketches, instead of detailed observations. Hence arises, as I have found to my cost, a constant tendency to fill up the wide gaps of knowledge, by inaccurate and superficial hypotheses.

But I have too deeply enjoyed the voyage, not to recommend any naturalist, although he must not expect to be so fortunate in his companions as I have been, to take all chances, and to start, on travels by land if possible, if otherwise on a long voyage. He may feel assured, he will meet with no difficulties or dangers, excepting in rare cases, nearly so bad as he beforehand anticipates. In a moral point of view, the effect ought to be, to teach him good-humoured patience, freedom from selfishness, the habit of acting for himself, and of making the best of every occurrence. In short, he ought to partake of the characteristic qualities of most sailors. Travelling ought also to teach him distrust; but at the same time he will discover, how many truly kind-hearted people there are, with whom he never before had, or ever again will have any further communication, who yet are ready to offer him the most disinterested assistance.

RALPH WALDO EMERSON
1803–1882

Educated at Harvard and raised in the Unitarian tradition of Boston, Emerson was honest and stubborn enough to relinquish his post as minister of the Second Church of Boston when he disagreed with his congregation over Christ's presumed intentions in performing the Last Supper. In his search for a quasi-religious philosophy he could embrace, he devoured the writings of Coleridge, Wordsworth, and Carlyle (the

"C." of his visit to Stonehenge), and enjoyed conversations with them during two trips to England, one in 1832, one in 1847. And late in life, in 1872, he went on a final journey abroad, to the Near East as far as Egypt. But most of his time he spent in Concord, Massachusetts, working up the lectures on intellect and ethics he gave first in Boston and then all over the country. These, stressing "self-reliance" and a due skepticism toward received forms, established his reputation as the esteemed "Sage of Concord."

As a traveler and a travel writer he is unique, an itinerant ethical philosopher prone to effuse constant metaphors, interested in places largely as providing insights into people, customs, usages, identities. A sophisticated wonder is his customary tone, an unremitting curiosity about man and his emblematic environment is his constant impulse. As Henry van Dyke, one of Emerson's early twentieth-century admirers, wrote, "On his pages, close beside the Parthenon, the Sphinx, Etna and Vesuvius, you will find the White Mountains, Monadnock, Katahdin, the pickerel weed in bloom, the wild geese honking through the sky, Wall Street, cotton mills, and Quincy granite. For an abstract thinker, he was strangely in love with the concrete facts of life."

From ENGLISH TRAITS
(1856)

VOYAGE TO ENGLAND

The occasion of my second visit to England was an invitation from some Mechanics' Institutes in Lancashire and Yorkshire, which separately are organised much in the same way as our New England Lyceums, but, in 1847, had been linked into a "Union," which embraced twenty or thirty towns and cities, and presently extended into the middle counties, and northward into Scotland. I was invited, on liberal terms, to read a series of lectures in them all. The request was urged with every kind suggestion, and every assurance of aid and comfort, by friendliest parties in Manchester, who, in the sequel, amply redeemed their word. The remuneration was equivalent to the fees at that time paid in this country for the like services. At all events, it was sufficient to cover any travelling expenses, and the proposal offered an excellent opportunity of seeing the interior of England and Scotland, by means of a home, and a committee of intelligent friends, awaiting me in every town.

I did not go very willingly. I am not a good traveller, nor have I found that long journeys yield a fair share of reasonable hours. But the invitation was repeated and pressed at a moment of more leisure, and when I was a little spent by some unusual studies. I wanted a change and a tonic, and England was proposed to me. Besides, there were, at least, the dread attraction and salutary influences of the sea. So I took my berth in the packet-ship *Washington Irving*, and sailed from Boston on Tuesday, 5th October, 1847.

On Friday at noon, we had only made one hundred and thirty-four miles. A nimble Indian would have swum as far; but the captain affirmed that the ship would show us in time all her paces, and we crept along through the floating drift of boards, logs, and chips, which the rivers of Maine and New Brunswick pour into the sea after a freshet.

At last, on Sunday night, after doing one day's work in four, the storm came, the winds blew, and we flew before a north-wester, which strained every rope and sail. The good ship darts through the water all day, all night, like a fish, quivering with speed, gliding through liquid leagues, sliding from horizon to horizon. She has passed Cape Sable; she has reached the Banks; the land-birds are left; gulls, haglets, ducks, petrels, swim, dive, and hover around; no fishermen; she has passed the Banks, left five sail behind her, far on the edge of the west at sundown, which were far east of us at morn,—though they say at sea a stern chase is a long race,—and still we fly for our lives. The shortest sea-line from Boston to Liverpool is 2850 miles. This a steamer keeps, and saves 150 miles. A sailing ship can never go in a shorter line than 3000, and usually it is much longer. Our good master keeps his kites up to the last moment, studding-sails alow and aloft, and, by incessant straight steering, never loses a rod of way. Watchfulness is the law of the ship,—watch on watch, for advantage and for life. Since the ship was built, it seems, the master never slept but in his dayclothes whilst on board. "There are many advantages," says Saadi, "in sea-voyaging, but security is not one of them." Yet in hurrying over these abysses, whatever dangers we are running into, we are certainly running out of the risks of hundreds of miles every day, which have their own chances of squall, collision, sea-stroke, piracy, cold, and thunder. Hour for hour, the risk on a steamboat is greater; but the speed is safety, or, twelve days of danger, instead of twenty-four.

Our ship was registered 750 tons, and weighed perhaps, with all her freight, 1500 tons. The mainmast, from the deck to the top-bottom, measured 115 feet; the length of the deck, from stem to stern, 155. It is impossible not to personify a ship; everybody does, in everything they say:—she behaves well; she minds her rudder; she swims like a duck; she runs her nose into the water; she looks into a port. Then that wonderful *esprit du corps*, by which we adopt into our self-love everything we touch, makes us all champions of her sailing qualities.

The conscious ship hears all the praise. In one week she has made 1467 miles, and now, at night, seems to hear the steamer behind her, which left Boston to-day at two, has mended her speed, and is flying before the gray south wind eleven and a half knots the hour. The sea-fire shines in her wake, and far around wherever a wave breaks. I read the hour, 9h.45', on my watch by this light. Near the equator, you can read small print by it; and the mate describes the phosphoric insects, when taken up in a pail, as shaped like a Carolina potato.

I find the sea-life an acquired taste, like that for tomatoes and olives. The confinement, cold, motion, noise, and odour are not to be dispensed with. The floor of your room is sloped at an angle of twenty or thirty degrees, and I waked every morning with the belief that some one was tipping up my berth. Nobody likes to be treated ignominiously, upset, shoved against the side of the house, rolled over, suffocated with bilge, mephitis, and stewing oil. We get used to these annoyances at last, but the dread of the sea remains longer. The sea is masculine, the type of active strength. Look, what egg-shells are drifting all over it, each one, like ours, filled with men in ecstasies of terror, alternating with cockney conceit, as the sea is rough or smooth. Is this sad-coloured circle an eternal cemetery? In our graveyards we scoop a pit, but this aggressive water opens mile-wide pits and chasms, and makes a mouthful of a fleet. To the geologist, the sea is the only firmament; the land is in perpetual flux and change, now blown up like a tumour, now sunk in a chasm, and the registered observations of a few hundred years find it in a perpetual tilt, rising and falling. The sea keeps its old level; and 'tis no wonder that the history of our race is so recent, if the roar of the ocean is silencing our traditions. A rising of the sea, such as has been observed, say an inch in a century, from east to west on the land, will bury all the towns, monuments, bones, and knowledge of mankind, steadily and insensibly. If it is capable of these great and secular mischiefs, it is quite as ready at private and local damage; and of this no landsman seems so fearful as the seaman. Such discomfort and such danger as the narratives of the captain and mate disclose are bad enough as the costly fee we pay for entrance to Europe; but the wonder is always new that any sane man can be a sailor. And here, on the second day of our voyage, stepped out a little boy in his shirtsleeves, who had hid himself, whilst the ship was in port, in the bread-closet, having no money, and wishing to go to England. The sailors have dressed him in Guernsey frock, with a knife in his belt, and he is climbing nimbly about after them, "likes the work first-rate, and, if the captain will take him, means now to come back again in the ship." The mate avers that this is the history of all sailors; nine out of ten are runaway boys; and adds, that all of them are sick of the sea, but stay in it out of pride. Jack has a life of risks, incessant abuse, and the worst pay. It is a little better with the mate, and not very much better with the captain. A hundred dollars a month is reckoned high pay. If sailors were contented, if they had not resolved again and again not to go to sea any more, I should respect them.

Of course, the inconveniences and terrors of the sea are not of any account to those whose minds are pre-occupied. The water-laws, arctic frost, the mountain, the mine, only shatter Cockneyism; every noble activity makes room for itself. A great mind is a good sailor, as a great heart is. And the sea is not slow in disclosing inestimable secrets to a good naturalist.

'Tis a good rule in every journey to provide some piece of liberal study to rescue the hours which bad weather, bad company, and taverns steal from the best economist. Classics which at home are drowsily read have a strange charm in a country inn, or in the transom of a merchant brig. I remember that some of the happiest and most valuable hours I have owed to books, passed, many years ago, on shipboard. The worst impediment I have found at sea is the want of light in the cabin.

We found on board the usual cabin library; Basil Hall, Dumas, Dickens, Bulwer, Balzac, and Sand, were our seagods. Among the passengers, there was some variety of talent and profession; we exchanged our experiences, and all learned something. The busiest talk with leisure and convenience at sea, and sometimes a memorable fact turns up, which you have long had a vacant niche for, and seize with the joy of a collector. But under the best conditions, a voyage is one of the severest tests to try a man. A college examination is nothing to it. Sea-days are long,—these lack-lustre, joyless days which whistled over us; but they were few,—only fifteen, as the captain counted, sixteen according to me. Reckoned from the time when we left soundings, our speed was such that the captain drew the line of his course in red ink on his chart, for the encouragement or envy of future navigators.

It has been said that the King of England would consult his dignity by giving audience to foreign ambassadors in the cabin of a man-of-war. And I think the white path of an Atlantic ship the right avenue to the palace front of this seafaring people, who for hundreds of years claimed the strict sovereignty of the sea, and exacted toll and the striking sail from the ships of all other peoples. When their privilege was disputed by the Dutch and other junior marines, on the plea that you could never anchor on the same wave, or hold property in what was always flowing, the English did not stick to claim the channel or bottom of all the main.

"As if," said they, "we contended for the drops of the sea, and not for its situation, or the bed of those waters. The sea is bounded by His Majesty's empire."

As we neared the land, its genius was felt. This was inevitably the British side. In every man's thought arises now a new system, English sentiments, English loves and fears, English history and social modes. Yesterday, every passenger had measured the speed of the ship by watching the bubbles over the ship's bulwarks. To-day, instead of bubbles, we measure by Kinsale, Cork, Waterford, and Ardmore. There lay the green shore of Ireland, like some coast of plenty. We could see towns, towers, churches, harvests; but the curse of eight hundred years we could not discern.

MANNERS

I find the Englishman to be him of all men who stands firmest in his shoes. They have in themselves what they value in their horses, mettle and bottom. On the day of my arrival at Liverpool, a gentleman, in describing to me the Lord Lieutenant of Ireland, happened to say, "Lord Clarendon has pluck like a cock, and will fight till he dies;" and, what I heard first I heard last; the one thing the English value is pluck. The cabmen have it; the merchants have it; the bishops have it; the women have it; the journals have it; the *Times* newspaper, they say, is the pluckiest thing in England, and Sydney Smith had made it a proverb that little Lord John Russell, the minister, would take the command of the Channel fleet to-morrow.

They require you to dare to be of your own opinion, and they hate the practical cowards who cannot in affairs answer directly yes or no. They dare to displease, nay, they will let you break all the commandments, if you do it natively, and with spirit. You must be somebody; then you may do this or that, as you will.

Machinery has been applied to all work, and carried to such perfection, that little is left for the men but to mind the engines and feed the furnaces. But the machines require punctual service, and, as they never tire, they prove too much for their tenders. Mines, forges, mills, breweries, railroads, steam-pump, steam-plough, drill of regiments, drill of police, rule of court, and shop-rule, have operated to give a mechanical regularity to all the habit and action of men. A terrible machine has possessed itself of the ground, the air, the men and women, and hardly even thought is free.

The mechanical might and organisation requires in the people constitution and answering spirits: and he who goes among them must have some weight of metal. At last, you take your hint from the fury of life you find, and say, one thing is plain, this is no country for fainthearted people; don't creep about diffidently; make up your mind; take your own course, and you shall find respect and furtherance.

It requires, men say, a good constitution to travel in Spain. I say as much of England, for other cause, simply on account of the vigour and brawn of the people. Nothing but the most serious business could give one any counterweight to these Baresarks, though they were only to order eggs and muffins for their breakfast. The Englishman speaks with all his body. His elocution is stomachic—as the American's is labial. The Englishman is very petulant and precise about his accommodation at inns, and on the roads; a quiddle about his toast and his chop, and every species of convenience, and loud and pungent in his expressions of impatience at any neglect. His vivacity betrays itself, at all points, in his manners, in his respiration, and the inarticulate noises he makes in clearing the throat;—all significant of burly strength. He has stamina; he can take the initiative in emergencies. He has that *aplomb* which results from a good adjustment of the moral and physical nature, and the obedience of all the powers to the will; as if the axes of his eyes were united to his backbone, and only moved with the trunk.

This vigour appears in the incuriosity, and stony neglect, each of every other. Each man walks, eats, drinks, shaves, dresses, gesticulates, and, in every manner, acts and suffers without reference to the bystanders, in his own fashion, only careful not to interfere with them, or annoy them; not that he is trained to neglect the eyes of his neighbours—he is really occupied with his own affair, and does not think of them. Every man in this polished country consults only his convenience, as much as a solitary pioneer in Wisconsin. I know not where any personal eccentricity is so freely allowed, and no man gives himself any concern with it. An Englishman walks in a pouring rain, swinging his closed umbrella like a walking-stick; wears a wig, or a shawl, or a saddle, or stands on his head, and no remark is made. And as he has been doing this for several generations, it is now in the blood.

In short, every one of these islanders is an island himself, safe, tranquil, incommunicable. In a company of strangers, you would think him deaf: his eyes never wander from his table and newspaper. He is never betrayed into any curiosity or unbecoming emotion. They have all been trained in one severe school of manners, and never put off the harness. He does not give his hand. He does not let you meet his eye. It is almost an affront to look a man in the face, without being introduced. In mixed or in select companies they do not introduce persons; so that a presentation is a circumstance as valid as a contract. Introductions are sacraments. He withholds his name. At the hotel he is hardly willing to whisper it to the clerk at the book-office. If he give you his private address on a card, it is like an avowal of friendship; and his bearing, on being introduced, is cold, even though he is seeking your acquaintance, and is studying how he shall serve you.

It was an odd proof of this impressive energy, that, in my lectures, I hesitated to read and threw out for its impertinence many a disparaging phrase, which I had been accustomed to spin, about poor, thin, unable mortals;—so much had the fine physique and the personal vigour of this robust race worked on my imagination.

I happened to arrive in England at the moment of a commercial crisis. But it was evident, that, let who will fail, England will not. These people have sat here a thousand years, and here will continue to sit. They will not break up, or arrive at any desperate revolution, like their neighbours; for they have as much energy, as much continence of character as they ever had. The power and possession which surround them are their own creation, and they exert the same commanding industry at this moment.

They are positive, methodical, cleanly, and formal, loving routine, and conventional ways; loving truth and religion, to be sure, but inexorable on points of form. All the world praises the comfort and private appointments of an English inn, and of English households. You are sure of neatness and of personal decorum. A Frenchman may possibly be clean; an Englishman is conscientiously clean. A certain order and complete propriety is found in his dress and in his belongings.

Born in a harsh and wet climate, which keeps him indoors whenever he is at rest, and being of an affectionate and loyal temper, he dearly loves his house. If he is rich, he buys a demesne, and builds a hall; if he is in middle condition, he spares no expense on his house. Without, it is all planted: within, it is wainscoted, carved, curtained, hung with pictures, and filled with good furniture. 'Tis a passion which survives all others, to deck and improve it. Hither he brings all that is rare and costly, and with the national tendency to sit fast in the same spot for many generations, it comes to be, in the course of time, a museum of heirlooms, gifts, and trophies of the adventures and exploits of the family. He is very fond of silver plate, and, though he have no gallery of portraits of his ancestors, he has of their punch-bowls and porringers. Incredible amounts of plate are found in good houses, and the poorest have some spoon or saucepan, gift of a godmother, saved out of better times.

An English family consists of a few persons, who, from youth to age, are found revolving within a few feet of each other, as if tied by some invisible ligature, tense as that cartilage which we have seen attaching the two Siamese. England produces under favourable conditions of ease and culture the finest women in the world. And as the men are affectionate and true-hearted, the women inspire and refine them. Nothing can be more delicate without being fantastical, nothing more firm and based in nature and sentiment, than the courtship and mutual carriage of the sexes. The song of 1596 says, "The wife of every Englishman is counted blest." The sentiment of Imogen in "Cymbeline" is copied from English nature; and not less the Portia of Brutus, the Kate Percy, and the Desdemona. The romance does not exceed the height of noble passion in Mrs. Lucy Hutchinson, or in Lady Russell, or even as one discerns through the plain prose of "Pepys's Diary" the sacred habit of an English wife. Sir Samuel Romilly could not bear the death of his wife. Every class has its noble and tender examples.

Domesticity is the tap-root which enables the nation to branch wide and high. The motive and end of their trade and empire is to guard the independence and privacy of their homes. Nothing so much marks their manners as the concentration on their household ties. This domesticity is carried into court and camp. Wellington governed India and Spain and his own troops, and fought battles, like a good family man, paid his debts, and, though general of an army in Spain, could not stir abroad for fear of public creditors. This taste for house and parish merits has of course its doting and foolish side. Mr. Cobbett attributes the huge popularity of Perceval, prime minister in 1810, to the fact that he was wont to go to church, every Sunday, with a large quarto gilt prayer-book under one arm, his wife hanging on the other, and followed by a long brood of children.

They keep their old customs, costumes, and pomps, their wig and mace, sceptre and crown. The middle ages still lurk in the streets of London. The Knights of the Bath take oath to defend injured ladies; the gold-stick-in-waiting survives. They repeated the ceremonies of the eleventh century in the coronation of the present Queen. A hereditary tenure is natural to them. Offices, farms, trades, and traditions descend so. Their leases run for a hundred and a thousand years. Terms of service and partnership are lifelong, or are inherited. "Holdship has been with me," said Lord Eldon, "eight-and-twenty years, knows all my business and books." Antiquity of usage is sanction enough. Wordsworth says of the small freeholders of Westmoreland, "Many of these humble sons of the hills had a consciousness that the land which they tilled had for more than five hundred years been possessed by men of the same name and blood." The ship-carpenter in the public yards, my lord's gardener and porter, have been there for more than a hundred years, grandfather, father, and son.

The English power resides also in their dislike of change. They have difficulty in bringing their reason to act, and on all occasions use their memory first. As soon as they have rid themselves of some grievance, and settled the better practice, they make haste to fix it as a finality, and never wish to hear of alteration more.

Every Englishman is an embryonic chancellor. His instinct is to search for a precedent. The favourite phrase of their law, is, "a custom whereof the memory of man runneth not back to the contrary." The barons say, *"Nolumus mutari* [We will not change];" and the cockneys stifle the curiosity of the foreigner on the reason of any practice, with "Lord, sir, it was always so!" They hate innovation. Bacon told them, Time was the right reformer; Chatham, that "confidence was a plant of slow growth;" Canning, to "advance with the times;" and Wellington, that "habit was ten times nature." All their statesmen learn the resistibility of the tide of custom, and have invented many fine phrases to cover this slowness of perception, and prehensility of tail.

A sea-shell should be the crest of England, not only because it represents a power built on the waves, but also the hard finish of the men. The Englishman is finished like a cowry or a murex. After the spire and the spines are formed, or, with the formation, a juice exudes, and a hard enamel varnishes every part. The keeping of the properties is as indispensable as clean linen. No merit quite countervails the want of this, whilst this sometimes stands in lieu of all. " 'Tis in bad taste," is the most formidable word an Englishman can pronounce. But this japan costs them dear. There is a prose in certain Englishmen which exceeds in wooden deadness all rivalry with other countrymen. There is a knell in the conceit and externality of their voice which seems to say, *Leave all hope behind.* In this Gibraltar of propriety, mediocrity gets intrenched, and consolidated, and founded in adamant. An Englishman of fashion is like one of those souvenirs, bound in gold vellum, enriched with delicate engravings on thick hot-pressed paper, fit for the hands of ladies and princes, but with nothing in it worth reading or remembering.

A severe decorum rules the court and the cottage. When Thalberg, the pianist, was one evening performing before the Queen, at Windsor, in a private party, the Queen accompanied him with her voice. The circumstance took air, and all England shuddered from sea to sea. The indecorum was never repeated. Cold, repressive manners prevail. No enthusiasm is permitted except at the opera. They avoid everything marked. They require a tone of voice that excites no attention in the room. Sir Philip Sidney is one of the patron saints of England, of whom Wotton said, "His wit was the measure of congruity."

Pretension and vapouring are once for all distasteful. They keep to the other extreme of low tone in dress and manners. They avoid pretension and go right to the heart of the thing. They hate nonsense, sentimentalism, and highflown expression; they use a studied plainness. Even Brummel their fop was marked by the severest simplicity in dress. They value themselves on the absence of everything theatrical in the public business, and on conciseness and going to the point in private affairs.

In an aristocratical country, like England, not the Trial by Jury, but the dinner, is the capital institution. It is the mode of doing honour to a stranger, to invite him to eat—and has been for many hundred years. "And they think," says the Venetian traveller of 1500, "no greater honour can be conferred or received, than to invite others to eat with them, or to be invited themselves, and they would sooner give five or six ducats to provide an entertainment for a person, than a groat to assist him in any distress." It is reserved to the end of the day, the family hour being generally six, in London, and, if any company is expected, one or two hours later. Every one dresses for dinner, in his own house, or in another man's. The guests are expected to arrive within half an hour of the time fixed by card of invitation, and nothing but death or mutilation is permitted to detain them. The English dinner is precisely the model on which our own are constructed in the Atlantic cities. The company sit one or two hours, before the ladies leave the table. The gentlemen remain over their wine an hour longer, and rejoin the ladies in the drawing-room, and take coffee. The dress-dinner generates a talent of table-talk which reaches great perfection: the stories are so good that one is sure they must have been often told before, to have got such happy turns. Hither come all manner of clever projects, bits of popular science, of practical invention, of miscellaneous humour; political, literary, and personal news; railroads, horses, diamonds, agriculture, horticulture, pisciculture and wine.

English stories, bon-mots, and the recorded table-talk of their wits, are as good as the best of the French. In America, we are apt scholars, but have not yet attained the same perfection: for the range of nations from which London draws, and the steep contrasts of condition, create the picturesque in society, as broken country makes picturesque landscape, whilst our prevailing equality makes a prairie tameness: and secondly, because the usage of a dress-dinner every day at dark has a tendency to hive and produce to advantage everything good. Much attrition has worn every sentence into a bullet. Also one meets now and then with polished men, who know everything, have tried everything, can do everything, and are quite superior to letters and science. What could they not, if only they would?

STONEHENGE

It had been agreed between my friend Mr. C. and me, that before I left England, we should make an excursion together to Stonehenge, which neither of us had seen; and the project pleased my fancy with the double attraction of the monument and the companion. It seemed a bringing together of extreme points, to visit the oldest religious monument in Britain, in company with her latest thinker, and one whose influence may be traced in every contemporary book. I was glad to sum up a little my experiences, and to exchange a few reasonable words on the aspects of England, with a man on whose genius I set a very high value, and who had as much penetration, and as severe a theory of duty, as any person in it. On Friday, 7th July, we took the South Western Railway through Hampshire to Salisbury, where we found a carriage to convey us to Amesbury. The fine weather and my friend's local knowledge of Hampshire, in which he is wont to spend a part of every summer, made the way short. There was much to say, too, of the travelling Americans, and their usual objects in London. I thought it natural that they should give some time to works of art collected here which they cannot find at home, and a little to scientific clubs and museums, which, at this moment, make London very attractive. But my philosopher was not contented. Art and "high art" is a favourite target for his wit. "Yes, *Kunst* is a great delusion, and Goethe and Schiller wasted a great deal of good time on it:"—and he thinks he discovers that old Goethe found this out, and, in his later writings, changed his tone. As soon as men begin to talk of art, architecture, and antiquities, nothing good comes of it. He wishes to go through the British Museum in silence, and thinks a sincere man will see something, and say nothing. In these days, he thought, it would become an architect to consult only the grim necessity, and say, "I can build you a coffin for such dead persons as you are, and for such dead purposes as you have, but you shall have no ornament." For the science, he had, if possible, even less tolerance, and compared the savants of Somerset House to the boy who asked Confucius "How many stars in the sky?" Confucius replied, "He minded things near him." Then said the boy, "How many hairs are there in your eyebrows?" Confucius said, "He didn't know and didn't care."

Still speaking of the Americans, C. complained that they dislike the coldness and exclusiveness of the English, and run away to France, and go with their countrymen, and are amused, instead of manfully staying in London, and confronting Englishmen, and acquiring their culture, who really have much to teach them.

I told C. that I was easily dazzled, and was accustomed to concede readily all that an Englishman would ask; I saw everywhere in the country proofs of sense and spirit, and success of every sort: I like the people: they are as good as they are handsome; they have everything, and can do everything: but meantime, I surely know, that, as soon as I return to Massachusetts, I shall lapse at once into the feeling, which the geography of America inevitably inspires, that we play the game with immense advantage; that there and not here is the seat and centre of the British race; and that no skill or activity can long compete with the prodigious natural advantages of that country, in the hands of the same race; and that England, an old and exhausted island, must one day be contented, like other parents, to be strong only in her children. But this was a proposition which no Englishman of whatever condition can easily entertain.

We left the train at Salisbury, and took a carriage to Amesbury, passing by Old Sarum, a bare, treeless hill, once containing the town which sent two members to Parliament—now, not a hut;—and, arriving at Amesbury, stopped at the George Inn. After dinner, we walked to Salisbury Plain. On the broad downs, under the gray sky, not a house was visible, nothing but Stonehenge, which looked like a group of brown dwarfs in the wide expanse—Stonehenge and the barrows—which rose like green bosses about the plain, and a few hayricks. On the top of a mountain, the old temple would not be more impressive. Far and wide a few shepherds with their flocks sprinkled the plain, and a bagman drove along the road. It looked as if the wide margin given in this crowded isle to this primeval temple was accorded by the veneration of the British race to the old egg out of which all their ecclesiastical structures and history had proceeded. Stonehenge is a circular colonnade with a diameter of a hundred feet, and enclosing a second and a third colonnade within. We walked round the stones, and clambered over them, to wont ourselves with their strange aspect and groupings, and found a nook sheltered from the wind among them, where C. lighted his cigar. It was pleasant to see, that, just this simplest of all simple structures—two upright stones and a lintel laid across—had long outstood all later churches, and all history, and were like what is most permanent on the face of the planet: these, and the barrows—mere mounds (of which there are a hundred and sixty within a circle of three miles about Stonehenge), like the same mound on the plain of Troy, which still makes good to the passing mariner on Hellespont the vaunt of Homer and the fame of Achilles. Within the enclosure, grow buttercups, nettles, and, all around, wild thyme, daisy, meadowsweet, goldenrod, thistle, and the carpeting grass. Over us, larks were soaring and singing—as my friend said, "the larks which were hatched last year, and the wind which was hatched many thousand years ago." We counted and measured by paces the biggest stones, and soon knew as much as any man can suddenly know of the inscrutable temple. There are ninety-four stones, and there were once probably one hundred and sixty. The temple is circular, and uncovered, and the situation fixed astronomically—the grand entrances here, and at Abury, being placed exactly north-east, "as all the gates of the old cavern temples are." How came the stones here? for these *sarsens*, or Druidical sandstones, are not found in this neighbourhood. The *sacrificial stone*, as it is called, is the only one in all these blocks that can resist the action of fire, and as I read in the books, must have been brought one hundred and fifty miles.

On almost every stone we found the marks of the mineralogist's hammer and chisel. The nineteen smaller stones of the inner circle are of granite. I, who had just come from Professor Sedgwick's Cambridge Museum of megatheria and mastodons, was ready to maintain that some cleverer elephants or mylodonta had borne off and laid these rocks one on another. Only the good beasts must have known how to cut a well-wrought tenon and mortise, and to smooth the surface of some of the stones. The chief mystery is that any mystery should have been allowed to settle on so remarkable a monument, in a country on which all the muses have kept their eyes now for eighteen hundred years. We are not yet too late to learn much more than is known of this structure. Some diligent Fellowes or Layard will arrive, stone by stone, at the whole history, by that exhaustive British sense and perseverance, so whimsical in its choice of objects, which leaves its own Stonehenge or Choir Gaur to the rabbits, whilst it opens pyramids, and uncovers Nineveh. Stonehenge, in virtue of the simplicity of its plan, and its good preservation, is as if new and recent; and, a thousand years hence, men will thank this age for the accurate history it will yet eliminate. We walked in and out, and took again and again a fresh look at the uncanny stones. The old sphinx put our petty differences of nationality out of sight. To these conscious stones we two pilgrims were alike known and near. We could equally well revere their old British meaning. My philosopher was subdued and gentle. In this quiet house of destiny, he happened to say, "I plant cypresses wherever I go, and if I am in search of pain, I cannot go wrong." The spot, the gray blocks, and their rude order, which refuses to be disposed of, suggested to him the flight of ages, and the succession of religions. The old times of England impress C. much: he reads little, he says, in these last years, but *"Acta Sanctorum,"* the fifty-three volumes of which are in the London Library. He finds all English history therein. He can see, as he reads, the old saint of Iona sitting there, and writing, a man to men. The *Acta Sanctorum* show plainly that the men of those times believed in God, and in the immortality of the soul, as their abbeys and cathedrals testify: now, even the puritanism is all gone. London is pagan. He fancied that greater men had lived in England than any of her writers; and, in fact, about the time when those writers appeared, the last of these were already gone.

We left the mound in the twilight, with the design to return the next morning, and coming back two miles to our inn, we were met by little showers, and late as it was, men and women were out attempting to protect their spread wind-rows. The grass grows rank and dark in the showery England. At the inn, there was only milk for one cup of tea. When we called for more, the girl brought us three drops. My friend was annoyed who stood for the credit of an English inn, and still more, the next morning, by the dog-cart, sole procurable vehicle, in which we were to be sent to Wilton. I engaged the local antiquary, Mr. Brown to go with us to Stonehenge, on our way, and show us what he knew of the "astronomical" and "sacrificial" stones. I stood on the last, and he pointed to the upright, or rather, inclined stone, called the "astronomical," and bade me notice that its top ranged with the sky-line. "Yes." Very well. Now, at the summer solstice, the sun rises exactly over the top of that stone, and, at the Druidical temple at Abury, there is also an astronomical stone, in the same relative positions.

In the silence of tradition, this one relation to science becomes an important clue; but we were content to leave the problem with the rocks. Was this the "Giants' Dance" which Merlin brought from Killaraus, in Ireland, to be Uther Pendragon's monument to the British nobles whom Hengist slaughtered here, as Geoffrey of Monmouth relates? or was it a Roman work, as Inigo Jones explained to King James; or identical in design and style with the East Indian temples of the sun as Davies in the "Celtic Researches" maintains? Of all the writers, Stukeley is the best. The heroic antiquary, charmed with the geometric perfections of his ruin, connects it with the oldest monuments and religion of the world, and with the courage of his tribe, does not stick to say, "The Deity who made the world by the scheme of Stonehenge." He finds that the *cursus* [broad avenue] on Salisbury Plain stretches across the downs, like a line of latitude upon the globe, and the meridian line of Stonehenge passes exactly through the middle of this *cursus*. But here is the high point of the theory: the Druids had the magnet; laid their courses by it; their cardinal points in Stonehenge, Ambresbury, and elsewhere, which vary a little from true east and west, followed the variations of the compass. The Druids were Phœnicians. The name of the magnet is *lapis Heracleus* [stone of Hercules], and Hercules was the god of the

Phœnicians. Hercules, in the legend, drew his bow at the sun, and the sungod gave him a golden cup, with which he sailed over the ocean. What was this, but a compass-box? This cup or little boat, in which the magnet was made to float on water, and so show the north, was probably its first form, before it was suspended on a pin. But science was an *arcanum* [secret], and, as Britain was a Phœnician secret, so they kept their compass a secret, and it was lost with the Tyrian commerce. The golden fleece, again, of Jason, was the compass—a bit of loadstone, easily supposed to be the only one in the world, and therefore naturally awakening the cupidity and ambition of the young heroes of a maritime nation to join in an expedition to obtain possession of this wise stone. Hence the fable that the ship Argo was loquacious and oracular. There is also some curious coincidence in the names. Apollodorus makes *Magnes* the son of *Æolus*, who married *Nais*. On hints like these, Stukeley builds again the grand colonnade into historic harmony, and computing backward by the known variations of the compass, bravely assigns the year 406 before Christ for the date of the temple.

For the difficulty of handling and carrying stones of this size, the like is done in all cities, every day, with no other aid than horse power. I chanced to see a year ago men at work on the substructure of a house in Bowdoin Square, in Boston, swinging a block of granite of the size of the largest of the Stonehenge columns with an ordinary derrick. The men were common masons, with Paddies to help, nor did they think they were doing anything remarkable. I suppose there were as good men a thousand years ago. And we wonder how Stonehenge was built and forgotten. After spending half an hour on the spot, we set forth in our dogcart over the downs for Wilton, C. not suppressing some threats and evil omens on the proprietors, for keeping these broad plains a wretched sheep-walk, when so many thousands of English men were hungry and wanted labour. But I heard afterwards that it is not an economy to cultivate this land, which only yields one crop on being broken up and is then spoiled.

We came to Wilton and to Wilton Hall,—the renowned seat of the Earls of Pembroke, a house known to Shakespeare and Massinger, the frequent home of Sir Philip Sidney where he wrote the "Arcadia"; where he conversed with Lord Brooke, a man of deep thought, and a poet, who caused to be engraved on his tombstone, "Here lies Fulke Greville Lord Brooke, the friend of Sir Philip Sidney." It is now the property of the Earl of Pembroke, and the residence of his brother, Sidney Herbert, and is esteemed a noble specimen of the English manor-hall. My friend had a letter from Mr. Herbert to his housekeeper, and the house was shown. The state drawing-room is a double cube, 30 feet high, by 30 feet wide, by 60 feet long: the adjoining room is a single cube of 30 feet every way. Although these apartments and the long library were full of good family portraits, Vandykes and other; and though there were some good pictures, and a quadrangle cloister full of antique and modern statuary,—to which C., catalogue in hand, did all too much justice,—yet the eye was still drawn to the windows, to a magnificent lawn, on which grew the finest cedars in England. I had not seen more charming grounds. We went out, and walked over the estate. We crossed a bridge built by Inigo Jones over a stream, of which the gardener did not know the name, (*Qu. Alph?*); watched the deer; climbed to the lonely sculptured summer-house, on a hill backed by a wood; came down into the Italian garden, and into a French pavilion, garnished with French busts; and so again, to the house, where we found a table laid for us with bread, meats, peaches, grapes, and wine.

On leaving Wilton House, we took the coach for Salisbury. The Cathedral, which was finished 600 years ago, has even a spruce and modern air, and its spire is the highest in England. I know not why, but I have been more struck with one of no fame at Coventry, which rises 300 feet from the ground, with the lightness of a mullein-plant, and not at all implicated with the church. Salisbury is now esteemed the culmination of the Gothic art in England, as the buttresses are fully unmasked, and honestly detailed from the sides of the pile. The interior of the Cathedral is obstructed by the organ in the middle, acting like a screen. I know not why in real architecture the hunger of the eye for length of line is so rarely gratified. The rule of art is that a colonnade is more beautiful the longer it is, and that *ad infinitum*. And the nave of a church is seldom so long that it need be divided by a screen.

We loitered in the church, outside the choir, whilst service was said. Whilst we listened to the organ, my friend remarked, the music is good, and yet not quite religious, but somewhat as if a monk were panting to some fine Queen of Heaven. C. was unwilling, and we did not ask to have the choir shown us, but returned to our inn, after seeing another old church of the place. We passed in the train Clarendon Park, but could see little but the edge of a wood, though C. had wished to pay closer attention to the birthplace of the Decrees of Clarendon. At Bishopstoke we stopped, and found Mr. H., who received us in his carriage, and took us to his house at Bishops Waltham.

On Sunday, we had much discourse on a very rainy day. My friends asked whether there were any Americans?—any with an American idea,—any theory of the right future of that country? Thus challenged, I bethought myself neither of caucuses nor congress, neither of presidents nor of cabinet-ministers, nor of such as would make of America another Europe. I thought only of the simplest and purest minds; I said, "Certainly yes; but those who hold it are fanatics of a dream which I should hardly care to relate to your English ears, to which it might be only ridiculous,—and yet it is the only true." So I opened the dogma of no-government and non-resistance, and anticipated the objections and the fun, and procured a kind of hearing for it. I said it is true that I have never seen in any country a man of sufficient valour to stand for this truth, and yet it is plain to me, that no less valour than this can command my respect. I can easily see the bankruptcy of the vulgar musket-worship,—though great men be musket-worshippers;—and 'tis certain, as God liveth, the gun that does not need another gun; the law of love and justice alone can effect a clean revolution. I fancied that one or two of my anecdotes made some impression on C., and I insisted, that the manifest absurdity of the view to English feasibility could make no difference to a gentleman; that as to our secure tenure of our mutton-chop and spinage in London or in Boston, the soul might quote Talleyrand, *"Monsieur, je n'en vois pas la necessité* [Sir, I don't see why]." As I had thus taken in the conversation the saint's part, when dinner was announced, C. refused to go out before me,—"He was altogether too wicked." I planted my back against the wall, and our host wittily rescued us from the dilemma, by saying, he was the wickedest, and would walk out first, then C. followed, and I went last.

On the way to Winchester, whither our host accompanied us in the afternoon, my friends asked many questions respecting American landscape, forests, houses,—my house, for example. It is not easy to answer these queries well. There I thought, in America, lies nature sleeping, over-growing, almost conscious, too much by half for man in the picture, and so giving a certain *tristesse* [melancholy], like the rank vegetation of swamps and forests seen at night, steeped in dews and rains, which it loves; and on it man seems not able to make much impression. There, in that great sloven continent, in high Allegheny pastures, in the sea-wide, sky-skirted prairie, still sleeps and murmurs and hides the great mother, long since driven away from the trim hedge-rows and over-cultivated garden of England. And, in England, I am quite too sensible of this. Every one is on his good behaviour, and must be dressed for dinner at six. So I put off my friends with very inadequate details, as best I could.

Just before entering Winchester, we stopped at the Church of Saint Cross, and, after looking through the quaint antiquity we demanded a piece of bread and a draught of beer, which the founder, Henry de Blois, in 1136, commanded should be given to everyone who should ask it at the gate. We had both, from the old couple who take care of the church.

Some twenty people, every day, they said, make the same demand. This hospitality of seven hundred years' standing did not hinder C. from pronouncing a malediction on the priest who receives £2,000 a year, that were meant for the poor, and spends a pittance on this small beer and crumbs.

In the Cathedral, I was gratified at least by the ample dimensions. The length of line exceeds that of any other English church; being 556 feet by 250 in breadth of transept. I think I prefer this church to all I have seen, except Westminster and York. Here was Canute buried, and here Alfred the Great was crowned and buried, and here the Saxon kings; and, later, in his own church, William of Wykeham. It is very old: part of the crypt into which we went down and saw the Saxon and Norman arches of the old church on which the present stands, was built fourteen or fifteen hundred years ago. Sharon Turner says, "Alfred was buried at Winchester, in the Abbey he had founded there, but his remains were removed by Henry I. to the new Abbey in the meadows at Hyde, on the northern quarter of the city, and laid under the high altar. The building was destroyed at the Reformation, and what is left of Alfred's body now lies covered by modern buildings, or buried in the ruins of the old." William of Wykeham's shrine tomb was unlocked for us, and C. took hold of the recumbent statue's marble hands, and patted them affectionately, for he rightly values the brave man who built Windsor, and this Cathedral, and the School here, and New College at Oxford. But it was growing late in the afternoon. Slowly we left the old house, and parting with our host, we took the train for London.

MARK TWAIN
1835–1910

Samuel Langhorne Clemens, born in Missouri, adopted his pseudonym while a young newspaper reporter in Virginia City, Nevada, in 1862, and used it to good effect in his career as a rowdy journalist and "serio-humorous lecturer," which followed on earlier vocations as printer and river-boat pilot.

In 1867 he was in New York, contributing sketches about life there to the San Francisco newspaper Daily Alta California. *It was as its correspondent that he enthusiastically joined a would-be genteel cruise aboard the sailing steamer* Quaker City. *The ultimate goal was the Holy Land—some parishioners of Henry Ward Beecher's Plymouth Church, in Brooklyn, were the originators of the venture—but there were to be attractive stopovers in France, where the Paris Exposition beckoned, as well as in Italy, Spain, Greece, Constantinople, and Egypt.*

Seventy-nine travelers embarked, many of them pious, and although Twain tried to be one of them and sometimes succeeded, the atmosphere of complacency, Sunday observance, and total abstinence got him down, and well before the Atlantic had been crossed he was seen conspicuously champagne drinking and poker playing, not to mention voicing sarcasms and blasphemies. He was locked up with a boatload of hypocrites, he came to believe, and with a small group of good old boys like himself he regarded with scorn the deadly shipboard routine of "solemnity, decorum, dinner, dominoes, prayers, slander."

But ashore, as these innocent self-improvers revealed a courageous stamina and met European snobberies with their open, democratic ways, Twain often became their sympathetic spokesman while remaining, on occasion, their mocker.

The book he made from his collected dispatches—jokey, half-irreverent toward European culture and customs, half awed by them— was an immediate success. Within three years it had sold 100,000 copies, unprecedented for a travel book then. And for decades afterwards Americans touring Europe and the Near East relied on it as a uniquely skeptical guidebook. Its insistence that the traveler see for himself, unfrightened by the received views of authority, was very much in the American grain.

From The Innocents Abroad
(1869)

PREFACE

This book is a record of a pleasure trip. If it were a record of a solemn scientific expedition, it would have about it that gravity, that profundity, and that impressive incomprehensibility which are so proper to works of that kind, and withal so attractive. Yet notwithstanding it is only a record of a picnic, it has a purpose, which is, to suggest to the reader how *he* would be likely to see Europe and the East if he looked at them with his own eyes instead of the eyes of those who traveled in those countries before him. I make small pretence of showing any one how he *ought* to look at objects of interest beyond the sea—other books do that, and therefore, even if I were competent to do it, there is no need.

I offer no apologies for any departures from the usual style of travel-writing that may be charged against me—for I think I have seen with impartial eyes, and I am sure I have written at least honestly, whether wisely or not.

In this volume I have used portions of letters which I wrote for the *Daily Alta California,* of San Francisco, the proprietors of that journal having waived their rights and given me the necessary permission.

I have also inserted portions of several letters written for the New York *Tribune* and the New York *Herald.*

THE AUTHOR.

SAN FRANCISCO.

CHAPTER I

For months the great Pleasure Excursion to Europe and the Holy Land was chatted about in the newspapers everywhere in America, and discussed at countless firesides. It was a novelty in the way of excursions—its like had not been thought of before, and it compelled that interest which attractive novelties always command. It was to be a picnic on a gigantic scale. The participants in it, instead of freighting an ungainly steam ferry-boat with youth and beauty and pies and doughnuts, and paddling up some obscure creek to disembark upon a grassy lawn and wear themselves out with a long summer day's laborious frolicking under the impression that it was fun, were to sail away in a great steamship with flags flying and cannon pealing, and take a royal holiday beyond the broad ocean, in many a strange clime and in many a land renowned in history! They were to sail for months over the breezy Atlantic and the sunny Mediterranean; they were to scamper about the decks by day, filling the ship with shouts and laughter—or read novels and poetry in the shade of the smoke-stacks, or watch for the jelly-fish and the nautilus, over the side, and the shark, the whale, and other strange monsters of the deep; and at night they were to dance in the open air, on the upper deck, in the midst of a ballroom that stretched from horizon to horizon, and was domed by the bending heavens and lighted by no meaner lamps than the stars and the magnificent moon—dance, and promenade, and smoke, and sing, and make love, and search the skies for constellations that never associate with the "Big Dipper" they were so tired of: and they were to see the ships of twenty navies—the customs and costumes of twenty curious peoples—the great cities of half a world—they were to hobnob with nobility and hold friendly converse with kings and princes, Grand Moguls, and the anointed lords of mighty empires!

It was a brave conception; it was the offspring of a most ingenious brain. It was well advertised, but it hardly needed it: the bold originality, the extraordinary character, the seductive nature, and the vastness of the enterprise provoked comment everywhere and advertised it in every household in the land. Who could read the program of the excursion without longing to make one of the party? I will insert it here. It is almost as good as a map. As a text for this book, nothing could be better:

EXCURSION TO THE HOLY LAND, EGYPT, THE CRIMEA,

GREECE, AND INTERMEDIATE POINTS OF INTEREST.

BROOKLYN, *February 1st, 1867.*

The undersigned will make an excursion as above during the coming season, and begs to submit to you the following programme:

A first-class steamer, to be under his own command, and capable of accommodating at least one hundred and fifty cabin passengers, will be selected, in which will be taken a select company, numbering not more than three-fourths of the ship's capacity. There is good reason to believe that this company can be easily made up in this immediate vicinity, of mutual friends and acquaintances.

The steamer will be provided with every necessary comfort, including library and musical instruments.

An experienced physician will be on board.

Leaving New York about June 1st, a middle and pleasant route will be taken across the Atlantic, and, passing through the group of Azores, St. Michael will be reached in about ten days. A day or two will be spent here, enjoying the fruit and wild scenery of these islands, and the voyage continued, and Gibraltar reached in three or four days.

A day or two will be spent here in looking over the wonderful subterraneous fortifications, permission to visit these galleries being readily obtained.

From Gibraltar, running along the coasts of Spain and France, Marseilles will be reached in three days. Here ample time will be given not only to look over the city, which was founded six hundred years before the Christian era, and its artificial port, the finest of the kind in the Mediterranean, but to visit Paris during the Great Exhibition; and the beautiful city of Lyons, lying intermediate, from the heights of which, on a clear day, Mont Blanc and the Alps can be distinctly seen. Passengers who may wish to extend the time at Paris can do so, and, passing down through Switzerland, rejoin the steamer at Genoa.

From Marseilles to Genoa is a run of one night. The excursionists will have an opportunity to look over this, the "magnificent city of palaces," and visit the birthplace of Columbus, twelve miles off, over a beautiful road built by Napoleon I. From this point, excursions may be made to Milan, Lakes Como and Maggiore, or to Milan, Verona (famous for its extraordinary fortifications), Padua, and Venice. Or, if passengers desire to visit Palma (famous for Correggio's frescoes) and Bologna, they can by rail go on to Florence, and rejoin the steamer at Leghorn, thus spending about three weeks amid the cities most famous for art in Italy.

From Genoa the run to Leghorn will be made along the coast in one night, and time appropriated to this point in which to visit Florence, its palaces and galleries: Pisa, its Cathedral and "Leaning Tower," and Lucca and its baths and Roman amphitheater; Florence, the most remote, being distant by rail about sixty miles.

From Leghorn to Naples (calling at Civita Vecchia to land any who may prefer to go to Rome from that point) the distance will be made in about thirty-six hours; the route will lay along the coast of Italy, close by Caprera, Elba, and Corsica. Arrangements have been made to take on board at Leghorn a pilot for Caprera, and, if practicable, a call will be made there to visit the home of Garibaldi.

Rome (by rail), Herculaneum, Pompeii, Vesuvius, Virgil's tomb, and possibly, the ruins of Paestum, can be visited, as well as the beautiful surroundings of Naples and its charming bay.

The next point of interest will be Palermo, the most beautiful city of Sicily, which will be reached in one night from Naples. A day will be spent here, and, leaving in the evening, the course will be taken towards Athens.

Skirting along the north coast of Sicily, passing through the group of Aeolian Isles, in sight of Stromboli and Vulcania, both active volcanoes, through the Straits of Messina, with "Scylla" on the one hand and "Charybdis" on the other, along the east coast of Sicily, and in sight of Mount Aetna, along the south coast of Italy, the west and south coast of Greece, in sight of ancient Crete, up Athens Gulf, and into the Piraeus, Athens will be reached in two and a half or three days. After tarrying here awhile, the Bay of Salamis will be crossed, and a day given to Corinth, whence the voyage will be continued to Constantinople, passing on the way through the Grecian Archipelago, the Dardanelles, the Sea of Marmora, and the mouth of the Golden Horn, and arriving in about forty-eight hours from Athens.

After leaving Constantinople, the way will be taken out through the beautiful Bosphorus, across the Black Sea to Sebastopol and Balaklava, a run of about twenty-four hours. Here it is proposed to remain two days, visiting the harbors, fortifications, and battlefields of the Crimea; thence back through the Bosphorus, touching at Constantinople to take in any who may have preferred to remain there; down through the Sea of Marmora and the Dardanelles, along the coasts of ancient Troy and Lydia in Asia, to Smyrna, which will be reached in two or two and a half days from Constantinople. A sufficient stay will be made here to give opportunity of visiting Ephesus, fifty miles distant by rail.

From Smyrna towards the Holy Land the course will lay through the Grecian Archipelago, close by the Isle of Patmos, along the coast of Asia, ancient Pamphylia, and the Isle of Cyprus. Beirout will be reached in three days. At Beirout time will be given to visit Damascus; after which the steamer will proceed to Joppa.

From Joppa, Jerusalem, the River Jordan, the Sea of Tiberias, Nazareth, Bethany, Bethlehem, and other points of interest in the Holy Land can be visited, and here those who may have preferred to make the journey from Beirout *through* the country, passing through Damascus, Galilee, Capernaum, Samaria, and by the River Jordan and Sea of Tiberias, can rejoin the steamer.

Leaving Joppa, the next point of interest to visit will be Alexandria, which will be reached in twenty-four hours. The ruins of Caesar's Palace, Pompey's Pillar, Cleopatra's Needle, the Catacombs, and ruins of ancient Alexandria, will be found worth the visit. The journey to Cairo, one hundred and thirty miles by rail, can be made in a few hours, and from which can be visited the site of ancient Memphis, Joseph's Granatles, and the Pyramids.

From Alexandria the route will be taken homeward, calling at Malta, Cagliari (in Sardinia), and Palma (in Majorca), all magnificent harbors, with charming scenery, and abounding in fruits.

A day or two will be spent at each place, and leaving Palma in the evening, Valencia in Spain will be reached the next morning. A few days will be spent in this, the finest city of Spain.

From Valencia, the homeward course will be continued, skirting along the coast of Spain, Alicante, Carthagena, Palos, and Malaga will be passed but a mile or two distant, and Gibraltar reached in about twenty-four hours.

A stay of one day will be made here, and the voyage continued to Madeira, which will be reached in about three days. Captain Marryatt writes: "I do not know a spot on the globe which so much astonishes and delights upon first arrival as Madeira." A stay of one or two days will be made here, which, if time permits, may be extended, and passing on through the islands, and probably in sight of the Peak of Teneriffe, a southern track will be taken, and the Atlantic crossed within the latitudes of the Northeast trade winds, where mild and pleasant weather and a smooth sea can always be expected.

A call will be made at Bermuda, which lies directly in this route homeward, and will be reached in about ten days from Madeira, and after spending a short time with our friends the Bermudians, the final departure will be made for home, which will be reached in about three days.

Already, applications have been received from parties in Europe wishing to join the Excursion there.

The ship will at all times be a home, where the excursionists, if sick, will be surrounded by kind friends, and have all possible comfort and sympathy.

Should contagious sickness exist in any of the ports named in the programme, such ports will be passed, and others of interest substituted.

The price of passage is fixed at $1,250, currency, for each adult passenger. Choice of rooms and of seats at the tables apportioned in the order in which passages are engaged, and no passage considered engaged until ten per cent of the passage money is deposited with the treasurer.

Passengers can remain on board of the steamer at all ports, if they desire, without additional expense, and all boating at the expense of the ship.

All passages must be paid for when taken, in order that the most perfect arrangements be made for starting at the appointed time.

Applications for passage must be approved by the committee before tickets are issued, and can be made to the undersigned.

Articles of interest or curiosity, procured by the passengers during the voyage, may be brought home in the steamer free of charge.

Five dollars per day, in gold, it is believed, will be a fair calculation to make for *all* traveling expenses on shore, and at the various points where passengers may wish to leave the steamer for days at a time.

The trip can be extended, and the route changed, by *unanimous* vote of the passengers.

CHAS. C. DUNCAN,
117 WALL STREET, NEW YORK.

R. R. G******, Treasurer.

COMMITTEE ON APPLICATIONS.

J. T. H******, ESQ.,   R. R. G******, ESQ.,   C. C. DUNCAN.

COMMITTEE ON SELECTING STEAMER.

CAPT. W. W. S******, *Surveyor for Board of Underwriters.*
C. W. C******, *Consulting Engineer for U.S. and Canada.*
J. T. H******, ESQ.
C. C. DUNCAN.

P.S.—The very beautiful and substantial side-wheel steamship *Quaker City* has been chartered for the occasion, and will leave New York June 8th. Letters have been issued by the government commending the party to courtesies abroad.

What was there lacking about that program, to make it perfectly irresistible? Nothing, that any finite mind could discover. Paris, England, Scotland, Switzerland, Italy—Garibaldi! The Grecian archipelago! Vesuvius! Constantinople! Smyrna! The Holy Land! Egypt and "our friends the Bermudians"! People in Europe desiring to join the Excursion—contagious sickness to be avoided—boating at the expense of the ship—physician on board—the circuit of the globe to be made if the passengers unanimously desired it—the company to be rigidly selected by a pitiless "Committee on Applications"—the vessel to be as rigidly selected by as pitiless a "Committee on Selecting Steamer." Human nature could not withstand these bewildering temptations. I hurried to the Treasurer's office and deposited my ten per cent. I rejoiced to know that a few vacant staterooms were still left. I *did* avoid a critical personal examination into my character, by that bowelless committee, but I referred to all the people of high standing I could think of in the community who would be least likely to know anything about me.

Shortly a supplementary program was issued which set forth that the Plymouth Collection of Hymns would be used on board the ship. I then paid the balance of my passage money.

I was provided with a receipt, and duly and officially accepted as an excursionist. There was happiness in that, but it was tame compared to the novelty of being "select."

This supplementary program also instructed the excursionists to provide themselves with light musical instruments for amusement in the ship; with saddles for Syrian travel; green spectacles and umbrellas; veils for Egypt; and substantial clothing to use in rough pilgrimizing in the Holy Land. Furthermore, it was suggested that although the ship's library would afford a fair amount of reading matter, it would still be well if each passenger would provide himself with a few guide-books, a Bible, and some standard works of travel. A list was appended, which consisted chiefly of books relating to the Holy Land, since the Holy Land was part of the excursion and seemed to be its main feature.

Rev. Henry Ward Beecher was to have accompanied the expedition, but urgent duties obliged him to give up the idea. There were other passengers who could have been spared better, and would have been spared more willingly. Lieutenant-General Sherman was to have been of the party, also, but the Indian war compelled his presence on the plains. A popular actress had entered her name on the ship's books, but something interfered, and *she* couldn't go. The "Drummer Boy of the Potomac" deserted, and lo, we had never a celebrity left!

However, we were to have a "battery of guns" from the Navy Department (as per advertisement), to be used in answering royal salutes; and the document furnished by the Secretary of the Navy, which was to make "General Sherman and party" welcome guests in the courts and camps of the old world, was still left to us, though both document and battery, I think, were shorn of somewhat of their original august proportions. However, had not we the seductive program, still, with its Paris, its Constantinople, Smyrna, Jerusalem, Jericho, and "our friends the Bermudians"? What did we care?

CHAPTER II

Occasionally, during the following month, I dropped in at 117 Wall Street to inquire how the repairing and refurnishing of the vessel was coming on; how additions to the passenger list were averaging; how many people the committee were decreeing not "select," every day, and banishing in sorrow and tribulation. I was glad to know that we were to have a little printing-press on board and issue a daily newspaper of our own. I was glad to learn that our piano, our parlor organ, and our melodeon were to be the best instruments of the kind that could be had in the market. I was proud to observe that among our excursionists were three ministers of the gospel, eight doctors, sixteen or eighteen ladies, several military and naval chieftains with sounding titles, an ample crop of "Professors" of various kinds, and a gentleman who had "COMMISSIONER OF THE UNITED STATES OF AMERICA TO EUROPE, ASIA, AND AFRICA" thundering after his name in one awful blast! I had carefully prepared myself to take rather a back seat in that ship, because of the uncommonly select material that would alone be permitted to pass through the camel's eye of that committee on credentials; I had schooled myself to expect an imposing array of military and naval heroes, and to have to set that back seat still further back in consequence of it, may be; but I state frankly that I was all unprepared for *this* crusher.

I fell under that titular avalanche a torn and blighted thing. I said that if that potentate *must* go over in our ship, why, I supposed he must—but that to my thinking, when the United States considered it necessary to send a dignitary of that tonnage across the ocean, it would be in better taste, and safer, to take him apart and cart him over in sections, in several ships.

Ah, if I had only known, then, that he was only a common mortal, and that his mission had nothing more overpowering about it than the collecting of seeds and uncommon yams and extraordinary cabbages and peculiar bullfrogs for that poor, useless, innocent, mildewed old fossil, the Smithsonian Institute, I would have felt *so* much relieved.

During that memorable month I basked in the happiness of being for once in my life drifting with the tide of a great popular movement. Everybody was going to Europe—I, too, was going to Europe. Everybody was going to the famous Paris Exposition—I, too, was going to the Paris Exposition. The steamship lines were carrying Americans out of the various ports of the country at the rate of four or five thousand a week, in the aggregate. If I met a dozen individuals, during that month, who were not going to Europe shortly, I have no distinct remembrance of it now. I walked about the city a good deal with a young Mr. Blucher, who was booked for the excursion. He was confiding, good-natured, unsophisticated, companionable; but he was not a man to set the river on fire. He had the most extraordinary notions about this European exodus, and came at last to consider the whole nation as packing up for emigration to France. We stepped into a store in Broadway, one day, where he bought a handkerchief, and when the man could not make change, Mr. B. said:

"Never mind, I'll hand it to you in Paris."

"But I am not going to Paris."

"How is—what did I understand you to say?"

"I said I am not going to Paris."

"Not going to *Paris!* Not g—well then, where in the nation *are* you going to?"

"Nowhere at all."

"Not anywhere whatsoever?—not any place on earth but this?"

"Not any place at all but just this—stay here all summer."

My comrade took his purchase and walked out of the store without a word—walked out with an injured look upon his countenance. Up the street apiece he broke silence and said impressively: "It was a lie—that is my opinion of it!"

In the fullness of time the ship was ready to receive her passengers. I was introduced to the young gentleman who was to be my room-mate, and found him to be intelligent, cheerful of spirit, unselfish, full of generous impulses, patient, considerate, and wonderfully good-natured. Not any passenger that sailed in the *Quaker City* will withhold his endorsement of what I have just said. We selected a stateroom forward of the wheel, on the starboard side, "below decks." It had two berths in it, a dismal dead-light, a sink with a wash-bowl in it, and a long sumptuously cushioned locker, which was to do service as a sofa—partly, and partly as a hiding place for our things. Notwithstanding all this furniture, there was still room to turn around in, but not to swing a cat in, at least with entire security to the cat. However, the room was large, for a ship's stateroom, and was in every way satisfactory.

The vessel was appointed to sail on a certain Saturday early in June. A little after noon, on the distinguished Saturday, I reached the ship and went on board. All was bustle and confusion. (I have seen that remark before, somewhere.) The pier was crowded with carriages and men; passengers were arriving and hurrying on board; the vessel's decks were encumbered with trunks and valises; groups of excursionists, arrayed in unattractive traveling costumes, were moping about in a drizzling rain and looking as droopy and woebegone as so many molting chickens. The gallant flag was up, but it was under the spell, too, and hung limp and disheartened by the mast. Altogether, it was the bluest, bluest spectacle! It was a pleasure excursion—there was no gainsaying that, because the program said so—it was so nominated in the bond— but it surely hadn't the general aspect of one.

Finally, above the banging, and rumbling, and shouting and hissing of steam, rang the order to "cast off!"—a sudden rush to the gangways— a scampering ashore of visitors—a revolution of the wheels, and we were off—the picnic was begun! Two very mild cheers went up from the dripping crowd on the pier; we answered them gently from the slippery decks; the flag made an effort to wave, and failed; the "battery of guns" spake not—the ammunition was out.

We steamed down to the foot of the harbor and came to anchor. It was still raining. And not only raining, but storming. "Outside" we could see, ourselves, that there was a tremendous sea on. We must lie still, in the calm harbor, till the storm should abate. Our passengers hailed from fifteen states; only a few of them had ever been to sea before; manifestly it would not do to pit them against a full-blown tempest until they had got their sea-legs on. Towards evening the two steam tugs that had accompanied us with a rollicking champagne party of young New Yorkers on board who wished to bid farewell to one of our number in due and ancient form, departed, and we were alone on the deep. On deep five fathoms, and anchored fast to the bottom. And out in the solemn rain, at that. This was pleasuring with a vengeance.

It was an appropriate relief when the gong sounded for prayer-meeting. The first Saturday night of any other pleasure excursion might have been devoted to whist and dancing; but I submit it to the unprejudiced mind if it would have been in good taste for *us* to engage in such frivolities, considering what we had gone through and the frame of mind we were in. We would have shone at a wake, but not at anything more festive.

However, there is always a cheering influence about the sea; and in my berth, that night, rocked by the measured swell of the waves, and lulled by the murmur of the distant surf, I soon passed tranquilly out of all consciousness of the dreary experiences of the day and damaging premonitions of the future.

CHAPTER XII

We have come five hundred miles by rail through the heart of France. What a bewitching land it is! What a garden! Surely the leagues of bright green lawns are swept and brushed and watered every day and their grasses trimmed by the barber. Surely the hedges are shaped and measured and their symmetry preserved by the most architectural of gardeners. Surely the long, straight rows of stately poplars that divide the beautiful landscape like the squares of a checker-board are set with line and plummet, and their uniform height determined with a spirit level. Surely the straight, smooth, pure white turnpikes are jack-planed and sand-papered every day. How else are these marvels of symmetry, cleanliness, and order attained? It is wonderful. There are no unsightly stone walls, and never a fence of any kind. There is no dirt, no decay, no rubbish anywhere—nothing that even hints at untidiness—nothing that ever suggests neglect. All is orderly and beautiful—everything is charming to the eye.

We had such glimpses of the Rhone gliding along between its grassy banks; of cosy cottages buried in flowers and shrubbery; of quaint old red-tiled villages with mossy mediaeval cathedrals looming out of their midst; of wooded hills with ivy-grown towers and turrets of feudal castles projecting above the foliage; such glimpses of Paradise, it seemed to us, such visions of fabled fairy-land!

We knew, then, what the poet meant, when he sang of—

> —thy cornfields green, and sunny vines,
> O pleasant land of France!

And it *is* a pleasant land. No word described it so felicitously as that one. They say there is no word for "home" in the French language. Well, considering that they have the article itself in such an attractive aspect, they ought to manage to get along without the word. Let us not waste too much pity on "homeless" France. I have observed that Frenchmen abroad seldom wholly give up the idea of going back to France some time or other. I am not surprised at it now.

We are not infatuated with these French railway cars, though. We took first-class passage, not because we wished to attract attention by doing a thing which is uncommon in Europe, but because we could make our journey quicker by so doing. It is hard to make railroading pleasant, in any country. It is too tedious. Stage-coaching is infinitely more delightful. Once I crossed the plains and deserts and mountains of the West, in a stage-coach, from the Missouri line to California, and since then all my pleasure-trips must be measured to that rare holiday frolic. Two thousand miles of ceaseless rush and rattle and clatter, by night and by day, and never a weary moment, never a lapse of interest! The first seven hundred miles a level continent, its grassy carpet greener and softer and smoother than any sea, and figured with designs fitted to its magnitude—the shadows of the clouds. Here were no scenes but summer scenes, and no disposition inspired by them but to lie at full length on the mail sacks, in the grateful breeze, and dreamily smoke the pipe of peace—what other, where all was repose and contentment? In cool mornings, before the sun was fairly up, it was worth a lifetime of city toiling and moiling to perch in the foretop with the driver and see the six mustangs scamper under the sharp snapping of a whip that never touched them; to scan the blue distances of a world that knew no lords but us; to cleave the wind with uncovered head and feel the sluggish pulses rousing to the spirit of a speed that pretended to the resistless rush of a typhoon! Then thirteen hundred miles of desert solitudes; of limitless panoramas of bewildering perspective; of mimic cities, of pinnacled cathedrals, of massive fortresses, counterfeited in the eternal rocks and splendid with the crimson and gold of the setting sun; of dizzy altitudes among fog-wreathed peaks and never-melting snows, where thunders and lightnings and tempests warred magnificently at our feet and the storm-clouds above swung their shredded banners in our very faces!

But I forgot. I am in elegant France, now, and not scurrying through the great South Pass and the Wind River Mountains, among antelopes and buffaloes, and painted Indians on the warpath. It is not meet that I should make too disparaging comparisons between humdrum travel on a railway and that royal summer flight across a continent in a stage-coach. I meant, in the beginning, to say that railway journeying is tedious and tiresome, and so it is—though at the time, I was thinking particularly of a dismal fifty-hour pilgrimage between New York and St. Louis. Of course our trip through France was not really tedious, because all its scenes and experiences were new and strange; but as Dan says, it had its "discrepancies."

The cars are built in compartments that hold eight persons each. Each compartment is partially subdivided, and so there are two tolerably distinct parties of four in it. Four face the other four. The seats and backs are thickly padded and cushioned, and are very comfortable; you can smoke, if you wish; there are no bothersome peddlers; you are saved the infliction of a multitude of disagreeable fellow-passengers. So far, so well. But then the conductor locks you in when the train starts; there is no water to drink in the car; there is no heating apparatus for night travel; if a drunken rowdy should get in, you could not remove a matter of twenty seats from him, or enter another car; but, above all, if you are worn out and must sleep, you must sit up and do it in naps, with cramped legs and in a torturing misery that leaves you withered and lifeless the next day—for behold, they have not that culmination of all charity and human kindness, a sleeping car, in all France. I prefer the American system. It has not so many grievous "discrepancies."

In France, all is clockwork, all is order. They make no mistakes. Every third man wears a uniform, and whether he be a marshal of the empire or a brakeman, he is ready and perfectly willing to answer all your questions with tireless politeness, ready to tell you which car to take, yea, and ready to go and put you into it to make sure that you shall not go astray. You cannot pass into the waiting-room of the depot till you have secured your ticket, and you cannot pass from its only exit till the train is at its threshold to receive you. Once on board, the train will not start till your ticket has been examined—till every passenger's ticket has been inspected. This is chiefly for your own good. If by any possibility you have managed to take the wrong train, you will be handed over to a polite official who will take you whither you belong, and bestow you with many an affable bow. Your ticket will be inspected every now and then along the route, and when it is time to change cars you will know it. You are in the hands of officials who zealously study your welfare and your interest, instead of turning their talents to the invention of new methods of discommoding and snubbing you, as is very often the main employment of that exceedingly self-satisfied monarch, the railroad conductor of America.

But the happiest regulation in French railway government, is—thirty minutes to dinner! No five-minute boltings of flabby rolls, muddy coffee, questionable eggs, gutta-percha beef, and pies whose conception and execution are a dark and bloody mystery to all save the cook who created them! No; we sat calmly down—it was in old Dijon, which is so easy to spell and so impossible to pronounce, except when you civilize it and call it Demijohn—and poured out rich Burgundian wines and munched calmly through a long table d'hote bill of fare, snail patties, delicious fruits and all, then paid the trifle it cost and stepped happily aboard the train again, without once cursing the railroad company. A rare experience, and one to be treasured forever.

They say they do not have accidents on these French roads, and I think it must be true. If I remember rightly, we passed high above wagon roads, or through tunnels under them, but never crossed them on their own level. About every quarter of a mile, it seemed to me, a man came out and held up a club till the train went by, to signify that everything was safe ahead. Switches were changed a mile in advance, by pulling a wire rope that passed along the ground by the rail, from station to station. Signals for the day and signals for the night gave constant and timely notice of the position of switches.

No, they have no railroad accidents to speak of in France. But why? Because when one occurs, *somebody* has to hang for it! Not hang, maybe, but be punished at least with such vigor of emphasis as to make negligence a thing to be shuddered at by railroad officials for many a day thereafter. "No blame attached to the officers"—that lying and disaster-breeding verdict so common to our soft-hearted juries, is seldom rendered in France. If the trouble occurred in the conductor's department, that officer must suffer if his subordinate cannot be proven guilty; if in the engineer's department, and the case be similar, the engineer must answer.

The Old Travelers—those delightful parrots who have "been here before," and know more about the country than Louis Napoleon knows now or ever will know—tell us these things, and we believe them because they are pleasant things to believe, and because they are plausible and savor of the rigid subjection to law and order which we behold about us everywhere.

But we love the Old Travelers. We love to hear them prate and drivel and lie. We can tell them the moment we see them. They always throw out a few feelers: they never cast themselves adrift till they have sounded every individual and know that he has not traveled. Then they open their throttle-valves, and how they do brag, and sneer, and swell, and soar, and blaspheme the sacred name of Truth! Their central idea, their grand aim, is to subjugate you, keep you down, make you feel insignificant and humble in the blaze of their cosmopolitan glory! They will not let you know anything. They sneer at your most inoffensive suggestions; they laugh unfeelingly at your treasured dreams of foreign lands; they brand the statements of your traveled aunts and uncles as the stupidest absurdities; they deride your most trusted authors and demolish the fair images they have set up for your willing worship with the pitiless ferocity of the fanatic iconoclast! But still I love the Old Travelers. I love them for their witless platitudes; for their supernatural ability to bore; for their delightful asinine vanity; for their luxuriant fertility of imagination; for their startling, their brilliant, their overwhelming mendacity!

By Lyons and the Saône (where we saw the Lady of Lyons and thought little of her comeliness); by Villa Franca, Tonnerre, venerable Sens, Melun, Fontainebleau, and scores of other beautiful cities, we swept, always noting the absence of hog-wallows, broken fences, cowlots, unpainted houses, and mud, and always noting, as well, the presence of cleanliness, grace, taste in adorning and beautifying, even to the disposition of a tree or the turning of a hedge, the marvel of roads in perfect repair, void of ruts and guiltless of even an inequality of surface—we bowled along, hour after hour, that brilliant summer day, and as nightfall approached we entered a wilderness of odorous flowers and shrubbery, sped through it, and then, excited, delighted, and half persuaded that we were only the sport of a beautiful dream, lo, we stood in magnificent Paris!

What excellent order they kept about that vast depot! There was no frantic crowding and jostling, no shouting and swearing, and no swaggering intrusion of services by rowdy hackmen. These latter gentry stood outside—stood quietly by their long line of vehicles and said never a word. A kind of hackman-general seemed to have the whole matter of transportation in his hands. He politely received the passengers and ushered them to the kind of conveyance they wanted, and told the driver where to deliver them. There was no "talking back," no dissatisfaction about overcharging, no grumbling about anything. In a little while we were speeding through the streets of Paris, and delightfully recognizing certain names and places with which books had long ago made us familiar. It was like meeting an old friend when we read *Rue de Rivoli* on the street corner; we knew the genuine vast palace of the Louvre as well as we knew its picture; when we passed by the Column of July we needed no one to tell us what it was, or to remind us that on its site once stood the grim Bastille, that grave of human hopes and happiness, that dismal prison-house within whose dungeons so many young faces put on the wrinkles of age, so many proud spirits grew humble, so many brave hearts broke.

We secured rooms at the hotel, or rather, we had three beds put into one room, so that we might be together, and then we went out to a restaurant, just after lamp-lighting, and ate a comfortable, satisfactory, lingering dinner. It was a pleasure to eat where everything was so tidy, the food so well cooked, the waiters so polite, and the coming and departing company so moustached, so frisky, so affable, so fearfully and wonderfully Frenchy! All the surroundings were gay and enlivening. Two hundred people sat at little tables on the sidewalk, sipping wine and coffee; the streets were thronged with light vehicles and with joyous pleasure-seekers; there was music in the air, life and action all about us, and a conflagration of gaslight everywhere!

After dinner we felt like seeing such Parisian specialties as we might see without distressing exertion, and so we sauntered through the brilliant streets and looked at the dainty trifles in variety stores and jewelry shops. Occasionally, merely for the pleasure of being cruel, we put unoffending Frenchmen on the rack with questions framed in the incomprehensible jargon of their native language, and while they writhed, we impaled them, we peppered them, we scarified them, with their own vile verbs and participles.

We noticed that in the jewelry stores they had some of the articles marked "gold," and some labeled "imitation." We wondered at this extravagance of honesty, and inquired into the matter. We were informed that inasmuch as most people are not able to tell false gold from the genuine article, the government compels jewelers to have their gold work assayed and stamped officially according to its fineness, and their imitation work duly labeled with the sign of its falsity. They told us the jewelers would not dare to violate this law, and that whatever a stranger bought in one of their stores might be depended upon as being strictly what it was represented to be. Verily, a wonderful land is France!

Then we hunted for a barber-shop. From earliest infancy it had been a cherished ambition of mine to be shaved some day in a palatial barber-shop of Paris. I wished to recline at full length in a cushioned invalid-chair, with pictures about me, and sumptuous furniture; with frescoed walls and gilded arches above me, and vistas of Corinthian columns stretching far before me; with perfumes of Araby to intoxicate my senses, and the slumbrous drone of distant noises to soothe me to sleep. At the end of an hour I would wake up regretfully and find my face as smooth and as soft as an infant's. Departing, I would lift my hands above that barber's head and say, "Heaven bless you, my son!"

So we searched high and low, for a matter of two hours, but never a barber-shop could we see. We saw only wig-making establishments, with shocks of dead and repulsive hair bound upon the heads of painted waxen brigands who stared out from glass boxes upon the passer-by, with their stony eyes, and scared him with the ghostly white of their countenances. We shunned these signs for a time, but finally we concluded that the wig-makers must of necessity be the barbers as well, since we could find no single legitimate representative of the fraternity. We entered and asked, and found that it was even so.

I said I wanted to be shaved. The barber inquired where my room was. I said, never mind where my room was, I wanted to be shaved—there, on the spot. The doctor said he would be shaved also. Then there was an excitement among those two barbers! There was a wild consultation, and afterward a hurrying to and fro and a feverish gathering up of razors from obscure places and a ransacking for soap. Next they took us into a little mean, shabby back room; they got two ordinary sitting-room chairs and placed us in them, with our coats on. My old, old dream of bliss vanished into thin air!

I sat bolt upright, silent, sad, and solemn. One of the wig-making villains lathered my face for ten terrible minutes and finished by plastering a mass of suds into my mouth. I expelled the nasty stuff with a strong English expletive and said, "Foreigner, beware!" Then this outlaw stropped his razor on his boot, hovered over me ominously for six fearful seconds, and then swooped down upon me like the genius of destruction. The first rake of his razor loosened the very hide from my face and lifted me out of the chair. I stormed and raved, and the other boys enjoyed it. Their beards are not strong and thick. Let us draw the curtain over this harrowing scene. Suffice it that I submitted, and went through with the cruel infliction of a shave by a French barber; tears of exquisite agony coursed down my cheeks, now and then, but I survived. Then the incipient assassin held a basin of water under my chin and slopped its contents over my face, and into my bosom, and down the back of my neck, with a mean pretense of washing away the soap and blood. He dried my features with a towel, and was going to comb my hair; but I asked to be excused. I said, with withering irony, that it was sufficient to be skinned—I declined to be scalped.

I went away from there with my handkerchief about my face, and never, never, never desired to dream of palatial Parisian barbershops any more. The truth is, as I believe I have since found out, that they have no barber-shops worthy of the name in Paris—and no barbers, either, for that matter. The impostor who does duty as a barber brings his pans and napkins and implements of torture to your residence and deliberately skins you in your private apartments. Ah, I have suffered, suffered, suffered, here in Paris, but never mind—the time is coming when I shall have a dark and bloody revenge. Some day a Parisian barber will come to my room to skin me, and from that day forth that barber will never be heard of more.

At eleven o'clock we alighted upon a sign which manifestly referred to billiards. Joy! We had played billiards in the Azores with balls that were not round, and on an ancient table that was very little smoother than a brick pavement—one of those wretched old things with dead cushions, and with patches in the faded cloth and invisible obstructions that made the balls describe the most astonishing and unsuspected angles, and perform feats in the way of unlooked-for and almost impossible "scratches," that were perfectly bewildering. We had played at Gibraltar with balls the size of a walnut, on a table like a public square— and in both instances we achieved far more aggravation than amusement. We expected to fare better here, but we were mistaken. The cushions were a good deal higher than the balls, and as the balls had a fashion of always stopping under the cushions, we accomplished very little in the way of caroms. The cushions were hard and unelastic, and the cues were so crooked that in making a shot you had to allow for the curve or you would infallibly put the "English" on the wrong side of the ball. Dan was to mark while the doctor and I played. At the end of an hour neither of us had made a count, and so Dan was tired of keeping tally with nothing to tally, and we were heated and angry and disgusted. We paid the heavy bill—about six cents—and said we would call around some time when we had a week to spend, and finish the game.

We adjourned to one of those pretty cafés and took supper and tested the wines of the country, as we had been instructed to do, and found them harmless and unexciting. They might have been exciting, however, if we had chosen to drink a sufficiency of them.

To close our first day in Paris cheerfully and pleasantly, we now sought our grand room in the Grand Hotel du Louvre and climbed into our sumptuous bed, to read and smoke—but alas!

> It was pitiful,
> In a whole city-full,
> Gas, we had none.

No gas to read by—nothing but dismal candles. It was a shame. We tried to map out excursions for the morrow; we puzzled over French "Guides to Paris"; we talked disjointedly, in a vain endeavor to make head or tail of the wild chaos of the day's sights and experiences; we subsided to indolent smoking; we gaped and yawned, and stretched—then feebly wondered if we were really and truly in renowned Paris, and drifted drowsily away into that vast mysterious void which men call sleep.

CHAPTER XXXII

Home again! For the first time, in many weeks, the ship's entire family met and shook hands on the quarter-deck. They had gathered from many points of the compass and from many lands, but not one was missing; there was no tale of sickness or death among the flock to dampen the pleasure of the reunion. Once more there was a full audience on deck to listen to the sailors' chorus as they got the anchor up, and to wave an adieu to the land as we sped away from Naples.

The seats were full at dinner again, the domino parties were complete, and the life and bustle on the upper deck in the fine moonlight at night was like old times—old times that had been gone weeks only, but yet they were weeks so crowded with incident, adventure, and excitement, that they seemed almost like years. There was no lack of cheerfulness on board the *Quaker City*. For once, her title was a misnomer.

At seven in the evening, with the western horizon all golden from the sunken sun, and specked with distant ships, the full moon sailing high over head, the dark blue of the sea under foot, and a strange sort of twilight affected by all these different lights and colors around us and about us, we sighted superb Stromboli. With what majesty the monarch held his lonely state above the level sea! Distance clothed him in a purple gloom, and added a veil of shimmering mist that so softened his rugged features that we seemed to see him through a web of silver gauze. His torch was out; his fires were smoldering; a tall column of smoke that rose up and lost itself in the growing moonlight was all the sign he gave that he was a living Autocrat of the Sea and not the specter of a dead one.

At two in the morning we swept through the Straits of Messina, and so bright was the moonlight that Italy on the one hand and Sicily on the other seemed almost as distinctly visible as though we looked at them from the middle of a street we were traversing. The city of Messina, milk-white, and starred and spangled all over with gaslights, was a fairy spectacle. A great party of us were on deck smoking and making a noise, and waiting to see famous Scylla and Charybdis. And presently the Oracle stepped out with his eternal spy-glass and squared himself on the deck like another Colossus of Rhodes. It was a surprise to see him abroad at such an hour. Nobody supposed he cared anything about an old fable like that of Scylla and Charybdis. One of the boys said:

"Hello, doctor, what are you doing up here at this time of night?— What do you want to see this place for?"

"What do *I* want to see this place for? Young man, little do you know me, or you wouldn't ask such a question. I wish to see *all* the places that's mentioned in the Bible."

"Stuff! This place isn't mentioned in the Bible."

"It ain't mentioned in the Bible!—*this* place ain't—well now, what place *is* this, since you know so much about it?"

"Why it's Scylla and Charybdis."

"Scylla and Cha—confound it, I thought it was Sodom and Gomorrah!"

And he closed up his glass and went below. The above is the ship story. Its plausibility is marred a little by the fact that the Oracle was not a biblical student, and did not spend much of his time instructing himself about Scriptural localities. They say the Oracle complains, in this hot weather, lately, that the only beverage in the ship that is passable is the butter. He did not mean butter, of course, but inasmuch as that article remains in a melted state now since we are out of ice, it is fair to give him the credit of getting one long word in the right place, anyhow, for once in his life. He said, in Rome, that the Pope was a noble-looking old man, but he never *did* think much of his Iliad.

We spent one pleasant day skirting along the Isles of Greece. They are very mountainous. Their prevailing tints are gray and brown, approaching to red. Little white villages, surrounded by trees, nestle in the valleys or roost upon the lofty perpendicular sea-walls.

We had one fine sunset—a rich carmine flush that suffused the western sky and cast a ruddy glow far over the sea. Fine sunsets seem to be rare in this part of the world—or at least, striking ones. They are soft, sensuous, lovely—they are exquisite, refined, effeminate, but we have seen no sunsets here yet like the gorgeous conflagrations that flame in the track of the sinking sun in our high northern latitudes.

But what were sunsets to us, with the wild excitement upon us of approaching the most renowned of cities! What cared we for outward visions, when Agamemnon, Achilles, and a thousand other heroes of the great Past were marching in ghostly procession through our fancies? What were sunsets to us, who were about to live and breathe and walk in actual Athens; yea, and go far down into the dead centuries and bid in person for the slaves, Diogenes and Plato, in the public market-place, or gossip with the neighbors about the siege of Troy or the splendid deeds of Marathon? We scorned to consider sunsets.

We arrived, and entered the ancient harbor of the Piraeus at last. We dropped anchor within half a mile of the village. Away off, across the undulating Plain of Attica, could be seen a little square-topped hill with a something on it, which our glasses soon discovered to be the ruined edifices of the citadel of the Athenians, and most prominent among them loomed the venerable Parthenon. So exquisitely clear and pure is this wonderful atmosphere that every column of the noble structure was discernible through the telescope, and even the smaller ruins about it assumed some semblance of shape. This at a distance of five or six miles. In the valley, near the Acropolis (the square-tipped hill before spoken of), Athens itself could be vaguely made out with an ordinary lorgnette. Everybody was anxious to get ashore and visit these classic localities as quickly as possible. No land we had yet seen had aroused such universal interest among the passengers.

But bad news came. The commandant of the Piraeus came in his boat, and said we must either depart or else get outside the harbor and remain imprisoned in our ship, under rigid quarantine, for eleven days!

So we took up the anchor and moved outside, to lie a dozen hours or so, taking in supplies, and then sail for Constantinople. It was the bitterest disappointment we had yet experienced. To lie a whole day in sight of the Acropolis, and yet be obliged to go away without visiting Athens! Disappointment was hardly a strong enough word to describe the circumstances.

All hands were on deck, all the afternoon, with books and maps and glasses, trying to determine which "narrow rocky ridge" was the Areopagus, which sloping hill the Pynx, which elevation the Museum Hill, and so on. And we got things confused. Discussion became heated, and party spirit ran high. Church members were gazing with emotion upon a hill which they said was the one St. Paul preached from, and another faction claimed that that hill was Hymettus, and another that it was Pentelicon! After all the trouble, we could be certain of only one thing—the square-topped hill was the Acropolis, and the grand ruin that crowned it was the Parthenon, whose picture we knew in infancy in the schoolbooks.

We inquired of everybody who came near the ship, whether there were guards in the Piraeus, whether they were strict, what the chances were of capture should any of us slip ashore, and in case any of us made the venture and were caught, what would be probably done to us? The answers were discouraging: there was a strong guard or police force; the Piraeus was a small town, and any stranger seen in it would surely attract attention—capture would be certain. The commandant said the punishment would be "heavy"; when asked "How heavy?" he said it would be "very severe"—that was all we could get out of him.

At eleven o'clock at night, when most of the ship's company were abed, four of us stole softly ashore in a small boat, a clouded moon favoring the enterprise, and started two and two, and far apart, over a low hill, intending to go clear around the Piraeus, out of the range of its police. Picking our way so stealthily over that rocky, nettle-grown eminence, made me feel a good deal as if I were on my way somewhere to steal something. My immediate comrade and I talked in an undertone about quarantine laws and their penalties, but we found nothing cheering in the subject. I was posted. Only a few days before, I was talking with our captain, and he mentioned the case of a man who swam ashore from a quarantined ship somewhere, and got imprisoned six months for it; and when he was in Genoa a few years ago, a captain of a quarantined ship went in his boat to a departing ship, which was already outside of the harbor, and put a letter on board to be taken to his family, and the authorities imprisoned him three months for it, and then conducted him and his ship fairly to sea, and warned him never to show himself in that port again while he lived. This kind of conversation did no good, further than to give a sort of dismal interest to our quarantine-breaking expedition, and so we dropped it. We made the entire circuit of the town without seeing anybody but one man, who stared at us curiously, but said nothing, and a dozen persons asleep on the ground before their doors, whom we walked among and never woke—but we woke up dogs enough, in all conscience—we always had one or two barking at our heels, and several times we had as many as ten and twelve at once. They made such a preposterous din that persons aboard our ship said they could tell how we were progressing for a long time, and where we were, by the barking of the dogs. The clouded moon still favored us. When we had made the whole circuit, and were passing among the houses on the further side of the town, the moon came out splendidly, but we no longer feared the light. As we approached a well, near a house, to get a drink, the owner merely glanced at us and went within. He left the quiet, slumbering town at our mercy. I record it here proudly, that we didn't do anything to it.

Seeing no road, we took a tall hill to the left of the distant Acropolis for a mark, and steered straight for it over all obstructions, and over a little rougher piece of country than exists anywhere else outside of the State of Nevada, perhaps. Part of the way it was covered with small, loose stones—we trod on six at a time, and they all rolled. Another part of it was dry, loose, newly-plowed ground. Still another part of it was a long stretch of low grapevines, which were tanglesome and troublesome, and which we took to be brambles. The Attic Plain, barring the grapevines, was a barren, desolate, unpoetical waste—I wonder what it was in Greece's Age of Glory, five hundred years before Christ?

In the neighborhood of one o'clock in the morning, when we were heated with fast walking and parched with thirst, Denny exclaimed, "Why, these weeds are grapevines!" and in five minutes we had a score of bunches of large, white, delicious grapes, and were reaching down for more when a dark shape rose mysteriously up out of the shadows beside us and said "Ho!" And so we left.

In ten minutes more we struck into a beautiful road, and unlike some others we had stumbled upon at intervals, it led in the right direction. We followed it. It was broad and smooth and white—handsome and in perfect repair, and shaded on both sides for a mile or so with single ranks of trees, and also with luxuriant vineyards. Twice we entered and stole grapes, and the second time somebody shouted at us from some invisible place. Whereupon we left again. We speculated in grapes no more on that side of Athens.

Shortly we came upon an ancient stone aqueduct, built upon arches, and from that time forth we had ruins all about us—we were approaching our journey's end. We could not see the Acropolis now or the high hill, either, and I wanted to follow the road till we were abreast of them, but the others overruled me, and we toiled laboriously up the stony hill immediately in our front—and from its summit saw another—climbed it and saw another! It was an hour of exhausting work. Soon we came upon a row of open graves, cut in the solid rock—(for a while one of them served Socrates for a prison)—we passed around the shoulder of the hill, and the citadel, in all its ruined magnificence, burst upon us! We hurried across the ravine and up a winding road, and stood on the old Acropolis, with the prodigious walls of the citadel towering above our heads. We did not stop to inspect their massive blocks of marble, or measure their height, or guess at their extraordinary thickness, but passed at once through a great arched passage like a railway tunnel, and went straight to the gate that leads to the ancient temples. It was locked! So, after all, it seemed that we were not to see the great Parthenon face to face. We sat down and held a council of war. Result: The gate was only a flimsy structure of wood—we would break it down. It seemed like desecration, but then we had traveled far, and our necessities were urgent. We could not hunt up guides and keepers—we must be on the ship before daylight. So we argued. This was all very fine, but when we came to break the gate, we could not do it. We moved around an angle of the wall and found a low bastion—eight feet high without—ten or twelve within. Denny prepared to scale it, and we got ready to follow. By dint of hard scrambling he finally straddled the top, but some loose stones crumbled away and fell with a crash into the court within. There was instantly a banging of doors and a shout. Denny dropped from the wall in a twinkling, and we retreated in disorder to the gate. Xerxes took that mighty citadel four hundred and eighty years before Christ, when his five millions of soldiers and camp-followers followed him to Greece, and if we four Americans could have remained unmolested five minutes longer, we would have taken it too.

The garrison had turned out—four Greeks. We clamored at the gate, and they admitted us. (Bribery and corruption.)

We crossed a large court, entered a great door, and stood upon a pavement of purest white marble, deeply worn by footprints. Before us, in the flooding moonlight, rose the noblest ruins we had ever looked upon—the Propylaea; a small temple of Minerva; the Temple of Hercules, and the grand Parthenon. (We got these names from the Greek guide, who didn't seem to know more than seven men ought to know.) These edifices were all built of the whitest Pentelic marble, but have a pinkish stain upon them now. Where any part is broken, however, the fracture looks like fine loaf sugar. Six caryatides, or marble women, clad in flowing robes, support the portico of the Temple of Hercules, but the porticoes and colonnades of the other structures are formed of massive Doric and Ionic pillars, whose flutings and capitals are still measurably perfect, notwithstanding the centuries that have gone over them and the sieges they have suffered. The Parthenon, originally, was two hundred and twenty-six feet long, one hundred wide, and seventy high, and had two rows of great columns, eight in each, at either end, and single rows of seventeen each down the sides, and was one of the most graceful and beautiful edifices ever erected.

Most of the Parthenon's imposing columns are still standing, but the roof is gone. It was a perfect building two hundred and fifty years ago, when a shell dropped into the Venetian magazine stored here, and the explosion which followed wrecked and unroofed it. I remember but little about the Parthenon, and I have put in one or two facts and figures for the use of other people with short memories. Got them from the guide-book.

As we wandered thoughtfully down the marble-paved length of this stately temple, the scene about us was strangely impressive. Here and there, in lavish profusion, were gleaming white statues of men and women, propped against blocks of marble, some of them armless, some without legs, others headless—but all looking mournful in the moon-light, and startlingly human! They rose up and confronted the midnight intruder on every side—they stared at him with stony eyes from un-looked-for nooks and recesses; they peered at him over fragmentary heaps far down the desolate corridors; they barred his way in the midst of the broad forum, and solemnly pointed with handless arms the way from the sacred fane; and through the roofless temple the moon looked down, and banded the floor and darkened the scattered fragments and broken statues with the slanting shadows of the columns.

What a world of ruined sculpture was about us! Set up in rows—stacked up in piles—scattered broadcast over the wide area of the Acrop-olis—were hundreds of crippled statues of all sizes and of the most exquisite workmanship; and vast fragments of marble that once be-longed to the entablatures, covered with bas-reliefs representing battles and sieges, ships of war with three and four tiers of oars, pageants and processions—everything one could think of. History says that the tem-ples of the Acropolis were filled with the noblest works of Praxiteles and Phidias, and of many a great master in sculpture besides—and surely these elegant fragments attest it.

We walked out into the grass-grown, fragment-strewn court beyond the Parthenon. It startled us, every now and then, to see a stony white face stare suddenly up at us out of the grass with its dead eyes. The place seemed alive with ghosts. I half expected to see the Athenian heroes of twenty centuries ago glide out of the shadows and steal into the old temple they knew so well and regarded with such boundless pride.

The full moon was riding high in the cloudless heavens now. We sauntered carelessly and unthinkingly to the edge of the lofty battlements of the citadel, and looked down—a vision! And such a vision! Athens by moonlight! The prophet that thought the splendors of the New Jerusalem were revealed to him surely saw this instead! It lay in the level plain right under our feet—all spread abroad like a picture—and we looked down upon it as we might have looked from a balloon. We saw no semblance of a street, but every house, every window, every clinging vine, every projection, was as distinct and sharply marked as if the time were noonday; and yet there was no glare, no glitter, nothing harsh or repulsive—the noiseless city was flooded with the mellowest light that ever streamed from the moon, and seemed like some living creature wrapped in peaceful slumber. On its further side was a little temple, whose delicate pillars and ornate front glowed with a rich luster that chained the eye like a spell; and nearer by, the palace of the king reared its creamy walls out of the midst of a great garden of shrubbery that was flecked all over with a random shower of amber lights—a spray of golden sparks that lost their brightness in the glory of the moon, and glinted softly upon the sea of dark foliage like the pallid stars of the milky-way. Overhead the stately columns, majestic still in their ruin—under foot the dreaming city—in the distance the silver sea—not on the broad earth is there another picture half so beautiful!

As we turned and moved again through the temple, I wished that the illustrious men who had sat in it in the remote ages could visit it again and reveal themselves to our curious eyes—Plato, Aristotle, Demosthenes, Socrates, Phocion, Pythagoras, Euclid, Pindar, Xenophon, Herodotus, Praxiteles and Phidias, Zeuxis the painter. What a constellation of celebrated names! But more than all, I wished that old Diogenes, groping so patiently with his lantern, searching so zealously for one solitary honest man in all the world, might meander along and stumble on our party. I ought not to say it, may be, but still I suppose he would have put out his light.

We left the Parthenon to keep its watch over old Athens, as it had kept it for twenty-three hundred years, and went and stood outside the walls of the citadel. In the distance was the ancient but still almost perfect Temple of Theseus, and close by, looking to the West, was the Bema, from whence Demosthenes thundered his philippics and fired the wavering patriotism of his countrymen. To the right was Mars Hill, where the Areopagus sat in ancient times, and where St. Paul defined his position, and below was the market-place where he "disputed daily" with the gossip-loving Athenians. We climbed the stone steps St. Paul ascended, and stood in the square-cut place he stood in, and tried to recollect the Bible account of the matter—but for certain reasons, I could not recall the words. I have found them since:

> Now while Paul waited for them at Athens, his spirit was stirred in him, when he saw the city wholly given up to idolatry.
> Therefore disputed he in the synagogue with the Jews, and with the devout persons, and in the market daily with them that met with him.
>
> * * *
>
> And they took him and brought him unto Areopagus, saying, May we know what this new doctrine whereof thou speakest is?
>
> * * *
>
> Then Paul stood in the midst of Mars hill, and said, Ye men of Athens, I perceive that in all things ye are too superstitious;
> For as I passed by and beheld your devotions, I found an altar with this inscription: TO THE UNKNOWN GOD. Whom, therefore, ye ignorantly worship, him declare I unto you.—*Acts*, ch. xvii.

It occurred to us, after a while, that if we wanted to get home before daylight betrayed us, we had better be moving. So we hurried away. When far on our road, we had a parting view of the Parthenon, with the moonlight streaming through its open colonnades and touching its capitals with silver. As it looked then, solemn, grand, and beautiful, it will always remain in our memories.

As we marched along, we began to get over our fears, and ceased to care much about quarantine scouts or anybody else. We grew bold and reckless; and once, in a sudden burst of courage, I even threw a stone at a dog. It was a pleasant reflection, though, that I did not hit him, because his master might just possibly have been a policeman. Inspired by this happy failure, my valor became utterly uncontrollable, and at intervals I absolutely whistled, though on a moderate key. But boldness breeds boldness, and shortly I plunged into a vineyard, in the full light of the moon, and captured a gallon of superb grapes, not even minding the presence of a peasant who rode by on a mule. Denny and Birch followed my example. Now I had grapes enough for a dozen, but then Jackson was all swollen up with courage, too, and he was obliged to enter a vineyard presently. The first bunch he seized brought trouble. A frowsy, bearded brigand sprang into the road with a shout, and flourished a musket in the light of the moon! We sidled toward the Piraeus—not running, you understand, but only advancing with celerity. The brigand shouted again, but still we advanced. It was getting late, and we had no time to fool away on every ass that wanted to drivel Greek platitudes to us. We would just as soon have talked with him as not if we had not been in a hurry. Presently Denny said, "Those fellows are following us!"

We turned, and, sure enough, there they were—three fantastic pirates armed with guns. We slackened our pace to let them come up, and in the meantime I got out my cargo of grapes and dropped them firmly but reluctantly into the shadows by the wayside. But I was not afraid. I only felt that it was not right to steal grapes. And all the more so when the owner was around—and not only around, but with his friends around also. The villains came up and searched a bundle Dr. Birch had in his hand, and scowled upon him when they found it had nothing in it but some holy rocks from Mars Hill, and these were not contraband. They evidently suspected him of playing some wretched fraud upon them, and seemed half inclined to scalp the party. But finally they dismissed us with a warning, couched in excellent Greek, I suppose, and dropped tranquilly in our wake. When they had gone three hundred yards they stopped, and we went on rejoiced. But behold, another armed rascal came out of the shadows and took their place, and followed us two hundred yards. Then he delivered us over to another miscreant, who emerged from some mysterious place, and he in turn to another! For a mile and a half our rear was guarded all the while by armed men. I never traveled in so much state before in all my life.

It was a good while after that before we ventured to steal any more grapes, and when we did we stirred up another troublesome brigand, and then we ceased all further speculation in that line. I suppose that fellow that rode by on the mule posted all the sentinels, from Athens to the Piraeus, about us.

Every field on that long route was watched by an armed sentinel, some of whom had fallen asleep, no doubt, but were on hand, nevertheless. This shows what sort of a country modern Attica is—a community of questionable characters. These men were not there to guard their possessions against strangers, but against each other; for strangers seldom visit Athens and the Piraeus, and when they do, they go in daylight, and can buy all the grapes they want for a trifle. The modern inhabitants are confiscators and falsifiers of high repute, if gossip speaks truly concerning them, and I freely believe it does.

Just as the earliest tinges of the dawn flushed the eastern sky and turned the pillared Parthenon to a broken harp hung in the pearly horizon, we closed our thirteenth mile of weary, round-about marching, and emerged upon the seashore abreast the ships, with our usual escort of fifteen hundred Piraean dogs howling at our heels. We hailed a boat that was two or three hundred yards from shore, and discovered in a moment that it was a police-boat on the lookout for any quarantine breakers that might chance to be abroad. So we dodged—we were used to that by this time—and when the scouts reached the spot we had so lately occupied, we were absent. They cruised along the shore, but in the wrong direction, and shortly our own boat issued from the gloom and took us aboard. They had heard our signal on the ship. We rowed noiselessly away, and before the police-boat came in sight again, we were safe at home once more.

Four more of our passengers were anxious to visit Athens, and started half an hour after we returned; but they had not been ashore five minutes till the police discovered and chased them so hotly that they barely escaped to their boat again, and that was all. They pursued the enterprise no further.

We set sail for Constantinople to-day, but some of us little care for that. We have seen all there was to see in the old city that had its birth sixteen hundred years before Christ was born, and was an old town before the foundations of Troy were laid—and saw it in its most attractive aspect. Wherefore, why should *we* worry?

Two other passengers ran the blockade successfully last night. So we learned this morning. They slipped away so quietly that they were not missed from the ship for several hours. They had the hardihood to march into the Piraeus in the early dusk and hire a carriage. They ran some danger of adding two or three months' imprisonment to the other novelties of their Holy Land Pleasure Excurion. I admire "cheek." But they went and came safely, and never walked a step.

CHAPTER XXXIII

From Athens all through the islands of the Grecian Archipelago, we saw little but forbidding sea-walls and barren hills, sometimes surmounted by three or four graceful columns of some ancient temple, lonely and deserted—a fitting symbol of the desolation that has come upon all Greece in these latter ages. We saw no plowed fields, very few villages, no trees or grass or vegetation of any kind, scarcely, and hardly ever an isolated house. Greece is a bleak, unsmiling desert, without agriculture, manufactures, or commerce, apparently. What supports its poverty-stricken people or its government is a mystery.

I suppose that ancient Greece and modern Greece compared, furnish the most extravagant contrast to be found in history. George I, an infant of eighteen, and a scraggy nest of foreign office-holders, sit in the places of Themistocles, Pericles, and the illustrious scholars and generals of the

Golden Age of Greece. The fleets that were the wonder of the world when the Parthenon was new are a beggarly handful of fishing-smacks now, and the manly people that performed such miracles of valor at Marathon are only a tribe of unconsidered slaves today. The classic Ilissus has gone dry, and so have all the sources of Grecian wealth and greatness. The nation numbers only eight hundred thousand souls, and there is poverty and misery and mendacity enough among them to furnish forty millions and be liberal about it. Under King Otho the revenues of the state were five millions of dollars—raised from a tax of *one-tenth* of all the agricultural products of the land (which tenth the farmer had to bring to the royal granaries on pack-mules any distance not exceeding six leagues) and from extravagant taxes on trade and commerce. Out of that five millions the small tyrant tried to keep an army of ten thousand men, pay all the hundreds of useless Grand Equerries in Waiting, First Grooms of the Bed-chamber, Lord High Chancellors of the Exploded Exchequer, and all the other absurdities which these puppy-kingdoms indulge in, in imitation of the great monarchies; and in addition he set about building a white marble palace to cost about five millions itself. The result was, simply: Ten into five goes no times and none over. All these things could not be done with five millions, and Otho fell into trouble.

The Greek throne, with its unpromising adjuncts of a ragged population of ingenious rascals who were out of employment eight months in the year because there was little for them to borrow and less to confiscate, and a waste of barren hills and weed-grown deserts, went begging for a good while. It was offered to one of Victoria's sons, and afterward to various other younger sons of royalty who had no thrones and were out of business, but they all had the charity to decline the dreary honor, and veneration enough for Greece's ancient greatness to refuse to mock her sorrowful rags and dirt with a tinsel throne in this day of her humiliation—till they came to this young Danish George, and he took it. He had finished the splendid palace I saw in the radiant moonlight the other night, and is doing many other things for the salvation of Greece, they say.

We sailed through the barren Archipelago, and into the narrow channel they sometimes call the Dardanelles and sometimes the Hellespont. This part of the country is rich in historic reminiscences, and poor as Sahara in everything else. For instance, as we approached the Dardanelles, we coasted along the Plains of Troy and past the mouth of the Scamander; we saw where Troy had stood (in the distance), and where it does not stand now—a city that perished when the world was young. The poor Trojans are all dead now. They were born too late to see

Noah's ark, and died too soon to see our menagerie. We saw where Agamemnon's fleets rendezvoused, and away inland a mountain which the map said was Mount Ida. Within the Hellespont we saw where the original first shoddy contract mentioned in history was carried out, and the "parties of the second part" gently rebuked by Xerxes. I speak of the famous bridge of boats which Xerxes ordered to be built over the narrowest part of the Hellespont (where it is only two or three miles wide). A moderate gale destroyed the flimsy structure, and the King, thinking that to publicly rebuke the contractors might have a good effect on the next set, called them out before the army and had them beheaded. In the next ten minutes he let a new contract for the bridge. It has been observed by ancient writers that the second bridge was a very good bridge. Xerxes crossed his host of five millions of men on it, and if it had not been purposely destroyed, it would probably have been there yet. If our government would rebuke some of our shoddy contractors occasionally, it might work much good. In the Hellespont we saw where Leander and Lord Byron swam across, the one to see her upon whom his soul's affections were fixed with a devotion that only death could impair, and the other merely for a flyer, as Jack says. We had two noted tombs near us, too. On one shore slept Ajax, and on the other Hecuba.

We had water batteries and forts on both sides of the Hellespont, flying the crimson flag of Turkey, with its white crescent, and occasionally a village, and sometimes a train of camels; we had all these to look at till we entered the broad sea of Marmora, and then the land soon fading from view, we resumed euchre and whist once more.

We dropped anchor in the mouth of the Golden Horn at daylight in the morning. Only three or four of us were up to see the great Ottoman capital. The passengers do not turn out at unseasonable hours, as they used to, to get the earliest possible glimpse of strange foreign cities. They are well over that. If we were lying in sight of the Pyramids of Egypt, they would not come on deck until after breakfast, nowadays.

The Golden Horn is a narrow arm of the sea, which branches from the Bosporus (a sort of broad river which connects the Marmora and Black Seas), and, curving around, divides the city in the middle. Galata and Pera are on one side of the Bosporus, and the Golden Horn; Stamboul (ancient Byzantium) is upon the other. On the other bank of the Bosporus is Scutari and other suburbs of Constantinople. This great city contains a million inhabitants, but so narrow are its streets, and so crowded together are its houses, that it does not cover much more than half as much ground as New York City. Seen from the anchorage or from a mile or so up the Bosporus, it is by far the handsomest city we have seen. Its dense array of houses swells upward from the water's edge, and spreads over the domes of many hills; and the gardens that peep out here and there, the great globes of the mosques, and the countless minarets that meet the eye everywhere, invest the metropolis with the quaint Oriental aspect one dreams of when he reads books of Eastern travel. Constantinople makes a noble picture.

But its attractiveness begins and ends with its picturesqueness. From the time one starts ashore till he gets back again, he execrates it. The boat he goes in is admirably miscalculated for the service it is built for. It is handsomely and neatly fitted up, but no man could handle it well in the turbulent currents that sweep down the Bosporus from the Black Sea, and few men could row it satisfactorily even in still water. It is a long, light canoe (caique), large at one end and tapering to a knife blade at the other. They make that long sharp end the bow, and you can imagine how these boiling currents spin it about. It has two oars, and sometimes four, and no rudder. You start to go to a given point and you run in fifty different directions before you get there. First one oar is backing water, and then the other; it is seldom that both are going ahead at once. This kind of boating is calculated to drive an impatient man mad in a week. The boatmen are the awkwardest, the stupidest, and the most unscientific on earth, without question.

Ashore, it was—well, it was an eternal circus. People were thicker than bees, in those narrow streets, and the men were dressed in all the outrageous, outlandish, idolatrous, extravagant, thunder-and-lightning costumes that every a tailor with the delirium tremens and seven devils could conceive of. There was no freak in dress too crazy to be indulged in; no absurdity too absurd to be tolerated; no frenzy in ragged diabolism too fantastic to be attempted. No two men were dressed alike. It was a wild masquerade of all imaginable costumes—every struggling throng in every street was a dissolving view of stunning contrasts. Some patriarchs wore awful turbans, but the grand mass of the infidel horde wore the fiery red skull-cap they call a fez. All the remainder of the raiment they indulged in was utterly indescribable.

The shops here are mere coops, mere boxes, bathrooms, closets— anything you please to call them—on the first floor. The Turks sit cross-legged in them, and work and trade and smoke long pipes, and smell like—like Turks. That covers the ground. Crowding the narrow streets in front of them are beggars, who beg forever, yet never collect anything; and wonderful cripples, distorted out of all semblance of humanity, almost; vagabonds driving laden asses; porters carrying dry-goods boxes as large as cottages on their backs; peddlers of grapes, hot corn, pumpkin seeds, and a hundred other things, yelling like fiends; and sleeping happily, comfortably, serenely, among the hurrying feet, are the famed dogs of Constantinople; drifting noiselessly about are squads of Turkish women, draped from chin to feet in flowing robes, and with snowy veils bound about their heads, that disclose only the eyes and a vague, shadowy notion of their features. Seen moving about, far away in the dim, arched aisles of the Great Bazaar, they look as the shrouded dead must have looked when they walked forth from their graves amid the storms and thunders and earthquakes that burst upon Calvary that awful night of the Crucifixion. A street in Constantinople is a picture which one ought to see once—not oftener.

And then there was the goose-rancher—a fellow who drove a hundred geese before him about the city, and tried to sell them. He had a pole ten feet long, with a crook in the end of it, and occasionally a goose would branch out from the flock and make a lively break around the corner, with wings half lifted and neck stretched to its utmost. Did the goose-merchant get excited? No. He took his pole and reached after that goose with unspeakable *sang froid*—took a hitch round his neck, and "yanked" him back to his place in the flock without an effort. He steered his geese with that stick as easily as another man would steer a yawl. A few hours afterward we saw him sitting on a stone at a corner, in the midst of the turmoil, sound asleep in the sun, with his geese squatting around him, or dodging out of the way of asses and men. We came by again, within the hour, and he was taking account of stock, to see whether any of his flock had strayed or been stolen. The way he did it was unique. He put the end of his stick within six or eight inches of a stone wall, and made the geese march in single file between it and the wall. He counted them as they went by. There was no dodging that arrangement.

If you want dwarfs—I mean just a few dwarfs for a curiosity—go to Genoa. If you wish to buy them by the gross, for retail, go to Milan. There are plenty of dwarfs all over Italy, but it did seem to me that in Milan the crop was luxuriant. If you would see a fair average style of assorted cripples, go to Naples, or travel through the Roman states. But if you would see the very heart and home of cripples and human monsters, both, go straight to Constantinople. A beggar in Naples who can show a foot which has all run into one horrible toe, with one shapeless nail on it, has a fortune—but such an exhibition as that would not provoke any notice in Constantinople. The man would starve. Who would pay any attention to attractions like his among the rare monsters that throng the bridges of the Golden Horn and display their deformities in the gutters of Stamboul? Oh, wretched impostor! How could he stand against the three-legged woman, and the man with his eye in his cheek? How would he blush in presence of the man with fingers on his elbow? Where would he hide himself when the dwarf with seven fingers on each hand, no upper lip, and his under-jaw gone, came down in his majesty? Bismillah! The cripples of Europe are a delusion and a fraud. The truly gifted flourish only in the byways of Pera and Stamboul.

That three-legged woman lay on the bridge, with her stock in trade so disposed as to command the most striking effect—one natural leg, and two long, slender, twisted ones with feet on them like somebody else's forearm. Then there was a man further along who had no eyes, and whose face was the color of a fly-blown beefsteak, and wrinkled and twisted like a lava-flow—and verily so tumbled and distorted were his features that no man could tell the wart that served him for a nose from his cheekbones. In Stamboul was a man with a prodigious head, an uncommonly long body, legs eight inches long, and feet like snow-shoes. He traveled on those feet and his hands, and was as sway-backed as if the Colossus of Rhodes had been riding him. Ah, a beggar has to have exceedingly good points to make a living in Constantinople. A blue-faced man, who had nothing to offer except that he had been blown up in a mine, would be regarded as a rank impostor, and a mere damaged soldier on crutches would never make a cent. It would pay him to get a piece of his head taken off, and cultivate a wen like a carpet sack.

The Mosque of St. Sophia is the chief lion of Constantinople. You must get a firman and hurry there the first thing. We did that. We did not get a firman, but we took along four or five francs apiece, which is much the same thing.

I do not think much of the Mosque of St. Sophia. I suppose I lack appreciation. We will let it go at that. It is the rustiest old barn in heathendom. I believe all the interest that attaches to it comes from the fact that it was built for a Christian church and then turned into a mosque, without much alteration, by the Mohammedan conquerors of the land. They made me take off my boots and walk into the place in my stocking feet. I caught cold, and got myself so stuck up with a complication of gums, slime, and general corruption, that I wore out more than two thousand pair of boot-jacks getting my boots off that night, and even then some Christian hide peeled off with them. I abate not a single boot-jack.

St. Sophia is a colossal church, thirteen or fourteen hundred years old, and unsightly enough to be very, very much older. Its immense dome is said to be more wonderful than St. Peter's, but its dirt is much more wonderful than its dome, though they never mention it. The church has a hundred and seventy pillars in it, each a single piece, and all of costly marbles of various kinds, but they came from ancient temples at Baalbec, Heliopolis, Athens, and Ephesus, and are battered, ugly, and repulsive. They were a thousand years old when this church was new, and then the contrast must have been ghastly—if Justinian's architects did not trim them any. The inside of the dome is figured all over with a monstrous inscription in Turkish characters, wrought in gold mosaic, that looks as glaring as a circus bill; the pavements and the marble balustrades are all battered and dirty; the perspective is marred everywhere by a web of ropes that depend from the dizzy height of the dome, and suspend countless dingy, coarse oil lamps, and ostrich-eggs, six or seven feet above the floor. Squatting and sitting in groups, here and there and far and near, were ragged Turks reading books, hearing sermons, or receiving lessons like children, and in fifty places were more of the same sort bowing and straightening up, bowing again and getting down to kiss the earth, muttering prayers the while, and keeping up their gymnastics till they ought to have been tired, if they were not.

Everywhere was dirt and dust and dinginess and gloom; everywhere were signs of a hoary antiquity, but with nothing touching or beautiful about it; everywhere were those groups of fantastic pagans; overhead the gaudy mosaics and the web of lampropes—nowhere was there anything to win one's love or challenge his admiration.

The people who go into ecstasies over St. Sophia must surely get them out of the guide-book (where every church is spoken of as being "considered by good judges to be the most marvelous structure, in many respects, that the world has ever seen"). Or else they are those old connoisseurs from the wilds of New Jersey who laboriously learn the difference between a fresco and a fire-plug, and from that day forward feel privileged to void their critical bathos on painting, sculpture, and architecture forevermore.

We visited the Dancing Dervishes. There were twenty-one of them. They wore a long, light-colored loose robe that hung to their heels. Each in his turn went up to the priest (they were all within a large circular railing) and bowed profoundly and then went spinning away deliriously and took his appointed place in the circle, and continued to spin. When all had spun themselves to their places, they were about five or six feet apart—and so situated, the entire circle of spinning pagans spun itself three separate times around the room. It took twenty-five minutes to do it. They spun on the left foot, and kept themselves going by passing the right rapidly before it and digging it against the waxed floor. Some of them made incredible "time." Most of them spun around forty times in a minute, and one artist averaged about sixty-one times a minute, and kept it up during the whole twenty-five. His robe filled with air and stood out all around him like a balloon.

They made no noise of any kind, and most of them tilted their heads back and closed their eyes, entranced with a sort of devotional ecstasy. There was a rude kind of music, part of the time, but the musicians were not visible. None but spinners were allowed within the circle. A man had to either spin or stay outside. It was about as barbarous an exhibition as we have witnessed yet. Then sick persons came and lay down, and beside them women laid their sick children (one a babe at the breast), and the patriarch of the Dervishes walked upon their bodies. He was supposed to cure their diseases by trampling upon their breasts or backs or standing on the back of their necks. This is well enough for a people who think all their affairs are made or marred by viewless spirits of the air—by giants, gnomes, and genii—and who still believe, to this day, all the wild tales in the Arabian Nights. Even so an intelligent missionary tells me.

We visited the Thousand and One Columns. I do not know what it was originally intended for, but they said it was built for a reservoir. It is situated in the center of Constantinople. You go down a flight of stone steps in the middle of a barren place, and there you are. You are forty feet underground, and in the midst of a perfect wilderness of tall, slender, granite columns, of Byzantine architecture. Stand where you would, or change your position as often as you pleased, you were always a center from which radiated a dozen long archways and colonnades that lost themselves in distance and the somber twilight of the place. This old dried-up reservoir is occupied by a few ghostly silk-spinners now, and one of them showed me a cross cut high up in one of the pillars. I suppose he meant me to understand that the institution was there before the Turkish occupation, and I thought he made a remark to that effect; but he must have had an impediment in his speech, for I did not understand him.

We took off our shoes and went into the marble mausoleum of the Sultan Mahmoud, the neatest piece of architecture, inside, that I have seen lately. Mahmoud's tomb was covered with a black velvet pall, which was elaborately embroidered with silver railing; at the sides and corners were silver candlesticks that would weigh more than a hundred pounds, and they supported candles as large as a man's leg; on the top of the sarcophagus was a fez, with a handsome diamond ornament upon it, which an attendant said cost a hundred thousand pounds, and lied like a Turk when he said it. Mahmoud's whole family were comfortably planted around him.

We went to the Great Bazaar in Stamboul, of course, and I shall not describe it further than to say it is a monstrous hive of little shops—thousands, I should say—all under one roof, and cut up into innumerable little blocks by narrow streets which are arched overhead. One street is devoted to a particular kind of merchandise, another to another, and so on. When you wish to buy a pair of shoes you have the swing of the whole street—you do not have to walk yourself down hunting stores in different localities. It is the same with silks, antiquities, shawls, etc. The place is crowded with people all the time, and as the gay-colored Eastern fabrics are lavishly displayed before every shop, the Great Bazaar of Stamboul is one of the sights that are worth seeing. It is full of life, and stir, and business, dirt, beggars, asses, yelling peddlers, porters, dervishes, high-born Turkish female shoppers, Greeks, and weird-looking and weirdly-dressed Mohammedans from the mountains and the far provinces—and the only solitary thing one does not smell when he is in the Great Bazaar, is something which smells good.

ROBERT LOUIS STEVENSON
1850–1894

"Charming" is the term attaching most readily to the writings of this immensely talented and productive Scottish personality. Soon after his birth in Edinburgh, it was apparent that his health would be fragile, and his whole life was a struggle against "lung trouble." He started as a civil engineer, but the outdoor rigors of this profession were too much for him, and he turned to the law instead. Meanwhile he found that he could write, and soon he was supplying the magazines with numerous essays and stories while cultivating personally a style of behavior that struck Edinburgh as Bohemian.

It proved hard to be a Bohemian in Edinburgh, so he took himself abroad, to Belgium, France, and Germany, looking both for a climate kinder to his health and for situations that might produce copy for travel books and essays. Subsequently he traveled even to San Francisco—as a passenger on a crowded and squalid emigrant ship, an experience that resulted in another travel book. In 1883 he turned to the romantic novel (Treasure Island) *and in 1886 to the science-horror story* (The Strange Case of Dr. Jekyll and Mr. Hyde). *The Scottish romances* Kidnapped *(1886) and* The Master of Ballantrae *(1889) soon followed.*

In 1887 he left Britain for good, journeying to Hawaii and then

*settling with his family in Samoa, where he vigorously identified himself
with the cause of the Samoans against their exploiters.*

*His travel books are of the subjective, personal sort suggestive of
Sterne's* Sentimental Journey, *and Sterne would probably not dissent
from Stevenson's kind observation that "We are all travellers in what
John Bunyan calls the wilderness of this world."*

From TRAVELS WITH A DONKEY
IN THE CÉVENNES
(1879)

VELAY

THE DONKEY, THE PACK, AND THE PACK-SADDLE

In a little place called Le Monastier, in a pleasant highland valley fifteen
miles from Le Puy, I spent about a month of fine days. Monastier is
notable for the making of lace, for drunkenness, for freedom of language,
and for unparalleled political dissension. There are adherents of each of
the four French parties—Legitimists, Orleanist, Imperialists, and
Republicans—in this little mountain-town; and they all hate, loathe,
decry, and calumniate each other. Except for business purposes, or to
give each other the lie in a tavern brawl, they have laid aside even the
civility of speech. 'Tis a mere mountain Poland. In the midst of this
Babylon I found myself a rallying-point; every one was anxious to be kind
and helpful to the stranger. This was not merely from the natural
hospitality of mountain people, nor even from the surprise with which
I was regarded as a man living of his own free will in Monastier, when
he might just as well have lived anywhere else in this big world; it arose
a good deal from my projected excursion southward through the Cévennes. A traveller of my sort was a thing hitherto unheard of in that
district. I was looked upon with contempt, like a man who should project
a journey to the moon, but yet with a respectful interest, like one setting
forth for the inclement Pole. All were ready to help in my preparations;
a crowd of sympathisers supported me at the critical moment of a
bargain; not a step was taken but was heralded by glasses round and
celebrated by a dinner or a breakfast.

It was already hard upon October before I was ready to set forth, and
at the high altitudes over which my road lay there was no Indian summer

to be looked for. I was determined, if not to camp out, at least to have the means of camping out in my possession; for there is nothing more harassing to an easy mind than the necessity of reaching shelter by dusk, and the hospitality of a village inn is not always to be reckoned sure by those who trudge on foot. A tent, above all for a solitary traveller, is troublesome to pitch, and troublesome to strike again; and even on the march it forms a conspicuous feature in your baggage. A sleeping-sack, on the other hand, is always ready—you have only to get into it; it serves a double purpose—a bed by night, a portmanteau by day; and it does not advertise your intention of camping out to every curious passer-by. This is a huge point. If the camp is not secret, it is but a troubled resting-place; you become a public character; the convivial rustic visits your bedside after an early supper; and you must sleep with one eye open, and be up before the day. I decided on a sleeping-sack; and after repeated visits to Le Puy, and a deal of high living for myself and my advisers, a sleeping-sack was designed, constructed, and triumphally brought home.

This child of my invention was nearly six feet square, exclusive of two triangular flaps to serve as a pillow by night and as the top and bottom of the sack by day. I call it "the sack," but it was never a sack by more than courtesy: only a sort of long roll or sausage, green waterproof cart cloth without and blue sheep's fur within. It was commodious as a valise, warm and dry for a bed. There was luxurious turning-room for one; and at a pinch the thing might serve for two. I could bury myself in it up to the neck; for my head I trusted to a fur cap, with a hood to fold down over my ears and a band to pass under my nose like a respirator; and in case of heavy rain I proposed to make myself a little tent, or tentlet, with my waterproof coat, three stones, and a bent branch.

It will readily be conceived that I could not carry this huge package on my own, merely human, shoulders. It remained to choose a beast of burthen. Now, a horse is a fine lady among animals, flighty, timid, delicate in eating, of tender health; he is too valuable and too restive to be left alone, so that you are chained to your brute as to a fellow galley-slave; a dangerous road puts him out of his wits; in short, he's an uncertain and exacting ally, and adds thirty-fold to the troubles of the voyager. What I required was something cheap and small and hardy, and of a stolid and peaceful temper; and all these requisites pointed to a donkey.

There dwelt an old man in Monastier, of rather unsound intellect according to some, much followed by street-boys, and known to fame as Father Adam. Father Adam had a cart, and to draw the cart a diminutive she-ass, not much bigger than a dog, the colour of a mouse, with a kindly eye and a determined under-jaw. There was something neat and high-bred, a quakerish elegance, about the rogue that hit my fancy on the spot. Our first interview was in Monastier market-place. To prove her good temper, one child after another was set upon her back to ride, and one after another went head over heels into the air; until a want of confidence began to reign in youthful bosoms, and the experiment was discontinued from a dearth of subjects. I was already backed by a deputation of my friends; but as if this were not enough, all the buyers and sellers came round and helped me in the bargain; and the ass and I and Father Adam were the centre of a hubbub for near half an hour. At length she passed into my service for the consideration of sixty-five francs and a glass of brandy. The sack had already cost eighty francs and two glasses of beer; so that Modestine, as I instantly baptised her, was upon all accounts the cheaper article. Indeed, that was as it should be; for she was only an appurtenance of my mattress, or self-acting bedstead on four castors.

I had a last interview with Father Adam in a billiard-room at the witching hour of dawn, when I administered the brandy. He professed himself greatly touched by the separation, and declared he had often bought white bread for the donkey when he had been content with black bread for himself; but this, according to the best authorities, must have been a flight of fancy. He had a name in the village for brutally misusing the ass; yet it is certain that he shed a tear, and the tear made a clean mark down one cheek.

By the advice of a fallacious local saddler, a leather pad was made for me with rings to fasten on my bundle; and I thoughtfully completed my kit and arranged my toilette. By way of armoury and utensils, I took a revolver, a little spirit-lamp and pan, a lantern and some halfpenny candles, a jack-knife and a large leather flask. The main cargo consisted of two entire changes of warm clothing—besides my travelling wear of country velveteen, pilot-coat, and knitted spencer—some books, and my railway-rug, which, being also in the form of a bag, made me a double castle for cold nights. The permanent larder was represented by cakes of chocolate and tins of Bologna sausage. All this, except what I carried about my person, was easily stowed into the sheepskin bag; and by good fortune I threw in my empty knapsack, rather for convenience of carriage than from any thought that I should want it on my journey. For more immediate needs, I took a leg of cold mutton, a bottle of Beaujolais, an empty bottle to carry milk, an egg-beater, and a considerable quantity of black bread and white, like Father Adam, for myself and donkey, only in my scheme of things the destinations were reversed.

Monastrians, of all shades of thought in politics, had agreed in threatening me with many ludicrous misadventures, and with sudden death in many surprising forms. Cold, wolves, robbers, above all the nocturnal practical joker, were daily and eloquently forced on my attention. Yet in these vaticinations, the true, patent danger was left out. Like Christian, it was from my pack I suffered by the way. Before telling my own mishaps, let me, in two words, relate the lesson of my experience. If the pack is well strapped at the ends, and hung at full length—not doubled, for your life—across the pack-saddle, the traveller is safe. The saddle will certainly not fit, such is the imperfection of our transitory life; it will assuredly topple and tend to overset; but there are stones on every roadside, and a man soon learns the art of correcting any tendency to overbalance with a well-adjusted stone.

On the day of my departure I was up a little after five; by six, we began to load the donkey; and ten minutes after, my hopes were in the dust. The pad would not stay on Modestine's back for half a moment. I returned it to its maker, with whom I had so contumelious a passage that the street outside was crowded from wall to wall with gossips looking on and listening. The pad changed hands with much vivacity; perhaps it would be more descriptive to say that we threw it at each other's heads; and, at any rate, we were very warm and unfriendly, and spoke with a deal of freedom.

I had a common donkey pack-saddle—a *barde*, as they call it—fitted upon Modestine; and once more loaded her with my effects. The double sack, my pilot-coat (for it was warm, and I was to walk in my waistcoat), a great bar of black bread, and an open basket containing the white bread, the mutton, and the bottles, were all corded together in a very elaborate system of knots, and I looked on the result with fatuous content. In such a monstrous deck-cargo, all poised above the donkey's shoulders, with nothing below to balance, on a brand-new pack-saddle that had not yet been worn to fit the animal, and fastened with brand-new girths that might be expected to stretch and slacken by the way, even a very careless traveller should have seen disaster brewing. That elaborate system of knots, again, was the work of too many sympathisers to be very artfully designed. It is true they tightened the cords with a will; as many as three at a time would have a foot against Modestine's quarters, and be hauling with clenched teeth; but I learned afterwards that one thoughtful person, without any exercise of force, can make a more solid job than half-a-dozen heated and enthusiastic grooms. I was then but a novice; even after the misadventure of the pad nothing could disturb my security, and I went forth from the stable-door as an ox goeth to the slaughter.

THE GREEN DONKEY-DRIVER

The bell of Monastier was just striking nine as I got quit of these preliminary troubles and descended the hill through the common. As long as I was within sight of the windows, a secret shame and the fear of some laughable defeat withheld me from tampering with Modestine. She tripped along upon her four small hoofs with a sober daintiness of gait; from time to time she shook her ears or her tail; and she looked so small under the bundle that my mind misgave me. We got across the ford without difficulty—there was no doubt about the matter, she was docility itself—and once on the other bank, where the road begins to mount through pinewoods, I took in my right hand the unhallowed staff, and with a quaking spirit applied it to the donkey. Modestine brisked up her pace for perhaps three steps, and then relapsed into her former minuet. Another application had the same effect, and so with the third. I am worthy the name of an Englishman, and it goes against my conscience to lay my hand rudely on a female. I desisted, and looked her all over from head to foot; the poor brute's knees were trembling and her breathing was distressed; it was plain that she could go no faster on a hill. God forbid, thought I, that I should brutalise this innocent creature; let her go at her own pace, and let me patiently follow.

What that pace was, there is no word mean enough to describe; it was something as much slower than a walk as a walk is slower than a run; it kept me hanging on each foot for an incredible length of time; in five minutes it exhausted the spirit and set up a fever in all the muscles of the leg. And yet I had to keep close at hand and measure my advance exactly upon hers; for if I dropped a few yards into the rear, or went on a few yards ahead, Modestine came instantly to a halt and began to browse. The thought that this was to last from here to Alais nearly broke my heart. Of all conceivable journeys, this promised to be the most tedious. I tried to tell myself it was a lovely day; I tried to charm my foreboding spirit with tobacco; but I had a vision ever present to me of the long, long roads, up hill and down dale, and a pair of figures ever infinitesimally moving, foot by foot, a yard to the minute, and, like things enchanted in a nightmare, approaching no nearer to the goal.

In the meantime there came up behind us a tall peasant, perhaps forty years of age, of an ironical snuffy countenance, and arrayed in the green tailcoat of the country. He overtook us hand over hand, and stopped to consider our pitiful advance.

"Your donkey," says he, "is very old?"

I told him, I believed not.

Then, he supposed, we had come far.

I told him, we had but newly left Monastier.

"*Et vous marchez comme ça* [And you're moving along like that]!" cried he; and, throwing back his head, he laughed long and heartily. I watched him, half prepared to feel offended, until he had satisfied his mirth; and then, "You must have no pity on these animals," said he; and, plucking a switch out of a thicket, he began to lace Modestine about the stern-works, uttering a cry. The rogue pricked up her ears and broke into a good round pace, which she kept up without flagging, and without exhibiting the least symptom of distress, as long as the peasant kept beside us. Her former panting and shaking had been, I regret to say, a piece of comedy.

My *deus ex machina*, before he left me, supplied some excellent, if inhumane, advice; presented me with the switch, which he declared she would feel more tenderly than my cane; and finally taught me the true cry or masonic word of donkey-drivers, "Proot!" All the time, he regarded me with a comical incredulous air, which was embarrassing to confront; and smiled over my donkey-driving, as I might have smiled over his orthography, or his green tail-coat. But it was not my turn for the moment.

I was proud of my new lore, and thought I had learned the art to perfection. And certainly Modestine did wonders for the rest of the forenoon, and I had a breathing space to look about me. It was Sabbath; the mountain-fields were all vacant in the sunshine; and as we came down through St. Martin de Frugères, the church was crowded to the door, there were people kneeling without upon the steps, and the sound of the priest's chanting came forth out of the dim interior. It gave me a home feeling on the spot; for I am a countryman of the Sabbath, so to speak, and all Sabbath observances, like a Scotch accent, strike in me mixed feelings, grateful and the reverse. It is only a traveller, hurrying by like a person from another planet, who can rightly enjoy the peace and beauty of the great ascetic feast. The sight of the resting country does his spirit good. There is something better than music in the wide unusual silence; and it disposes him to amiable thoughts, like the sound of a little river or the warmth of sunlight.

In this pleasant humour I came down the hill to where Goudet stands in the green end of a valley, with Château Beaufort opposite upon a rocky steep, and the stream, as clear as crystal, lying in a deep pool between them. Above and below, you may hear it wimpling over the stones, an amiable stripling of a river, which it seems absurd to call the

Loire. On all sides, Goudet is shut in by mountains; rocky foot-paths, practicable at best for donkeys, join it to the outer world of France; and the men and women drink and swear, in their green corner, or look up at the snow-clad peaks in winter from the threshold of their homes, in an isolation, you would think, like that of Homer's Cyclops. But it is not so; the postman reaches Goudet with the letter-bag; the aspiring youth of Goudet are within a day's walk of the railway at Le Puy; and here in the inn you may find an engraved portrait of the host's nephew, Régis Senac, "Professor of Fencing and Champion of the two Americas," a distinction gained by him, along with the sum of five hundred dollars, at Tammany Hall, New York, on the 10th April, 1876.

I hurried over my midday meal, and was early forth again. But, alas, as we climbed the interminable hill upon the other side, "Proot!" seemed to have lost its virtue. I prooted like a lion, I prooted mellifluously like a sucking-dove; but Modestine would be neither softened nor intimidated. She held doggedly to her pace; nothing but a blow would move her, and that only for a second. I must follow at her heels, incessantly belabouring. A moment's pause in this ignoble toil, and she relapsed into her own private gait. I think I never heard of any one in as mean a situation. I must reach the lake of Bouchet, where I meant to camp, before sundown, and, to have even a hope of this, I must instantly maltreat this uncomplaining animal. The sound of my own blows sickened me. Once, when I looked at her, she had a faint resemblance to a lady of my acquaintance who formerly loaded me with kindness; and this increased my horror of my cruelty.

To make matters worse, we encountered another donkey, ranging at will upon the roadside; and this other donkey chanced to be a gentleman. He and Modestine met nickering for joy, and I had to separate the pair and beat down their young romance with a renewed and feverish bastinado. If the other donkey had had the heart of a male under his hide, he would have fallen upon me tooth and hoof; and this was a kind of consolation—he was plainly unworthy of Modestine's affection. But the incident saddened me, as did everything that spoke of my donkey's sex.

It was blazing hot up the valley, windless, with vehement sun upon my shoulders; and I had to labour so consistently with my stick that the sweat ran into my eyes. Every five minutes, too, the pack, the basket, and the pilot-coat would take an ugly slew to one side or the other; and I had to stop Modestine, just when I had got her to a tolerable pace of about two miles an hour, to tug, push, shoulder, and readjust the load. And at last, in the village of Ussel, saddle and all, the whole hypothec turned round and grovelled in the dust below the donkey's belly. She, none better pleased, incontinently drew up and seemed to smile; and a party of one man, two women, and two children came up, and, standing round me in a half-circle, encouraged her by their example.

I had the devil's own trouble to get the thing righted; and the instant I had done so, without hesitation, it toppled and fell down upon the other side. Judge if I was hot! And yet not a hand was offered to assist me. The man, indeed, told me I ought to have a package of a different shape. I suggested, if he knew nothing better to the point in my predicament, he might hold his tongue. And the good-natured dog agreed with me smilingly. It was the most despicable fix. I must plainly content myself with the pack for Modestine, and take the following items for my own share of the portage: a cane, a quart flask, a pilot-jacket heavily weighted in the pockets, two pounds of black bread, and an open basket full of meats and bottles. I believe I may say I am not devoid of greatness of soul; for I did not recoil from this infamous burden. I disposed it, Heaven knows how, so as to be mildly portable, and then proceeded to steer Modestine through the village. She tried, as was indeed her invariable habit, to enter every house and every courtyard in the whole length; and, encumbered as I was, without a hand to help myself, no words can render an idea of my difficulties. A priest, with six or seven others, was examining a church in process of repair, and he and his acolytes laughed loudly as they saw my plight. I remembered having laughed myself when I had seen good men struggling with adversity in the person of a jackass, and the recollection filled me with penitence. That was in my old light days, before this trouble came upon me. God knows at least that I shall never laugh again, thought I. But O, what a cruel thing is a farce to those engaged in it!

A little out of the village, Modestine, filled with the demon, set her heart upon a by-road, and positively refused to leave it. I dropped all my bundles, and, I am ashamed to say, struck the poor sinner twice across the face. It was pitiful to see her lift up her head with shut eyes, as if waiting for another blow. I came very near crying; but I did a wiser thing than that, and sat squarely down by the roadside to consider my situation under the cheerful influence of tobacco and a nip of brandy. Modestine, in the meanwhile, munched some black bread with a contrite hypocritical air. It was plain that I must make a sacrifice to the gods of shipwreck. I threw away the empty bottle destined to carry milk; I threw away my own white bread, and, disdaining to act by general average, kept the black bread for Modestine; lastly, I threw away the cold leg of mutton and the egg-whisk, although this last was dear to my heart. Thus I found room for everything in the basket, and even stowed the boating-coat on the top. By means of an end of cord I slung it under one arm; and although the cord cut my shoulder, and the jacket hung almost to the ground, it was with a heart greatly lightened that I set forth again.

I had now an arm free to thrash Modestine, and cruelly I chastised her. If I were to reach the lakeside before dark, she must bestir her little shanks to some tune. Already the sun had gone down into a windy-looking mist; and although there were still a few streaks of gold far off to the east on the hills and the black fir-woods, all was cold and grey about our onward path. An infinity of little country by-roads led hither and thither among the fields. It was the most pointless labyrinth. I could see my destination overhead, or rather the peak that dominates it; but choose as I pleased, the roads always ended by turning away from it, and sneaking back towards the valley, or northward along the margin of the hills. The failing light, the waning colour, the naked, unhomely, stony country through which I was travelling threw me into some despondency. I promise you, the stick was not idle; I think every decent step that Modestine took must have cost me at least two emphatic blows. There was not another sound in the neighbourhood but that of my unwearying bastinado.

Suddenly, in the midst of my toils, the load once more bit the dust, and, as by enchantment, all the cords were simultaneously loosened, and the road scattered with my dear possessions. The packing was to begin again from the beginning; and as I had to invent a new and better system, I do not doubt but I lost half an hour. It began to be dusk in earnest as I reached a wilderness of turf and stones. It had the air of being a road which should lead everywhere at the same time; and I was falling into something not unlike despair when I saw two figures stalking towards me over the stones. They walked one behind the other like tramps, but their pace was remarkable. The son led the way, a tall, ill-made, sombre, Scotch-looking man; the mother followed, all in her Sunday's best, with an elegantly-embroidered ribbon to her cap, and a new felt hat atop, and proffering, as she strode along with kilted petticoats, a string of obscene and blasphemous oaths.

I hailed the son and asked him my direction. He pointed loosely west and north-west, muttered an inaudible comment, and, without slacking his pace for an instant, stalked on, as he was going, right athwart my path. The mother followed without so much as raising her head. I shouted and shouted after them, but they continued to scale the hillside, and turned a deaf ear to my outcries. At last, leaving Modestine by herself, I was constrained to run after them, hailing the while. They stopped as I drew near, the mother still cursing; and I could see she was a handsome, motherly, respectable-looking woman. The son once more answered me roughly and inaudibly, and was for setting out again. But this time I simply collared the mother, who was nearest me, and, apologising for my violence, declared that I could not let them go until they had put me on my road. They were neither of them offended—rather mollified than otherwise; told me I had only to follow them; and then the mother asked me what I wanted by the lake at such an hour. I replied, in the Scotch manner, by inquiring if she had far to go herself. She told me, with another oath, that she had an hour and a half's road before her. And then, without salutation, the pair strode forward again up the hillside in the gathering dusk.

I returned for Modestine, pushed her briskly forward, and, after a sharp ascent of twenty minutes, reached the edge of a plateau. The view, looking back on my day's journey, was both wild and sad. Mount Mézenc and the peaks beyond St. Julien stood out in trenchant gloom against a cold glitter in the east; and the intervening field of hills had fallen together into one broad wash of shadow, except here and there the outline of a wooded sugar-loaf in black, here and there a white irregular patch to represent a cultivated farm, and here and there a blot where the Loire, the Gazeille, or the Lausonne wandered in a gorge.

Soon we were on a highroad, and surprise seized on my mind as I beheld a village of some magnitude close at hand; for I had been told that the neighbourhood of the lake was uninhabited except by trout. The road smoked in the twilight with children driving home cattle from the fields; and a pair of mounted stride-legged women, hat and cap and all, dashed past me at a hammering trot from the canton where they had been to church and market. I asked one of the children where I was. At Bouchet St. Nicolas, he told me. Thither, about a mile south of my destination, and on the other side of a respectable summit, had these confused roads and treacherous peasantry conducted me. My shoulder was cut, so that it hurt sharply; my arm ached like toothache from perpetual beating; I gave up the lake and my design to camp, and asked for the *auberge* [inn].

*   *   *

WALT WHITMAN
1819–1892

Born on Long Island, Whitman lived variously in Brooklyn, New Orleans, Washington D. C., and finally, for eighteen years, in Camden, N. J., but except for a visit to Canada in 1880 he never left the United States.

SONG OF THE OPEN ROAD
(1856)

1

Afoot and light-hearted I take to the open road,
Healthy, free, the world before me,
The long brown path before me leading wherever I choose.

Henceforth I ask not good-fortune, I myself am good-fortune,
Henceforth I whimper no more, postpone no more, need nothing,
Done with indoor complaints, libraries, querulous criticisms,
Strong and content I travel the open road.

The earth, that is sufficient,
I do not want the constellations any nearer,
I know they are very well where they are,
I know they suffice for those who belong to them.

(Still here I carry my old delicious burdens,
I carry them, men and women, I carry them with me wherever I go,
I swear it is impossible for me to get rid of them,
I am fill'd with them, and I will fill them in return.)

2

You road I enter upon and look around, I believe you are not all
    that is here,
I believe that much unseen is also here.
Here the profound lesson of reception, nor preference nor denial,
The black with his woolly head, the felon, the diseas'd, the illiterate
    person, are not denied;
The birth, the hasting after the physician, the beggar's tramp, the
    drunkard's stagger, the laughing party of mechanics,
The escaped youth, the rich person's carriage, the fop, the eloping
    couple,
The early market-man, the hearse, the moving of furniture into the
    town, the return back from the town,
They pass, I also pass, any thing passes, none can be interdicted,
None but are accepted, none but shall be dear to me.

3

You air that serves me with breath to speak!
You objects that call from diffusion my meanings and give them
    shape!
You light that wraps me and all things in delicate equable showers!
You paths worn in the irregular hollows by the roadsides!
I believe you are latent with unseen existences, you are so dear to
    me.

You flagg'd walks of the cities! you strong curbs at the edges!
You ferries! you planks and posts of wharves! you timber-lined sides!
    you distant ships!
You rows of houses! you window-pierc'd façades! you roofs!
You porches and entrances! you copings and iron guards!
You windows whose transparent shells might expose so much!
You doors and ascending steps! you arches!
You gray stones of interminable pavements! you trodden crossings!
From all that has touch'd you I believe you have imparted to
    yourselves, and now would impart the same secretly to me,
From the living and the dead you have peopled your impassive
    surfaces, and the spirits thereof would be evident and
    amicable with me.

4

The earth expanding right hand and left hand,
The picture alive, every part in its best light,
The music falling in where it is wanted, and stopping where it is
     not wanted,
The cheerful voice of the public road, the gay fresh sentiment of
     the road.

O highway I travel, do you say to me *Do not leave me?*
Do you say *Venture not—if you leave me you are lost?*
Do you say *I am already prepared, I am well-beaten and undenied,
     adhere to me?*

O public road, I say back I am not afraid to leave you, yet I love
     you,
You express me better than I can express myself,
You shall be more to me than my poem.

I think heroic deeds were all conceiv'd in the open air, and all free
     poems also,
I think I could stop here myself and do miracles,
I think whatever I shall meet on the road I shall like, and whoever
     beholds me shall like me,
I think whoever I see must be happy.

5

From this hour I ordain myself loos'd of limits and imaginary lines,
Going where I list, my own master total and absolute,
Listening to others, considering well what they say,
Pausing, searching, receiving, contemplating,
Gently, but with undeniable will, divesting myself of the holds that
     would hold me.

I inhale great draughts of space,
The east and the west are mine, and the north and the south are
     mine.

I am larger, better than I thought,
I did not know I held so much goodness.

All seems beautiful to me,
I can repeat over to men and women You have done such good to
        me I would do the same to you,
I will recruit for myself and you as I go,
I will scatter myself among men and women as I go,
I will toss a new gladness and roughness among them,
Whoever denies me it shall not trouble me,
Whoever accepts me he or she shall be blessed and shall bless me.

6

Now if a thousand perfect men were to appear it would not amaze
        me,
Now if a thousand beautiful forms of women appear'd it would not
        astonish me.

Now I see the secret of the making of the best persons,
It is to grow in the open air and to eat and sleep with the earth.

Here a great personal deed has room,
(Such a deed seizes upon the hearts of the whole race of men,
Its effusion of strength and will overwhelms law and mocks all
        authority and all argument against it.)

Here is the test of wisdom,
Wisdom is not finally tested in schools,
Wisdom cannot be pass'd from one having it to another not having it,
Wisdom is of the soul, is not susceptible of proof, is its own proof,
Applies to all stages and objects and qualities and is content,
Is the certainty of the reality and immortality of things, and the
        excellence of things;
Something there is in the float of the sight of things that provokes
        it out of the soul.

Now I re-examine philosophies and religions,
They may prove well in lecture-rooms, yet not prove at all under the
        spacious clouds and along the landscape and flowing currents.

Here is realization,
Here is a man tallied—he realizes here what he has in him,
The past, the future, majesty, love—if they are vacant of you, you
        are vacant of them.

Only the kernel of every object nourishes;
Where is he who tears off the husks for you and me?
Where is he that undoes stratagems and envelopes for you and me?

Here is adhesiveness, it is not previously fashion'd, it is apropos;
Do you know what it is as you pass to be loved by strangers?
Do you know the talk of those turning eye-balls?

7

Here is the efflux of the soul,
The efflux of the soul comes from within through embower'd gates,
      ever provoking questions,
These yearnings why are they? these thoughts in the darkness why
      are they?
Why are there men and women that while they are nigh me the
      sunlight expands my blood?
Why when they leave me do my pennants of joy sink flat and lank?
Why are there trees I never walk under but large and melodious
      thoughts descend upon me?
(I think they hang there winter and summer on those trees and
      always drop fruit as I pass;)
What is it I interchange so suddenly with strangers?
What with some driver as I ride on the seat by his side?
What with some fisherman drawing his seine by the shore as I walk
      by and pause?
What gives me to be free to a woman's and man's good-will? what
      gives them to be free to mine?

8

The efflux of the soul is happiness, here is happiness,
I think it pervades the open air, waiting at all times,
Now it flows unto us, we are rightly charged.
Here rises the fluid and attaching character,
The fluid and attaching character is the freshness and sweetness of
      man and woman,
(The herbs of the morning sprout no fresher and sweeter every day
      out of the roots of themselves, than it sprouts fresh and
sweet continually out of itself.)

Toward the fluid and attaching character exudes the sweat of the
      love of young and old,

From it falls distill'd the charm that mocks beauty and attainments,
Toward it heaves the shuddering longing ache of contact.

9

Allons [Let's go]! whoever you are come travel with me!
Traveling with me you find what never tires.

The earth never tires,
The earth is rude, silent, incomprehensible at first, Nature is rude
    and incomprehensible at first,
Be not discouraged, keep on, there are divine things well envelop'd,
I swear to you there are divine things more beautiful than words can
    tell.

Allons! we must not stop here,
However sweet these laid-up stores, however convenient this
    dwelling we cannot remain here,
However shelter'd this port and however calm these waters we must
    not anchor here,
However welcome the hospitality that surrounds us we are permitted
    to receive it but a little while.

10

Allons! the inducements shall be greater,
We will sail pathless and wild seas,
We will go where winds blow, waves dash, and the Yankee clipper
    speeds by under full sail.
Allons! with power, liberty, the earth, the elements,
Health, defiance, gayety, self-esteem, curiosity;
Allons! from all formules!
From your formules, O bat-eyed and materialistic priests.

The stale cadaver blocks up the passage—the burial waits no longer.

Allons! yet take warning!
He traveling with me needs the best blood, thews, endurance,
None may come to the trial till he or she bring courage and health,
Come not here if you have already spent the best of yourself,
Only those may come who come in sweet and determin'd bodies,
No diseas'd person, no rum-drinker or venereal taint is permitted
    here.

(I and mine do not convince by arguments, similes, rhymes,
We convince by our presence.)

11

Listen! I will be honest with you,
I do not offer the old smooth prizes, but offer rough new prizes,
These are the days that must happen to you:
You shall not heap up what is call'd riches,
You shall scatter with lavish hand all that you earn or achieve,
You but arrive at the city to which you were destin'd, you hardly
    settle yourself to satisfaction before you are call'd by an
irresistible call to depart,
You shall be treated to the ironical smiles and mockings of those
    who remain behind you,
What beckonings of love you receive you shall only answer with
    passionate kisses of parting,
You shall not allow the hold of those who spread their reach'd
    hands toward you.

12

Allons! after the great Companions, and to belong to them!
They too are on the road—they are the swift and majestic
    men—they are the greatest women,
Enjoyers of calms of seas and storms of seas,
Sailors of many a ship, walkers of many a mile of land,
Habituès of many distant countries, habituès of far-distant dwellings,
Trusters of men and women, observers of cities, solitary toilers,
Pausers and contemplators of tufts, blossoms, shells of the shore,
Dancers at wedding-dances, kissers of brides, tender helpers of
    children, bearers of children,
Soldiers of revolts, standers by gaping graves, lowerers-down of
    coffins,
Journeyers over consecutive seasons, over the years, the curious years
    each emerging from that which preceded it,
Journeyers as with companions, namely their own diverse phases,
Forth-steppers from the latent unrealized baby-days,
Journeyers gayly with their own youth, journeyers with their bearded
    and well-grain'd manhood,
Journeyers with their womanhood, ample, unsurpass'd, content,
Journeyers with their own sublime old age of manhood or
    womanhood,

Old age, calm, expanded, broad with the haughty breadth of the
    universe,
Old age, flowing free with the delicious near-by freedom of
    death.

13

Allons! to that which is endless as it was beginningless,
To undergo much, tramps of days, rests of nights,
To merge all in the travel they tend to, and the days and nights
    they tend to,
Again to merge them in the start of superior journeys,
To see nothing anywhere but what you may reach it and pass it,
To conceive no time, however distant, but what you may reach it
    and pass it,
To look up or down no road but it stretches and waits for you,
    however long but it stretches and waits for you,
To see no being, not God's or any, but you also go thither,
To see no possession but you may possess it, enjoying all without
    labor or purchase, abstracting the feast yet not abstracting
    one particle of it,
To take the best of the farmer's farm and the rich man's elegant
    villa, and the chaste blessings of the well-married couple, and
    the fruits of orchards and flowers of gardens,
To take to your use out of the compact cities as you pass through,
To carry buildings and streets with you afterward wherever you go,
To gather the minds of men out of their brains as you encounter
    them, to gather the love out of their hearts,
To take your lovers on the road with you, for all that you leave
    them behind you,
To know the universe itself as a road, as many roads, as roads for
    traveling souls.

All parts away for the progress of souls,
All religion, all solid things, arts, governments—all that was or is
    apparent upon this globe or any globe, falls into niches and
    corners before the procession of souls along the grand roads
    of the universe.

Of the progress of the souls of men and women along the grand
    roads of the universe, all other progress is the needed
    emblem and sustenance.

Forever alive, forever forward,
Stately, solemn, sad, withdrawn, baffled, mad, turbulent, feeble,
    dissatisfied,   ·
Desperate, proud, fond, sick, accepted by men, rejected by men,
They go! they go! I know that they go, but I know not where they
    go,
But I know that they go toward the best—toward something great.

Whoever you are, come forth! or man or woman come forth!
You must not stay sleeping and dallying there in the house, though
    you built it, or though it has been built for you.

Out of the dark confinement! out from behind the screen!
It is useless to protest, I know all and expose it.

Behold through you as bad as the rest,
Through the laughter, dancing, dining, supping, of people,
Inside of dresses and ornaments, inside of those wash'd and trimm'd
    faces,
Behold a secret silent loathing and despair.
No husband, no wife, no friend, trusted to hear the confession,
Another self, a duplicate of every one, skulking and hiding it goes,
Formless and wordless through the streets of the cities, polite and
    bland in the parlors,
In the cars of railroads, in steamboats, in the public assembly,
Home to the houses of men and women, at the table, in the
    bedroom, everywhere,
Smartly attired, countenance smiling, form upright, death under the
    breast-bones, hell under the skull-bones,
Under the broadcloth and gloves, under the ribbons and artificial
    flowers,
Keeping fair with the customs, speaking not a syllable of itself,
Speaking of any thing else but never of itself.

14

Allons! through struggles and wars!
The goal that was named cannot be countermanded.

Have the past struggles succeeded?
What has succeeded? yourself? your nation? Nature?
Now understand me well—it is provided in the essence of things

that from any fruition of success, no matter what, shall come
forth something to make a greater struggle necessary.

My call is the call of battle, I nourish active rebellion,
He going with me must go well arm'd,
He going with me goes often with spare diet, poverty, angry
enemies, desertions.

15

Allons! the road is before us!
It is safe—I have tried it—my own feet have tried it well—be not
detain'd!
Let the paper remain on the desk unwritten, and the book on the
shelf unopen'd!
Let the tools remain in the workshop! let the money remain
unearn'd!
Let the school stand! mind not the cry of the teacher!
Let the preacher preach in his pulpit! let the lawyer plead in the
court, and the judge expound the law.

Camerado, I give you my hand!
I give you my love more precious than money,
I give you myself before preaching or law;
Will you give me yourself? will you come travel with me?
Shall we stick by each other as long as we live?

A. E. HOUSMAN
1859–1936

*Here this lonely, erotically frustrated classical scholar invokes images of
travel and tenderly recalled topography as he transforms time into space
to mourn the loss of youth.*

Into My Heart an Air That Kills
(1896)

Into my heart an air that kills
From yon far country blows:
What are those blue remembered hills,
What spires, what farms are those?

That is the land of lost content,
I see it shining plain,
The happy highways where I went
And cannot come again.

HENRY JAMES
1843–1916

*James was born in New York into an intellectual and artistic family
anxious to forward the progress of its two older sons, Henry and William,
both of whom distinguished themselves by their psychological acuteness, the one in serious fiction, the other in philosophy. Henry was
educated in Geneva and at the Harvard Law School. While in Cambridge he began contributing to* The Atlantic Monthly, *of which William Dean Howells was editor.*

*His acquaintance with Europe began in 1868, when he wandered
widely and, in Paris and London, scrutinized "society" closely. He undertook a deep study of the techniques of fiction in Flaubert, Zola,
Maupassant, and Daudet, and started producing novels on "the international theme"—largely dealing with the predicaments abroad of innocent Americans in contact with more sophisticated, if not actively
wicked, Europeans. Settling in London, he was close to such fellow
literary sensibilities as Edmund Gosse and Robert Louis Stevenson, but
he found he needed a quieter environment for work, and in 1896 he
moved out to the town of Rye. Furious with the Americans for not*

immediately entering the Great War, in 1915 he became a British subject.

France and Italy were the main arenas of his travels, which he pursued with a painterly eye and with a complete sympathetic humanity. Where others might use the term traveler, *he likes the word* visitor—*suggesting something of the comfortable intimacy he develops toward the scenes and objects he lovingly frequents.*

Italian Hours collects the travel essays James produced during tours in the 1860s and 1870s. Of an early "visit" to Italy, he wrote: "At last—for the first time—I live!"

From ITALIAN HOURS
(1909)

ITALY REVISITED

I waited in Paris until after the elections for the new Chamber (they took place on the 14th of October); as only after one had learned that the famous attempt of Marshal MacMahon and his ministers to drive the French nation to the polls like a flock of huddling sheep, each with the white ticket of an official candidate round his neck, had not achieved the success which the energy of the process might have promised—only then it was possible to draw a long breath and deprive the republican party of such support as might have been conveyed in one's sympathetic presence. Seriously speaking too, the weather had been enchanting— there were Italian fancies to be gathered without leaving the banks of the Seine. Day after day the air was filled with golden light, and even those chalkish vistas of the Parisian *beaux quartiers* [formal neighborhoods] assumed the iridescent tints of autumn. Autumn-weather in Europe is often such a very sorry affair that a fair-minded American will have it on his conscience to call attention to a rainless and radiant October.

The echoes of the electoral strife kept me company for a while after starting upon that abbreviated journey to Turin which, as you leave Paris at night, in a train unprovided with encouragements to slumber, is a singular mixture of the odious and the charming. The charming indeed I think prevails; for the dark half of the journey is the least interesting. The morning light ushers you into the romantic gorges of the Jura, and after a big bowl of *café au lait* at Culoz you may compose yourself comfortably for the climax of your spectacle. The day before leaving

Paris I met a French friend who had just returned from a visit to a Tuscan country-seat where he had been watching the vintage. "Italy," he said, "is more lovely than words can tell, and France, steeped in this electoral turmoil, seems no better than a bear-garden." The part of the bear-garden through which you travel as you approach the Mont-Cenis seemed to me that day very beautiful. The autumn colouring, thanks to the absence of rain, had been vivid and crisp, and the vines that swung their low garlands between the mulberries round about Chambéry looked like long festoons of coral and amber. The frontier station of Modane, on the further side of the Mont-Cenis Tunnel, is a very ill-regulated place; but even the most irritable of tourists, meeting it on his way southward, will be disposed to consider it good-naturedly. There is far too much bustling and scrambling, and the facilities afforded you for the obligatory process of ripping open your luggage before the officers of the Italian custom-house are much scantier than should be; but for myself there is something that deprecates irritation in the shabby green and grey uniforms of all the Italian officials who stand loafing about and watching the northern invaders scramble back into marching order. Wearing an administrative uniform doesn't necessarily spoil a man's temper, as in France one is sometimes led to believe; for these excellent under-paid Italians carry theirs as lightly as possible, and their answers to your inquiries don't in the least bristle with rapiers, buttons and cockades. After leaving Modane you slide straight downhill into the Italy of your desire; from which point the road edges, after the grand manner, along those great precipices that stand shoulder to shoulder, in a prodigious perpendicular file, till they finally admit you to a distant glimpse of the ancient capital of Piedmont.

Turin is no city of a name to conjure with, and I pay an extravagant tribute to subjective emotion in speaking of it as ancient. But if the place is less bravely peninsular than Florence and Rome, at least it is more in the scenic tradition than New York and Paris; and while I paced the great arcades and looked at the fourth-rate shop windows I didn't scruple to cultivate a shameless optimism. Relatively speaking, Turin touches a chord; but there is after all no reason in a large collection of shabbily-stuccoed houses, disposed in a rigidly rectangular manner, for passing a day of deep, still gaiety. The only reason, I am afraid, is the old superstition of Italy—that property in the very look of the written word, the evocation of a myriad images, that makes any lover of the arts take Italian satisfactions on easier terms than any others. The written word stands for something that eternally tricks us; we juggle to our credulity even with such inferior apparatus as is offered to our hand at Turin. I roamed all the morning under the tall porticoes, thinking it sufficient joy to take note of the soft, warm air, of that local colour of things that is at once so broken and so harmonious, and of the comings and goings, the physiognomy and manners, of the excellent Turinese. I had opened the old book again; the old charm was in the style; I was in a more delightful world. I saw nothing surpassingly beautiful or curious; but your true taster of the most seasoned of dishes finds well-nigh the whole mixture in any mouthful. Above all on the threshold of Italy he knows again the solid and perfectly definable pleasure of finding himself among the traditions of the grand style in architecture. It must be said that we have still to go there to recover the sense of the domiciliary mass. In northern cities there are beautiful houses, picturesque and curious houses; sculptured gables that hang over the street, charming bay-windows, hooded doorways, elegant proportions, a profusion of delicate ornament; but a good specimen of an old Italian palazzo has a nobleness that is all its own. We laugh at Italian "palaces," at their peeling paint, their nudity, their dreariness; but they have the great palatial quality— elevation and extent. They make of smaller things the apparent abode of pigmies; they round their great arches and interspace their huge windows with a proud indifference to the cost of materials. These grand proportions—the colossal basements, the doorways that seem meant for cathedrals, the far away cornices—impart by contrast a humble and *bourgeois* expression to interiors founded on the sacrifice of the whole to the part, and in which the air of grandeur depends largely on the help of the upholsterer. At Turin my first feeling was really one of renewed shame for our meaner architectural manners. If the Italians at bottom despise the rest of mankind and regard them as barbarians, disinherited of the tradition of form, the idea proceeds largely, no doubt, from our living in comparative mole-hills. They alone were really to build their civilisation.

An impression which on coming back to Italy I find even stronger than when it was first received is that of the contrast between the fecundity of the great artistic period and the vulgarity there of the genius of to-day. The first few hours spent on Italian soil are sufficient to renew it, and the question I allude to is, historically speaking, one of the oddest. That the people who but three hundred years ago had the best taste in the world should now have the worst; that having produced the noblest, loveliest, costliest works, they should now be given up to the manufacture of objects at once ugly and paltry; that the race of which Michael Angelo and Raphael, Leonardo and Titian were characteristic should have no other title to distinction than third-rate *genre* pictures and catchpenny statues—all this is a frequent perplexity to the observer of actual Italian life. The flower of "great" art in these latter years ceased to bloom very powerfully anywhere; but nowhere does it seem so drooping and withered as in the shadow of the immortal embodiments of the old Italian genius. You go into a church or a gallery and feast your fancy upon a splendid picture or an exquisite piece of sculpture, and on issuing from the door that has admitted you to the beautiful past are confronted with something that has the effect of a very bad joke. The aspect of your lodging—the carpets, the curtains, the upholstery in general, with their crude and violent colouring and their vulgar material—the trumpery things in the shops, the extreme bad taste of the dress of the women, the cheapness and baseness of every attempt at decoration in the cafés and railway-stations, the hopeless frivolity of everything that pretends to be a work of art—all this modern crudity runs riot over the relics of the great period.

We can do a thing for the first time but once; it is but once for all that we can have a pleasure in its freshness. This is a law not on the whole, I think, to be regretted, for we sometimes learn to know things better by not enjoying them too much. It is certain, however, at the same time, that a visitor who has worked off the immediate ferment for this inexhaustibly interesting country has by no means entirely drained the cup. After thinking of Italy as historical and artistic it will do him no great harm to think of her for a while as panting both for a future and for a balance at the bank; aspirations supposedly much at variance with the Byronic, the Ruskinian, the artistic, poetic, æsthetic manner of considering our eternally attaching peninsula. He may grant—I don't say it is absolutely necessary—that its actual aspects and economics are ugly, prosaic, provokingly out of relation to the diary and the album; it is nevertheless true that, at the point things have come to, modern Italy in a manner imposes herself. I hadn't been many hours in the country before that truth assailed me; and I may add that, the first irritation past, I found myself able to accept it. For, if we think, nothing is more easy to understand than an honest ire on the part of the young Italy of to-day at being looked at by all the world as a kind of soluble pigment. Young Italy, preoccupied with its economical and political future, must be heartily tired of being admired for its eyelashes and its pose. In one of Thackeray's novels occurs a mention of a young artist who sent to the Royal Academy a picture representing "A Contadino dancing with a Trasteverina at the door of a Locanda, to the music of a Pifferaro." ["A peasant dancing with a working-girl from Trastevere at the door of an inn to the music of a piper."] It is in this attitude and with these conventional accessories that the world has hitherto seen fit to represent young Italy, and one doesn't wonder that if the youth has any spirit he should at last begin to resent our insufferable æsthetic patronage. He has established a line of tram-cars in Rome, from the Porta del Popolo to the Ponte Molle, and it is on one of these democratic vehicles that I seem to see him taking his triumphant course down the vista of the future. I won't pretend to rejoice with him any more than I really do; I won't pretend, as the sentimental tourists say about it all, as if it were the setting of an intaglio or the border of a Roman scarf, to "like" it. Like it or not, as we may, it is evidently destined to be; I see a new Italy in the future which in many important respects will equal, if not surpass, the most enterprising sections of our native land. Perhaps by that time Chicago and San Francisco will have acquired a pose, and their sons and daughters will dance at the doors of *locande.*

However this may be, the accomplished schism between the old order and the new is the promptest moral of a fresh visit to this ever-suggestive part of the world. The old has become more and more a museum, preserved and perpetuated in the midst of the new, but without any further relation to it—it must be admitted indeed that such a relation is considerable—than that of the stock on his shelves to the shopkeeper, or of the Siren of the South to the showman who stands before his booth. More than once, as we move about nowadays in the Italian cities, there seems to pass before our eyes a vision of the coming years. It represents to our satisfaction an Italy united and prosperous, but altogether scientific and commercial. The Italy indeed that we sentimentalise and romance about was an ardently mercantile country; though I suppose it loved not its ledgers less, but its frescoes and altar-pieces more. Scattered through this paradise regained of trade—this country of a thousand ports—we see a large number of beautiful buildings in which an endless series of dusky pictures are darkening, dampening, fading, failing, through the years. By the doors of the beautiful buildings are little turnstiles at which there sit a great many uniformed men to whom the visitor pays a tenpenny fee. Inside, in the vaulted and frescoed chambers, the art of Italy lies buried as in a thousand mausoleums. It is well taken care of; it is constantly copied; sometimes it is "restored" —as in the case of that beautiful boy-figure of Andrea del Sarto at Florence, which may be seen at the gallery of the Uffizi with its honourable duskiness quite peeled off and heaven knows what raw, bleeding cuticle laid bare. One evening lately, near the same Florence, in the soft twilight, I took a stroll among those encircling hills on which the massive villas are mingled with the vaporous olives. Presently I arrived where three roads met at a wayside shrine, in which, before some pious daub of an old-time Madonna, a little votive lamp glimmered through the evening air. The hour, the atmosphere, the place, the twinkling taper, the sentiment of the observer, the thought that some one had been

rescued here from an assassin or from some other peril and had set up
a little grateful altar in consequence, against the yellow-plastered wall of
a tangled *podere* [farm]; all this led me to approach the shrine with a
reverent, an emotional step. I drew near it, but after a few steps I paused.
I became aware of an incongruous odour; it seemed to me that the
evening air was charged with a perfume which, although to a certain
extent familiar, had not hitherto associated itself with rustic frescoes and
wayside altars. I wondered, I gently sniffed, and the question so put left
me no doubt. The odour was that of petroleum; the votive taper was
nourished with the essence of Pennsylvania. I confess that I burst out
laughing, and a picturesque contadino, wending his homeward way in
the dusk, stared at me as if I were an iconoclast. He noticed the petroleum only, I imagine, to snuff it fondly up; but to me the thing served
as a symbol of the Italy of the future. There is a horse-car from the Porta
del Popolo to the Ponte Mole, and the Tuscan shrines are fed with
kerosene.

A ROMAN HOLIDAY

It is certainly sweet to be merry at the right moment; but the right
moment hardly seems to me the ten days of the Roman Carnival. It was
my rather cynical suspicion perhaps that they wouldn't keep to my
imagination the brilliant promise of legend; but I have been justified by
the event and have been decidedly less conscious of the festal influences
of the season than of the inalienable gravity of the place. There was a
time when the Carnival was a serious matter—that is a heartily joyous
one; but, thanks to the seven-league boots the kingdom of Italy has lately
donned for the march of progress in quite other directions, the fashion
of public revelry has fallen woefully out of step. The state of mind and
manners under which the Carnival was kept in generous good faith I
doubt if an American can exactly conceive: he can only say to himself
that for a month in the year there must have been things—things
considerably of humiliation—it was comfortable to forget. But now that
Italy is made the Carnival is unmade; and we are not especially tempted
to envy the attitude of a population who have lost their relish for play
and not yet acquired to any striking extent an enthusiasm for work. The
spectacle on the Corso has seemed to me, on the whole, an illustration
of that great breach with the past of which Catholic Christendom felt
the somewhat muffled shock in September 1870. A traveller acquainted
with the fully papal Rome, coming back any time during the past winter,
must have immediately noticed that something momentous had happened—something hostile to the elements of picture and colour and

"style." My first warning was that ten minutes after my arrival I found myself face to face with a newspaper stand. The impossibility in the other days of having anything in the journalistic line but the *Osservatore Romano* and the *Voce della Verità* used to seem to me much connected with the extraordinary leisure of thought and stillness of mind to which the place admitted you. But now the slender piping of the Voice of Truth is stifled by the raucous note of eventide vendors of the *Capitale*, the *Libertà* and the *Fanfulla;* and Rome reading unexpurgated news is another Rome indeed. For every subscriber to the *Libertà* there may well be an antique masker and reveller less. As striking a sign of the new régime is the extraordinary increase of population. The Corso was always a well-filled street, but now it's a perpetual crush. I never cease to wonder where the new-comers are lodged, and how such spotless flowers of fashion as the gentlemen who stare at the carriages can bloom in the atmosphere of those *camere mobiliate* [furnished rooms] of which I have had glimpses. This, however, is their own question, and bravely enough they meet it. They proclaimed somehow, to the first freshness of my wonder, as I say, that by force of numbers Rome had been secularised. An Italian dandy is a figure visually to reckon with, but these goodly throngs of them scarce offered compensation for the absent monsignori, treading the streets in their purple stockings and followed by the solemn servants who returned on their behalf the bows of the meaner sort; for the mourning gear of the cardinals' coaches that formerly glittered with scarlet and swung with the weight of the footmen clinging behind; for the certainty that you'll not, by the best of traveller's luck, meet the Pope sitting deep in the shadow of his great chariot with uplifted fingers like some inaccessible idol in his shrine. You may meet the King indeed, who is as ugly, as imposingly ugly, as some idols, though not so inaccessible. The other day as I passed the Quirinal he drove up in a low carriage with a single attendant; and a group of men and women who had been waiting near the gate rushed at him with a number of folded papers. The carriage slackened pace and he pocketed their offerings with a business-like air—that of a good-natured man accepting hand-bills at a street-corner. Here was a monarch at his palace gate receiving petitions from his subjects—being adjured to right their wrongs. The scene ought to have thrilled me, but somehow it had no more intensity than a woodcut in an illustrated newspaper. Homely I should call it at most; admirably so, certainly, for there were lately few sovereigns standing, I believe, with whom their people enjoyed these filial hand-to-hand relations. The King this year, however, has had as little to do with the Carnival as the Pope, and the innkeepers and Americans have marked it for their own.

It was advertised to begin at half-past two o'clock of a certain Saturday, and punctually at the stroke of the hour, from my room across a wide court, I heard a sudden multiplication of sounds and confusion of tongues in the Corso. I was writing to a friend for whom I cared more than for any mere romp; but as the minutes elapsed and the hubbub deepened curiosity got the better of affection, and I remembered that I was really within eye-shot of an affair the fame of which had ministered to the day-dreams of my infancy. I used to have a scrap-book with a coloured print of the starting of the bedizened wild horses, and the use of a library rich in keepsakes and annuals with a frontispiece commonly of a masked lady in a balcony, the heroine of a delightful tale further on. Agitated by these tender memories I descended into the street; but I confess I looked in vain for a masked lady who might serve as a frontispiece, in vain for any object whatever that might adorn a tale. Masked and muffled ladies there were in abundance; but their masks were of ugly wire, perfectly resembling the little covers placed upon strong cheese in German hotels, and their drapery was a shabby water-proof with the hood pulled over their chignons. They were armed with great tin scoops or funnels, with which they solemnly shovelled lime and flour out of bushel-baskets and down on the heads of the people in the street. They were packed into balconies all the way along the straight vista of the Corso, in which their calcareous shower maintained a dense, gritty, unpalatable fog. The crowd was compact in the street, and the Americans in it were tossing back confetti out of great satchels hung round their necks. It was quite the "you're another" sort of repartee, and less seasoned than I had hoped with the airy mockery tradition hangs about this festival. The scene was striking, in a word; but somehow not as I had dreamed of its being. I stood regardful, I suppose, but with a peculiarly tempting blankness of visage, for in a moment I received half a bushel of flour on my too-philosophic head. Decidedly it was an ignoble form of humour. I shook my ears like an emergent diver, and had a sudden vision of how still and sunny and solemn, how peculiarly and undisturbedly themselves, how secure from any intrusion less sympathetic than one's own, certain outlying parts of Rome must just then be. The Carnival had received its death-blow in my imagination; and it has been ever since but a thin and dusky ghost of pleasure that has flitted at intervals in and out of my consciousness.

I turned my back accordingly on the Corso and wandered away to the grass-grown quarters delightfully free even from the possibility of a fellow-countryman. And so having set myself an example I have been keeping Carnival by strolling perversely along the silent circumference of Rome. I have doubtless lost a great deal. The Princess Margaret has occupied a balcony opposite the open space which leads into Via Condotti and, I believe, like the discreet princess she is, has dealt in no missiles but bonbons, bouquets and white doves. I would have waited half an hour any day to see the Princess Margaret hold a dove on her forefinger; but I never chanced to notice any preparation for that effect. And yet do what you will you can't really elude the Carnival. As the days elapse it filters down into the manners of the common people, and before the week is over the very beggars at the church-doors seem to have gone to the expense of a domino. When you meet these specimens of dingy drollery capering about in dusky back-streets at all hours of the day and night, meet them flitting out of black doorways between the greasy groups that cluster about Roman thresholds, you feel that a love of "pranks," the more vivid the better, must from far back have been implanted in the Roman temperament with a strong hand. An unsophisticated American is wonderstruck at the number of persons, of every age and various conditions, whom it costs nothing in the nature of an ingenuous blush to walk up and down the streets in the costume of a theatrical supernumerary. Fathers of families do it at the head of an admiring progeniture; aunts and uncles and grandmothers do it; all the family does it, with varying splendour but with the same good conscience. "A pack of babies!" the doubtless too self-conscious alien pronounces it for its pains, and tries to imagine himself strutting along Broadway in a battered tin helmet and a pair of yellow tights. Our vices are certainly different; it takes those of the innocent sort to be so ridiculous. A self-consciousness lapsing so easily, in fine, strikes me as so near a relation to amenity, urbanity and general gracefulness that, for myself, I should be sorry to lay a tax on it, lest these other commodities should also cease to come to market.

I was rewarded, when I had turned away with my ears full of flour, by a glimpse of an intenser life than the dingy foolery of the Corso. I walked down by the back streets to the steps mounting to the Capitol— that long inclined plane, rather, broken at every two paces, which is the unfailing disappointment, I believe, of tourists primed for retrospective raptures. Certainly the Capitol seen from this side isn't commanding. The hill is so low, the ascent so narrow, Michael Angelo's architecture in the quadrangle at the top so meagre, the whole place somehow so much more of a mole-hill than a mountain, that for the first ten minutes of your standing there Roman history seems suddenly to have sunk through a trap-door. It emerges however on the other side, in the Forum; and here meanwhile, if you get no sense of the sublime, you get gradually a sense of exquisite composition. Nowhere in Rome is more colour, more charm, more sport for the eye. The mild incline, during the winter months, is always covered with lounging sun-seekers, and especially with those more constantly obvious members of the Roman population—beggars, soldiers, monks and tourists. The beggars and peasants lie kicking their heels along that grandest of loafing-places, the great steps of the Ara Cœli. The dwarfish look of the Capitol is intensified, I think, by the neighbourhood of this huge blank staircase, mouldering away in disuse, the weeds thick in its crevices, and climbing to the rudely solemn façade of the church. The sunshine glares on this great unfinished wall only to light up its featureless despair, its expression of conscious, irremediable incompleteness. Sometimes, massing its rusty screen against the deep blue sky, with the little cross and the sculptured porch casting a clear-cut shadow on the bricks, it seems to have even more than a Roman desolation, it confusedly suggests Spain and Africa—lands with no latent *risorgimentz* [political renewals], with absolutely nothing but a fatal past. The legendary wolf of Rome has lately been accommodated with a little artificial grotto, among the cacti and the palms, in the fantastic triangular garden squeezed between the steps of the church and the ascent to the Capitol, where she holds a perpetual levee and "draws" apparently as powerfully as the Pope himself. Above, in the piazzetta before the stuccoed palace which rises so jauntily on a basement of thrice its magnitude, are more loungers and knitters in the sun, seated round the massively inscribed base of the statue of Marcus Aurelius. Hawthorne has perfectly expressed the attitude of this admirable figure in saying that it extends its arm with "a command which is in itself a benediction." I doubt if any statue of king or captain in the public places of the world has more to commend it to the general heart. Irrecoverable simplicity—residing so in irrecoverable Style—has no sturdier representative. Here is an impression that the sculptors of the last three hundred years have been laboriously trying to reproduce; but contrasted with this mild old monarch their prancing horsemen suggest a succession of riding-masters taking out young ladies' schools. The admirably human character of the figure survives the rusty decomposition of the bronze and the slight "debasement" of the art; and one may call it singular that in the capital of Christendom the portrait most suggestive of a Christian conscience is that of a pagan emperor.

You recover in some degree your stifled hopes of sublimity as you pass beyond the palace and take your choice of either curving slope to descend into the Forum. Then you see that the little stuccoed edifice is but a modern excrescence on the mighty cliff of a primitive construction, whose great squares of porous tufa, as they underlie each other, seem to resolve themselves back into the colossal cohesion of unhewn rock. There are prodigious strangenesses in the union of this airy and comparatively fresh-faced superstructure and these deep-plunging, hoary foundations; and few things in Rome are more entertaining to the eye than to measure the long plumb-line which drops from the inhabited windows of the palace, with their little over-peeping balconies, their muslin curtains and their bird-cages, down to the rugged constructional work of the Republic. In the Forum proper the sublime is eclipsed again, though the late extension of the excavations gives a chance for it.

Nothing in Rome helps your fancy to a more vigorous backward flight than to lounge on a sunny day over the railing which guards the great central researches. It "says" more things to you than you can repeat to see the past, the ancient world, as you stand there, bodily turned up with the spade and transformed from an immaterial, inaccessible fact of time into a matter of soils and surfaces. The pleasure is the same—in kind—as what you enjoy at Pompeii, and the pain the same. It wasn't here, however, that I found my compensation for forfeiting the spectacle on the Corso, but in a little church at the end of the narrow byway which diverges up the Palatine from just beside the Arch of Titus. This byway leads you between high walls, then takes a bend and introduces you to a long row of rusty, dusty little pictures of the stations of the cross. Beyond these stands a small church with a front so modest that you hardly recognise it till you see the leather curtain. I never see a leather curtain without lifting it; it is sure to cover a constituted *scene* of some sort—good, bad or indifferent. The scene this time was meagre— whitewash and tarnished candlesticks and mouldy muslin flowers being its principal features. I shouldn't have remained if I hadn't been struck with the attitude of the single worshipper—a young priest kneeling before one of the side-altars, who, as I entered, lifted his head and gave me a sidelong look so charged with the languor of devotion that he immediately became an object of interest. He was visiting each of the altars in turn and kissing the balustrade beneath them. He was alone in the church, and indeed in the whole region. There were no beggars even at the door; they were plying their trade on the skirts of the Carnival. In the entirely deserted place he alone knelt for religion, and as I sat respectfully by it seemed to me I could hear in the perfect silence the far-away uproar of the maskers. It was my late impression of these frivolous people, I suppose, joined with the extraordinary gravity of the young priest's face—his pious fatigue, his droning prayer and his isola- tion—that gave me just then and there a supreme vision of the religious passion, its privations and resignations and exhaustions and its terribly small share of amusement. He was young and strong and evidently of not too refined a fibre to enjoy the Carnival; but, planted there with his face pale with fasting and his knees stiff with praying, he seemed so stern a satire on it and on the crazy thousands who were preferring it to *his* way, that I half expected to see some heavenly portent out of a monastic legend come down and confirm his choice. Yet I confess that though I wasn't enamoured of the Carnival myself his seemed a grim preference and this forswearing of the world a terrible game—a gaining one only if your zeal never falters; a hard fight when it does. In such an hour, to a stout young fellow like the hero of my anecdote, the smell of incense must seem horribly stale and the muslin flowers and gilt candlesticks to figure no great bribe. And it wouldn't have helped him much to think that not so very far away, just beyond the Forum, in the Corso, there was sport for the million, and for nothing. I doubt on the other hand whether my young priest had thought of this. He had made himself a temple out of the very elements of his innocence, and his prayers followed each other too fast for the tempter to slip in a whisper. And so, as I say, I found a solider fact of human nature than the love of *coriandoli* [confetti].

One of course never passes the Colosseum without paying it one's respects—without going in under one of the hundred portals and crossing the long oval and sitting down awhile, generally at the foot of the cross in the centre. I always feel, as I do so, as if I were seated in the depths of some Alpine valley. The upper portions of the side toward the Esquiline look as remote and lonely as an Alpine ridge, and you raise your eyes to their rugged sky-line, drinking in the sun and silvered by the blue air, with much the same feeling with which you would take in a grey cliff on which an eagle might lodge. This roughly mountainous quality of the great ruin is its chief interest; beauty of detail has pretty well vanished, especially since the high-growing wild-flowers have been plucked away by the new government, whose functionaries, surely, at certain points of their task, must have felt as if they shared the dreadful trade of those who gather samphire. Even if you are on your way to the Lateran you won't grudge the twenty minutes it will take you, on leaving the Colosseum, to turn away under the Arch of Constantine, whose noble battered bas-reliefs, with the chain of tragic statues—fettered, drooping barbarians—round its summit, I assume you to have profoundly admired, toward the piazzetta of the church of San Giovanni e Paolo, on the slope of Cælian. No spot in Rome can show a cluster of more charming accidents. The ancient brick apse of the church peeps down into the trees of the little wooded walk before the neighbouring church of San Gregorio, intensely venerable beneath its excessive modernisation; and a series of heavy brick buttresses, flying across to an opposite wall, overarches the short, steep, paved passage which leads into the small square. This is flanked on one side by the long mediæval portico of the church of the two saints, sustained by eight time-blackened columns of granite and marble. On another rise the great scarce-widowed walls of a Passionist convent, and on the third the portals of a grand villa, whose tall porter, with his cockade and silver-topped staff, standing sublime behind his grating, seems a kind of mundane St. Peter, I suppose, to the beggars who sit at the church door or lie in the sun along the farther slope which leads to the gate of the convent. The place always seems to me the perfection of an out-of-the-way corner—a place you would think twice before telling people about, lest you should find them there the next time you were to go. It is such a group of objects, singly and in their happy combination, as one must come to Rome to find at one's house door; but what makes it peculiarly a picture is the beautiful dark red campanile of the church, which stands embedded in the mass of the convent. It begins, as so many things in Rome begin, with a stout foundation of antique travertine, and rises high, in delicately quaint mediæval brickwork—little tiers and apertures sustained on miniature columns and adorned with small cracked slabs of green and yellow marble, inserted almost at random. When there are three or four brown-breasted contadini sleeping in the sun before the convent doors, and a departing monk leading his shadow down over them, I think you will not find anything in Rome more *sketchable*.

If you stop, however, to observe everything worthy of your water-colours you will never reach St. John Lateran. My business was much less with the interior of that vast and empty, that cold clean temple, which I have never found peculiarly interesting, than with certain charming features of its surrounding precinct—the crooked old court beside it, which admits you to the Baptistery and to a delightful rear-view of the queer architectural odds and ends that may in Rome compose a florid ecclesiastical façade. There are more of these, a stranger jumble of chance detail, of lurking recesses and wanton projections and inexplicable windows, than I have memory or phrase for; but the gem of the collection is the oddly perched peaked turret, with its yellow travertine welded upon the rusty brickwork, which was not meant to be suspected, and the brickwork retreating beneath and leaving it in the odd position of a tower *under* which you may see the sky. As to the great front of the church overlooking the Porta San Giovanni, you are not admitted behind the scenes; the term is quite in keeping, for the archi-tecture has a vastly theatrical air. It is extremely imposing—that of St. Peter's alone is more so; and when from far off on the Campagna you see the colossal images of the mitred saints along the top standing distinct against the sky, you forget their coarse construction and their inflated draperies. The view from the great space which stretches from the church steps to the city wall is the very prince of views. Just beside you, beyond the great alcove of mosaic, is the Scala Santa, the marble staircase which (says the legend) Christ descended under the weight of Pilate's judgment, and which all Christians must forever ascend on their knees; before you is the city gate which opens upon the Via Appia Nuova, the long gaunt file of arches of the Claudian aqueduct, their jagged ridge stretching away like the vertebral column of some monstrous mouldering skeleton, and upon the blooming brown and purple flats and dells of the Campagna and the glowing blue of the Alban Mountains, spotted with their white, high-nestling towns; while to your left is the great grassy space, lined with dwarfish mulberry-trees, which stretches across to the damp little sister-basilica of Santa Croce in Gerusalemme. During a former visit to Rome I lost my heart to this idle tract, and wasted much time in sitting on the steps of the church and watching certain white-cowled friars who were sure to be passing there for the delight of my eyes. There are fewer friars now, and there are a great many of the king's recruits, who inhabit the ex-conventual barracks adjoining Santa Croce and are led forward to practise their goose-step on the sunny turf. Here too the poor old cardinals who are no longer to be seen on the Pincio descend from their mourning-coaches and relax their venerable knees. These members alone still testify to the traditional splendour of the princes of the Church; for as they advance the lifted black petticoat reveals a flash of scarlet stockings and makes you groan at the victory of civilisation over colour.

If St. John Lateran disappoints you internally, you have an easy compensation in pacing the long lane which connects it with Santa Maria Maggiore and entering the singularly perfect nave of that most delightful of churches. The first day of my stay in Rome under the old dispensation I spent in wandering at random through the city, with accident for my *valet-de-place* [guide]. It served me to perfection and introduced me to the best things; among others to an immediate happy relation with Santa Maria Maggiore. First impressions, memorable impressions, are generally irrecoverable; they often leave one the wiser, but they rarely return in the same form. I remember, of my coming uninformed and unprepared into the place of worship and of curiosity that I have named, only that I sat for half an hour on the edge of the base of one of the marble columns of the beautiful nave and enjoyed a perfect revel of—what shall I call it?—taste, intelligence, fancy, perceptive emotion? The place proved so endlessly suggestive that perception became a throbbing confusion of images, and I departed with a sense of knowing a good deal that is not set down in Murray. I have seated myself more than once again at the base of the same column; but you live your life only once, the parts as well as the whole. The obvious charm of the church is the elegant grandeur of the nave—its perfect shapeliness and its rich simplicity, its long double row of white marble columns and its high flat roof, embossed with intricate gildings and mouldings. It opens into a choir of an extraordinary splendour of effect, which I recommend you to look out for of a fine afternoon. At such a time the glowing western light, entering the high windows of the tribune, kindles the scattered masses of colour into sombre brightness, scintillates on the great solemn mosaic of the vault, touches the porphyry columns of the superb baldachino with ruby lights, and buries its shining shafts in the deep-toned shadows that hang about frescoes and sculptures and mouldings. The deeper charm even than in such things, however, is the social or historic note or tone or atmosphere of the church—I fumble, you see, for my right expression; the sense it gives you, in common with most of the Roman churches, and more than any of them, of having been prayed in for several centuries by an endlessly curious and complex society. It takes no great attention to let it come to you that the authority of Italian Catholicism has lapsed not a little in these days; not less also perhaps than to feel that, as they stand, these deserted temples were the fruit of a society leavened through and through by ecclesiastical manners, and that they formed for ages the constant background of the human drama. They are, as one may say, the *churchiest* churches in Europe—the fullest of gathered memories, of the experience of their office. There's not a figure one has read of in old-world annals that isn't to be imagined on proper occasion kneeling before the lamp-decked Confession beneath the altar of Santa Maria Maggiore. One sees after all, however, even among the most palpable realities, very much what the play of one's imagination projects there; and I present my remarks simply as a reminder that one's constant excursions into these places are not the least interesting episodes of one's walks in Rome.

I had meant to give a simple illustration of the church-habit, so to speak, but I have given it at such a length as leaves scant space to touch on the innumerable topics brushed by the pen that begins to take Roman notes. It is by the aimless *flânerie* [strolling] which leaves you free to follow capriciously every hint of entertainment that you get to know Rome. The greater part of the life about you goes on in the streets; and for an observer fresh from a country in which town scenery is at the least monotonous incident and character and picture seem to abound. I become conscious with compunction, let me hasten to add, that I have launched myself thus on the subject of Roman churches and Roman walks without so much as a preliminary allusion to St. Peter's. One is apt to proceed thither on rainy days with intentions of exercise—to put the case only at that—and to carry these out body and mind. Taken as a walk not less than as a church, St. Peter's of course reigns alone. Even for the profane "constitutional" it serves where the Boulevards, where Piccadilly and Broadway, fall short, and if it didn't offer to our use the grandest area in the world it would still offer the most diverting. Few great works of art last longer to the curiosity, to the perpetually transcended attention. You think you have taken the whole thing in, but it expands, it rises sublime again, and leaves your measure itself poor. You never let the ponderous leather curtain bang down behind you—your weak lift of a scant edge of whose padded vastness resembles the liberty taken in folding back the parchment corner of some mighty folio page—without feeling all former visits to have been but missed attempts at apprehension and the actual to achieve your first real possession. The conventional question is ever as to whether one hasn't been "disappointed in the size," but a few honest folk here and there, I hope, will never cease to say no. The place struck me from the first as the hugest thing conceivable—a real exaltation of one's idea of space; so that one's entrance, even from the great empty square which either glares beneath the deep blue sky or makes of the cool far-cast shadow of the immense front something that resembles a big slate-coloured country on a map, seems not so much a going in somewhere as a going out. The mere man of pleasure in quest of new sensations might well not know where to better his encounter there of the sublime shock that brings him, within the threshold, to an immediate gasping pause. There are days when the vast nave looks mysteriously vaster than on others and the gorgeous baldachino a longer journey beyond the far-spreading tessellated plain of the pavement, and when the light has yet a quality which lets things loom their largest, while the scattered figures—I mean the human, for there are plenty of others—mark happily the scale of items and parts. Then you have only to stroll and stroll and gaze and gaze; to watch the glorious altar-canopy lift its bronze architecture, its colossal embroidered contortions, like a temple within a temple, and feel yourself, at the bottom of the abysmal shaft of the dome, dwindle to a crawling dot.

Much of the constituted beauty resides in the fact that it is all general beauty, that you are appealed to by no specific details, or that these at least, practically never importunate, are as taken for granted as the lieutenants and captains are taken for granted in a great standing army— among whom indeed individual aspects may figure here the rather shifting range of decorative dignity in which details, when observed, often prove poor (though never not massive and substantially precious) and sometimes prove ridiculous. The sculptures, with the sole exception of Michael Angelo's ineffable "Pièta," which lurks obscurely in a side-chapel—this indeed to my sense the rarest artistic *combination* of the greatest things the hand of man has produced—are either bad or indifferent; and the universal incrustation of marble, though sumptuous enough, has a less brilliant effect than much later work of the same sort, that for instance of St. Paul's without the Walls. The supreme beauty is the splendidly sustained simplicity of the whole. The thing represents a prodigious imagination extraordinarily strained, yet strained, at its happiest pitch, without breaking. Its happiest pitch I say, because this is the only creation of its strenuous author in presence of which you are in presence of serenity. You may invoke the idea of ease at St. Peter's without a sense of sacrilege—which you can hardly do, if you are at all spiritually nervous, in Westminster Abbey or Notre Dame. The vast enclosed clearness has much to do with the idea. There are no shadows to speak of, no marked effects of shade; only effects of light innumerable—points at which this element seems to mass itself in airy density and scatter itself in enchanting gradations and cadences. It performs the office of gloom or of mystery in Gothic churches; hangs like a rolling mist along the gilded vault of the nave, melts into bright interfusion the mosaic scintillations of the dome, clings and clusters and lingers, animates the whole huge and otherwise empty shell. A good Catholic, I suppose, is the same Catholic anywhere, before the grandest as well as the humblest altars; but to a visitor not formally enrolled St. Peter's speaks less of aspiration than of full and convenient assurance. The soul infinitely expands there, if one will, but all on its quite human level. It marvels at the reach of our dream and the immensity of our resources. To be so impressed and put in our place, we say, is to be sufficiently "saved"; we can't be more than that in heaven itself; and what specifically celestial beauty such a show or such a substitute may lack it makes up for in certainty and tangibility. And yet if one's hours on the scene are not actually spent in praying, the spirit seeks it again as for the finer comfort, for the blessing, exactly, of its example, its protection and its exclusion. When you are weary of the swarming democracy of your fellow-tourists, of the unremunerative aspects of human nature on Corso and Pincio, of the oppressively frequent combination of coronets on carriage panels and stupid faces in carriages, of addled brains and lacquered boots, of ruin and dirt and decay, of priests and beggars and takers of advantage, of the myriad tokens of a halting civilisation, the image of the great temple depresses the balance of your doubts, seems to rise above even the highest tide of vulgarity and make you still believe in the heroic will and the heroic act. It's a relief, in other words, to feel that there's nothing but a cab-fare between your pessimism and one of the greatest of human achievements.

*   *   *

One grows to feel the collection of pictures at the Pitti Palace splendid rather than interesting. After walking through it once or twice you catch the key in which it is pitched—you know what you are likely not to find on closer examination; none of the works of the uncompromising period, nothing from the half-groping geniuses of the early time, those whose colouring was sometimes harsh and their outlines sometimes angular. Vague to me the principle on which the pictures were originally gathered and of the æsthetic creed of the princes who chiefly selected them. A princely creed I should roughly call it—the creed of people who believed in things presenting a fine face to society; who esteemed showy results rather than curious processes, and would have hardly cared more to admit into their collection a work by one of the laborious precursors of the full efflorescence than to see a bucket and broom left standing in a state saloon. The gallery contains in literal fact some eight or ten paintings of the early Tuscan School—notably two admirable specimens of Filippo Lippi and one of the frequent circular pictures of the great Botticelli—a Madonna, chilled with tragic prescience, laying a pale cheek against that of a blighted Infant. Such a melancholy mother as this of Botticelli would have strangled her baby in its cradle to rescue it from the future. But of Botticelli there is much to say. One of the Filippo Lippis is perhaps his masterpiece—a Madonna in a small rose-garden (such a "flowery close" as Mr. William Morris loves to haunt), leaning over an Infant who kicks his little human heels on the grass while half-a-dozen curly-pated angels gather about him, looking back over their shoulders with the candour of children in *tableaux vivants* ["living pictures"], and one of them drops an armful of gathered roses one by one upon the baby. The delightful earthly innocence of these winged youngsters is quite inexpressible. Their heads are twisted about toward the spectator as if they were playing at leap-frog and were expecting a companion to come and take a jump. Never did "young" art, never did subjective freshness, attempt with greater success to represent those phases. But these three fine works are hung over the tops of doors in a dark back room—the bucket and broom are thrust behind a curtain. It seems to me, nevertheless, that a fine Filippo Lippi is good enough company for an Allori or a Cigoli, and that that too deeply sentient Virgin of Botticelli might happily balance the flower-like irresponsibility of Raphael's "Madonna of the Chair."

Taking the Pitti collection, however, simply for what it pretends to be, it gives us the very flower of the sumptuous, the courtly, the grand-ducal. It is chiefly official art, as one may say, but it presents the fine side of the type—the brilliancy, the facility, the amplitude, the sovereignty of good taste. I agree on the whole with a nameless companion and with what he lately remarked about his own humour on these matters; that, having been on his first acquaintance with pictures nothing if not critical, and held the lesson incomplete and the opportunity slighted if he left a gallery without a headache, he had come, as he grew older, to regard them more as the grandest of all pleasantries and less as the most strenuous of all lessons, and to remind himself that, after all, it is the privilege of art to make us friendly to the human mind and not to make us suspicious of it. We do in fact as we grow older unstring the critical bow a little and strike a truce with invidious comparisons. We work off the juvenile impulse to heated partisanship and discover that one spontaneous producer isn't different enough from another to keep the all-knowing Fates from smiling over our loves and our aversions. We perceive a certain human solidarity in all cultivated effort, and are conscious of a growing accommodation of judgment—an easier disposition, the fruit of experience, to take the joke for what it is worth as it passes. We have in short less of a quarrel with the masters we don't delight in, and less of an impulse to pin all our faith on those in whom, in more zealous days, we fancied that we made out peculiar meanings. The meanings no longer seem quite so peculiar. Since then we have arrived at a few in the depths of our own genius that are not sensibly less striking.

And yet it must be added that all this depends vastly on one's mood— as a traveller's impressions do, generally, to a degree which those who give them to the world would do well more explicitly to declare. We have our hours of expansion and those of contraction, and yet while we follow the traveller's trade we go about gazing and judging with unadjusted confidence. We can't suspend judgment; we must take our notes, and the notes are florid or crabbed, as the case may be. A short time ago I spent a week in an ancient city on a hill-top, in the humour, for which I was not to blame, which produces crabbed notes. I knew it at the time, but couldn't help it. I went through all the motions of liberal appreciation; I uncapped in all the churches and on the massive ramparts stared all the views fairly out of countenance; but my imagination, which I suppose at bottom had very good reasons of its own and knew perfectly what it was about, refused to project into the dark old town and upon the yellow hills that sympathetic glow which forms half the substance of our genial impressions. So it is that in museums and palaces we are alternate radicals and conservatives. On some days we ask but to be somewhat sensibly affected; on others, Ruskin-haunted, to be spiritually steadied. After a long absence from the Pitti Palace I went back there the other morning and transferred myself from chair to chair in the great golden-roofed saloons—the chairs are all gilded and covered with faded silk—in the humour to be diverted at any price. I needn't mention the things that diverted me; I yawn now when I think of some of them. But an artist, for instance, to whom my kindlier judgment has made permanent concessions is that charming Andrea del Sarto. When I first knew him, in my cold youth, I used to say without mincing that I didn't like him. *Cet âge est sans pitié* [That stage of life has no pity]. The fine sympathetic, melancholy, pleasing painter! He has a dozen faults, and if you insist pedantically on your rights the conclusive word you use about him will be the word *weak*. But if you are a generous soul you will utter it low—low as the mild grave tone of his own sought harmonies. He is monotonous, narrow, incomplete; he has but a dozen different figures and but two or three ways of distributing them; he seems able to utter but half his thought, and his canvases lack apparently some final return on the whole matter—some process which his impulse failed him before he could bestow. And yet in spite of these limitations his genius is both itself of the great pattern and lighted by the air of a great period. Three gifts he had largely: an instinctive, unaffected, unerring grace; a large and rich, and yet a sort of withdrawn and indifferent, sobriety; and best of all, as well as rarest of all, an indescribable property of relatedness as to the moral world. Whether he was aware of the connection or not, or in what measure, I cannot say; but he gives, so to speak, the taste of it. Before his handsome vague-browed Madonnas; the mild, robust young saints who kneel in his foregrounds and look round at you with a conscious anxiety which seems to say that, though in the picture, they are not of it, but of your own sentient life of commingled love and weariness; the stately apostles, with comely heads and harmonious draperies, who gaze up at the high-seated Virgin like early astronomers at a newly seen star—there comes to you the brush of the dark wing of an inward life. A shadow falls for the moment, and in it you feel the chill of moral suffering. Did the Lippis suffer, father or son? Did Raphael suffer? Did Titian? Did Rubens suffer? Perish the thought—it wouldn't be fair to *us* that they should have had everything. And I note in our poor second-rate Andrea an element of interest lacking to a number of stronger talents.

Interspersed with him at the Pitti hang the stronger and the weaker in splendid abundance. Raphael is there, strong in portraiture—easy, various, bountiful genius that he was—and (strong here isn't the word, but) happy beyond the common dream in his beautiful "Madonna of the Chair." The general instinct of posterity seems to have been to treat this lovely picture as a semi-sacred, an almost miraculous, manifestation. People stand in a worshipful silence before it, as they would before a taper-studded shrine. If we suspend in imagination on the right of it the solid realistic, unidealised portrait of Leo the Tenth (which hangs in another room) and transport to the left the fresco of the School of Athens from the Vatican, and then reflect that these were three separate fancies of a single youthful, amiable genius we recognise that such a producing consciousness must have been a "treat." My companion already quoted has a phrase that he "doesn't care for Raphael," but confesses, when pressed, that he was a most remarkable young man. Titian has a dozen portraits of unequal interest. I never particularly noticed till lately—it is very ill hung—that portentous image of the Emperor Charles the Fifth. He was a burlier, more imposing personage than his usual legend figures, and in his great puffed sleeves and gold chains and full-skirted overdress he seems to tell of a tread that might sometimes have been inconveniently resonant. But the *purpose* to have his way and work his will is there—the great stomach for divine right, the old monarchical temperament. The great Titian, in portraiture, however, remains that formidable young man in black, with the small compact head, the delicate nose and the irascible blue eye. Who was he? What was he? *"Ritratto virile* [masculine portrait]" is all the catalogue is able to call the picture. "Virile!" Rather! you vulgarly exclaim. You may weave what romance you please about it, but a romance your dream must be. Handsome, clever, defiant, passionate, dangerous, it was not his own fault if he hadn't adventures and to spare. He was a gentleman and a warrior, and his adventures balanced between camp and court. I imagine him the young orphan of a noble house, about to come into mortgaged estates. One wouldn't have cared to be his guardian, bound to paternal admonitions once a month over his precocious transactions with the Jews or his scandalous abduction from her convent of such and such a noble maiden.

The Pitti Gallery contains none of Titian's golden-toned groups; but it boasts a lovely composition by Paul Veronese, the dealer in silver hues—a Baptism of Christ. W——— named it to me the other day as the picture he most enjoyed, and surely painting seems here to have proposed to itself to discredit and annihilate—and even on the occasion of such a subject—everything but the loveliness of life. The picture bedims and enfeebles its neighbours. We ask ourselves whether painting as such can go further. It is simply that here at last the art stands complete. The early Tuscans, as well as Leonardo, as Raphael, as Michael, saw the great spectacle that surrounded them in beautiful sharp-edged elements and parts. The great Venetians felt its indissoluble unity and recognised that form and colour and earth and air were equal members of every possible subject; and beneath their magical touch the hard outlines melted together and the blank intervals bloomed with meaning. In this beautiful Paul Veronese of the Pitti everything is part of the charm—the atmosphere as well as the figures, the look of radiant morning in the white-streaked sky as well as the living human limbs, the cloth of Venetian purple about the loins of the Christ as well as the noble humility of his attitude. The relation to Nature of the other Italian schools differs from that of the Venetian as courtship—even ardent courtship—differs from marriage.

SELECTIONS FROM TRAVEL HANDBOOKS

A glimpse into a very special world is provided by the handbooks travelers used a century or so ago. For one thing, these guides assume without question that society is divided by the laws of human variety into fixed classes and that only the upper, the upper-middle, and the middle class travel. The others who serve them, on ships and railways and in hotels and post offices, are assumed to be not just "low" but dishonest, dirty, and rapacious, and generally so class peevish as to be kept from open insult only by fear of the law or the sack.

In contrast to the tourists of a century later, the travelers posited by these handbooks seem surprisingly "inner-directed." They know precisely what they want. Far from desiring to merge into groups attended by guides and leaders, they want to proceed by themselves. Their wish is to be assisted only by literature, and their goal is art and architecture, never consumer goods. Thus Karl Baedeker addresses these travelers in the opening paragraph of his Russia *(1914):*

> *The Handbook to Russia . . . is intended to supply the traveler with such information as will render him as nearly as possible independent of hotelkeepers, commissionnaires, and guides, and thus enable him the more thoroughly to enjoy and appreciate the objects of interest he meets with on his tour.*

(With tourism, on the other hand, it is the very multiplicity and variety of guides, attendants, recreation directors, and the like that is emphasized.)

There are other interesting archaisms here as well. One is the command of the subjunctive—a device of rhetorical subtlety now virtually extinct—shown by many of these authors. But most conspicuous is their sharp, tart, unillusioned view of things, which seems today, in our insecure and sentimental age, hopelessly out of date. If the guidebook used to be critical, today it seems largely a celebratory adjunct to the publicity operations of hotels, resorts, and even countries. Only rarely today does the old skeptical tone surface, as in the last example in this section.

From W. Pembroke Fetridge, *Harper's Handbook for Travelers in Europe and The East,* New York, 1862.

The best guidebooks that the author found in Europe were most decidedly "Murray's;" and he would, by all means, advise their purchase in case of a lengthened stay at any one place.

INTRODUCTION

CONTAINING HINTS TO TRAVELERS WHICH SHOULD BE CAREFULLY READ BEFORE LEAVING THE UNITED STATES.

Not the least important requisite for a traveler is a ready stock of good temper and forbearance. Let your motto be, "Keep cool." Good-humor will procure more comforts than gold. If you think you are imposed upon, be firm; custom has established certain charges; . . . any deviation from them is soon detected, and, unless unnecessary trouble has been given, firmness and good temper will lower your bill more readily than violence.

We, as a nation, have unfortunately acquired a reputation abroad of great prodigality in our expenditures, and in the East we are charged twenty per cent, more than any other nation. . . .

Wherever you are, it is best to fall into the manners and customs of the place; it may be inconvenient, but it is less so than running counter to them.

* * *

The author's advice is, to avoid guides as much as possible. . . . By wandering about and trusting to your own observations, you will become much more readily acquainted with places, and your impressions will be stronger.

* * *

The author most decidedly advises travelers never to omit calling on the minister resident, or the consul, at any place he may visit. It is a duty they owe themselves, as well as their representatives. . . .

* * *

Fire-arms. As nearly all travelers carry some kind of fire-arms with them, more especially if they visit the East, where they are indispensable, it behooves them to take the best that are manufactured. . . .

From MURRAY'S HANDBOOK FOR TRAVELLERS IN NORTHERN ITALY, LONDON, 1874.

Caution to Innkeepers and Others. The Editor of the Handbooks has learned from various quarters that persons have been extorting money from innkeepers, tradespeople, artists, and others, on the Continent, under pretext of procuring favorable notices of them and their establishments in the Handbooks for Travellers, or in guides which, being artfully styled *"livres* rouges," are passed off by these imposters as the *red* handbooks published by Mr. Murray. The Publisher, therefore, thinks proper to warn all whom it may concern, that recommendations in the Handbooks are not to be obtained by such means, and that the persons alluded to are not only unauthorized, but being totally unknown to him are little better than swindlers. All those, therefore, who place confidence in such promises, or in persons who assume to be agents of the Publisher, demanding money as the price of recommendations in the Handbooks, may rest assured that they will be defrauded without attaining their object.

* * *

No attention can be paid to letters from Hotel-keepers in praise of their inns; the postage of them being onerous, they will be refused.

* * *

Throughout N. Italy, but especially at Verona and Venice, no one should think of paying the price *asked* for any article in the shops. Bargaining, unpleasant though it be, is usual, and is expected; and if the English traveller will quietly specify the sum he considers just, and which he is prepared to give, at least no offence will be taken by the shop-keeper, even if he does not accept the offer.

* * *

Post Office; Letters and Postage. . . . A cautious traveller will take important letters to the post-office himself . . . , since if given to an untrustworthy person to carry to the post-office they run the risk of being made away with for the sake of the stamps.

* * *

Sight-Seeing. Laquais de Place and Ciceroni. If you hire a laquais de place—1st, Make him take you to every place *you* wish to see, for . . . caprice, or some plan of his own, or mere laziness, will often make him try to put you off. 2nd, If you have plenty of time on your hands, it is as well to see every object which *he* recommends, unless it evidently should be something quite absurd. For though in so doing he may have a job in view—some shop kept by a friend into which he wishes to seduce you, some ally of a custode for whom he wants to secure a *buona mano*, and thus usually occasions you a waste of time and money—yet he is sometimes the means of conducting you to an object which you would have been sorry not to have seen. A laquais de place should not be allowed to make bargains for you, as the commissions which the shop-keeper allows him will be, of course, paid out of your pocket.

* * *

The clergy do not like to have their churches considered as shows, nor are the congregations at all indifferent, as has been asserted, to the conduct of strangers, in walking about and talking during Divine service. It might perhaps, too, be suggested to our Protestant countrymen, that they are not protesting against Roman Catholic errors by behaving indecorously in churches. . . .

* * *

Inns and Accommodation. Ask the price of everything beforehand. . . . A traveller will frequently be put into a room for which five or six francs will be charged for the night, when one of three francs will suit him just as well. Never scruple to bargain. . . . In ordering dinner it is the best plan for the traveller to mention the price he will pay, with or without ordinary wine. . . . If exorbitant charges be made, the best plan, if you have nerve enough, is to refuse to pay them, putting down a reasonable sum upon the table. . . .

* * *

Books; Maps. A traveller whose mind is not previously prepared for a visit to Italy is deprived of the greatest portion of the pleasure (to say nothing of the instruction) which he would otherwise derive. This obser-vation is true of every part of the world; but the extent and variety of interest attaching to the scenery, the cities, the churches, the castles, the palaces, the works of art in Italy, renders the amount of loss much greater than in any other country. . . .

The reputation acquired by Roscoe's *Lorenzo de' Medici* was, in some degree, owing to the novelty of the subject. But Roscoe is always elegant and, so far as literary history is concerned, fairly correct. . . .

From THOMAS W. KNOX, *HOW TO TRAVEL: HINTS, ADVICE, AND SUGGESTIONS TO TRAVELERS BY LAND AND SEA ALL OVER THE GLOBE*, NEW YORK, 1881.

If you have been reared in the belief that your own country, or your own state, town, or hamlet, contains all that is good in the world, whether of moral excellence, mental development, or mechanical skill, you must prepare to eradicate that belief at an early date. . . . To an observant and thoughtful individual the invariable effect of travel is to teach respect for the opinions, the faith, or the ways of others, and to convince him that other civilizations than his own are worthy of consideration.

* * *

Close all your business and have everything ready the day before your departure. It is better to sit around and be idle for a few hours than to have the worry of a lot of things that have been deferred to the last.

* * *

Do not disturb yourself with unpleasant thoughts of what may happen [to transatlantic ships] in the fog. Remember, rather, that of the thousands of voyages that have been made across the Atlantic only a few dozens have been unfortunate, and of all the steamers that have plowed these waters only the *President, City of Glasgow, Pacific, Tempest, United Kingdom, City of Boston,* and *Ismailia*—seven in all—are unheard from. The chances are thousands to one in your favor. . . .

* * *

When the ship is pitching violently in a head sea, avoid going forward on deck, as you may get a drenching unexpectedly, and possibly may be washed overboard. Be cautious about leaning over the taffrail or stern at any time, and especially in rough weather, as the ship may "jump from under you" without the least warning, and drop you in the sea.

* * *

The moist climate of the British Islands is apt to leave a disagreeable dampness on bed-linen, and makes it very detrimental to the general health. Many a man has taken a severe cold by sleeping in damp sheets on his arrival in England, and discovered to his sorrow that his recovery was a thing of several weeks, if not longer.

* * *

Sometimes even a careful bargain will not protect the traveler from trouble. Italian boatmen will agree for a certain sum, and while on the

Established 1832.
THE ORIGINAL GUIDE AND TRAVELLERS' DEPÔT.
and
Passport and Couriers' Agency,

L E E ℰ C A R T E R, 440 West Strand, London
(Nearly opposite the Charing Cross Hotel).

KNAPSACKS	PORTMANTEAUX	BAGS
Stiff or Limp.	Of All Patterns.	Of All Kinds.

Intending Tourists are respectfully invited to visit this Establishment
before making purchases for their journey.

AN EXTENSIVE STOCK OF TRAVELLERS' REQUISITES TO
SELECT FROM:—

Guide Books (in pocket bindings).
Maps and Plans of All Parts.
Foreign Dictionaries.
Dialogues and Grammars.
Polyglot Washing Books.
Journals and Diaries.
Pocket Books and Note Cases.
Purses, Sov. and Nap. Cases.
Money Bags and Belts.
Writing Cases and Blotters.
Ink Stands and Light Boxes.
Foreign Stationery.
Travelling Chess Boards, ℰc.
Knives, Scissors, ℰ Corkscrews.
Barometers and
Thermometers.
Field Glasses and Compasses.
Eye Preservers and Spectacles.
Railway Rugs and Straps.

Hat Cases and Bonnet Boxes.
Luggage Straps and Labels.
Travelling Lamps.
Camp Candlesticks.
Flasks and Drinking Cups.
Sandwich Cases.
Luncheon Baskets.
Dressing Cases and Housewives.
Soap and Brush Boxes.
Sponge and Sponge Bags.
Baths and Air Cushions.
Waterproofs and Foot Warmers.
Camp Stools and Leg Rests.
Portable Closet Seats.
Etnas for Boiling Water.
Combs, Brushes, and Mirrors.
Glycerine and Insect Powder.
Door Fasteners, ℰc., ℰc., ℰc.

way they demand more. If you are going on board a steamer at Naples they are apt to be extortionate, as they know you are leaving port and are not likely to give them trouble with the police. A boatman agrees to carry you and your baggage for two francs; you enter his boat and off you go. Half way to the ship he stops rowing and demands four, or perhaps five, francs, and threatens to return to shore unless you comply. If you are strong, and carry a cane or good umbrella, a threat to break his head, accompanied with a gesture to that effect, will generally cause him to proceed. If you are weak and timid, the best way is to say nothing, and if you are tough in conscience and don't mind meeting downright rascality with a white lie, you can nod assent and let him go on. Before he gets to the ship he will increase his demand, and you may nod again. When you reach the vessel do not show your money till your baggage is safe on board, the heavy trunks in the hold, and the lighter things in your cabin. Then pay the sum you first agreed to give, and not a centime more, and, having discharged the obligation, descend to the saloon. The boatman is not allowed to follow you there, but he will give vent to a volley of imprecations that fall harmless on your devoted head if you happen to be ignorant of Italian. When these fellows get too noisy they are ordered away from the ship, and after their departure you may mount again to the deck and enjoy the wonderfully beautiful panorama of the Bay of Naples.

* * *

The American who visits Europe for the first time is apt to be in a hurry, and to endeavor to see too much. . . . Instances have occurred of tourists who could not tell whether St. Paul's Cathedral was in London or Rome, and who had a vague impression that the tomb of Napoleon was beneath the Arc de Triomphe. They told of the wonderful wood-carving to be seen at Venice, and thought that Michael Angelo, John Titian, and Sir Christopher Wren were among the most famous painters Switzerland had ever produced. . . .

Moral—Don't be in a hurry.

* * *

There is no pleasanter steamship life anywhere than in the East, so far as the associations are concerned. The brainless idiots that add a pang to existence on the transatlantic voyage are rarely seen so far away from home as the coast of China; the majority of the people you meet there are the possessors of at least a fair amount of intelligence, and know how to use it.

From Karl Baedeker, *Paris and Environs, Handbook for Travellers*, Leipzig, 1907.

As a rule the Parisian may be said to invite and deserve the confidence of travellers. Accustomed by long usage to their presence, he is skilful in catering for their wants, and recommends himself to them by his politeness and complaisance. In return the traveller in France should accustom himself to the inevitable *"s'il vous plaît"* when ordering refreshments at a café or restaurant, or making any request. It is also customary to address persons even of humble station as *"Monsieur," "Madame,"* or *"Mademoiselle."*

* * *

Visitors should avoid the less-frequented districts after night-fall. . . . They should also be on their guard against the huge army of pickpockets and other rogues, who are quick to recognize the stranger and skilful in taking advantage of his ignorance. It is perhaps unnecessary specially to mention the card-sharpers sometimes met with in the suburban and other trains, or the various other dangers to purse and health which the French metropolis shares with other large towns.

* * *

Cabs whose drivers wear *white hats* are usually the most comfortable and the quickest. India-rubber tires are indicated by small bells on the horse's neck.

* * *

Theatres. Music Halls. Balls. Circuses. Paris possesses some 20 large theatres, in the proper sense of the word, and the traveller doing the "sights" of Paris should not omit to visit some at least of the principal houses. . . .

The *Claque*, or paid applauders, form an annoying, although time-honored and characteristic feature in most of the theatres. They occupy the center seats in the pit . . . and are easily recognized by the obtrusive and simultaneous vigor of their exertions. There are even *"entrepreneurs de succès dramatiques"* who furnish theatres with *claques* at stated terms. . . . Strange as it may seem to the visitor, all attempts to abolish this nuisance have hitherto failed. . . .

Cabarets Artistiques. . . . The entertainments, which consist of songs, mystic illusions, shadow-plays, etc., are often clever, but presuppose a considerable knowledge of colloquial French. These cabarets are scarcely suitable for ladies. . . .

Balls. Bals Publics. . . . It need hardly be said that ladies cannot attend these balls.

From KARL BAEDEKER, *SOUTHERN FRANCE, INCLUDING CORSICA. HANDBOOK FOR TRAVELLERS.* LEIPZIG, 1907.

A slight acquaintance with French is indispensable for those who desire to explore the more remote districts of Southern France, but tourists who do not deviate from the beaten track will generally find English spoken at the principal hotels and the usual resorts of strangers. If, however, they are entirely ignorant of the French language, they must be prepared occasionally to submit to the extortions practiced by porters, cab-drivers, and others of a like class, which even the data furnished by the Handbook will not always enable them to avoid.

* * *

The pedestrian of moderate requirements, who is tolerably proficient in the language and avoids the beaten track as much as possible, may limit his expenditure to 12–15 fr. per day, while those who prefer driving to walking, choose the dearest hotels, and employ the services of guides and commissionaires must be prepared to spend at least 20–30 fr. daily. Two or three gentlemen travelling together will be able to journey more economically than a single tourist, but the presence of ladies generally adds considerably to the expense of the party.

* * *

Sketching, photographing, or making notes near fortified places sometimes exposes innocent travellers to disagreeable suspicions or worse, and should therefore be avoided.

* * *

Custom House. . . . Books and newspapers occasionally give rise to suspicion and may in certain cases be confiscated.

* * *

When the traveller remains for a week or more at a hotel, it is advisable to pay, or at least call for the account, every two or three days, in order that erroneous insertions may be at once detected. Verbal reckonings are objectionable. . . . A waiter's mental arithmetic is faulty, and the faults are seldom in favor of the traveller. A habit too often prevails of presenting the bill at the last moment, when mistakes or wilful impositions cannot easily be detected or rectified. . . . Doors should be locked at night. . . .

Travellers who are not fastidious as to their table-companions will often find an excellent cuisine, combined with moderate charges, at the hotels frequented by commercial travellers. . . .

* * *

Cafés. . . . Ladies may visit the better-class cafés without dread, at least during the day.

* * *

Walking Tours. Many fine points in the part of France of which the present Handbook treats are accessible to pedestrians alone, and even where riding or driving is practicable, walking is often more enjoyable. For a short tour a couple of flannel shirts, a pair of worsted stockings, slippers, the articles of the toilette, a light waterproof, and a stout umbrella will generally be found a sufficient equipment. . . . A pocket-knife with a corkscrew, a leather drinking-cup, a spirit-flask, stout gloves, and a piece of green crape or colored spectacles to protect the eyes from the glare of the snow should not be forgotten. . . . Glaciers should be traversed as early in the morning as possible, before the sun softens the crust of ice formed during the night over the crevasses. . . . Glacier-water should not be drunk except in small quantities, mixed with wine or cognac. Cold milk is also safer when qualified with spirits. . . .

Guides. A glacier should never be crossed without an experienced guide. Good guides are unfortunately rare. . . .

Horses and Mules. On the whole, unless the ascent be very long, it is less fatiguing to ascend on foot than on horseback; while a descent on horseback is almost invariably uncomfortable and fatiguing, and cannot be recommended to those who are subject to dizziness.

* * *

NICE

Apartments. Houses and apartments to let . . . are easily found, best with the aid of a house-agent. A doctor should be consulted as to situation, etc.

From KARL BAEDEKER, *RUSSIA, WITH TEHERAN, PORT ARTHUR, AND PEKING. HANDBOOK FOR TRAVELLERS.* LEIPZIG, 1914.

To hotel-keepers, tradesmen, and others the Editor begs to intimate that a character for fair dealing towards travellers is the sole passport to his commendation, and that no advertisements of any kind are admitted to his Handbooks. Persons calling themselves agents for Baedeker's Handbooks are imposters.

* * *

The cost of travelling in Russia is considerably higher than in Central Europe. . . . Even the slightest acquaintance with the language is a considerable help, and all who visit the country should at least learn the Russian alphabet, in order to be able to read street-names, etc. . . .

Clothing should not be too light, for even in summer the nights are often chilly, and changes of temperature are frequent and extreme. Woollen underwear is recommended. The traveller should be provided with a pillow or an air-cushion, linen sheets (useful on long railway journeys and in provincial hotels), towels, a coverlet or rug, a small india-rubber bath, and some insect-powder. . . . *Unboiled Water* should be avoided.

* * *

The passport is demanded at the frontier. . . . If a passport is not in order, its unhappy owner has to recross the frontier, the train by which he came waiting for this purpose.

* * *

Customs. Whether at the railway frontier-station or at a seaport the customs examination of passengers' luggage is generally thorough. . . . Unprinted paper only should be used for packing, to avoid any cause of suspicion. . . . Books in large quantities are submitted to a censor. Travellers should avoid works of a political, social, or historical nature.

* * *

The *Railway Book Stalls* of the larger stations generally offer a small assortment of English, French, and German books (not cheap), but foreign newspapers are seldom met with.

* * *

The large *Hotels* . . . are little inferior to those of Western Europe. . . . The hotels in provincial towns, especially the older ones, satisfy as a rule only the most moderate demands, and they often leave much to be desired in point of cleanliness. In spite of these failings they frequently have high-sounding names, such as Grand-Hôtel, etc. The traveller is thrown back upon Russian, as no other language is understood. . . . No notice should be taken if the izvóshtchick declares there is no room in the hotel he has been told to drive to.

* * *

Concerts are given daily in summer in the parks and pleasure resorts near the larger towns by military and other bands. . . . Those who do not shrink from an expensive supper and somewhat Bohemian society should make a point of hearing one of the Russian or Gipsy Choirs. The very characteristic performances of these choirs are generally given in the fashionable restaurants on the outskirts of the large towns, which on winter evenings are much frequented by the jeunesse dorée in their three-horse sleighs.

The Russians are great lovers of *Music*. Social entertainments without singing are almost unheard of. The workman also lightens his labor and the soldier his long marches with characteristic songs. The concertina or accordion is very common, but the old *Balaláika*, a kind of three-stringed zither, has lately become again very popular.

* * *

The smoking of cigarettes is common among all classes of society and both sexes; the Russian smokes even at meals, between the courses. The Old Believers . . . do not smoke.

* * *

The Great Russians . . . , of whom there are 52,000,000 in European Russia, now occupy not only 'Great Russia' . . . but also E. and S.E. Russia. . . . Their speech, customs, and character are spread over the whole empire. Physically they are blond, blue-eyed, and vigorous, with broad shoulders and bull necks, often somewhat clumsy and with a strong tendency to obesity. Their character has been influenced not only by a long history of subjugation to feudal despotism, but also by the gloomy forests, the unresponsive soil, and the rigorous climate, and especially by the enforced inactivity of the long winters. In disposition they are melancholy and reserved, clinging obstinately to their traditions, and full of self-sacrificing devotion to Tzar, Church, and feudal superior. They are easily disciplined, and so make excellent soldiers, but have little power of independent thinking or of initiation. The normal Great Russian is thus the mainstay of political and economic inertia and reaction. Even the educated Russian gives comparatively little response to the actual demands of life; he is more or less the victim of fancy and temperament, which sometimes leads him to a despondent slackness, sometimes to emotional outbursts. Here we have the explanation of the want of organization, the disorder, and the waste of time which strike the western visitor to Russia.

* * *

A unique position is held by the *Poles*, a Slav race occupying the Russian part of the old kingdom of Poland. Their total number is about 8,000,000. . . . The Poles are of the middle height, with slender but muscular bodies and light hair. The contrast between the lower classes and the noblesse is very striking, the latter being physically and in character refined to an almost excessive pitch of elegance.

* * *

The total population of Russia, apart from the Jews and the Nomads in the East and North, is divided into four classes: nobles and officials, clergy, citizens or townspeople, and peasants, the last including the laborers. The really sharp distinction, however, is that between the great mass of the people on the one side and the hereditary and official nobility and the burgess class on the other. Even in the upper ranks of society the consequences of the sudden transition from the Old Russian civilization to that of W. Europe are easily discernible. Alongside of admirable achievements in all spheres of intellectual activity, we find also a great deal of merely outward imitation of western forms, with a tendency to rest content with a veneer of western culture and a stock of western catchwords. . . . The upper classes are noted for their luxury and extravagance and for their reckless gambling, their better side showing itself in their unlimited hospitality. The lower classes live in unspeakable poverty and destitution. Beggars are very troublesome, especially in the vicinity of churches.

* * *

The relations between the clergy and the laymen are very different from those obtaining elsewhere. The function of the parish priest is not so much the cure of souls as the regular performance of the ceremonial duties of his office. He is more honored in his status than in his person.

Every foreigner will be struck by the frequency with which the people cross themselves, by their obeisances or prostrations before every open church door, and by the kissing of the floor and the relics . . . inside the churches. The pious Russian also salutes the ikon on entering a room.

ST. PETERSBURG

The Streets of St. Petersburg are much less animated than those of other European capitals, though they are a little less dull on Sun. and holidays. . . . The scarlet liveries of the royal carriages are conspicuous. Nearly one-tenth of the male population . . . wear some kind of uniform, including not only the numerous military officers, but civil officials, and even students, schoolboys, and others. Characteristic street figures, which are, however, fast disappearing, are the vendors of ices . . . and kvass . . . , who carry their pails and glass jugs on their heads; the itinerant cooks . . . ; the vendors of old clothes . . . and linen. . . .

The wet nurses, dressed in bright and rich national costume (blue, when their charges are boys, and pink for girls) are a conspicuous feature.

*　*　*

The climate of St. Petersburg is raw, damp, and very unsettled; woollen underclothing is the best protection against chills. *Unboiled water should on no account be drunk.*

From Bob Green, in *Fodor's South-East Asia*, 1978

Cruise ships [calling at Hong Kong] dock at the Ocean Terminal, one of the world's best facilities for cruise passengers. This modern, 30-acre, air-conditioned shopping center is the biggest in Hong Kong and perhaps in the entire region. . . . There are facilities for cabling or making overseas telephone calls, exchanging currency, mailing parcels or forwarding baggage, and hiring a car or launch. The traveler arriving by ship can also usually count on being welcomed to Hong Kong by a cluster of pimps and touts.

THOMAS HARDY 1840–1928

That life is a "journey" is one of the oldest clichés lodged in the human imagination. That life is a railway journey became easily conceivable during the age of steam and electricity. But it took Hardy, with his flair for the portentous, the dangerous, and the uncertain, to imagine life as a risky and mysterious rail journey—despite the straight tracks and the public stations and the ticket bought for a specific destination— "towards a world unknown."

MIDNIGHT ON THE GREAT WESTERN
(1917)

In the third-class seat sat the journeying boy,
        And the roof-lamp's oily flame
Played down on his listless form and face,
Bewrapt past knowing to what he was going,
        Or whence he came.

In the band of his hat the journeying boy
        Had a ticket stuck; and a string
Around his neck bore the key of his box,
That twinkled gleams of the lamp's sad beams
        Like a living thing.

What past can be yours, O journeying boy
        Towards a world unknown,
Who calmly, as if incurious quite
On all at stake, can undertake
        This plunge alone?

Knows your soul a sphere, O journeying boy,
        Our rude realms far above,
Whence with spacious vision you mark and mete
This region of sin that you find you in,
        But are not of?

D. H. LAWRENCE
1885–1930

For Lawrence, as for most travelers in the modern industrial age, travel was both an escape and a search—an escape in his case from an England he despised for its prudence and emotional atrophy, a search for any place more vivid, elemental, and un-selfconscious. His life consisted of a series of impatient acts of travel, to Germany and Italy, to Sardinia and Switzerland and France, to Ceylon and Australia and Tahiti, to New and Old Mexico, and back to France again, where he died in a tuberculosis sanitarium at Vence, on the Riviera, observing with virtually his last breath, "This place no good."

In January, 1921, with his wife Frieda (designated the q-b, for Queen Bee*), he toured Sardinia for only twelve days. Back in Taormina, in Sicily, he is said to have written* Sea and Sardinia *in six weeks. The book, which sometimes seems less about a specific place than about the principle of variety, registers Lawrence's sheer delight in movement and colors and intense perception, virtually for their own sake. As the traveler H. M. Tomlinson noted, Lawrence was "a delicate sensorium, quivering and vociferating to every physical fact." And to Aldous Huxley he seemed "a kind of mystical materialist." But there is little mysticism in* Sea and Sardinia, *the merriest of Lawrence's travel books, a book remarkably sensitive to social comedy and the magic of an unfamiliar place. And couched in a bold, impulsive style, which seems the corollary of the joyous travel emotion itself. As he blurts out on the boat carrying him toward this new place, "Oh, God, what a joy it is to the wild innermost soul. One is free at last."*

From SEA AND SARDINIA
(1921)

Comes over one an absolute necessity to move. And what is more, to move in some particular direction. A double necessity then: to get on the move, and to know whither.

Why can't one sit still? Here in Sicily it is so pleasant: the sunny Ionian sea, the changing jewel of Calabria, like a fire-opal moved in the light; Italy and the panorama of Christmas clouds, night with the dog-star laying a long luminous gleam across the sea, as if baying at us, Orion marching above; how the dog-star Sirius looks at one, looks at one! he is the hound of heaven, green, glamorous and fierce!—and then, oh, regal evening star, hung westward flaring over the jagged dark precipices of tall Sicily: then Etna, that wicked witch, resting her thick white snow under heaven, and slowly, slowly rolling her orange-coloured smoke. They called her the Pillar of Heaven, the Greeks. It seems wrong at first, for she trails up in a long, magical, flexible line from the sea's edge to her blunt cone, and does not seem tall. She seems rather low, under heaven. But as one knows her better, oh, awe and wizardry! Remote under heaven, aloof, so near, yet never with us. The painters try to paint her, and the photographers to photograph her, in vain. Because why? Because the near ridges, with their olives and white houses, these are with us. Because the river-bed, and Naxos under the lemon groves, Greek Naxos deep under dark-leaved, many-fruited lemon groves, Etna's skirts and skirt-bottoms, these still are our world, our own world. Even the high villages among the oaks on Etna. But Etna herself, Etna of the snow and secret changing winds, she is beyond a crystal wall. When I look at her, low, white, witch-like under heaven, slowly rolling her orange smoke and giving sometimes a breath of rose-red flame, then I must look away from earth, into the ether, into the low empyrean. And there, in that remote region, Etna is alone. If you would see her, you must slowly take off your eyes from the world and go a naked seer to the strange chamber of the empyrean. Pedestal of heaven! The Greeks had a sense of the magic truth of things. Thank goodness one still knows enough about them to find one's kinship at last. There are so many photographs, there are so infinitely many water-colour drawings and oil paintings which purport to render Etna. But pedestal of heaven! You must cross the invisible border. Between the foreground, which is our own, and Etna, pivot of winds in lower heaven, there is a dividing line. You must change your state of mind. A metempsychosis. It is no use thinking you can see and behold Etna and the foreground both at once. Never. One or the other. Foreground and a transcribed Etna. Or Etna, pedestal of heaven.

Why, then, must one go? Why not stay? Ah, what a mistress, this Etna! with her strange winds prowling round her like Circe's panthers, some black, some white. With her strange remote communications and her terrible dynamic exhalations. She makes men mad. Such terrible vibrations of wicked and beautiful electricity she throws about her, like a deadly net! Nay, sometimes, verily, one can feel a new current of her demon magnetism seize one's living tissue and change the peaceful life of one's active cells. She makes a storm in the living plasm and a new adjustment. And sometimes it is like a madness.

This timeless Grecian Etna, in her lower-heaven loveliness, so lovely, so lovely, what a torturer! Not many men can really stand her without losing their souls. She is like Circe. Unless a man is very strong, she takes his soul away from him and leaves him not a beast, but an elemental creature, intelligent and soulless. Intelligent, almost inspired, and soulless, like the Etna Sicilians. Intelligent daimons, and humanly, according to us, the most stupid people on earth. Ach, horror! How many men, how many races, has Etna put to flight? It was she who broke the quick of the Greek soul. And after the Greeks, she gave the Romans, the Normans, the Arabs, the Spaniards, the French, the Italians, even the English, she gave them all their inspired hour and broke their souls. Perhaps it is she one must flee from. At any rate, one must go: and at once. After having come back only at the end of October, already one must dash away. And it is only the third of January. And one cannot afford to move. Yet there you are: at the Etna bidding one goes.

Where does one go? There is Girgenti by the south. There is Tunis at hand. Girgenti, and the sulphur spirit and the Greek guarding temples, to make one madder? Never. Neither Syracuse and the madness of its great quarries. Tunis? Africa? Not yet, not yet. Not the Arabs, not yet. Naples, Rome, Florence? No good at all. Where then?

Where then? Spain or Sardinia. Spain or Sardinia. Sardinia, which is like nowhere. Sardinia which has no history, no date, no race, no offering. Let it be Sardinia. They say neither Romans nor Phoenicians, Greeks nor Arabs ever subdued Sardinia. It lies outside; outside the circuit of civilization. Like the Basque lands. Sure enough, it is Italian now, with its railways and its motor omnibuses. But there is an uncaptured Sardinia still. It lies within the net of this European civilization, but it isn't landed yet. And the net is getting old and tattered. A good many fish are slipping through the net of the old European civilization. Like that great whale of Russia. And probably even Sardinia. Sardinia then. Let it be Sardinia.

* * *

And so we steam out. And almost at once the ship begins to take a long, slow, dizzy dip, and a fainting swoon upwards, and a long, slow, dizzy dip, slipping away from beneath one. The q-b turns pale. Up comes the deck in that fainting swoon backwards—then down it fades in that indescribable slither forwards. It is all quite gentle—quite, quite gentle. But oh, so long, and so slow, and so dizzy.

"Rather pleasant!" say I to the q-b.

"Yes. Rather lovely *really!*" she answers wistfully. To tell the truth there is something in the long, slow lift of the ship, and her long, slow slide forwards which makes my heart beat with joy. It is the motion of freedom. To feel her come up—then slide slowly forward, with the sound of the smashing of waters, is like the magic gallop of the sky, the magic gallop of elemental space. That long, slow, waveringly rhythmic rise and fall of the ship, with waters snorting as it were from her nostrils, oh, God, what a joy it is to the wild innermost soul. One is free at last—and lilting in a slow flight of the elements, winging outwards. Oh, God, to be free of all the hemmed-in life—the horror of human tension, the absolute insanity of machine persistence. The agony which a train is to me, really. And the long-drawn-out agony of a life among tense, resistant people on land. And then to feel the long, slow lift and drop of this almost empty ship, as she took the waters. Ah, God, liberty, liberty, elemental liberty. I wished in my soul the voyage might last forever, that the sea had no end, that one might float in this wavering, tremulous, yet long and surging pulsation while ever time lasted: space never exhausted, and no turning back, no looking back, even.

The ship was almost empty—save of course for the street-corner louts who hung about just below, on the deck itself. We stood alone on the weather-faded little promenade deck, which had old oak seats with old, carved little lions at the ends, for arm-rests—and a little cabin mysteriously shut, which much peeping determined as the wireless office and the operator's little curtained bed-niche.

Cold, fresh wind, a black-blue, translucent, rolling sea on which the wake rose in snapping foam, and Sicily on the left: Monte Pellegrino, a huge, inordinate mass of pinkish rock, hardly crisped with the faintest vegetation, looming up to heaven from the sea. Strangely large in mass and bulk Monte Pellegrino looks: and bare, like a Sahara in heaven: and old-looking. These coasts of Sicily are very imposing, terrific, fortifying the interior. And again one gets the feeling that age has worn them bare: as if old, old civilizations had worn away and exhausted the soil, leaving a terrifying blankness of rock, as at Syracuse in plateau, and here in great mass.

There seems hardly anyone on board but ourselves: we alone on the little promenade deck. Strangely lonely, floating on a bare old ship past the great bare shores on a rolling sea, stooping and rising in the wind. The wood of the fittings is all bare and weather-silvered, the cabin, the seats, even the little lions of the seats. The paint wore away long ago: and this timber will never see paint any more. Strange to put one's hand on the old oaken wood, so sea-fibred. Good old delicate-threaded oak: I swear it grew in England. And everything so carefully done, so solid and everlastingly. I look at the lions, with the perfect-fitting pins through their paws chinching them down, and their little mouths open. They are as solid as they were in Victorian days, as immovable. They will never wear away. What a joy in the careful, thorough, manly, everlasting work put into a ship: at least into this sixty-year-old vessel. Every bit of this oak wood so sound, so beautiful: and the whole welded together with joints and wooden pins far more beautifully and livingly than iron welds. Rustless, life-born, living-tissued old wood: rustless as flesh is rustless, and happy-seeming as iron never can be. She rides so well, she takes the sea so beautifully, as a matter of course.

Various members of the crew wander past to look at us. This little promenade deck is over the first-class quarters, full in the stern. So we see first one head then another come up the ladder—mostly bare heads: and one figure after another slouches past, smoking a cigarette. All crew. At last the q-b stops one of them—it is what they are all waiting for, an opportunity to talk—and asks if the weird object on the top of Pellegrino is a ruin. Could there be a more touristy question! No, it is the semaphore station. Slap in the eye for the q-b! She doesn't mind, however, and the member of the crew proceeds to converse. He is a weedy, hollow-cheeked town-product: a Palermitan. He wears faded blue overalls and informs us he is the ship's carpenter: happily unemployed for the rest of his life, apparently, and taking it as rather less than his dues. The ship once did the Naples–Palermo course—a very important course—in the old days of the General Navigation Company. The General Navigation Company sold her for eighty thousand liras years ago, and now she was worth two million. We pretended to believe: but I make a poor show. I am thoroughly sick to death of the sound of liras. No man can overhear ten words of Italian today without two thousand or two million or ten or twenty or two liras flying like venomous mosquitoes round his ears. Liras—liras—liras—nothing else. Romantic, poetic, cypress-and-orange-tree Italy is gone. Remains an Italy smothered in the filthy smother of innumerable lira notes: ragged, unsavoury paper money so thick upon the air that one breathes it like some greasy fog. Behind this greasy fog some people may still see the Italian sun. I find it hard work. Through this murk of liras you peer at Michael Angelo and at Botticelli and the rest, and see them all as through a glass, darkly. For heavy around you is Italy's after-the-war atmosphere, darkly pressing you, squeezing you, milling you into dirty paper notes. King Harry was lucky that they only wanted to coin him into gold. Italy wants to mill you into filthy paper liras.

Another head—and a black alpaca jacket and a serviette this time—to tell us coffee is ready. Not before it is time, too. We go down into the subterranean state-room and sit on the screw-pin chairs, while the ship does the slide-and-slope trot under us, and we drink a couple of cups of coffee and milk, and eat a piece of bread and butter. At least one of the innumerable members of the crew gives me one cup, then casts me off. It is most obviously his intention that I shall get no more: because of course the innumerable members of the crew could all just do with another coffee and milk. However, though the ship heaves and the alpaca coats cluster menacingly in the doorway, I balance my way to the tin buffet and seize the coffee pot and the milk pot, and am quite successful in administering to the q-b and myself. Having restored the said vessels to their tin altar, I resume my spin-chair at the long and desert board. The q-b and I are alone—save that in the distance a very fat back with gold-braid collar sits sideways and a fat hand disposes of various papers—he is part of the one-and-only table, of course. The tall lean alpaca jacket, with a face of yellow stone and a big black moustache, moves from the outer doorway, glowers at our filled cups, and goes to the tin altar and touches the handles of the two vessels: just touches them to an arrangement: as one who should say: These are mine. What dirty foreigner dares help himself!

As quickly as possible we stagger up from the long dungeon where the alpaca jackets are swooping like blue-bottles upon the coffee pots, into the air. There the carpenter is waiting for us, like a spider.

"Isn't the sea a little quieter?" says the q-b wistfully. She is growing paler.

"No, Signora—how should it be?" says the gaunt-faced carpenter. "The wind is waiting for us behind Cape Gallo. You see that Cape?" he points to a tall black cliff-front in the sea ahead. "When we get to that Cape we get the wind and the sea. Here"—he makes a gesture—"it is quite moderate."

"Ugh!" says the q-b, turning paler. "I'm going to lie down."

She disappears. The carpenter, finding me stony ground, goes forward, and I see him melting into the crowd of the innumerable crew that hovers on the lower-deck passage by the kitchen and the engines.

The clouds are flying fast overhead: and sharp and isolated come drops of rain, so that one thinks it must be spray. But no, it is a handful of rain. The ship swishes and sinks forward, gives a hollow thudding and rears slowly backward, along this pinkish lofty coast of Sicily that is just retreating into a bay. From the open sea comes the rain, come the long waves.

No shelter. One must go down. The q-b lies quietly in her bunk. The state-room is stale like a passage on the underground railway. No shelter, save near the kitchen and the engines, where there is a bit of warmth. The cook is busy cleaning fish, making the whiting bite their tails venomously at a little board just outside his kitchen-hole. A slow stream of kitchen filth swilkers back and forth along the ship's side. A gang of the crew leans near me—a larger gang further down. Heaven knows what they can all be—but they never do anything but stand in gangs and talk and eat and smoke cigarettes. They are mostly young—mostly Palermitan—with a couple of unmistakable Neapolitans, having the peculiar Neapolitan hangdog good looks, the chiselled cheek, the little black moustache, the large eyes. But they chew with their cheeks bulged out, and laugh with their fine, semi-sarcastic noses. The whole gang looks continually sideways. Nobody ever commands them—there seems to be absolutely no control. Only the fat engineer in grey linen looks as clean and as competent as his own machinery. Queer how machine-control puts the pride and self-respect into a man.

* * *

It is market day. We turn up the Largo Carlo-Felice, the second wide gap of a street, a vast but very short boulevard, like the end of something. Cagliari is like that: all bits and bobs. And by the side of the pavement are many stalls, stalls selling combs and collar-studs, cheap mirrors, handkerchiefs, shoddy Manchester goods, bed-ticking, boot-paste, poor crockery and so on. But we see also Madame of Cagliari going market-ing, with a servant accompanying her, carrying a huge grass-woven basket: or returning from marketing, followed by a small boy supporting one of these huge grasswoven baskets—like huge dishes—on his head, piled with bread, eggs, vegetables, a chicken, and so forth. Therefore we follow Madame going marketing, and find ourselves in the vast market-house, and it fairly glows with eggs: eggs in these great round dish-baskets of golden grass: but eggs in piles, in mounds, in heaps, a Sierra Nevada of eggs, glowing warm white. How they glow! I have never noticed it before. But they give off a pearly effulgence into the air, almost a warmth. A pearly-gold heat seems to come out of them. Myriads of eggs, glowing avenues of eggs.

And they are marked—60 centimes, 65 centimes. Ah, cries the q-b, I must live in Cagliari—for in Sicily the eggs cost 1.50 each.

This is the meat and poultry and bread market. There are stalls of new, various-shaped bread, brown and bright: there are tiny stalls of marvellous native cakes, which I want to taste; there is a great deal of meat and kid: and there are stalls of cheese, all cheeses, all shapes, all whitenesses, all the cream colours, on into daffodil yellow. Goat's cheese, sheep's cheese, Swiss cheese, Parmeggiano, stracchino, caciocavallo, torolone, how many cheeses I don't know the names of! But they cost about the same as in Sicily, eighteen francs, twenty francs, twenty-five francs the kilo. And there is lovely ham—thirty and thirty-five francs the kilo. There is a little fresh butter too—thirty or thirty-two francs the kilo. Most of the butter, however, is tinned in Milan. It costs the same as the fresh. There are splendid piles of salted black olives, and huge bowls of green salted olives. There are chickens and ducks and wildfowl: at eleven and twelve and fourteen francs a kilo. There is mortadella, the enormous Bologna sausage, thick as a church pillar: 16 francs: and there are various sorts of smaller sausage, salami, to be eaten in slices. A wonderful abundance of food, glowing and shining. We are rather late for fish, especially on Friday. But a bare-footed man offers us two weird objects from the Mediterranean, which teems with marine monsters.

The peasant women sit behind their wares, their homewoven linen skirts, hugely full, and of various colours, ballooning round them. The yellow baskets give off a glow of light. There is a sense of profusion once more. But alas, no sense of cheapness: save the eggs. Every month up goes the price of everything.

"I must come and live in Cagliari, to do my shopping here," says the q-b. "I must have one of those big grass baskets."

We went down to the little street—but saw more baskets emerging from a broad flight of stone stairs, enclosed. So up we went—and found ourselves in the vegetable market. Here the q-b was happier still. Peasant women, sometimes barefoot, sat in their tight little bodices and voluminous, coloured skirts behind the piles of vegetables, and never have I seen a lovelier show. The intense deep green of spinach seemed to predominate, and out of that came the monuments of curd-white and black-purple cauliflowers: but marvelous cauliflowers, like a flower show, the purple ones intense as great bunches of violets. From this green, white, and purple massing struck out the vivid rose-scarlet and blue-crimson of radishes, large radishes like little turnips in piles. Then the long, slim, grey-purple buds of artichokes, and dangling clusters of dates, and piles of sugar-dusty white figs and sombre-looking black figs, and bright burnt figs: basketfuls and basketfuls of figs. A few baskets of almonds, and many huge walnuts. Basket-pans of native raisins. Scarlet peppers like trumpets: magnificent fennels, so white and big and succulent: baskets of new potatoes: scaly kohlrabi: wild asparagus in bunches, yellow-budding sparacelli: big, clean-fleshed carrots: feathery salads with white hearts: long, brown-purple onions, and then, of course, pyramids of big oranges, pyramids of pale apples, and baskets of brilliant shiny mandarini, the little tangerine oranges with their green-black leaves. The green and vivid-coloured world of fruit-gleams I have never seen in such splendour as under the market roof at Cagliari: so raw and gorgeous. And all quite cheap, the one remaining cheapness, except potatoes. Potatoes of any sort are 1.40 or 1.50 the kilo.

"Oh!" cried the q-b, "if I don't live at Cagliari and come and do my shopping here, I shall die with one of my wishes unfulfilled."

But out of the sun it was cold, nevertheless. We went into the streets to try and get warm. The sun was powerful. But alas, as in southern towns generally, the streets are as sunless as wells.

So the q-b and I creep slowly along the sunny bits, and then perforce are swallowed by shadow. We look at the shops. But there is not much to see. Little frowsy provincial shops, on the whole.

But a fair number of peasants in the streets, the peasant women in rather ordinary costume: tight-bodiced, volume-skirted dresses of hand-woven linen or thickish cotton. The prettiest is of dark-blue-and-red, stripes-and-lines, intermingled, so made that the dark blue gathers round the waist into one colour, the myriad pleats hiding all the rosy red. But when she walks, the full-petticoated peasant woman, then the red goes flash-flash-flash, like a bird showing its colours. Pretty that looks in the sombre street. She has a plain light bodice with a peak: sometimes a little vest, and great full white sleeves, and usually a handkerchief or shawl loose knotted. It is charming the way they walk, with quick, short steps. When all is said and done, the most attractive costume for women, in my eye, is the tight little bodice and the many-pleated skirt, full and vibrating with movement. It has a charm which modern elegance lacks completely—a bird-like play in movement.

They are amusing, these peasant girls and women: so brisk and defiant. They have straight backs like little walls, and decided, well-drawn brows. And they are amusingly on the alert. There is no Eastern creeping. Like sharp, brisk birds they dart along the streets, and you feel they would fetch you a bang over the head as lief as look at you. Tenderness, thank heaven, does not seem to be a Sardinian quality. Italy is so tender—like cooked macaroni—yards and yards of soft tenderness ravelled round everything. Here men don't idealize women, by the look of things. Here they don't make those great leering eyes, the inevitable yours-to-command look of Italian males. When the men from the country look at these women, then it is mind-yourself, my lady. I should think the grovelling Madonna-worship is not much of a Sardinian feature. These women have to look out for themselves, keep their own backbone stiff and their knuckles hard. Man is going to be male lord if he can. And woman isn't going to give him too much of his own way either. So there you have it, the fine old martial split between the sexes. It is tonic and splendid, really, after so much sticky intermingling and backbone-less Madonna-worship. The Sardinian isn't looking for the "noble woman nobly planned." No, thank you. He wants that young madam over there, a young stiff-necked generation that she is. Far better sport than with the nobly-planned sort: hollow frauds that they are. Better sport too than with a Carmen, who gives herself away too much. In these women there is something shy and defiant and unget-at-able. The defiant, splendid split between the sexes, each absolutely determined to defend his side, her side from assault. So the meeting has a certain wild salty savour, each the deadly unknown to the other. And at the same time, each his own, her own native pride and courage taking the dangerous leap and scrambling back.

Give me the old salty way of love. How I am nauseated with sentiment and nobility, the macaroni slithery-slobbery mess of modern adorations.

* * *

The night was cold, the blankets flat and heavy, but one slept quite well till dawn. At seven o'clock it was a clear, cold morning, the sun not yet up. Standing at the bedroom window looking out, I could hardly believe my eyes, it was so like England, like Cornwall in the bleak parts, or Derbyshire uplands. There was a little paddock-garden at the back of the station, rather tumble-down, with two sheep in it. There were several forlorn-looking outbuildings, very like Cornwall. And then the wide, forlorn country road stretched away between borders of grass and low, drystone walls, towards a greystone farm with a tuft of trees, and a naked stone village in the distance. The sun came up yellow, the bleak country glimmered bluish and reluctant. The low, green hill-slopes were divided into fields, with low drystone walls and ditches. Here and there a stone barn rose alone, or with a few bare, windy trees attached. Two rough-coated winter horses pastured on the rough grass, a boy came along the naked, wide, grass-bordered high-road with a couple of milk cans, drifting in from nowhere: and it was all Cornwall, or a part of Ireland, that the old nostalgia for the Celtic regions began to spring up in me. Ah, those old, drystone walls dividing the fields—pale and granite-blenched! Ah, the dark, sombre grass, the naked sky! the forlorn horses in the wintry morning! Strange is a Celtic landscape, far more moving, disturbing, than the lovely glamour of Italy and Greece. Before the curtains of history lifted, one feels the world was like this—this Celtic bareness and sombreness and *air*. But perhaps it is not Celtic at all: Iberian. Nothing is more unsatisfactory than our conception of what is Celtic and what is not Celtic. I believe there were never any Celts, as a race.—As for the Iberians—!

Wonderful to go out on a frozen road, to see the grass in shadow bluish with hoar-frost, to see the grass in the yellow winter sunrise beams melting and going cold-twinkly. Wonderful the bluish, cold air, and things standing up in cold distance. After two southern winters, with roses blooming all the time, this bleakness and this touch of frost in the ringing morning go to my soul like an intoxication. I am so glad, on this lonely naked road, I don't know what to do with myself. I walk down in the shallow grassy ditches under the loose stone walls. I walk on the little ridge of grass, the little bank on which the wall is built, I cross the road across the frozen cow-droppings: and it is all so familiar to my *feet*, my very feet in contact, that I am wild as if I had made a discovery. And I realize that I hate limestone, to live on limestone or marble or any of those limy rocks. I hate them. They are dead rocks, they have no life—thrills for the feet. Even sandstone is much better. But granite! Granite is my favourite. It is so live under the feet, it has a deep sparkle of its own. I like its roundnesses—and I hate the jaggy dryness of limestone, that burns in the sun, and withers.

* * *

These automobiles in Italy are splendid. They take the steep, looping roads so easily, they seem to run so naturally. And this one was comfortable too.

The roads of Italy always impress me. They run undaunted over the most precipitous regions, and with curious ease. In England almost any such road, among the mountains at least, would be labelled three times dangerous and would be famous throughout the land as an impossible climb. Here it is nothing. Up and down they go, swinging about with complete sangfroid. There seems to have been no effort in their construction. They are so good, naturally, that one hardly notices what splendid gestures they represent. Of course, the surface is now often intolerably bad. And they are most of them roads which, with ten years' neglect, will become ruins. For they are cut through overhanging rock and scooped out of the sides of hills. But I think it is marvellous how the Italians have penetrated all their inaccessible regions, of which they have so many, with great high-roads: and how along these high-roads the omnibuses now keep up a perfect communication. The precipitous and craggily-involved land is threaded through and through with roads. There seems to be a passion for high-roads and for constant communication. In this the Italians have a real Roman instinct, *now*. For the roads are new.

The railways, too, go piercing through rock for miles and miles, and nobody thinks anything of it. The coast railway of Calabria, down to Reggio, would make us stand on our heads if we had it in England. Here it is a matter of course. In the same way I always have a profound admiration for their driving—whether of a great omnibus or of a motor-car. It all seems so easy, as if the man were part of the car. There is none of that beastly grinding, uneasy feeling one has in the north. A car behaves like a smooth, live thing, sensibly.

All the peasants have a passion for a high-road. They want their land opening out, opening out. They seem to hate the ancient Italian remoteness. They all want to be able to get out at a moment's notice, to get away—quick, quick. A village which is two miles off the high-road, even if it is perched like a hawk's nest on a peak, still chafes and chafes for the great road to come to it, chafes and chafes for the daily motor-bus connection with the railway. There is no placidity, no rest in the heart of the land. There is a fever of restless irritation all the time.

And yet the permanent way of almost every railway is falling into bad disrepair; the roads are shocking. And nothing seems to be done. Is our marvellous mechanical era going to have so short a bloom? Is the marvellous openness, the opened-out wonder of the land going to collapse quite soon, and the remote places lapse back into inaccessibility again? Who knows! I rather hope so.

The automobile took us rushing and winding up the hill, sometimes through cold, solid-seeming shadow, sometimes across a patch of sun. There was thin bright ice in the ruts, and deep grey hoar-frost on the grass. I cannot tell how the sight of the grass and bushes, heavy with frost and wild—in their own primitive wildness—charmed me. The slopes of the steep wild hills came down shaggy and bushy, with a few berries lingering, and the long grass stalks sere with the frost. Again, the dark valley sank below like a ravine, but shaggy, bosky, unbroken. It came upon me how I loved the sight of the blue-shadowed, tawny-tangled winter with its frosty standstill. The young oaks keep their brown leaves. And doing so, surely they are best with a thin edge of rime.

One begins to realize how old the real Italy is, how man-gripped and how withered. England is far more wild and savage and lonely, in her country parts. Here since endless centuries man has tamed the impossible mountain-side into terraces, he has quarried the rock, he has fed his sheep among the thin woods, he has cut his boughs and burnt his charcoal, he has been half domesticated even among the wildest fastnesses. This is what is so attractive about the remote places, the Abruzzi, for example. Life is so primitive, so pagan, so strangely heathen and half-savage. And yet it is human life. And the wildest country is half humanized, half brought under. It is all conscious. Wherever one is in Italy, either one is conscious of the present, or of the medieval influences, or of the far, mysterious gods of the early Mediterranean. Wherever one is, the place has its conscious genius. Man has lived there and brought forth his consciousness there and in some way brought that place to consciousness, given it its expression, and, really, finished it. The expression may be Proserpine, or Pan, or even the strange "shrouded gods" of the Etruscans or the Sikels, none the less it is an expression.

The land has been humanized, through and through: and we in our own tissued consciousness bear the results of this humanization. So that for us to go to Italy and to *penetrate* into Italy is like a most fascinating act of self-discovery—back, back down the old ways of time. Strange and wonderful chords awake in us, and vibrate again after many hundreds of years of complete forgetfulness.

And then—and then—there is a final feeling of sterility. It is all worked out. It is all known: *connu, connu!*

This Sunday morning, seeing the frost among the tangled, still savage bushes of Sardinia, my soul thrilled again. This was not all known. This was not all worked out. Life was not only a process of rediscovering backwards. It is that, also; and it is that intensely. Italy has given me back I know not what of myself, but a very, very great deal. She has found for me so much that was lost: like a restored Osiris. But this morning in the omnibus I realize that, apart from the great rediscovery backwards, which one *must* make before one can be whole at all, there is a move forwards. There are unknown, unworked lands where the salt has not lost its savour. But one must have perfected oneself in the great past first.

* * *

We descended into a deep narrow valley, to the road-junction and the canteen house, then up again, up and up sharp to Tonara, our village we had seen in the sun yesterday. But we were approaching it from the back. As we swerved into the sunlight, the road took a long curve on to the open ridge between two valleys. And there in front we saw a glitter of scarlet and white. It was in slow motion. It was a far-off procession, scarlet figures of women, and a tall image moving away from us, slowly, in the Sunday morning. It was passing along the level sunlit ridge above a deep, hollow valley. A close procession of women glittering in scarlet, white and black, moving slowly in the distance beneath the grey-yellow buildings of the village on the crest, towards an isolated old church: and all along this narrow upland saddle as on a bridge of sunshine itself.

Were we not going to see any more? The bus turned and rushed along the now level road and then veered. And there beyond, a little below, we saw the procession *coming.* The bus faded to a standstill, and we climbed out. Above us, old and mellowed among the smooth rocks and the bits of flat grass, was the church, tangling its bell. Just in front, above, were old half-broken houses of stone. The road came gently winding up to us, from what was evidently two villages ledged one above the other upon the steep summit of the south slope. Far below was the south valley, with a white puff of engine steam.

And slowly chanting in the near distance, curving slowly up to us on the white road between the grass, came the procession. The high morning was still. We stood all on this ridge above the world, with the deeps of silence below on the right. And in a strange, brief, staccato monody chanted the men, and in quick, light rustle of women's voices came the responses. Again the men's voices! The white was mostly men, not women. The priest in his robes, his boys near him, was leading the chanting. Immediately behind him came a small cluster of bare-headed, tall, sunburnt men all in golden-velveteen corduroy, mountain peasants, bowing beneath a great life-size seated image of Saint Anthony of Padua. After these a number of men in the costume, but with the white linen breeches hanging wide and loose almost to the ankles, instead of being tucked into the black gaiters. So they seemed very white beneath the black kilt frill. The black frieze body-vest was cut low, like an evening suit, and the stocking-caps were variously perched. The men chanted in low, hollow, melodic tones. Then came the rustling chime of the women. And the procession crept slowly, aimlessly forward in time with the chant. The great image rode, rigid, and rather foolish.

After the men was a little gap—and then the brilliant wedge of the women. They were packed two by two, close on each other's heels, chanting inadvertently when their turn came, and all in brilliant, beautiful costume. In front were the little girl-children, two by two, immediately following the tall men in peasant black-and-white. Children demure and conventional, in vermilion, white and green—little girl-children with long skirts of scarlet cloth down to their feet, green-banded near the bottom: with white aprons bordered with vivid green and mingled colour: having little scarlet, purple-bound, open boleros over the full white skirts: and black head-cloths folded across their little chins, just leaving the lips clear, the face framed in black. Wonderful little girl-children, perfect and demure in the stiffish, brilliant costume, with black headdress! Stiff as Velasquez princesses! The bigger girls followed, and then the mature women, a close procession. The long vermilion skirts with their green bands at the bottom flashed a solid moving mass of colour, softly swinging, and the white aprons with their bands of brilliant mingled green seemed to gleam. At the throat the full-bosomed white shirts were fastened with big studs of gold filigree, two linked filigree globes: and the great white sleeves billowed from the scarlet, purplish-and-green-edged boleros. The faces came nearer to us, framed all round in the dark cloths. All the lips still sang responses, but all the eyes watched us. So the softly-swaying coloured body of the procession came up to us. The poppy-scarlet smooth cloth rocked in fusion, the bands and bars of emerald green seemed to burn across the red and the showy white, the dark eyes peered and stared at us from under the black snood, gazed back at us with raging curiosity, while the lips moved automatically in chant. The bus had run into the inner side of the road, and the procession had to press round it, towards the sky-line, the great valley lying below.

The priest stared, hideous St Anthony cockled a bit as he passed the butt end of the big grey automobile, the peasant men in gold-coloured corduroy, old, washed soft, were sweating under the load and still singing with opened lips, the loose white breeches of the men waggled as they walked on with their hands behind their backs, turning again, to look at us. The big, hard hands, folded behind black kilt-frill! The women, too, shuffled slowly past, rocking the scarlet and the bars of green, and all twisting as they sang, to look at us still more. And so the procession edged past the bus, and was trailing upwards, curved solid against the skyline towards the old church. From behind, the geranium scarlet was intense; one saw the careful, curiously cut backs of the shapen boleros, poppy-red, edged with mauve-purple and green, and the white of the shirt just showing at the waist. The full sleeves billowed out, the black head-cloths hung down to a point. The pleated skirts swung slowly, the broad band of green accentuating the motion. Indeed that is what it must be for, this thick, rich band of jewel green, to throw the wonderful horizontal motion back and forth, back and forth, of the suave vermil-ion, and give that static, Demeter splendour to a peasant motion, so magnificent in colour, geranium and malachite.

All the costumes were not exactly alike. Some had more green, some had less. In some the sleeveless boleros were of a darker red, and some had poorer aprons, without such gorgeous bands at the bottom. And some were evidently old; probably thirty years old: still perfect and in keeping, reserved for Sunday and high holidays. A few were darker, ruddier than the true vermilion. This varying of the tone intensified the beauty of the shuffling woman-host.

When they had filed into the grey, forlorn little church on the ridge-top just above us, the bus started silently to run on to the rest-point below, whilst we climbed back up the little rock-track to the church. When we came to the side-door we found the church quite full. Level with us as we stood in the open side doorway, we saw kneeling on the bare stone flags the little girl-children, and behind them all the women clustered kneeling upon their aprons, with hands negligently folded, filling the church to the further doorway, where the sun shone: the bigger west-end doorway. In the shadow of the whitewashed, bare church all these kneeling women with their colour and their black head-cloths looked like some thick bed of flowers, geranium, black-hooded above. They all knelt on the naked, solid stone of the pavement.

There was a space in front of the geranium little girl-children, then the men in corduroys, gold-soft, with dark round heads, kneeling awkwardly in reverence; and then the queer, black cuirasses and full white sleeves of grey-headed peasant men, many bearded. Then just in front of them the priest in his white vestment, standing exposed, and just baldly beginning an address. At the side of the altar was seated, large and important, the modern, simpering, black-gowned Anthony of Padua, nursing a boy-child. He looked a sort of male Madonna.

"Now," the priest was saying, "blessed Saint Anthony shows you in what way you can be Christians. It is not enough that you are not Turks. Some think they are Christians because they are not Turks. It is true you are none of you Turks. But you have still to learn how to be good Christians. And this you can learn from our blessed Saint Anthony. Saint Anthony, etc., etc. . . ."

The contrast between Turks and Christians is still forceful in the Mediterranean, where the Mohammedans have left such a mark. But how the word *cristiani, cristiani,* spoken with a peculiar priestly unction, gets on my nerves. The voice is barren in its homily. And the women are all intensely watching the q-b and me in the doorway, their folded hands are very negligently held together.

"Come away!" say I. "Come away, and let them listen."

We left the church crowded with its kneeling host, and dropped down past the broken houses towards the omnibus, which stood on a sort of level outlook place, a levelled terrace with a few trees, standing silent over the valley. It should be picketed with soldiers having arquebuses. And I should have welcomed a few thorough-paced infidels, as a leaven to this dreary Christianity of ours.

But it was a wonderful place. Usually, the life-level is reckoned as sea-level. But here, in the heart of Sardinia, the life-level is high as the golden-lit plateau, and the sea-level is somewhere far away, below, in the gloom, it does not signify. The life-level is high up, high and sun-sweetened and among rocks.

We stood and looked below, at the puff of steam, far down the wooded valley where we had come yesterday. There was an old, low house on this eagle-perching piazza. I would like to live there. The real village—or rather two villages, like an earring and its pendant—lay still beyond, in front, ledging near the summit of the long, long steep wooded slope, that never ended till it ran flush to the depths away below there in shadow.

CYRIL CONNOLLY
1903–1974

Essayist, journalist, lover of food and wine and of France, distinguished editor and reviewer, Connolly has been called by Kenneth Clark "without doubt the most gifted man of his generation." Yet he severely disappointed expectation, and ended less as a great writer than a wit and critic and gossip, a hedonist skilled in deep secret self-contempt.

He came from a well-to-do background and was educated at Eton and at Balliol College, Oxford. Very early his fantasies began to take travel form. His grandmother remembered his sitting on her knee and "making out a lovely tour for me on the map." His early travels were with his family to Tangier and Corsica, and by the age of eighteen he had had his first taste of France, especially Provence. Soon, largely during school and college vacations, he became acquainted with Germany and Austria, Hungary, Italy, Spain, Switzerland, North Africa, Greece, and Turkey. At twenty he asserted: "My love of traveling is a consuming passion."

During the late 1920s he became a literary journalist in London, writing for the New Statesman *and later the* Sunday Times. *Despite his numerous, flagrantly intelligent books of criticism and literary commentary, his most distinguished achievement may prove to be his editorship of the monthly journal* Horizon, *which from 1939 to 1950 kept alive in the midst of wartime privations and brutalities the most elegant traditional values of art, literature, and travel. In 1944 he brought out* The Unquiet Grave *(by "Palinurus"), an intense collection of opinions and aperçus designed as a counterweight to the corruption of taste and the coarsening of perception occasioned by the war. His standards, for books, people, and places, as well as for food and drink, were high, and he did not exempt himself. "I have always disliked myself at any given moment," he wrote. "The total of such moments is my life."*

To Noel Blakiston

February 13, 1927
Madrid Palace Hotel.

Dear Noel,

Thank you so much for your letter, send me some more. They make half the joy of arriving at places so do send some to the Hotel de Madrid Seville and the Reina Cristina Algeciras. I am writing to you after dinner smoking a large cigar. This is a very grand hotel, all light and carpets and a melodious tango band. A Jack Hotel—as opposed to a Jake hotel with its large selection of English books or a Gabby Hotel with its glass cases of diamonds and pyjamas and love among the lift boys. A Cyril hotel should have a Moor who makes coffee, a Sligger Hotel is always jolly and the 3rd on the list in Baedeker then there is the Roach hotel with its stables and steaks and strangers arriving at midnight. Of the Cyril-Noel hotels I will not speak for they are shining and inaccessible peaks that the average millionaire is content to look at with a wild surmise—did you know (which I did not) that the place we had tea at in Paris is the dearest hotel in Europe and the hardest to get a room in—I have been thinking of the hotel in Seo where we overslept our dinner and you read Wuthering Heights. The more I think of Tripoli, the more I think we must go there, the more I think of where we must go the more I think of Tripoli—it was mooted that I should go there before we arranged the Seo trip do you remember and I can think of nothing nicer than to hold Africa and the desert and a real oasis in your company with a few Greek temples to soften our return—could you try and find out about boats, which go chiefly from Syracuse, also sometimes from Naples, I think once a week from S. If you could find out if it is possible to go and spend 2 or 3 days in Tarabulus (el Gharb) and get back to Syracuse you could arrange your exeat better. The line is the Societa Italia, the fares not excessive. I think we may have over fifty pounds for our jaunt so we should be able to manage it, if there is any left we could spend an Athanasian day in Munich on the way back with Jack. I can't say how lovely it is to be in Spain again—I sat and ecstasied in the wagon restaurant after Irun, to think that it surrounded me as thick as the darkness we (you, me, Jack) so much assume that it is the best country that one forgets how hard it is to explain why the sleeper reminded me of ours to Toulouse and I woke to see the sun rise over the snows of Guadarrama and the tableland as broad and bracing as the Spanish carriages. Avila was impressive, gaunt and desolate "of barren acres simple minded King"—the snow lay in wisps under its Romanesque towers and an icy wind blew through its high crusader gateways "realm nobly poor and proudly desolate" where Santayana and Santa Teresa first saw the light—the drive was exciting, over the usual tawny waste with shepherds shivering in the winter sun and muffled herdsmen staring from among the rocks, the cape carts, or the flocks beside the frozen pools—the sun shone all the way and the snow and forests of the Guadarrama rise in front like a wall, we climbed a very good pass with Font Romeu country all round and descended to the bleak Escorial, a mixture of Princetown gaol and the Brompton Oratory. I was not disappointed for I had not expected more and the last vestiges of Logan's independence (he had insisted on seeing it) vanished like Chilling celery—the El Greco however was magnificent and I bought a reproduction of it for you. I also have our railway tickets and will send you mine for Pat's museum—(only in Spain could one escape with two unpunched Cooks tickets from Bordeaux to Irun, Irun to Medina, Medina to Avila, and a supplementary one!) There were no photos worth buying alas— the approach to Madrid was lovely with no suburbs only a distant view of it across the plain and a climb through woods and public gardens to the heart of the town. O wild and bubbly tangos and their long forsaken Sidney Shusha wails! We stay here till Tuesday when we go to Toledo and thence by the Mancha and the Cervantes country—(fancy living like Don Quixote at Argamasilla!) to the Sierra Morena and the south. Ronnie has a record called the Danse Macabre (Saint Saens) which somehow seems to give the atmosphere of the tableland of the Castiles. I expect my high water mark of feeling to be the ride from Granada to Motril and Malaga—I shall do it alone, by bus—and spend a night at Motril among the cocoanuts and sugar cane (*el mes era de Mayo quando hace la calor!* the month was May when it began to get hot!) I hope the Theocritus arrived—do read him before we go as it is impossible to read anything in the South I think, imaginary worlds pale before the reality. As to Blake I think he is an indispensable. I worshipped the Marriage at Eton and have worshipped almost everything of his since but stuck in the prophetic books. I think he has the rare Eliot-Isaiah quality of earthy mysticism as opposed to the ethereal apocalyptic kind, songs of experience are the best I think and he has the perfect desultory lyric gift like Chinese poems and the Coplas. Rimbaud is the French Blake— *oisive jeunesse* is like a song of experience and *la Saison* like Heaven and Hell. Then Blake is superbly English and rural without being artificial and blends the wisdom of the serpent with the innocence and spontaneity of childhood, in fact he is a good man, subtly childish and brightly cruel. Spain one loves for what it is and takes the wrinkled sulky little millionaires with the forlorn peasants or the ruddy perspiring parish priests. In time I will like you in this way and am surely nearer to it than I was and in this way you probably like me with my drear pedantry and morning beard. Roach I feel was something of a gaunt caballero and at home in the straw strewn venta or the noisy parador. He was often heard mumbling strange lists of names, Covarrúbias, Guadalajara, Beniajan, Jimenes de Libar—most lonely mountains, the Libar, I feel rather sick from mixing cigar and lemonade so I don't think this letter will last out the page—it is amazing how often one feels sick, especially travelling. I was sick at Messina station when last in Sicily don't let's go there. I think Tripoli and Astrakhan are the only places that have inspired images as vivid as places I haven't seen in Spain so it will be a real pilgrimage to go there. I don't much mind if we do quarrel all the time, it will come to the same afterwards and presence—you know the Athanasian saw. I too can't say how I wish you were with me but if you read between the lines you will see I have been saying nothing else, and you appear almost continually sometimes as a vast green overcoat and a red scarf and sometimes as a soothing glow. Thank you very much for the photo by the way *quamvis ille niger, quamvis tu candidus esses* [although it was black, you were white]. Send me any more that you find—the band is waxing gayer and the harsh babel of Castilian voices rages around me. I think I shall soon be beginning to understand you, but by then, I expect, you will have changed! What about a tower at Motril? by the sea and in an African huerta of steaming fruit trees with a view down the hill to the blue fields of cane which smell sweet at night and back to the snows of the Sierra Nevada from whence cool breezes blow—would it be too luscious or would the wildness (40 miles from a railway station) and the absence of the academic blessing make it durable? I feel a villa in Italy would be death—if you like Italy better than Spain will you tell me—it will be a terrible scene.

To Noel Blakiston

Magdalene College,
Cambridge,   *February 15, 1927*
Inglaterra.   [Postcard of Toledo.].

We have been here all day which is rather wet but the town very fine and the gorge of the Tajo lovely and some of the cloisters and Moorish walls—I don't think it goes into the holy places though and it is too trippery to be as exciting as Seo or Trujillo looks. I have a superb guide book the Murray's Spain of 1845 done by Richard Ford in superb English and fine romantic efficiency—it is a book to read at Cambridge even more than in Spain. O Tripoli.

To Noel Blakiston

February 1927
Granja Nacional, Granada.

Dear Noel,

This washy ink proclaims Abroad. Thank you so much for your letters, I sent an Armada to you between Paris and Toledo. I hope some arrived. Tell me the result of the career conference which is worrying me—I am afraid the feast of St. Pepys is ill propitious to any romantic conclusion. There has been a lovely sunset which I have watched over the superb snows of the Sierra Nevada and later among the peasant carts and trains of mules winding across the bridge of the Genil. I am drinking some incredible kind of tea, infusion of garbage, which they have given me in mistake for something else—I will wait till after dinner where there is a better pen and try and translate coplas till then.

We had a lovely journey here from Madrid first over the desolate Mancha which was white and sunny, we saw Argamarilla in the distance and then came the Sierra Morena green and aromatic and deserted mountains stretching away in the sun, then a good gorge and Andalusia represented by a beggar boy singing a trailing song beside the carriage and a thousand miles of green corn rising along the Guadalquivir like English tropics and transfigured downs till they vanished in a golden Claude like haze, most soothing and so wide. Then more mountains and the dark and finally here with a full moon, a splitting headache, a letter from you, and bed to the noise of rushing streams. This is really one of the best places in the world, the air is crisp and bright and though it is still winter it is such gaudy winter and so warm to sit in the sun. The moorish park of the Alhambra is all oaks and elms and ivy and you would think it England till you see the white houses, slot windows, caves, prickly pears, and precipices of the Albaicin or the green vega of Granada still as a lake below or the snows and glaciers of the Sierra Nevada behind or the Alhambra perched above like an apricot. Inside it is a miracle of warmth and grace and the myrtles smell in the sun and the gold fish swim in the tanks and the doves coo. We walked down the cypress avenue to the Generalife of which you have the post card this afternoon but after the Alhambra the best place is Granada itself where every street has some unknown palace or grim prison and all seem different temperatures, white and narrow and ending in green sky or broad and brown and arcaded with the white snow mountains at the end. Assuredly we will come here on our grand tour. It is odd being here again and remembering places where I missed you and where I wrote to you or sent frantic wires. Psalm tunes recur at sunset but it is hot and southern and I can do nothing to lessen your odium, for it is not even too hot but deliciously fresh and good walking weather as at Font Romeu. I think a lot of our voyage but so far no image is clear but a warm deck smelling of tar and us under an awning and over the jade Syrtis awaiting palms. I am much moved by the Spanish coplas which I have been finding and which seem to rival Greek epigrams and Catullus or Waley for passion, subtlety and desultory song.

To Noel Blakiston

March 7, 1927
Café Central, Tangier.

Dear Noel,

I write in the Petit Socco, a square about as big as chamber on allowance night to contain Jews, Arabs, Berbers, Spaniards, French, English and Americans—it is dusk and I am sitting out on the pavement having my boots cleaned, in a moment the cannon will be fired for the Arabs to break their fast—They do not eat from 3.30 in the morning to half past six nor smoke nor drink all Ramadan and do all their ordinary work. It is rather a lesson in fasting as they never talk about it and don't seem to be any the worse for it besides doing it whether they are rich men or Americanised touts—there is a romance don't you think about the rich Jews and Moslems whose houses are of mud outside and gold within; who dress and feed like paupers and are held in respect like the patriarchs and the sons of the patriarchs, there are good Arabs here who play roulette and baccarat all the evening quite impassively. They have thin faces, large eyes and moustaches that turn down like Bellini's Mahommed II. At Tetuan live many Jews with the keys of their old

houses in Cordova and Granada, from when they left with the Moors—
the Jewish girls are very lovely in the biblical way and in Fez wear
gorgeous mediaeval dresses of green velvet and gold braid like pictures
on bible markers. Arab women look more like oxen than you would think
it possible for human beings, the good point about Spanish I think is
their homely wit, the "aire y gracia" that sits so well and earthily on their
matronly shoulders. The worst types round here without exception seem
to be young English officers who glare, English women of the sour,
drawling, militant, gray haired type (there are few Florences), American
men and French Bourgeoisie who don't penetrate N. of Rabat luckily—
there you may see the papa, red and round and black and bloated
gobbling like a turkey cock, there is madame mean and managing, there
is le petit in his velvet shorts, his beret, and his exhibitionism, and there
is the dreary boulevard, the grand magasins du Louvre, the officialism
and sordidity of their native land—a bitter letter but I have been anti-
French for some time and am always surprised to confirm it, I feel like
a good patriot of the 1820's—then English really are intolerable abroad.
The cannon has just gone amid cheers and soon the children carrying
bowls of stew home will fill the street. About nationalities I think the
French are rather awful, the Italians, at least the Fascists (cynical,
theatrical, bête) worse and America, at least U.S.A. the private view of
the ruin of the world—at least of all the things one likes in the world
but if one accepts this absolutely, e.g. that it has got to be and will be
ruined (standardised) and that America is not necessarily the cause but
only the most advanced case of material civilisation wedded to vulgarity,
there remain consolations, such as finding places that aren't spoilt and
not being surprised by their destruction into the attitude of the grumbling, sentimental, oldie worldie type—on the other hand Spaniards one
likes without explanations, Germans are clean and decent and reasonable and artistic even in factories, Austrians are gay and northern,
Russians probably interesting, Arabs charming, Greeks sanctified and
Bulgarians are nice too because they are not Roumanians. The Portuguese we allow because they have carried Dagoism to its highest point
and because they have good costumes, the trouble is what to make of
the English, hypocrites, bores, fools, glarers and yet the most just and
wholesome and honourable people in the world—one must distinguish
between England and the English, between the English abroad and the
English at home, between the English who have made liberty practicable and the public school bigot "service" class—then there are more
exceptions to the type in England than anywhere else in the world don't
you think—it is the stronghold of individualism which is the only quality

that Americans cannot buy (distinction comes with the third generation)—I think Americans are the cure for Anglophobia—a dry letter this
but I must dogmate on this subject—of course French language is good
and Italians are not always a nation of Babington Smiths popping paper
bags. Greenness is vital isn't it—

Cyril

To Noel Blakiston

April 21, 1927
Hotel Astoria, Wien.

Dear Noel,

I am afraid you must have had a bloody night. I had a large and
lugubrious dinner and stayed in the Mitropa till Regensburg and then
found 3rd so full and painful that I changed in to first till the Austrian
frontier and then was too tired to leave it—after I had been marched
through miles of corridors to get my 2 visas—which only my lonely glory
in the empty first class carriage made obtainable at all I think—then I
stayed on it till Vienna so I start with an enormous deficit—my feet
ached so—did yours—however I had a good night and dreamt you were
an angel—you were barely recognisable and flew about "looking after"
me in a more than mortal way, very bright and straight and wearing the
fixed unreal smile of royalty. Still it was stirring at least the moment I
recognised you was. I have been low to-day and loneliness is gnawing.
quid valet omne decus, desit is cura sodalis [what good is all beauty if
a friend's interest is lacking]? I looked at pictures in the morning and
was very moved by Brueghel, chiefly as a satirist, he makes a ghastly
presentation of Renaissance Nordic bourgeoisie, puppet figures against
a dull cold sky, mirthless enjoyment, snivelling children, grovelling men
and nagging women, all the loves of all the Harry's and gluttonous beery
professional entertainments on faces blank and cold—he draws human
beings like little fat bugs and they look like Japanese paintings but does
northern landscape with superb insight and sympathy, especially some
cattle going along a road on an autumn evening. I will try and get you
a post card of it—His realism with people, "surrealisme" with places,
is like Crabbe with his dowdy villains and inspiring views—Vienna
seems a nice town and much less domineering than Munich—the people seem frank and idle and the parks and streets are good—but I pine,

I don't know what I shall do—rush back to England in a day or so probably and then wish I had stayed abroad. I am in for a bad backwash after Sicily like an elderly man who has suddenly lost his job. . . . I shall only tell people we went to Sicily unless questioned, so jealous do I feel of Taggiura and the market—which-is-not-to-be-named. What was good I think was that travelling in luxury we yet managed to live austerely—at any rate in spirit—for we were never bloated, satiated, or over-weening as rich people when young often are. I think the places were largely responsible for this, Castelvetrano for instance seems as if we went there on a walking tour—but I think all the same we have concurred with our sage and serious poet Spenser, and behaved like the true flag wagging Christian—I am skilfully writing this letter from 7 1/2–9 P.M. so as to save by having no dinner—the more I think of our Eden conversations the more coherent and valuable they seem. I do believe we have really reached a system and can begin to be great poets in the Santayanic sense—I mean I think we had noticed all these things before but only in one island did we really estimate their importance which was a discovery in itself—let us keep it secret till Chilling and then see how we can make it . . .

I have written enough I feel and have saved the price of a dinner! Thank you for coming to Sicily and for contributing to the most sustained ecstasy of my life and its most perfect αυτάρχεια [self-sufficiency]—o words, words, words—but thanks all the same—you know though glib I am not self-delusive and I don't tell everyone with perfect sincerity that I shall never be able to travel with anyone else again. (Of course I shall travel with them probably but I mean that there will be a reservation in every moment and a condescension in every enthusiasm)—for I on honey dew have fed and drunk the milk of paradise. Don't gush.

I send you the stamps—it seems a pity to halve them and my father will be satisfied with the snails. How was Cologne? You must be just about at Cambridge. O Noel!

Love from Cyril

From THE UNQUIET GRAVE
(1944)

A CHARM AGAINST THE GROUP MAN
THE MAGIC CIRCLE

[*Hic est quod petis*: Here is something to be desired]

Streets of Paris, pray for me; beaches in the sun, pray for me; ghosts of the lemurs, intercede for me; planetree and laurel-rose, shade me; summer rain on quays of Toulon, wash me away.

* * *

In the break-up of religions and creeds there is but one deity whose worshippers have multiplied without a set-back. The Sun. In a few years there will be a stampede towards this supreme anæsthetic. Scotland will pour itself into Southern England, Canada into the U.S.A., the U.S.A, dwindle to Florida, California and New Mexico, while Southern Englanders will have migrated en masse to the Mediterranean. The temperate zone, especially for women, is becoming uninhabitable. Let us leave England to retired Generals and culture-diffusionists, goose-fleshed politicians and bureaucrats, while the rest of us heliotropes cluster nearer to the great bronze disk of church-emptying Apollo, hardener of heart and skin.

*   *   *

Peeling off the kilometres to the tune of "Blue Skies", sizzling down the long black liquid reaches of Nationale Sept, the plane trees going sha-sha-sha through the open window, the windscreen yellowing with crushed midges, she with the Michelin beside me, a handkerchief binding her hair . . .

"Le coeur a ses raisons [The heart has its reasons]"—and so have rheumatism and 'flu. The sole of the foot, the nape of the neck still recollect the embrace of the Mediterranean—pale water streaked with sapphirine sea-shadow, translucent under the Esterel.

REVISITING GREECE
(1963)

After examining a clutch of well-made travel books, I have sometimes wondered for how many pages one could keep it up by setting out to tell the truth, not only about places but about the inadequacy of our feelings. (I have known the Acropolis to resemble a set of false teeth in a broken palate.) When at last we take our long-wished-for holiday what really happens?

There is, first, the period of preparation (in a sense the only time we are abroad); guidebooks are compared; experts are consulted; a mirage of a brown, lean summer self descending on an obese island dances before our eyes and we are convincingly importuned by the wrong clothes, the wrong books, the wrong introductions. "Of course you will need a white dinner jacket and a cummerbund"; "you must take the *whole* of Pausanias"; "an ultra-violet filter"; "stout walking shoes"; "the rubber flippers should be made to measure."

At twenty we travel to discover ourselves, at thirty for love, at forty out of greed and curiosity, at fifty for a revelation. Irresponsible, illiterate, shedding all ties and cares, we await the visitation, the rebirth. Gradually the present dissolves, England becomes totally unreal; we have in fact already left, not yet airborne but anxiety-cradled; "if the flippers are not ready, they cannot possibly be sent on"; "you quite understand that these traveler's checks are not negotiable on Mount Athos"; "don't go to the new hotel but the other one"; "don't go to the old hotel"; "there are three new hotels"; "Corfu is the place for you: it has everything"; "yes, if you like a green island. I prefer Mikonos"; "it's never too hot on Corfu"; "you would hate Corfu."

D-Day. Running in the new dark glasses in the car to the airport. Livid clouds, infra-red buses, a lurid day-of-judgment air about the hoardings along the clotted avenue. Signs of panic, cleverly concealed, as I board the plane, where I suffer from a private phobia, dispelled only by champagne, that the signal "Fasten your safety-belts" is staying on for the whole voyage.

Paris: the heat advances across the tarmac, our gaoler for the next six weeks. "Thick brown overcoat, stout walking shoes, whole of Pausanias," it mumbles; "Mr. Connolly? I think we can take care of all that." Inevitable contrast between London and Paris, the one muffled under its summer cloud-cap, all Wimbledon and roses, the other with a migraine of politics, bleached and persilled in the heat. The bookstall at London Airport for a nation of magazine readers—if that; at Le Bourget full of expensive works on art and philosophy. The paralysis of suburbia contrasted with the animation of the *banlieue* [outskirts] where a fair is in progress and a horse-drawn dray of children jingles under the catalpas.

How much of a holiday is spent lying gasping on one's back, in planes, trains, cabins, beaches, and hotel bedrooms, the guidebook held aloft like an awning? We really travel twice—as a physical object resembling a mummy or small wardrobe-trunk which is shuttled about at considerable expense; and as a mind married to a "Guide Bleu," always reading about the last place or the next one.

It is suddenly apparent that the heat permits no reading of any kind; whole areas of consciousness must be evacuated, the perimeter of sensation shortened; no past, no future. Only the guidebook survives and the other books we have brought sneak to the bottom of the suitcase. And now the Seven Indispensables perform their ghostly jig from pocket to pocket. The passport, the traveler's checks, the tickets, the dark glasses, the reading glasses, the pen, the comb. Where are they? I could have sworn I had them a moment ago.

A flying visit to Versailles to see the *petits appartements* rendered famous by the Pompadour, the Dubarry and Madame de Mitford. Intense disappointment; so much redecoration, and everywhere the milling multitudes, locusts of the post-war summer. Illumination: *The human eye deteriorates all it looks at.* Why is the decoration of the House of the Vettii at Pompeii so much less exciting than the new excavations? Because the human eye has faded the colors, vulgarized the painting. The camera also enfeebles its subject, and being photographed too often I believe to cause cancer of the soul.

And now, Venice, city of sore throats, frayed tempers, and leaking wallets; alas, never the same for me since I reviewed Hemingway's last novel but one. Much as I disliked the book I remain obsessed by his terrible colonel. I drink Valpolicella and take the fatal stroll to Harry's Bar, stopping on the little bridge where the colonel had a heart attack on his way from his wine to his martinis. How he would have hated the Biennale! So much painting that should never have come South of the Alps, North of the Po, West of Suez, or East of Saint Louis, all maltreated by the heat, the humidity, and the merciless light—except the paintings which have some secret poster quality, Delvaux's clustering cowlike nudes or Bacon's agonizing tycoons. Art is bottled sunshine and should never be exposed to it.

And everywhere art critics, never a painter; symbol of the age of culture-diffusion when publishers and village-explainers travel while authors have to stay at home, when painters in Maida Vale hear from their dealers in Mozambique or Mogador, when Byron would have received a postcard: "Dear B. London must be very hot. Just off to Ravenna to join the Galignanis and then to meet some Greek publishers at Missolonghi. Hope to be able to do something for you. How goes the Canto?—Yrs., John Murray."

Revisit the equestrian statue of Colleone in its dingy square. The base is too high. Better in a photograph. Failure to experience any emotion over Tintoretto. Horror of Surrealist masters in Biennale. Moved by nothing later than Pompeii. Great paintings should be kept under lock and key and shown as seldom as wonder working images. The real connoisseurs of art were the Pharaohs; they took it with them. Intoxication with Venetian gardens, the oleander drooping over the canal at some scabrous corner, the ubiquitous freshwater sea smell and the best drink in Europe, a tumbler of ice-cold peach juice in the colonel's bar. More hordes of milling tourists, squeaking *lederhosen;* Clapham Junction of the mechanized masses in the Piazza. Everybody is somebody. Nobody is anybody. Everyone is everywhere.

At last the boat: survival of an earlier form of travel, obeying the strange psychology of "on board ship." Whom we hate on the first day we shall love on the last, whom we greet on the first we shall not bid farewell; boredom will become its own reward and change suddenly to ecstasy. The *Achilleus* is a charmed vessel, trim, white, gay, its inmates friendly and delightful. The islands of the lagoon bob at their moorings as we churn through the warm night and the next blue day past Monte Gargano and Brindisi, with its lemon ices and Roman column, and across to Corfu where we stay for three hours instead of a week, just time to see the famous view at Canoni, so called because the tourist is fired at it like a cannonball.

That evening we are streaking through the Corinth Canal like mercury rising in a thermometer. The *Achilleus* has now gone completely Greek. The food is interesting and local, the crew sings, the married couples no longer flash their signals of distress, "save me, rescue me." The passengers crane over the rail to where the distant corona of Athens glows above the dark bulk of Salamis. We enter the sooty bustle of Piraeus as the last evening steamers beetle forth to fertilize the expectant islands and are extracted from our carefree cabin like ticks from a dog's ear. Nothing on shore will quite come up to it, even as Nice is never worthy of the Blue Train or New York of the *Queen Mary. Arriver, c'est déjà partir un peu.* [To arrive is already to depart a little bit.]

Great heat, like a smart doctor, begins every sentence "You'll have to cut out. . . ." With the temperature always around ninety, generalities alone can be appreciated, details and detours must be ignored; we are but fit for the simplest forms of sightseeing.

Air throbs, marble hisses, the sea glistens with malice, the exhausted landscape closes at lunchtime and does not reopen before six o'clock when the sun ceases its daily interrogation. We stagger across the grilled slabs of the Propylaea with only one idea—which is both idea and sensation—the juice of a lemon and an orange in equal proportions poured again and again over cubes of ice. After this postwar duty visit we flee the Parthenon and rush to take the first boat at the Piraeus. It is crowded and unbelievably noisy but there is a cool breeze as we round Sunium.

Bathed in lemon-yellow light like Rabat or Casablanca, Rhodes has some claim to be the perfect island. Neither too large nor too small, too hot nor too cold, fertile, hilly, legendary and exotic, it lives in the present as well as the past. The medieval city of the knights has been so perfectly restored by the Italians as to outdo Carcassonne; it is a golden flypaper for tourists who are led to it like bombers to a dummy target, leaving the real town uninjured. Between the austerity of the medieval fortress and the flamboyant Fascist concrete outside the walls the old Turkish quarter sprawls in exquisite decay.

The few simple elements required by the Moslem conception of beauty, the dome and minaret, fountain, plane tree, and arcaded court-yard are here combined into a dozen similar but never monotonous patterns . . . we are in a tiny Stamboul, a sixteenth and seventeenth century quarter of dignified exiles with their Persian tiles and Arabic inscriptions, their memories of fallen grandeur. No farther from the comfortable but hideous Hôtel des Roses than you can spit a pomegranate seed stands the little mosque of Murad-Reïz, its cemetery planted with mulberry and oleander. Few places are more soothing than a

Turkish graveyard, where the turbaned tombs are jumbled like spillikins
around the boles of cypresses and the cicadas zizz above the silent
koubbas.

Here sleeps the commander who captured Tripoli, and probably the
administrators who lost it, heroes and footlers together, the generals and
admirals, the Beys and Pashas of that cruel, clean, pious, frugal horticul-
tural community. The great admiral's grave is well kept-up and hung
with Mecca-green cloth; otherwise the nodding conversation pieces are
abandoned to shade and sun, each stone turban proudly proclaiming its
owner's status or bearing a verse from the Koran by which we linger in
bewilderment—even as one day in some far-flung graveyard a passing
Chinese may halt, baffled by the enumeration of our meager virtues.

Mikonos by contrast is a rude stone altar erected to the stern god of
summer. The town is a white African sneer arching brightly round the
bay where a row of little restaurants vie with each other in disappointments. The heat swaggers through the spotless alleys where bearded
Danish painters seal every exit with their easels.

To swim one must bump across the bay to some blinding cove or
trudge the iron-hot mountain path, paved with mule-dung and brown
thistle. The sun needles the brain cavity, desiccates the lung and obtains
a garnishee upon the liver. Doors bang, nerves jangle, little waves bristle
and buffet through the afternoon and in our sleep fashionable voices cry
"Mikonos for me," "*il y a toujours du vent à Mikonos* [there's always
a wind on Mikonos]."

After this stony sanatorium its humble neighbor seems to flower with
statues, tremendous in its exuberant and irretrievable collapse. Whereas
Delphi's mountain womb remains one of the holy places of the human
spirit, Delos is complex and baffling, irreverent even in its piety. With
its swans and geese and cafeteria, the sacred lake where Apollo was born
must have been not unlike the Round Pond in Kensington Gardens; the
commercial Roman town survives in better shape than the Greek; the
shrines of Isis and the phalloi of Dionysus have stood up better than
Apollo's altars. In this center of the ancient slave trade, this eclectic
battener on the world's religions whose moneylending priesthood were
the Rothschilds of antiquity, the god of man's fulfilment in this world,
the wielder of the lyre and the bow, is noticeably absent.

Yet Delos is magical. According to the admirable Greek usage, no
fence surrounds the ruins nor is there an entrance fee; black with tourists
and lizards, prostrate in the sunshine, the ancient stones are part of the
world's daily life. Among the Roman pavements is the mysteriously
haunting mosaic of anchor and dolphin which was found on the seals
of the wine jars on the Greek ship salvaged outside Marseilles by M.

Cousteau, and which aided him to identify his Sextius, owner of the vessel, with the proprietor of this sumptuous villa. By such means are we enabled to creep backward into time, liberated by significant detail such as the hand, in the museum, from that colossal archaic Apollo which was broken off by the fall of the sculptor Nikias's fabulous bronze palm tree.

Delphi remains sacred to Apollo while Delos had permission to exploit him; both became enormously rich, both tottered to destruction after Julian's reign in A.D. 363 with full treasuries, gold ceilings and colonnades of marble statues (Delos had 3,000 intact under the opprobrium of the Christians). Abandoned to pirates through the Dark Ages, Delos must still have been one of the wonders of the world, a desert island carpeted with temples and matchless private buildings, a thousand years of sanctity still clinging to the shrines and avenues while Delphi, pillaged by Byzantium, issued its despairing last oracle and the bronze horses of St. Mark's, as I like to think, were reft from the impassive Charioteer.

We may walk across the sacred lake or stand on Apollo's temple at Delphi where the earth-dragon fumed and fretted and the priestess gave out incoherent moans for the priest to polish into the double meanings which answered our desire. But it is difficult to feel aware of the terrible god of youthful strength and intellectual beauty. He exists only in museums. For though Greek architecture has barely survived, and Greek music and painting not at all, we have at last learned how to display sculpture at its best.

In the new museum at Athens we no longer need to pretend to ourselves; here the chain of masterpieces signal to each other down the ages. This is how Greece was; this is what man can do. Apollo is manifest at last with his smile which seems instantly to annihilate all time and all suffering. Joy is under everything and if we feel pain it is our fault because we are not divine enough. Death has an appropriateness which transcends sorrow; the world belongs to the beautiful charm; is welded to courage, thought to action—even the serpent is a friend.

But humanity could not grow up without a religion of the mother; the world could not always belong to the graceful tactless hearties with red curls, bulging eyeballs, stocky behinds, a try-anything-once look below their waving helmets. Can one think of any archaic sculpture which takes even Zeus beyond early middle age? In this art "Hippocleides doesn't care" triumphs over the maxims of the seven sages. Irresponsible perfection went out about 475 B.C.; yet is it my imagination or are not the contemporary Greeks one of the happiest as well as the most friendly nations in the world?

EVELYN WAUGH
1903–1966

If poets like Blake and Keats and Housman and Hardy tend to use travel as material for metaphor, novelists are different: they like to hurl themselves into it and then refract it in travel books. Waugh's six travel books indicate what delights can ensue when the novelistic imagination, skilled in narrative resources and in Waugh's case brimming with critical intelligence and a relish for the absurd, takes charge. Indeed, Waugh claimed membership in "that small circle . . . who prefer all but the very worst travel books to all but the very best novels." What counted for him, he said, was "the flavor of first-hand experience . . . , unmistakable and intoxicating."

"From 1918 until 1937," he says, "I had no fixed home and no possessions which would not conveniently go on a porter's barrow. I travelled continuously." His first travel report, an account of a trip through the Mediterranean aboard the comfortable Norwegian cruise vessel Stella Polaris, *he titled* Labels *because, he explained, "All the places I visited on this trip are already fully labelled." A few years later he undertook a very different kind of travel, its hardships resembling those of actual exploration—a rugged horse and foot expedition through British Guiana and Brazil, with the city of Manaos the target. For the reason he never got there, see the selection here from* Ninety-Two Days.

Like Graham Greene and Peter Fleming and Robert Byron, Waugh was one of those young British writers who helped make the period between the two world wars seem the Modern Age of Literary Traveling. "I never aspired to being a great traveler," Waugh recalled. "I was simply a young man, typical of my age; we traveled as a matter of course. I rejoice that I went when the going was good."

From LABELS: A MEDITERRANEAN JOURNAL
(1930)

One day I went alone to Sakkara, the enormous necropolis some way down the Nile from Mena. There are two pyramids there, and a number of tombs; one of them, named unpronounceably the Mastaba of Ptah-hotep, is exquisitely decorated in low relief. Another still more beauti-fully sculptured chamber is called more simply the Mastaba of Ti. As I emerged from this vault I came upon a large party of twenty or thirty indomitable Americans dragging their feet, under the leadership of a dragoman, across the sand from a charabanc. I fell in behind this party and followed them underground again, this time into a vast subterranean tunnel called the Serapeum, which, the guide explained, was the burial-place of the sacred bulls. It was like a completely unilluminated tube-railway station. We were each given a candle, and our guide marched on in front with a magnesium flare. Even so, the remote corners were left in impenetrable darkness. On either side of our path were ranged the vast granite sarcophagi; we marched very solemnly the full length of the tunnel, our guide counting the coffins aloud for us; there were twenty-four of them, each so massive that the excavating engineers could devise no means of removing them. Most of the Americans counted aloud with him.

One is supposed, I know, to think of the past on these occasions; to conjure up the ruined streets of Memphis and to see in one's mind's eye the sacred procession as it wound up the avenue of sphinxes, mourning the dead bull; perhaps even to give licence to one's fancy and invent some personal romance about the lives of these garlanded hymn-singers, and to generalize sagely about the mutability of human achievement. But I think we can leave all that to Hollywood. For my own part I found the present spectacle infinitely stimulating. What a funny lot we looked, trooping along that obscure gallery! First the Arab with his blazing white ribbon of magnesium, and behind him, clutching their candles, like penitents in procession, this whole rag-tag and bobtail of self-improvement and uplift. Some had been bitten by mosquitoes and bore swollen, asymmetrical faces; many were footsore, and limped and stumbled as they went; one felt faint and was sniffing "salts"; one coughed with dust; another had her eyes inflamed by the sun; another wore his arm in a sling, injured in heaven knows what endeavour; every one of the party in some way or another was bruised and upbraided by the thundering surf of education. And still they plunged on. One, two, three, four . . . twenty-four dead bulls; not twenty-three or twenty-five. How could they remember twenty-four? Why, to be sure, it was the number of Aunt Mabel's bedroom at Luxor. "How did the bulls die?" one of them asks.

"What did he ask?" chatter the others.

"What did the guide answer?" they want to know.

"How *did* the bulls die?"

"How much did it cost?" asks another. 'You can't build a place like this for nothing."

"We don't spend money that way nowadays."

"Fancy spending all that burying bulls . . ."

Oh, ladies and gentlemen, I longed to declaim, dear ladies and gentlemen, fancy crossing the Atlantic Ocean, fancy coming all this way in the heat, fancy enduring all these extremities of discomfort and exertion; fancy spending all this money, to see a hole in the sand where, three thousand years ago, a foreign race whose motives must for ever remain inexplicable interred the carcasses of twenty-four bulls. Surely the laugh, dear ladies and gentlemen, is on us.

But I remembered I was a gate-crasher in this party and remained silent.

* * *

I left Port Said in the P. & O. ship *Ranchi* for Malta. On leaving Egypt, as a final nip of avarice, one is obliged to pay a few shillings "quarantine tax." No one seems to know anything about this imposition, what statute authorized it and how much of what is collected ever finds its way into the treasury, or what bearing it has upon "quarantine." Many residents maintain that it is purely a bit of fun on the part of the harbour officials, who have no legal right to it whatever.

Thanks to the kind offices of the local manager, I was able to obtain a second-class berth. The residents in Port Said said: "You meet a first-rate lot of people travelling second class since the war. A jolly sight better than in the first class, particularly on the ships from India—the first class is all *nouveaux riches*. You'll find second class on the *Ranchi* as good as first class on a foreign line. My wife travels second class when she goes home."

But my motive really was less the ambition to meet nice people than to save money. After my extravagances at Mena House I was beginning to get worried about money, so I thought of an ingenious device. Before leaving Cairo I wrote—on the notepaper of the Union Club, Port Said—to the managers of the two leading hotels in Valletta, the Great

Britain and the Osborne, between whom, I was told, there existed a relationship of acute rivalry, and enclosed a publisher's slip of Press cuttings about my last book; I said to each that I proposed to publish a travel diary on my return to England; I had heard that his was the best hotel in the island. Would he be willing to give me free accommodation during my visit to Malta in return for a kind reference to his establishment in my book? They had not had time to answer by the time I embarked at Port Said, but I went on board hoping that at Valletta I should experience some remission of the continual draining of money that I had suffered for the last two months.

The *Ranchi* was advertised to sail some time on Sunday and was expected early in the afternoon. On Sunday morning she was announced for nine o'clock that evening. Finally she came in well after midnight and stayed only two hours. During those two hours the town, which, as usual, was feeling the ill-effects of its Saturday night at the Casino, suddenly woke again into life. Simon Arzt's store opened; the cafés turned on their lights and dusted the tables; out came the boot-cleaners and postcard sellers; the passengers who had stayed on board through the canal came ashore and drove round in two-horse carriages; those who had left the ship at Aden for a few hours at Cairo, and had spent all that afternoon on the quay in a fever of apprehension that they might miss her, scuttled on board to their cabins; half the residents of Port Said had business of some kind to transact on board. I went down to the harbour in a bustle that was like noon in the city of London. The sudden brightness of the streets and the animation on all sides seemed quite unreal. I went on board, found my steward and my cabin, disposed of my luggage, and went on deck for a little. The passengers who had done the Suez-Cairo-Port Said dash were drinking coffee, eating sandwiches, and describing the pyramids and Shepheard's Hotel. "Two pounds ten, simply for a single bed and no bathroom. Think of that!" they said with obvious pride. "And we rode on camels—you should just have seen me. How Katie would have laughed, I said. And the camel-boy told my fortune, and we had a coffee made actually in the temple of the Sphinx. You *ought* to have come. Well, yes, perhaps it was a little exhausting, but then we've plenty of time at sea to make up for it. And there was the sweetest little boy who cleaned our shoes. And we went into a mosque where the Mohammedans were all saying their prayers—so quaint. And would you believe it—at Shepheard's they charged 15 piastres—that's over three shillings—for a cup of early morning tea, and not very good tea at that. You *ought* to have come, Katie!"

Before we sailed, I went down to my cabin and went to bed. The man who was sharing it with me, a kindly, middle-aged civil engineer, was already undressing; he wore combinations. I woke once when the engines started, dozed and woke again as we ran clear of the breakwater and began to roll, and then fell soundly asleep, to wake next morning on the high seas with a hundred Englishmen all round me, whistling as they shaved.

We had cold, sunless weather and fairly heavy seas during the next two days. I rather wished that I had gone first class. It was not that my fellow passengers were not every bit as nice as the Port Said residents had told me they would be, but that there were so many of them. There was simply nowhere to sit down. The lounge and smoking-room were comfortable and clean and well ventilated and prettily decorated and all that, but they were always completely full. On the decks there were no deck-chairs except those the passengers provided for themselves; the three or four public seats were invariably occupied by mothers doing frightful things to their babies with jars of vaseline. It was not even possible to walk round with any comfort, so confined and crowded was the single promenade deck. Children were everywhere. It was the beginning of the hot season in India, and the officers' wives were taking them back to England in shoals; the better sort lay and cried in perambulators; the worse ones fell all over the deck and were sick; these, too, appeared in the dining-room for breakfast and luncheon and were encouraged by their mothers to eat. There was an awful hour every evening at about six o'clock, when the band came down from the first-class deck to play Gilbert and Sullivan to us in the saloon; this visitation coincided exactly with the bathing of the elder children below; the combination of soap and salt water is one of the more repugnant features of sea travel, and the lusty offspring of sahib and memsahib shrieked their protest till the steel rafters and match-board partitions echoed and rang. There was no place above or below for a man who values silence.

The other passengers were mostly soldiers on leave or soldiers' wives, leavened with a few servants of first-class passengers, some clergymen, and three or four nuns. The valets wore neat blue suits throughout the voyage, but the soldiers had an interesting snobbism. During the day, though cleanly shaved and with carefully brushed hair, they cultivated an extreme freedom of dress, wearing khaki shorts and open tennis shirts and faded cricket blazers. At dinner, however, they all appeared in dinner jackets and stiff shirts. One of them told me that the reason he travelled second class was that he need not trouble about clothes, but that he had to draw the line somewhere. On the other side of the barrier we could see the first-class passengers dressed very smartly in white flannels and parti-coloured brown and white shoes. Among them there was a youth who knew me hurrying back to contest a seat in the Conservative interest at the General Election. He kept popping over the rail to have cocktails with me and tell me about the lovely first-class girls he danced and played quoits with. He cost me quite a lot in cocktails. He often urged me to come over and see all the lovely girls and have cocktails with him. "My dear chap," he used to say, "no one will dare to say anything to you while you're with *me*. I'd soon fix it up with the Captain if they did." But I kept to my own bar. Later this young man, in his zeal to acquit himself splendidly before the first-class girls, clambered up one of the davits on the boat deck. He was reported to the Captain and seriously reprimanded. P. & O. ships are full of public school spirit. He did very badly indeed in the election, I believe, reducing an already meagre Conservative poll almost to extinction.

Just before luncheon on the third morning, we came in sight of Malta. There was some delay about landing because one of the passengers had developed chicken-pox. There was only one other passenger disembarking. We had to go and see the medical officer in the first-class saloon. He had infinite difficulties about the pronunciation of my name. He wanted to know the address I was going to in Malta. I would only tell him that I had not yet decided between the two hotels. He said, "Please decide now. I have to fill in this form."

I said I could not until I had seen the managers.

He said, "They are both good hotels, what does it matter?"

I said, "I want to get in free."

He thought I was clearly a very suspicious character, and told me that on pain of imprisonment, I must report daily at the Ministry of Health during my stay at Valletta. If I did not come the police would find me and bring me. I said I would come, and he gave me a quarantine form to keep. I lost the form that evening and never went near the Ministry of Health and heard no more about it.

We went ashore in a lighter and landed at the Custom House. Here I was met by two young men, both short, swarthy, and vivacious, and each wearing a peaked cap above a shiny English suit. One had "The Osborne Hotel" in gold on his cap, the other "The Great Britain Hotel." Each held in his hand a duplicate letter from me, asking for accommodation. Each took possession of a bit of my luggage and handed me a printed card. One card said:

THE OSBORNE HOTEL
STRADA MEZZODI

Every modern improvement. Hot water. Electric light.
Excellent Cuisine.

PATRONISED BY H.S.H. PRINCE LOUIS OF
BATTENBERG AND THE DUKE OF BRONTE

The other said:

THE GREAT BRITAIN HOTEL
STRADA MEZZODI

Every modern improvement. Hot and cold water. Electric light.
Unrivalled cuisine. Sanitation.

THE ONLY HOTEL UNDER ENGLISH MANAGEMENT

(a fact, one would have thought, more fit to be concealed than advertised).

I had been advised in Cairo that the Great Britain was really the better of the two, so I directed its representative to take charge of my luggage. The porter of the Osborne fluttered my letter petulantly before my eyes.

"A forgery," I explained, shocked at my own duplicity. "I am afraid that you have been deluded by a palpable forgery."

The porter of the Great Britain chartered two little horse-carriages, conducted me to one, and sat with the luggage in the other. There were low, fringed canopies over our heads so that it was impossible to see out very much. I was aware of a long and precipitous ascent, with many corners to turn. At some of these I got a glimpse of a baroque shrine, at others a sudden bird's-eye view of the Grand Harbour, full of shipping, with fortifications beyond. We went up and round, along a broad street of shops and more important doorways. We passed groups of supremely ugly Maltese women wearing an astonishing black headdress, half veil and half umbrella, which is the last legacy to the island of the conventional inclinations of the Knights of St John. Then we turned off down a narrow side street and stopped at the little iron and glass porch of the Great Britain Hotel. A little dark passage led into a little dark lounge, furnished like an English saloon bar, with imitation leather arm-chairs, bowls of aspidistra on fumed oak stands, metal-topped tables, and tables with plush coverings, Benares brass work, framed photographs, and ashtrays stamped with the trade-marks of various brands of whisky and gin. Do not mistake me; it was not remotely like an old-fashioned hotel in an English market town; it was a realization of the picture I have always in my mind of the interiors of those hotels facing on to Paddington station, which advertise "5s. Bed and Breakfast" over such imposing names as Bristol, Clarendon, Empire, etc. My heart fell rather as I greeted my host in this dingy hall, and continued to fall as I ascended, storey by storey, to my bedroom. The worst of it, however, was in this first impression, and I think I am really doing my duty honourably to the proprietor in warning people of it and exhorting them not to be deterred. For I can quite conscientiously say that the Great Britain *is* the best hotel in the island. I went later to look at the Osborne and felt that I had done better than H.S.H. Prince Louis of Battenberg and the Duke of Bronte. The food at the Great Britain was good; the servants particularly willing and engaging. One evening, being tired and busy, I decided to dine in my room. At Mena House, where there were hosts of servants and a lift, the dinner was brought up in one load and left outside the door; at the Great Britain every course was carried separately up three flights of stairs by the panting but smiling *valet de chambre.*

Before I left, the proprietor of the hotel asked me, rather suspiciously, what I intended to say about him.

They had had another writer, he told me, who had come to stay as his guest; he wrote for a paper called *Town and Country Life;* he had written a very nice piece indeed about the Great Britain. They had had the article reprinted for distribution.

The proprietor gave me a copy.

That, he said, was the kind of article that did a house good. He hoped mine would be as much like that as I could make it.

It began: "The beautiful and prolific foliage, exotic skies, and glorious blue waters, a wealth of sunshine that spells health and happiness, and the facilities for enjoying outdoor sports, all the year round, are a few of the reasons that has made Malta so popular. Picturesque scenery, and people, complete as fascinating an array of attractions as the heart of the most blasé, could wish for." It continued in this way for a column, with the same excess of punctuation; then it gave a brief survey of Maltese history and a description of the principal sights, for another column. Then it started on the Great Britain Hotel. "No expense," it said, "has been spared to make the Public Rooms as comfortable as possible . . . the Management boasts that its meals equal in the excellence of its food, cooking and serving, those served at London's hostelries and restaurants . . . special pains are taken to see that all beds are most comfortable and only best material used . . ." and so on for a column and a half. It finished: "The luxuries of modern civilization have all been embodied in the building and organization of the Great Britain Hotel, Valletta, Malta, where the visitor is able to revel in the joys of a healthy happy stay amidst the fascinations of a modern palace set in Nature's own setting of sea and foliage, and here are to be obtained sunshine and warmth the whole year round."

I will not be outdone in gratitude. If my appreciation is more temperately expressed it is none the less genuine. Let me state again, the Great Britain may be less suitably placed for golfers than Gleneagles; the gambling may be better from the Normandie; one can shop more conveniently from the Crillon, the Russie is set in a prettier square, one meets more amusing company at the Cavendish, one can dance better at the Berkeley and sleep better at Mena and eat better at the Ritz, but *the Great Britain Hotel, Valletta, Malta, is the best on the island;* further comparisons seem rather to confuse the issue.

I spent too little time in Malta. Most of my days were spent in exploring Valletta, with the aid of a small book called *Walks in Malta*, by F. Weston, which I bought for two shillings at Critien's, the big stationer's shop. I found it a slightly confusing book at first until I got used to the author's method; after that I became attached to it, not only for the variety of information it supplied, but for the amusing Boy-Scout game it made of sightseeing. "Turning sharply to your left you will notice . . ." Mr Weston prefaces his comments, and there follows a minute record of detailed observation. On one occasion, when carrying his book, I landed at the Senglea quay, taking it for Vittoriosa, and walked on for some time in the wrong town, hotly following false clues and identifying "windows with fine old mouldings," "partially defaced escutcheons," "interesting ironwork balustrades," etc., for nearly a mile, until a clearly non-existent cathedral brought me up sharp to the realization of my mistake.

From Ninety-Two Days: The Account of
a Tropical Journey Through British
Guiana and Part of Brazil
(1934)

Since the evening at Kurupukari when Mr Bain had first mentioned its name, Boa Vista had come to assume greater and greater importance to me. Father Mather had been there only once, and then in the worst stage of malignant malaria, so that he had been able to tell me little about it except that some German nuns had proved deft and devoted nurses. Everybody else, however, and particularly David, had spoken of it as a town of dazzling attraction. Whatever I had looked for in vain at Figuiredo's store was, he told me, procurable at "Boa Vist' "; Mr Daguar had extolled its modernity and luxury—electric light, cafés, fine buildings, women, politics, murders. Mr Bain had told of the fast motor launches, plying constantly between there and Manaos. In the discomfort of the journey there, I had looked forward to the soft living of Boa Vista, feeling that these asperities were, in fact, a suitable contrast, preparing my sense for a fuller appreciation of the good things in store. So confident was I that when we first came in sight of the ramshackle huddle of buildings on the further bank, I was quite uncritical and conscious of no emotion except delight and expectation.

The river was enormously broad and very low; so low that as we gazed at the town across sand dunes and channels and a fair-sized island it seemed to be perched on a citadel, instead of being, as was actually the case, at the same dead level as the rest of the plain. Two *vaqueiros* [cowboys] were lying in hammocks by the bank, and from these David elicited the information that a boat was expected some time in the next few hours to ferry them across. The *vaqueiros* studied us with an air that I came to recognize as characteristic of Boa Vista; it was utterly unlike the open geniality of the ranches; conveying, as it did, in equal degrees, contempt, suspicion and the suggestion that only listlessness kept them from active insult.

With David's assistance, I began some enquiries about accommodation. There was none, they said.

"But I understood there were two excellent hotels."

"Ah, that was in the days of the Company. There was all kinds of foolishness in the days of the Company. There is nowhere now. There has not been an hotel for two years."

"Then where do strangers stay?"

"Strangers do not come to Boa Vist'. If they come on business, the people they have business with put them up."

I explained that I was on the way to Manaos and had to wait for a boat. They showed complete indifference, only remarking that they did not know of any boat to Manaos. Then one of them added that possibly the foreign priests would do something for me—unless they had left; last time he was in Boa Vist' the foreign priests were all sick; most people were sick in Boa Vist'. Then the two men started talking to each other.

My enthusiasm had already cooled considerably by the time we saw a boat put out from the opposite shore and make slowly towards us. We all got in, David, Francisco, I, the two surly *vaqueiros*, the saddles and the baggage, so that the gunwales were only an inch clear of the water. Then partly paddling, partly wading and pushing, we made our way across. There were women squatting on the further shore, pounding dirty linen on the rocks at the water's edge. We hauled our possessions up the steep bank and found ourselves in the main street of the town. It was very broad, composed of hard, uneven mud, cracked into wide fissures in all directions and scored by several dry gulleys. On either side was a row of single-storeyed, whitewashed mud houses with tiled roofs; at each doorstep sat one or more of the citizens staring at us with eyes that were insolent, hostile and apathetic; a few naked children rolled about at their feet. The remains of an overhead electric cable hung loose from a row of crazy posts, or lay in coils and loops about the gutter.

The street rose to a slight hill and half-way up we came to the Benedictine Mission. This at any rate presented a more imposing aspect than anything I had seen since leaving Georgetown. It was built of concrete with a modestly ornamented façade, a row of unbroken glass windows, a carved front door with an electric bell, a balustraded veran-dah with concrete urns at either end; in front of it lay a strip of garden marked out into symmetrical beds with brick borders.

We approached rather diffidently, for we were shabby and stained with travelling and lately unaccustomed to carved front doors and electric bells. But the bell need have caused us no misgiving, for it was out of order. We pressed and waited and pressed again. Then a head appeared from a window and told us, in Portuguese, to knock. We knocked several times until the head reappeared; it was Teutonic in character, blond and slightly bald, wrinkled, with a prominent jaw and innocent eyes.

"The gentleman is a stranger too. He speaks Portuguese in a way I do not understand," said David. "He says there is a priest but that he is probably out."

I was used to waiting by now, so we sat on the doorstep among our luggage until presently an emaciated young monk in white habit appeared up the garden path. He seemed to accept our arrival with resignation, opened the door and led us into one of those rooms found only in religious houses, shuttered, stuffy and geometrically regular in arrangement; four stiff chairs ranged round four walls; devotional oleographs symmetrically balanced; a table in the exact centre with an embroidered cloth and a pot of artificial flowers; everything showing by its high polish of cleanliness that nuns had been at work there.

The monk was a German-Swiss. We spoke in halting French and I explained my situation. He nodded gloomily and said that it was impossible to predict when another boat would leave for Manaos; on the other hand a new Prior was expected some time soon and that boat must presumably return one day. Meanwhile I was at liberty to stay in the house if I chose.

"Will it be a question of days or weeks?"

"A question of weeks or months."

David thought the Boundary Commission had a boat going down in a few days; he would go into the town and enquire. With rather lugubrious courtesy the monk, who was named Father Alcuin, showed me a room and a shower bath; explained that he and the other guest had already breakfasted; sent across to the convent for food for me. I ate the first palatable meal since I had left St Ignatius, changed and slept. Presently David returned with reassuring information. The Commission boat was passing through in four or five days; a week after that there would be a trade launch. He smiled proudly both at bringing good news and because he had bought a startling new belt out of his wages. Then he and Francisco bade me good-bye and went to rest with the horses on the other bank of the river.

Already, in the few hours of my sojourn there, the Boa Vista of my imagination had come to grief. Gone; engulfed in an earthquake, uprooted by a tornado and tossed sky-high like chaff in the wind, scorched up with brimstone like Gomorrah, toppled over with trumpets like Jericho, ploughed like Carthage, bought, demolished and transported brick by brick to another continent as though it had taken the fancy of Mr Hearst; tall Troy was down. When I set out on a stroll of exploration, I no longer expected the city I had had in mind during the thirsty days of approach; the shady boulevards; kiosks for flowers and cigars and illustrated papers; the hotel terrace and the cafés; the baroque church built by seventeenth-century missionaries; the bastions of the old fort; the bandstand in the square, standing amidst fountains and flowering shrubs; the soft, slightly swaggering citizens, some uniformed and spurred, others with Southern elegance twirling little canes, bowing from the waist and raising boater hats, flicking with white gloves indiscernible particles of dust from their white linen spats; dark beauties languorous on balconies, or glancing over fans at the café tables. All that extravagant and highly improbable expectation had been obliterated like a sand castle beneath the encroaching tide.

Closer investigation did nothing to restore it. There was the broad main street up which we had come; two parallel, less important streets and four or five more laid at right angles to them. At a quarter of a mile in every direction they petered out into straggling footpaths. They were all called Avenidas and labelled with names of politicians of local significance. The town had been planned on an ambitious scale, spacious, rectangular, but most of the building lots were still unoccupied. There was one fair-sized store, a little larger and a little better stocked than Figuiredo's, half a dozen seedy little shops; an open booth advertising the services of a barber-surgeon who claimed to wave women's hair, extract teeth and cure venereal disease; a tumble-down house inhabited by the nuns, an open schoolhouse where a fever-stricken teacher could be observed monotonously haranguing a huge class of listless little boys; a wireless office, and a cottage where they accepted letters for the post; there were two cafés; one on the main street was a little shed, selling *farine* [dried pieces of starchy cassava root], bananas and fish, there were three tables in front of it, under a tree, where a few people collected in the evening to drink coffee in the light of a single lantern; the second, in a side street, was more attractive. It had a concrete floor and a counter where one could buy cigarettes and nuts, there were dominoes for the use of habitués and, besides coffee, one could drink warm and expensive beer.

The only place, besides the Benedictine Priory, which had any pretensions to magnificence was the church, a modern building painted in yellow and orange horizontal stripes, with ornate concrete mouldings; there were old bells outside, and inside three sumptuous altars, with embroidered frontals and veils, carved reredoses, large, highly coloured statues, artificial flowers and polished candlesticks, decorated wooden pews, a marble font bearing in enormous letters the name of the chief merchant of the town, a harmonium; everything very new, and clean as a hospital—not a hen or a pig in the building. I was curious to know by what benefaction this expensive church had come into being and was told that, like most things, it had started "in the days of the Company."

I discovered one English-speaking person in the town; a singularly charmless youth, the illegitimate son of a prominent Georgetown citizen whom I had met there at Christmas time. This served as a fragile link between us, for the young man told me that he hated his father and had thought of shooting him on more than one occasion. "Now I have been married and have written five times for money and had no answer."

He was completely fleshless like all the inhabitants of Boa Vista, with dank, black hair hanging over his eyes, which were of slightly lighter yellow than the rest of his face. He spoke in a melancholy drawl. He was almost the only person I saw doing any work in the whole town. He owned a small blacksmith's shop where he made branding irons and mended guns. Most of the other inhabitants seemed to have no occupation of any kind, being caught up in the vicious circle of semi-starvation. Perhaps they picked up a few casual wages during the flood season when boats ran from Manaos fairly frequently and the ranchers came in for stores and needed labour for shipping their cattle. All the time that I was there I scarcely saw anyone except the school teacher earn anything—or spend anything. Even in the café the majority of customers came to gossip and play dominoes and went away without ordering a cup of coffee. At some miles distance was a settlement of soldiers who brought a few shillings into the town; they were reservists bedded out with wives on small allotments. An aged town clerk presumably received some sort of wages; so no doubt did the itinerant government vet, who appeared from time to time; so did the wireless operator and an official of villainous aspect called the "Collector." But the other thousand odd inhabitants spent the day lying indoors in their hammocks and the evenings squatting on their doorsteps gossiping. Land was free, and, as the nuns proved, could produce excellent vegetables, but the diet of the town was *farine, tasso* [salted dried meat] and a little fish, all of which were of negligible cost. But it was far from being a care-free, idyllic improvidence. Everyone looked ill and discontented. There was not a fat man or woman anywhere. The women, in fact, led an even drearier life than the men. They had no household possessions to care for, no cooking to do, they left their children to sprawl about the streets naked or in rags. They were pretty—very small and thin, small-boned and with delicate features; a few of them took trouble with their appearance and put in an appearance at Mass on Sundays in light dresses, stockings and shoes, and cheap, gay combs in their hair.

From fragmentary and not altogether reliable sources I picked up a little history of Boa Vista. It was a melancholy record. The most patriotic Brazilian can find little to say in favour of the inhabitants of Amazonas; they are mostly descended from convicts, loosed there after their term of imprisonment as the French loose their criminals in Cayenne, to make whatever sort of living they can in an inhospitable country. Practically all of them are of mixed Indian and Portuguese blood. There is no accurate census, but a recent medical survey in the *Geographical Magazine* reports that they are dying out, families usually becoming sterile in three generations; alien immigrants, mostly German and Japanese, are gradually pushing what is left of them up country; Boa Vista is their final halting place before extinction. The best of them go out into the ranches; the worst remain in the town.

They are naturally homicidal by inclination, and every man, however poor, carries arms; only the universal apathy keeps them from frequent bloodshed. There were no shootings while I was there; in fact there had not been one for several months, but I lived all the time in an atmosphere that was novel to me, where murder was always in the air. The German at the Priory constantly slept with a loaded gun at his bedside and expressed surprise at seeing me going shopping without a revolver; the blacksmith, partly no doubt owing to his avocation, spoke of little else; one of his main preoccupations was altering trigger springs so that they could be fired quick on the draw.

There was rarely a conviction for murder. The two most sensational trials of late years had both resulted in acquittals. One was the case of a young Britisher who had come across from Guiana, panning gold. He had no right there and one evening in the café tipsily expressed his willingness to shoot anyone who interfered with him. The boast was accepted as constituting provocation when, a few nights later, he was shot in the back and robbed, while entering his house.

The other case was more remarkable. Two respected citizens, a Dr Zany and a Mr Homero Cruz, were sitting on a verandah talking, when a political opponent rode up and shot Dr Zany. His plea of innocence, when brought to trial, was that the whole thing had been a mistake; he had meant to kill Mr Cruz. The judges accepted the defence and brought in a verdict of death from misadventure.

From time to time attempts have been made to raise the condition of the town. A little before the War a German appeared with ample capital and began buying cattle. He offered and paid a bigger price than the ranchers had ever before received; he fitted out a fleet of large motor launches to take the beasts down to market at Manaos. The project was perfectly sound financially and would have brought considerable advantage to the district, but it was destined to failure. Before the first convoy had reached the market, he had been shot and killed by an official whom he had neglected to bribe. The defence was that he had been shot while evading arrest on a charge of collecting turtles' eggs out of season. The murderer was exonerated and the boats never reappeared at Boa Vista.

A more recent enterprise had been that of "the Company," so frequently referred to. I never learned the full story of this fiasco, for the Benedictines were deeply involved in it and I did not like to press the question at the Priory. The blacksmith gravely assured me that the scandal had been so great that the Archbishop had been taken to Rome and imprisoned by the Pope. There certainly seemed to have been more than ordinary mismanagement of the affair. Father Alcuin never mentioned it except to say that things had not gone as well as they had hoped.

* * *

I found very little to occupy my time. There was an edition of Bossuet's sermons and a few lives of the Saints in French for me to read; I could walk to the wireless office and learn that no news had been heard of the Boundary Commissioner's boat; I could visit the English-speaking blacksmith and watch him tinkering with antiquated automatic pistols. This young man would not come with me to the café on account of his having recently beaten the proprietor—an act of which he was inordinately proud, though it can have required no great courage since he was a very old man and slightly crippled. I could give bananas to the captive monkey and I could study the bottled worms in the laboratory; I could watch the carpenter in his rare moments of industry, sawing up lengths of planks. There was really quite a number of things for me to do, but, in spite of them all, the days seemed to pass slowly.

The blacksmith, who knew all that was going on in the town, promised to tell me as soon as the Commissioner's boat was sighted, but it so happened that he forgot to do so, and I only learned from Mr Steingler, one morning after I had been six days in the Priory, that it had arrived the previous evening and was due to leave in an hour; the Commissioner was at that moment at the wireless station. I hurried off to interview him. Things might have been less difficult if Father Alcuin had been able to accompany me, but it was one of the days when he was down with fever. Alone I was able to make no impression. The Commissioner was an amicable little man, in high good humour at the prospect of a few days' leave in Manaos, but he flatly refused to have me in his boat. I cannot hold it against him. Everyone in that district is a potential fugitive from justice and he knew nothing of me except my dishevelled appearance and my suspicious anxiety to get away from Boa Vista. I showed my passport and letters of credit, but he was not impressed. I besought him to cable to Georgetown for my credentials, but he pointed out that it might take a week to get an answer. I offered him large wads of greasy notes. But he was not having any. He knew too much about foreigners who appeared alone and unexplained in the middle of Amazonas; the fact of my having money made me the more sinister. He smiled, patted my shoulder, gave me a cigarette, and sharp on time left without me.

I cannot hold it against him. I do not think that the British Commissioners would have done any more for a stray Brazilian. But it was in a despondent and rather desperate mood that I heard his boat chugging away out of sight down the Rio Branco.

From then onwards my only concern was to find some other means of getting away from Boa Vista. The trade boat of which David had spoken became increasingly elusive as I tried to pin its proprietor down to any definite statement of its departure. He was the manager of the chief store, a low-spirited young man named Martinez. I went to see him every day to talk about it; he seemed glad of a chat but could hold out only the vaguest hopes for me. The boat had to arrive first. It should be on its way with the new Prior; when it came, there would be time enough to discuss its departure. All sorts of things had to be considered—cargo, mail, other passengers. Day after day went by until all faith I had ever cherished in the trade boat slowly seeped away. Ordinary vexation at the delay began to give place to anxiety, for everyone in the town seemed to spend at least three days a week in fever. It seemed to me a poor gamble to risk becoming semi-invalid for life for the dubious interest of a voyage down the Rio Branco. So I abandoned the idea of Manaos and decided to return to Guiana.

This journey, so simple from British territory, where one was supported by the good will of the mission and the ranchers, presented endless difficulties from the other side. Mr Martinez said he could arrange it, but days passed and no horses appeared. He found me a guide, however, in the person of a good-natured boy named Marco; he was fifteen or sixteen, in from the country, and had been hanging round the store for some weeks in search of employment; this youth, after a house to house enquiry lasting several days, eventually secured the hire of a horse for himself, belonging, as it turned out, to Mr Martinez and quartered at the ranch on the other side of the river. I still needed another horse—if possible two—and provisions. Mr Martinez had some tins of sweet biscuits and sardines, another shop had two tins of sausage; the nuns made bread and cheese. These would comfortably take us the three days' ride to Dadanawa. Horses were still an unsolved difficulty when help came from an unexpected quarter.

Mr Steingler had hitherto listened apathetically to my complaints, merely remarking from time to time, "Les peuples ici sont tous bêtes, tous sauvages; il faut toujours de patience [People here are all animals, all savages; you must be patient.]," until one day the thought came to him that there might be something in it for him. He opened the subject cautiously, saying one evening that even if I secured a horse, it would be impossible to get a saddle; both were equally important. I agreed. He then went on to say that it so happened that he had a very good saddle himself, one that he would not readily part with to anyone, a particularly fine, new saddle of European workmanship, a rare and invaluable possession in a country like this. However, seeing my difficulty, and feeling the kinship that one European feels for another in a savage country, he was willing to part with it to me.

He took me to his room and dragged it out from under his bed. It was made on the English pattern but clearly of the most slipshod local workmanship; moreover, it was of great age and in deplorable condition, half unsewn, with padding as hard as metal, every leather frayed and half worn through, several buckles missing. I asked him what he wanted for it.

Between European gentlemen, he said, it was impossible to bargain over money. He would call in a friend to make an assessment. The friend was the carpenter from the next room who was transparently in the racket up to his eyes. He turned over the saddle, praised it (embarrassing himself and Mr Steingler by inadvertently detaching another buckle while he spoke) and said that, all things considered, 20,000 *Reis* (£5) would be a moderate price. I accepted the assessment and then began, in my turn, to point out that, necessary as a saddle was, and much as I admired this particular one of Mr Steingler's, it was of very little use to me without a horse. I would buy it at his price, if he would find me a mount to put under it.

From that moment onwards Mr Steingler worked for me indefatigably. He set out there and then in his boater hat, twirling his ridiculous cane, and by evening was able to report that the Collector had the very horse for me; a beast of some age, he admitted, but immensely strong, big boned, well-conditioned; just what was needed for savannah travelling. We went to see him. He was of much the same quality as the saddle and, curiously enough, commanded exactly the same price. Presumably 20,000 *Reis* was a unit in their minds, the highest figure to which avarice could aspire. I bought him on the spot. I do not know what rake-off Mr Steingler got on the transaction, or whether he merely wished to keep in with the Collector. I preferred to be thought a mug and get away, rather than to achieve a reputation for astuteness and risk spending an unnecessary hour in Boa Vista.

That evening Mr Steingler did a further bit of business, by producing the town clerk, a venerable old man with a long white beard, who was willing to hire me a pack horse he owned in the corral on the further bank—4,000 *Reis* for the journey to Dadanawa. I paid him and went to bed well contented with the prospect of immediate escape.

Next morning I bade farewell to Father Alcuin. The plans for my departure had been freely discussed at table for over a week, but had not penetrated the feverish trance in which the poor monk lived. He was greatly surprised, and when I handed him a donation to the house to cover my board and lodging, he woke suddenly to the fact that he had exerted himself very little on my behalf; it was then that he revealed, what before he had kept carefully hidden, that he had a wooden pack saddle which he could put at my disposal. Thus equipped and blessed I felt that I was at last on my way.

But it was not to be as easy as that; the forces of chaos were still able to harass my retreat and inflict some damaging attacks. The next two days, in fact, were slapstick farce, raised at moments to the heights of fantasy by the long-awaited appearance of the Prior.

News of his approach and imminent arrival came on the morning of the day that I had fixed for my departure. Instantly the Priory was overrun by nuns. They worked in the way nuns have, which is at the same time sub-human and superhuman; poultry and angels curiously compounded in a fluttering, clucking, purposeful scurry of devoted industry; they beat up the Prior's mattresses and dusted every crevice of his quarters, they trotted to and fro with wicker rocking-chairs and clean sheets, they lined the corridor to his room with potted shrubs, put palm leaves behind all the pictures, arranged embroidered tablecloths on every available shelf and ledge, decorated the bookcase with artificial flowers, built a triumphal arch over the front door and engrossed programmes for a hastily organized concert. I regretted very much that I should not be there to see his reception.

My plans were that I should cross the river in the afternoon with the grey cob I had bought from the Collector; see to the rounding in of the other two horses, sleep by the corral on the further side and start for Dadanawa first thing the next morning.

Mr Martinez had organized the crossing, for which he had hired me a canoe and another boy, whom I was to meet with Marco at three o'clock. At half past four they arrived; the other boy turned out to be a child of eight or nine. Mr Martinez explained that he was taking the place of his elder brother who had fever that day.

We carried the saddles and baggage down the bank, found the canoe, which when loaded was dangerously low in the water. The descent at the usual landing place was too steep for a horse, so it was arranged that the small boy and I should paddle to a point up stream where the bank shelved down more gently, where Marco would meet us with the horse.

It was half past five when we reached the place and found no sign of Marco. The sun sets at six. For half an hour the small boy and I sat hunched in the canoe—I cramped and fretful, he idly playful with my belongings—then we paddled back in the darkness to the landing place. Sundry whistlings and catcalls ensued until presently Marco loomed up through the shadows riding the grey. We neither spoke a word of the other's language but by repetitions and gestures, and that telepathy which seems to function between two people who have something of urgency to communicate, we got to understand that the horse had taken some catching, that Marco was quite ready to try swimming him across in the dark, that I thought this lunacy, that the baggage was to be left where it was, that Marco was to sling his hammock by the bank and guard it all night, that I would come at dawn and we would cross over then. I cannot explain how we discussed all this, but in the end the situation was well understood. Then I hurried back to the Priory which I had left a few hours before with so many formal thanks and good wishes.

In my vexation I had entirely forgotten about the Prior. I now came to the refectory, ten minutes late for dinner, out of breath and wet to the knees, to find him sitting at table. He was, as it happens, in the middle of the story of his own sufferings on the way up. It was a problem of good manners of the kind that are solved so astutely on the women's pages of the Sunday papers. What should I do? It was clearly impossible to escape unobserved, for the Prior had already fixed me with a look of marked aversion. I could not slip into a chair with a murmured apology for my lateness, because some explanation of my reappearance was due to Father Alcuin, and of my existence to my new host, the Prior. There was nothing for it but to interrupt the Prior's story with one of my own. He did not take it too kindly. Father Alcuin attempted to help me out, explaining rather lamely that I was an Englishman who had waited here on the way to Manaos.

Then what was I doing attempting to cross the Rio Branco in the dark? the Prior demanded sternly.

I said I was on my way to Dadanawa.

"But Dadanawa is nowhere near Manaos."

Clearly the whole thing seemed to him highly unsatisfactory and suspicious. However, with the charity of his Order he bade me sit down. The idiot boy removed the soup plates and the Prior resumed his story. In honour of his arrival a fish course had been added to the dinner; nothing could have been less fortunate, for he had lived on fish for the last ten days and on that particular sort of coarse and tasteless fish that was now offered him. He glared at it resentfully over his spectacles and ordered it to be removed. Mr Steingler watched it go with evident distress.

The Prior was no doubt a very good man, but he did not add to the ease of the refectory. He was thoroughly exhausted by his journey and in no mood to bustle off to the nuns' concert. He had already formed a low opinion of Mr Steingler and my arrival confirmed him in his general disapproval. He was there on a mission of reorganization and Mr Steingler and myself were obviously the kind of thing that had to be investigated and cleaned up. He finished his narration of delays and discomforts, took a dislike to the pudding, and before Mr Steingler had nearly finished his first helping, rose to recite an immensely long grace. Then, with hostile adieux, stumped away grumbling to the celebrations at the school.

Next day at dawn I saw him on his way to Mass and he was more amicable. I bade him good-bye with renewed thanks and went down to the river. The small boy and Marco were there; the baggage was intact; after an hour's perilous and exhausting work we got the canoe and the horse across to the other side; the child paddled back and I settled down to wait until Marco had collected the other horses. The pack horse was easily identified by some *vaqueiros* who were waiting there. He was a wretched creature, down in the pasterns, but our baggage was very light and it seemed probable that he would get it to Dadanawa. Mr Martinez's horse could not be found. After two hours Marco returned, smiling and shrugging and shaking his head.

Back to Boa Vista once more. We had to wait until noon for a canoe. I arrived at the Priory once more, a good quarter of an hour late for luncheon. The Prior's doubts of my honesty became doubts of my sanity. Once more I made my adieux, repeating the same thanks with increased apologies. Mr Martinez, at last roused to activity, decided to accompany me himself to the other side and find the horse. He issued a number of peremptory orders which were lethargically obeyed. His motor launch was brought up, four or five men were recruited, and a formidable expedition set out. After some hours, the horse was discovered straying some miles distant, lassoed and led in. Then a further disaster occurred. A large sow which had been nosing round the baggage for some time discovered a way into the kit bag and ate the whole of the bread and cheese on which I had been counting as my main sustenance in the next few days.

Back to Boa Vista; back to the Priory, just as they were finishing dinner. The Prior now regarded me with undisguised despair. I was able, however, to buy another loaf and more cheese from the convent. Next morning, without further contact with my hosts, I slipped out of the Priory and left Boa Vista for the last time.

ROBERT BYRON
1905–1941

This passionate, brilliant, and intense young eccentric—a distant relative of Lord Byron's—came from a substantial family in Wiltshire and went to Eton and Merton College, Oxford. There he rebelled against the veneration of all things Greek and Roman and came to prefer the less ideal, more "human" sinuosities and unpredictabilities of the Byzantine style, which he studied in the architecture and mosaics of Greece and the Near East and celebrated in books like The Station: Athos, Treasures and Men *(1928),* The Byzantine Achievement *(1929), and* The Birth of Western Painting *(1930).*

It was in search of a lively, un-grey "chromatic" architecture that he journeyed to the USSR and Tibet in the early 1930s, and in his report on that trip, First Russia, Then Tibet, *he included this classic defense of travel as a form of knowledge, indeed as one of the liberal arts:*

> The *pleasures* of travel need no reiteration. But when the impulse is so imperious that it amounts to a spiritual necessity, then travel must rank with the more serious forms of endeavour.

He continued his quest for stunning examples of non-Western architecture in the trip he and his friend Christopher Sykes took in 1933 and 1934 to Persia—then ruled by a Shah so sensitive to Western criticism that they felt safe in referring to him only as "Marjoriebanks." The journey, recounted in The Road to Oxiana, *took them near the River Oxus, part of the border between Afghanistan and the USSR; hence Oxiana, the land of the Oxus. The main object of the trip was to behold the Gumbad-i-Kabus, a remarkable brick burial tower dating from the early eleventh century. Consisting not of the usual seamless narration but of a great variety of heterogeneous materials—clippings, public*

notices, letters, official forms, comic dialogues—The Road to Oxiana *is
in method one of the most Modernist of travel books, applying* The
Waste Land's *and* Ulysses' *mode of "collage" and ironic juxtaposition
to the experiences of travel.*

*In 1941 Byron was killed at the age of thirty-six when the ship
carrying him to an official assignment in Persia (Intelligence, naturally)
was sunk by enemy action.*

From First Russia, Then Tibet
(1933)

The supreme moments of travel are born of beauty and strangeness in
equal parts: the first panders to the senses, the second to the mind; and
it is the rarity of this coincidence which makes the rarity of these
moments. Such a moment was mine, when, at the age of three, I
ventured on to a beach in Anglesey, and found a purple scabious; such
again, when I stood on the Jelep La and surveyed the peaks of Tibet;
and such once more, as I walked up the side of the River Moskva late
in the afternoon of my second day in Russia. The Red Capital in winter
is a silent place. Like black ghouls on the soundless snow the Muscovites
went their way, hatted in fur, lamb, leather, and velvet, each with a great
collar turned up against the wind that sweeps down the river from the
east. With bent heads they hurried past, impervious to collision with one
another, or myself, as though desensitized by a decade of mass-living.
Farther on, at the corner by the bridge, stood a line of hackney sledges,
whose owners, the rearguard of capitalism, sat huddled in their portentous blue coats. Other sledges of robuster build trailed by, bearing piles
of hay and boxes. When they came to the slope by the bridge, they all
began to go sideways, while their horses scrabbled at the ice.

This, at last, was Red Russia; this horde of sable ghosts the Bolshe-
vists, the cynosure of an agitated world. It was more than Russia, it was
the capital of the Union, the very pulse of proletarian dictatorship, the
mission-house of Dialectical Materialism. I looked across the river. Before me stood the inmost sanctuary of all: the Kremlin.

A curious irony has dowered the creed of utilitarianism with this
edifice as the symbol of outward power. While collective man sits
within, the walls deny him and the domes laugh aloud. Fantastic one
has always known it to be from photographs. But the reality embodies
fantasy on an unearthly scale—a mile and a half of weathered, rose-

coloured brick in the form of a triangle that rises uphill from its base along the river. These airy walls, which in places attain a height of forty feet, are hedged with deep crenellations, cloven and coped in white stone after the Venetian fashion. Their impalpable tint and texture might suggest rather the protection of some fabled kitchen-garden than the exigencies of medieval assault. But from their mellow escarpments bursts a succession of nineteen towers, arbitrarily placed, and exhibiting such an accumulation of architectural improbability as might have resulted had the Brobdingnagians, during a game of chess, suddenly built a castle for Gulliver with the pieces. As my eye moved westward, seven of these unbelievable structures marked the half-mile prospective, itself slightly askew, of the base-wall. At either end the angle-towers were taller than the rest, each a cylinder finished with a machicolated balcony and surmounted by an octagonal cone, a kind of dormered cracker-hat tapering skywards to a bronze pennant. Between these two marched five squatter towers—steep, rectangular cones of dark green tiles, broken by a middle storey of the same rosy brick, but varying in height and breadth. These five towers, though they vary in particular dimensions, reflect a pattern introduced by the Tartars. Thus the historian may distinguish a Sino-Byzantine fusion accomplished under the aegis of Italian architects. Be that as it may—my attention was elsewhere. For now, within the walls, rose a white hill, as it were a long table covered with a cloth of snow, lifting up to the winter sky the residences of those vanished potentates, Tsar and God: to the west the two palaces, nineteenth-century Russo-Venetian, cream-coloured against the presage of snow in the sky; the little Italian palace of the fifteenth century, whose grey-stone façade of diamond rustications conceals the tiny apartments of the early Tsars; and then the Cathedrals: that of the Annunciation with nine onion-domes; that of the Dormition, where the coronations took place, with five helm-shaped domes; and that of the Archangel Michael, whose central bulb stands high above its four smaller companions; nineteen domes in all, each finished with a cross, most of them thinly gilt; and then, higher than all, the massive belfry, crowned with a flat onion; yet still overtopped by the ultimate cupola of the tower of Ivan Veliki, colossal in solitude, the climax of this Caesaropapist fantasia. I looked down to the river below me; I looked up to the sky; I looked to the right and I looked to the left: horizontally and vertically, towers and domes, spires, cones, onions, crenellations, filled the whole view. It might have been the invention of Dante, arrived in a Russian heaven.

And then as the lights came out and the snowflakes, long imminent, began to wander down in front of them, the scene became alive. As I reached the turn to the bridge, a company of soldiers came marching up the opposite street; the Red Army! visible agent of proletarian power and hardly less fantastic to my eyes than its fortress over the river. In their grey serge dressing-gowns swinging right down to the feet, and their grey serge helmets with pointed Tartar crowns, they looked like so many goblins on an infernal errand. Tramp! tramp! swung the grey serge skirts; but not a footfall sounded. From the shoulders of each goblin slanted a pair of skis, taller than the man himself, and ready to whisk him down upon some country churchyard to prod the dead. As they wheeled round to cross the bridge, they broke into a ringing chorus, taking those earnest, melancholy parts which are associated with all Russian singing. The theme of the words was doubtless Revolutionary, and, if so, not ill-suited to the effect achieved—as though the troops of ancient Russia were sallying out to a Holy War. It was quite dark now; the snow falling fast. Behind the chanting goblins the Kremlin rose aglow with electricity, like some ghostly back-cloth to the hurrying city, tower upon tower, dome upon dome, piling up from the rose-red ramparts and the snowy eminence within them, to the last gigantic onion of Ivan Veliki, 450 feet above the black river.

I followed the soldiers, and, climbing a steep road parallel with the east wall of the Kremlin, reached the Red Square. Half-way across the expanse of floodlit snow a queue had formed, ant-like in the distance, to see Lenin. The tomb was open.

I took my place next to a young Turcoman. His pale, aquiline features, properly moulded and furnished with bones, were those of an individual, and seemed companionable, despite the outlandish fleece that crowned them, among these casual-bred Slavs. But for a group of peasants clad in leather and shod with birch-bark, they presented the usual characterless appearance of all urban populations—the mass-man about to pay his Russian homage to his new and Russian Christ.

A halt preceded our entry while they swept out the snow left by the previous pilgrims. Then, two by two, the Turcoman with me, we entered the bronze wicket in the low balustrade. Two sentries, with fixed bayonets and sheepskin ruffs, stood on either side of the door. The vestibule was blank, but for the Soviet emblem—hammer and sickle on a globe supported by sheaves of wheat—in silver relief on the grey stone. Turning to the left, a flight of stairs and a subterranean corridor led us down to the vault.

In the midst of this tall, dim interior, sheeted with sombre, close-grained stones, the mummy lay on a tall pedestal sheltered by an inverted cradle of plate-glass, and brightly lit. Below, in pairs at either end, stood four sentries. We lengthened into single file. Mounting a flight of steps, I took my view and, in virtue of the atmosphere, paid my homage. Round the walls, I noticed, ran a frieze of vitreous scarlet lightning.

Lenin must have been a very small man. He rests on a bed of dun-coloured draperies, which engulf his legs with the tasteful negligence of a modiste's window. His upper part wears a khaki jacket buttoned at the neck. The finely modelled hands and features are of waxen texture, like the petals of a magnolia flower. The beard and moustache turn from straw-colour to brown, a fact which caused Bernard Shaw more surprise (so he told me) than anything else in his self-patented Russian Elysium. One might have said: A nice little man, fond of his grandchildren, and given to pruning his trees. I wondered whether a countenance so placid and benign was not really made of wax. For rumour insists that the sewers of the Kremlin recently overflowed into the shrine, to the detriment of its keepsake. But when I got outside, I had not walked a hundred yards before I met an old man with features, beard, and expression exactly similar to those I had just examined. So that there need be nothing inherently false about the present appearance of the relic.

The Red Square was so called long before the Revolution, since the Russian words for "red" and "beautiful" are the same. Still the snow falls, each flake softly sparkling in the electric haze. At the north end of the great white oblong rises the blood-coloured bulk of the Historical Museum, a building in Ye Olde Russian style, but now transformed into something fairy-like by the snow filigree on its twin steeples and twisting rooflets. Along the Kremlin side runs the same crenellated rose-red wall, interrupted by three towers. That near the Museum, which carries a slender, cold green spire, was blown up by Napoleon, but rebuilt according to the old design after his departure. At the other end of the square, to the south, stands the famous Spassky tower, a castle of brick surmounted by Gothic pinnacles and finials of white stone, which remind one of Wren's Tom Tower, and were actually built by an Englishman, Christopher Holloway, in 1625. This bears a rich octagonal steeple, decorated with a gilt clock-face. From the topmost apex shines the emblem of the Tsars, a golden eagle, whose glinting double heads act as a signpost to the stranger lost in the "China Town" opposite.

These two towers, with one other on the west side, are the chief entrances to the Kremlin. Between them the wall is broken by a blind tower of the rectangular double-cone type, above which appears a flat dome of green copper, in the austere Greek style of the later Catherine period. From this dome floats a plain red flag, emblem no longer of the rowdy May-Day farce in other capitals, but invested with the dignity of its architectural surroundings. Beneath the wall runs a series of low tribunes in grey-white granite. These are interrupted, immediately below the tower, by Lenin's tomb, which is backed by a screen of small black fir-trees.

The tomb is squat and powerful, instepped like a Ziggurat, and polished like a public-house. It is built of red Ukrainian granite and black and grey Ukrainian labrador, which contains flecks of iridescent blue like those on a butterfly's wing. The lantern is surmounted by a monolith of red Karelian porphyry, 26 1/4 feet in length and weighing 59 tons. The colour of the granite is not our anaemic pink, but a deep rhubarb-red, slightly tinged with ochre. This colour strikes a mean between the scarlet flag and the pink walls, and fits the monument harmoniously upon its ancient stage.

The architect of the mausoleum is Stchousev. His original design, which stood for five years, was of wood. The present, though similar in character, is stronger and more ruthless. It is constructed—or gives the illusion of being constructed—of superb blocks of stone, whose gigantic size is reminiscent of the Inca walls. The form is gained partly by the use of the three colours, black, grey, and red, as an instrument of proportion, and partly by the irregular succession of steps on which these colours are employed. But these steps, though irregular, are far from haphazard. Their ratios, both of height and width, are calculated with the utmost nicety, so as to increase the effect of power and strength. The base of the monument is slightly above the level of the Square, and is enclosed within a low parapet, whose front corners are rounded, and whose rear corners are finished with two small pavilions. This parapet, these pavilions, as well as the long rows of tribunes which run parallel with the Kremlin Wall, are built of a greyish white granite, only semi-polished, and having a very close and hard texture. Within the parapet on either side of the entrance have been planted small fir-trees, which, it must be hoped, will not be allowed to grow too high.

Last of all, at the far end where the ground begins to slope down to the river, rises the famous church of Basil Blajenny—Basil the Blessed. Lying slightly below the general level of the square, yet with no other buildings behind it, it closes the panorama like some phantom ship ice-bound against the skyline. Or in circus mood one might compare it with a giant's cocoanut-shy, whose drab nuts have been replaced by sea-urchins, leeks, pineapples, and peeled pomegranates at different levels—multicoloured fruits, spiral, spiked and fluted, that tempt Lenin's ghost to warm itself on cold nights by potting snowballs at them. There are always a few nocturnal drunks about the Red Square. Perhaps some staggering mystic, or a frozen cabman, or a posse of G.P.U. raiders, passing by in the small hours, have already seen that all-familiar figure clambering wraithlike up its mausoleum for one more shot at the embodied past. I can hardly be sure that I myself, after a certain party at the Metropole, did not discern one or two extra-human missiles hurtling through the air towards that green pineapple with the red scales. . . . But the less of this the better. When I emerged from inspecting Lenin's more solid remains on this particular afternoon it was barely tea-time. Suddenly the Spassky clock rang out the hour on the last of the Moscow bells, whose deep melodious chimes never failed, so long as I stayed in the town, to give me a little start of melancholy and pleasure. And as the first clang echoed over the snow and along the red walls, a black smoke of crows shot up into the sky, cawing and croaking their contempt for that motionless anachronism, the Tsar's eagle.

The vision was over. I had exchanged the experience of a moment for a memory that will support me till I die. I shall never see Moscow again as I saw it on that afternoon.

From The Road to Oxiana
(1937)

PALESTINE: Jerusalem (2,800 ft.), September 6th.—A Nicaraguan leper would have fared better with the port authorities of a British Mandate than we did yesterday. They came on board at 5 A.M. After waiting two hours in a queue, they asked me how I could land without a visa and when my passport was not even endorsed for Palestine. I said I could buy a visa, and explained that the system of endorsement was merely one of the cruder forms of dishonesty practised by our Foreign Office, which had no real bearing on the validity of a passport. Another busybody then discovered I had been to Russia. When? and why? O, for pleasure was it? Was it pleasurable? And where was I going now? To Afghanistan? Why? Pleasure again, indeed. I was on a pleasure-trip round the world, he supposed. Then they grew so absorbed with Christopher's diplomatic visa that they forgot to give him a card of disembarkation.

A frenzied crowd seethed round the head of the gangway. Physically, Jews can look the best or the worst bred people in the world. These were the worst. They stank, stared, shoved, and shrieked. One man, who had been there five hours, began to weep. When his rabbi failed to comfort him, Christopher offered him a whisky and soda out of the bar window. He refused it. Our luggage, by degrees, was handed into a boat. I followed it. Christopher had to go back for his card of disembarkation.

There was a heavy swell, as we negotiated the surf-bound reef which constitutes the "port" of Jaffa. A woman was sick over my hand. Her husband nursed their child, while supporting in his other arm a tall plant of veronica in a pot.

"Upstairs, please!" The sweating, malformed mob divided into two queues. After half an hour I reached the doctor. He apologised for delay, and gave me a medical certificate without an examination. Downstairs the boatmen were clamouring for money. The transport of ourselves and luggage cost £1 2s. "Do you write books?" asked the customs officer, scenting an author of dutiable obscenities. I said I was not Lord Byron, and suggested he should get on with his business. At length we found a car, and putting the hood down in compliment to the Holy Land, set out for Jerusalem.

The King David Hotel is the only good hotel in Asia this side of Shanghai. We treasure every moment spent in it. The general decoration is harmonious and restrained, almost severe. But you might not think so from this notice which hangs in the hall:

NOTICE FOR THE INTERIOR DECORATION OF
THE KING DAVID HOTEL, JERUSALEM

The object was to evoke by reminiscence of ancient Semitic styles the ambience of the glorious period of King David.
A faithful reconstruction was impossible, so the artist tried to adopt to modern taste different old Jew styles.
Entrance Hall: Period of King David (Assyrian influence).
Main-Lounge: Period of King David (Hittite influence).
Reading-room: Period of King Salomon.
Bar: Period of King Salomon.
Restaurant: Greek-Syrian-Style.
Banquet Hall: Phenician Style (Assyrian influence), etc.

G. A. HUFSCHMID
Decorator, O.E.V. & S.W.B.
Geneva

The beauty of Jerusalem in its landscape can be compared with that of Toledo. The city stands in the mountains, a scape of domes and towers enclosed by crenellated walls and perched on a table of rock above a deep valley. As far as the distant hills of Moab the contours of the country resemble those of a physical map, sweeping up the slopes in regular, stratified curves, and casting grand shadows in the sudden valleys. Earth and rock reflect the lights of a fire-opal. Such an essay in urban emplacement, whether accidental or contrived, has made a work of art.

In detail, even Toledo offers no comparison with the steep winding streets, cobbled in broad steps and so narrow that a single camel causes as much disturbance as a motor coach in an English lane. Jostling up and down King David Street, from dawn to sunset, the crowd is still a picture of "the East," immune as yet from the tide of lounge suits and horn spectacles. Here comes the desert Arab, furiously moustached, sailing by in his voluminous robes of gold-worked camel hair; the Arab woman, with her face tattooed and her dress embroidered, bearing a basket on her head; the priest of Islam, trim of beard and sporting a neat white turban round his fez; the Orthodox Jew, in ringlets, beaver hat, and black frock coat; the Greek priest and Greek monk, bearded and bunned beneath their tall black chimney-pots; priests and monks from Egypt, Abyssinia, and Armenia; the Latin father in brown robe and white topee; the woman of Bethlehem, whose backward-sloping head-dress beneath a white veil is said to be a legacy of the Norman kingdom; and among them all, as background of the essential commonplace, the occasional lounge suit, the cretonne frock, the camera-strapped tourist.

Yet Jerusalem is more than picturesque, more than shoddy in the style of so many Oriental towns. There may be filth, but there is no brick or plaster, no crumbling and discolourment. The buildings are wholly of stone, a whitish cheese-like stone, candid and luminous, which the sun turns to all tones of ruddy gold. Charm and romance have no place. All is open and harmonious. The associations of history and belief, deep-rooted in the first memories of childhood, dissolve before the actual apparition. The outpourings of faith, the lamentations of Jew and Christian, the devotion of Islam to the holy Rock, have enshrouded the *genius loci* [spirit of the place] with no mystery. That spirit is an imperious emanation, evoking superstitious homage, sustained thereby perhaps, but existing independently of it. Its sympathy is with the centurions rather than the priests. And the centurions are here again. They wear shorts and topees, and answer, when addressed, with a Yorkshire accent.

* * *

Damascus, September 18th.—Since our arrival on these coasts, Christopher and I have learned that the cost of everything from a royal suite to a bottle of soda water can be halved by the simple expedient of saying it must be halved. Our technique was nicely employed in the hotel at Baalbek.

"Four hundred piastres for *that* room? *Four hundred* did you say? Good God! Away! Call the car. Three hundred and fifty? *One* hundred and fifty you mean. Three hundred? Are you deaf, can't you hear? I said a hundred and fifty. We must go. There are other hotels. Come, load the luggage. I doubt if we shall stay in Baalbek at all."

"But, sir, this is first-class hotel. I give you very good dinner, five courses. This is our best room, sir, it has bath and view of ruins, very fine."

"God in heaven, are the ruins yours? Must we pay for the very air? Five courses for dinner is too much, and I don't suppose the bath works. You still say three hundred? Come down. I say, come down a bit. That's better, two hundred and fifty. I said a hundred and fifty. I'll say two hundred. You'll have to pay the other fifty out of your own pocket, will you? Well *do*, please. I shall be delighted. Two hundred then? No? Very good. *(We run downstairs and out of the door.)* Goodbye. What? I didn't hear. Two hundred. I thought so.

"And now a whisky and soda. What do you charge for that? Fifty piastres. Fifty piastres indeed. Who do you think we are? Anyhow you always give too much whisky. I'll pay *fifteen* piastres, not fifty. Don't laugh. Don't go away either. I want exactly this much whisky, no more, no less; that's only half a full portion. Thirty, you say? Is thirty half fifty? Can you do arithmetic? Soda water indeed. Twenty now. No *not* twenty-five. Twenty. There is all the difference, if you could only realise it. Bring the bottle at once, and for heaven's sake don't argue."

During the five-course dinner, we complimented the man on some succulent birds.

"Partridges, sir," he replied, "I make them fat in little houses."

Admission to the ruins costs five shillings per person per visit. Having secured a reduction of this charge by telephoning to Beyrut, we walked across to visit them.

"Guide, Monsieur?"

Silence.

"Guide, Monsieur?"

Silence.

"Qu'est-ce que vous désirez, Monsieur?"

Silence.

"D'où venez-vous, Monsieur?"

Silence.

"Où allez-vous, Monsieur?"

Silence.

"Vous avez des affaires ici, Monsieur?"

"Non."

"Vous avez des affaires à Baghdad, Monsieur?"

"Non."

"Vous avez des affaires à Téhéran, Monsieur?"

"Non."
"Alors, qu'est-ce que vous faites, Monsieur?"
"Je fais un voyage en Syrie."
"Vous êtes un officier naval, Monsieur?"
"Non."
"Alors, qu'est-ce que vous êtes, Monsieur?"
"Je suis homme."
"Quoi?"
"Homme."
"Je comprends. Touriste."
["What do you wish, Sir?"
"Where are you from Sir?"
"Where are you headed, Sir?"
"Do you have business here, Sir?"
"Do you have business in Baghdad, Sir?"
"Do you have business in Teheran, Sir?"
"Then what are you doing here, Sir?"
"I'm traveling in Syria."
"Are you a naval officer, Sir?"
"Then what are you, Sir?"
"I am a person."
"What?"
"A *person.*"
"I understand. A tourist."]

Even "voyageur" [traveller] is obsolete; and with reason: the word has a complimentary air. The traveller of old was one who went in search of knowledge and whom the indigènes were proud to entertain with their local interests. In Europe this attitude of reciprocal appreciation has long evaporated. But there at least the "tourist" is no longer a phenomenon. He is part of the landscape, and in nine cases out of ten has little money to spend beyond what he has paid for his tour. Here, he is still an aberration. If you can come from London to Syria on business, you must be rich. If you can come so far without business, you must be very rich. No one cares if you like the place, or hate it, or why. You are simply a tourist, as a skunk is a skunk, a parasitic variation of the human species, which exists to be tapped like a milch cow or a gum tree.

At the turnstile, that final outrage, a palsied dotard took ten minutes to write out each ticket. After which we escaped from these trivialities into the glory of Antiquity.

Baalbek is the triumph of stone; of lapidary magnificence on a scale whose language, being still the language of the eye, dwarfs New York into a home of ants. The stone is peach-coloured, and is marked in ruddy gold as the columns of St. Martin-in-the-Fields are marked in soot. It has a marmoreal texture, not transparent, but faintly powdered, like bloom on a plum. Dawn is the time to see it, to look up at the Six Columns, when peach-gold and blue air shine with equal radiance, and even the empty bases that uphold no columns have a living, sun-blest identity against the violet deeps of the firmament. Look up, look up; up this quarried flesh, these thrice-enormous shafts, to the broken capitals and the cornice as big as a house, all floating in the blue. Look over the walls, to the green groves of white-stemmed poplars; and over them to the distant Lebanon, a shimmer of mauve and blue and gold and rose. Look along the mountains to the void: the desert, that stony, empty sea. Drink the high air. Stroke the stone with your own soft hands. Say goodbye to the West if you own it. And then turn, *tourist,* to the East.

We did, when the ruins closed. It was dusk. Ladies and gentlemen in separate parties were picnicking on a grass meadow, beside a stream. Some sat on chairs by marble fountains, drawing at their hubble-bubbles; others on the grass beneath occasional trees, eating by their own lanterns. The stars came out and the mountain slopes grew black. I felt the peace of Islam. And if I mention this commonplace experience, it is because in Egypt and Turkey that peace is now denied; while in India Islam appears, like everything else, uniquely and exclusively In-dian. In a sense it is so; for neither man nor institution can meet that overpowering environment without a change of identity. But I will say this for my own sense: that when travelling in Mohammedan India without previous knowledge of Persia, I compared myself to an Indian observing European classicism, who had started on the shores of the Baltic instead of the Mediterranean.

* * *

In Kazvin next morning we hired another car, whose driver refused to lower the hood. When, therefore, he took a dip at forty miles an hour and my forehead came crack against a wooden strut, I gave him a sharp prod in the back. The car stopped dead. We bade him go on. He did so, at ten miles an hour. We bade him go faster. He did so for a little, then slowed down again.

Christopher: Faster! Faster!
Driver: How can I drive if you all hit me?
R.B.: Go on!
Driver: How can I drive if the aga doesn't like me?
Christopher: Drive carefully. We don't dislike you, but we hate danger-
ous driving.

Driver: Alas, how can I drive? The aga hates me. My times are
   bitter.
Christopher: The aga does like you.
Driver: How can he if I have broken his head?

And so on for miles, till we came to a police-post. Here he stopped dead,
saying he must register a complaint. There was only one thing to do:
complain first. We jumped from the car and strode towards the office.
This alarmed the man; for it was evident that if we sought the police
with such alacrity they must be on our side instead of his. He suggested
going on instead. We agreed.

The incident was an illustration, and a warning, of the acute horror
which Persians feel towards even the pretence of physical violence.

*   *   *

Tabriz (4,500 ft.), October 15th.—In Zinjan at last we picked up a
lorry. As Christopher was taking a photograph of me sitting in the back,
a policeman stepped up and said photographing was forbidden. The
driver was an Assyrian from near Lake Urmiya, and by his side sat an
Assyrian schoolmistress, who was returning from a missionary conference in Teheran. She regaled us with slices of quince. They were much
interested in my acquaintance with Mar Shimun, and advised me to say
nothing about it in Tabriz, since there was a persecution of Christians
at the moment, and Mrs. Cochran's Women's Club in Urmiya had been
shut by the police. At the thought of this, they sang *Lead, Kindly Light*
in unison, the school-mistress informing me that she had taught the
driver this to prevent his singing the usual drivers' songs. I said I should
have preferred the drivers' songs. She added that she had also persuaded
him to remove the blue beads from his radiator-cap; they were a superstition of "these Moslems." When I told her they were a superstition
generally practised by Christians of the Orthodox Church, she was
dumbfounded. She admitted then that superstitions sometimes worked:
there was a devil named Mehmet, for instance, with a human wife,
through whom he had prophesied the War in her father-in-law's parlour.
She called herself a bible-worker, and wanted to know if most people in
England smoked or did not smoke. Why doctors did not forbid smoking
and drinking, instead of doing so themselves, she could not understand.

I began to sympathise with the Persian authorities. Missionaries do
noble work. But once they make converts, or find indigenous Christians,
their usefulness is not so great.

Christopher, at this stage, was reading in the back of the lorry, where
his companions were a Teherani, an Isfahani, two muleteers, and the
driver's assistant.

Teherani: What's this book?

Christopher: A book of history.

Teherani: What history?

Christopher: The history of Rum and the countries near it, such as Persia, Egypt, Turkey, and Frankistan.

Assistant (opening the book): Ya Ali! What characters!

Teherani: Can you read it?

Christopher: Of course. It's my language.

Teherani: Read it to us.

Christopher: But you cannot understand the language.

Isfahani: No matter. Read a little.

Muleteers: Go on! Go on!

Christopher: "It may occasion some surprise that the Roman pontiff should erect, in the heart of France, the tribunal from whence he hurled his anathemas against the king; but our surprise will vanish so soon as we form a just estimate of a king of France in the eleventh century."

Teherani: What's that about?

Christopher: About the Pope.

Teherani: The Foof? Who's that?

Christopher: The Caliph of Rum.

Muleteer: It's a history of the Caliph of Rum.

Teherani: Shut up! Is it a new book?

Assistant: Is it full of clean thoughts?

Christopher: It is without religion. The man who wrote it did not believe in the prophets.

Teherani: Did he believe in God?

Christopher: Perhaps. But he despised the prophets. He said that Jesus was an ordinary man *(general agreement)* and that Mohammad was an ordinary man *(general depression)* and that Zoroaster was an ordinary man.

Muleteer (who speaks Turkish and doesn't understand well): Was he called Zoroaster?

Christopher: No, Gibbon.

Chorus: Ghiboon! Ghiboon!

Teherani: Is there any religion which says there is no god?

Christopher: I think not. But in Africa they worship idols.

Teherani: Are there many idolaters in England?

The road led into mountains, where a great gorge brought us to the river of the Golden Swimmer. He was a shepherd, a Leander, who used to swim across to visit his beloved, until at last she built the truly magnificent bridge by which we also crossed. A herd of gazelle frisked along beside us. At length we came out on the Azerbaijan highlands, a dun sweeping country like Spain in winter. We passed through Miana, which is famous for a bug that bites only strangers, and spent the night in a lonely caravanserai where a wolf was tethered in the courtyard. At Tabriz the police asked us for five photographs each (they did not get them) and the following information:

AVIS

Je soussigné   { Robert Byron
                   Christopher Sykes

Sujet   { anglais
            anglais

et exerçant la profession de   { peintre
                                   philosophe

déclare être arrivé en date du   { 13me octobre
                                     13me octobre

accompagné de   { un djinn
                    un livre par Henry James

etc.

[NOTICE

The undersigned   { Robert Byron
                      Christopher Sykes

Nationality   { British
                  British

Profession   { Painter
                 Philosopher

Arrived   { October 13
              October 13

Accompanied by   { A genie
                     A book by Henry James]

* * *

Wadsworth, the American chargé d'affaires, introduced me to Farquharson. I beheld an unattractive countenance, prognathous yet weedy, with hair growing to a point on the bridge of the nose. From the mouth issued a whining monotone. Still, I thought, one must make allowances.

Now that Christopher is laid up, it will be difficult to find anyone else to travel with.

R.B.: I hear you're thinking of going to Afghanistan. Perhaps we could join up, if you really—
Farquharson: Now I must explain to you first of all that I'm here to make a *vurry* hurried trip. I've already spent two days in Teheran. They tell me I ought to see the Peacock Throne, whatever that may be. I don't know that I'm particularly keen on seeing it. Frankly I'm naht interested in seeing things, I'm interested in history. I'm interested in liberty. Even in America liberty is naht what it was. I'd have you understand of course that I am *vurry* pressed for time. My parents were naht anxious for me to come on this trip. My father has recently founded an advertising business in Memphis, and he said he hoped I'd be back home by Christmas. Perhaps I'll stay over till January. It depends how things work out. There's the southern trip, with a day in Isfahann, and another in Shiraz. There's Tabriz. And there's Afghanistan. Frankly, if Afghanistan is pahssible, I should like to go there. My plans aren't fixed. I wasn't sure even, when I left, if I'd come to Persia. People in the States told me it was dangerous. People here say the same about Afghanistan. They may be right. I doubt it. I've travelled considerably. There's no European country, including Iceland and excepting Russia, I haven't visited. I once slept in a ditch in Albania. Of course that wasn't *vurry* difficult, though I talked about it afterwards in Memphis a good deal. So if it is pahssible, I should like to go to Afghanistan. But I could only make a *vurry* hurried trip. We might get through to Kabul, we might not. If we did, I might rent a plane back here. I'm naht anxious to see India for the moment. It's a big place and I'm saving it for another fall. I've already spent two days in Teheran. Those two days have been mainly occupied socially. I've enjoyed them. But that's naht what I came for. I'm here, you understand, to make a *vurry* hurried trip. Now if Afghanistan is pahssible, I should like to start tomorrow. Mr. Wadsworth, who also comes from Memphis, gave me a letter to the Afghan Ambassador. When I lost it, he gave me another. I went round this morning, but the Ambassador couldn't see me. He had some ladies with him. I saw a secretary instead, but he didn't speak English, and my French is only college French, so we didn't get *vurry* far. I may get the visa, I may naht. In any case I should like to start tomorrow morning. You see, I'm here to make a *vurry* hurried trip.

R.B.: I was going to suggest that if you wanted a companion, I might come with you and share expenses. It would suit me, because I can't afford to take a car of my own.

Farquharson: I must admit I'm naht exactly pressed for money. At the same time I work, like everyone else in the States. With you in Europe it's different. But over there we have no leisured class. Everyone works, even if he hasn't gaht to. It would hurt you socially if you didn't. I've set aside four thousand dollars for this trip. But that doesn't mean I'm particularly anxious to throw money away. I expect I can *afford* to go to Afghanistan if I can spare the time. You see I'm here to make a *vurry* hurried trip.

R.B.: If you could tell me exactly how long you do want to spend over the journey, perhaps we could work out a plan.

Farquharson: That all depends. *(Repeats all he has previously said at greater length.)*

Eventually I went myself to the Afghan Embassy, to see whether I would assist Farquharson's application for a visa. Meanwhile, we had arranged to meet next day. He came to the Coq d'Or while Christopher and I were lunching with Herzfeld, who had just returned from Europe.

Farquharson (breathlessly, as he lopes across the dining-room): I believe my plans have taken a turn for the better. I haven't actually gaht the visa yet. But I think I shall get it. Now there are one or two points I'm *vurry* anxious to discuss with you—

R.B.: May I introduce Professor Herzfeld?

Farquharson: . . . I'm vurry glad to meet you, sir. You see I'm here to make a *vurry* hurried trip and I was going to say—

Christopher: Won't you sit down?

Farquharson: I was going to say, first of all, that I'm vurry anxious to start tomorrow morning if pahssible. Of course it may naht be pahssible. But if it is, that's my plan.

Herzfeld (trying to dissipate the boredom): I see you have a tame fox in the courtyard here.

Christopher: There used to be a wild boar as well. But it had to be killed because it would get into the guests' beds when they were asleep. Why they should have minded, Madame Pitrau said, she couldn't imagine; it only wanted its stomach scratching. But they did, and that was the end of it.

R.B.: The fox gets into the beds too, and wets them.

Farquharson: Of course this is vurry amusing, though I'm afraid I don't get the joke. Now there are one or two points I'm *vurry* anxious to discuss with you.

Herzfeld: I keep a porcupine at Persepolis. It is very domesticated. If tea is one minute late it becomes furious, and its spikes, what do you call them, quills, stand up.

Farquharson: There are one or two points I'm *vurry*—

Herzfeld: Also it uses the W.C. like a human being. Every morning I have to wait for it. We all have to wait for it.

Farquharson (wanly): That's extremely interesting, though I'm afraid I don't quite get there. Now there are one or two—

R.B.: We'd better go to my room. *(We go.)*

Farquharson: There are one or two points I'm *vurry* anxious to discuss with you. I want to make it clear that if I do go to Afghanistan, I shall have to make a *vurry* hurried trip. Now I want to speak vurry frankly. You don't know me and I don't know you. I think we'll get on. I hope we will. But we must try and get things clear beforehand. I've written down a few points on a bit of paper which I'll just read out. Number one I've called Personal Relationships. I've travelled a considerable amount. I know therefore that travelling brings out the worst in people. For instance I have a brother in Memphis. He's vurry fond of music. I am naht fond of music. We were together in Paris. After dinner he'd go to a concert. I did naht. I'm fond of my brother, but even so certain difficulties of this class are apt to arise. Now I don't know you and you don't know me. We may have hardships, we may fall sick. In sickness we can't expect to be cheerful. Otherwise I think we should remember this question of Personal Relationships. The second point I've called Political. I'm going to speak *vurry* frankly. I'm pressed for time over here, you understand, and if we go to Afghanistan together, as I hope we will, I want to make it clear that I must have the power on this trip. That's why I've called this second point Political. If I decide I don't want to go anywhere, well then we just shan't be able to go. I shall do my best to meet your wishes. I shall try and be fair. I think I shall be fair. Mr. Wadsworth, who also comes from Memphis, knows my family and I think he'll tell you I'm likely to be fair. But I must be the boss politically. The third point is Financial. Since I've taken so much power on this trip, I'm prepared to pay a little more than half the car. But you realise I'm pressed for time, I have to make a *vurry* hurried trip, and it's pahssible I may go right through to India and take a boat from there. Now I understand you're pressed for money, from what you said. I couldn't leave a fellow-traveller stranded in India. So before we start I've gaht to

know you've enough money to get back to Persia, and I've gaht to
see the notes actually in your hand—
R.B.: What?
Farquharson: I've gaht to see the notes actually in your hand—
R.B.: Goodbye.
Farquharson: . . . before leaving, so's I can be quite sure you can shift
for yourself in the event of—
R.B.: Get out, if you're not deaf.

Farquharson fled. On the way out, he ran into Herzfeld and Christopher, and wrung their hands warmly. "I'm vurry glad to have met you.
Goodbye. I must be getting along. You see I have to make a *vurry*
hurried trip. . . ."

He had. I was at his heels. Not that I would have touched him without
rubber gloves and a bottle of disinfectant. But he was good to threaten.
I had seen him dressing the day before, and had noted a *vurry* poor
muscular development.

* * *

A Hungarian has arrived here. He has just spent a month in hospital
at Kandahar, and his stomach is still so deranged that he cannot eat. In
fact he is starving to death. I gave him some soup and ovaltine which
cheered him up and made him talk in bad French.

"Five years, Monsieur, I have been travelling. I shall travel five years
more. Then perhaps I shall write something."

"You like travelling?"

"Who could like travelling in Asia, Monsieur? I had a good education.
What would my parents say if they saw me in such a place as this? It
is not like Europe. Beyrut is like Europe. Beyrut I could support. But
this country, these people . . . the things I have seen! I cannot tell you
of them. I cannot. Aaaaah!" And overcome by the recollection of them,
he buried his head in his hands.

"Come, Monsieur," I said, giving him a gentle pat, "confide in me
these terrible experiences. You will feel better for it.'

"I am not the type, Monsieur, who thinks himself superior to the rest
of humanity. Indeed I am no better than others. Perhaps I am worse.
But these people, these Afghans, they are not human. They are dogs,
brutes. They are lower than the animals."

"But why do you say that?"

"You don't see why, Monsieur? Have you eyes? Look at those men
over there. Are they not eating with their hands? With their *hands!* It
is frightful. I tell you, Monsieur, in one village I saw a madman, and he
was naked . . . naked."

He was silent for a little. Then he asked me in a solemn voice: "You know Stambul, Monsieur?"

"Yes."

"I lived in Stambul a year, and I tell you, Monsieur, it is a hell from which there is no way out."

"Really. But you, since you are here, did you find a way out?"

"Thank God, Monsieur, I did."

* * *

Teheran, January 25th.—Still here. Still snow.

* * *

Walking into the local stationer's to buy some drawing paper, I found the Papal Nuncio at the counter, and could think of nothing to say outside my own train of thought.

"Bonjour, Monseigneur."

"Bonjour, Monsieur."

Silence.

"Vous êstes artiste, Monseigneur?"

"Quoi?"

"Vous êtes peintre? Vous achetez des crayons, des couleurs?"

Horror ravaged his saintly countenance.

"Certainement non. J'achète des cartes d'invitation."

["Good day, Monsignor."

"Good day, Sir."

"Are you an artist, Monsignor?"

"What?"

"Are you a painter, perhaps? Are you buying some crayons, some paints?"

"Certainly not. I'm buying some invitation cards."]

Shir Ahmad and Tommy Jacks, the resident director of the Anglo-Persian Oil Company, came to dinner at the club. It was a good dinner: caviare, beetroot, bortsch, grilled salmon, roast partridge with mushrooms, potato chips and salad, hot meringue pudding with an ice in the middle, and mulled claret.

Shir Ahmad (mf): Madame Jacks where is she? *(dim)* She is pretty lady.

Jacks: She could not come.

Shir Ahmad (roaring ff): WHY NOT? *(Purring furiously mf)* I am very angree, *(cr)* very angree.

We played bridge afterwards, but could not finish a rubber, as Shir Admad continually left the table to illustrate his stories by acting. The history of the Afghan royal family took half an hour, in which it transpired that Shir Ahmad's cousinship to both Amanullah and the present king was due to its founder's having had 120 children. After the next hand, he proceeded to Amanullah's tour of Europe. Attended by various noble Italians they were in a box at the Roman opera.

> *(m)* Italian lady she sit beside me. She is *(eyes blazing ff)* big lady, yah! great? no, fat. *(mf)* She more fat than Madame Egypt [the Egyptian Ministress] and her breast is *(cr)* too big. *(mf)* It fall out of box, so. Much diamonds and gold on it. *(pp)* I am frightened. I see if it shall be in my face *(f)* I suffocate.

The scene moved to the State Banquet at Buckingham Palace.

> *(m)* Prince of Wales he talk to me. *(p)* I tell him, "Your Royal Highness *(ff)* you are fool! *(roaring)* You are FOOL!" *(m)* Prince of Wales he say, *(p)* "Why am I fool?" *(m)* I tell him, "Sir, because you steeple-jump. It is dangerous, *(cr)* dangerous. *(p)* English peoples not pleased if Your Royal Highness die." *(m)* King he hear. He tell Queen, "Mary, His Excellency call our son fool." He very angree, *(cr)* very angree. *(mf)* Queen she ask me why her son fool. I say because he steeple-jump. Queen say to me, *(dim)* "Your Excellency, Your Excellency, you are right, *(cr)* you are right." *(m)* Queen thank me. King thank me.

Teheran. January 29th.—Still here.

Yesterday morning we got up at three and were out of the town by six, intending to make Isfahan in one day. After ten miles the road became an ice-floe; a drift had thawed and frozen again. I accelerated. We crashed on twenty yards, nearly overturned, and came to a lugubrious full-stop. At this moment the sun rose, a twinkle of fire lit the snowy plain, the white range of the Elbuzr was suffused with blue and gold, and a breath of warmth endeared the icy wind. Cheered by the beauty of the scene, we returned to the capital.

* * *

At Bandar Shah, the new Caspian port where the railway ends, a regular seaside crowd met the train. Among them were the local Chief of Police and a representative of the War Office, who asked us where we were going.

Gumbad-i-Kabus?

Certainly. And we could also, if we liked, motor on to Meshed by the new military road through Bujnurd and the Turcoman country.

This was a welcome surprise. When I asked for permission to visit

Gumbad-i-Kabus in Teheran, Jam, the Minister of the Interior, sent me a private message begging me to withdraw the request, since the place was in a military zone and he could not grant it. Hearing this, Pybus, our Military Attaché, offered to put in a word for us with the General Staff. But he had had no answer when we left, and we had come thus far on chance. It was Diez's picture of Gumbad-i-Kabus that decided me to come to Persia, and I would sooner, as far as I know, have missed any other building in the country.

Even in the dark, we could perceive the steppe. The headlights died in space, finding nothing to reveal but a passing boar. There came a scent of sweet grass, as on a night in June at home before the hay is cut. At Asterabad the populace were celebrating Mohurram, marching through the streets behind a draped coffin and bearing aloft triangular banners of lights. Many wept and groaned, and such as had their hands free were tearing their clothes and beating themselves, as Shir Ahmad had described. We are staying with an old Turk, who used to be British vice-consul here, and offers to arrange a tiger-shoot for us.

Gumbad-i-Kabus (200 ft.), April 24th.—After following the Bandar Shah road a little way back, we turned to the right down a track between wattle fences. High reeds obscured the view. Suddenly, as a ship leaves an estuary, we came out on to the steppe: a dazzling open sea of green. I never saw that colour before. In other greens, of emerald, jade, or malachite, the harsh deep green of the Bengal jungle, the sad cool green of Ireland, the salad green of Mediterranean vineyards, the heavy full-blown green of English summer beeches, some element of blue or yellow predominates over the others. This was the pure essence of green, indissoluble, the colour of life itself. The sun was warm, the larks were singing up above. Behind us rose the misty Alpine blue of the wooded Elburz. In front, the glowing verdure stretched out to the rim of the earth.

Bearings, landmarks, disappeared, as they would from a skiff in mid-Atlantic. We seemed to be always below the surrounding level, caught in the trough of a green swell. Sitting down, we might see for twenty feet: standing up, for twenty miles—and even then, twenty miles away, the curve of the earth was as green as the bank that touched the wheels, so that it was hard to tell which was which. Our only chart was by things whose scale we knew: groups of white-topped kibitkas, dotted like mushrooms on a lawn—though even in their case it needed an effort of reason to believe they were not mushrooms; and droves of cattle, mares with their foals, black and brown sheep, kine and camels—though the camels were deceptive in the opposite sense, seeming so tall that it needed another effort to believe they were not antediluvian monsters. As the huts and animals varied in size, we could plot their distances: half a mile, a mile; five miles. But it was not this that conveyed the size of the steppe so much as the multiplicity of these nomadic encampments, cropping up wherever the eye rested, yet invariably separate by a mile or two from their neighbours. There were hundreds of them, and the sight, therefore, seemed to embrace hundreds of miles.

As plans of cities are inset on maps of countries, another chart on a larger scale lay right beneath our wheels. Here the green resolved, not into ordinary grass, but into wild corn, barley, and oats, which accounted for that vivid fire, as of a life within the green. And among these myriad bearded alleys lived a population of flowers, buttercups and poppies, pale purple irises and dark purple campanulas, and countless others, exhibiting all the colours, forms, and wonders that a child finds in its first garden. Then a puff of air would come, bending the corn to a silver ripple, while the flowers leaned with it; or a cloud-shadow, and all grow dark, as if for a moment's sleep; though a few feet off there would be no ripple and no darkness; so that this whole inner world of the steppe was mapped on a system of infinite minute recessions, having just those gradations of distance that the outer lacked.

Our spirits had risen when we left the plateau. Now they effervesced. We shouted for joy, stopping the car lest the minutes that were robbing us of the unrepeatable first vision should go faster. Even the larks in this paradise had lost their ordinary aloofness. One almost hit my hat in its inquisitiveness.

We found the Gurgan river in a cutting thirty feet deep, whose bare earth cliffs traced a gash of desolation through the green. It was as wide as the Severn in its upper reaches, and we crossed it by an old brick bridge on tall pointed arches. This was defended, on the north bank, by a gate-house, whose overhanging upper storey had a broad-eaved tiled roof such as one sees in the Apennines. From here smooth green tracks began to radiate over the steppe in all directions, and we could hardly have found the way but for the occasional traffic of riders on horses and camels and high-wheeled gigs who pointed it out to us. They were all Turcomans, the ladies in red chintz covered with flowers, the men in plain red or more rarely in gorgeous multi-coloured silks woven with lightning zigzags. But there were not many fleece hats. Most of the men wore Marjoribanks's substitute, or at least a cardboard peak attached to a fleece cap.

The Elburz now began to curve round in front of us, enclosing a green bay. In the middle of this, twenty miles away, a small cream needle stood up against the blue of the mountains, which we knew for the tower of Kabus. An hour later, steering by this point, we reached a small market town, whose broad straight streets recall the Russian occupation of the district before the War. The tower stands on the north of the town, helped into the sky by a green hillock of irregular shape, but artificial, and of great age.

A tapering cylinder of café-au-lait brick springs from a round plinth to a pointed grey-green roof, which swallows it up like a candle extinguisher. The diameter at the plinth is fifty-feet; the total height about a hundred and fifty. Up the cylinder, between plinth and roof, rush ten triangular buttresses, which cut across two narrow garters of Kufic text, one at the top underneath the cornice, one at the bottom over the slender back entrance.

The bricks are long and thin, and as sharp as when they left the kiln, thus dividing the shadow from the sunshine of each buttress with knife-like precision. As the buttresses recede from the direction of the sun, the shadows extend on to the curving wall of the cylinder between them, so that the stripes of light and shade, varying in width, attain an extraordinary momentum. It is the opposition of this vertical momentum to the lateral embrace of the Kufic rings that gives the building its character, a character unlike anything else in architecture.

There is nothing inside. The body of Kabus used to hang there, suspended from the roof in a glass coffin. He died in 1007. For more than a thousand years this lighthouse has announced his memory, and the genius of Persia, to the nomads of the Central Asian sea. Today it has a larger audience, which must wonder how the use of brick, at the beginning of the second millennium after Christ, came to produce a more heroic monument, and a happier play of surfaces and ornament, than has ever been seen in that material since.

(Superlatives applied by travellers to objects which they have seen, but most people have not, are generally suspect; I know it, having been guilty of them. But re-reading this diary two years later, in as different an environment as possible (Pekin), I still hold the opinion I formed before going to Persia, and confirmed that evening on the steppe: that the Gumbad-i-Kabus ranks with the great buildings of the world.)

The military Governor called at dinner-time, and told us of the tradition that something used to flash from the roof of the tower; it was of glass or crystal, and was believed to hold a lamp. The Russians, he said, took it away; though he did not explain how they reached it. This tradition may contain a distorted reference to Kabus's glass coffin, which seems to have been genuine fact, as it was recorded by the Arab historian Jannabi soon after Kabus's death.

The country round here is covered with antiquities, if only we had time to stop and look for them. "Alexander's Wall" is only a few miles north of the Gurgan, and the swamps along the river to the east are said to be crowded with ruins that no one has explored. There are also prehistoric remains. Not long ago some Turcoman families found a tumulus filled with bronze vessels, which they abstracted and put into domestic use. Then bad luck overtook them, and ascribing it to their desecration of a grave they returned to the tumulus and re-buried the vessels. One imagines the rush of professors to this archaeological Klondyke, if they knew where it was.

The Governor also brings us the bad news that the road to Bujnurd is blocked by rain and landslides. We might get through, but a lorry has just crawled in here half wrecked, after spending five days on the journey, and we dare not risk the car, with Afghanistan before it. In consequence, we are considering a ride over the mountains to Shahrud, while the car goes back by Firuzkuh.

Bandar Shah (sea-level), April 26th.— Under arrest! I am writing on a bed in the police-station.

FREYA STARK
1893–

Freya Stark is among the most memorable of modern women explorer-travelers, distinguished by her learning, resource, stubbornness (she earned a reputation of being "difficult"), and courage. "Pretty tough" is the way she once described herself. She has always been concerned not just with travel but with its meaning for human life in general. At her aphoristic best she resembles a peripatetic female Emerson, but a resolutely British one.

She was born of artistic parents in Paris and lived and traveled widely in Italy during holidays from the University of London and the School of Oriental and African Studies. During the Great War she was a nurse in northern Italy, and it is there that she has chosen mainly to live when not exploring on donkey- or camel-back remote areas of Persia (the region of the original Assassins), Turkey, Greece, and the Arab countries. She has produced over two dozen travel books and volumes of memoirs and letters. In her travel writing, as one reader has noted, she focuses simultaneously on "past and present, as it were stereoscopically, in a single image," and she is skilled at inferring general human principles from the observed data of travel. For example: "Curiosity ought to increase as one grows older. The earth grows bigger, it ceases to contain itself, it laps beyond its sphere; and Time comes less and less to be confined in this tangible air." And wondering what it is that urges people to travel seriously, she finds that "Travel does what good novelists also do to the life of everyday, placing it like a picture in a frame or a gem in its setting, so that the intrinsic qualities are made more clear. Travel does this with the very stuff that everyday life is made of, giving to it the sharp contour and meaning of art."

The following selections have been made from the books indicated by Freya Stark, with the assistance of Lawrence Durrell.

From THE VALLEYS OF THE ASSASSINS
(1934)

This is a great moment, when you see, however distant, the goal of your wandering. The thing which has been living in your imagination suddenly becomes a part of the tangible world. It matters not how many ranges, rivers or parching dusty ways may lie between you: it is yours now for ever. So did those old Barbarians feel who first from the Alpine wall looked down upon the Lombard plain, and saw Verona and its towers and the white river bed below them: so did Xenophon and Cortez, and every adventurer and pilgrim, however humble, before them or after: and so did I as I looked over that wide country, intersected by red and black ranges, while the group of hillmen around me, delighted with my delight, pointed out the way to the Rock of Alamut in a pale green cleft made small by distance far below.

* * *

The mountain shape, first seen as a dream in the distance, alarming as you approach, lost perhaps altogether as you become involved in its outworks and ramifying valleys, appears again suddenly, unexpected as some swift light upon a face beloved to which custom has blunted our eyes. Like a human being, the mountain is a composite creature, only to be known after many a view from many a different point, and repaying this loving study, if it is anything of a mountain at all, by a gradual revelation of personality, an increase of significance: until, having wandered up in its most secret places, you will know it ever after from the plains, though from there it is but one small blue flame among the sister ranges that press their delicate teeth into the evening sky.

* * *

People who know nothing about these things will tell you that there is no addition of pleasure in having a landscape to yourself. But this is not true. It is a pleasure exclusive, unreasoning, and real: it has some of the quality and some of the intensity of love: it is a secret shared: a communion which an intruder desecrates: and to go to the lonely and majestic places of the world for poor motives, to turn them to cheap advertisement or flashy journalism, jars like a spiritual form of prostitution on your true lover of the hills. The solitary rapture must be disinterested. And often it is stumbled upon unthinkingly by men whose business takes them along remoter ways: who suddenly find enchantment on their path and carry it afterwards through their lives with a secret sense of exile.

* * *

What a delicate plant is our civilization, I thought, as I sat in the shade with the circle of the tribesmen around me, in that short silence which is good manners in the East. You would imagine that these people, who know the life of cities and its comforts, would reproduce it in some measure when they return to their own hills. Far from it. They return and live just as they lived two thousand years ago or more. The force of primitive circumstance is too great for them. And these amenities are not, like freedom, or religion, authority or leisure, among the indispensable necessities of mankind.

* * *

Out in the sunset the homing flocks poured like honey down the hill-side with their shepherds behind them; beyond the cries and greetings, the barking and noises of the camp, lay the silence of uninhabited mountains, a high and lonely peace.

* * *

Solitude, I reflected, is the one deep necessity of the human spirit to which adequate recognition is never given in our codes. It is looked upon as a discipline or a penance, but hardly ever as the indispensable, pleasant ingredient it is to ordinary life; and from this want of recognition come half our domestic troubles. The fear of an unbroken tête-à-tête for the rest of his life should, you would think, prevent any man from getting married. (Women are not so much affected, since they can usually be alone in their houses for most of the day if they wish.) Modern education ignores the need for solitude: hence a decline in religion, in poetry, in all the deeper affections of the spirit: a disease to be *doing* something always, as if one could never sit quietly and let the puppet show unroll itself before one: an inability to lose oneself in mystery and wonder while, like a wave lifting us into new seas, the history of the world develops around us. I was thinking these thoughts when Husein, out of breath and beating the grey mare for all he was worth with the plaited rein, came up behind me, and asked how I could bear to go on alone for over an hour, with everyone anxious behind me.

* * *

Danger is interesting and necessary to the human spirit, but to do something that will be generally disapproved of, if found out, must be humiliating unless one is so hardened that other people's opinions can have no influence at all. Only a fanatic can be happily a criminal.

* * *

It is pleasant now and then to go among people who carry their lives lightly, who do not give too much importance to this transitory world, and are not so taken up with the means of living that no thought and time is left over for the enjoyment of life itself.

* * *

It is a remarkable thing, when one comes to consider it, that indifference should be so generally considered a sign of superiority the world over; dignity or age, it is implied, so fill the mind with matter that other people's indiscriminate affairs glide unperceived off that profound abstraction: that at any rate is the impression given not only by village *mullas* [Islamic scholars], but by ministers, bishops, dowagers and well-bred people all over the world, and the village of Shahristan was no exception, except that the assembled dignitaries found it more difficult to conceal the strain which a total absence of curiosity entails.

* * *

We came down into Khava in the sunset when the cliffs of Kuh Garu shine like opals in a light of their own. Mist lay in the hollows and the air was cold. In the village of Beira where we lodged, in the north-eastern part of the plain beside another ancient mound, the tribesmen had not yet moved from their tents into the winter houses, so that we had another evening in the open, roasting pleasantly round a fire of thorn bushes in the middle of the headman's tent, where his carpets were spread in our honour. One side was open: a long line of black oxen with felt rugs on their backs blocked it and acted as a windscreen: they chewed their feed gently through the night, while we slept as well as we could with rivulets of cold air creeping down our spines: now and then some tribesman, pirate-faced in the half-darkness, would rouse himself, heap an armful of thorns on the embers, and fill the tent with strange shadows and a fleeting warmth.

LURISTAN

* * *

As we rode back, and the valley lay shining before us with the mounds of its cemeteries, or habitations perhaps, plainly visible under the folds of the ground, the great age of the world seemed to be revealed with a sudden poignancy: here men had wandered for thousands of years, their origin and their end unknown. Their dead lie thicker than the living amid these hills.

LURISTAN

* * *

Zora used to look after me for fourpence a day. With her rags, which hung in strips about her, she had the most beautiful and saddest face I have ever seen. She would sit on the grass by my bedside with her knees drawn up, silent by the hour, looking out with her heavy-lidded eyes to the valley below and the far slopes where the shadows travelled, like some saint whose Eternity is darkened by the remote voice of sorrow in the world.

SHAHRISTAN VALLEY

* * *

A worse shock met me as I came down into the courtyard. The sergeant, on his face on a blue rug on the ground, was being bastinadoed: one policeman sat on his ankles and another on his shoulders, and two more were hitting him alternately from either side with leather thongs. The Sardari sat close by on an overturned saddle, and called to me in a friendly way to come up too. The man, he said, had been stealing government cartridges. By this time I had come to the conclusion that he was not really being hurt, though calling lustily on one Imam after the other: perhaps privates are careful how they beat their own sergeants. When the Sardari had counted forty strokes, the two men got off their kicking superior, the executioners folded away their lashes, and the victim himself rose a little stiffly, but cheerfully, and saluted as if to suggest that bygones should be bygones.

LURISTAN

* * *

"Are there any police?" asked *Hajji*, who had been spoilt again by travelling with an escort.

"There were two; they have been shot," said Keram carelessly, unconscious of the havoc he caused.

He was a charming man. I think he was never afraid, though the country seemed to be thick with relatives of people he had killed, and this was a serious drawback to his usefulness as a guide outside his own tribe. On the other hand, there is a certain advantage in travelling with someone who has a reputation for shooting rather than being shot: as Keram said, in a self-satisfied way, they might kill me, but they would know that, if I was with him, there would be unpleasantness afterwards.

He had a great sense of humour and was excellent at telling a story. He told me how he had been deprived of his gun for shooting the seven pet pigs of the Armenian Governor of Alishtar, the same who had betrayed Mir Ali Khan. The pigs were grazing near the castle, and Keram, like a good Moslem, never imagined that anyone would go to the trouble of keeping such animals; he amused himself by shooting six and laming the seventh. It limped back to the castle just as the Governor came out of the gate for his evening ride. "What is this?" said the Governor. "I shot six pigs in the wood," Keram explained innocently. Whereupon his gun was taken from him, "and since then," said he, "I have had to take to opium; my heart is so sad for the long days in the hills."

It was the time for his pipe, and I offered to sit by the roadside and wait while he smoked it—a suggestion which evidently touched him, for he repeated it over and over again to his friends as an illustration of the "Akhlaq-i-shirin" or sweetness of character of women in Europe.

* * *

The uncle of Amanulla Khan appeared from the next settlement; he looked a villain, but at least a cheerful one; he had a short, thick, red beard, and a roving eye which settled at frequent intervals on my luggage. I had brought very little with me—and nothing in the way of cloaks, bed, field-glasses, or weapons that might tempt a Lur: but even so I always felt there was a certain danger in the few possessions I carried, for there was no mistaking the looks that were cast upon them even among the friendly tribes. My hat was always a great attraction, being made of finer felt than any in Luristan, and I had several times to explain that it was a woman's hat and that men would be ashamed to be seen in it; whereupon it would regretfully be put down.

* * *

Distant fires of Ittivend camps twinkled in the shadows of the valley and the lower slopes: the cliffs of Peri Kuh rose flooded in moonlight from the darkness: there was an immense and beautiful silence. Just as I was dozing off, *Hajji* crept up, and whispered to me to sleep lightly, for there would be trouble in the night: I opened one eye to watch him creep back and sit, a wakeful and forlorn little figure, guarding his horses in the moonlight: and I heard him no more till, somewhere about the middle of the night, the two men woke me with shouts which frightened away a woman who was creeping from under the back of the tent towards the luggage I was sleeping on.

LURISTAN

* * *

It is unlucky to reach a nomad's tent in the master's absence.

The laws of hospitality are based on the axiom that a stranger is an enemy until he has entered the sanctuary of somebody's tent: after that, his host is responsible, not only for his safety, but for his general acceptability with the tribe. He is treated at first with suspicion, and gradually with friendliness as he explains himself—very much as if he were trying to enter a county neighbourhood in England, for the undeveloped mind is much the same in Lincolnshire or Luristan. From the very first, however, once he is a guest, he is safe, in every district I have ever been in except the wilder regions of Lakistan.

* * *

Poor as they were, these people had two guests poorer than themselves, a widow woman and her daughter from Lakistan across the river. "The widow and the fatherless and the stranger." Among the nomad one realizes the Bible sorrow of these words; the absolute want of protection, the bitter coldness of charity when obligations of kinship or hospitality have ceased to count. These two women worked about the fields for their small share of the household bread, until they must wander on, weak, helpless, and indifferent to their own fate as driftwood.

* * *

"It was a fight," said he, "two years ago. I used to live in Harsin then, as I had married a Harsini woman and had a house there. One evening in the *Chaikhana* [tea house] there was an argument, and I shot someone dead. I was right, but perhaps I did not think before shooting. Anyway, when I had gone home to bed, those accursed Harsinis came round to my house and shouted out that they did not want tribesmen in their town and I was to leave. I got up on to the roof and said I would not leave. They then began to shoot, and I shot back and hit some of them. Then they all surrounded the house, and I went into the upper room which had a small window good for firing from, and we kept at it till the morning and all through that day. The house had high walls so that the people could not get in anywhere; and I had a friend among them outside, and in the dusk he crept up and spoke to me, and I told him to go into the mountain and call the tribe. Meanwhile the Harsinis knew that I always smoked my pipe of opium in the evening, and counted on getting into the house when I had to stop firing. But my wife was a good woman: I put her at the window with the gun, and she continued to shoot while I smoked, and hit a man, she says. Anyway, we kept it up all that night as well, and next morning just at dawn, *tik tak*, we heard shots all around in the hills, and we knew that the Kakavends were coming. Our tribe numbered 8,000 fighting men then before these last year's wars. Well, the Harsinis also knew that the tribe was coming down upon them, and they scattered like rabbits. My wife saddled my horse, and I rode out alone to meet the tribe, and came back with them up here into the hills. And I have never been into Harsin since."

"And what did you do with your wife?" said I. "I hope you took her with you. She seems to have been a useful sort of person."

"I sent for her afterwards," said Keram. "I have her still," he added, as if it were a rather remarkable fact. "I am fond of her. She is as good as a man."

* * *

The dust-storm raged all through that night. Tired out with the sound of talking, of which the day seemed to have been more full than usual, I left the Zardushtis early and took refuge in a mud-walled cubicle both from the tribesmen, who sat on their carpets outside in the moonlight, and from their women, of whom only two or three ventured from their own part of the tent to watch my evening toilet. When I had undressed and washed, and had tried, to their rather fearful delight, the effect of cold cream on the faces of two gay young brides, I was left in solitude and darkness, while the dust swished in showers through the dry leaves of the roof above my head. The slight mud wall, here in the waste of open spaces, turned into the very emblem of solidity; no comfortable safety of London houses, with shuttered curtained windows and draught-proof doors, has ever seemed to me so sheltering as those six feet of upright earth buffeted by the Arabian wind.

PUSHT-I-KUH

* * *

Shah Riza is really a maker of quilts, but he looks like a philosopher, which, in his way, he is. His philosophy is one of passive resistance to the slings and arrows of fortune as they hurtle round him: he sits among them looking as if he thought of something else, but ready, in his quiet way, to make the most of any lull in the general perversity of things. As an attendant he left much to be desired—everything in fact if an attendant is supposed, as I take it, to attend. But he was a charming old man, and would sit for hours, while all was bustle around him, filling little tubes of paper with native tobacco, lost in what one might take to be the ultimate perfection of resignation, but which was really a happy daydream, far from the toilsome world in which I was looking for keys or dinner, or any of the other things he was supposed to see to.

* * *

Thieves were around after dates, which hung in moonlit clusters on the palm trees, and Mahmud would wake at the slightest noise and go prowling round. But as a matter of fact there was little enough chance of sleep for anyone, for the moon went into eclipse, and a beating of tins from every roof, a wailing of women and frenzy of dogs, and occasional high yelp of jackal made chaos of the night. I sat up at last and tried to explain the solar system to Shah Riza, who was smoking meditatively, squatting on his hams.

"They say," said I noncommittally, as befitted so unlikely a theory, "that it is the shadow of our world which hides the moon."

Even the Philosopher's mild abstraction was roused.

"That," said he, "is quite impossible. Anyone can see from here that it is an insect which eats the moon. It is alive. It has a spirit. It means war and trouble coming. But it is only a sign, and Allah will not allow it to go too far."

As if in answer to his words, the moon, a red and sullen ember, began to reappear: the blackness of sky dissolved again slowly into luminous spaces: the rattle of tines subsided: and, leaving the matter of the solar system unsettled, we were able to sleep.

PUSHT-I-KUH

* * *

The handsomest people in Baghdad are the Lurs of Pusht-i-Kuh. They stride about among the sallow-faced city Shi'as in sturdy nakedness, a sash round the waist keeping their rags together, a thick felt padded affair on their backs to carry loads, and their native felt cap surrounded by a wisp of turban. They crouch in groups against a sunny wall in winter, or sleep in the shade of the pavement, careless of the traffic around them, and speaking their own language among themselves: and you will think them the veriest beggars, until some day you happen to see them shaved and washed and in their holiday clothes, and hear that they belong to this tribe or that tribe in the mountainous region that touches Iraq's eastern border, and find that they are as proud, and have as much influence in their own lonely districts as any member of a county family in his.

* * *

It is only the unexpected that ever makes a customs officer think.

* * *

The valley was now full of loveliness. A last faint sense of daylight lingered in its lower reaches, beyond the village houses whose flat roofs, interspersed with trees, climb one above the other up the slope. Behind the great mountain at our back the moon was rising, not visible yet, but flooding the sky with gentle waves of light ever increasing, far, far above our heads. Here was more than beauty. We were remote, as in a place closed by high barriers from the world. No map had yet printed its name for the eyes of strangers. A sense of quiet life, unchanging, centuries old and forgotten, held our pilgrim souls in its peace.

SHAHRISTAN

* * *

The dawn crept dove-coloured over the solitary landscape, subduing the high ridge before us to a uniform shadowy gentleness; even as the mind of men, growing in wisdom, may yet subdue and smooth away by very excess of light the obstacles before it.

* * *

The Mirza was an ascetic—one of those sad-faced Persians with tired eyes and gentle manners, pathetically thin, who spend their lives meditating inaccurately on abstruse subjects, and are roused to mild enthusiasm over beautiful and harmless things like calligraphy.

They knew about Hasan-i-Sabbah: they thought it natural that one should journey from England to see his castle. The Persian's mind, like his illuminated manuscripts, does not deal in perspective: two thousand years, if he happens to know anything about them, are as exciting as the day before yesterday; and the country is full of obscure worshippers of leaders and prophets whom the rest of the world has long ago forgotten.

* * *

The Persian love for the ornaments of life pierces through religion in the domes of Shah Abbas: mistily lost in their blue patterns they melt above our heads like flights of birds into an atmosphere part heaven and part the pale Iranian spring. The seasons of this world are ever remembered: in the Masjid-i-Shah, the "Royal Mosque," at the bottom of the oldest polo ground that is now the open space of Isfahan, the four liwans (the covered spaces) are built for the four seasons, one by an artist from

Kerman, the other three by Isfahanis; the differences of their carpets are visible in the pattern of their domes, and the temper of meditation rises from its sectarian hedges into the air of peace. Walking there under the building of the craftsman, "the humble one, the Servant of God, the Isfahani, who requires your prayers," one thinks of mosques and tombs scattered over Asia, fragments of a splintered turquoise sky that covers the Muslim world.

* * *

The great religious leaders have all come from Asia: it is the more spiritual continent, we are fond of saying. But perhaps it is also because the woes of mankind are here so much more evident; the need for reliance on something more universal than human charity is so much greater; and the deep and tender hearts of the prophets are more inevitably awakened by the sight of human suffering. The Ages of Darkness produced saints: perhaps their relative scarcity at the present day is the result of a higher standard in ordinary comfort and kindness.

* * *

There were three charming women. I left the men outside and came to them by the fire out of the night wind. An older woman with a sweet and gay face, was mistress of the tent; it was her daughter, and a daughter-in-law, and a friend, who had brought us in, and showed us off as a delightful find picked up by rare good fortune. I soon discovered that I carried a kind of radiance about me, a magic not my own, derived from the city of Baghdad from where I came. The two young women had spent a few months there when their husbands worked as coolies, and the memory lived with them in a glorified vision. They stroked my clothes with a wistfulness pathetic to see.

"Kahraba," electricity! I lit my torch and they murmured the word as if it held a whole heartful of longings. The worship of the East for mechanical things seems to us deplorable and shallow; but seen here against so naked a background, the glamour of the machine, of something that gives comfort without effort in a place where bare necessities themselves are precarious, and every moment of ease comes as a boon and a miracle; seen here by the fire in the tent that swayed in the cold night, the light that sprang at will from the palm of my hand did indeed hold a divinity about it—a Promethean quality as of lightning snatched from heaven and made gentle and submissive to the uses of man. So their eyes saw it, more truly, perhaps, than ours, who buy the thing as soulless glass and wire.

* * *

The tomatoes were cooking in a pot while our hunger in the meanwhile was being stayed with raw cucumbers. Our meal was evidently looked on in the nature of a banquet. Every now and then the mother of the family gave it a stir, tasted it, and nodded with an appreciation beyond mere powers of speech. Four little boys, subdued with expectation, sat in a silent row, while a smaller infant amused himself with two lambs, tied up in the tent near the fire out of the way of wolves, and evidently used to being treated as members of the family. The little daughter, the prettiest woman's eldest child, busied herself with household jobs, knowing well that her chance of the feast was remote.

And presently the dinner was cooked: the tomatoes were poured out steaming: they had dwindled, alas, and now only just looked presentable on three small pewter plates, one for me, one for the Philosopher, and one for the two muleteers. Such as they were, they were put before us, while the family looked on in admirable silence: only one boy, unable as yet quite to control his feelings, followed the plates with his eyes; his tears rose slowly, the corners of his little mouth turned down. His mother, ashamed, gave him a small slap and then, surreptitiously, offered him her fingers to lick, on which some savour of tomato still lingered.

I myself was hungry enough to have demolished all three dishes at once with the greatest ease; but who could withstand so heart-rending a spectacle? To say anything was impossible: our hostess would have been humiliated beyond words: but one could leave part of the dinner on one's plate. I pretended to be satisfied half-way through the microscopic meal, and the four little boys lapped up what remained. As for the daughter, she had learnt already what is what in this world. She neither got nor expected a share.

* * *

Two weddings were now in progress. The bride from Pichiban was expected at any moment. She had a three hours' ride down the precipitous track from Salambar to negotiate under her *chadur*. She was coming: a beating of wooden sticks and drums announced her; *"Chub chini ham Iaria. Chub chini ham Iaria,"* the boys cried, dancing round her. A vague and helpless look of discomfort made itself felt from under the *chadur* which hid the lady on her mule, all except her elastic-sided boots. Two uncles, one on each side, kept her steady on the extremely bumpy path. So, in complete blindness, the modest female is expected to venture into matrimony. The village seethed around, waiting. The lady approached, riding her mule like a galleon in a labouring sea. At a few yards from the door she was lifted down: a lighted candle was put into either hand: in front of her on trays they carried her mirror, her Quran and corn and coloured rice in little saucers, with lighted candles: these were all borne into her new home, but she herself paused on the threshold with her two lights held up in white cotton-gloved hands; and her bridegroom from the roof above took small coins and corn and coloured rice, and flung it all over her as she stood. The little boys of Garmrud were on the look out: a great scrum ensued for the pennies: the bride, unable to see what was going on and with the responsibility of the candles, which must not blow out, in her hands, swayed about, pushed hither and thither, and only sustained by the buttressing uncles: it is as well to have relatives at such moments.

With a great heave the threshold was transcended: in the shelter of her new home the lady unveiled, while the bridegroom, paying her not the slightest attention now he had got her, devoted himself to our reception.

GARMRUD

* * *

Love, like broken porcelain, should be wept over and buried, for nothing but a miracle will resuscitate it: but who in this world has not for some wild moments thought to recall the irrecoverable with words?

CHRISTOPHER ISHERWOOD
1904–1986

Novelist, memoirist, and self-styled "chronic wanderer," Isherwood seems to have lived as little as possible in England, where he was born. He attended Cambridge University until expelled for his brilliant, quietly ironic insolence. After his first novel All the Conspirators *(1928) he removed to Berlin, where he gave English lessons and wrote another novel,* The Memorial *(1932). When Hitler came to power in 1933, he vacated Germany and began traveling, but he recalled the absurdity, turmoil, and menace of the German scene in* Mr. Norris Changes Trains *(1935) and* Goodbye to Berlin *(1939). During these years he moved about briskly, motivated perhaps less by curiosity than by the desire to escape threats to his personal freedom. He lived in Austria and Greece, in Holland, Belgium, and Denmark, in the Canary Islands and North Africa, in Portugal and France. In 1938 he traveled with his old school friend W. H. Auden to China to write a book about the Sino–Japanese War (Isherwood wrote the prose, Auden added poems), and just before*

*World War II the two abandoned England for permanent residence in
the United States, both eventually becoming citizens. This apparent
flight from Europe and her troubles many Britons found hard to forgive.*

*Isherwood settled near Hollywood, grew friendly with Gerald Heard
and the Aldous Huxleys, and developed an enthusiasm for Hindu philosophy and religion while writing for the films. He traveled extensively
again in 1948, to South America, where he wrote an impressionistic
travel book,* The Condor and the Cows *(1949), in his view not a success
because it failed to specify a goal or point for the whole trip. "The ideal
travel book," he says, "should be perhaps a little like a crime story in
which you're in search of something." His late memoirs* Kathleen and
Frank *(1971) and* Christopher and His Kind *(1976) revealed, with a new
frankness, how autobiographical his fiction had always been.*

LOS ANGELES
(1947)

In order to get the worst possible first impression of Los Angeles one
should arrive there by bus, preferably in summer and on a Saturday
night. That is what I did, eight years ago, having crossed the country
via Washington, New Orleans, El Paso, Albuquerque and Flagstaff,
Arizona. As we passed over the state-line at Needles (one of the hottest
places, outside Arabia, in the world) a patriotic lady traveller started to
sing "California, here I come!" In America you can do this kind of thing
unselfconsciously on a long-distance bus: a good deal of the covered
wagon atmosphere still exists. Nevertheless, the effect was macabre. For
ahead of us stretched the untidy yellow desert, quivering in its furnace-
glare, with, here and there, among the rocks at the roadside, the rusty
skeleton of an abandoned automobile, modern counterpart of the pioneer's dead mule. We drove forward into the Unpromising Land.

Beyond the desert, the monster market-garden begins: thousands of
acres of citrus-groves, vineyards, and flat fields planted with tomatoes
and onions. The giant billboards reappear. The Coca Cola advertisement: "Thirst ends here." The girl telling her friend: "He's tall, dark
. . . and owns a Ford V-8." The little towns seem almost entirely built
of advertisements. Take these away, you feel, and there would be
scarcely anything left: only drugstores, filling-stations and unpainted
shacks. And fruit: Himalayas of fruit. To the European immigrant, this

rude abundance is nearly as depressing as the desolation of the wilderness. The imagination turns sulky. The eye refuses to look and the ear to listen.

Downtown Los Angeles is at present one of the most squalid places in the United States. Many of the buildings along Main Street are comparatively old but they have not aged gracefully. They are shabby and senile, like nasty old men. The stifling sidewalks are crowded with sailors and Mexicans, but there is none of the glamour of a port and none of the charm of a Mexican city. In twenty-five years this section will probably have been torn down and rebuilt; for Los Angeles is determined to become at all costs a metropolis. Today, it is still an uncoordinated expanse of townlets and suburbs, spreading wide and white over the sloping plain between the mountains and the Pacific Ocean. The Angeleno becomes accustomed to driving great distances in his car between his work, his entertainment and his home: eighty miles a day would not be very unusual. Most people have a car or the use of one. It is an essential, not a luxury, for the bus services are insufficient and there is no subway. I would scarcely know how to "show" Los Angeles to a visitor. Perhaps the best plan would be to drive quite aimlessly, this way and that, following the wide streets of little stucco houses, gorgeous with flowering trees and bushes—jacaranda, oleander, mimosa and eucalyptus—beneath a technicolour sky. The houses are ranged along communal lawns, unfenced, staring into each other's bedroom windows, without even a pretence of privacy. Such are the homes of the most inquisitive nation in the world; a nation which demands, as its unquestioned right, the minutest details of the lives of its movie stars, politicians and other public men. There is nothing furtive or unfriendly about this American curiosity, but it can sometimes be merciless.

It should not be supposed, from what I have written above, that the architecture of Los Angeles is uniform or homogeneous. On the contrary, it is strongly, and now and then insanely, individualistic. Aside from all the conventional styles—Mexican, Spanish, French Chateau, English Tudor, American Colonial and Japanese—you will find some truly startling freaks: a witch's cottage with nightmare gables and eaves almost touching the ground, an Egyptian temple decorated with hieroglyphics, a miniature medieval castle with cannon on the battlements. Perhaps the influence of the movies is responsible for them. Few of the buildings look permanent or entirely real. It is rather as if a gang of carpenters might be expected to arrive with a truck and dismantle them next morning.

North of Hollywood rises a small steep range of hills. In the midst of the city, they are only half-inhabited; many of their canyons are still

choked with yuccas, poison oak and miscellaneous scrub. You find rattle-
snakes there and deer and coyotes. At dusk, or in the first light of dawn,
the coyotes can be mistaken for dogs as they come trotting along the
trail in single file, and it is strange and disconcerting to see them
suddenly turn and plunge into the undergrowth with the long, easy leap
of the wild animal. Geologically speaking, the Hollywood hills will not
last long. Their decomposed granite breaks off in chunks at a kick and
crumbles in your hand. Every year the seasonal rains wash cartloads of
it down into the valley.

In fact, the landscape, like Los Angeles itself, is transitional. Imper-
manence haunts the city, with its mushroom industries—the aircraft
perpetually becoming obsolete, the oil which must one day be exhausted,
the movies which fill America's theatres for six months and are forgotten. Many of its houses—especially the grander ones—have a curiously
disturbing atmosphere, a kind of psychological dankness which smells of
anxiety, overdrafts, uneasy lust, whisky, divorce and lies. "Go away," a
wretched little ghost whispers from the closet, "go away before it is too
late. I was vain. I was silly. They flattered me. I failed. You will fail, too.
Don't listen to their promises. Go away. Now, at once." But the new
occupant seldom pays any attention to such voices. Indeed he is deaf to
them, just as the pioneers were deaf to the ghosts of the goldfields. He
is quite sure that he knows how to handle himself. He will make his pile;
and he will know when to stop. No stupid mistakes for *him*. No extravagance, no alimony, no legal complications. . . . And then the lawyer says:
"Never mind all that small print: it doesn't mean a thing. All you have
to do is sign here." And he signs.

California is a tragic country—like Palestine, like every Promised
Land. Its short history is a fever-chart of migrations—the land rush, the
gold rush, the oil rush, the movie rush, the Okie fruit-picking rush, the
wartime rush to the aircraft factories—followed, in each instance, by
counter-migrations of the disappointed and unsuccessful, moving sor-
rowfully homeward. You will find plenty of people in the Middle West
and in the East who are very bitter against California in general and Los
Angeles in particular. They complain that the life there is heartless,
materialistic, selfish. But emigrants to Eldorado have really no right to
grumble. Most of us come to the Far West with somewhat cynical
intentions. Privately, we hope to get something for nothing—or, at any
rate, for very little. Well, perhaps we shall. But if we don't, we have no
one to blame but ourselves.

The movie industry—to take the most obvious example—is still very
like a goldmining camp slowly and painfully engaged in transforming
itself into a respectable, ordered community. Inevitably, the process is

violent. The anarchy of the old days, with every man for himself and winner take the jackpot, still exercises an insidious appeal. It is not easy for the writer who earns 3,000 dollars a week to make common cause with .his colleague who only gets 250. The original tycoons were not monsters; they were merely adventurers, in the best and worst sense of the word. They had risked everything and won—often after an epic and ruthless struggle—and they thought themselves entitled to every cent of their winnings. Their attitude toward their employees, from stars down to stagehands, was possessive and paternalistic. Knowing nothing about art and very little about technique, they did not hesitate to interfere in every stage of film production—blue-pencilling scripts, dictating casting, bothering directors and criticizing camera-angles. The spectre of the Box Office haunted them night and day. This was their own money, and they were madly afraid of losing it. "There's nothing so cowardly," a producer once told me, "as a million dollars." The paternalist is a sentimentalist at heart, and the sentimentalist is always potentially cruel. When the studio operatives ceased to rely upon their bosses' benevolence and organized themselves into unions, the tycoon became an injured papa, hurt and enraged by their ingratitude. If the boys did not trust him—well, that was just too bad. He knew what was good for them, and to prove it he was ready to use strike-breakers and uniformed thugs masquerading as special police. But the epoch of the tycoons is now, happily, almost over. The financier of today has learnt that it pays better to give his artists and technicians a free hand, and to concentrate his own energies on the business he really understands; the promotion and distribution of the finished product. The formation of independent units within the major studios is making possible a much greater degree of co-operation between directors, writers, actors, composers and art-directors. Without being childishly optimistic, one can foresee a time when quite a large proportion of Hollywood's films will be entertainment fit for adults, and when men and women of talent will come to the movie colony not as absurdly overpaid secretaries resigned to humouring their employers but as responsible artists free and eager to do their best. Greed is, however, only one of two disintegrating forces which threaten the immigrant's character: the other, far more terrible, is sloth. Out there, in the eternal lazy morning of the Pacific, days slip away into months, months into years; the seasons are reduced to the faintest nuance by the great central fact of the sunshine; one might pass a lifetime, it seems, between two yawns, lying bronzed and naked on the sand. The trees keep their green, the flowers perpetually bloom, beautiful girls and superb boys ride the foaming breakers. They are not always the same boys, girls, flowers and trees; but that you scarcely notice. Age and death are very discreet there; they seem as improbable as the Japanese submarines which used to lurk up and down the coast during the war and sometimes sink ships within actual sight of the land. I need not describe the de luxe, parklike cemeteries which so hospitably invite you to the final act of relaxation: Aldous Huxley has done this classically already in *After Many a Summer*. But it is worth recalling one of their advertisements, in which a charming, well-groomed elderly lady (presumably risen from the dead) assured the public: "It's better at Forest Lawn. *I speak from experience.*"

To live sanely in Los Angeles (or, I suppose, in any other large American city) you have to cultivate the art of staying awake. You must learn to resist (firmly but not tensely) the unceasing hypnotic suggestions of the radio, the billboards, the movies and the newspapers; those demon voices which are forever whispering in your ear what you should desire, what you should fear, what you should wear and eat and drink and enjoy, what you should think and do and be. They have planned a life for you—from the cradle to the grave and beyond—which it would be easy, fatally easy, to accept. The least wandering of the attention, the least relaxation of your awareness, and already the eyelids begin to droop, the eyes grow vacant, the body starts to move in obedience to the hypnotist's command. Wake up, wake up—before you sign that seven-year contract, buy that house you don't really want, marry that girl you secretly despise. Don't reach for the whisky, that won't help you. You've got to think, to discriminate, to exercise your own free will and judgment. And you must do this, I repeat, without tension, quite rationally and calmly. For if you give way to fury against the hypnotists, if you smash the radio and tear the newspapers to shreds, you will only rush to the other extreme and fossilize into defiant eccentricity. Hollywood's two polar types are the cynically drunken writer aggressively nursing a ten-year-old reputation and the theatrically self-conscious hermit who strides the boulevard in sandals, home-made shorts and a prophetic beard, muttering against the Age of the Machines.

An afternoon drive from Los Angeles will take you up into the high mountains, where eagles circle above the forests and the cold blue lakes, or out over the Mojave Desert, with its weird vegetation and immense vistas. Not very far away are Death Valley, and Yosemite, and the Sequoia Forest with its giant trees which were growing long before the Parthenon was built; they are the oldest living things in the world. One should visit such places often, and be conscious, in the midst of the city, of their surrounding presence. For this is the real nature of California and the secret of its fascination; this untamed, undomesticated, aloof, prehistoric landscape which relentlessly reminds the traveller of his human condition and the circumstances of his tenure upon the earth. "You are perfectly welcome," it tells him, "during your short visit. Everything is at your disposal. Only, I must warn you, if things go wrong, don't blame me. I accept no responsibility. I am not part of your neurosis. Don't cry to me for safety. There is no home here. There is no security in your mansions or your fortresses, your family vaults or your banks or your double beds. Understand this fact, and you will be free. Accept it, and you will be happy."

Coming to London
(1957)

I don't remember exactly how or when I first came to London; it was probably while I was still a baby, on a visit to my grandmother. She had a flat at the lower end of Buckingham Street in the Adelphi, overlooking the old watergate, and for many years this seemed to me to be the very hub of the city. On entering, you breathed in the fine dust of potpourri and the musk of my grandmother's furs: the odour was like an incense offered before the divinity of Sarah Bernhardt, whom she adored and constantly spoke of, and it came to evoke for me the whole magic of the theatre, past and present. At the same time, the watercolours and etchings on her sitting-room walls—of Venice, Granada, Avignon and the Panama Canal—quickened my earliest longings to travel and made me see London as a gateway to the world. Reclining in a deck-chair on the roof of this flat, during the first Great War, my grandmother liked to watch the daylight raids through her lorgnette. No doubt she described the enemy as "odious creatures," it was her favourite phrase of condemnation—and she was later to apply it, in the singular, to George Moore, as she tore from a copy of *The Brook Kerith* the pages she considered blasphemous. She kept the rest of the book, however, because she greatly admired his descriptions of the Holy Land. She was the grandest *grande dame* I have ever known.

As a young man I lived in London myself, and left it and came back to it often. But, of all these returns, I think that only one will remain with me vividly for the rest of my life. It is my return from the United States at the beginning of 1947. I had been away from England for eight years, almost to the day.

On January 21, around noon, our plane took off from New York. It was nearly dark when we reached Newfoundland and circled over the snow-woods and the frozen lakes to Gander, a tiny sparkle of lights in the wilderness. Transatlantic air travel was somewhat more of an adventure in those days, and less elegantly conducted. The big bare white waiting-hall, with its table of simple refreshments, seemed very much a frontier-post; here were the last cup of coffee and the last bun in the Western Hemisphere.

I did not sleep at all that night. Not because I was unduly nervous; it was rather a kind of awe that kept me awake. If you are old enough, as I am, to remember Blériot—not to mention Lindbergh—it seems incredible to find yourself actually flying the Atlantic. I sat at my little window with its doll's house curtains; vibrating with the changing rhythms of the aircraft and peering out for glimpses of the stars. Fragments of ice, dislodged from the wings, kept rattling against the pane. The cabin was dark, except for a few pin-rays of light from overhead reading lamps. Although all the seats around me were occupied, I felt curiously alone—for the journey I was making was back through time rather than forward through space, and it concerned no one on board except myself.

And then—in palest saffron, in pink, in scarlet, in stabbing gold—the sunrise. It gleamed dully on our wet metal and on the cloudfield below us, which was blue-grey like dirty snow. We were flying over an arctic aerial landscape; weirdly solid, with terraces, erosions, valleys and great rounded rugged hills. The roar of our engines, which had been so loud through the night, now sank, or seemed to sink, to a soft hushing sigh. We were gradually coming lower. The plane skimmed the cloud-drifts like a motor boat, and you had a sudden terrific sense of speed and impact, as though it would surely be dashed to pieces. We raced over them, through them, with the thick vapour whirling back in shreds from our propellors, massing, towering above us, bursting upon us in furious silent breakers. Then, through a wide rift, we saw Ireland—a country of bogs and stony fields, green and mournful in the showery morning, crossed by the winding estuary of the Shannon.

A few miles up the Shannon is Limerick, where I had lived for three years, as a little boy, because my father was stationed there. In those days, it now seems to me, I accepted our unwelcomeness as a matter of course; it did not seem particularly shocking to me that children of my own age should spit and shout "dirty Protestant!" as I walked down the street, or that my father's regiment should occasionally be sniped at from rooftops on its march to church.

And now the green and orange flag of independence fluttered over the airport hangars, and an announcement in Gaelic was coming through the loudspeakers as we entered the dining-room. But if the political situation had changed, the local atmosphere had not. I encountered, with happy recognition, the faded grandeur of velvet curtains and the breakfast of under-cooked, disembowelled sausage and strong but tepid tea. In a brogue as rich as a 'cello, my waiter described the terrible accident of a few weeks back—pointing, as he did so, to the fuselage of the wrecked plane which could still be seen sticking out of a bog beside the airfield. "The minute I set eyes on them coming down—Mother of God, I said to myself, they're all lost entirely!" His charming, sympathetic eyes were moist and sparkling with enjoyment of his story.

And now, for the first time in my life, I began to feel American—or, at any rate, more American than European. Standing at the bar with a fellow passenger, a businessman from New Jersey, I watched the other travellers and suddenly found myself seeing them through his eyes. There was a group of tweedy fox-hunting ladies who did not look as if they were going anywhere in particular; they might well have stopped in here for a drink after a meet. There was a party of Italian emigrants who had been waiting twenty-four hours to take off for the States; when their plane was announced, they embraced each other and cheered. And there was Sir Somebody Someone, who appeared to be running the British Empire single-handed. He had crossed the Atlantic with us, and was now in an audible state of impatience because we were delayed by the weather and London's failure to "open." "They're waiting for me in Whitehall," he kept repeating. "All I can say is, I intend to be in India on Monday." I was afraid he might have sufficient authority to order our departure, regardless of the risk. But it seemed that he had not.

When we finally started it must have been near two o'clock in the afternoon. We climbed steeply into the clouds and saw no more land until the coast of the Bristol Channel. This was my first opportunity to compare bird's eye views of England and the States. What a contrast between the vast rectangular sections of the Middle West and the jigsaw pattern of this countryside! Even from the air, one gets a sense of the complexity of the past—of the Domesday Book. And of smallness. How small and vulnerable it all looks—wide open to the bitter east wind of history! The churches and the little towns, where three or four straggling roads converge as if expressly to lead a bomber to its target. The all-too-evident factories and landing strips. An eighteenth-century country house with a portico, standing out tiny but sharply distinct against a wood in which clearings have been cut to form the initials G. V. R. We flew quite low, beneath the overcast; and it was cosy, like a room in the winter light of tea-time. London appeared, a long smudge of brown haze, far ahead. The plane landed at Bovingdon Airport.

Here was the scenery of the war—but already it was falling into disuse.

Weeds were growing from cracks in the concrete runways; the Army signposts and the camouflage on the hangars were weather-beaten and faded. Some Germans were strolling around with spades on their shoulders—no longer with the air of prisoners but of accepted inhabitants. And here were the representatives of officialdom; an elderly gentleman and a young lady doctor of birdlike cheerfulness, waiting to examine us and our belongings in a draughty hut with an iron stove. The lady doctor was sorry I had no certificate of vaccination, but remarked consolingly: "Oh well, never mind—you've got a jolly good sunburn!" I told her that I had been swimming in the Pacific three days before. I could scarcely believe it myself.

Throughout the years I had spent in Hollywood, I had never tired of protesting against the American film presentation of English life. What caricature! What gross exaggeration! But now—and increasingly during the weeks that followed—I began to reverse my judgment. *Is* it possible to exaggerate the Englishness of England? Even the bus which took us from the airport into London seemed grotesquely "in character"; one almost suspected that it had been expressly designed to amaze foreign visitors. By nature a single-decker, it had had a kind of greenhouse grafted insecurely on to its back. Riding in this was much more alarming than flying. We whizzed down narrow lanes with barely room enough to pass a pram, scraping with our sides the notorious English hedgerows; then slowed with a jerk to circle a roundabout—an Alice-in-Wonderland death trap guaranteed to wreck any driver doing more than five miles an hour. And then we would pass through an English village complete with a village church in a country churchyard; so absurdly authentic that it might have been lifted bodily off a movie-lot at MGM. And as for the accents that I now began to hear around me—I could scarcely trust my ears. Surely they were playing it *very* broad? Half of the population appeared to be talking like Richard Haydn as a Cockney bank clerk, the other half like Basil Rathbone as Sherlock Holmes.

I saw little of London that night, for I went straight to John Lehmann's house; and there a welcome awaited me that I shall never forget. Looking around me at the faces of my old friends, I discovered a happy paradox—namely that, while England seemed fascinatingly strange, my friends and our friendship seemed to be essentially what they had always been, despite the long separation. That was what was to make my visit so wonderful and memorable.

During my re-exploration of London, I got two strong impressions; of shabbiness and of goodwill. The Londoners themselves were shabby—many of them staring longingly at my new overcoat—and their faces were still wartime faces, lined and tired. But they did not seem depressed or sullen. This may sound like a stupidly sweeping statement by a casual visitor; but I have seen a thoroughly depressed nation—the German in 1932. The English were not in the least like that. For instance, the girls at the ration board, which surely must have been the most exasperating of jobs, were gratuitously pleasant. "It seems so silly," one of them remarked to me, "to have to call Americans *aliens.*" And this was not just a chance encounter with a solitary xenophile, for I heard another girl being extremely sympathetic to a native lady with an obviously unreasonable grievance. On another occasion, when I was on a train, a young couple sat next to me who were about to emigrate to Australia; their baggage, already labelled for the voyage, proclaimed this fact. The other passengers in my compartment congratulated the couple on their decision and questioned them eagerly about their plans—all this without the slightest hint of bitterness or criticism. Of course, this goodwill was somewhat of the grin-and-bear-it variety which is produced by national emergencies; but it had certainly made London a much friendlier place for a stranger to visit. The only negative aspect of it was, perhaps, that the English had become a little too docile in their attitude toward official regulations. "We're a nation of queue-formers," someone said. I experienced the truth of this for myself, one afternoon, when I went to a cinema, found that the film I wanted to see had five minutes left to run, and decided to wait outside till it was over. When next I turned my head I saw that a line of half-a-dozen people had grown behind me.

London's shabbiness was another matter; it did not seem to me to have a cheerful side. The actual bomb damage gave you a series of sudden shocks—as when, one evening, I spent some time ringing the doorbell of a house, until I happened to look up through the fanlight and saw that the place was an empty shell, smashed wide open to the stars. Yet the shabbiness was more powerfully and continually depressing. Plaster was peeling from even the most fashionable squares and crescents; hardly a building was freshly painted. In the Reform Club, the wallpaper was hanging down in tatters. The walls of the National Gallery showed big unfaded rectangles, where pictures had been removed and not yet rehung. Many once stylish restaurants were now reduced to drabness and even squalor. The shortage of materials made all but the most urgent repairs illegal. I heard some weird tales of builders who were smuggled into private homes in their Sunday suits as "guests" and who did not emerge until their "visit"—with much record-playing to drown the noise of hammering—was over. London's shabbiness was so sad, I thought, because it was unwilling—quite unlike the cheerful down-at-heel air of some minor Latin American capital. London remembered the past and was ashamed of its present appearance.

Several Londoners I talked to at that time believed it would never recover. "This is a dying city," one of them told me.

Few of my English readers will need to be reminded that this was the winter of the coal shortage and the great blizzards. The snow started about a week after my arrival, and it soon assumed the aspect of an invading enemy. Soldiers turned out to fight it with flame-throwers. The newspapers spoke of it in quasi-military language: "Scotland Isolated," "England Cut in Half." Even portions of London were captured; there was a night when no taxi-driver would take you north of Regent's Park. With coal strictly rationed, gas reduced to a blue ghost and electricity often cut off altogether, everybody in England was shivering. I remember how the actors played to nearly empty houses, heroically stripped down to their indoor clothes, while we their audience huddled together in a tight clump, muffled to the chins in overcoats, sweaters and scarves. I remember a chic lunch party composed of the intellectual *beau monde* [elite], at which an animated discussion of existentialism was interrupted by one of the guests exclaiming piteously: "Oh, I'm so *cold!*" Two or three of my friends said to me then: "Believe us, this is worse than the war!" By which I understood them to mean that the situation could not, by any stretch of the imagination, be viewed as a challenge to self-sacrifice or an inspiration to patriotism; it was merely hell.

PAUL BOWLES
1911–

Bowles was born in New York City and early revealed his precocity, producing short stories by the age of four and composing music before leaving grade school. He spent two semesters at the University of Virginia but quit to study music with Aaron Copland and Virgil Thompson and, in Paris, to frequent Gertrude Stein, who encouraged him to stick to writing. He installed himself in Tangier, where over the years he has lived a varied creative life, generating poems, short stories, and novels, journalistic pieces, translations, musicological studies, opera librettos and film and theater scores. His novel The Sheltering Sky *(1949) explores the psychology of contemporaries who use travel to exotic or primitive places as a form of escape from the monotony and constriction of modern life.* Let It Come Down *(1952) goes further in considering modes of escape from the modern dullness, and here Bowles adds drugs to travel, finding in kif a way of extending the adventure.*

Although solidly identified with the exoticism of Tangier, he has traveled widely, to South America, Ceylon, India, and, as this selection indicates, Turkey. He recalls what he felt upon setting off for Ceylon: "I had the illusion of being about to add another country, another culture, to my total experience, and the further illusion that to do so would be in itself of value. My curiosity about alien cultures was avid and obsessive. I had a placid belief that it was good for me to live in the midst of people whose motives I did not understand." In addition to his travels and writing, he will be remembered as one of the most assiduous collectors—for the Library of Congress—of the native music of North Africa.

From THEIR HEADS ARE GREEN AND THEIR HANDS ARE BLUE
(1957)

A MAN MUST NOT BE VERY MOSLEM

Aboard m/s Tarsus, Turkish Maritime Lines
September 25, 1953

When I announced my intention of bringing Abdeslam along to Istanbul, the general opinion of my friends was that there were a good many more intelligent things to do in the world than to carry a Moroccan Moslem along with one to Turkey. I don't know. He may end up as a dead weight, but my hope is that he will turn out instead to be a kind of passkey to the place. He knows how to deal with Moslems, and he has the Moslem sense of seemliness and protocol. He has also an intuitive gift for the immediate understanding of a situation and at the same time is completely lacking in reticence or inhibitions. He can lie so well that he convinces himself straightway, and he is a master at bargaining; it is a black day for him when he has to pay the asking price for anything. He never knows what is printed on a sign because he is totally illiterate; besides, even if he did know he would pay no attention, for he is wholly deficient in respect for law. If you mention that this or that thing is forbidden, he is contemptuous: "Agh! a decree for the wind!" Obviously he is far better equipped than I to squeeze the last drop of adventure out of any occasion. I, unfortunately, *can* read signs but can't lie or bargain effectively, and will forgo any joy rather than risk unpleasantness or reprimand from whatever quarter. At all events, the die is cast: Abdeslam is here on the ship.

My first intimation of Turkey came during tea this afternoon, as the ship was leaving the Bay of Naples. The orchestra was playing a tango which finally established its identity, after several reprises, as the "Indian Love Call," and the cliffs of Capri were getting in the way of the sunset. I glanced at a biscuit that I was about to put into my mouth, then stopped the operation to examine it more closely. It was an ordinary little arrowroot tea-biscuit, and on it were embossed the words HAYD PARK. Contemplating this edible tidbit, I recalled what friends had told me of the amusing havoc that results when the Turks phoneticize words borrowed from other languages. These metamorphosed words have a way of looking like gibberish until you say them aloud, and then more likely than not they resolve themselves into perfectly comprehensible English or French or, even occasionally, Arabic. skoç tuid looks like nothing; suddenly it becomes Scotch Tweed. tualet, trençkot, ototeknik and seksoloji likewise reveal their messages as one stares at them. Synthetic orthography is a constantly visible reminder of Turkey's determination to be "modern." The country has turned its back on the East and Eastern concepts, not with the simple yearning of other Islamic countries to be European or to acquire American techniques, but with a conscious will to transform itself from the core outward—even to destroy itself culturally, if need be.

Tarabya, Bosporus

This afternoon it was blustery and very cold. The water in the tiny Sea of Marmara was choppy and dark, laced with froth; the ship rolled more heavily than it had at any time during its three days out on the open Mediterranean. If the first sight of Istanbul was impressive, it was because the perfect hoop of a rainbow painted across the lead-colored sky ahead kept one from looking at the depressing array of factory smokestacks along the western shore. After an hour's moving backward and forward in the harbor, we were close enough to see the needles of the minarets (and how many of them!) in black against the final flare-up of the sunset. It was a poetic introduction, and like the introductions to most books, it had very little to do with what followed. "Poetic" is not among the adjectives you would use to describe the disembarkation.

The pier was festive; it looked like an elegant waterside restaurant or one of the larger Latin-American airports—brilliantly illumined, awnings flapping, its decks mobbed with screaming people.

The customs house was the epitome of confusion for a half-hour or so; when eventually an inspector was assigned us, we were fortunate enough to be let through without having to open anything. The taxis were parked in the dark on the far side of a vast puddle of water, for it had been raining. I had determined on a hotel in Istanbul proper, rather than one of those in Beyoğlu, across the Golden Horn, but the taxi driver and his front-seat companion were loath to take me there. "All hotels in Beyoğlu," they insisted. I knew better and did some insisting of my own. We shot into the stream of traffic, across the Galata Bridge, to the hotel of my choosing. Unhappily I had neglected, on the advice of various friends back in Italy, to reserve a room. There was none to be had. And so on, from hotel to hotel there in Istanbul, back across the bridge and up the hill to every establishment in Beyoğlu. Nothing, nothing. There are three international conventions in progress here, and besides, it is vacation time in Turkey; everything is full. Even the m/s *Tarsus,* from which we just emerged, as well as another ship in the harbor, has been called into service tonight to be used as a hotel. By half past ten I accepted the suggestion of being driven twenty-five kilometers up the Bosporus to a place, where they had assured me by telephone that they had space.

"Do you want a room with bath?" they asked.

I said I did.

"We haven't any," they told me.

"Then I want a room without bath."

"We have one." That was that.

Once we had left the city behind and were driving along the dark road, there was nothing for Abdeslam to do but catechize the two Turks in front. Obviously they did not impress him as being up-to-the-mark Moslems, and he started by testing their knowledge of the Koran. I thought they were replying fairly well, but he was contemptuous. "They don't know anything," he declared in Moghrebi. Going into English, he asked them: "How many times one day you pray?"

They laughed.

"People can sleep in mosque?" he pursued. The driver was busy navigating the curves in the narrow road, but his companion, who spoke a special brand of English all his own, spoke for him. "Not slep in mosque many people every got hoss," he explained.

"You make sins?" continued Abdeslam, intent on unearthing the hidden flaws in the behavior of these foreigners. "Pork, wine?"

The other shrugged his shoulders. "Muslim people every not eat pork not drink wine but maybe one hundred year ago like that. Now different."

"*Never* different!" shouted Abdeslam sternly. "You not good Moslems here. People not happy. You have bad government. Not like Egypt. Egypt have good government. Egypt one-hundred-percent Moslem."

The other was indignant. "Everybody happy," he protested. "Happy with Egypt too for religion. But the Egypts sometimes fight with Egypts. Arab fight Arabs. Why? I no like Egypt. I in Egypt. I ask my way. They put me say bakhshish [tip]. If you ask in Istanbul, you say I must go my way, he can bring you, but he no say give *bakhshish*. Before, few people up, plenty people down. Now, you make your business, I make my business. You take your money, I take my money. Before, *you* take *my* money. You rich with *my* money. Before, Turkey like Egypt with Farouk." He stopped to let all this sink in, but Abdeslam was not interested.

"Egypt very good country," he retorted, and there was no more conversation until we arrived. At the hotel the driver's comrade was describing a fascinating new ideology known as democracy. From the beginning of the colloquy I had my notebook out, scribbling his words in the dark as fast as he spoke them. They express the average uneducated Turk's reaction to the new concept. It was only in 1950 that the first completely democratic elections were held. (Have there been any since?) To Abdeslam, who is a traditionally-minded Moslem, the very idea of democracy is meaningless. It is impossible to explain it to him; he will not listen. If an idea is not explicitly formulated in the Koran, it is wrong; it came either directly from Satan or via the Jews, and there is no need to discuss it further.

This hotel, built at the edge of the lapping Bosporus, is like a huge wooden box. At the base of the balustrade of the grand staircase leading up from the lobby, one on each side, are two life-sized ladies made of lead and painted with white enamel in the hope of making them look like marble. The dining room's decorations are of a more recent period—the early 'twenties. There are high murals that look as though the artist had made a study of Boutet de Monvel's fashion drawings of the era; long-necked, low-waisted females in cloches and thigh-length skirts, presumably picnicking on the shores of the Bosporus.

At dinner we were the only people eating, since it was nearly midnight. Abdeslam took advantage of this excellent opportunity by delivering an impassioned harangue (partly in a mixture of Moghrebi and Standard Arabic and partly in English), with the result that by the end of the meal we had fourteen waiters and bus boys crowded around the table listening. Then someone thought of fetching the chef. He arrived glistening with sweat and beaming; he had been brought because he spoke more Arabic than the others, which was still not very much. "Old-fashioned Moslem," explained the headwaiter. Abdeslam immediately put him through the *chehade,* and he came off with flying colors, reciting it word for word along with Abdeslam: *"Achhaddouanlaillahainallah. . . ."* The faces of the younger men expressed unmistakable admiration, as well as pleasure at the approval of the esteemed foreigner, but none of them could perform the chef's feat. Presently the manager of the hotel came in, presumably to see what was going on in the dining room at this late hour. Abdeslam asked for the check, and objected when he saw that it was written with Roman characters. "Arabic!" he demanded. "You Moslem? Then bring check in Arabic." Apologetically the manager explained that writing in Arabic was "dangerous," and had been known on occasion to put the man who did it into jail. To this he added, just to make things quite clear, that any man who veiled his wife also went to jail. "A man must not be *very* Moslem," he said. But Abdeslam had had enough. "I *very very* Moslem," he announced. We left the room.

The big beds stand high off the floor and haven't enough covers on them. I have spread my topcoat over me; it is cold and I should like to leave the windows shut, but the mingled stenches coming from the combined shower-lavatory behind a low partition in the corner are so powerful that such a course is out of the question. The winds moving down from the Black Sea will blow over me all night. Sometime after we had gone to bed, following a long silence during which I thought he had fallen asleep, Abdeslam called over to me: "That Mustapha Kemal was carrion! He ruined his country. The son of a dog!" Because I was writing, and also because I am not sure exactly where I stand in this philosophical dispute, I said: "You're right. *Allah imsik bekhir* [May Allah keep you safe]."

Sirkeci, September 29

We are installed at Sirkeci on the Istanbul side, in the hotel I had first wanted. Outside the window is a taxi stand. From early morning onward there is the continuous racket of men shouting and horns being blown in a struggle to keep recently arrived taxis from edging in ahead of those that have been waiting in line. The general prohibition of horn-blowing, which is in effect everywhere in the city, doesn't seem to apply here. The altercations are bitter, and everyone gets involved in them. Taxi drivers in Istanbul are something of a race apart. They are the only social group who systematically try to take advantage of the foreign visitor. In the shops, restaurants, cafés, the prices asked of the newcomer are the same as those paid by the inhabitants. (In the bazaars buying is automatically a matter of wrangling; that is understood.) The cab drivers, however, are more actively acquisitive. For form's sake, their vehicles are equipped with meters, but their method of using them is such that they might better do without them. You get into a cab whose meter registers seventeen liras thirty kuruş, ask the man to turn it back to zero and start again, and he laughs and does nothing. When you get out it registers eighteen liras eighty kuruş. You give him the difference—one lira and a half. Never! He may want two and a half or three and a half or a good deal more, but he will not settle for what seems equitable according to the meter. Since most tourists pay what they are asked and go on their way, he is not prepared for an argument, and he is likely to let his temper run away with him if you are recalcitrant. There is also the pre-arranged-price system of taking a cab. Here the driver goes as slowly and by as circuitous a route as possible, calling out the general neighborhood of his destination for all in the streets to hear, so that he can pick up extra fares en route. He will, unless you assert yourself, allow several people to pile in on top of you until there is literally no room left for you to breathe.

The streets are narrow, crooked and often precipitous; traffic is very heavy, and there are many tramcars and buses. The result is that the taxis go like the wind whenever there is a space of a few yards ahead, rushing to the extreme left to get around obstacles before oncoming traffic reaches them. I am used to Paris and Mexico, both cities of evil repute where taxis are concerned, but I think Istanbul might possibly win first prize for thrill-giving.

One day our driver had picked up two extra men and mercifully put them in front with him, when he spied a girl standing on the curb and slowed down to take her in, too. A policeman saw his maneuver and did not approve: one girl with five men seemed too likely to cause a disturbance. He blew his whistle menacingly. The driver, rattled, swerved sharply to the left, to pretend he had never thought of such a thing as stopping to pick up a young lady. There was a crash and we were thrown forward off the seat. We got out; the last we saw of the driver, he was standing in the middle of the street by his battered car, screaming at the man he had hit, and holding up all traffic. Abdeslam took down his license number in the hope of persuading me to instigate a lawsuit.

Since the use of the horn is proscribed, taxi drivers can make their presence known only by reaching out the window and pounding violently on the outside of the door. The scraping of the tramcars and the din of the enormous horse-drawn carts thundering over the cobbled pavements make it difficult to judge just how much the horn interdiction reduces noise. The drivers also have a pretty custom of offering cigarettes at the beginning of the journey; this is to soften up the victim for the subsequent kill. On occasion they sing for you. One morning I was entertained all the way from Sulemaniye to Taksim with "Jezebel" and "Come On-a My House." In such cases the traffic warnings on the side of the car are done in strict rhythm.

Istanbul is a jolly place; it's hard to find any sinister element in it, notwithstanding all the spy novels for which it provides such a handsome setting. A few of the older buildings are of stone; but many more of them are built of wood which looks as though it had never been painted. The cupolas and minarets rise above the disorder of the city like huge gray fungi growing out of a vast pile of ashes. For disorder is the visual keynote of Istanbul. It is not slovenly—only untidy; not dirty—merely dingy and drab. And just as you cannot claim it to be a beautiful city, neither can you accuse it of being uninteresting. Its steep hills and harbor views remind you a little of San Francisco; its overcrowded streets recall Bombay; its transportation facilities evoke Venice, for you can go many places by boats which are continually making stops. (It costs threepence to get across to Üsküdar in Asia.) Yet the streets are strangely reminiscent of an America that has almost disappeared. Again and again I have been reminded of some New England mill town in the time of my childhood. Or a row of little houses will suggest a back street in Stapleton, on Staten Island. It is a city whose esthetic is that of the unlikely and incongruous, a photographer's paradise. There is no native quarter, or, if you like, it is all native quarter. Beyoğlu, the site of the so-called better establishments, concerns itself as little with appearances as do the humbler regions on the other side of the bridges.

You wander down the hill toward Karaköy. Above the harbor with its thousands of caïques, rowboats, tugs, freighters and ferries, lies a pall of smoke and haze through which you can see the vague outline of the domes and towers of Aya Sofia, Sultan Ahmet, Süleyimaniye; but to the left and far above all that there is a pure region next to the sky where the mountains in Asia glisten with snow. As you descend the alleys of steps that lead to the water's level, there are more and more people around you. In Karaköy itself just to make progress along the sidewalk requires the best part of your attention. You would think that all of the city's million and a quarter inhabitants were in the streets on their way to or from Galata Bridge. By Western European standards it is not a well-dressed crowd. The chaotic sartorial effect achieved by the populace in Istanbul is not necessarily due to poverty, but rather to a divergent conception of the uses to which European garments should be put. The mass is not an ethnically homogeneous one. The types of faces range from Levantine through Slavic to Mongoloid, the last belonging principally to the soldiers from eastern Antolia. Apart from language there seems to be no one common element, not even shabbiness, since there are usually a few men and women who do understand how to wear their clothing.

Galata Bridge has two levels, the lower of which is a great dock whence the boats leave to go up the Golden Horn and the Bosporus, across to the Asiatic suburbs, and down to the islands in the Sea of Marmara. The ferries are there, of all sizes and shapes, clinging to the edge like water beetles to the side of a floating stick. When you get across to the other side of the bridge there are just as many people and just as much traffic, but the buildings are older and the streets narrower, and you begin to realize that you are, after all, in an oriental city. And if you expect to see anything more than the "points of interest," you are going to have to wander for miles on foot. The character of Istanbul derives from a thousand disparate, nonevident details; only by observing the variations and repetitions of such details can you begin to get an idea of the patterns they form. Thus the importance of wandering. The dust is bad. After a few hours of it I usually have a sore throat. I try to get off the main arteries, where the horses and drays clatter by, and stay in the alleyways, which are too narrow for anything but foot traffic. These lanes occasionally open up into little squares with rugs hanging on the walls and chairs placed in the shade of the grapevines overhead. A few Turks will be sitting about drinking coffee; the *narghilehs* [water-pipes] bubble. Invariably, if I stop and gaze a moment, someone asks me to have some coffee, eat a few green walnuts and share his pipe. An irrational disinclination to become involved keeps me from accepting, but today Abdeslam did accept, only to find to his chagrin that the narghileh contained tobacco, and not kif or hashish as he had expected.

Cannabis sativa and its derivatives are strictly prohibited in Turkey, and the natural correlative of this proscription is that alcohol, far from being frowned upon as it is in other Moslem lands, is freely drunk; being a government monopoly it can be bought at any cigarette counter. This fact is no mere detail; it is of primary social importance, since the psychological effects of the two substances are diametrically opposed to each other. Alcohol blurs the personality by loosening inhibitions. The drinker feels, temporarily at least, a sense of participation. Kif abolishes no inhibitions; on the contrary it reinforces them, pushes the individual further back into the recesses of his own isolated personality, pledging him to contemplation and inaction. It is to be expected that there should be a close relationship between the culture of a given society and the means used by its members to achieve release and euphoria. For Judaism and Christianity the means has always been alcohol; for Islam it has been hashish. The first is dynamic in its effects, the other static. If a nation wishes, however mistakenly, to Westernize itself, first let it give up hashish. The rest will follow, more or less as a matter of course. Conversely, in a Western country, if a whole segment of the population desires, for reasons of protest (as has happened in the United States), to isolate itself in a radical fashion from the society around it, the quickest and surest way is for it to replace alcohol by cannabis.

October 2

Today in our wanderings we came upon the old fire tower at the top of the hill behind Süleymaniye, and since there was no sign at the door forbidding entry, we stepped in and began to climb the one hundred and eighty rickety wooden steps of the spiral staircase leading to the top. (Abdeslam counted them.) When we were almost at the top, we heard strains of Indian music; a radio up there was tuned in to New Delhi. At the same moment a good deal of water came pouring down upon us through the cracks above. We decided to beat a retreat, but then the boy washing the stairs saw us and insisted that we continue to the top and sit awhile. The view up there was magnificent; there is no better place from which to see the city. A charcoal fire was burning in a brazier, and we had tea and listened to some Anatolian songs which presently came over the air. Outside the many windows the wind blew, and the city below, made quiet by distance, spread itself across the rolling landscape on every side, its roof tiles pink in the autumn sun.

Later we sought out Pandeli's, a restaurant I had heard about but not yet found. This time we managed to discover it, a dilapidated little building squeezed in among harness shops and wholesale fruit stores, unprepossessing but cozy, and with the best food we have found in Istanbul. We had *pirinç çorba, beyendeli kebap, barbunya fasulya* and other good things. In the middle of the meal, probably while chewing on the *taze makarna*, I bit my lip. My annoyance with the pain was not mitigated by hearing Abdeslam remark unsympathetically, "If you'd keep your mouth open when you chew, like everybody else, you wouldn't have accidents like this." Pandeli's is the only native restaurant I have seen which doesn't sport a huge refrigerated showcase packed with food. You are usually led to this and told to choose what you want to eat. In the glare of the fluorescent lighting the food looks pallid and untempting, particularly the meat, which has been hacked into unfamiliar-looking cuts. During your meal there is usually a radio playing ancient jazz; occasionally a Turkish or Syrian number comes up. Although the tea is good, it is not good enough to warrant its being served as though it were nectar, in infinitesimal glasses that can be drained at one gulp. I often order several at once, and this makes for confusion. When you ask for water, you are brought a tiny bottle capped with tinfoil. Since it is free of charge, I suspect it of being simple tap water; perhaps I am unjust.

In the evening we went to the very drab red-light district in Beyoğlu, just behind the British Consulate General. The street was mobbed with men and boys. In the entrance door of each house was a small square opening, rather like those through which one used to be denied access to American speak-easies, and framed in each opening, against the dull yellow light within, was a girl's head.

The Turks are the only Moslems I have seen who seem to have got rid of that curious sentiment (apparently held by all followers of the True Faith), that there is an inevitable and hopeless difference between themselves and non-Moslems. Subjectively, at least, they have managed to bridge the gulf created by their religion, that abyss which isolates Islam from the rest of the world. As a result the visitor feels a specific connection with them which is not the mere one-sided sympathy the well-disposed traveler has for the more basic members of other cultures, but is something desired and felt by them as well. They are touchingly eager to understand and please—so eager, indeed, that they often neglect to listen carefully and consequently get things all wrong. Their good will, however, seldom flags, and in the long run this more than compensates for being given the breakfast you did not order, or being sent in the opposite direction from the one you in which you wanted to go. Of course, there is the linguistic barrier. One really needs to know Turkish to live in Istanbul and because my ignorance of all Altaic languages is total, I suffer. The chances are nineteen in twenty that when I give an order things will go wrong, even when I get hold of the housekeeper who speaks French and who assures me calmly that all the other employees are idiots. The hotel is considered by my guidebook to be a "de luxe" establishment—the highest category. Directly after the "de luxe" listings come the "first class" places, which it describes in its own mysterious rhetoric: "These hotels have somewhat luxury, but are still comfortable with every convenience." Having seen the lobbies of several of the hostelries thus pigeonholed, complete with disemboweled divans and abandoned perambulators, I am very thankful to be here in my de-luxe suite, where the telephone is white so that I can see the cockroaches on the instrument before I lift it to my lips. At least the insects are discreet and die obligingly under a mild blast of DDT. It is fortunate I came here: my two insecticide bombs would never have lasted out a sojourn in a first-class hotel.

October 6

Santa Sophia? Aya Sofya now, not a living mosque but a dead one, like those of Kairouan which can no longer be used because they have been profaned by the feet of infidels. Greek newspapers have carried on propaganda campaigns designed to turn the clock back, reinstate Aya Sofya as a tabernacle of the Orthodox Church. The move was obviously foredoomed to failure; after having used it as a mosque for five centuries the Moslems would scarcely relish seeing it put back into the hands of the Christians. And so now it is a museum which contains nothing but its own architecture. Sultan Ahmet, the mosque just across the park, is more to my own taste; but then, a corpse does not bear comparison to a living organism. Sultan Ahmet is still a place of worship, the *imam* is allowed to wear the classical headgear, the heavy final syllable of Allah's name reverberates in the air under the high dome, boys *dahven* [recite] in distant corners as they memorize surat from the Koran. When the tourists stumble over the prostrate forms of men in prayer, or blatantly make use of their light meters and Rolleiflexes, no one pays any attention. To Abdeslam this incredible invasion of privacy was tantamount to lack of respect for Islam; it fanned the coals of his resentment into flame. (In his country no unbeliever can put even one foot into a mosque.) As he wandered about, his exclamations of indignation became increasingly audible. He started out with the boys by suggesting to them that it was their great misfortune to be living in a country of widespread sin. They looked at him blankly and went on with their litanies. Then in a louder voice he began to criticize the raiment of the worshipers, because they wore socks and slippers on their feet and on their heads berets or caps with the visors at the back. He knows that the wearing of the *tarboosh* is forbidden by law, but his hatred of Kemal Ataturk, which has been growing hourly ever since his arrival, had become too intense, I suppose, for him to be able to repress it any longer. His big moment came when the imam entered. He approached the venerable gentleman with elaborate salaams which were enthusiastically reciprocated. Then the two retired into a private room, where they remained for ten minutes or so. When Abdeslam came out there were tears in his eyes and he wore an expression of triumph. "Ah, you see?" he cried, as we emerged into the street. "That poor man is very, *very* unhappy. They have only one day of Ramadan in the year." Even I was a little shocked to hear that the traditional month had been whittled down to a day. "This is an accursed land," he went on. "When we get power we'll soak it in petrol and set it afire and burn everyone in it. May it forever be damned! And all these dogs living in it, I pray Allah they may be thrown into the fires of Gehennem. Ah, if we only had our power back for one day, we Moslems! May Allah speed that day when we shall ride into Turkey and smash their government and all their works of Satan!" The imam, it seems, had been delighted beyond measure to see a young man who still had the proper respect for religion; he had complained bitterly that the youth of Turkey was spiritually lost.

Today I had lunch with a woman who has lived here a good many years. As a Westerner, she felt that the important thing to notice about Turkey is the fact that from having been in the grip of a ruthless dictatorship it has slowly evolved into a modern democracy, rather than having followed the more usual reverse process. Even Ataturk was restrained by his associates from going all the way in his iconoclasm, for what he wanted was a Turkish adaptation of what he had seen happen in Russia. Religion was to him just as much of an opiate in one country as in another. He managed to deal it a critical blow here, one which may yet prove to have been fatal. Last year an American, a member of Jehovah's Witnesses, arrived, and as is the custom with members of that sect, stood on the street handing out brochures. But not for long. The police came, arrested him, put him in jail, and eventually effected his expulsion from the country. This action, insisted my lunch partner, was not taken because the American was distributing Christian propaganda; had he been distributing leaflets advocating the reading of the Koran, it's likely that his punishment would have been more severe.

October 10

At the beginning of the sixteenth century, Selim the Grim captured from the Shah of Persia one of the most fantastic pieces of furniture I have ever seen. The trophy was the poor Shah's throne, a simple but massive thing made of chiseled gold, decorated with hundreds of enormous emeralds. I went to see it today at the Topkapi Palace. There was a bed to match, also of emerald-studded gold. After a moment of looking, Abdeslam ran out of the room where these incredible objects stood into the courtyard, and could not be coaxed back in. "Too many riches are bad for the eyes," he explained. I could not agree; I thought them beautiful. I tried to make him tell me the exact reason for his sudden flight, but he found it difficult to give me a rational explanation of his behavior. "You know that gold and jewels are sinful," he began.

To get him to go on, I said I knew. "And if you look at sinful things for very long you can go crazy; you know that. And I don't want to go crazy." I was willing to take the chance, I replied, and I went back in to see more.

October 16

These last few days I have spent entirely at the covered souks. I discovered the place purely by accident, since I follow no plan in my wanderings about the city. You climb an endless hill; whichever street you take swarms with buyers and sellers who take up all the room between the shops on either side. It isn't good form to step on the merchandise, but now and then one can't avoid it.

The souks are all in one vast ant hill of a building, a city within a city whose avenues and streets, some wide, some narrow, are like the twisting hallways of a dream. There are more than five thousand shops under its roof, so they assure me; I have not wondered whether it seems a likely number or not, nor have I passed through all its forty-two entrance portals or explored more than a small number of its tunneled galleries. Visually the individual shops lack the color and life of the *kissarias* of Fez and Marrakech, and there are no painted Carthaginian columns like those which decorate the souks in Tunis. The charm of the edifice lies in its vastness and, in part, precisely from its dimness and clutter. In the middle of one open space where two large corridors meet, there is an outlandish construction, in shape and size not unlike one of the old traffic towers on New York's Fifth Avenue in the 'twenties. On the ground floor is a minute kitchen. If you climb the crooked outside staircase, you find yourself in a tiny restaurant with four miniature tables. Here you sit and eat, looking out along the tunnels over the heads of the passers-by. It is a place out of Kafka's *Amerika*.

The antique shops here in the souks are famous. As one might expect, tourists are considered to be a feeble-minded and nearly defenseless species of prey, and there are never enough of them to go around. Along the sides of the galleries stand whole tribes of merchants waiting for them to appear. These men have brothers, fathers, uncles and cousins, each of whom operates his own shop, and the tourist is passed along from one member of the family to the next with no visible regret on anyone's part. In one shop I heard the bearded proprietor solemnly assuring a credulous American woman that the amber perfume she had just bought was obtained by pressing beads of amber like those in the necklace she was examining. Not that it would have been much more truthful of him had he told her that it was made of ambergris; the amber I have smelled here never saw a whale, and consists almost entirely of benzoin.

If you stop to look into an antiquary's window you are lost. Suddenly you are aware that hands are clutching your clothing, pulling you gently toward the door, and honeyed voices are experimenting with greetings in all the more common European languages, one after the other. Unless you offer physical resistance you find yourself being propelled forcibly within. Then as you face your captors over arrays of old silver and silk, they begin to work on you in earnest, using all the classic clichés of Eastern sales-patter. "You have such a fine face that I want my merchandise to go with you." "We need money today; you are the first customer to come in all day long." A fat hand taps the ashes from a cigarette. "Unless I do business with you, I won't sleep tonight. I am an old man. Will you ruin my health?" "Just buy one thing, no matter what. Buy the cheapest thing in the store, if you like, but buy something. . . ." If you get out of the place without making a purchase, you are entitled to add ten to your score. A knowledge of Turkish is not necessary here in the bazaars. If you prefer not to speak English or French or German, you find that the Moslems love to be spoken to in Arabic, while the Jews speak a corrupt Andalucían version of Spanish.

Today I went out of the covered souks by a back street that I had not found before. It led downward toward the Rustempaşa Mosque. The shops gave the street a strange air: they all looked alike from the outside. On closer inspection I saw that they were all selling the same wildly varied assortment of unlikely objects. I wanted to examine the merchandise, and since Abdeslam had been talking about buying some rubber-soled shoes, we chose a place at random and went into it. While he tried on sneakers and sandals I made a partial inventory of the objects in the big, gloomy room. The shelves and counters exhibited footballs, Moslem rosaries, military belts, reed mouthpieces for native oboes, doorhooks, dice of many sizes and colors, narghilehs, watchstraps of false cobraskin, garden shears, slippers of untanned leather—hard as stone, brass taps for kitchen sinks, imitation ivory cigarette holders—ten inches long, suitcases made of pressed paper, tambourines, saddles, assorted medals for the military and plastic game counters. Hanging from the ceiling were revolver holsters, lutes, and zipper fasteners that looked like strips of flypaper. Ladders were stacked upright against the wall, and on the floor were striped canvas deck chairs, huge tin trunks with scenes of Mecca stamped on their sides, and a great pile of wood shavings among whose comfortable hills nestled six very bourgeois cats. Abdeslam bought no shoes, and the proprietor began to stare at me and my notebook with unconcealed suspicion, having decided, perhaps, that I was a member of the secret police looking for stolen goods.

October 19

Material benefits may be accrued in this worldwide game of refusing to be oneself. Are these benefits worth the inevitable void produced by such destruction? The question is apposite in every case where the traditional beliefs of a people have been systematically modified by its government. Rationalizing words like "progress," "modernization," or "democracy" mean nothing because, even if they are used sincerely, the imposition of such concepts by force from above cancels whatever value they might otherwise have. There is little doubt that by having been made indifferent Moslems, the younger generation in Turkey has become more like our idea of what people living in the twentieth century should be. The old helplessness in the face of *mektoub* (it is written) is gone, and in its place is a passionate belief in man's ability to alter his destiny. That is the greatest step of all; once it has been made, anything, unfortunately, can happen.

Abdeslam is not a happy person. He sees his world, which he knows is a good world, being assailed from all sides, slowly crumbling before his eyes. He has no means of understanding me should I try to explain to him that in this age what he considers to be religion is called superstition, and that religion today has come to be a desperate attempt to integrate metaphysics with science. Something will have to be found to replace the basic wisdom which has been destroyed, but the discovery will not be soon; neither Abdeslam nor I will ever know of it.

JACK KEROUAC

1922–1969

Jean Louis Lebris de Kerouac was born in Lowell, Massachusetts, into a French–Canadian working-class family. A hot football player, he prepared at Horace Mann School in New York for entrance to Columbia

University on an athletic scholarship. At Columbia he dropped out after a year and entered the Navy, where, at the end of six months, he was discharged because of inability to accede to the discipline. During World War II he served in the Merchant Marine and on leaves in New York got to know such Beats-to-Be as Allen Ginsberg and William Burroughs. Drink, drugs, and emotional intensity were the thing then, and Kerouac delighted in all three.

He soon found himself electrified by one Neal Cassady, a reform-school alumnus and "hipster intellectual," notable in Kerouac's eyes for compellingly representing the values of "the West"—the western part of the United States. He conducted Kerouac on exciting travels there, and Kerouac also traveled abroad, to Tangier, London, and Paris.

He began—in imitation of Thomas Wolfe—producing "spontaneous fiction." (Said Truman Capote: "It isn't writing at all—it's typing.") One of the best of his novels is the travel book On the Road (1957), whose over-stimulated brand of descriptive excitement gives it a tone all its own. The book is written from the viewpoint of Sal Paradise (i.e., Kerouac). The character Dean Moriarty is an echo of Neal Cassady. "What'll we do? What'll we do?" asks Dean-Neal. His answer: "Let's move."

From ON THE ROAD
(1957)

It was May. And how can homely afternoons in Colorado with its farms and irrigation ditches and shady dells—the places where little boys go swimming—produce a bug like the bug that bit Stan Shephard? He had his arm draped over the broken door and was riding along and talking happily when suddenly a bug flew into his arm and embedded a long stinger in it that made him howl. It had come out of an American afternoon. He yanked and slapped at his arm and dug out the stinger, and in a few minutes his arm had begun to swell and hurt. Dean and I couldn't figure what it was. The thing was to wait and see if the swelling went down. Here we were, heading for unknown southern lands, and barely three miles out of hometown, poor old hometown of childhood, a strange feverish exotic bug rose from secret corruptions and sent fear into our hearts. "What is it?"

"I've never known of a bug around here that can make a swelling like that."

"Damn!" It made the trip seem sinister and doomed. We drove on. Stan's arm got worse. We'd stop at the first hospital and have him get a shot of penicillin. We passed Castle Rock, came to Colorado Springs at dark. The great shadow of Pike's Peak loomed to our right. We bowled down the Pueblo highway. "I've hitched thousands and thousands of times on this road," said Dean. "I hid behind that exact wire fence there one night when I suddenly took fright for no reason whatever."

We all decided to tell our stories, but one by one, and Stan was first. "We've got a long way to go," preambled Dean, "and so you must take every indulgence and deal with every single detail you can bring to mind—and still it won't all be told. Easy, easy," he cautioned Stan, who began telling his story, "you've got to relax too." Stan swung into his life story as we shot across the dark. He started with his experiences in France but to round out ever-growing difficulties he came back and started at the beginning with his boyhood in Denver. He and Dean compared times they'd seen each other zooming around on bicycles. "One time you've forgotten, I know—Arapahoe Garage? Recall? I bounced a ball at you on the corner and you knocked it back to me with your fist and it went in the sewer. Grammar days. Now recall?" Stan was nervous and feverish. He wanted to tell Dean everything. Dean was now arbiter, old man, judge, listener, approver, nodder. "Yes, yes, go on please." We passed Walsenburg; suddenly we passed Trinidad, where Chad King was somewhere off the road in front of a campfire with perhaps a handful of anthropologists and as of yore he too was telling our own stories. O sad American night! Then we were in New Mexico and passed the rounded rocks of Raton and stopped at a diner, ravingly hungry for hamburgers, some of which we wrapped in a napkin to eat over the border below. "The whole vertical state of Texas lies before us, Sal," said Dean. "Before we made it horizontal. Every bit as long. We'll be in Texas in a few minutes and won't be out till tomorrow this time and won't stop driving. Think of it."

We drove on. Across the immense plain of night lay the first Texas town, Dalhart, which I'd crossed in 1947. It lay glimmering on the dark floor of the earth, fifty miles away. The land by moonlight was all mesquite and wastes. On the horizon was the moon. She fattened, she grew huge and rusty, she mellowed and rolled, till the morning star contended and dews began to blow in our windows—and still we rolled. After Dalhart—empty crackerbox town—we bowled for Amarillo, and reached it in the morning among windy panhandle grasses that only a few years ago waved around a collection of buffalo tents. Now there were gas stations and new 1950 jukeboxes with immense ornate snouts and ten-cent slots and awful songs. All the way from Amarillo to Childress, Dean and I pounded plot after plot of books we'd read into Stan, who asked for it because he wanted to know. At Childress in the hot sun we turned directly south on a lesser road and highballed across abysmal wastes to Paducah, Guthrie, and Abilene, Texas. Now Dean had to sleep, and Stan and I sat in the front seat and drove. The old car burned and bopped and struggled on. Great clouds of gritty wind blew at us from shimmering spaces. Stan rolled right along with stories about Monte Carlo and Cagnes-sur-Mer and the blue places near Menton where dark-faced people wandered among white walls.

Texas is undeniable: we burned slowly into Abilene and all woke up to look at it. "Imagine living in this town a thousand miles from cities. Whoop, whoop, over there by the tracks, old town Abilene where they shipped the cows and shot it up for gumshoes and drank red-eye. Look out there!" yelled Dean out the window with his mouth contorted like W. C. Fields. He didn't care about Texas or any place. Red-faced Texans paid him no mind and hurried along the burning sidewalks. We stopped to eat on the highway south of town. Nightfall seemed like a million miles away as we resumed for Coleman and Brady—the heart of Texas, only, wildernesses of brush with an occasional house near a thirsty creek and a fifty-mile dirt road detour and endless heat. "Old dobe Mexico's a long way away," said Dean sleepily from the back seat, "so keep her rolling, boys, and we'll be kissing señoritas b'dawn 'cause this old Ford can roll if y'know how to talk to her and ease her along— except the back end's about to fall but don't worry about it till we get there." And he went to sleep.

I took the wheel and drove to Fredericksburg, and here again I was crisscrossing the old map again, same place Marylou and I had held hands on a snowy morning in 1949, and where was Marylou now? "Blow!" yelled Dean in a dream and I guess he was dreaming of Frisco jazz and maybe Mexican mambo to come. Stan talked and talked; Dean had wound him up the night before and now he was never going to stop. He was in England by now, relating adventures hitchhiking on the English road, London to Liverpool, with his hair long and his pants ragged, and strange British truck-drivers giving him lifts in glooms of the Europe void. We were all red-eyed from the continual mistral-winds of old Tex-ass. There was a rock in each of our bellies and we knew we were getting there, if slowly. The car pushed forty with shuddering effort. From Fredericksburg we descended the great western high plains. Moths began smashing our windshield. "Getting down into the hot country now, boys, the desert rats and the tequila. And this is my first time this far south in Texas," added Dean with wonder.

"Gawd-damn! this is where my old man comes in the wintertime, sly old bum."

Suddenly we were in absolutely tropical heat at the bottom of a five-mile-long hill, and up ahead we saw the lights of old San Antonio. You had the feeling all this used to be Mexican territory indeed. Houses by the side of the road were different, gas stations beater, fewer lamps. Dean delightedly took the wheel to roll us into San Antonio. We entered town in a wilderness of Mexican rickety southern shacks without cellars and with old rocking chairs on the porch. We stopped at a mad gas station to get a grease job. Mexicans were standing around in the hot light of the overhead bulbs that were blackened by valley summerbugs, reaching down into a soft-drink box and pulling out beer bottles and throwing the money to the attendant. Whole families lingered around doing this. All around there were shacks and drooping trees and a wild cinnamon smell in the air. Frantic teenage Mexican girls came by with boys. "Hoo!" yelled Dean. "*Si! Mañana!*" Music was coming from all sides, and all kinds of music. Stan and I drank several bottles of beer and got high. We were already almost out of America and yet definitely in it and in the middle of where it's maddest. Hotrods blew by. San Antonio, ah-haa!

"Now, men, listen to me—we might as well goof a coupla hours in San Antone and so we will go and find a hospital clinic for Stan's arm and you and I, Sal, will cut around and get these streets dug—look at those houses across the street, you can see right into the front room and all the purty daughters layin around with *True Love* magazines, whee! Come, let's go!"

We drove around aimlessly awhile and asked people for the nearest hospital clinic. It was near downtown, where things looked more sleek and American, several semi-skyscrapers and many neons and chain drugstores, yet with cars crashing through from the dark around town as if there were no traffic laws. We parked the car in the hospital driveway and I went with Stan to see an intern while Dean stayed in the car and changed. The hall of the hospital was full of poor Mexican women, some of them pregnant, some of them sick or bringing their little sick kiddies. It was sad. I thought of poor Terry and wondered what she was doing now. Stan had to wait an entire hour till an intern came along and looked at his swollen arm. There was a name for the infection he had, but none of us bothered to pronounce it. They gave him a shot of penicillin.

Meanwhile Dean and I went out to dig the streets of Mexican San Antonio. It was fragrant and soft—the softest air I'd ever known—and dark, and mysterious, and buzzing. Sudden figures of girls in white bandannas appeared in the humming dark. Dean crept along and said

not a word. "Oh, this is too wonderful to do anything!" he whispered.
"Let's just creep along and see everything. Look! Look! A crazy San
Antonio pool shack." We went in. A dozen boys were shooting pool at
three tables, all Mexicans. Dean and I bought Cokes and shoved nickels
in the jukebox and played Wynonie Blues Harris and Lionel Hampton
and Lucky Millinder and jumped. Meanwhile Dean warned me to
watch.

"Dig, now, out of the corner of your eye and as we listen to Wynonie
blow about his baby's pudding and as we also smell the soft air as you
say—dig the kid, the crippled kid shooting pool at table one, the butt
of the joint's jokes, y'see, he's been the butt all his life. The other fellows
are merciless but they love him."

The crippled kid was some kind of malformed midget with a great big
beautiful face, much too large, in which enormous brown eyes moistly
gleamed. "Don't you see, Sal, a San Antonio Mex Tom Shark, the same
story the world over. See, they hit him on the ass with a cue? Ha-ha-ha!
hear them laugh. You see, he wants to win the game, he's bet four bits.
Watch! Watch!" We watched as the angelic young midget aimed for
a bank shot. He missed. The other fellows roared. "Ah, man," said
Dean, "and now watch." They had the little boy by the scruff of the
neck and were mauling him around, playful. He squealed. He stalked out
in the night but not without a backward bashful, sweet glance. "Ah,
man, I'd love to know that gone little cat and what he thinks and what
kind of girls he has—oh, man, I'm high on this air!" We wandered out
and negotiated several dark, mysterious blocks. Innumerable houses hid
behind verdant, almost jungle-like yards; we saw glimpses of girls in front
rooms, girls on porches, girls in the bushes with boys. "I never knew this
mad San Antonio! Think what Mexico'll be like! Lessgo! Lessgo!" We
rushed back to the hospital. Stan was ready and said he felt much better.
We put our arms around him and told him everything we'd done.

And now we were ready for the last hundred and fifty miles to the
magic border. We leaped into the car and off. I was so exhausted by now
I slept all the way through Dilley and Encinal to Laredo and didn't wake
up till they were parking the car in front of the lunchroom at two o'clock
in the morning. "Ah," sighed Dean, "the end of Texas, the end of
America, we don't know no more." It was tremendously hot: we were
all sweating buckets. There was no night dew, not a breath of air,
nothing except billions of moths smashing at bulbs everywhere and the
low, rank smell of a hot river in the night nearby—the Rio Grande, that
begins in cool Rocky Mountain dales and ends up fashioning world-
valleys to mingle its heats with the Mississippi muds in the great Gulf.

Laredo was a sinister town that morning. All kinds of cabdrivers and border rats wandered around, looking for opportunities. There weren't many; it was too late. It was the bottom and dregs of America where all the heavy villains sink, where disoriented people have to go to be near a specific elsewhere they can slip into unnoticed. Contraband brooded in the heavy syrup air. Cops were red-faced and sullen and sweaty, no swagger. Waitresses were dirty and disgusted. Just beyond, you could feel the enormous presence of whole great Mexico and almost smell the billion tortillas frying and smoking in the night. We had no idea what Mexico would really be like. We were at sea level again, and when we tried to eat a snack we could hardly swallow it. I wrapped it up in napkins for the trip anyway. We felt awful and sad. But everything changed when we crossed the mysterious bridge over the river and our wheels rolled on official Mexican soil, though it wasn't anything but carway for border inspection. Just across the street Mexico began. We looked with wonder. To our amazement, it looked exactly like Mexico. It was three in the morning, and fellows in straw hats and white pants were lounging by the dozen against battered pocky storefronts.

"Look—at—those—cats!" whispered Dean, "Oo," he breathed softly, "wait, wait." The Mexican officials came out, grinning, and asked please if we would take out our baggage. We did. We couldn't take our eyes from across the street. We were longing to rush right up there and get lost in those mysterious Spanish streets. It was only Nuevo Laredo but it looked like Holy Lhasa to us. "Man those guys are up all night," whispered Dean. We hurried to get our papers straightened. We were warned not to drink tapwater now we were over the border. The Mexicans looked at our baggage in a desultory way. They weren't like officials at all. They were lazy and tender. Dean couldn't stop staring at them. He turned to me. "See how the *cops* are in this country. I can't believe it!" He rubbed his eyes. "I'm dreaming." Then it was time to change our money. We saw great stacks of pesos on a table and learned that eight of them made an American buck, or thereabouts. We changed most of our money and stuffed the big rolls in our pockets with delight.

Then we turned our faces to Mexico with bashfulness and wonder as those dozens of Mexican cats watched us from under their secret hat-brims in the night. Beyond were music and all-night restaurants with smoke pouring out of the door. "Whee," whispered Dean very softly.

"Thassall!" A Mexican official grinned. "You boys all set. Go ahead. Welcome Mehico. Have good time. Watch you money. Watch you driving. I say this to you personal, I'm Red, everybody call me Red. Ask for Red. Eat good. Don't worry. Everything fine. Is not hard enjoin yourself in Mehico."

"*Yes!*" shuddered Dean and off we went across the street into Mexico on soft feet. We left the car parked, and all three of us abreast went down the Spanish street into the middle of the dull brown lights. Old men sat on chairs in the night and looked like Oriental junkies and oracles. No one was actually looking at us, yet everybody was aware of everything we did. We turned sharp left into the smoky lunchroom and went in to music of campo guitars on an American 'thirties jukebox. Shirt-sleeved Mexican cabdrivers and straw-hatted Mexican hipsters sat at stools, devouring shapeless messes of tortillas, beans, tacos, whatnot. We bought three bottles of cold beer—*cerveza* was the name of beer—for about thirty Mexican cents or ten American cents each. We bought packs of Mexican cigarettes for six cents each. We gazed and gazed at our wonderful Mexican money that went so far, and played with it and looked around and smiled at everyone. Behind us lay the whole of America and everything Dean and I had previously known about life, and life on the road. We had finally found the magic land at the end of the road and we never dreamed the extent of the magic. "*Think* of these cats staying up all hours of the night," whispered Dean. "And think of this big continent ahead of us with those enormous Sierra Madre mountains we saw in the movies, and the jungles all the way down and a whole desert plateau as big as ours and reaching clear down to Guatemala and God knows where, whoo! What'll we do? What'll we do? Let's move!" We got out and went back to the car. One last glimpse of America across the hot lights of the Rio Grande bridge, and we turned our back and fender to it and roared off.

Instantly we were out in the desert and there wasn't a light or a car for fifty miles across the flats. And just then dawn was coming over the Gulf of Mexico and we began to see the ghostly shapes of yucca cactus and organpipe on all sides. "What a wild country!" I yelped. Dean and I were completely awake. In Laredo we'd been half dead. Stan, who'd been to foreign countries before, just calmly slept in the back seat. Dean and I had the whole of Mexico before us.

"Now, Sal, we're leaving everything behind us and entering a new and unknown phase of things. All the years and troubles and kicks—and now *this!* so that we can safely think of nothing else and just go on ahead with our faces stuck out like this, you see, and *understand* the world as, really and genuinely speaking, other Americans haven't done before us—they were here, weren't they? The Mexican war. Cutting across here with cannon."

"This road," I told him, "is also the route of old American outlaws who used to skip over the border and go down to old Monterrey, so if you'll look out on that graying desert and picture the ghost of an old

Tombstone hellcat making his lonely exile gallop into the unknown, you'll see further. . . ."

"It's the world," said Dean. "My God!" he cried, slapping the wheel. "It's the world! We can go right on to South America if the road goes. Think of it! Son-of-a-*bitch!* Gawd-*damn!*" We rushed on. The dawn spread immediately and we began to see the white sand of the desert and occasional huts in the distance off the road. Dean slowed down to peer at them. "Real beat huts, man, the kind you only find in Death Valley and much worse. These people don't *bother* with appearances." The first town ahead that had any consequence on the map was called Sabinas Hidalgo. We looked forward to it eagerly. "And the road don't look any different than the American road," cried Dean, "except one mad thing and if you'll notice, right here, the mileposts are written in kilometers and they click off the distance to Mexico City. See, it's the only city in the entire land, everything points to it." There were only 767 more miles to that metropolis; in kilometers the figure was over a thousand. "Damn! I gotta go!" cried Dean. For a while I closed my eyes in utter exhaustion and kept hearing Dean pound the wheel with his fists and say, "Damn," and "What kicks!" and "Oh, what a land!" and "Yes!" We arrived at Sabinas Hidalgo, across the desert, at about seven o'clock in the morning. We slowed down completely to see this. We woke up Stan in the back seat. We sat up straight to dig. The main street was muddy and full of holes. On each side were dirty broken-down adobe fronts. Burros walked in the street with packs. Barefoot women watched us from dark doorways. The street was completely crowded with people on foot beginning a new day in the Mexican countryside. Old men with handle-bar mustaches stared at us. The sight of three bearded, bedraggled American youths instead of the usual well-dressed tourists was of unusual interest to them. We bounced along over Main Street at ten miles an hour, taking everything in. A group of girls walked directly in front of us. As we bounced by, one of them said, "Where you going, man?"

I turned to Dean, amazed. "Did you hear what she said?"

Dean was so astounded he kept on driving slowly and saying, "Yes, I heard what she said. I certainly damn well did, oh me, oh my, I don't know what to do I'm so excited and sweetened in this morning world. We've finally got to heaven. It couldn't be cooler, it couldn't be grander, it couldn't be any*thing.*"

"Well, let's go back and pick em up!" I said.

"Yes," said Dean and drove right on at five miles an hour. He was knocked out, he didn't have to do the usual things he would have done in America. "There's millions of them all along the road!" he said.

Nevertheless he U-turned and came by the girls again. They were headed for work in the fields; they smiled at us. Dean stared at them with rocky eyes. "Damn," he said under his breath. "*Oh!* This is too great to be true. Gurls, gurls. And particularly right now in my stage and condition, Sal, I am digging the interiors of these homes as we pass them—these gone doorways and you look inside and see beds of straw and little brown kids sleeping and stirring to wake, their thoughts congealing from the empty mind of sleep, their selves rising, and the mothers cooking up breakfast in iron pots, and dig them shutters they have for windows and the old men, the *old men* are so cool and grand and not bothered by anything. There's no *suspicion* here, nothing like that. Everybody's cool, everybody looks at you with such straight brown eyes and they don't say anything, just *look,* and in that look all of the human qualities are soft and subdued and still there. Dig all the foolish stories you read about Mexico and the sleeping gringo and all that crap—and crap about greasers and so on—and all it is, people here are straight and kind and don't put down any bull. I'm so amazed by this." Schooled in the raw road night, Dean was come into the world to see it. He bent over the wheel and looked both ways and rolled along slowly. We stopped for gas the other side of Sabinas Hidalgo. Here a congregation of local straw-hatted ranchers with handlebar mustaches growled and joked in front of antique gas-pumps. Across the fields an old man plodded with a burro in front of his switch stick. The sun rose pure on pure and ancient activities of human life.

Now we resumed the road to Monterrey. The great mountains rose snow-capped before us; we bowled right for them. A gap widened and wound up a pass and we went with it. In a matter of minutes we were out of the mesquite desert and climbing among cool airs in a road with a stone wall along the precipice side and great whitewashed names of presidents on the cliffsides—ALEMAN! We met nobody on this high road. It wound among the clouds and took us to the great plateau on top. Across this plateau the big manufacturing town of Monterrey sent smoke to the blue skies with their enormous Gulf clouds written across the bowl of day like fleece. Entering Monterrey was like entering Detroit, among great long walls of factories, except for the burros that sunned in the grass before them and the sight of thick city adobe neighborhoods with thousands of shifty hipsters hanging around doorways and whores looking out of windows and strange shops that might have sold anything and narrow sidewalks crowded with Hongkong-like humanity. "Yow!" yelled Dean. "And all in that sun. Have you dug this Mexican sun, Sal? It makes you high. Whoo! I want to get on and on—this road drives *me!!*" We mentioned stopping in the excitements of Monterrey, but Dean wanted to make extra-special time to get to Mexico City, and besides he knew the road would get more interesting, especially ahead, always ahead. He drove like a fiend and never rested. Stan and I were completely bushed and gave it up and had to sleep. I looked up outside Monterrey and saw enormous weird twin peaks beyond Old Monterrey, beyond where the outlaws went.

Montemorelos was ahead, a descent again to hotter altitudes. It grew exceedingly hot and strange. Dean absolutely had to wake me up to see this. "Look, Sal, you *must* not miss." I looked. We were going through swamps and alongside the road at ragged intervals strange Mexicans in tattered rags walked along with machetes hanging from their rope belts, and some of them cut at the bushes. They all stopped to watch us without expression. Through the tangled bush we occasionally saw thatched huts with African-like bamboo walls, just stick huts. Strange young girls, dark as the moon, stared from mysterious verdant doorways. "Oh, man, I want to stop and twiddle thumbs with the little darlings," cried Dean, "but notice the old lady or the old man is always somewhere around—in the back usually, sometimes a hundred yards, gathering twigs and wood or tending animals. They're never alone. Nobody's ever alone in this country. While you've been sleeping I've been digging this road and this country, and if I could only tell you all the thoughts I've had, man!" He was sweating. His eyes were red-streaked and mad and also subdued and tender—he had found people like himself. We bowled right through the endless swamp country at a steady forty-five. "Sal, I think the country won't change for a long time. If you'll drive, I'll sleep now."

I took the wheel and drove among reveries of my own, through Linares, through hot, flat swamp country, across the steaming Rio Soto la Marina near Hidalgo, and on. A great verdant jungle valley with long fields of green crops opened before me. Groups of men watched us pass from a narrow old-fashioned bridge. The hot river flowed. Then we rose in altitude till a kind of desert country began reappearing. The city of Georgia was ahead. The boys were sleeping, and I was alone in my eternity at the wheel, and the road ran straight as an arrow. Not like driving across Carolina, or Texas, or Arizona, or Illinois; but like driving across the world and into the places where we would finally learn ourselves among the Fellahin Indians of the world, the essential strain of the basic primitive, wailing humanity that stretches in a belt around the equatorial belly of the world from Malaya (the long fingernail of China) to India the great subcontinent to Arabia to Morocco to the selfsame deserts and jungles of Mexico and over the waves to Polynesia to mystic Siam of the Yellow Robe and on around, on around, so that you hear the same mournful wail by the rotted walls of Cádiz, Spain, that you hear 12,000 miles around in the depths of Benares the Capital of the World. These people were unmistakably Indians and were not at all like the Pedros and Panchos of silly civilized American lore—they had high cheekbones, and slanted eyes, and soft ways; they were not fools, they were not clowns; they were great, grave Indians and they were the source of mankind and the fathers of it. The waves are Chinese, but the earth is an Indian thing. As essential as rocks in the desert are they in the desert of "history." And they knew this when we passed, ostensibly self-important moneybag Americans on a lark in their land; they knew who was the father and who was the son of antique life on earth, and made no comment. For when destruction comes to the world of "history" and the Apocalypse of the Fellahin returns once more as so many times before, people will still stare with the same eyes from the caves of Mexico as well as from the caves of Bali, where it all began and where Adam was suckled and taught to know. These were my growing thoughts as I drove the car into the hot, sunbaked town of Gregoria.

* * *

Immediately outside Gregoria the road began to drop, great trees arose on each side, and in the trees as it grew dark we heard the great roar of billions of insects that sounded like one continuous high-screeching cry. "Whoo!" said Dean, and he turned on his headlights and they weren't working. "What! what! damn now what?" And he punched and fumed at his dashboard. "Oh, my, we'll have to drive through the jungle without lights, think of the horror of that, the only time I'll see is when another car comes by and there just *aren't* any cars! And of course no lights? Oh, what'll we do, dammit?"

"Let's just drive. Maybe we ought to go back, though?"

"No, never-never! Let's go on. I can barely see the road. We'll make it." And now we shot in inky darkness through the scream of insects, and the great, rank, almost rotten smell descended, and we remembered and realized that the map indicated just after Gregoria the beginning of the Tropic of Cancer. "We're in a new tropic! No wonder the smell! Smell it!" I stuck my head out the window; bugs smashed at my face; a great screech rose the moment I cocked my ear to the wind. Suddenly our lights were working again and they poked ahead, illuminating the lonely road that ran between solid walls of drooping, snaky trees as high as a hundred feet.

"Son-of-a-*bitch!*" yelled Stan in the back. "Hot *damn!*" He was still so high. We suddenly realized he was still high and the jungle and troubles made no difference to his happy soul. We began laughing, all of us.

"To hell with it! We'll just throw ourselves on the gawd-damn jungle, we'll sleep in it tonight, let's go!" yelled Dean. "Old Stan is right. Ole Stan don't care! He's so high on those women and that tea and that crazy out-of-this-world impossible-to-absorb mambo blasting so loud that my eardrums still beat to it—whee! he's so high he knows what he's doing!" We took off our T-shirts and roared through the jungle, bare-chested. No towns, nothing, lost jungle, miles and miles, and down-going, getting hotter, the insects screaming louder, the vegetation growing higher, the smell ranker and hotter until we began to get used to it and like it. "I'd just like to get naked and roll and roll in that jungle," said Dean. "No, hell, man, that's what I'm going to do soon's I find a good spot." And suddenly Limón appeared before us, a jungle town, a few brown lights, dark shadows, enormous skies overhead, and a cluster of men in front of a jumble of woodshacks—a tropical cross-roads.

We stopped in the unimaginable softness. It was as hot as the inside of a baker's oven on a June night in New Orleans. All up and down the street whole families were sitting around in the dark, chatting; occasional girls came by, but extremely young and only curious to see what we looked like. They were barefoot and dirty. We leaned on the wooden porch of the broken-down general store with sacks of flour and fresh pineapple rotting with flies on the counter. There was one oil lamp in here, and outside a few more brown lights, and the rest all black, black, black. Now of course we were so tired we had to sleep at once and moved the car a few yards down a dirt road to the backside of town. It was so incredibly hot it was impossible to sleep. So Dean took a blanket and laid it out on the soft, hot sand in the road and flopped out. Stan was stretched on the front seat of the Ford with both doors open for a draft, but there wasn't even the faintest puff of a wind. I, in the back seat, suffered in a pool of sweat. I got out of the car and stood swaying in the blackness. The whole town had instantly gone to bed; the only noise now was barking dogs. How could I ever sleep? Thousands of mosquitoes had already bitten all of us on chest and arms and ankles. Then a bright idea came to me: I jumped up on the steel roof of the car and stretched out flat on my back. Still there was no breeze, but the steel had an element of coolness in it and dried my back of sweat, clotting up thousands of dead bugs into cakes on my skin, and I realized the jungle takes you over and you become it. Lying on the top of the car with my face to the black sky was like lying in a closed trunk on a summer night. For the first time in my life the weather was not something that touched me, that caressed me, froze or sweated me, but became me. The atmosphere and I became the same. Soft infinitesimal showers of microscopic bugs fanned down on my face as I slept, and they were extremely pleasant and soothing. The sky was starless, utterly unseen and heavy. I could lie there all night long with my face exposed to the heavens, and it would do me no more harm than a velvet drape drawn over me. The dead bugs mingled with my blood; the live mosquitoes exchanged further portions; I began to tingle all over and to smell of the rank, hot, and rotten jungle, all over from hair and face to feet and toes. Of course I was barefoot. To minimize the sweat I put on my bug-smeared T-shirt and lay back again. A huddle of darkness on the blacker road showed where Dean was sleeping. I could hear his snoring. Stan was snoring too.

Occasionally a dim light flashed in town, and this was the sheriff making his rounds with a weak flashlight and mumbling to himself in the jungle night. Then I saw his light jiggling toward us and heard his footfalls coming soft on the mats of sand and vegetation. He stopped and flashed the car. I sat up and looked at him. In a quivering, almost querulous, and extremely tender voice he said, *"Dormiendo?"* indicating Dean in the road. I knew this meant "sleep."

"Si, dormiendo."

"Bueno, bueno," he said to himself and with reluctance and sadness turned away and went back to his lonely rounds. Such lovely policemen God hath never wrought in America. No suspicions, no fuss, no bother: he was the guardian of the sleeping town, period.

I went back to my bed of steel and stretched out with my arms spread. I didn't even know if branches or open sky were directly above me, and it made no difference. I opened my mouth to it and drew deep breaths of jungle atmosphere. It was not air, never air, but the palpable and living emanation of trees and swamp. I stayed awake. Roosters began to crow the dawn across the brakes somewhere. Still no air, no breeze, no dew, but the same Tropic of Cancer heaviness held us all pinned to earth, where we belonged and tingled. There was no sign of dawn in the skies. Suddenly I heard the dogs barking furiously across the dark, and then I heard the faint clip-clop of a horse's hooves. It came closer and closer. What kind of mad rider in the night would this be? Then I saw an apparition: a wild horse, white as a ghost, came trotting down the road directly toward Dean. Behind him the dogs yammered and contended. I could not see them, they were dirty old jungle dogs, but the horse was white as snow and immense and almost phosphorescent and easy to see. I felt no panic for Dean. The horse saw him and trotted right by his head, passed the car like a ship, whinnied softly, and continued on through town, bedeviled by the dogs, and clip-clopped back to the jungle on the other side, and all I heard was the faint hoofbeat fading away in the woods. The dogs subsided and sat to lick themselves. What was this horse? What myth and ghost, what spirit? I told Dean about it when he woke up. He thought I'd been dreaming. Then he recalled faintly dreaming of a white horse, and I told him it had been no dream. Stan Shephard slowly woke up. The faintest movements, and we were sweating profusely again. It was still pitch dark. "Let's start the car and blow some air!" I cried "I'm dying of heat."

"Right!" We roared out of town and continued along the mad highway with our hair flying. Dawn came rapidly in a gray haze, revealing dense swamps sunk on both sides, with tall, forlorn, viny trees leaning and bowing over tangled bottoms. We bowled right along the railroad tracks for a while. The strange radio-station antenna of Ciudad Mante appeared ahead, as if we were in Nebraska. We found a gas station and loaded the tank just as the last of the jungle-night bugs hurled themselves in a black mass against the bulbs and fell fluttering at our feet in huge wriggly groups, some of them with wings a good four inches long, others frightful dragonflies big enough to eat a bird, and thousands of immense yangling mosquitoes and unnamable spidery insects of all sorts. I hopped up and down on the pavement for fear of them; I finally ended up in the car with my feet in my hands, looking fearfully at the ground where they swarmed around our wheels. "Lessgo!" I yelled. Dean and Stan weren't perturbed at all by the bugs; they calmly drank a couple of bottles of Mission Orange and kicked them away from the water cooler. Their shirts and pants, like mine, were soaked in the blood and black of thousands of dead bugs. We smelled our clothes deeply.

"You know, I'm beginning to like this smell," said Stan. "I can't smell myself any more."

"It's a strange, good smell," said Dean. "I'm not going to change my shirt till Mexico City, I want to take it all in and remember it." So off we roared again, creating air for our hot, caked faces.

Then the mountains loomed ahead, all green. After this climb we would be on the great central plateau again and ready to roll ahead to Mexico City. In no time at all we soared to an elevation of five thousand feet among misty passes that overlooked streaming yellow rivers a mile below. It was the great River Moctezuma. The Indians along the road began to be extremely weird. They were a nation in themselves, mountain Indians, shut off from everything else but the Pan-American Highway. They were short and squat and dark, with bad teeth; they carried immense loads on their backs. Across enormous vegetated ravines we saw patchworks of agriculture on steep slopes. They walked up and down those slopes and worked the crops. Dean drove the car five miles an hour to see. "Whooee, this I never thought existed!" High on the highest peak, as great as any Rocky Mountain peak, we saw bananas growing. Dean got out of the car to point, to stand around rubbing his belly. We were on a ledge where a little thatched hut suspended itself over the precipice of the world. The sun created golden hazes that obscured the Moctezuma, now more than a mile below.

In the yard in front of the hut a little three-year-old Indian girl stood with her finger in her mouth, watching us with big brown eyes. "She's probably never seen anybody parked here before in her entire life!" breathed Dean. "Hel-lo, little girl. How are you? Do you like us?" The little girl looked away bashfully and pouted. We began to talk and she again examined us with finger in mouth. "Gee, I wish there was something I could give her! *Think of it*, being born and living on this ledge—this ledge representing all you know of life. Her father is probably groping down the ravine with a rope and getting his pineapples out of a cave and hacking wood at an eighty-degree angle with all the bottom below. She'll never, never leave here and know anything about the outside world. It's a nation. Think of the wild chief they must have! They probably, off the road, over that bluff, miles back, must be even wilder and stranger, yeah, because the Pan-American Highway partially civilizes this nation on this road. Notice the beads of sweat on her brow," Dean pointed out with a grimace of pain. "It's not the kind of sweat we have, it's oily and it's *always there* because it's *always* hot the year round and she knows nothing of non-sweat, she was born with sweat and dies with sweat." The sweat on her little brow was heavy, sluggish; it didn't run; it just stood there and gleamed like a fine olive oil. "What that must do to their souls! How different they must be in their private concerns and evaluations and wishes!" Dean drove on with his mouth hanging in awe, ten miles an hour, desirous to see every possible human being on the road. We climbed and climbed.

As we climbed, the air grew cooler and the Indian girls on the road wore shawls over their heads and shoulders. They hailed us desperately; we stopped to see. They wanted to sell us little pieces of rock crystal. Their great brown, innocent eyes looked into ours with such soulful intensity that not one of us had the slightest sexual thought about them; moreover they were very young, some of them eleven and looking almost thirty. "Look at those eyes!" breathed Dean. They were like the eyes of the Virgin Mother when she was a child. We saw in them the tender and forgiving gaze of Jesus. And they stared unflinching into ours. We rubbed our nervous blue eyes and looked again. Still they penetrated us with sorrowful and hypnotic gleam. When they talked they suddenly became frantic and almost silly. In their silence they were themselves.

"They've only *recently* learned to sell these crystals, since the highway was built about ten years back—up until that time this entire nation must have been *silent.*"

The girls yammered around the car. One particularly soulful child gripped at Dean's sweaty arm. She yammered in Indian. "Ah yes, ah yes, dear one," said Dean tenderly and almost sadly. He got out of the car and went fishing around in the battered trunk in the back—the same old tortured American trunk—and pulled out a wristwatch. He showed it to the child. She whimpered with glee. The others crowded around with amazement. Then Dean poked in the little girl's hand for "the sweetest and purest and smallest crystal she has personally picked from the mountain for me." He found one no bigger than a berry. And he handed her the wristwatch dangling. Their mouths rounded like the mouths of chorister children. The lucky little girl squeezed it to her ragged breast-robes. They stroked Dean and thanked him. He stood among them with his ragged face to the sky, looking for the next and highest and final pass, and seemed like the Prophet that had come to them. He got back in the car. They hated to see us go. For the longest time, as we mounted a straight pass, they waved and ran after us. We made a turn and never saw them again, and they were still running after us. "Ah, this breaks my heart!" cried Dean, punching his chest. "How far do they carry out these loyalties and wonders! What's going to happen to them? Would they try to follow the car all the way to Mexico City if we drove slow enough?"

"Yes," I said, for I knew.

We came into the dizzying heights of the Sierra Madre Oriental. The banana trees gleamed golden in the haze. Great fogs yawned beyond stone walls along the precipice. Below, the Moctezuma was a thin golden thread in a green jungle mat. Strange crossroad towns on top of the world rolled by, with shawled Indians watching us from under hatbrims and *rebozos.* Life was dense, dark, ancient. They watched Dean, serious and insane at his raving wheel, with eyes of hawks. All had their hands outstretched. They had come down from the back mountains and higher places to hold forth their hands for something they thought civilization could offer, and they never dreamed the sadness and the poor broken delusion of it. They didn't know that a bomb had come that could crack all our bridges and roads and reduce them to jumbles, and we would be as poor as they someday, and stretching out our hands in the same, same way. Our broken Ford, old thirties upgoing America Ford, rattled through them and vanished in dust.

We had reached the approaches of the last plateau. Now the sun was golden, the air keen blue, and the desert with its occasional rivers a riot of sandy, hot space and sudden Biblical tree shade. Now Dean was sleeping and Stan driving. The shepherds appeared, dressed as in first times, in long flowing robes, the women carrying golden bundles of flax, the men staves. Under great trees on the shimmering desert the shepherds sat and convened, and the sheep moiled in the sun and raised dust beyond. "Man, man," I yelled to Dean, "wake up and see the shepherds, wake up and see the golden world that Jesus came from, with your own eyes you can tell!"

He shot his head up from the seat, saw one glimpse of it all in the fading red sun, and dropped back to sleep. When he woke up he described it to me in detail and said, "Yes, man, I'm glad you told me to look. Oh, Lord, what shall I do? Where will I go?" He rubbed his belly, he looked to heaven with red eyes, he almost wept.

The end of our journey impended. Great fields stretched on both sides of us; a noble wind blew across the occasional immense tree groves and over old missions turning salmon pink in the late sun. The clouds were close and huge and rose. "Mexico City by dusk!" We'd made it, a total of nineteen hundred miles from the afternoon yards of Denver to these vast and Biblical areas of the world, and now we were about to reach the end of the road.

"Shall we change our insect T-shirts?"

"Naw, let's wear them into town, hell's bells." And we drove into Mexico City.

A brief mountain pass took us suddenly to a height from which we saw all of Mexico City stretched out in its volcanic crater below and spewing city smokes and early dusklights. Down to it we zoomed, down Insurgentes Boulevard, straight toward the heart of town at Reforma. Kids played soccer in enormous sad fields and threw up dust. Taxi-drivers overtook us and wanted to know if we wanted girls. No, we didn't want girls now. Long, ragged adobe slums stretched out on the plain; we saw lonely figures in the dimming alleys. Soon night would come. Then the city roared in and suddenly we were passing crowded cafes and theaters and many lights. Newsboys yelled at us. Mechanics slouched by, barefoot, with wrenches and rags. Mad barefoot Indian drivers cut across us and surrounded us and tooted and made frantic traffic. The noise was incredible. No mufflers are used on Mexican cars. Horns are batted with glee continual. "Whee!" yelled Dean. "Look out!" He staggered the car through the traffic and played with everybody. He drove like an Indian. He got on a circular glorietta drive on Reforma Boulevard and rolled around it with its eight spokes shooting cars at us from all directions, left, right, *izquierda,* dead ahead, and yelled and jumped with joy. "This is traffic I've always dreamed of! Everybody *goes!*" An ambulance came balling through. American ambulances dart and weave through traffic with siren blowing; the great world-wide Fellahin Indian ambulances merely come through at eighty miles an hour in the city streets, and everybody just has to get out of the way and they don't pause for anybody or any circumstances and fly straight through. We saw it reeling out of sight on skittering wheels in the breaking-up moil of dense downtown traffic. The drivers were Indians. People, even old ladies, ran for buses that never stopped. Young Mexico City businessmen made bets and ran by squads for buses and athletically jumped them. The bus-drivers were barefoot, sneering and insane and sat low and squat in T-shirts at the low, enormous wheels. Ikons burned over them. The lights in the buses were brown and greenish, and dark faces were lined on wooden benches.

In downtown Mexico City thousands of hipsters in floppy straw hats and long-lapeled jackets over bare chests padded along the main drag, some of them selling crucifixes and weed in the alleys, some of them kneeling in beat chapels next to Mexican burlesque shows in sheds. Some alleys were rubble, with open sewers, and little doors led to closet-size bars stuck in adobe walls. You had to jump over a ditch to get your drink, and in the bottom of the ditch was the ancient lake of the Aztec. You came out of the bar with your back to the wall and edged back to the street. They served coffee mixed with rum and nutmeg. Mambo blared from everywhere. Hundreds of whores lined themselves along the dark and narrow streets and their sorrowful eyes gleamed at us in the night. We wandered in a frenzy and a dream. We ate beautiful steaks for forty-eight cents in a strange tiled Mexican cafeteria with genera-tions of marimba musicians standing at one immense marimba—also wandering singing guitarists, and old men on corners blowing trumpets. You went by the sour stink of pulque saloons; they gave you a water glass of cactus juice in there, two cents. Nothing stopped; the streets were alive all night. Beggars slept wrapped in advertising posters torn off fences. Whole families of them sat on the sidewalk, playing little flutes and chuckling in the night. Their bare feet stuck out, their dim candles burned, all Mexico was one vast Bohemian camp. On corners old women cut up the boiled heads of cows and wrapped morsels in tortillas and served them with hot sauce on newspaper napkins. This was the great and final wild uninhibited Fellahin-childlike city that we knew we would find at the end of the road.

ERIC NEWBY
1919-

Eric Newby's most risky traveling occurred during the Second World War when as a lieutenant in the British army on a secret mission to Italy, he was captured and imprisoned but escaped to be hidden by sympathizers, one of whom, Wanda Skof, he later married. That whole experience, later revisited by Newby in Love and War in the Apennines *(1971), suggests the anomaly and resourcefulness of all his enterprises.*

He was born in London and educated at St. Paul's School. At nineteen he signed on as an apprentice aboard the four-masted Finnish grain ship Moshulu, *plying between England and Australia, an adventure he recalled in* The Last Grain Race *(1956). When the war broke out he was working for an advertising agency, and after his return to civilian life he entered his father's business—the wholesale women's garment trade, first as a cutter, button sorter, and traveler, later as an executive.* Something Wholesale: My Life and Times in the Rag Trade *(1962) delivers his comic, amiably skeptical view of haute couture. In 1956 he was invited to accompany his friend Hugh Carless on an amateur mountain-climbing trip to Afghanistan. The comic consequences are the subject of* A Short Walk in the Hindu Kush *(1958). He worked in the fashion business until 1964, when he became travel editor of* The Observer, *turning out regular travel pieces as well as travel books like* Slowly Down the Ganges *(1966).*

Considering Newby as a travel writer, Evelyn Waugh specified as typically British qualities "the understatement, the self-ridicule, the delight in the foreignness of foreigners, the complete denial of any attempt to enlist the sympathies of his readers in the hardships he has capriciously invited." And for Newby, clearly a large part of the joy of traveling is the plethora of comic misunderstandings occasioned by any attempt really to fathom the world of Abroad.

From A Short Walk in the Hindu Kush
(1958)

PERA PALACE

I arrived with Wanda in Istanbul. As we drove along the last long stretch of road, lurching into the potholes, the Sea of Marmara appeared before us, green and windswept, deserted except for a solitary caique beating up towards the Bosphorus under a big press of sail. Our spirits rose at the thought of seeing Istanbul when the sun was setting, but when we reached the outskirts it was already quite dark. We had planned to enter the city by the Golden Gate on the seaward side, for it sounded romantic and appropriate and we had been stoking ourselves all the way across Europe with the thought of it, not knowing that for several hundred years the gate had been sealed up. Instead we found ourselves on an interminable by-pass lined with luminous advertisements for banks and razor blades. Of the wall constructed by Theodosius there was no sign. It was a fitting end to an uncomfortable journey.

We left the car in the courtyard of the old Embassy and changed our money with one of the gatekeepers. We asked him where we should stay.

"Star *Oteli*, clean *Oteli*, cheap *Oteli*, good *Oteli*, *Oteli* of my brodder."

"Is it far?"

"Not so far; take taxi, always taxi. Bad place, at night bad menses and girlses."

"Order a taxi."

He uttered some strange cries. As if by magic a taxi appeared. It was driven by a huge brute with a shaven head; sitting next to him was another smaller man. They were a sinister pair.

"What's the other one for?"

"He is not for anything. He is brodder."

"They don't look like brothers."

"He is brodder by other woman."

With a roar the taxi shot forward. After fifty yards it stopped and the brother opened the door.

"Star *Oteli.*"

With sinking hearts we followed him up a nearly vertical flight of stairs to the reception desk. I prayed that the hotel would be full but it wasn't. We set off down a long brilliantly lit passage, the brother of the gatekeeper leading and the brother of the taxi man bringing up the rear to cut off our retreat. The doors on either side were open, and we could see into the rooms. The occupants all seemed to be men who were lying on their beds fully clothed, gazing at the ceiling. Everywhere, like a miasma, was the unforgettable grave-smell of Oriental plumbing.

"Room with bed for two," said the proprietor, flinging open a door at the extreme end. He contrived to invest it with an air of extreme indelicacy, which in no way prepared us for the reality.

It was a nightmare room, the room of a drug fiend or a miscreant or perhaps both. It was illuminated by a forty-watt bulb and looked out on a black wall with something slimy growing on it. The bed was a fearful thing, almost perfectly concave. Underneath it was a pair of old cloth-topped boots. The sheets were almost clean but on them there was the unmistakable impress of a human form and they were still warm. In the corner there was a washbasin with one long red hair in it and a tap which leaked. Somewhere nearby a fun-fair was testing its loud-hailing apparatus, warming up for a night of revelry. The smell of the room was the same as the corridor outside with some indefinable additions.

After the discomforts of the road it was too much. In deep gloom we got back into the taxi. The driver was grinning.

"Pera Palace!"

As we plunged down the hill through the cavern-like streets, skidding on the tramlines, the brothers screwed their heads round and carried on a tiresome conversation with their backs to the engine.

"Pera very good."

Never had a city affected me with such an overpowering sense of melancholy.

"No."

"Very good Istanbul."

"Very good taxi." We were heading straight for a tram that was groaning its way up the hill but passed it safely on the wrong side of the road.

I asked if anyone was ever killed. "Many, many, every day."

"How many?"

"Two million."

At the Pera Palace we took a large room. Originally it must have had a splendid view of the Golden Horn; now there was a large building in the way. We sent our clothes to the laundry and went to bed.

There had been no news of Hugh at the Embassy, but before sinking into a coma of fatigue, we both uttered a prayer that he would be delayed.

Early on the following morning he was battering on our door. He had just arrived by air and was aggressively fit and clean. Between his teeth was a Dunhill pipe in which some luxurious mixture was burning; under his arm was a clip board full of maps and lists. His clothes had just the right mixture of the elegant and the dashing. He was the epitome of a young explorer. We knew what he would say. It was an expression that we were to hear with ever-increasing revulsion in the weeks to come.

"We must leave at once."

"We can't, the wagon's got to be serviced."

"I've already arranged that. It'll be ready at noon."

Like survivors of an artillery bombardment we were still shaking from the spine-shattering road we had taken through Bulgaria. What the pre-war guide had described as "another route."

"It's been rather a long drive." We enumerated the hardships we had undergone, how we had been stripped by customs officials on the Yugoslav frontier, the hailstones as big as pigeons' eggs in the Balkans, the floods, landslips, mosquitoes, all the tedious mishaps of our journey; but lying in our splendid bed we were not objects for obvious sympathy.

"I shall drive. You two can rest."

"You don't seem to realize," I said, "there's no rest in that machine, there's so much stuff in it. After a bit we were fighting one another to drive. Besides, damn it, we want to see Istanbul."

"You can always see Istanbul some other time. It's been here for two thousand years."

"You mean *you* can always see it another time."

He looked at his watch reluctantly.

"How long do you want?"

Only Wanda had the courage to answer. "Three days," she said.

We grew fond of the Pera Palace; the beds had big brass knobs on and were really comfortable. Our room seemed the setting for some ludicrous comedy that was just about to begin. Probably it had already been played many times. It was easy to imagine some bearded minister of Abdul Hamid pursuing a fat girl in black stockings and garters round it and hurting himself on the sharp bits of furniture. In the bathroom the bath had the unusual facility of filling itself by way of the waste pipe without recourse to the taps. We watched this process enthralled.

"I think it's when the current's running strongly in the Bosphorus."

"It can't be that. It's warm."

"Why don't you taste it?"

"I can't remember whether the Bosphorus is salt or not. Besides it's a very curious colour sometimes."

It was Wanda who discovered the truth. I found her with her ear jammed hard against the wall of the bathroom.

"It's the man next door. He's just had a bath. Now he's pulled out the plug. Here it comes."

For the second time that day the bath began to fill silently.

By contrast the staff were mostly very old and very sad and, apart from our friend in the next bathroom, we never saw anyone. There was a restaurant where we ate interminable meals in an atmosphere of really dead silence. It was the hotel of our dreams.

Three days later we left Istanbul. The night porter at the Pera Palace had been told to call us at a quarter to four; knowing that he wouldn't, I willed myself to wake at half past three. I did so but immediately fell into a profound slumber until Hugh arrived an hour later from his modern *Oteli* up the hill, having bathed, shaved, breakfasted and collected the vehicle. It was not an auspicious beginning to our venture. He told us so.

There was a long wait for the ferry to take us to Scutari and when it did finally arrive embarkation proceeded slowly. Consumed by an urgent necessity, I asked the ferry master who bowed me into his own splendidly appointed quarters, where I fell into a delightful trance, emerging after what seemed only a moment to see the ferry boat disappearing towards the Asian shore with the motor-car and my ticket. At the barrier there was a great press of people and one of three fine-looking porters stole my wallet. It was the ferry master himself who escorted me on to the next boat, *"pour tirer d'embarras notre client distingue* [to solve the problem of our valuable passenger]" as he ironically put it. For the second time in my life I left Europe penniless.

THE DYING NOMAD

On the road from Istanbul we were detained by a series of misadventures in Armenia. At Horasan, a small one-street town on the Aras river, instead of turning right for Agri and the Persian frontier, Hugh roared straight on. There was a long climb, followed by a descent on hairpin bends into a canyon of red, silver and green cliffs, with a castle perched on the top, down to a village where the air was cool under the trees and women were treading something underfoot in a river, and a level stretch under an overhanging cliff where gangs working on a narrow gauge railway were bringing down avalanches of stones. On the right was the same fast running river.

We were tired and indescribably dirty. In the last of the sunlight we crossed a green meadow and bathed in a deep pool. It was very cold.

"What river do you think this is?" Bathed and shaved we sat in the meadow putting on clean socks. Behind a rock, further downstream Wanda was washing her hair.

"It's the Aras."

"But the Aras flows west to east; this one's going in the opposite direction."

"How very peculiar. What do you make of it?"

"It can't be the Aras."

With night coming down we drove on beside the railway, over a wooden bridge that thundered and shuddered under our weight, through a half-ruined village built of great stone blocks where two men were battering one another to death and the women, black-skirted and wearing white head-scarves, minded their own business, up and up through a ravine with the railway always on our left, into pine forests where the light was blue and autumnal-partisan, Hemingway country, brooding and silent—past a sealed-up looking house, with Hugh's dreadful radio blaring all the time louder and louder until suddenly we realized that what we were listening to was Russian, crystal clear and getting stronger every minute.

Hugh stopped the car and switched on the light and we huddled over the map, which Wanda had been studying with a torch.

"Do you know where we are?" He looked very serious.

"About sixty kilometres from Kars," she said.

"But we're on the wrong road. That's on the Russian Frontier."

"Not quite on it. The frontier's here"—she pointed to the map—"on the river, a long way from the town."

"How long have you known this?" I had never seen him so worried.

"Since we had that swim: the current was going the wrong way. I thought you realized it."

At first I thought he was going to hit her. Finally, he said in a strangled sort of voice, "We must go back immediately."

"Whatever for? Look, there's a road along the Turkish side of the river, south to Argadsh, just north of Ararat. It's a wonderful chance. If we're stopped all we've got to say is that we took the wrong road."

"It's all very well for you. Do you realize *my* position? I'm a member of the Foreign Service but I haven't got a diplomatic visa for Turkey. We have permission to cross Anatolia by the shortest possible route. In this vehicle we've got several cameras, one with a long-focus lens, a telescope, prismatic compasses, an aneroid and several large-scale maps."

"The maps are all of Afghanistan."

"Do you think they'll know the difference at a road block? We've even got half a dozen daggers."

"They weren't *my* idea. I always said daggers were crazy."

"That's not the point. You saw what the Turks were like in Erzerum. We shall all be arrested. We may even get shot. It's got all the makings of an incident. And you're not even British."

"By marriage," said Wanda, "but I think you're making it sound much worse than it really is."

We argued with him in the growing darkness, even made fun of him, but it was no use, he was beyond the reach of humour. On his face was a look that I had never seen. He spoke with an air of absolute certainty, like a man under the influence of drugs. Like the Mole in *The Wind in the Willows* picking up the scent of his old home, Hugh was in direct contact with the Foreign Office, s w 1, and the scent was breast-high.

We were ninety kilometers from Horasan. Finally he agreed to continue to the next town, Sarikamis, and return the following day.

But the next day had brought disaster and tragedy. Towards evening we had arrived at Bayazid. "Fortress town on the Persian Frontier; close to Ararat on the great caravan road from Tabriz to Erzerum with the Serail of Ezak Pasha on a rock." The ancient guide to Turkey had made it sound romantic, but the splendours of the caravan road had departed and several earthquakes and countless massacres had made of Bayazid a sad, shanty town without a skyline, full of soldiers clumping down the single street in great boots, and debased-looking civilians in tattered western suits and cloth caps.

Determined to sleep in Persia we set off at breakneck speed towards the east. Night was coming on. The road was deserted; it ran through an arid plain; to the right were low mountains with, close under them, the black tents of the nomad people. All day, in the upland country about Ararat, we had seen bands of them on the march, driving their bullocks loaded with tent poles and big tribal cooking pots; vicious-looking donkeys with pack saddles, flocks of goats and sheep; the men and women on foot, the women in full red skirts with a sort of black surcoat and black balaclavas, the younger ones in pill-box hats and plaits, the boys wearing lambskin caps, the smallest children sitting, on white cushions, astride lean little horses; all moving westward along the line of the telegraph poles, each family enveloped in its own cloud of dust.

Less than a mile from the Customs House on the Turkish side, travelling in the last of the light, something dark loomed up on the road in front. Wanda shouted but Hugh was already braking hard. There was going to be an accident and it was going to take a long time to happen. I wondered whether he would swerve off the road and whether we should turn over when he did. He shouted to us to hold on, the wheels locked and we went into a long tearing skid with the horn blaring and all our luggage falling on us, pressing us forward on to the windscreen, everything happening at once as we waited for the smash but instead coming to a standstill only a few feet from whatever it was in the road.

There was a moment of silence broken only by awful groans. We were fearful of what we should see but the reality was worse than anything we imagined. Lying in the road, face downwards, a shapeless black bundle covered with dust, was one of the nomads. He was an old man of about seventy, blackened by the sun, with a cropped grizzled head. Something had run him down from behind and his injuries were terrible; his nose was almost completely torn off and swelling up through a tear in the back of his shirt was a great liquid bulge; but he was still conscious and breathing like a steam engine.

We wrapped him in a blanket, put a big shell dressing on the maw where his nose had been, stopped the bleeding from the back of his head and wondered what to do next. We dared not move him off the road because we had no idea what internal injuries he had, nor could we give him morphia because it seemed certain that his brain must have been injured.

Now the men of the tribe came running, attracted by the lights. They were followed by the children and then by the women. With the women came the man's wife, a windswept black-haired creature of about thirty, who flung herself down in the dust with a jangling of gold ornaments and set up a great wailing. The rest stood in a half-circle in the light of the headlamps and looked at us silently.

At the same moment a jeep arrived, full of soldiers. One of them was a doctor who spoke English. It seemed a miracle.

He lifted the shell dressing and winced. Then he saw the great blue swelling, now growing bigger.

"You must take him to the camp." (There was a military camp five miles back on the road.)

"But if he's moved he may die."

"He is going to die. You see that"—he pointed at the bulge— "haemorrhage. He may live till morning. He is strong old man but there is nothing to do."

"You will come with us?"

"I am going to—" (He named a place none of us had ever heard of.) "It is you must take him."

We told him that we were going to Persia. Still we did not realize our predicament.

Then it came, like a bombshell.

"YOU CANNOT KILL MAN AND GO AWAY. THERE WILL BE INQUIRY."

"BUT WE DIDN'T. WE FOUND HIM. LOOK HERE." We showed him the tyre marks. They ended about seven feet from the body.

"To do such damage you must travel fast." He pointed to the crushed offside wing, legacy of Hugh's encounter with a London taxi. "But do not worry, *he* is only nomad. I am sorry for *you.*"

His men helped us place the wounded man in the back seat. When he had gone we realized that we didn't know his name.

At the camp, a few huts under the mountain, there was no doctor. Nor could anyone speak Persian, French or German—only Turkish.

"Bayazid, Bayazid," was all they could say, waving us on. With the groans of the old man in our ears and the heartrending cries of his wife from the back seat where she supported him, we drove the fifteen miles to the town.

All night we sat under the electric light in the corridor of the military hospital, smoking cigarettes, dozing, going into the room where he was, to listen to his breathing as it became louder and louder. He died horribly, early the next morning on a canvas stretcher just as it was growing light, surrounded by judges and prosecutors and interpreters screaming at him, trying to find out what had run him down, the members of his family elbowed out by official observers.

As soon as the man was dead, the nightmare of the day began. In a convoy of vehicles we returned to the scene of the accident. In ours was a Judge, who seemed hostile; a young Public Prosecutor, who didn't; a tall Colonel with a broken nose, hard as nails like a Liverpool policeman; a Captain, who was indifferent, neither unamiable nor amiable— nothing; an interpreter, who looked as though he had been routed out of a house of ill-fame, who spoke extraordinarily bad Levantine French of a purely declamatory kind; a number of really smelly policemen and two or three soldiers. Apart from the Interpreter, the Prosecutor spoke a few words of French but tried hard with them; the Captain not more than a dozen words of English but he was useless. All the rest spoke nothing but their native tongue. By a paradox it was the Prosecutor who seemed to offer the greatest hope. Worst of all was the Interpreter, who seemed intent on destroying us.

"*Vous étes Carless?*" he inquired sardonically as I was getting into the car to drive to the place of the accident. With all the more important officials in our car, which had been emptied of luggage in order to transport them, it seemed better that Hugh shouldn't drive.

"*Non, M'sieur.*"

"*Il faut que M. Carless conduit l'automobile.*"

"*Pourquoi?*"

"*M. le 'Juge l'a dit.*" ["Are you Carless?"

"No, sir."

"Mr. Carless must drive the car."

"Why?"

"The judge has ordered it."]

All the way to the scene of the accident they watched Hugh like a hawk. It looked very bad for him. There on the gravel road was the long swerving mark of the skid ending practically where the body had been. The space between was already ploughed up by countless footmarks, but if we had hit the old man, the force of the blow would have thrown his body almost precisely into the position in which we found it.

The interrogation went on right through the baking noonday heat until evening. Half a dozen times we were made to re-enact the accident; the road was measured; the nomad children were made to collect stones to mark the key points; drawings were made; statements were taken. All we could say was that we had found him and that there had been no other witnesses—the nearest nomads had been nearly a mile from the road. It was not our fault, we said, you must believe us. But then there were the men of the tribe committing perjury, describing the accident, offering flowers to the Judge; while the Interpreter, sensing the dislike that we were trying so hard to conceal, redoubled his own efforts to destroy us by garbling everything we said. Worst of all they told us that ours was the only vehicle travelling towards the Customs House from the Turkish side on the evening of the accident.

Hugh was in a spot. The only hope seemed to be the Prosecutor, who had ordered the beating of several members of the tribe. "They are lying," he said, as he watched the policeman thumping them in the incandescent heat. "I am only interested in the *truth*. And I shall discover it." He was a remarkable man. But when we were alone we begged Hugh to send a cable to Ankara. He was absolutely immovable.

"I'm going to see it through myself," he said. "If it comes to a trial there's going to be the most shocking scandal at any rate. Whether they find me guilty or innocent, somebody will always bring it up. The only thing is to convince them that I didn't do it at this stage before they charge me. Besides, what will my Ambassador think if I arrive in Persia under a cloud."

Exhausted we returned to the town. On the way one of the jeeps full of policemen broke down. The Judge ordered us to abandon them. No one was sorry; they were a brutal lot. We left them honking despairingly in the darkness; the soldiers were delighted.

But there were inexhaustible supplies of policemen; at the station in Bayazid half a dozen more poured out of the building, surrounding us.

"My God, they're going to lock me up for the night." All day Hugh had behaved with the most admirable calmness. Now for the first time he showed signs of strain.

"*Malheureusement,*" said the Interpreter, turning to Wanda and myself and showing a set of broken yellow teeth, "*M. Carless doit rester ici mais VOUS, 'VOUS étes libre."* ["Unfortunately, Mr. Carless must stay here, but you, you are free."]

"I don't need a policeman," Hugh said. I had never seen him so angry. "You have my word. I shan't run away."

"You are not arrested yet. It is to protect you from incidents. Perhaps people will be angry."

With a policeman outside the inn shooing away the passersby, the three of us ate rice and kebab and some very odd vegetables and drank a whole bottle of raki. We were famished, having eaten nothing since the previous night.

At the next table was a medical officer in battledress. He was an Armenian and had the facility with languages of his race. "My name is Niki," he said. After dinner we sat with him on the roof under a rusty-looking moon. "This is a town of no-women," he said, pointing at the soldiery milling in the street below. "Look, there are thousands of them. They are all becoming mad because there is nothing here for them—or for me," he added more practically.

"This is your country?"

"This was my country. There is no Armenia any more. All those shops"—pointing at the shop fronts now shuttered and barred— "Armenian—dead, dead, all dead. Tomorrow they will decide whether you will be tried or not," he went on to Hugh. "If you need me I will come. I think it is better that you should not be tried. I have heard that there is a German from Tehran here, a lorry driver who has cut off a child's foot with his lorry. He has been three months awaiting a trial. They keep him without trousers so that he shall not escape."

Next morning all three of us took pains with our appearance. The internal arrangements at the inn were so loathsome that I shared a kerosene tin of water with Hugh and shaved on the roof, the cynosure of the entire population who were out in force. Wanda, debarred from public appearance, was condemned to the inside. As a final touch our shoes were cleaned by a bootblack who refused to charge. I was impressed but not Hugh.

"I don't suppose they charge anything at the Old Bailey." Nothing could shake his invincible gloom.

At nine o'clock, sweltering in our best clothes, we presented ourselves at the Courthouse and joined a queue of malefactors.

After a short wait we were called. The room was simple, whitewashed, with half a dozen chairs and a desk for the Prosecutor. On it was a telephone at which we looked lovingly. Behind the Prosecutor lurked his evil genius, the Interpreter.

The Prosecutor began to speak. It was obvious that one way or the other he had made his mind up. He was, he said, interested only in Justice and Justice would be done. It was unfortunate for M. Carless that he did not possess a Diplomatic Visa for Turkey otherwise it would be difficult to detain him. We now knew that Hugh was doomed. But, he went on, as his visa only applied to Iran, he proposed to ask for proceedings to be stayed for a week while he consulted the authorities in Ankara.

"*Malheureusement, c'est pas possible pour M. Carless,*" said the Interpreter winding up with relish, "*mais vous étes libre d'aller en Iran.*" ["Unfortunately, it is not possible for Mr. Carless, but you are free to go on to Iran."]

For two hours we argued; when Hugh flagged I intervened; then Wanda took up the struggle; arguments shot backwards and forwards across the room like tennis balls: about diplomatic immunity, children languishing in Europe without their mother, ships and planes missed, expeditions ruined, the absence of witnesses.

"Several beatings were given yesterday for the discouragement of false witnesses and their evidence is inadmissible," said the Prosecutor, but he was remote, immovable.

"*Malheureusement vous devez rester ici sept jours pour qu'arrive une réponse à notre telegramme,*" said the Interpreter in his repulsive French.

"*Monsieur le Procureur a envoyé une telegramme?*"

"*Pas encore,*" replied the Interpreter, leering triumphantly.

["Unfortunately you must stay here a week until an answer to our telegram arrives."

"Has the Prosecutor sent a telegram?"

"Not yet."]

I had never seen him look happier.

We implored Hugh to send a telegram to Ankara. He was adamant but he did agree to send for Niki, the Armenian doctor. It was not easy to find an un-named Armenian M.O. in a garrison town but he arrived in an hour, by jeep, round and fat but to us a knight in armour. The Interpreter was banished and Niki began translating sentence by sentence, English to Turkish, Turkish to English. Hugh spoke of N.A.T.O. and there was a flicker of interest, of how the two countries had fought together on the same side in Korea, of the great qualities of the Turkish Nation, of the political capital that the Russians would make when the news became known, that such a situation would not happen in England. Finally, Hugh said he wanted to send a telegram. We knew what agony this decision cost him.

"It is extremely difficult. There is no direct communication. We shall first have to send to Erzerum."

"Then send it to Ezerum."

"It will take three days. You still wish?"

"Yes, I wish."

Hugh wrote the telegram. It looked terrible on paper. I began to understand why he had been so reluctant to send it.

Detained Bayazid en route Tehran awaiting formulation of charge killing civilian stop Diplomatic visa applicable Iran only.

Niki translated it into Turkish; holding the message, the Prosecutor left the room. After a few minutes he returned with a heavily moustached clerk in shirt-sleeves. For more than ten minutes he dictated with great fluency. It was a long document. When it was finished Niki read it aloud. It gave an account of the entire affair and expressed Hugh's complete innocence.

The last stamp was affixed; the Prosecutor clapped his hands, coffee was brought in.

It all happened so quickly that it was difficult to believe that it was all over.

"But what made him change his mind?" It was an incredible volte-face.

"The Public Prosecutor asks me to say," said Niki, "that it is because M. Carless was gentlemanly in this thing, because you were all gentlemanly," bowing to Wanda, "that he has decided not to proceed with it."

AIRING IN A CLOSED CARRIAGE

In Tehran Wanda left us to return to Europe.

On 30 June, eleven days from Istanbul, Hugh and I reached Meshed, the capital of the province of Khurasan, in north-east Persia, and drove through streets just dark to the British Consulate-General, abandoned since Mussadiq's coup and the breaking off of diplomatic relations in 1953.

After a long wait at the garden gate we were admitted by an old, grey-bearded sepoy of the Hazarah Pioneers. He had a Mongolian face and was dressed in clean khaki drill with buttons polished. Here we were entertained kindly by the Hindu caretaker.

The place was a dream world behind high walls, like a property in the Deep South of the United States. Everywhere lush vegetation reached out long green arms to destroy what half a century of care had built up. The great bungalows with walls feet thick were collapsing room by room, the wire gauze fly nettings over the windows were torn and the five-year-old bath water stagnant in the bathrooms. In the living rooms were great Russian stoves, standing ceiling high, black and banded like cannon set in the walls, warming two rooms at once, needing whole forests of wood to keep them going.

The Consulate building itself was lost and forgotten; arcades of Corinthian columns supported an upper balcony, itself collapsing. The house was shaded by great trees, planted perhaps a century ago, now at their most magnificent. Behind barred windows were the big green safes with combination locks in the confidential registry. I asked Hugh how they got them there.

"In the days of the *Raj* you could do anything."

"But they must weigh tons. There's no railway."

"If Curzon had anything to do with it, they were probably dragged overland from India."

On the wall in one of the offices we found a map of Central Asia. It was heavily marked in coloured pencil. One such annotation well inside Russian Territory, beyond a straggling river, on some sand dunes in the Kara-Kum desert read, "Captain X, July, '84" and was followed by a cryptic question mark.

"The Great Game," said Hugh. It was a sad moment for him, born nearly a century too late to participate in the struggle that had taken place between the two great powers in the no-man's-land between the frontiers of Asiatic Russia and British India.

Apart from Hugh and myself, everyone inside the Consulate firmly believed that the British would return. In the morning when we met the old man from Khurasan who had been in the Guides Cavalry, the younger one who had been in a regiment of Punjabis and the old, old man who was the caretaker's cook, I felt sad under their interrogation about my health and regiment. To them it was as though the Indian Army as they had known it still existed.

"*Apka misaj kaisa hai, Sahib?*"

"*Bilkul tik hai.*"

"*Apka paltan kya hai?*"

I had acquired Urdu rapidly sixteen years before. It had vanished as quickly as it came. Soon I dried up completely and was left mouthing affirmatives. "*Han, han.*"

"For God's sake don't keep on saying, "*Han, han.*" They'll think you're crazy."

"I've said everything I can remember. What do you want me to say. That we're not coming back, ever?"

With all the various delights of Meshed to sample it was late when we set off. Driving in clouds of dust and darkness beyond the outer suburbs the self-starter began to smoke. Grovelling under the vehicle among the ants and young scorpions, fearful of losing our feet when the great American lorries roared past, we attained the feeling of comradeship that only comes in moments of adversity.

The starter motor was held in place by two inaccessible screws that must have been tightened by a giant. It was a masterpiece of British engineering. With the ants marching and counter-marching over me, I held a guttering candle while Hugh groped with the tinny spanner that was part of the manufacturers' "tool-kit."

"What does the book say?"

It was difficult to read it with my nose jammed into the earth.

"The starter is pre-packed with grease and requires no maintenance during the life of the vehicle."

"That's the part about lubrication but how do you GET IT OFF?"

It was like trying to read a first folio in a crowded train. I knocked over the candle and for a time we were in complete darkness.

"It says: 'Loosen the retaining screws and slide it.' "

"There must be a place in hell for the man who wrote that."

"Perhaps you have to take the engine out first."

Late at night we returned unsuccessful to the city and in the *Shāri Tehran*, the Warren Street of Meshed, devoted to the motor business, hammered on the wooden doors of what until recently had been a çaravanserai, until the night watchman came with stave and lantern and admitted us.

In the great court, surrounded by broken-down droshkies and the skeletons of German motor-buses, we spread our sleeping-bags on the oily ground beside our vehicle. For the first time since leaving Istanbul we had achieved Hugh's ambition to sleep "under the stars."

Early the next morning the work was put in hand at a workshop which backed on to the courtyard. It was the sort of place where engines are dismembered and never put together again. The walls of the shop were covered with the trophies of failure, which, together with the vast, inanimate skeletons outside, gave me the same curious feelings of fascination and horror that I still experience in that part of the Natural History Museum devoted to prehistoric monsters.

The proprietor Abdul, a broken-toothed demon of a man, conceived a violent passion for Hugh. We sat with him drinking coffee inside one of the skeletons while his assistant, a midget ten-year-old, set to work on the starter with a spanner as big as himself, shaming us by the ease with which he removed it.

"Arrrh, CAHARLESS, soul of your father. You have ill-used your motor-car." He hit Hugh a violent blow of affection in the small of the back, just as he was drinking his coffee.

"Urggh!"

"What do you say, o CAHARLESS?"

Hugh was mopping thick black coffee from his last pair of clean trousers.

"I say nothing."

"What shall I say?"

"How should I know."

"You are angry with me. Let us go to my workshop and I shall make you happy."

He led us into the shop. There he left us. In a few minutes he returned with a small blind boy, good-looking but with an air of corruption. Abdul threw down his spanner with a clang and began to fondle him.

"CAHARLESS!" he roared, beckoning Hugh.

"NO!"

Presently Abdul pressed the boy into a cupboard and shut the door. There followed a succession of nasty stifled noises that drove us out of the shop.

Later, when we returned, Hugh was given a tremendous welcome.

"CAHARLESS, I thought you were departed for ever. You have come back!"

"You still have my motor-car."

To me he was less demonstrative but also less polite, snatching my pipe from my mouth and clenching it between his awful broken teeth in parody of an Englishman.

"CAHARLESS, when you take me to *Englestan* I shall smoke the pipe."

All through the hot afternoon he worked like a demon with his midget assistant, every few minutes beseeching Hugh to take him to England. After two hours the repairs were finished. Now he wanted to show us how he had driven to Tehran in fourteen hours, a journey that had taken us two days and most of one night.

In breathless heat he whirled us through the streets, tyres screeching at the corners. We were anxious to pay the bill and be off. Never had we met anyone more horrible than Abdul, more energetic and more likely to succeed.

"How much?"

"CAHARLESS, my heart, CAHARLESS, my soul, you will transport me to *Englestan*?"

"Yes, of course."

"We shall drive together?"

What a pair they would make on the Kingston By-Pass.

"Yes, of course, Bastard" (in English). "How much?"

The machine almost knocked down a heavily swathed old lady descending from a droshky and screamed to a halt outside a café filled with evil-looking men, all of whom seemed to be smitten with double small-pox.

"CAHARLESS, I am your slave. I will drive you to Tehran."

"Praise be to God for your kindness (and I hope you drop dead). THE BILL."

"CAHARLESS, soul of your father, I shall bring you water. Ho, there, Mohammed Gholi. Oh, bring water for CAHARLESS, my soul, my love. He is thirsty."

He screamed at the robbers in the shop, who came stumbling out with a great *chatti* which they slopped over Carless.

"Thank you, that is sufficient."

"CAHARLESS, I love you as my son."

"This bill is enormous."

It was enormous but probably correct.

A little beyond Meshed we stopped at a police post in a miserable hamlet to ask the way to the Afghan Frontier and Herat. I was already afflicted with the gastric disorders that were to hang like a cloud over our venture, a pale ghost of the man who had climbed the *Spiral Stairs* on Dinas Cromlech less than a month before. Hugh seemed impervious to bacilli and, as I sat in the vehicle waiting for him to emerge from the police station, I munched sulphaguanadine tablets gloomily and thought of the infected ice-cream he had insisted on buying at Kazvin on the road from Tabriz to Tehran.

"We must accustom our stomachs to this sort of thing," he had said and had shared it with Wanda, who had no need to accustom herself to anything as she was returning to Italy.

The germs had been so virulent that she had been struck down almost at once; only after three days in bed at the Embassy with a high temperature had she been able to totter to the plane on the unwilling arm of a Queen's Messenger. I had rejected the ice-cream. Hugh had eaten it and survived. It was unjust; I hated him; now I wondered whether my wife was dead, and who would look after my children.

I had succumbed much later. In the fertile plain between Neishapur and Meshed we had stopped at a *qanat* for water. The *qanat*, a subterranean canal, was in a grove of trees and this was the place where it finally came to the surface after its journey underground. It was a magical spot, cool and green in the middle of sunburnt fields. There was a mound grown with grass like a tumulus with a mill room hollowed out of it and a leat into which the water gushed from a brick conduit, the *qanat* itself flowing under the mill. In several different spouts the water issued from the far side of the mound. It was as complex as a telephone exchange.

"Bound to be good," Hugh said, confronted by the crystal jets. "*Qanat* water. Comes from the hills."

It was delicious. After we had drunk a couple of pints each we discovered that the water didn't come from the *qanat* but from the conduit which came overland from a dirty-looking village less than a mile away.

"I can't understand why you're so fussy," he said, "it doesn't affect me."

Now, as I sat outside the police station brooding over these misfortunes, there was a sudden outburst of screams and moans from the other side of the road, becoming more and more insistent and finally mounting to such a crescendo that I went to investigate.

Gathered round a well or shaft full of the most loathsome sewage was a crowd of gendarmes in their ugly sky-blue uniforms and several women in a state of happy hysteria, one screaming more loudly than the rest.

"What is it?"

"*Bābā,*" said one of the policemen, pointing to the seething mess at our feet and measuring the length of quite a small baby. He began to keen; presumably he was the father. I waited a little, no one did anything.

This was the moment I had managed to avoid all my life; the rescue of the comrade under fire, the death-leaper from Hammersmith Bridge saved by Newby, the tussle with the lunatic with the cut-throat razor.

Feeling absurd and sick with anticipation I plunged head first into the muck. It was only four feet deep and quite warm but unbelievable, a real eastern sewer. The first time I got hold of something cold and clammy that was part of an American packing case. The second time I found nothing and came up spluttering and sick to find the mother beating a serene little boy of five who had watched the whole performance from the house next door into which he had strayed. The crowd was already dispersing; the policeman gave me tea and let me change in the station house but the taste and smell remained.

Five miles beyond the police post the road forked left for the Afghan Frontier. It crossed a dry river bed with banks of gravel and went up past a large fortified building set on a low hill. After my pointless immersion I had become cold and my teeth were chattering. It seemed a good enough reason to stop the vehicle and have a look. Only some excuse such as this could halt our mad career, for whoever was driving seemed possessed of a demon who made it impossible ever to stop. Locked in the cab we were prisoners. We could see the country we passed through but not feel it and the only smells, unless we put our heads out of the window (a hazardous business if we both did it at the same time), were the fumes of the exhaust and our foul pipes; vistas we would gladly have lingered over had we been alone were gone in an instant and for ever. If there is any way of seeing less of a country than from a motor-car I have yet to experience it.

The building was a caravanserai, ruined and deserted, built of thin flat bricks. The walls were more than twenty feet high, decorated on the side where the gate was with blind, pointed arches. Each corner was defended by a smooth round tower with a crumbling lip.

Standing alone in a wilderness of scrub, it was an eerie place. The wind was strong and under the high gateway, flanked by embrasures, it whistled in the machicolations. Inside it was a warren of dark, echoing tunnels and galleries round a central court, open to the sky, with the same pointed arches as on the outer wall but here leading into small cells for the accommodation of more important travellers. In time of need this was a place that might shelter a thousand men and their animals.

The roof was grown thick with grass and wild peas, masking open chimney holes as dangerous as oubliettes. The view from the ramparts was desolate.

The air was full of dust and, as the sun set, everything was bathed in a blinding saffron light. There was not a house or a village anywhere, only a whitewashed tomb set on a hill and far up the river bed, picking their way across the grey shingle, a file of men and donkeys. Here for me, rightly or wrongly, was the beginning of Central Asia.

We drove on and on and all the time I felt worse. Finally we reached a town called Fariman. A whole gale of wind was blowing, tearing up the surface of the main street. Except for two policemen holding hands and a dog whose hind legs were paralysed it was deserted. Through waves of nausea I saw that Hugh had stopped outside some sort of café.

"I think we'd better eat here." To my diseased imagination he seemed full of bounce.

"I don't think I can manage any more."

"You are a funny fellow; always talking about food, now you don't want any."

"You forget I've already eaten."

He disappeared for a moment, then I saw him in the doorway semaphoring at me. With my last remaining strength I tottered into the building. It was a long room, brilliantly lit, empty except for the proprieter. He was bald, but for a grubby-looking frizz of grey curls, and dressed in a long, prophetic sort of garment. Hanging like a miasma over him and everything else in the building was a terrible smell of grease.

"*Ovis aries*, fat-tailed sheep, they store it up in their tails for the winter."

"I've never smelt a sheep like this, dead or alive."

"It's excellent for cooking," Hugh said. Nevertheless, he ordered boiled eggs.

I had "*mast.*" Normally an innocuous dish of curdled milk fit for the most squeamish stomach, it arrived stiff as old putty, the same colour and pungent.

While I was being noisily ill in the street, a solitary man came to gaze. "*Shekam dard,*" I said, pointing to my stomach, thinking to enlist his sympathy, and returned to the work in hand. When next I looked at him he had taken off his trousers and was mouthing at me. With my new display of interest, he started to strip himself completely until a relative led him away struggling.

That night we huddled in our sleeping-bags at the bottom of a dried-out watercourse. It seemed to offer some protection from the wind, which howled about us, but in the morning we woke to find ourselves buried under twin mounds of sand like dead prospectors. But for the time being I was cured: sixteen sulphaguanadine tablets in sixteen hours had done it.

Full of sand we drove to the frontier town, Taiabad. It was only eight o'clock but the main street was already an oven. The military commander, a charming colonel, offered us sherbet in his office. It was delicious and tasted of honey. Hugh discussed the scandals of the opium smuggling with him. "It is a disgraceful habit," the Colonel said. "Here, of course, it is most rigorously repressed but it is difficult to control the traffic at more remote places." (In the Customs House the clerks were already at this hour enveloped in clouds of smoke.) "You are going to Kabul. Which route are you proposing to take?"

We asked him which he thought the best.

"The northern is very long; the centre, through the Hazara country, is very difficult; the way by Kandahar is very hot. We are still awaiting the young American, Winant. He set off to come here by the northern route in May."

"But today's the second of July."

"There was a Swedish nurse with him. Also he was very religious. It was a great mistake—a dangerous combination. Now we shall never see them again. In some respects it is a disagreeable country. Unless you are bound to go there, I counsel you to remain in Iran. I shall be delighted to put you up here for as long as you wish. It is very lonely for me here."

We told him our plans.

"You are not armed? You are quite right. It is inadvisable; so many travellers are, especially Europeans. It only excites the cupidity of the inhabitants. I should go by Kandahar. Your visas are for Kandahar and that is the only route they will permit anyway. That is if anyone at the customs post can read," he added mischievously.

Reluctantly we took leave of this agreeable man and set off down the road through a flat wilderness, until we came to a road block formed by a solitary tree-trunk. In the midst of this nothingness, pitched some distance from the road, was a sad little tent shuddering in the wind. After we had sounded the horn for some minutes a sergeant appeared and with infinite slowness drew back the tree-trunk to let us pass and without speaking returned to the flapping tent. Whatever indiscretion the Colonel may have been guilty of to land himself in such a place as Taiabad paled into utter insignificance when one considered the nameless crimes that this sergeant must have been expiating in his solitary tent.

After eight miles in a no-man's-land of ruined mud forts and nothing else we came to a collection of buildings so deserted-looking that we thought they must be some advanced post evacuated for lack of amenity. This time the tree-trunk was whitewashed. As Hugh got down to remove it, angry cries came from the largest and most dilapidated building and a file of soldiers in hairy uniforms that seemed to have been made from old blankets poured out of it and hemmed us in. As we marched across the open space towards the building, the wind was hot like an electric hair dryer and strong enough to lean on.

Inside the customs house in a dim corridor several Pathans squatted together sharing a leaky hubble-bubble. They had semitic, feminine faces but were an uncouth lot, full of swagger, dressed in saffron shirts and *chaplis* with rubber soles made from the treads of American motor tyres. In charge of them was a superior official in a round hat and blue striped pyjamas whom they completely ignored. It was he who stamped our passports without formality.

The customs house was rocking in the wind which roared about it so loud that conversation was difficult.

"Is it always like this?" I screamed in Hugh's ear.

"It's the *Bād-i-Sad-o-Bist*," 'the Wind of Hundred and Twenty Days.' "

"Yes," said one of the Pathans, "for a hundred and twenty days it blows. It started ten days ago. It comes from the north-west, but God only knows where it goes to."

After the half-light of the building, the light in the courtyard was blinding, incandescent; the dust in it thick and old and bitter-tasting, as if it had been swirling there for ever.

We were in Afghanistan.

PATRICK LEIGH FERMOR
1915–

This bright, brave, and literary British traveler came from an Anglo–Irish background and was early regarded as a "difficult child," headstrong and frequently very naughty. After passing through special schools for anarchic children, he landed at King's School, Canterbury, where his transgressions earned for him his housemaster's designation, "a dangerous mixture of sophistication and recklessness." Expelled because of an affair with a local girl, he entered a cramming program in London aiming at admission to the Royal Military College. But study proved intolerably boring, and in the winter of 1933, when he was eighteen, he decided to take a long walk—to Constantinople. He recalled his journey in 1977 in A Time of Gifts, *pronounced by Jan Morris to be "nothing short of a masterpiece."*

During World War II, as a young officer of the Irish Guards, he took part in the daring abduction from Crete to Cairo of the German General Karl Kreipe, commander of the 22nd Panzer Grenadier Division. The whole amazing story is told by W. Stanley Moss in Ill Met by Moonlight *(1950), a combination military memoir and travel book.*

After the war Fermor traveled in the Caribbean and the remoter parts of Greece, and three highly successful travel books resulted: The Traveller's Tree *(1950),* Mani *(1958), and* Roumeli *(1966). Like all his travel writings, these books are distinguished by his prolific use of fascinating detail. Freya Stark has celebrated, in his books, "the felicitous profusion, the exuberance of learning and information." He has promised that some day he will publish the remainder of his journey to Constantinople.*

From A TIME OF GIFTS
(1977)

I struck the board and cried, "No more; I will abroad."
What, shall I ever sigh and pine?
My life and lines are free; free as the road,
Loose as the wind.

George Herbert

* * *

My scheme was not working well. That improvident flight from the rooms and meals and all that went with them at my tutor's had reduced my funds to a pound a week and the way things were shaping, it looked as though opulence from writing might be delayed for a time. I managed somehow, but gloom and perplexity descended with the start of winter. Fitful streaks of promise and scrapes and upheavals had marked my progress so far; they still continued; but now I seemed to be floating towards disintegration in a tangle of submerged and ill-marked reefs. The outlook grew steadily darker and more overcast. About lamplighting time at the end of a wet November day, I was peering morosely at the dog-eared pages on my writing table and then through the panes at the streaming reflections of Shepherd Market, thinking as *Night and Day* succeeded *Stormy Weather* on the gramophone in the room below, that *Lazybones* couldn't be far behind; when, almost with the abruptness of Herbert's lines at the beginning of these pages, inspiration came. A plan unfolded with the speed and the completeness of a Japanese paper flower in a tumbler.

To change scenery; abandon London and England and set out across Europe like a tramp—or, as I characteristically phrased it to myself, like a pilgrim or a palmer, an errant scholar, a broken knight or the hero of *The Cloister and the Hearth!* All of a sudden, this was not merely the obvious, but the only thing to do. I would travel on foot, sleep in hayricks in summer, shelter in barns when it was raining or snowing and only consort with peasants and tramps. If I lived on bread and cheese and apples, jogging along on fifty pounds a year like Lord Durham with a few noughts knocked off, there would even be some cash left over for paper and pencils and an occasional mug of beer. A new life! Freedom! Something to write about!

Even before I looked at a map, two great rivers had already plotted the itinerary in my mind's eye: the Rhine uncoiled across it, the Alps rose up and then the wolf-harbouring Carpathian watersheds and the cordilleras of the Balkans; and there, at the end of the windings of the Danube, the Black Sea was beginning to spread its mysterious and lopsided shape; and my chief destination was never in a moment's doubt. The levitating skyline of Constantinople pricked its sheaves of thin cylinders and its hemispheres out of the sea-mist; beyond it Mount Athos hovered; and the Greek archipelago was already scattering a paper-chase of islands across the Aegean. (These certainties sprang from reading the books of Robert Byron; dragon-green Byzantium loomed serpent-haunted and gong-tormented; I had even met the author for a moment in a blurred and saxophone-haunted night club as dark as Tartarus.)

I wondered during the first few days whether to enlist a companion; but I knew that the enterprise had to be solitary and the break complete. I wanted to think, write, stay or move on at my own speed and unencumbered, to gaze at things with a changed eye and listen to new tongues that were untainted by a single familiar word. With any luck the humble circumstances of the journey would offer no scope for English or French. Flights of unknown syllables would soon be rushing into purged and attentive ears.

The idea met obstruction at first: why not wait till spring? (London by now was shuddering under veils of December rain.) But when they understood that all was decided, most of the objectors became allies. Warming to the scheme after initial demur, Mr Prideaux undertook to write to India putting my démarche in a favourable light; I determined to announce the *fait accompli* by letter when I was safely on the way, perhaps from Cologne . . . Then we planned the dispatch of those weekly pounds—each time, if possible, after they had risen to a monthly total of four—by registered letter to suitably spaced-out *postes restantes* [general deliveries.] (Munich would be the first; then I would write and suggest a second.) I next borrowed fifteen pounds off the father of a school friend, partly to buy equipment and partly to have something in hand when I set out. I telephoned to my sister Vanessa, back from India again a few years before, and married and settled in Gloucestershire. My mother was filled with apprehension to begin with; we pored over the atlas, and, bit by bit as we pored, the comic possibilities began to unfold in absurd imaginary scenes until we were falling about with laughter; and by the time I caught the train to London next morning, she was infected with my excitement.

During the last days, my outfit assembled fast. Most of it came from Millet's army surplus store in The Strand: an old Army greatcoat, different layers of jersey, grey flannel shirts, a couple of white linen ones for best, a soft leather windbreaker, puttees, nailed boots, a sleeping bag (to be lost within a month and neither missed nor replaced); notebooks and drawing blocks, rubbers, an aluminum cylinder full of Venus and Golden Sovereign pencils; an old *Oxford Book of English Verse*. (Lost likewise, and, to my surprise—it had been a sort of Bible—not missed much more than the sleeping bag.) The other half of my very conventional travelling library was the Loeb *Horace*, Vol. I, which my mother, after asking what I wanted, had bought and posted in Guildford. (She had written the translation of a short poem by Petronius on the flyleaf, chanced on and copied out, she told me later, from another volume on the same shelf: "Leave thy home, O youth, and seek out alien shores . . . Yield not to misfortune: the far-off Danube shall know thee, the cold North-wind and the untroubled kingdom of Canopus and the men who gaze on the new birth of Phoebus or upon his setting . . ." She was an enormous reader, but Petronius was not in her usual line of country and he had only recently entered mine. I was impressed and touched.) Finally I bought a ticket on a small Dutch steamer sailing from Tower Bridge to the Hook of Holland. All this had taken a shark's bite out of my borrowed cash, but there was still a wad of notes left over.

At last, with a touch of headache from an eve-of-departure party, I got out of bed on the great day, put on my new kit and tramped south-west under a lowering sky. I felt preternaturally light, as though I were already away and floating like a djinn escaped from its flask through the dazzling middle air while Europe unfolded. But the grating hobnails took me no farther than Cliveden Place, where I picked up a rucksack left for me there by Mark Ogilvie-Grant. Inspecting my stuff, he had glanced with pity at the one I had bought. (His—a superior Bergen affair resting on a lumbar semicircle of metal and supported by a triangular frame, had accompanied him—usually, he admitted, slung on a mule—all round Athos with Robert Byron and David Talbot-Rice when *The Station* was being written. Weathered and faded by Macedonian suns, it was rife with *mana*.) Then I bought for nine-pence a well-balanced ashplant at the tobacconist's next to the corner of Sloane Square and headed for Victoria Street and Petty France to pick up my new passport. Filling in the form the day before—born in London, 11 February 1915; height 5' 9 3/4"; eyes, brown; hair, brown; distinguishing marks, none—I had left the top space empty, not knowing what to write. Profession? "Well, what shall we say?" the Passport Official had asked, pointing to the void. My mind remained empty. A few years earlier, an American hobo song called *Hallelujah I'm a bum!* had been on many lips; during the last days it had been haunting me like a private *leitmotif* and without realizing I must have been humming the tune as

I pondered, for the Official laughed. "You can't very well put *that*," he said. After a moment he added: "I should just write 'student';" so I did. With the stiff new document in my pocket, stamped "8 December 1933," I struck north over the Green Park under a dark massing of cloud. As I crossed Piccadilly and entered the crooked chasm of White Horse Street, there were a few random splashes and, glistening at the end of it, Shepherd Market was prickly with falling drops. I would be just in time for a good-bye luncheon with Miss Stewart and three friends—two fellow lodgers and a girl: then, away. The rain was settling in.

*   *   *

On the far side of the bridge I abandoned the Rhine for its tributary and after a few miles alongside the Neckar the steep lights of Heidelberg assembled. It was dark by the time I climbed the main street and soon softly-lit panes of coloured glass, under the hanging sign of a Red Ox, were beckoning me indoors. With freezing cheeks and hair caked with snow, I clumped into an entrancing haven of oak beams and carving and alcoves and changing floor levels. A jungle of impedimenta encrusted the interior—mugs and bottles and glasses and antlers—the innocent accumulation of years, not stage props of forced conviviality—and the whole place glowed with a universal patina. It was more like a room in a castle and, except for a cat asleep in front of the stove, quite empty.

This was the moment I longed for every day. Settling at a heavy inn-table, thawing and tingling, with wine, bread, and cheese handy and my papers, books and diary all laid out; writing up the day's doings, hunting for words in the dictionary, drawing, struggling with verses, or merely subsiding in a vacuous and contented trance while the snow thawed off my boots. An elderly woman came downstairs and settled by the stove with her sewing. Spotting my stick and rucksack and the puddle of melting snow, she said, with a smile, "Wer reitet so spät durch Nacht und Wind?" My German, now fifteen days old, was just up to this: "Who rides so late through night and wind?" But I was puzzled by *reitet.* (How was I to know that it was the first line of Goethe's famous *Erlkönig*, made more famous still by the music of Schubert?) *What, a foreigner?* I knew what to say at this point, and came in on cue: . . . "Englischer Student . . . zu Fuss nach Konstantinopel" [hiking to Constantinople] . . . I'd got it pat by now. "Konstantinopel?" she said. "*Oh Weh!*" O Woe! So far! And in midwinter too. She asked where I would be the day after, on New Year's Eve. Somewhere on the road, I said. "You can't go wandering about in the snow on Sylvesterabend!" she answered. "And where are you staying tonight, pray?" I hadn't thought yet. Her husband had come in a little while before and overheard our exchange. "Stay with us," he said. "You must be our guest."

They were the owner and his wife and their names were Herr and Frau Spengel. Upstairs, on my hostess's orders, I fished out things to be washed—it was my first laundry since London—and handed them over to the maid: wondering, as I did so, how a German would get on in Oxford if he turned up at The Mitre on a snowy December night.

One of the stained-glass armorial shields in the windows bore the slanting zigzag of Franken. This old stronghold of the Salian Franks is a part of northern Bavaria now, and the Red Ox Inn was the headquarters of the Franconia student league. All the old inns of Heidelberg had these regional associations, and the most exalted of them, the Saxoborussia, was Heidelberg's Bullingdon and the members were Prussia's and Saxony's haughtiest. They held their sessions at Seppl's next door, where the walls were crowded with faded daguerrotypes of slashed and incipiently side-whiskered scions of the *Hochjunkertum* [petty nobility] defiant in high boots and tricoloured sashes. Their gauntlets grasped basket-hilted sabres. Askew on those faded pates little caps like collapsed képis were tilted to display the initial of the Corps embroidered on the crown—a contorted Gothic cypher and an exclamation mark, all picked out in gold wire. I pestered Fritz Spengel, the son of my hosts, with questions about student life: songs, drinking ritual, and above all, duelling, which wasn't duelling at all of course, but tribal scarification. Those dashing scars were school ties that could never be taken off, the emblem and seal of a ten-years' cult of the humanities. With a sabre from the wall, Fritz demonstrated the stance and the grip and described how the participants were gauntleted, gorgeted and goggled until every exposed vein and artery, and every inch of irreplaceable tissue, were upholstered from harm. Distance was measured; the sabres crossed at the end of outstretched arms; only the wrists moved; to flinch spelt disgrace; and the blades clashed by numbers until the razor-sharp tips sliced gashes deep enough, tended with rubbed-in salt, to last a lifetime. I had noticed these academic stigmata on the spectacled faces of doctors and lawyers; brow, cheek or chin, and sometimes all three, were ripped up by this haphazard surgery in puckered or gleaming lines strangely at odds with the wrinkles that middle age had inscribed there. I think Fritz, who was humane, thoughtful and civilized and a few years older than me, looked down on this antique custom, and he answered my question with friendly pity. He knew all too well the dark glamour of the Mensur [ritual duel] among foreigners.

The rather sad charm of a university in the vacation pervaded the beautiful town. We explored the academic buildings and the libraries and the museum and wandered round the churches. Formerly a stronghold of the Reform, the town now harbours the rival faiths in peaceful juxtaposition and if it is a Sunday, Gregorian plainsong escapes through the doors of one church and the Lutheran strains of *Ein' feste Burg* from the next.

That afternoon, with Fritz and a friend, I climbed through the woods to look at the ruins of the palace that overhangs the town: an enormous complex of dark red stone which turns pink, russet or purple with the vagaries of the light and the hour. The basic mass is medieval, but the Renaissance bursts out again and again in gateways and courtyards and galleries and expands in the delicate sixteenth-century carving. Troops of statues posture in their scalloped recesses. Siege and explosion had partly wrecked it when the French ravaged the region. When? In the Thirty Years War; one might have guessed . . . But who had built it? *Didn't I know? Die Kurfürsten von der Pfalz!* The Electors Palatine . . . We were in the old capital of the Palatinate . . .

Distant bells, ringing from faraway English class-rooms, were trying to convey a forgotten message; but it was no good. "Guess what this gate is called!", Fritz said, slapping a red column. "The Elizabeth, or English Gate! Named after the English princess." "*Of course!* I was there at last! The Winter Queen! Elizabeth, the high-spirited daughter of James I, Electress Palatine and, for a year, Queen of Bohemia! She arrived here as a bride of seventeen and for the five years of her reign, Heidelberg, my companions said, had never seen anything like the masques and the revels and the balls. But soon, when the Palatinate and Bohemia were both lost and her brother's head was cut off and the Commonwealth had reduced her to exile and poverty, she was celebrated as the Queen of Hearts by a galaxy of champions. Her great-niece, Queen Anne, ended the reigning line of the Stuarts and Elizabeth's grandson, George I, ascended the throne where her descendant still sits. My companions knew much more about it than I did.

In spite of its beauty, it was a chill, grey prospect at this moment. Lagged in sacking for the winter, desolate rose trees pierced the snow-muffled terraces. These were bare of all footprints but our own and the tiny arrows of a robin. Below the last balustrade, the roofs of the town clustered and beyond it flowed the Neckar and then the Rhine, and the Haardt Mountains, and the Palatine Forest rippled away beyond. A sun like an enormous crimson balloon was about to sink into the pallid landscape. It recalled, as it does still, the first time I saw this wintry portent. In a sailor-suit with *H.M.S. Indomitable* on my cap-ribbon, I was being hurried home to tea across Regent's Park while the keepers

were calling closing time. We lived so close to the zoo that one could
hear the lions roaring at night.

This Palatine sun was the dying wick of 1933; the last vestige of that
ownerless rump of the seasons that stretches from the winter solstice to
the New Year. " 'Tis the year's midnight . . . the world's whole sap is
sunk." On the way back we passed a group of youths sitting on a low
wall and kicking their heels as they whistled the *Horst Wessel Lied*
between their teeth. Fritz said, "I *think*, perhaps, I've heard that tune
before . . ."

That night at the inn, I noticed that a lint-haired young man at the
next table was fixing me with an icy gleam. Except for pale blue eyes
set flush with his head like a hare's, he might have been an albino. He
suddenly rose with a stumble, came over, and said: "So? Ein Eng-
länder?" with a sardonic smile. "*Wunderbar!*" Then his face changed
to a mask of hate. Why had we stolen Germany's colonies? Why
shouldn't Germany have a fleet and a proper army? Did I think Germany was going to take orders from a country that was run by the Jews?
A catalogue of accusations followed, not very loud, but clearly and
intensely articulated. His face, which was almost touching mine, raked
me with long blasts of schnapps-breath. "Adolf Hitler will change all
that," he ended. "*Perhaps you've heard the name?*" Fritz shut his eyes
with a bored groan and murmured "Um Gottes willen!" Then he took
him by the elbow with the words, "Komm, Franzi!" and, rather, surprisingly, my accuser allowed himself to be led to the door. Fritz sat down
again, saying: "I'm so sorry. You see what it's like." Luckily, none of the
other tables had noticed and the hateful moment was soon superseded
by feasting and talk and wine and, later, by songs to usher in St Sylv-
ester's Vigil; and by the time the first bells of 1934 were clashing outside,
everything had merged in a luminous haze of music and toasts and
greetings.

Frau Spengel insisted that it was absurd to set off on New Year's Day;
so I spent another twenty-four hours wandering about the town and the
castle and reading and writing and talking with this kind and civilized
family. (My sojourn at the Red Ox, afterwards, was one of several high
points of recollection that failed to succumb to the obliterating moods
of war. I often thought of it.)

"Don't forget your *treuer Wanderstab* [trusty walking-staff]" Frau
Spengel said, handing me my gleaming stick as I was loading up for
departure on the second of January. Fritz accompanied me to the edge
of the town. Ironed linen lay neatly in my rucksack; also a large parcel
of Gebäck [baked goods], special Sylvestrine cakes rather like shortbread,
which I munched as I loped along over the snow. All prospects glowed,

for the next halt—at Bruchsal, a good stretch further—was already fixed
up. Before leaving London, a friend who had stayed there the summer
before and canoed down the Neckar by *faltboot* [collapsable boat] with
one of the sons of the house, had given me an introduction to the mayor.
Fritz had telephoned; and by dusk I was sitting with Dr Arnold and his
family drinking tea laced with brandy in one of the huge baroque rooms
of Schloss Bruchsal. I couldn't stop gazing at my magnificent surroundings. Bruchsal is one of the most beautiful baroque palaces in the whole
of Germany. It was built in the eighteenth century by the Prince-
Bishops of Spires, I can't remember when their successors stopped living
in it; perhaps when their secular sovereignty was dissolved. But for many
decades it had been the abode of the Burgomasters of Bruchsal. I stayed
here two nights, sleeping in the bedroom of an absent son. After a long
bath, I explored his collection of Tauchnitz editions and found exactly
what I wanted to read in bed—*Leave it to Psmith*—and soon I wasn't
really in a German schloss at all, but in the corner seat of a first class
carriage on the 3.45 from Paddington to Market Blandings, bound for
a different castle.

It was the first time I had seen such architecture. The whole of next
day I loitered about the building; hesitating half-way up shallow staircases balustraded by magnificent branching designs of wrought metal;
wandering through double doors that led from state room to state room;
and gazing with untutored and marvelling eyes down perspectives
crossed by the diminishing slants of winter sunbeams. Pastoral scenes
unfolded in light-hearted colours across ceilings that were enclosed in
a studiously asymmetrical icing of scrolls and sheaves; shells and garlands
and foliage and ribands depicted myths extravagant enough to stop an
unprepared observer dead in his tracks. The sensation of wintry but
glowing interior space, the airiness of the snowy convolutions, the twirl
of the metal foliage and the gilt of the arabesques were all made more
buoyant still by reflections from the real snow that lay untrodden outside; it came glancing up through the panes, diffusing a still and muted
luminosity: a northern variant (I thought years later) of the reflected
flicker that canals, during Venetian siestas, send up across the cloud-
born apotheoses and rapes that cover the ceilings. Only statues and
skeleton trees broke the outdoor whiteness, and a colony of rooks.

In England, the Burgomaster, with his white hair and moustache, his
erect bearing and grey tweeds, might have been colonel of a good line
regiment. After dinner he tucked a cigar in a holder made of a cardboard
cone and a quill, changed spectacles and, hunting through a pile of
music on the piano, sat down and attacked the Waldstein Sonata with

authority and verve. The pleasure was reinforced by the player's enjoyment of his capacity to wrestle with it. His expression of delight, as he peered at the notes through a veil of cigar smoke and tumbling ash, was at odds with the gravity of the music. It was a surprise; so different was it from an evening spent with his putative English equivalent; and when the last chord had been struck, he leapt from the stool with a smile of youthful and almost ecstatic enjoyment amid the good-humoured applause of his family. A rush of appraisal broke out, and hot argument about possible alternative interpretations.

There was no doubt about it, I thought next day: I'd taken a wrong turning. Instead of reaching Pforzheim towards sunset, I was plodding across open fields with snow and the night both falling fast. My new goal was a light which soon turned out to be the window of a farmhouse by the edge of a wood. A dog had started barking. When I reached the door a man's silhouette appeared in the threshold and told the dog to be quiet and shouted: "Wer ist da?" ["Who's there?"] Concluding that I was harmless, he let me in.

A dozen faces peered up in surprise, their spoons halted in mid air, and their features, lit from below by a lantern on the table, were as gnarled and grained as the board itself. Their clogs were hidden in the dark underneath, and the rest of the room, except for the crucifix on the wall, was swallowed by shadow. The spell was broken by the unexpectedness of the irruption: *A stranger from Ausland!* Shy, amazed hospitality replaced earlier fears and I was soon seated among them on the bench and busy with a spoon as well.

The habit of grasping and speaking German had been outpaced during the last few days by another change of accent and idiom. These farmhouse sentences were all but out of reach. But there was something else here that was enigmatically familiar. Raw knuckles of enormous hands, half clenched still from the grasp of ploughs and spades and bill-hooks, lay loose among the cut onions and the chipped pitchers and a brown loaf broken open. Smoke had blackened the earthenware tureen and the light caught its pewter handle and stressed the furrowed faces, and the bricky cheeks of young and hemp-haired giants . . . A small crone in a pleated coif sat at the end of the table, her eyes bright and timid in their hollows of bone and all these puzzled features were flung into relief by a single wick from below. Supper at Emmaus or Bethany? Painted by whom?

Dog-tired from the fields, the family began to stretch and get down the moment the meal was over and to amble bedwards with dragging clogs. A grandson, apologizing because there was no room indoors, slung a pillow and two blankets over his shoulder, took the lantern and led the way across the yard. In the barn the other side, harrows, ploughshares, scythes and sieves loomed for a moment, and beyond, tethered to a manger that ran the length of the barn, horns and tousled brows and liquid eyes gleamed in the lantern's beam. The head of a cart-horse, with a pale mane and tail and ears pricked at our advent, almost touched the rafters.

When I was alone I stretched out on a bed of sliced hay like a crusader on his tomb, snugly wrapped up in greatcoat and blankets, with crossed legs still putteed and clodhoppered. Two owls were within earshot. The composite smell of snow, wood, dust, cobwebs, mangolds, beetroots, fodder, cattlecake and the cows' breath was laced with an ammoniac tang from the plip-plop and the splash that sometimes broke the rhythm of the munching and the click of horns. There was an occasional grate of blocks and halters through their iron rings, a moo from time to time, or a huge horseshoe scraping or clinking on the cobbles. This was more like it!

The eaves were stiff with icicles next morning. Everyone was out of the kitchen and already at work, except the old woman in the coif. She gave me a scalding bowl of coffee and milk with dark brown bread broken in it. Would an offer to pay be putting my foot in it, I wondered; and then tentatively proposed it. There was no offence; but, equally, it was out of the question: "Nee, nee!" she said, with a light pat of her transparent hand. (It sounded the same as the English "Nay.") The smile of her totally dismantled gums had the innocence of an infant's. "Gar nix!" ["Not at all!"] After farewells, she called me back with a shrill cry and put a foot-long slice of buttered black bread in my hand; I ate my way along this gigantic and delicious butterbrot as I went, and after a furlong, caught sight of all the others. They waved and shouted "Gute Reise!" ["good Journey!"] They were hacking at the frostbitten grass with mattocks, delving into a field that looked and sounded as hard as iron.

*   *   *

Of the town of Pforzheim, where I spent the next night, I remember nothing. But the evening after I was in the heart of Stuttgart by lamp-lighting time, sole customer in a café opposite the cubistic mass of the Hotel Graf Zeppelin. Snow and sleet and biting winds had emptied the streets of all but a few scuttling figures, and two cheerless boys doggedly rattling a collection box. Now they had vanished as well and the proprietor and I were the only people in sight in the whole capital of Württemberg. I was writing out the day's doings and vaguely wondering where to find lodging when two cheerful and obviously well-brought up girls came in, and began buying groceries at the counter. They were amusingly dressed in eskimo hoods, furry boots and gauntlets like grizzly bears which they clapped together to dispel the cold. I wished I knew them. The sleet, turning to hail, rattled on the window like grapeshot. One of the girls, who wore horn-rimmed spectacles, catching sight of my German-English dictionary, daringly said "How do you do, do, Mister Brown?" (This was the only line of an idiotic and now mercifully forgotten song, repeated ad infinitum like *Lloyd George Knew My Father*, it had swept across the world two years before.) Then she laughed in confusion at her boldness, under a mild reproof from her companion. I jumped up and implored them to have a coffee, or anything. They suddenly became more reserved: "Nein, nein, besten Dank, aber wir müssen weg!" ["No, no, thanks a lot, but we must leave!]" I looked crestfallen; and after an exchange of "Warum nicht?" ["Why not?"] they consented to stay five minutes, but refused coffee.

The line of the song was almost the only English they knew. My first interlocutrix, who had taken her spectacles off, asked how old I was. I said "Nineteen," though it wouldn't be quite true for another five weeks. "We too!" they said. "And what do you do?" "I'm a student." "We too! *Wunderbar!*" They were called Elizabeth-Charlotte, shortened to Liselotte or Lise—and Annie. Lise was from Donaueschingen, where the Danube rises, in the Black Forest, but she was living in Annie's parents' house in Stuttgart, where they were studying music. Both were pretty. Lise had unruly brown hair and a captivating and lively face, from which a smile was never absent for long; her glance, with her spectacles off, was wide, unfocused and full of trusting charm. Annie's fair hair was plaited and coiled in earphones, a fashion I'd always hated; but it suited her pallor and long neck and gave her the look of a Gothic effigy from the door of an abbey. They told me they were buying things for a young people's party in celebration of the *Dreikönigsfest*. It was Epiphany, the 6th of January, the feast of the Three Kings. After some whispered confabulation, they decided to have pity on me and take me with them. Lise enterprisingly suggested we could invent a link with her family— "falls sie fragen, wo wire Sie aufgegabelt haben" ("Just in case they ask where we forked you out from"). Soon, in the comfortable bathroom of Annie's absent parents—he was a bank manager and they were away in Basel on business—I was trying to make myself presentable: combing my hair, putting on the clean shirt and flannel bags I had extracted before leaving my rucksack in charge of the café. I hadn't fixed up anything for the night yet, they said, when I rejoined them: it was unorthodox and would be uncomfortable—but would I like to doss down on the sofa? "No, no, no!" I cried: far too much of a nuisance for them, after all their kindness; but I didn't insist too long. "Don't say you're staying here!" Annie said. "You know how silly people are." There was a feeling of secrecy and collusion in all this, like plans for a midnight feast. They were thrilled by their recklessness. So was I.

Collusion looked like breaking down when we got to the party. "Can I introduce," Annie began. "Darf ich Ihnen vorstellen—." Her brow puckered in alarm; we hadn't exchanged surnames. Lise quickly chimed in with "Mr Brown, a family friend." She might have been a captain of hussars, turning the tide of battle by a brilliant swoop. Later a cake was ceremoniously cut, and a girl was crowned with a gold cardboard crown. Songs were sung in honour of Epiphany and the Magi, some in unison, some solo. Asked if there were any English ones (as I had hoped, in order to show Lise and Annie I wasn't a godless barbarian), I sang *We Three Kings of Orient Are*. A later song, celebrating the Neckar Valley and Swabia, was sung in complex harmony.

* * *

When I woke up on the sofa—rather late; we had sat up talking and drinking Annie's father's wine before going to bed—I had no idea where I was; it was a frequent phenomenon on this journey. But when I found my hands muffled like a pierrot's in the scarlet silk sleeves of Annie's father's pyjamas, everything came back to me. He must have been a giant (a photograph on the piano of a handsome ski-booted trio in the snow—my host with his arms round his wife and daughter—bore this out). The curtains were still drawn and two dressing-gowned figures were tiptoeing about the shadows. When they realized I was awake at last, greetings were exchanged and the curtains drawn. It only seemed to make the room very few degrees lighter. "Look!" Lise said, "no day for walking!" It was true: merciless gusts of rain were thrashing the roof-scape outside. Nice weather for young ducks. "Armer Kerl!—Poor chap!" she said, "you'll have to be our prisoner till tomorrow." She put on another log and Annie came in with coffee. Half-way through break-fast, Sunday morning bells began challenging each other from belfry to belfry. We might have been in a submarine among sunk cathedrals. "O Weh!" Lise cried, "I ought to be in church!;" then, peering at the streaming panes: "Too late now." "Zum Beichten, perhaps," Annie said. (*Beichten* is confession.) Lise asked: "What for?" "Picking up strangers." (Lise was Catholic, Annie Protestant; there was a certain amount of sectarian banter.) I urged their claim to every dispensation for sheltering the needy, clothing the naked—a flourish of crimson sleeve supported this—and feeding the hungry. Across the boom of all these bells a marvellous carillon broke out. It is one of the most famous things in Stuttgart. We listened until its complicated pattern faded into silence.

The evening presented a problem in advance. They were ineluctably bidden to a dinner party by a business acquaintance of Annie's father, and though they didn't like him they couldn't plausibly chuck it. But what was to become of me? At last, screwing up their courage, Annie rang his wife up: could they bring a young English friend of Lise's family—informally clad, because he was on a winter walking tour across Europe? (It sounded pretty thin.) There was a twitter of assent from the other end; the receiver was replaced in triumph. She, it seemed, was very nice; he was an industrialist—*steinreich* [enormously rich], rolling— "You'll get plenty to eat and drink!"—Annie said he was a great admirer of Lise's. "No, no!" Lise cried, "of Annie's!" "He's awful! You'll see! You must defend us both."

We were safe till ten o'clock next morning, when the maid's bus got back; she had gone to her Swabian village for the Dreikönigsfest. We drew the curtains to block out the deluge and put on the lights—it was best to treat the dismal scene outside as if it were night—and lolled in dishabille all the morning talking by the fire. I played the gramophone— *St Louis Blues, Stormy Weather, Night and Day*—while the girls ignored their dresses for the dinner party and the submarine morning sped by, until it was time for Annie and me to face the weather outdoors: she for luncheon—a weekly fixture with relations—me to collect my stuff and to buy some eggs for an omelette. Out of doors, even in a momentary lull, the rain was fierce and hostile and the wind was even worse. When Annie got back about five, I was doing a sketch of Lise; an attempt at Annie followed; then I taught them how to play Heads-Bodies-and-Legs. They took to this with a feverish intensity and we played until tolling bells reminded us how late it was. In my case, all that a flat-iron and a brush and comb could achieve had been done. But the girls emerged from their rooms like two marvellous swans. The door bell rang. It was the first sign of the outer world since my invasion, and a bit ominous. "It's the car! He always sends one. Everything in style!"

Downstairs, a chauffeur in leggings held his cap aloft as he opened the door of a long Mercedes. When we had rustled in he enveloped us in bearskin from the waist down. "You see?" the girls said, "High life!"

We soared through the liquid city and up into the wooded hills and alighted at a large villa of concrete and plate glass. Our host was a blond, heavy man with bloodshot eyes and a scar across his forehead. He hailed my companions with gallantry; me, much more guardedly. His dinner-jacket made me feel still more of a ragamuffin. (I cared passionately about these things; but the fact of being called Michael Brown—we had to stick to it now—induced a consoling sense of disembodiment.) Perhaps to account for my lowly outfit among these jewelled figures, he introduced me to the women as "der englische Globetrotter," which I didn't like much. Men guests who were unacquainted toured the room in the German way, shaking hands and reciprocally announcing their names: I did the same "Muller!" "Brown!" "Ströbel!" "Brown!" "Tschudi!" "Brown!" "Röder!" "Brown!" "Altmeier!" "Brown!" "von Schröder!" "Brown!" . . . An old man—a professor from Tübingen, I think, with heavy glasses and a beard—was talking to Lise. We wrung each other's hands, barking "Braun!" and "Brown!" simultaneously. *Snap!* I avoided the girls' glance.

Except for the panorama of the lights of Stuttgart through the plate glass, the house was hideous—prosperous, brand new, shiny, and dispiriting. Pale woods and plastics were juggled together with stale and pretentious vorticism, and the chairs resembled satin boxing-gloves and nickel plumbing. Carved dwarfs with red noses stoppered all the bottles on the oval bar and glass ballerinas pirouetted on ashtrays of agate that rose from the beige carpets on chromium stalks. There were paintings—or tinted photographs—of the Alps at sunset and of naked babies astride Great Danes. Everything looked better, however, after I'd swallowed two White Ladies taken from a tray that was carried about by a white-gloved butler. I helped myself to cigarettes from a seventeenth-century vellum-bound Dante, with the pages glued together and scooped hollow, the only book in sight. Down the dinner table, beside napkins that were half mitres and half Rajput turbans, glittered a promising arsenal of glasses, and by the time we had worked our way through them, the scene was delightfully blurred. From time to time during dinner, I intercepted a puzzled bloodhound scrutiny from the other end of the table. My host obviously found me a question mark; possibly a bit of a rotter, and up to no good; I didn't like him either. I bet he's a terrific Nazi, I thought. I asked the girls later, and they both exclaimed "Und wie!" in vehement unison: "And how!" I think he found something fishy, too, about my being on *Du* terms with his unwilling favourites, while he, most properly, was still restricted to *Sie*. (We had drunk threefold Brüderschaft [undying fellowship] and embraced in the Cologne style the night before.) When we were back in the *salon*, the men armed with cigars like truncheons and brandy rotating in glasses like transparent footballs, the party began to lose coherence. The host flogged it along with a jarring laugh even louder than the non-stop gramophone, between-whiles manoeuvring first Lise and then Annie into a window-bay whence each extricated herself in turn like a good-humoured Syrinx. I watched them as I listened to my namesake Dr Braun, a learned and delightful fogey who was telling me all about the Suevi and the Alemanni and the Hohenstaufens and Eberhardt the Bearded. When the evening broke up, and Lise and Annie were back in the car, our host stood leaning against the top of the car door, idiotically telling them they looked like two Graces. I ducked under his arm and slipped in between them. 'Three now!' Lise said. He looked at me with disfavour. "Ah! And where shall I tell him to drop *you*, junger Mann?"

"At the Graf Zeppelin, please." I sensed a tremor of admiration on either side: even Lise couldn't have done better.

"Ach so?" His opinion of me went up. "And how do you like our best hotel?"

"Clean, comfortable and quiet."

"Tell the manager if you have any complaints. He's a good friend of mine."

"I will! And thanks very much."

We had to take care about conversation because of the chauffeur. A few minutes later, he was opening the car with a flourish of his cockaded cap before the door of the hotel and after fake farewells, I strolled about the hall of the Graf Zeppelin for a last puff at the ogre cigar. When the coast was clear I hared through the streets and into the lift and up to the flat. They were waiting with the door open and we burst into a dance.

At half-past nine next morning, we were waving good-bye across a tide of Monday morning traffic. I kept looking upwards and back, flourishing my glittering wand and bumping into busy Stuttgarters until the diminishing torsos frantically signalling from the seventh-storey window were out of sight. I felt as Ulysses must have felt, gazing astern while some island of happy sojourn dropped below the horizon.

I followed the banks of the Neckar, crossed it, and finally left it for good. Suddenly, when it was much too late, I remembered the Kitsch-Museum in Stuttgart; a museum, that is, of German and international bad taste, which the girls had said I mustn't miss. (The décor last night—for this was how the subject had cropped up—could have been incorporated as it stood.) I slept at Göppingen and tried with the help of the dictionary to write three letters in German; to Heidelberg, Bruchsal and Stuttgart. Further on I got a funny joint answer from Lise and Annie; there was a rumpus when Annie's parents got back; not about my actually staying in the flat, which remained a secret to the end. But the bottles we had recklessly drained were the last of a fabulously rare and wonderful vintage that Annie's father had been particularly looking forward to. Heaven only knew what treasured Spätlese from the banks of the Upper Mosel: nectar beyond compare. They had prudently blamed the choice on me. Outrage had finally simmered down to the words: "Well, your thirsty friend must know a lot about wine." (Totally untrue.) "I hope he enjoyed it." (Yes.) It was years before the real enormity of our inroads dawned on me.

Now the track was running south-south-east across Swabia. Scattered conifers appeared, and woods sometimes overshadowed the road for many furlongs. They were random outposts, separated by leagues of pasture and ploughland, of the great mass, lying dark towards the south-west, of the Black Forest. Beyond it the land rippled away to the Alps.

On straight stretches of road where the scenery changed slowly, singing often came to the rescue; and when songs ran short, poetry. At home, and at my various schools, and among the people who took me in after scholastic croppers, there had always been a lot of reading aloud. (My mother was marvellously gifted in this exacting skill, and imaginative and far-ranging in choice; there had been much singing to the piano as well.) At school some learning by heart was compulsory, though not irksome. But this intake was out-distanced many times, as it always is among people who need poetry, by a private anthology, both of those automatically absorbed and of poems consciously chosen and memorized as though one were stocking up for a desert island or for a stretch of solitary. (I was at the age when one's memory for poetry or for languages—indeed for anything—takes impressions like wax and, up to a point, lasts like marble.)

*   *   *

Song is universal in Germany; it causes no dismay; *Shuffle off to Buffalo; Bye, Bye, Blackbird;* or *Shenandoah;* or *The Raggle Taggle Gypsies,* sung as I moved along, evoked nothing but tolerant smiles. But verse was different. Murmuring on the highway caused raised eyebrows and a look of anxious pity. Passages, uttered with gestures and sometimes quite loud, provoked, if one was caught in the act, stares of alarm. Regulus brushing the delaying populace aside as he headed for the Carthaginian executioner, as though to Lacedaemonian Tarentum or the Venafrian fields, called for a fairly mild flourish; but urging the assault-party at Harfleur to close the wall up with English dead would automatically bring on a heightened pitch of voice and action and double one's embarrassment if caught. When this happened I would try to taper off in a cough or weave the words into a tuneless hum and reduce all gestures to a feint at hair-tidying. But some passages demand an empty road as far as the eye can see before letting fly. The terrible boxing-match, for instance, at the funeral games of Anchises when Entellus sends Dares reeling and spitting blood and teeth across the Sicilian shore—"ore ejectantem mixtosque in sanguine dentes"!—and then, with his thonged fist, scatters a steer's brains with one blow between the horns—this needs care. As for the sword-thrust at the bridge-head that brings the great lord of Luna crashing among the augurs like an oak-tree on Mount Alvernus—here the shouts, the walking-stick slashes, the staggering gait and the arms upflung should never be indulged if there is anyone within miles, if then. To a strange eye, one is drunk or a lunatic.

So it was today. I was at this very moment of crescendo and climax, when an old woman tottered out of a wood where she had been gathering sticks. Dropping and scattering them, she took to her heels. I would have liked the earth to have swallowed me, or to have been plucked into the clouds.

Herrick would have been safer, Valéry, if I had known him, perfect: "'Calme . . .'"

PART IV

TOURISTIC TENDENCIES

"The age of independent travel is drawing to an end," said E. M. Forster way back in 1920. The mass production of travel, inevitable, it would seem, in the late-industrial era, has produced the phenomenon of tourism. It is to travel as plastic is to wood. It is, in the words of Patrick Leigh Fermor, "that gregarious passion which destroys the object of its love."

Tourism simulates travel, sometimes quite closely. You do pack a suitcase or two and proceed abroad with passport and travelers checks. But it is different in crucial ways. It is not self-directed but externally directed. You go not where you want to go but where the industry has decreed you shall go. Tourism soothes you by comfort and familiarity and shields you from the shocks of novelty and oddity. It confirms your prior view of the world instead of shaking it up. Tourism requires that you see conventional things, and that you see them in a conventional way.

Tourism can operate profitably only as a device of mass merchandising, fulfilling the great modern rule of mediocrity and uniformity, "Unless everybody wants it, nobody gets it." Anathema to it is the conviction of the sacredness of individuals (like Robert Byron, for example, or Freya Stark, or Eric Newby). It assumes a special docility in its participants, who conceive that actuality will be meaningless unless interpreted somehow and who assume that every question has a correct answer. Thus the tourist is at all times attended by his couriers, guides, and tour directors lecturing at him, telling him things, and insulating him from unmediated contact with abroad, its surprises, mysteries, and menaces. The "personalities" of these attendants, furthermore, are presumed to be part of the appeal of group touring. As one tour company was advertising in 1985, its guides "have bright, witty personalities, and love to share anecdotes and chit-chat with the family." Another tour company is careful to make the point that its guides are more than guides: they are "entertainers." (A long distance from the ideal of Baedeker, whose devotees travel largely to escape from things like that and who use the Baedeker guidebooks precisely to free themselves from such "entertainers.") In addition, the tourist is wholly protected from contingency. By contrast, the traveler, as Patrick White has noticed, often arrives "at the wrong moment: too hot, too cold, the opera, theatre, museum, is closed for the day, the season, or indefinitely for repairs, or else there is a strike, or an epidemic, or tanks are taking part in a political coup." None of that for the tourist, who is purchasing, as one 1985 travel brochure guarantees, "Absolute Peace of Mind."

An additional characteristic of the tourist is an obsession with things that are not travel—the mechanics of displacement, not its objects: the waiters and concierges, the currency exchanges and the swindles, the hotels and meals and their satisfactoriness or lack of it, the "value" of things, the tipping, and the oddities or charms of one's fellow groupers, often objects of concern as compelling as the sights themselves. "Making new friends is one of the joys of travel," asserts Caravan Tours. "With Caravan, you'll find congenial companions of all ages. . . . You'll likely feel right at home." There is irony there, to be sure, but there are ironies everywhere in the world of tourism. Even Eugene Fodor, whose guidebooks have been one of the most effective stimulators of mass international tourism, is now obliged to admit what he has done. In his guide to *Rome, 1986,* he recognizes ruefully that as a result in part of his efforts, 11,000 tourists a day swamp the Sistine Chapel, making a visit to it now "an equal blend of pleasure and torture," precisely illustrating Patrick Leigh Fermor's point and even suggesting that when tourism itself becomes hellish enough, it may come full circle and turn into something like travel again.

The intent of bringing together certain writers in this section is not to slander them as "tourists." It is rather to demonstrate their grasp of the psychological dimensions of tourism and to let them reveal some ways in which it differs from travel in the old sense. The first time abroad, everyone is more or less a tourist, for it's never certain that one is going to get to go again. Thus one does not miss the famous things, and even traveling alone rather than with a group, one hits the high spots of the Grand Tour and solicits the standard emotions at the standard sights. Thus W. C. William's "Dr. Evans" proceeds doggedly through Marseilles and the French Riviera to the sculptures of Florence.

Hemingway could perform as a tourist as well as a traveler. He was capable of enjoying the stereotyped as well as the outré. He was a master at understanding the tourist industry and its procedures, as his treatment of Swiss usages indicates, and he revelled unafraid in the traditional sentimentalities attaching to well-known foreign places and objects, like "the book stalls along the Seine," etc. (Hemingway here is a fine example of the truth noted by Alison Lurie, that when you function as a tourist your senses reduce to two only—sight and taste. What you do is "sightseeing," on the one hand, and eating and drinking, on the other.)

As an archetypal American, Sinclair Lewis understood fully the American's touristic excitement toward Europe and its culture together with the American's customary fear of it, and in his Sam Dodsworth he contrives an authentic and persuasive (because autobiographical?) vehicle of first-time tourist emotions, including, surprisingly but accurately, boredom. When Dodsworth first appears on the liner headed for Europe, it is inevitable that ultimately he will be brought to behold "twilight in Naples."

Like Hemingway, Truman Capote lived and traveled much overseas as well as touring there, but he seems especially good as a writer about abroad when moving from one place on the tourist circuit to another— from Venice to Lake Garda to Paris—or recalling standard touristic settings like the Orient Express or the islands ("beautiful") in the Bay of Naples. Likewise, Jan Morris has demonstrated her capacities as a traveler, moving courageously and resourcefully through many uncharted places and unhackneyed experiences. But much of her writing records times when she is behaving very like a tourist, registering her instinctive cheerfulness and optimism, her ability to look on the bright side, her conviction that it is all not a perceptual con-game, her gratitude at what she has been vouchsafed. "Cheer up," she exhorts the down-in-the-mouth immigration officer at the Yugoslav border. She likes to evoke the "magic" of an exotic place—you feel that the Vale of Kashmir has been just waiting for her to celebrate it properly—and she has never extinguished in herself that capacity for enjoyment which the more critical might find naive or even disingenuous. And Lawrence Durrell, himself a veteran traveler, decided to go on a corny group tour to see what it was like, and to write about it. As it turned out, he had no end of fun.

That's a salutary reminder of what Evelyn Waugh is getting at when he observes what a contemptible figure the tourist is. It is he, Waugh writes, who "debauches the great monuments of antiquity," who is "a comic figure, always inapt in his comments, incongruous in his appearance; . . . avarice and deceit attack him at every step; the shops that he patronizes are full of forgeries." But, he concludes, "we need feel no scruple or twinge of uncertainty; *we* are travellers and cosmopolitans; the tourist is the other fellow."

WILLIAM CARLOS WILLIAMS
1883-1963

A pediatrician by profession but an author by impulse, Williams set himself the lifelong task of making modern writing "Modernist." He spent most of his life in Rutherford, New Jersey, where he was born and where, after graduating from the Horace Mann School in New York and taking his medical degree at the University of Pennsylvania, he returned and practiced medicine.

He was devoted to local American actuality and was dismayed to see T. S. Eliot and his friend Ezra Pound remove to Europe, in his view an unnecessary and reactionary gesture. "Europe's enemy is the past," he said. "Our enemy is Europe." Remaining resolutely at home in New Jersey, he sought to refine an indigenous non-European idiom for American poetry and prose. Out of this effort came his best-known work, the long poem Paterson, about the past and present of the nearby New Jersey town, but he also produced memorable fiction as well as highly original literary criticism and cultural history.

Responding finally to Pound's taunt, "You'd better come across and broaden your mind," he and his wife Flossie spent six months in 1924 touring Europe—"Pagany," the place of Pagans, as Williams thought of it. The literary result was A Voyage to Pagany, a travel book disguised as a novel about a sensitive, romantic, forty-year-old American, "Dr. Evans" ("Dev"), and the women he meets (all of them Flossie, actually, even if named Lou, etc.) while pursuing the guide-book route. In Evans's experience of Europe for the first time, Williams registers honestly and sensitively the mingled awe and anxiety with which so many Americans have confronted the apparent cultural certainties of the Old World.

From A Voyage to Pagany (1928)

CHAPTER VII

MARSEILLES

The treeless plain about Carcassonne is covered with vineyards; through these the train started at noon to the south. Sticking their tongues out at the old gray fortifications as they went by, Evans and Lou went immediately into the diner.

There is in this part of France, in the neck that connects the peninsula of Spain with the rest of Europe, a constant feeling of the sea, the Atlantic on one side—at some distance—and on the other, the Mediterranean, the ancient Oceanus. As the two sat at lunch they looked curiously at the endless brown of the bare vineyards, in February, itself a rolling sea spread off in waves about them on all sides. It was an earth ocean seeming to break upon the very walls of the little châteaux which occupied the hill crests here and there at varying distances from the railroad in the background.

Lou had on a dark traveling suit of some shaggy material Evans did not recognize, a small black hat in the fashion, flesh-colored stockings, and French shoes decorative in cut and boldly buckled.

At least he did not have to consider her a baby.

He liked her because she was strong—and brave. Here were bravery and desire, misty and unquenchable; and she had the wit to desire what he could give her. Not that she weighed it, but she knew—how to want, to feel and to get—as in a game. Of love how much was there in her? But what did he care, really? He felt that she would not break her heart over anyone. But he had to add that in spite of the constancy of types—none knows what will happen when the time comes. At least, they were on their way. He believed it and he was happy.

The train was running with few stops through the cold squally weather. There were miles and yet miles of grape vines, brown waves, colored like a satyr.—But the soil, Evans explained, is good for little else than these small bitter grapes, useless for eating and best where the soil is worst. In a rich soil the wine-flavor is nothing. It is where there is sun, a height and the salts which make for flavor that the best grapes are found. Here and there are rare soils, then a wine will be famous, and the years will bring special favors from the weather and again the grapes record it by their flavor and richer yield. So the secret of the waving soil gathers in the names of the great châteaux, gathers and is gathered and solicitously preserved. A race of wine men has grown up flavoring this country, by the soil, as the soil flavors the grapes: skillful, dextrous and solicitous.—This was not what he wanted to say, but everything was burning for him in his present mood.

Warm again, they sat at table for more than an hour after the meal had been cleared away and the other diners had gone back to their compartments.

Shall we talk?

No, no, not just now, dear.

They smoked instead. He had not believed she could be this way.—So much more credit to her then for the escape. From what? A fury always made Evans' head swell with blood when he thought of the U.S. Anyhow, the sudden anger cured him of his mooning. She was magnificent, her kiddishness would pass.

Thank God, we're here.

You said it, she replied, We're in no hurry, are we?

Comparatively not, he said, and she looked out of the window quickly.

He laughed a good laugh which made her frown.

Evans studied his companion carefully. She had a round instinctive head, a good complexion, firm chin and a large mouth—he had never quite so looked at her before. Her lips, however, were really sensitive and her eyes blue but somewhat shadowed by her brows so that they showed not brilliance but reserve. The whole face was laughing—best of all, it was young.

How old? Evans guessed twenty-eight. She had never told him. Too old to be beginning this sort of thing—perhaps she is much younger.

More of a child than I thought—and he felt a quick pang of regret. Perhaps she would welch. He looked at her and did not think so. He admired her.

You're a miracle, Lou, he said.

Her reply was that the secret of the Sphinx is that she is shy!

Then for an hour they talked of France, of the grapes, of wheat, and Lou wondered about the wine, as if the French were curious addicts to some rite which kept them idolatrous before the wine drinking, amazed, when if they would but plant their ground to oats or wheat—they would be wiser.

No, the wine is cash, answered Evans, and the cash brings more wheat than would the ground itself. It is the intoxicating savor of the soil itself that's gifted for these things.

Finally, feeling strange and too conscious of each other in the deserted dining car, they returned to their compartment.

Now the vines had ceased. There were swampy meadows to the left, great stretches reaching in the middle distance to the glint of water beside which were shining white mounds of salt—or so Evans judged them to be.

But when in a lift of the tracks they saw, they saw, to the right, a sail, over the edge of a dune and then the blue! a great exultation seized the two companions.

The sea!

Evans saw: Grecian galleys; Africa just there, imminent; the blue, blue water. Then over the dunes, looking out to sea—the granite changelessness of time.

The train is annihilated, what of the window or the speed? It is the salt grass, it is the sand, it is the sea. There has been no change.

No change. The lovers were awed by the sea, giving up its history to the imagination. A richness, without loss, ran beside the train as if it had been a toy. It entered on invisible waves that played about their temples full of pleasure: Greece, Rome, Barbary: to-day the same—the accumulation of all time—perfect.

Especially to Americans does the Mediterranean bring memories—to Americans cut off from its good.

It was a bright interval, for as night came nearer, the train turned north again and a cold rain came with the darkness. It was cold and black by five o'clock.

At six they passed Arles but the determination to descend and spend a day there had faded with the forbidding weather. Across the Rhone the lights were shining at Avignon:

No, let us go on at once to Marseilles.

Marseilles, the city of sailor love!

At the Hôtel de France the steam radiator was ardently hugged. Oh boy! A wash. Marseilles! And they dashed out famished, and down the *Cannebière*—thronged by Algerians, French, Spanish, English, Americans, down to the old harbor to the shipping, feeing one of the many beggars sitting there by the water. This was fine. At a table of the *Restaurant au Port*, they ordered a *bouillabaisse*. A cat, outside the glassed-in porch overlooking the harbor, walked up and down, confused by the glass, smelling the fish and trying to get in.

They talked long over their plates and a bottle of Meursault. Lou told him intimately of herself much that he could not have guessed and had not known before, talking in a low voice. He was interested and forgot himself completely in her.

After a while it began to penetrate to them that they were being watched: at a table nearby were four drunken Americans—or two American men and two French girls whom they had in tow. Lou was nervous, more scared than Evans had imagined possible. A product of Melrose High, enervated by a lifelong unprofitable contact with boys and men—without issue—she was not taking it as easily as he had believed she would.

He put it down to just nerves and hoped she would get over it later.

A noisy party in the next room, the four at their backs, the masts of all nations in the basin and the cat weaving up and down on the roof of the porch outside the glass—in front of the ships and the lights—before them, they continued to eat, toward the end without saying a word.

Lou was very ill at ease.

But it was only that she was eager to be alone with him away from the ears of the heterogeneous crowd. Back in the hotel, she felt serious, alert, alarmed. Her eyes were round and startled when he came to her after the bath, but she was tender and clung to him quite out of her usual temper, but, as she had been all that day, like a small child.

CHAPTER VIII

THE RIVIERA

The next morning, windy, clear and still cold, but with a southern brightness of air. Ready for the trip eastward along the border of the sea, the two were in a mood of extreme exhilaration, more especially Lou whose constant warming glances and eager, simple questions. What's that? and Tell me, Tell me, soon had her companion nearly as alert and curious as was she herself. Oh look! It was her first mimosa tree in blossom.

Like your hair! smiled Dev. But she did not notice. Look, look!

All these things also will be discovered, said he half aloud but she did not hear; she was too busy looking from the train window—in this suddenly acquired south hitherto unsuspected.

Evans constructed a more conscious symbolism as they rode along by the sea.—So this is the new life, he said to himself. What would Bess think of me now?

Look, look, Lou kept saying, now darting to the sea side of the car—they were fortunate to have secured a compartment alone—now to the other. Olive trees and cactus and low palms; the sun caught in the protecting mountains; the pale blue sea—and Lou was all delight.

And still it was cold, but cold and sunny—a clear Mediterranean chill full of a crystallic light. So this is the Riviera! It was bare, as they edged along the sea. Scrub pine and oak clung to the towering gray rocks to the north. Now they would be running close by the sea with jagged gray promontories catching the low surges, then they would strike back into the coastal plain where some peninsula would jut out and near them at the left again they would see the low coastal range, the *Alpes Maritimes*, rugged, bare eminences of stratified gray rock, treeless for the most part—and then there at the peak of one, the tricolor of France. It capped a low concrete dome, the beginning of the fortifications about Toulon. Toulon whence Napoleon set sail for Egypt. Military roads zigzagged up the cliffs. A curious bare country into which the sun beat all day long.

Oh look, look, said Lou. It was an orange tree. How wonderful, and just the day before yesterday we were in Paris. It is miraculous.—At the stations men and women were going about in summer costumes and light top coats. In a little station garden there were flowers whose names they did not know. Tangerines were on the trees.

But again near the mountains a small brown village, startlingly apart from the new town, stood out to a peak on an isolated hill or there was one which clustered up the mountain side, reminiscent of the days of quick attack from the sea and the necessity for a mountain defense. Such was Cagnes—but the great town they first came to was Cannes. Should they get out and remain here for a few days?

At first Lou was for it. The tennis matches would be on, they could put up at some small place and see Lenglen and the rest. Tennis was Lou's great key with which, up to now, she had unlocked nearly every good which life had so far offered her. Through that means she had found her friends, formed her athletic opinions concerning life and built up her small talk. She played well.

Logically enough it was in a mood antithetic to her usual one, during a time of uncertainty, that she had fallen in with Evans. She wanted to stop and see the matches but as the train came to a standstill in the station of Cannes—the crowds waiting, the excitement, even the courts themselves to be seen from the window—she did not move.

Evans was already on his feet reaching for the luggage.

Well?

No.

Evans sat down. He put his arm about her waist and together they looked out at the jabbering mob rushing back and forth below them outside the car window: English faces, American faces, and the rest. It was easy to read in the compartment while the train was stopped; they picked up the map and located themselves, counting the stations before Villefranche where Dev had said they would get down. Another half hour.

Then they were in the station at Nice: Nice a smooth indentation of the coast line, the great hotels backing away from the town up on the hills, glass and bright towers. It was all a brilliant confirmation to Lou of her newly awakened insights into happiness. And then the mountains came close in and they were just at the sea's edge once more ducking through tunnels, with cliffs below them fringed by white foam.

In all crevices in the rocks were small gardens. In places high retaining walls had been constructed to hold the earth in place. These plots were planted especially with carnations against the time of the carnival approaching now. Few of the flowers were in bloom yet but here and there color would show.

Then after a moment they arrived at the lonesome little station on top of the high cliff, Villefranche, and there Dev bade her alight. Only a few others got down. The privacy, the light, the mountains, the sea, at once appealed to Lou; then as she turned she looked out over that narrow bay, far below her, with the wooded promontory behind which lay Beaulieu to the left and the old fishing port of Villefranche itself off to the right. Inaccessible, it seemed at first, approached, as she saw later, only by a footpath beside high walls stuck with cactus and overhung by flowering vines. It was a land of grave promise, gray rocks and the sea—but packed with brilliant light and a keen air.—No wonder they can play tennis in this country.

Three old men in blue blouses put their things into a small hand-cart and started off up the hill, over the bridge that crosses the railroad track and then up the path and down the path to the village. Lou and Dev came behind with their wraps and lighter grips.

To Lou it all continued an inexpressible joy. The old narrow streets by their quaintness seemed to be unlocking a long unused delight. She wanted to pat on the head the little boys whom they passed and who paid no attention to them. But she took tight hold of Dev's arm instead and kept looking into the small dark windows of shops down three steps below the street and below the natural level of the eye, with strings of onions and peppers—in the Italian style—hanging outside before them. The place was full of smells.

Evans explained that the city had belonged to Italy until modern times. In places the streets were precipitous, paved with flat stones, narrow, with the gutter in the center, and went often down irregular flights of steps, dark and not always sweet smelling—yet it was a delight to Lou.

The men they met wore round blue caps. Many were dressed as sailors, though as the lovers found later this was an affectation—for the most part—since few of them had more concern with boats than with those in which they took tourists for a good price on short rowing trips about the bay in summer.

Following the old men with the luggage they passed the central fountain in a tiny square with a strong smell of wine barrels about it; there were all manner of tiny stores with small windows showing caps, dried figs, and other handy merchandise for sale, but all small, dark. Now it would be a smell of cheese, or they'd come to a baker's shop—or it would be cloth in bolts they'd pass, emerging at last into a diminutive plaza with steps leading up to the right to the church and down to the left again to the wharf and the Hotel Boston by the sea.

Before stopping their march, the two Americans, unused to such a February, walked to the edge of the stone wharf and looked down into the blue clear water, seeing the pebbles and rusty débris below them under the movement of quiet waves.

Oh Dev, how wonderful it is just to be here.—At the back of the hotel were two old men smoking. Boats were fastened to iron rings in the massive stones of the wharf. The two were ever filled anew with the charm of the place, its diminutive self-sufficiency, its antique streets and the near lovely sea.

They ate supper in the quiet, rather English hotel which pleased them—with its family air—not at all, and went off on a ramble in the dark looking for a better lodging.

Finding none at that hour, all the inhabitants it seemed having gone to rest bird-like with the setting sun, they went down beyond the hotel keeping beside the sea on the little dock and there lay back across the still warm stones where the sun had beat an hour before. Phosphorus flashed in the water but from a third story window someone emptied some slops near them. A little sobered, they turned back to the hotel for that night at least. The beacon on the point beyond Beaulieu kept flashing its circular flare across the face of the village every forty seconds. It flashed into their room.

CHAPTER XIV

NIGHT

Genoa. The name sounded hollow, depressing as the coldly sulphurous gallery through which he was passing, baggage in hand, to the wicket. He had not wanted to stop here. It annoyed him not to have foreseen this compulsory arrest. He felt stiff of limb, stripped of all pleasure, bewildered.

No, I do not want a hotel. I want to check this stuff.

He knew no Italian. The porter shrugged and walked away. Evans wandered around aimlessly until he found the check room. 12:05 to Florence. Thank God. Only two hours to kill.

The waiting room was gloomy, deserted. He walked out into the fresh air. Two drunks exaggerated in size by their shadows were doing a slow motion wrestling match among the heavy columns of the station portico. Evans began to stray off in the dark into the space of the great *piazza* before the station. The whole neighborhood seemed desolate. He had no idea in what direction he was going. He feared he might get lost if he went too far.

The harbor, he said to himself walking on. It was the only thing about Genoa that stuck in his memory to attract him.

To the left the houses seemed to rise, one above the other in an endless embankment. He could not see the tops. They passed up into the murk. The stores near at hand were all shuttered. No one was in the streets. He wondered if he were going in the right direction. Didn't know how to ask. Gradually a nameless panic grew upon him. His heart beat fast. The sea can't lie this way. He turned back.

Behind him at the far end of the street whither he had been going a wild shouting burst out. Turning once more, he saw a small crowd passing under a street light, yelling and dancing. Boys, young men, they were. They were singing, hugging each other, running about, taking in the whole street, arm in arm. He caught the word—*Giovanezza,* many times repeated. For a moment they stopped, wavered, arguing loudly among themselves, then turned and hurried off whence they had come.

Evans resumed his way back to the station. Yes, one store was open, a shallow booth in the wall of dark houses. He smelled coffee and asked for a cup. Steam spouted with a roar from the nozzle,—he thought the machine had run dry: *Café expresso.* What a relief to get away from French coffee, the one thing he could not get used to in France. He swallowed the burning hot thimbleful of dark liquor gratefully.

His legs tingling now from the drink, he decided to strike in, to take one of the narrow streets leading among the tall houses, and climb the hill to see what he could see. Perhaps from there one might get a view of the lights of the harbor in the distance.

I'll never see the sun in Genoa.

Steps, hill upon hill, street lights at the bottoms of funnels. *Giovanezza*—arm in arm, drunk. *Giovanezza*—a mob shouting drunk— towers going up into night without top. No direction. No north, no south. Only the street to the railroad station; home. Lonely stairs, up. up—nowhere. Where is the sea Columbus sailed on?—He could see nothing but a very close darkness. He mounted. The way grew still. Two men in evening dress, one stout, the other smaller, passed down talking volubly. There was a desolate garden, empty benches, trees he did not know.

Alarmed lest he should miss his train, Evans sought to make certain his way out. Coming to a small open space at a certain level, with an electric bulb glowing above him at the far edge, he went to the edge which was a stone parapet, and looking down saw again the station sleeping below him. Up, up above were walls and lights. An overbearing weariness possessed him as if he were dead—and yet he must go on. He was dead yet his limbs, endlessly weary, would not lie down. They carried him—they would carry him now. He put his hand out as he had done at night to touch Lou's thigh and rest it there. His arm fell upon the stone.

Genoa! A city of nameless terror. From the parapet he looked down resting his breast against the stone, his heart pounding from the climb. The station! He leaned against the edge of the stone wall and looked down upon its roof, the cyclopean clock's eye marking the advancing hour yellowly.

There he leaned alone for eight thousand years, inexpressible weariness having overtaken him. His legs would not move further since there was nowhere to go. He would not go on. There they should find him in the morning. At first they would not notice him but after, they would take him to the hospital; they would notify the American Consul. The Consul came. He was high-minded, intelligent and well off. He looked and ordered the patient to be towed to America by the heels at the end of a line—thrown from the stern of the ship. Evans accepted it; dead he accepted everything thus cast at him. He accepted it. There was no reason why he should fear anything for he was dead. This was a proof.

Waking, he sensed vividly with open eyes the formlessness which terrified him asleep.

Night. Not even an animal. The uselessness of all things froze his heart. All art is terror; one makes in the night. It is still. There is nothing. One is no more a Christian. One does not believe in a life that will be endlessly the same. One does not want anything that life can bring. Life is an insult, an injury thrust upon us. What could have done that?

All knowledge is at an end. Soon we shall have a wakening against the schools and knowledge will begin again. He saw all knowledge vanishing into the apex of a hollow cone—spinning off. Philosophic solitude—a dear delight. But that is philosophy. Alone is not philosophy; it is despair.

The terror of emptiness had come about him, the terror of no form, the poet's ache, and he pressed harder against the stone wall.

What, then, is art? It is a cathedral. No: a cathedral is terror, painted with the four points of the compass. The Egyptians made the pyramids so that by looking through a hole in the rock one could see a certain star; thus it began with a star. But whether you forbid the delineation of animals and men, like the Arabs, or whether it be the image of the devil or a saint—it is nothing but a form of the night. Out of this we make—they make: this is the mother stuff.

It begins at the finger nails—it is these we see and begin with in anguish, the fingers which annoy us, being always in our sight. We pick at them. Or we make, to extend their length.

This is Genoa, they say, because the train stops here and the train never leaves the track. No. It is not Genoa. It is night, upon which the light begins to build but it is night first.

Night is not damned. It is the only thing which is not damned. Because out of it we make what we please. The sun makes the trees and the grass and cows and ourselves by day. But we make of the night arabesques, paintings on cloth, stones cut into shapes. Darkness and despair: These are my home. Here I have always retreated when I was beaten, to lie and breed with myself.

Their cathedrals and their chants are like buttercups to the night which puts them out or brings its stars to sing them to sleep—and adds its moon.

Night. It is the only thing that is sacred. It is ourselves.—And he felt that his body extended to the horizon. It is in the night that we love. It is the generative hour. Of this I am made.

He saw a desolate pantomime far up in the corner of his mind, a world empty and lost. It was not a Christian hell (this to which he had climbed) but one much older. And there sat Bess enthroned.

Weary, weary, weary, inhumanly, inexpressibly weary, he shook against the wall and waited for the train. More certainly now he began to take notice of his hands. He had forgotten that his arms were short. As when a child he woke terrified in his bed and strained to see, hating the dark, he would begin to think of definite things: a bird, a house—so now he looked at his fingers in the lamplight. They looked ghastly, as if dead. But he smiled knowingly and was satisfied. He felt his face.

The night is the body of someone else. Into which we have come.

Then he began to move. He found that leaning on the wall he had rested his legs. His elbows were stiff, aching but he walked down the hill to the station, checked out his baggage, found a compartment unoccupied (and warm) in the Florence train and stretched out. As the train began to glide forward, he fell asleep. Moving again, he slept—moving—slept without a dream.

CHAPTER XV

THE ARNO

By dawn they were at Pisa. The train was still, in a freight yard. The stars were not yet gone. There was a moon in what Evans thought must have been the west. He got up and looked about, as the train began to move again softly, slowly in the gray light, thinking he might see the famous tower. Nothing. They left Pisa behind. So much for Pisa. Again he slept.

He woke greatly refreshed. The sun was up.

Leaning into the window he saw the world of form once more, vineyards, trees in rows to which wires were fastened supporting grape vines newly pruned, long reddish canes awaiting the sun of summer to grow new shoots and grapes. Peasants were coming into the fields. There were magpies, a bird he knew, in the young trees, magpies and crows in the furrows. Now there was grain and garden truck, and orchards pruned and ready. Fields of mustard flower there were and cows and goats, by the light of the early blinding sun. Italy! He did not think of an ancient splendor but of morning and fields and vines.

Steadily the train took him into his delight.

The train which understands but a very few words and in the modern dialect only, was approaching that ancient Tuscan city of Florence—but without being impressed. Evans, however, was impressed and began to decorate his spirit with fitting clothes—saying to himself. They speak of these cities as if they were dusty or dead—or with scholarly abated voices.

The train was running beside a narrow winding rivulet.

It was the Arno flooding its banks, from whose liquorous bounty an army of sunbeams were drinking so that the air was luminous with mist and the grass and herbage everywhere was dripping. It was the Arno preparing to bring all its country charm to pass under the old bridge.

It was the Arno, before Florence, gathering tribute from the fields—a workaday river—countryman, maker, poet—poetic river. River, make new, always new—using rain, subterranean springs to make a great bounty.

Florence, city of makers.

To make, that's where we begin. Sooner or later, they call us in, to make up choir benches out of oak trees, make lace out of daisies, the circles out of roses, the white out of our despair—white as despair—totally colorless.

River, you make "the Arno" every day fresher than the greatest artists can make painted flowers: they may come to you every day for a lesson remembering only the sea that is greater.

Flow. Flow under the old bridge forever new and say to it that only that which is made out of nothing at all is forever new. Make new, make new.

And all the time he was watching the sun clearing the mists over the wild Arno and seeing it up to the top of its banks as if with ready fingers seeking to feel in among the grass. I know that feeling, he said, to be full of pleasure.

Flow new under the old bridge.

He was jealous of French painting and he was backing the river against it.

Make new. (And the river meanwhile was getting broader and going about its business.) One can put the best painting beside you and judge it by the place where the small stream joins your cool body. It is there! Nothing is more ordered, more certain nor more flexible, more passionate, yet chaste.

And all the time he was going to Florence, Dante's city, city of the old bridge, city of "the David," of Raphael—and a faint pang of worn beauty struck him. He wanted to say Giotto—Instead he called it: City of the Arno, and the Arno before there was a city, teaching from the fields of Proserpine, the fields of the Vernal gods. Botticelli, Donatello—now it was nearer. But he did not care for history. He knew only a river flowing through March in the sun, making, making, inviting the recreators—asking to be recreated.

It is the river god singing, that I hear, singing in the morning, asking if all making is ended. What to do?

He saw peasants leading animals, in the cold. Clickety click, clickety clack. People going into Florence began to get into his compartment. Be there by 8:30. They bowed to him, for the most part, with a momentary glance at his strangeness—perhaps; a foreigner. Then they looked out of the windows or talked, or read a paper.

If I were an agent come here to sell American shoes, or ploughs, that would be a common reason.

Idle as a river. Loafer.

I sing and loaf at my ease.

Loaf of bread. The Arno loafs and it is a loaf of which I drink. Pah.

It is drink nevertheless, the richest drink to me, in the morning this way. The natives of Bangkok drink the river and fish half-rotten drowned pigs out of it and roast them and eat them—and live.

Drink of the Arno like that; a kind of artist they are, the natives.

Drink. A kind of cholera it is to be wanting to make. Loaf. Catch it from the river.

I caught a little silver fish: Pah.

Throw out both conceptions; reality, romance: it sums up, to make—that's all. Make, and that's the end of it,—if you can.

Fine careful fields, these *are*, their hands are all over them, making the soil, patting it, tying up the vines. Mostly that now. They left off there by that tree yesterday; you can see the willow withes they left there in a bundle last night. Just starting again now. Willow withes they are using, the same willow withes. That's why they cut the trees off pompadour, the willow trees. Get the withes for tying up grapes. Smart men those. Habit. Always do the same thing, year after year. That's work, work is worship.

I'm not in their class. I work home. Cure bellyaches. Come to Italy for something else.

Work home gives me an excuse to loaf now. Does it? If I were a peasant the river wouldn't look so poetic, but it would look more god-like, more real. Poetic it is just the same, even if they can't see it.

Just the same it is the prototype of art. Useless river—as far as itself is concerned. Gathers dewdrops from flower petals just the same. Carries them just the same. Nobody gives a damn. Goes under the old bridge.

The prototype of art just the same. Don't have to describe everything that's in a river any more than we have to say—like Quevedo, when the girls dropped a rose at his feet from the balcony (Mother told me that): That's not the only thing you drop, ladies.

Arno! maker. He was jealous of French painters. Make it. Giotto made colors out of flowers. What of it? No help in that. You must begin with nothing, like a river in the morning and make, make new. Arno! I want you to say this, I want you to take me into Florence from upstream and that is all I want you to say. I want you to say *this* and this *only* for I am making of it my procession. I make my way out of nothing using what I find by chance: to make—new.

That's ALL I want it to say. I don't care what's in the river.—It was a fascinating view of a river from a train, a swift, bird's-eye view.

The presence of Florence so near now exhilarated him, flowing in his mind like the Arno, forever recreating its own loveliness. Florence and the Arno and the newness of his despair, his lust to make-fused into an excitement of architecture, painting. By the time the train reached the station, he was filled with eagerness to look at the older things of the city, full of excellence for him to gather, if he would.

CHAPTER XVI

FLORENCE

Too excited, expectant of too much, Florence came to him when his enjoyment was already exhausted. He saw it coldly, through an aura of returning disillusionment which was really a good thing, a lens which sharpened his wit—not always sufficiently discriminating. But for the most part he was bored—after all.

At Cook's in the Via Tornabuoni, after breakfast, he had picked up a card from his sister in Montreux. It was the lake with a Moroccan looking sailboat upon it—laden with brick in all probability, he thought. It said, Hotel Asterial, February is (has been lying here two weeks): Shall be here for two weeks longer, Bess.—Bah. He stuffed it into his pocket and went out, stopping to look at the torch-brackets on the Palazzo Massimo. He looked up, Buonarotti's cornice overhung the street, and felt himself affected by the scale of the great windows, the roughness of the structural stone, the mass of the whole façade played upon so softly by the finely felt proportions of everything. This angered him.

He had always been somewhat irritated by the Renaissance, anyhow. The crudeness of the material they used, the size, the coarseness even, he ate up with joy—but the touch of the delicate fingers bit into him like an acid.—God damn their impertinence, he cried aloud, to appease his own dullness and sorrow. It is too soft, *nouveau riche;* with their petty imitations of the Assyrian, the Egyptian and the Greek; soft and harsh, brutal and sweet. He found it lying, offensive, this unhappy American with nothing but the offense of New York in his mind to give him stability. Yet it was Florence he was seeing; the jewel of all Italian cities.

From Cook's he walked to the Duomo, with his eyes on the ground lifting them for a moment only at the flower market—But he went on from this as from a sickness.

With contradictory but rapidly mounting savagery his heart craved only that softness, if he must have softness, which might be in stones not flowers; stones cut, jointed—not haply irregular, like those of the Inca fortress walls, but not out of a machine either; made, each stone made. "I Matteo, made this column," he had once read. I'll accept that. So each stone had probably been made, selected first by some crafts-man—some peasant, that's it. Some manual man, *that is* "the rock" and the neurasthenic Master puts his softness on it after.

But then he lifted his eyes to Giotto's tower of colored stone, "the shepherd's tower," that quadrangular thrust out of the bare ground, and his delight sprung at once to a brief release. Here it is! No Rome here. No Greece. Pure Italy, tall, spare, severe, colored, flowerlike. He felt it powerfully—but from afar. It was too bare, too soon, he looked too hard and after all saw just the stones. At least it was hardly sentimental. Curious relic, he thought, finally. It seemed so obvious however that it fast became in his eyes like everything else, dulled.

Through all, he was conscious of the strange Christian influence in everything; he felt it with disgust, with despair. He tried to separate out Italy, the power itself, to tear it from this moss. The incense belonged to Apollo. They had copied their politics from Plato. It all worked so marvelously well, so smugly well. It had drawn in even the makers, warped them to its confounding delicacy.

Disturbed by his reflections, Evans wandered slowly back along the Via S. toward the Palazzo Vecchio on the way passing by chance Donatello's St. Michael, high in the Palazzo Medici east wall, quiet, in his shallow niche, holding his shield before him with womanly delicacy but good wrists; tall, fine of face—a face removed to heaven, contrasting rudely with his rested shield; a sensitive anguish whetting the taste for brutal combat. A wistful longing for contemplations beyond battle seemed just to burst from the moment of waiting.—Donatello has caught it, in his fashion. There it is, a moment, a balance, the time.— But the delicacy was strange to Dev's present mood. Through a mist he saw it and it angered him anew.

And so he came to the great marble David and stood beside that also. The false crudity of Angelo, the delicate torment drove him wild again. That's Christian, big with mental anguish, the genesis of which is the impossibility of fusing the old power with the new weakness. The pain, the weakening is the charm! Agh! He twisted the Greek; put the anguish of the soul into it. The Christian anguish. But why take *that* to torment; the Greek, the quiet, the perfect, the lovely. No, no!

Evans could not frame it. He felt only the offense in the David. The too big hand, the over-anxious Jewish eyes. The neurasthenic size of the thing standing there in the courtyard with the Judith not far off turning her face away.

This is not Italy. The David meant nothing to him. It is lying. It leans on the Greek, which it bastardizes, to give it a kind of permission. Had to have something to lean on—so it slimes the anguish over that, trying to unite two impossible themes.

The next morning he found it to be election day in Florence. Groups of working men were loafing about the streets in their Sunday clothes. They seemed orderly and more or less indifferent to the event; more a *festa* than a day devoted to serious civic and national duty. Here and there men stood before a voting place talking quietly: a small election most likely.

But *carabinieri* and police with guns in hand could be observed now and then in straw-paved carts going from place to place about the town: and at the far end of the Ponte Vecchio, where youths and girls clad in carnival attire were returning from the old city, the police were making them remove the masks and show their features before they could proceed further.

To this point Evans followed the crowd, stopping on the bridge half an hour to buy a green aquamarine for his sister at one of the booths. Then he came to the Pitti Palace whose simple fortress-like roughness delighted his mood. There and in the Boboli gardens he spent his time till noon.

In the afternoon he thought he'd take in the Santa Croce. Walking unexpectant across the bare piazza before it, he pushed upon the Cathedral's soiled red leather inner doors and letting them close behind him stood within, waiting for his eyes to penetrate the half light. And there he was overtaken by an emotional reaction, striking back upon him across that rolling floor, that lifted him into an enchantment he would never cease to recall thereafter as long as he should live—nor to enjoy.

He escaped wholly at that first moment the feeling of a church. A double row of widely spaced hexagonal columns held up the flat beamed middle ceiling painted with crude colors, a dark and intricate design of blue and red and gold, orange and green and red; it might have been the flat roof of an old temple. But the floor of worn mosaics, uneven, undulant, irregular, the tomb of saints over whose effigies in bronze and marble he walked; and in the side walls other famous tombs—of Dante, the Medici; the Pantheon of Florence; it seemed all to him a savage, spacious present; direct, puissant—overwhelming, free, free somehow of all that which he hated.

But, looking toward the room's far end with evergrowing ardor, he stopped in amazement at that wall. It remained a wall, a decorated wall. In the center of it was the altar, a tall, shallow, vaulted alcove molded into the plaster of the place, the plaster painted with a fresco from the history. But on each side of this, standing up, one close beside the other, were the chapels: further, narrower bare alcoves, a rank to right and left, high and pin arched. And on the plaster, here also, figures from the history were painted.

He could not tell the Giotto from the Cimabue, he liked the unknown best—and there he stayed, disturbed in exultation—carried away by awe and antiquity—a presence nearer than the nearest day that he had ever known. It was close, close to him—its simplicity walked about in him, as if he were its garden and by its side he saw himself as he had known he was, but never could draw near enough.

It was a key. It was beauty. The colors of the dark floor, the smoky ceiling—into them he gazed. He sat, he watched a priest unshaven, sick, miserable—he watched him kneel and pray or seem to pray on the steps before one of the narrow painted altars.

Bare, columnar, plaster alcoves, sharp-edged, pointed and un-decorated by construction or beading, molding or ledge—save only by the painting upon the plaster paneling, the back and sides: tall sentinels they were, of a strange deceptive holiness—whose fine aberrance from the Christian, Evans was feeling exultantly, a beauty that by its simplic-ity, not softened, reached back truly outside of church into a sunlight which he identified by his earliest uncaptured instincts—

To-day no resentment against the stucco of a church disturbed him; he drank as if the purity of the source could wash away all sins in fact—and he would come out clean, clean of the world: the bone-cracking, skin-muddying impacts of his life.

Clean! that was to him the purport of it all, a holiness will come out alone if we be clean.

Clean, stripped as were these chapels, colored with oranges and men from the streets—molded into figures—

It was with pain, as if leaving behind the best that was in his life, that he drew off at the warning of the sexton priest—it was dark. They were closing the church, he had been there all the afternoon.

But he had been purified past the walls of any church. Santa Croce held for him an unguessed holiness that had forever blessed him. Clean, the ugly tombs of the masters on the two lateral walls did not disturb him. *Clean, of all that!* It was none of theirs. Village worthies. Men of the place, sleeping. That was all. But a beauty had shone through their work, through it—through its Christian disguises. He, Evans, had been penetrated, he permitted it to penetrate him. A Greek beauty—a resur-gent paganism, still untouched.

He went back to the hotel, exhausted, tired, neurasthenic, in no ecstasy but a pale, fragile mood. But the supper tickled him. He had Lacrima Christi which still amused him by its name, he drank much. He bought a Corona Corona—thinking of the Indians who mixed tea berry leaves with their tobacco, and smoked himself dizzy. To bed. To sleep. A marvelous bed.

ERNEST HEMINGWAY
1898–1961

Hemingway's first flights away from his genteel family home in Oak Park, Illinois, took him to Kansas City and Toronto as a newspaper reporter, and after being wounded in northern Italy during the Great War he settled in Paris to write. Subsequently he traveled or lived in Switzerland, Germany, Austria, Spain, and Africa, following such tough sports as boxing and hunting and such dangerous rituals as bullfighting. He settled finally in Cuba, attracted by the marlin fishing. His novels are all set outside the United States, in Spain, Italy, or the Caribbean. He was an active supporter of the anti-Franco forces in the Spanish Civil War, and in World War II he served in Europe as an enthusiastically bellicose war correspondent, sometimes actually leading troops.

In his popular novel A Farewell to Arms, *the American Frederic Henry deserts from the Italian army, where he has served as an ambulance officer until unjustly accused of cowardice. He escapes into Switzerland by crossing Lake Maggiore in a rowboat with his pregnant sweetheart, the British nurse Catherine Barkley. Their arrival in Switzerland offers Hemingway an opportunity to register his satiric views about the Swiss tourist atmosphere.*

E. L. Doctorow has speculated that perhaps "Hemingway's real achievement in the early great novels was that of a travel writer who taught a provincial American audience what dishes to order, what drinks to prefer and how to deal with the European servant class."

From A Farewell to Arms (1929)

I rowed all night. Finally my hands were so sore I could hardly close them over the oars. We were nearly smashed up on the shore several times. I kept fairly close to the shore because I was afraid of getting lost on the lake and losing time. Sometimes we were so close we could see a row of trees and the road along the shore with the mountains behind. The rain stopped and the wind drove the clouds so that the moon shone through and looking back I could see the long dark point of Castagnola and the lake with white-caps and beyond, the moon on the high snow mountains. Then the clouds came over the moon again and the mountains and the lake were gone, but it was much lighter than it had been before and we could see the shore. I could see it too clearly and pulled out where they would not see the boat if there were custom guards along the Pallanza road. When the moon came out again we could see white villas on the shore on the slopes of the mountain and the white road where it showed through the trees. All the time I was rowing.

The lake widened and across it on the shore at the foot of the mountains on the other side we saw a few lights that should be Luino. I saw a wedgelike gap between the mountains on the other shore and I thought that must be Luino. If it was we were making good time. I pulled in the oars and lay back on the seat. I was very, very tired of rowing. My arms and shoulders and back ached and my hands were sore.

"I could hold the umbrella," Catherine said. "We could sail with that with the wind."

"Can you steer?"

"I think so."

"You take this oar and hold it under your arm close to the side of the boat and steer and I'll hold the umbrella." I went back to the stern and showed her how to hold the oar. I took the big umbrella the porter had given me and sat facing the bow and opened it. It opened with a clap. I held it on both sides, sitting astride the handle hooked over the seat. The wind was full in it and I felt the boat suck forward while I held as hard as I could to the two edges. It pulled hard. The boat was moving fast.

"We're going beautifully," Catherine said. All I could see was umbrella ribs. The umbrella strained and pulled and I felt us driving along with it. I braced my feet and held back on it, then suddenly, it buckled; I felt a rib snap on my forehead, I tried to grab the top that was bending with the wind and the whole thing buckled and went inside out and I was astride the handle of an inside-out, ripped umbrella, where I had been holding a wind filled pulling sail. I unhooked the handle from the seat, laid the umbrella in the bow and went back to Catherine for the oar. She was laughing. She took my hand and kept on laughing.

"What's the matter?" I took the oar.

"You looked so funny holding that thing."

"I suppose so."

"Don't be cross, darling. It was awfully funny. You looked about twenty feet broad and very affectionate holding the umbrella by the edges—" she choked.

"I'll row."

"Take a rest and a drink. It's a grand night and we've come a long way."

"I have to keep the boat out of the trough of the waves."

"I'll get you a drink. Then rest a little while, darling."

I held the oars up and we sailed with them. Catherine was opening the bag. She handed me the brandy bottle. I pulled the cork with my pocket-knife and took a long drink. It was smooth and hot and the heat went all through me and I felt warmed and cheerful. "It's lovely brandy," I said. The moon was under again but I could see the shore. There seemed to be another point going out a long way ahead into the lake.

"Are you warm enough, Cat?"

"I'm splendid. I'm a little stiff."

"Bail out that water and you can put your feet down."

Then I rowed and listened to the oarlocks and the dip and scrape of the bailing tin under the stern seat.

"Would you give me the bailer?" I said. "I want a drink."

"It's awful dirty."

"That's all right. I'll rinse it."

I heard Catherine rinsing it over the side. Then she handed it to me dipped full of water. I was thirsty after the brandy and the water was icy cold, so cold it made my teeth ache. I looked toward the shore. We were closer to the long point. There were lights in the bay head.

"Thanks," I said and handed back the tin pail.

"You're ever so welcome," Catherine said. "There's much more if you want it."

"Don't you want to eat something?"

"No. I'll be hungry in a little while. We'll save it till then."

"All right."

What looked like a point ahead was a long high headland. I went further out in the lake to pass it. The lake was much narrower now. The moon was out again and the *guardia di finanza* [border guards] could have seen our boat black on the water if they had been watching.

"How are you, Cat?" I asked.

"I'm all right. Where are we?"

"I don't think we have more than about eight miles more."

"That's a long way to row, you poor sweet. Aren't you dead?"

"No. I'm all right. My hands are sore is all."

We went on up the lake. There was a break in the mountains on the right bank, a flattening-out with a low shore line that I thought must be Cannobio. I stayed a long way out because it was from now on that we ran the most danger of meeting *guardia*. There was a high dome-capped mountain on the other shore a way ahead. I was tired. It was no great distance to row but when you were out of condition it had been a long way. I knew I had to pass that mountain and go up the lake at least five miles further before we would be in Swiss water. The moon was almost down now but before it went down the sky clouded over again and it was very dark. I stayed well out in the lake, rowing awhile, then resting and holding the oars so that the wind struck the blades.

"Let me row awhile," Catherine said.

"I don't think you ought to."

"Nonsense. It would be good for me. It would keep me from being too stiff."

"I don't think you should, Cat."

"Nonsense. Rowing in moderation is very good for the pregnant lady."

"All right, you row a little moderately. I'll go back, then you come up. Hold on to both gunwales when you come up."

I sat in the stern with my coat on and the collar turned up and watched Catherine row. She rowed very well but the oars were too long and bothered her. I opened the bag and ate a couple of sandwiches and took a drink of the brandy. It made everything much better and I took another drink.

"Tell me when you're tired," I said. Then a little later, "Watch out the oar doesn't pop you in the tummy."

"If it did"—Catherine said between strokes—"life might be much simpler."

I took another drink of the brandy.

"How are you going?"

"All right."

"Tell me when you want to stop."

"All right."

I took another drink of the brandy, then took hold of the two gunwales of the boat and moved forward.

"No. I'm going beautifully."

"Go on back to the stern. I've had a grand rest."

For a while, with the brandy, I rowed easily and steadily. Then I began to catch crabs and soon I was just chopping along again with a thin brown taste of bile from having rowed too hard after the brandy.

"Give me a drink of water, will you?" I said.

"That's easy," Catherine said.

Before daylight it started to drizzle. The wind was down or we were protected by mountains that bounded the curve the lake had made. When I knew daylight was coming I settled down and rowed hard. I did not know where we were and I wanted to get into the Swiss part of the lake. When it was beginning to be daylight we were quite close to the shore. I could see the rocky shore and the trees.

"What's that?" Catherine said. I rested on the oars and listened. It was a motor boat chugging out on the lake. I pulled close up to the shore and lay quiet. The chugging came closer; then we saw the motor boat in the rain a little astern of us. There were four *guardia di finanza* in the stern, their *alpini* hats pulled down, their cape collars turned up and their carbines slung across their backs. They all looked sleepy so early in the morning. I could see the yellow on their hats and the yellow marks on their cape collars. The motor boat chugged on and out of sight in the rain.

I pulled out into the lake. If we were that close to the border I did not want to be hailed by a sentry along the road. I stayed out where I could just see the shore and rowed on for three quarters of an hour in the rain. We heard a motor boat once more but I kept quiet until the noise of the engine went away across the lake.

"I think we're in Switzerland, Cat," I said.

"Really?"

"There's no way to know until we see Swiss troops."

"Or the Swiss navy."

"The Swiss navy's no joke for us. That last motor boat we heard was probably the Swiss navy."

"If we're in Switzerland let's have a big breakfast. They have wonderful rolls and butter and jam in Switzerland."

It was clear daylight now and a fine rain was falling. The wind was still blowing outside up the lake and we could see the tops of the white-caps going away from us and up the lake. I was sure we were in Switzerland now. There were many houses back in the trees from the shore and up the shore a way was a village with stone houses, some villas on the hills and a church. I had been looking at the road that skirted the shore for guards but did not see any. The road came quite close to the lake now and I saw a soldier coming out of a café on the road. He wore a gray-green uniform and a helmet like the Germans. He had a healthy-looking face and a little toothbrush mustache. He looked at us.

"Wave to him," I said to Catherine. She waved and the soldier smiled embarrassedly and gave a wave of his hand. I eased up rowing. We were passing the waterfront of the village.

"We must be well inside the border," I said.

"We want to be sure, darling. We don't want them to turn us back at the frontier."

"The frontier is a long way back. I think this is the customs town. I'm pretty sure it's Brissago."

"Won't there be Italians there? There are always both sides at a customs town."

"Not in war-time. I don't think they let the Italians cross the frontier."

It was a nice-looking little town. There were many fishing boats along the quay and nets were spread on racks. There was a fine November rain falling but it looked cheerful and clean even with the rain.

"Should we land then and have breakfast?"

"All right."

I pulled hard on the left oar and came in close, then straightened out when we were close to the quay and brought the boat alongside. I pulled in the oars, took hold of an iron ring, stepped up on the wet stone and was in Switzerland. I tied the boat and held my hand down to Catherine.

"Come on up, Cat. It's a grand feeling."

"What about the bags?"

"Leave them in the boat."

Catherine stepped up and we were in Switzerland together.

"What a lovely country," she said.

"Isn't it grand?"

"Let's go and have breakfast!"

"Isn't it a grand country? I love the way it feels under my shoes."

"I'm so stiff I can't feel it very well. But it feels like a splendid country. Darling, do you realize we're here and out of that bloody place?"

"I do. I really do. I've never realized anything before."

"Look at the houses. Isn't this a fine square? There's a place we can get breakfast."

"Isn't the rain fine? They never had rain like this in Italy. It's cheerful rain."

"And we're here, darling! Do you realize we're here?"

We went inside the café and sat down at a clean wooden table. We

were cockeyed excited. A splendid clean-looking woman with an apron
came and asked us what we wanted.

"Rolls and jam and coffee," Catherine said.

"I'm sorry, we haven't any rolls in war-time."

"Bread then."

"I can make you some toast."

"All right."

"I want some eggs fried too."

"How many eggs for the gentleman?"

"Three."

"Take four, darling."

"Four eggs."

The woman went away. I kissed Catherine and held her hand very
tight. We looked at each other and at the café.

"Darling, darling, isn't it lovely?"

"It's grand," I said.

"I don't mind there not being rolls," Catherine said. "I thought about
them all night. But I don't mind it. I don't mind it at all."

"I suppose pretty soon they will arrest us."

"Never mind, darling. We'll have breakfast first. You won't mind
being arrested after breakfast. And then there's nothing they can do to
us. We're British and American citizens in good standing."

"You have a passport, haven't you?"

"Of course. Oh let's not talk about it. Let's be happy."

"I couldn't be any happier," I said. A fat gray cat with a tail that lifted
like a plume crossed the floor to our table and curved against my leg to
purr each time she rubbed. I reached down and stroked her. Catherine
smiled at me very happily. "Here comes the coffee," she said.

They arrested us after breakfast. We took a little walk through the
village then went down to the quay to get our bags. A soldier was
standing guard over the boat.

"Is this your boat?"

"Yes."

"Where do you come from?"

"Up the lake."

"Then I have to ask you to come with me."

"How about the bags?"

"You can carry the bags."

I carried the bags and Catherine walked beside me and the soldier
walked along behind us to the old custom house. In the custom house
a lieutenant, very thin and military, questioned us.

"What nationality are you?"

"American and British."

"Let me see your passports."

I gave him mine and Catherine got hers out of her handbag.

He examined them for a long time.

"Why do you enter Switzerland this way in a boat?"

"I am a sportsman," I said. "Rowing is my great sport. I always row when I get a chance."

"Why do you come here?"

"For the winter sport. We are tourists and we want to do the winter sport."

"This is no place for winter sport."

"We know it. We want to go where they have the winter sport."

"What have you been doing in Italy?"

"I have been studying architecture. My cousin has been studying art."

"Why do you leave there?"

"We want to do the winter sport. With the war going on you cannot study architecture."

"You will please stay where you are," the lieutenant said. He went back into the building with our passports.

"You're splendid, darling," Catherine said. "Keep on the same track. You want to do the winter sport."

"Do you know anything about art?"

"Rubens," said Catherine.

"Large and fat," I said.

"Titian," Catherine said.

"Titian-haired," I said. "How about Mantegna?"

"Don't ask hard ones," Catherine said. "I know him though—very bitter."

"Very bitter," I said. "Lots of nail holes."

"You see I'll make you a fine wife," Catherine said. "I'll be able to talk art with your customers."

"Here he comes," I said. The thin lieutenant came down the length of the custom house, holding our passports.

"I will have to send you into Locarno," he said. "You can get a carriage and a soldier will go in with you."

"All right," I said. "What about the boat?"

"The boat is confiscated. What have you in those bags?"

He went all through the two bags and held up the quarter-bottle of brandy. "Would you join me in a drink?" I asked.

"No thank you." He straightened up. "How much money have you?"

"Twenty-five hundred lire."

He was favorably impressed. "How much has your cousin?"

Catherine had a little over twelve hundred lire. The lieutenant was pleased. His attitude toward us became less haughty.

"If you are going for winter sports," he said. "Wengen is the place. My father has a very fine hotel at Wengen. It is open all the time."

"That's splendid," I said. "Could you give me the name?"

"I will write it on a card." He handed me the card very politely.

"The soldier will take you into Locarno. He will keep your passports. I regret this but it is necessary. I have good hopes they will give you a visa or a police permit at Locarno."

He handed the two passports to the soldier and carrying the bags we started into the village to order a carriage. "Hi," the lieutenant called to the soldier. He said something in a German dialect to him. The soldier slung his rifle on his back and picked up the bags.

"It's a great country," I said to Catherine.

"It's so practical."

"Thank you very much," I said to the lieutenant. He waved his hand.

"*Service!*" he said. We followed our guard into the village.

We drove to Locarno in a carriage with the soldier sitting on the front seat with the driver. At Locarno we did not have a bad time. They questioned us but they were polite because we had passports and money. I do not think they believed a word of the story and I thought it was silly but it was like a law-court. You did not want something reasonable, you wanted something technical and then stuck to it without explanations. But we had passports and we would spend the money. So they gave us provisional visas. At any time this visa might be withdrawn. We were to report to the police wherever we went.

Could we go wherever we wanted? Yes. Where did we want to go?

"Where do you want to go, Cat?"

"Montreux."

"It is a very nice place," the official said. "I think you will like that place."

"Here at Locarno is a very nice place," another official said. "I am sure you would like it here very much at Locarno. Locarno is a very attractive place."

"We would like some place where there is winter sport."

"There is no winter sport at Montreux."

"I beg your pardon," the other official said. "I come from Montreux. There is very certainly winter sport on the Montreux Oberland Bernois railway. It would be false for you to deny that."

"I do not deny it. I simply said there is no winter sport at Montreux."

"I question that," the other official said. "I question that statement."

"I hold to that statement."

"I question that statement. I myself have *luge-ed* into the streets of Montreux. I have done it not once but several times. Luge-ing is certainly winter sport."

The other official turned to me.

"Is luge-ing your idea of winter sport, sir? I tell you you would be very comfortable here in Locarno. You would find the climate healthy, you would find the environs attractive. You would like it very much."

"The gentleman has expressed a wish to go to Montreux."

"What is luge-ing?" I asked.

"You see he has never even heard of luge-ing!"

That meant a great deal to the second official. He was pleased by that.

"Luge-ing," said the first official, "is tobogganing."

"I beg to differ," the other official shook his head. "I must differ again. The toboggan is very different from the luge. The toboggan is constructed in Canada of flat laths. The luge is a common sled with runners. Accuracy means something."

"Couldn't we toboggan?" I asked.

"Of course you could toboggan," the first official said. "You could toboggan very well. Excellent Canadian toboggans are sold in Montreux. Ochs Brothers sell toboggans. They import their own toboggans."

The second official turned away. "Tobogganing," he said, "requires a special *piste* [runway]. You could not toboggan into the streets of Montreux. Where are you stopping here?"

"We don't know," I said. "We just drove in from Brissago. The carriage is outside."

"You make no mistake in going to Montreux," the first official said. "You will find the climate delightful and beautiful. You will have no distance to go for winter sport."

"If you really want winter sport," the second official said, "you will go to the Engadine or to Mürren. I must protest against your being advised to go to Montreux for the winter sport."

"At Les Avants above Montreux there is excellent winter sport of every sort." The champion of Montreux glared at his colleague.

"Gentlemen," I said, "I am afraid we must go. My cousin is very tired. We will go tentatively to Montreux."

"I congratulate you," the first official shook my hand.

"I believe that you will regret leaving Locarno," the second official said. "At any rate you will report to the police at Montreux."

"There will be no unpleasantness with the police," the first official assured me. "You will find all the inhabitants extremely courteous and friendly."

"Thank you both very much," I said. "We appreciate your advice very much."

"Good-by," Catherine said. "Thank you both very much."

SINCLAIR LEWIS
1885-1951

Born in a small town in Minnesota, Lewis escaped first to Yale and then to journalism and editorial work in New York, where he began developing his talent as a satirist and iconoclast in the tradition of H. L. Mencken. After a few conventional novels, he became famous with Main Street *(1920), an exposé of the stultifying atmosphere of a small Middle Western town. This he followed with* Babbitt *(1922), a satire on a small businessman, in Lewis's day easily conceivable as a booster, a chauvinist, and a fraud, canting about "service" while shrewdly accumulating his conscienceless pile. Deeply researched like all Lewis's work,* Babbitt *fully revealed Lewis's gifts as a mimic, especially of American commercial rhetoric. In* Elmer Gantry *(1927) he turned to rip the wrappings off American religious evangelism, depicting his Fundamentalist hero as little more than a cunning hypocrite.*

One of his least satiric novels is Dodsworth *(1929), which presents sympathetically the marital problems of a retired automobile magnate eagerly but at the same time timidly encountering Europe for the first time. Lewis projects Dodsworth as the archetypal American tourist— half worshipful of the esteemed antiquities and formalities, half scornful of them. These novels, delineating so accurately the twentieth-century inhabitants of the new society of hustle and getting-on, brought Lewis the Nobel Prize for Literature in 1930. He was the first American to win it.*

From DODSWORTH
(1929)

The S. S. *Ultima*, thirty-two thousand tons burden, was four hours out of New York. As the winter twilight glowered on the tangle of gloomy waves, Samuel Dodsworth was aware of the domination of the sea, of the insignificance of the great ship and all mankind. He felt lost in the round of ocean, one universal gray except for a golden gash on the western horizon. His only voyaging had been on lakes, or on the New York ferries. He felt uneasy as he stood at the after rail and saw how the rearing mass of the sea loomed over the ship and threatened it when the stern dipped—down, unbelievably down, as though she were sinking. But he felt resolute again, strong and very happy, as he swung about the deck. He had been sickish only for the first hour. The wind filled his chest, exhilarated him. Only now, the messy details of packing and farewells over, and the artificially prolonged waving to friends on the dock endured, did he feel that he was actually delivered from duty, actually going—going to strange-colored, exciting places, to do unknown and heroic things.

He hummed (for Kipling meant something to Sam Dodsworth which no Shelley could, nor Dante)—he hummed "The Gipsy Trail":

> Follow the Romany patteran
>   North where the blue bergs sail,
> And the bows are gray with the frozen spray,
>   And the masts are shod with mail.
> Follow the Romany patteran
>   West to the sinking sun,
> Till the junk-sails lift through the houseless drift,
>   And the East and the West are one.
> Follow the Romany patteran
>   East where the silence broods
> By a purple wave on an opal beach
>   In the hush of the Mahim woods.

"Free!" he muttered.

He stopped abruptly by the line of windows enclosing the music-room, forward on the promenade deck, as he fumbled for the memory of the first time he had ever sung "The Gipsy Trail."

It must have been when the poem was first set to music. Anyway, Fran and he had been comparatively poor. The money that old Herman

Voelker had lent them had gone into the business. (A sudden, meaningless spatter of snow, out on that cold sea. How serene the lights in the music room! He began to feel the gallant security of the ship, his enduring home.) Yes, it was when they had gone off on a vacation—no chauffeur then, nor suites at the hotels, but Sam driving all day in their shabby Revelation, with sleep in an earth-scented, wind-stirred tent. They had driven West—West, two thousand miles toward the sunset, till it seemed they must indeed come on the Pacific and junk-sails lifting against the misted sun. They had no responsibilities of position. Together they chanted "The Gipsy Trail," vowing that some day they would wander together—

And they were doing it!

Such exultation filled him, such overwhelming tenderness, that he wanted to dash down to their cabin and assure himself that he still had the magic of Fran's companionship. But he remembered with what irritable efficiency she had been unpacking. He had been married for over twenty years. He stayed on deck.

He explored the steamer. It was to him, the mechanic, the most sure and impressive mechanism he had ever seen; more satisfying than a Rolls, a Delauney-Belleville, which to him had been the equivalents of a Velasquez. He marveled at the authoritative steadiness with which the bow mastered the waves; at the powerful sweep of the lines of the deck and the trim stowing of cordage. He admired the first officer, casually pacing the bridge. He wondered that in this craft which was, after all, but a floating iron egg-shell, there should be the roseate music room, the smoking-room with its Tudor fireplace—solid and terrestrial as a castle—and the swimming-pool, green-lighted water washing beneath Roman pillars. He climbed to the boat deck, and some never realized desire for sea-faring was satisfied as he looked along the sweep of gangways, past the huge lifeboats, the ventilators like giant saxophones, past the lofty funnels serenely dribbling black wooly smoke, to the forward mast. The snow-gusts along the deck, the mysteriousness of this new world but half seen in the frosty lights, only stimulated him. He shivered and turned up his collar, but he was pricked to imaginativeness, standing outside the wireless room, by the crackle of messages springing across bleak air-roads, ocean-bounded to bright snug cities on distant plains.

"I'm at sea!"

He tramped down to tell Fran—he was not quite sure what it was that he wanted to tell her, save that steamers were very fine things indeed, and that ahead of them, in the murk of the horizon, they could see the lanes of England.

She, in their cabin with its twin brass beds, its finicking imitations of gray-blue French prints on the paneled walls, was amid a litter of shaken-out frocks, heaps of shoes, dressing gowns, Coty powder, three gift copies of "The Perennial Bachelor," binoculars, steamer letters, steamer telegrams, the candy and the Charles & Company baskets of overgrown fruit and tiny conserves with which they were to help out the steamer's scanty seven meals a day, his dress-shirts (of which he was to, and certainly would not, put on a fresh one every evening), and French novels (which she was to, and certainly wouldn't read in a stately, aloof, genteel manner every day on deck.)

"It's terrible!" she lamented. "I'll get things put away just about in time for landing. . . . Oh, here's a wireless from Emily, the darling, from California. Harry and she seem to be standing the honeymoon about as well as most victims."

"Chuck the stuff. Come out on deck. I love this ship. It's so— Man certainly has put it over Nature for once! I think I could've built ships! Come out and see it."

"You do sound happy. I'm glad. But I must unpack. You skip along—"

It was not often, these years, that he was kittenish, but now he picked her up, while she kicked and laughed, he lifted her over a pile of sweaters and tennis shoes and bathing-suits and skates, kissed her, and shouted, "Come on! It's our own honeymoon! Eloping! Have I ever remembered to tell you that I adore you? Come up and see some ocean with me. There's an awful lot of ocean around this ship. . . . Oh, damn the unpacking!"

He sounded masterful, but it was always a satisfaction, when he was masterful, to have her consent to be mastered. He was pleased now when she stopped being efficient about this business of enjoying life, and consented to do something for no reason except that it was agreeable.

In her shaggy Burberry, color of a dead maple leaf, and her orange tam o' shanter, she suggested autumn days and brown uplands. She was a girl; certainly no mother of a married daughter. He was cumbersomely proud of her, of the glances which the men passengers snatched at her as they swung round the deck.

"Funny how it comes over a fellow suddenly I mean—this is almost the first time we've ever really started out like lovers—no job to call us back. You were dead right, Fran—done enough work—now we'll live! Together—always! But I'll have so much to learn, to keep up with you. You, and Europe! Hell, I'm so sentimental! D'you mind? Just come out of state prison! Did twenty years!"

Round and round the deck. The long stretch on the starboard side, filthy with deck chairs, with rug-wadded passengers turning a pale green as the sea rose, with wind-ruffled magazines, cups left from teatime, and children racing with toy carts. The narrow passage aft, where the wind swooped on them, pushing them back, and the steamer dipped so that they had to labor up-hill, bending forward, their limbs of lead. But, as they toiled, a glimpse of ship mysteries that were stirring to land-bound imaginations. They looked down into a hatchway—some one said there were half a dozen Brazilian cougars being shipped down there—and along a dizzy aerial gangway to the after deck and the wheelhouse and a lone light in the weaving darkness. They saw the last glimmer of the streaky wake stretching back to New York.

Then, blown round the corner, released from climbing upward, a dash along the cold port side, blessedly free of steamer chairs and of lady staring. Swinging at five miles an hour. The door of the smoking-room, with a whiff of tobacco smoke, a pleasant reek of beer, a sound of vocal Americans. The place where the deck widened into an alcove—thick walls of steel, dotted with lines of rivets smeared with thick white paint—and the door of the stewards' pantry from which, in the afternoon, came innumerable sandwiches and cakes and cups and pots of tea. The double door to the main stairway, where, somehow, a stewardess in uniform was always talking to a steward. The steel-gripped windows of the music room, with a glimpse of unhappy young-old women, accompanying their mothers abroad, sitting flapping through magazines. Where the deck was unenclosed, the yellow scoured rail and the white stanchions, bright in the deck light, brighter against the dark coil of sea. Always before them, the long straight lines of the decking planks, rigid as bars of music, divided by seams of glistening tar. Deck—ship—at sea!

Then forward, and the people along the rail—bold voyagers facing the midwinter Atlantic through glass windows—honeymooners quickly unclasping as the pestiferous deck-circlers passed—aged and sage gentlemen commenting on the inferiority of the steerage passengers who, on the deck below, altogether innocent of being condescendingly observed by the gentry-by-right-of-passage-money, jiggled beside a tarpaulin-covered hatch to the pumping music of an accordion, and blew blithely on frosted fingers.

And round all over again, walking faster, turning from casual pedestrians into competitors in the ocean marathon. Faster. Cutting corners more sharply. Superior to thrusting wind, to tilting deck. Gaining on that lone, lean, athletic girl, and passing her. . . .

"That's the way to walk! Say, Fran, I wonder if sometime we couldn't get away from hotels and sort of take a walking-trip along the Riviera—interesting. I should think. . . . Darling!"

Gaining on but never quite passing that monacle-flashing, tweed-coated man whom they detested on sight and who, within three days, was to prove the simplest and heartiest of acquaintances.

A racing view of all their companions of the voyage, their fellow-citizens in this brave village amid the desert of waters: strangers to be hated on sight, to be snubbed lest they snub first, yet presently to be known better and better loved and longer remembered than neighbors seen for a lifetime on the cautious land.

Their permanent home, for a week, to become more familiar, thanks to the accelerated sensitiveness which is the one blessing of travel, than rooms paced for years. Every stippling of soot on the lifeboats, every chair in the smoking-room, every table along one's own aisle in the dining salon, to be noted and recalled, in an exhilarated and heightened observation.

"I do feel awfully well," said Sam, and Fran: "So do I. So long since we've walked together like this! And we'll keep it up; we won't get caught by people. But I must arise now and go to Innisfree to finish the unpacking of the nine bean rows oh *why* did I bring so many clothes! Till dressing-time—*my dear!*"

He was first dressed for dinner. She had decided, after rather a lot of conversation about it, that the belief that our better people do not dress for dinner on the first night out was a superstition. He sauntered up to the smoking-room for his first cocktail aboard, feeling very glossy and handsome and much-traveled. Then he was feeling very lonely, for the smoking-room was filled with amiable-looking people who apparently all knew one another. And he knew nobody aboard save Fran.

"That's the one trouble. I'm going to miss Tub and Doc Hazzard and the rest horribly," he brooded. "I wish they were along! Then it would be about perfect."

He was occupying an alcove with a semi-circular leather settee, before a massy table. The room was crowded, and a square-rigged Englishman, blown into the room with a damp whiff of sea air, stopped at Sam's table asking abruptly, "Mind if I sit here?"

The Englishman ordered his cocktail with competence:

"Now be very careful about this, steward. I want half Booth gin and half French vermouth, and just four drops of orange bitters, and no Italian vermouth, remember, no Italian vermouth." As the Englishman gulped his drink, Sam enjoyed hating him. The man was perfectly expressionless, like a square-headed wooden idol, colored like an idol of cedar wood. "Supercilious as the devil. Never would be friendly, not till he'd known you ten years. Well, he needn't worry! I'm not going to speak to him! Curious how an Englishman like that can make you feel that you're small and skinny and your tie's badly tied without even looking at you! Well, he—"

The Englishman spoke, curtly:

"Decent weather, for a February crossing."

"Is it? I don't really know. Never crossed before."

"Really?"

"You've crossed often?"

"Oh, perhaps twenty times. I was with the British War Mission during the late argument. They were always chasing me across. Lockert's my name. I'm growing cocoa down in British Guiana now. Hot there! Going to stay in London?"

"I think so, for a while. I'm on an indefinite vacation."

Sam had the American yearning to become acquainted, to tell all about his achievements, not as boasting but to establish himself as a worthy fellow.

"I've been manufacturing motor cars—the Revelation—thought it was about time to quit and find out what the world was like. Dodsworth is my name."

"Pleased to meet you." (Like most Europeans, Lockert believed that all Americans of all classes always said "Pleased to meet you," and expected so to be greeted in turn.) "Revelation! Jolly good car. Had one in Kent. My cousin—live with him when I'm home—bouncing old retired general—he's dotty over motors. Roars around on a shocking old motor bike—mustache and dignity flying in the morning breeze—atrocious bills for all the geese and curates he runs over. He's insanely pro-American—am myself, except for your appalling ice water. Have another cocktail?"

In twenty minutes, Sam and Major Clyde Lockers had agreed that the "labor turnover" was too high, that driving by night into the brilliance of headlights was undesirable, that Bobby Jones was a player of golf, and that they themselves were men of the world and cheery companions.

* * *

On the horizon was a light, stationary, *on land*, after these days of shifting waters and sliding hulls. He waited to be certain. Yes! It was a lighthouse, swinging its blade of flame. They had done it, they had fulfilled the adventure, they had found their way across the blind immensity and, the barren sea miles over, they had come home to England. He did not know (he never knew) whether the light was on Bishop's Rock or the English mainland, but his released imagination saw the murkiness to northward there as England itself. Mother England! Land of his ancestors; land of the only kings who, to an American schoolboy, had been genuine monarchs—Charles I and Henry VIII and Victoria;

not a lot of confusing French and German rulers. Land where still, for the never quite matured Sammy Dodsworth, Coeur de Lion went riding, the Noir Faineant went riding, to rescue Ivanhoe, where Oliver Twist still crept through evil alleys, where Falstaff's belly-laugh discommoded the godly, where Uncle Ponderevo puffed and mixed, where Jude wavered by dusk across the moorland, where Old Jolyon sat with quiet eyes, in immortality more enduring than human life. And his own people—he had lost track of them, but he had far-off cousins in Wiltshire, in Durham. And all of them there—in a motor boat he could be ashore in half an hour! Perhaps there was a town just off there—He saw it, from pictures in *Punch* and the *Illustrated London News*, from Cruikshank illustrations of his childhood.

A seaside town: a crescent of flat-faced houses, the brass-sheathed door of a select pub and, countrywards, a governess-cart creeping among high hedges to a village green, a chalky hill with Roman earthworks up to which panted the bookish vicar beside a white-mustached ex-proconsul who had ruled jungles and maharajahs and lost temples where peacocks screamed.

Mother England! Home!

He dashed down to Fran. He had to share it with her. For all his training in providing suitable company for her and then not interrupting his betters, he burst through her confidences as Lockert and she stood aloof from the dance. He seized her shoulder and rumbled, "Light ahead! We're there! Come up on the top deck. Oh, hell, never *mind* a coat! Just a second, to see it!"

His insistence bore Fran away, and with her alone, unchaperoned by that delightful Major Lockert, he stood huddled by a lifeboat, in his shirtsleeves, his dress coat around her, looking at the cheery wink of the light that welcomed them.

They had full five minutes of romancing and of tenderness before Lockert came along, placidly bumbling that they would catch cold . . . that they would find Kent an estimable county . . . that Dodsworth must never make the mistake of ordering his street-boots and his riding-boots from the same maker.

The smell of London is a foggy smell, a sooty smell, a coal-fire smell, yet to certain wanderers it is more exhilarating, more suggestive of greatness and of stirring life, than springtime hillsides or the chill sweetness of autumnal nights; and that unmistakable smell, which men long for in rotting perfumes along the Orinoco, in the greasy reek of South Chicago, in the hot odor of dusty earth among locust-buzzing Alberta wheatfields, that luring breath of the dark giant among cities, reaches halfway to Southampton to greet the traveler. Sam sniffed at it, uneasily, restlessly, while he considered how strange was the British fashion of having railway compartments instead of an undivided car with a nice long aisle along which you could observe ankles, magazines, Rotary buttons, clerical collars, and all the details that made travel interesting.

And the strangeness of having framed pictures of scenery behind the seats; of having hand straps—the embroidered silk covering so rough to the finger tips, the leather inside so smooth and cool—beside the doors. And the greater strangeness of admitting that these seats were more comfortable than the flinty Pullman chairs of America. And of seeing outside, in the watery February sunshine, not snow-curdled fields but springtime greenness; pollarded willows and thatched roofs and half-timbered façades—

Just like in the pictures! England!

Like most people who have never traveled abroad, Sam had not emotionally believed that these "foreign scenes" veritably existed; that human beings really could live in environments so different from the front yards of Zenith suburbs; that Europe was anything save a fetching myth like the Venusberg. By finding it actually visible, he gave himself up to grasping it as enthusiastically as, these many years, he had given himself to grinding out motor cars.

* * *

A little melancholy at having to struggle through their Second Honeymoon unassisted, they dined at the hotel and went to the theater. In the taxicab, he had a confused timidity—no fear of violence, no sense of threatened death, but a feeling of incompetence in this strange land, of making a fool of himself, of being despised by Fran and by these self-assured foreigners; a fear of loneliness; a fear that he might never be restored to the certainties of Zenith. He saw his club, the office, the dear imprisonment of home, against the background of London, with its lines of severe façades, its roaring squares, corners clamorous with newspaper vendors, and a whole nest of streets that irritated him because they weren't reasonable—he didn't know where they led! And a tremendous restaurant that looked bigger than any clashing Childs' in New York, which was annoying in a land where he had expected to find everything as tiny and stiff and unambitious as a Japanese toy garden.

And the taxi-driver hadn't understood his pronunciation—he had had to let the hotel porter give the name of the theater—and what ought he to tip the fellow? He couldn't ask Fran's advice. He was making up for his negligence about the radiogram for hotel reservations by being brusque and competent—a man on whom she could rely, whom she would love the more as she saw his superiority in new surroundings. God, he loved her more than ever, now that he had the time for it!

And what was that about not confusing a half-crown (let's see: that was fifty cents, almost exactly, wasn't it?) and a florin? Why had Lockert gone and mixed him all up by cautioning him so much about them? Curse Lockert—nice chap—awfully kind, but treating him as though he were a baby who would be disgraced in decent English society unless he had a genteel guide to tell him what he might wear and what he might say in mixed society! He'd managed to become president of quite a fair-sized corporation without Lockert's aid, hadn't he!

He felt, at the theater, even more forlorn.

He did not understand more than two-thirds of what the actors said on the stage. He had been brought up to believe that the English language and the American language were one, but what could a citizen of Zenith make of "Ohs rath, eastill in labtry"?

What were they talking about? What was the play about?

He knew that in America, even in the Midwestern saneness of Zenith, where the factories and skyscrapers were not too far from the healing winds across the cornfields, an incredible anarchy had crept into the family life which, he believed, had been the foundation of American greatness. People that you knew, people like his own cousin, Jerry Loring, after a decent career as a banker had taken up with loose girls and had stood for his wife's having a lover without killing the fellow. By God if he, Sam Dodsworth, ever found *his* wife being too friendly with a man—

No, he probably wouldn't. Not kill them. She had a right to her own way. She was better than he—that slender, shining being, in the golden frock she had insisted on digging out of a wardrobe trunk. She was a divine thing, while he was a clodhopper—and how he'd like to kiss her, if it weren't for shocking all these people so chillily calm about him! If conceivably she *could* look at another man, he'd just leave her . . . and kill himself.

But he must attend to the play, considering that he was being educated, and so expensively.

He concluded that the play was nonsense. In America there was a criminal amount of divorcing and of meriting divorce, but surely that collapse of all the decencies was impossible in Old England, the one land that these hundreds of years had upheld the home, the church, the throne! Yet here on the stage, with no one hissing, an English gentleman was represented as being the lover of a decent woman, wife of a chemist, and as protesting against running away with her because then they would be unable to continue having tea and love together at the husband's expense. And the English audience, apparently good honest people, laughed.

The queer cold bewilderment crept closer to him in the entr'acte, when he paced the lobby with Fran. The people among whom he was strolling were so blankly indifferent to him. In Zenith, he would have been certain to meet acquaintances at the theater; even in New York there was a probability of meeting classmates or automobile men. But here—He felt li'.:e a lost dog. He felt as he had on the first day of his Freshman year in college.

And his evening clothes, he perceived, were all wrong.

They went to bed rather silently, Sam and Fran. He would have given a great deal if she had suggested that they take a steamer back to America tomorrow. What, actually, she was thinking, he did not know. She had retired into the mysteriousness which had hidden her essential self ever since the night when he had first made love to her, at the Kennpoos Canoe Club. She was pleasant now—too pleasant; she said, too easily, that she had enjoyed the play; and she said, without saying it, that she was far from him and that he was not to touch her body, her sacred, proud, passionately cared-for body, save in a fleeting good-night kiss. She seemed as strange to him as the London audience at the theater. It was inconceivable that he had lived with her for over twenty years; impossible that she should be the mother of his two children; equally impossible that it could mean anything to her to travel with him—he so old and tired and aimless, she so fresh and unwrinkled and sure.

Tonight, she wasn't forty-two to his fifty-one; she was thirty to his sixty.

He heard the jesting of Tub Pearson, the friendliness of his chauffeur at home, the respectful questions of his stenographer.

He realized that Fran was also lying awake and that, as quietly as possible, her face rammed into her pillow, she was crying.

And he was afraid to comfort her.

* * *

Sam had remained calm amid the frenzy of a Detroit Automobile Show; he had stalked through the crush of a New Year's Eve on Broadway, merely brushing off the bright young men with horns and feather ticklers; but in the Calais customs-house he was appalled. The porters shrieked ferocious things like "attonshion" as they elbowed past, walking mountains of baggage; the passengers jammed about the low baggage platform; the customs inspectors seemed to Sam cold-eyed and hostile; all of them bawled and bleated and wailed in what sounded to him like no language whatever; and he remembered that he had four hundred cigarettes in his smaller bag.

The porter who had taken their bags on the steamer had shouted something that sounded like "catravan deuce"—Fran said it meant that he was Porter Number ninety-two. Then Catravan Deuce had malignantly disappeared, with their possessions. Sam knew that it was all right, but he didn't believe it. He assured himself that a French porter was no more likely to steal their bags than a Grand Central red-cap— only, he was quite certain that Catravan Deuce had stolen them. Of course he could replace everything except Fran's jewelry without much expense but—Damn it, he'd hate to lose his old red slippers—

He was disappointed at so flabby an ending when he found Catravan Deuce at his elbow in the customs room, beaming in a small bearded way and shouldering aside the most important passengers to plank their baggage down on the platform for examination.

Sam was proud of Fran's French (of Stratford, Connecticut) when the capped inspector said something quite incomprehensible and she answered with what sounded like "reean." He felt that she was a scholar; he felt that he was untutored and rusty; he depended on her admiringly. And then he opened the smaller bag and the four hundred cigarettes were revealed to the inspector.

The inspector looked startled, he gaped, he spread out his arms, and protested in the name of liberty, equality, fraternity, and indemnities. Fran tried to answer, but her French stumbled and fell, and she turned to Sam, all her airy competence gone, wailing, "I can't understand what he says! He—he talks patois!"

At her appeal, Sam suddenly became competent, ready to face the entire European Continent, with all appertaining policemen, laws, courts, and penitentiaries.

"Here! I'll get somebody!" he assured her, and to the customs inspector, who was now giving a French version of the Patrick Henry oration, he remarked, "Just a *mo*-ment! Keep your shirt on!"

He had a notion of finding the English vicar to whom he had listened on the Channel steamer. "Fellow seems to know European languages." He wallowed through the crowd as though he were making a touchdown, and saw on a cap the thrice golden words "American Express Company." The American Express man beamed and leaped forward at something in the manner with which Mr. Samuel Dodsworth of the Revelation Motor Company suggested, "Can you come and do a little job of interpreting for me?" . . . Sam felt that for a moment he was being Mr. Samuel Dodsworth, and not Fran Dodsworth's husband. . . . And for something less than a moment he admitted that he was possibly being the brash Yankee of Mark Twain and Booth Tarkington. And he could not successfully be sorry for it.

The American Express man saw them on the waiting train (a very bleak and tall and slaty train it seemed to Sam); he prevented Sam from tipping the porter enough to set him up in a shop. And so Sam and Fran were alone in a compartment, safe again till Paris.

Sam chuckled, "Say, I guess I'll have to learn the French for two phrases: 'How much?' and 'Go to hell.' But—Sweet! We're in France—in Europe!"

She smiled at him; she let him off and didn't even rebuke him for his Americanism. They sat hand in hand, and they were more intimately happy than since the day they had sailed from America. They were pleased by everything: by the battery of red and golden bottles on their table at lunch, by the deftness with which the waiter sliced the cone of ice cream, by the mysterious widow who was trying to pick up the mysterious Frenchman who combined a checked suit and a red tie with a square black beard—such a beard, murmured Fran, as it was worth crossing the Atlantic to behold.

He was stimulated equally by the "foreignness" of the human spectacle flickering past the window of their compartment—women driving ox-carts, towns with sidewalk cafés, and atrocious new houses of yellow brick between lumpy layers of stone picked out in red mortar—and the lack of "foreignness" in the land itself. Somehow it wasn't quite right that French trees and grass should be of the same green, French earth of the same brown, French sky of the same blue, as in a natural, correct country like America. After the tight little fenced fields of England, the wide Picardy plains, green with approaching April, seemed to him extraordinarily like the prairies of Illinois and Iowa. If it was a little disappointing, not quite right and decent after he had gone and taken so long and expensive a journey, yet he was pleased by that sense of recognition which is one of the most innocent and egotistic of human diversions, that feeling of understanding and of mastering an observation. He was as pleased as a side-street nobody when in his newspaper he sees the name of a man he knows.

"I'm enjoying this!" said Sam.

He had been accustomed to "sizing up" American towns; he could look from a Pullman window at Kalamazoo or Titus Center and guess the population within ten per cent. He could, and with frequency he did; he was fascinated by figures of any sort, and for twenty years he had been trying to persuade Fran that there was nothing essentially ignoble in remembering populations and areas and grade-percentages and the average life of tires. He had been able to guess not too badly at the size of British towns; he had not been too greatly bewildered by anything in England, once he was over the shock of seeing postmen with funny hats, and taxicabs with no apparent speed above neutral. But in Paris, as they bumped and slid and darted from the Gare du Nord to their hotel, he could not be certain just what it was that he was seeing.

Fran was articulate enough about it. She half stood up in the taxi, crying, "Oh, look, Sam, look! Isn't it adorable! Isn't it too exciting! Oh, the darling funny little *zincs!* And the Cointreau ads, instead of chewing gum. These bald-faced high white houses! Everybody so noisy, and yet so gay! Oh, I *adore* it!"

But for Sam it was a motion picture produced by an insane asylum; it was an earthquake with a volcano erupting and a telephone bell ringing just after he'd gone to sleep; it was lightning flashes and steam whistles and newspaper extras and war.

Their taxicab, just missing an omnibus, sliding behind its rear platform. A policeman, absurdly little, with an absurd white baton. Two priests over glasses of beer at a café. Silver gray everywhere, instead of London's golden brown. Two exceedingly naked plaster ladies upholding a fifth-story balcony. Piles of shoddy rugs in front of a shop, and beside them a Frenchman looking utterly content with his little business, instead of yearning at the department store opposite and feeling guilty as he would in New York or Chicago or Zenith. Fish. Breads. Beards. Brandy. Artichokes. Apples. Etchings. Fish. A stinking-looking alley. A splendid sweeping boulevard. Circular tin structures whose use he dared not suspect and which gave him a shocking new notion of Latin proprieties and of the apparently respectable and certainly bearded gentlemen who dashed toward them. Many books, bound in paper of a thin-looking yellow. An incessant, nerve-cracking, irritating, exhilarating blat-blat-blat of nervous little motor horns. Buildings which in their blankness seemed somehow higher than American skyscrapers ten times as high. A tiny, frowsy, endearing façade of a house which suggested the French Revolution and crazed women in red caps and kirtled skirts. A real artist (Sam decided), a being in red beard, wide black hat, and a cloak, with a dog-eared marble-paper-covered portfolio under his arm. Gossiping women, laughing, denouncing, forgiving, laughing. Superb public buildings, solid-looking as Gibraltar. Just missing another taxi, and the most admirable cursing by both chauffeurs—

"This certainly is a busy town. But not much traffic control, looks to me," said Samuel Dodsworth, and his voice was particularly deep and solemn, because he was particularly confused and timid.

It was at the Grand Hôtel des Deux Hémisphères et Dijon that he was able to reassume the pleasant mastery with which (he hoped) he had been able to impress Fran at the Calais customs. The assistant manager of the hotel spoke excellent English, and Sam had never been entirely at a loss so long as his opponent would be decent and speak a recognizable language.

Lucile McKelvey, of Zenith, had told Fran that the Hémisphères was "such a nice, quiet hotel," and Sam had wired for reservations from London. By himself, he would doubtless have registered and taken meekly whatever room was given him. But Fran insisted on seeing their suite, and they found it a damp, streaked apartment looking on a sunless courtyard.

"Oh, this won't do at all!" wailed Fran. "Haven't you something decent?"

The assistant manager, a fluent Frenchman from Roumania via Algiers, looked them up and down with that contempt, that incomparable and enfeebling contempt, which assistant managers reserve for foreigners on their first day in Paris.

"We are quite full up," he sniffed.

"You haven't anything else at all?" she protested.

"No, Madame."

Those were the words, but the tune was, "No, you foreign nuisance—jolly lucky you are to be admitted here at all—I wonder if you two really *are* married—well, I'll overlook that, but I shan't stand any Yankee impertinence!"

Even the airy Fran was intimidated, and she said only, "Well. I don't like it—"

And then Samuel Dodsworth appeared again.

His knowledge of Parisian hotels and their assistant managers was limited, but his knowledge of impertinent employees was vast.

"Nope," he said. "No good. We don't like it. We'll look elsewhere."

"But Monsieur has engaged this suite!"

The internationalist and the provincial looked at each other furiously, and it was the assistant manager whose eyes fell, who looked embarrassed, as Sam's paws curled, as the back of his neck prickled with unholy wrath.

"Look here! You know this is a rotten hole! Do you want to send for the manager—the boss, whatever you call him?"

The assistant manager shrugged, and left them, coldly and with speed.

Rather silently, Sam lumbered beside Fran down to their taxi. He supervised the reloading of their baggage, and atrociously overtipped every one whom he could coax out of the hotel.

"Grand Universe!" he snapped at the taxi-driver, and the man seemed to understand his French.

In the taxi he grumbled, "I *told* you I had to learn the French for 'Go to hell.'"

A silence; then he ruminated. "Glad we got out of there. But I bullied that poor rat of a clerk. Dirty trick! I'm sorry! I'm three times as big as he is. Stealing candy from a kid! Dirty trick! I see why they get sore at Americans like me. Sorry, Fran."

"I adore you!" she said, and he looked mildly astonished.

At the Grand Universal, on the Rue de Rivoli, they found an agreeable suite overlooking the Tuileries, and twenty times an hour, as she unpacked, Fran skipped to the window to gloat over Paris, the Casanova among cities.

Their sitting-room seemed to him very pert and feminine in its paneled walls covered with silky yellow brocade, its fragile chairs upholstered in stripes of silver and lemon. Even the ponderous boule cabinet was frivolous, and the fireplace was of lively and rather indecorous pink marble. He felt that it was a light-minded room, a room for sinning in evening clothes. All Paris was like that, he decided.

Then he stepped out on the fretted iron balcony and looked to the right, to the Place de la Concorde and the beginning of the Champs Elysées, with the Chamber of Deputies across the Seine. He was suddenly stilled, and he perceived another Paris, stately, aloof, gray with history, eternally quiet at heart for all its superficial clamor.

Beneath the quacking of motor horns he heard the sullen tumbrils. He heard the trumpets of the Napoleon who had saved Europe from petty princes. He heard, without quite knowing that he heard them, the cannon of the Emperor who was a Revolutionist. He heard things that Samuel Dodsworth did not know he had heard or ever could hear.

"Gee, Fran, this town has been here a long time, I guess," he meditated. "This town knows a lot," said Samuel Dodsworth of Zenith. "Yes, it knows a lot."

And, a little sadly, "I wish I did!"

There are many Parises, with as little relation one to another as Lyons to Monte Carlo, as Back Bay to the Dakota wheatfields. There is the trippers' Paris: a dozen hotels, a dozen bars and restaurants, more American than French; three smutty revues; three railroad stations; the Café de la Paix; the Eiffel Tower; the Arc de Triomphe; the Louvre; shops for frocks, perfumes, snake-skin shoes, and silk pajamas; the regrettable manners of Parisian taxi-drivers; and the Montmartre dance-halls where fat, pink-skulled American lingerie-buyers get drunk on imitation but inordinately expensive champagne, to the end that they put on pointed paper hats, scatter confetti, conceive themselves as Great Lovers, and in general forget their unfortunate lot.

The students' Paris, round about the Sorbonne, very spectacled and steady. The fake artists' Paris, very literary and drunk and full of theories. The real artists' Paris, hidden and busy and silent. The cosmopolites'

Paris, given to breakfast in the Bois, to tea at the Ritz, and to reading the social columns announcing who has been seen dining with princesses at Ciro's—namely, a Paris whose chief joy is in being superior to the trippers.

There is also reported to be a Paris inhabited by no one save three million Frenchmen.

It is said that in this unknown Paris live bookkeepers and electricians and undertakers and journalists and grandfathers and grocers and dogs and other beings as unromantic as people Back Home.

Making up a vast part of all save this last of the Parises are the Americans.

Paris is one of the largest, and certainly it is the pleasantest, of modern American cities. It is a joyous town, and its chief joy is in its jealousies. Every citizen is in rivalry with all the others in his knowledge of French, of museums, of wine, and of restaurants.

The various castes, each looking down its nose at the caste below, are after this order: Americans really domiciled in Paris for years, and connected by marriage with the French noblesse. Americans long domiciled, but unconnected with the noblesse. Americans who have spent a year in Paris—those who have spent three months—two weeks—three days—half a day—just arrived. The American who has spent three days is as derisive toward the half-a-day tripper as the American resident with smart French relatives is toward the poor devil who has lived in Paris for years but who is there merely for business.

And without exception they talk of the Rate of Exchange.

And they are all very alike, and mostly homesick.

They insist that they cannot live in America, but, except for a tenth of them who have really become acclimated in Europe, they are so hungry for American news that they subscribe to the home paper, from Keokuk or New York or Pottsville, and their one great day each week is that of the arrival of the American mail, on which they fall with shouts of "Hey, Mamie, listen to this! They're going to put a new heating plant in the Lincoln School." They know quite as well as Sister Louisa, back home, when the Washington Avenue extension will be finished. They may ostentatiously glance daily at *Le Matin* or *Le Journal,* but the Paris editions of the New York *Herald* and the Chicago *Tribune* they read solemnly, every word, from the front page stories—"Congress to Investigate Election Expenses," and "Plans Transatlantic Aeroplane Liners" to the "News of Americans in Europe," with its tidings that Mrs. Whitney T. Auerenstein of Scranton entertained Geheimrat and Frau Bopp at dinner at the Bristol, and that Miss Mary Minks Meeton, author and lecturer, has arrived at the Hôtel Pédauque.

Each of these castes is subdivided according to one's preference for smart society or society so lofty that it need not be smart, society given to low bars and earnest drinking, the society of business exploitation, or that most important society of plain loafing. Happy is he who can cleave utterly to one of these cliques; he can find a group of fellow zealots and, drinking or shopping or being artistic, be surrounded with gloriously log-rolling comrades.

* * *

Since the days of Alexander the Great there has been a fashionable belief that travel is agreeable and highly educative. Actually, it is one of the most arduous yet boring of all pastimes and, except in the case of a few experts who go globe-trotting for special purposes, it merely provides the victim with more topics about which to show ignorance. The great traveler of the novelists is tall and hawk-nosed, speaking nine languages, annoying all right-thinking persons by constantly showing drawing-room manners. He has "been everywhere and done everything." He has shot lions in Siberia and gophers in Minnesota, and played tennis with the King at Stockholm. He can give you a delightful evening discoursing on Tut's tomb and the ethnology of the Maoris.

Actually, the great traveler is usually a small mussy person in a faded green fuzzy hat, inconspicuous in a corner of the steamer bar. He speaks only one language, and that gloomily. He knows all the facts about nineteen countries, except the home-lives, wage-scales, exports, religions, politics, agriculture, history and languages of those countries. He is as valuable as Baedeker in regard to hotels and railroads, only not so accurate.

He who has seen one cathedral ten times has seen something; he who has seen ten cathedrals once has seen but little; and he who has spent half an hour in each of a hundred cathedrals has seen nothing at all. Four hundred pictures all on a wall are four hundred times less interesting than one picture; and no one knows a café till he has gone there often enough to know the names of the waiters.

These are the laws of travel.

If travel were so inspiring and informing a business as the new mode of round-the-world-tour advertisements eloquently sets forth, then the wisest men in the world would be deck hands on tramp steamers, Pullman porters, and Morman missionaries.

It is the awful toil which is the most distressing phase of travel. If there is anything worse than the aching tedium of staring out of car windows, it is the irritation of getting tickets, packing, finding trains, lying in bouncing berths, washing without water, digging out passports, and fighting through customs. To live in Carlsbad is seemly and to loaf at San Remo healing to the soul, but to get from Carlsbad to San Remo is of the devil.

Actually, most of those afflicted with the habit of traveling merely lie about its pleasures and profits. They do not travel to see anything, but to get away from themselves, which they never do, and away from rowing with their relatives—only to find new relatives with whom to row. They travel to escape thinking, to have something to do, just as they might play solitaire, work cross-word puzzles, look at the cinema, or busy themselves with any other dreadful activity.

These things the Dodsworths discovered, though, like most of the world, they never admitted them.

More than cathedrals or castles, more even than waiters, Sam remembered the Americans he met along the way. Writers speak confidently, usually, insultingly, of an animal called "the typical American traveling abroad." One might as well speak of "a typical human being." The Americans whom Sam encountered ranged from Bostonian Rhodes scholars to Arkansas farmers, from Riviera tennis players to fertilizer salesmen.

There were Mr. and Mrs. Meece from Ottumwa, Iowa, at a palm-smothered hotel in Italy. Mr. Meece had been a druggist for forty-six years, and his wife looked like two apples set one on top of the other. They plodded at sightseeing all day long; they took things exactly in the order in which the guide-book gave them; and they missed nothing—art galleries, aquariums, the King Ludwig monument in two shades of pink granite, or the site of the house in which Gladstone spent two weeks in 1887. If they enjoyed anything, they did not show it. But neither did they look bored. Their expressions showed precisely nothing. They returned to the hotel at five daily, and always dined in the grill at six, and Mr. Meece was allowed one glass of beer. He was never heard to say anything whatever to his wife except, "Well, getting late."

In the same hotel with them were the Noisy Pair: two New Yorkers who at all hours were heard, widely heard, observing that all Europeans were inefficient, that they could get no hot water after midnight, that hotel prices were atrocious, that no revue in Europe was as good as Ziegfeld's Follies, that they couldn't buy Lucky Strike cigarettes or George Washington coffee in this doggone Wop town, and that lil ole Broadway was good enough for *them.*

They were followed by other Americans: Professor and Mrs. Whittle of Northern Wisconsin Baptist University—Professor Whittle taught Greek and knew more about stained glass and the manufacture of Benedictine than any American living, and Mrs. Whittle had taken her doctorate at Bonn on the philosophy of Spinoza but really preferred fruit-ranching. The Whittles were followed by Percy West, the explorer of Yucatan; by Mr. Roy Hoops, who sold motor tires; by Judge and Mrs. Cady of Massachusetts—the Cadys had lived in the same house for five generations; by Mr. Otto Kretch and Mr. Fred Larabee of Kansas City, two oil men who were on a golfing tour of the world, to take three years; by the brass-bound heel-clicking Colonel Thorne; by Mr. Lawrence Simton, who dressed like a lily and spoke like a lady; by Miss Addy T. Belcher, who was collecting material for a new lecture trip on foreign politics and finance and who, off stage, resembled a chorus girl; and by Miss Rose Love, the musical comedy star, who off stage resembled a short-sighted school teacher.

Typical Americans!

Sam never lost the adventurousness of seeing on a railway car a sign promising that the train was going from Paris to Milan, Venice, Trieste, Zagreb, Vinkovci, Sofia and Stamboul. Though he became weary of wandering, so that one museum was like another, so that when he awoke in the morning it took a minute to remember in what country he was, yet the names of foreign towns always beckoned him.

To Avignon, they wandered, to San Sebastian and Madrid and Toledo and Seville. To Arles, Carcassonne, Marseilles, Monte Carlo. To Genoa, Florence, Sienna, Venice, with two months divided between Naples and Rome and a jaunt to Sicily. To Vienna, Budapest, Munich, Nuremberg. And so, late in April, they came to Berlin.

Sam might not tell of it when he went home, nor years later remember it, but he found that to him the real characteristic of Making a Foreign Tour had nothing to do with towers or native costumes, galleries or mountain scenery. It was the tedium of almost every hotel, almost every evening, when they had completed their chore of sight-seeing. There was "nothing to do in the evening" save occasional movies, or cafés if they were not too far from the hotel in the foreign and menacing darkness.

Every evening the same. Back to the hotel, weary, a grateful cup of tea, and slow dressing. They never dared, after trying it once, to go down to dinner in tweeds and be stared at by the English tourists of the pay-in-guineas classes as though they were polluting the dining-room.

A melancholy cocktail in the bar. Dinner, always the same—white and gold dining-room, suavely efficient black-haired captain of waiters pulling out their chairs, a clear soup of parenthetic flavor, a fish not merely white but blanched, chicken with gloomy little carrots, crème caramel, cheese and fruit. The same repressed and whispering fellow-diners: the decayed American mother in silver with the almost equally decayed daughter in gold, staring pitifully at the large lone Englishman;

the young intellectual Prussian honeymoon couple, pretending to read and ignore each other, and the fat mature Bavarian couple, wanting to be cheery but not daring. The aged Britons—he with a spurt of eyebrows and positive opinions on artichokes and the rate of exchange; she always glaring over her glasses at you if you laughed or asked the head-waiter about trains to Grasse. The vicar of the local English church, moistly friendly, the one person who came and spoke to you but who, by his manner of inquiring after your health, made you feel guilty because you weren't going to his service next Sunday.

Then the real tedium.

Sitting till ten in the lounge, listening to an orchestra mildly celebrating the centenary of Verdi, reading an old Tauchnitz, peeping up uneasily as you felt more and more the tightening of personal ties with these too well-known, too closely studied strangers.

It was worse when the hotel was half empty and the desert of waiting chairs in the lounge looked so lonely.

Always the same, except in a few cities with casinos and cabarets and famous restaurants—the same in Florence and Granada, in Hyeres and Dresden.

Every evening after such a siege of boredom Sam guiltily inquired of himself why they hadn't gone out and looked at what was called the "Native Life" of the city—at the ways of that inconspicuous 99/100 of the population whom tourists ignored. But—Oh, they'd tried it. It wasn't a matter of dark-alley dangers; he would rather have liked a fight in a low bar. But foreign languages, the need of ordering a drink or asking a taxi fare in Italian or Spanish, was like crawling through a hedge of prickly thorns. And to go anywhere in dress clothes save the tourist-ridden restaurants was to be tormented by stares, comments, laughter. The frankness with which these Italians stared at Fran—

No, easier to stay in the hotel.

Once in a fortnight Sam was able to let himself be picked up in the bar by some American or English blade, and then he glowed and talked beamingly of motors, of Ross Ireland. And Fran welcomed and was gracious with such rescuers . . . whatever she said in the bedroom afterward about manners and vulgarity.

But it thrust them together, this aching tedium of marooned evenings, and they were often tender.

And Fran was getting tired of the isolation of travel. He gloated that before long now, she would be content to go home with him, to *stay*, and at last, fed up on the syrupy marshmallows of what she had considered Romance, to become his wife.

Twilight in Naples, and from their room at Bertolini's they looked across the bay. The water and the mountains in the water were the color of smoke, and a few little boats, far out, were fleeing home before dark. In the garden below them the fronds of a palm tree waved slowly, and lemon trees exhaled an acrid sweetness. The lights at the foot of Vesuvius were flickering steel points. Her hand slipped into his and she whispered, "I hope the boats get safely home!" They stood there till palms and sea had vanished and they could see only the lights of Naples. Some one afar was singing "Santa Lucia." Sam Dodsworth did not know the song was hackneyed.

"Tee—ta—tah, tee de dee, tee—ta—tah, taaaa—da," he hummed. Italy and Fran! The Bay of Naples! And they would go on—to sun-bright isles, to the moon-hushed desert, pagoda bells, and home! "Tee—ta—tah, tee de dee—Santaaaaa Lucia!" He had won her back to be his wife!

"And they still sing that horrible grind-organ garbage! Let's go eat," she said.

He started and sighed.

TRUMAN CAPOTE
1924–1984

Born in New Orleans, the only child of a marriage soon to break up in steamy acrimony, Capote attended schools in New York City and Connecticut but found the experience such "a waste" that he abjured further education and at the age of seventeen went to work at The New Yorker *cataloguing cartoons and occasionally writing a bit of the "Talk of the Town" section. Two years later he was back in the South writing highly imaginative short stories full of grotesque characters and neo-Gothic atmosphere. His novel* Other Voices, Other Rooms *appeared in 1948,* The Grass Harp *in 1951. In 1966, without abandoning melodrama, he turned to fact and produced his triumph of high journalism,* In Cold Blood, *a report and meditation on the infamous murder of a Kansas farm family by two pathetic young drifters.*

"I prefer travel to any other form of entertainment," Capote said once, and for most of his life he traveled or lived abroad, in the West

*Indies, France, Spain, Tangier, Venice, Switzerland, and Sicily, where
at Taormina he owned the villa once occupied by the D. H. Lawrences.
He was always an eccentric character, tiny, blond, and childish-looking,
with a wee voice, and he declined finally into a celebrity. But always he
remained a writer, concerned as much with the subtle management of
language as with "themes." "The content of my work," he explained,
"is literary; as opposed, that is, to writing inspired by political or religious
convictions, of which I have . . . none."*

To Europe
(1948)

Standing very still you could hear a harp. We climbed the wall, and
there, among the burning rain-drenched flowers of the castle's garden,
sat four mysterious figures, a young man who thumbed a hand harp and
three rusted old men who were dressed in patched-together black: how
stark they were against the storm-green air. And they were eating figs,
those Italian figs so fat the juice ran out of their mouths. At the garden's
edge lay the marble shore of Lago de Garda, its waters swarming in the
wind, and I knew then I would be always afraid to swim there, for, like
distortions beyond the beauty of ivy-glass, Gothic creatures must move
in the depths of water so ominously clear. One of the old men tossed
too far a fig peel, and a trio of swans, thus disturbed, rustled the reeds
of the waterway.

D. jumped off the wall and gestured for me to join him; but I couldn't,
not quite then: because suddenly it was true and I wanted the trueness
of it to last a moment longer—I could never feel it so absolutely again,
even the movement of a leaf and it would be lost, precisely as a cough
would forever ruin Tourel's high note. And what was this truth? Only
the truth of justification: a castle, swans and a boy with a harp, for all
the world out of a childhood storybook—before the prince has entered
or the witch has cast her spell.

It was right that I had gone to Europe, if only because I could look
again with wonder. Past certain ages or certain wisdoms it is very difficult
to look with wonder; it is best done when one is a child; after that, and
if you are lucky, you will find a bridge of childhood and walk across it.
Going to Europe was like that. It was a bridge of childhood, one that
led over the seas and through the forests straight into my imagination's
earliest landscapes. One way or another I had gone to a good many

places, from Mexico to Maine—and then to think I had to go all the way to Europe to go back to my hometown, my fire and room where stories and legends seemed always to live beyond the limits of our town. And that is where the legends were: in the harp, the castle, the rustling of the swans.

A rather mad bus ride that day had brought us from Venice to Sirmione, an enchanted, infinitesimal village on the tip of a peninsula jutting into Lago di Garda, bluest, saddest, most silent, most beautiful of Italian lakes. Had it not been for the gruesome circumstance of Lucia, I doubt that we should have left Venice. I was perfectly happy there, except of course that it is incredibly noisy: not ordinary city noise, but ceaseless argument of human voices, scudding oars, running feet. It was once suggested that Oscar Wilde retire there from the world. "And become a monument for tourists?" he asked.

It was an excellent advice, however, and others than Oscar have taken it: in the palazzos along the Grand Canal there are colonies of persons who haven't shown themselves publicly in a number of decades. Most intriguing of these was a Swedish countess whose servants fetched fruit for her in a black gondola trimmed with silver bells; their tinkling made a music atmospheric but eerie. Still, Lucia so persecuted us we were forced to flee. A muscular girl, exceptionally tall for an Italian and smelling always of wretched condiment oils, she was the leader of a band of juvenile gangsters, displaced roaming youths who had flocked north for the Venetian season. They could be delightful, some of them, even though they sold cigarettes that contained more hay than tobacco, even though they would short-circuit you on a currency exchange. The business with Lucia began one day in the Piazza San Marco.

She came up and asked us for a cigarette; whereupon D., whose heart doesn't know that we are off the gold standard, gave her a whole package of Chesterfields. Never were two people more completely adopted. Which at first was quite pleasant; Lucia shadowed us wherever we went, abundantly giving us the benefits of her wisdom and protection. But there were frequent embarrassments; for one thing, we were always being turned out of the more elegant shops because of her overwrought haggling with the proprietors; then, too, she was so excessively jealous that it was impossible for us to have any contact with anyone else whatever: we chanced once to meet in the piazza a harmless and respectable young woman who had been with us in the carriage from Milan. "Attention!" said Lucia in that hoarse voice of hers, "Attention!" and proceeded almost to persuade us that this was a lady of infamous past and shameless future. On another occasion D. gave one of her cohorts a dollar watch which he had much admired. Lucia was furious; the next time we saw her she had the watch suspended on a cord around her neck, and it was said the young man had left overnight for Trieste.

Lucia had a habit of appearing in our hotel at any hour that pleased her (she lived no place that we could divine); scarcely sixteen, she would sit herself down, drain a whole bottle of Strega, smoke all the cigarettes she could lay hold of, then fall into an exhausted sleep; only when she slept did her face resemble a child's. But then one dreadful day the hotel manager stopped her in the lobby and told her that she could no longer visit our rooms. It was, he said, an insupportable scandal. So Lucia, rounding up a dozen of her more brutish companions, laid such siege to the hotel that it was necessary to bring down iron shutters over the doors and call the carabinieri. After that we did our best to avoid her.

But to avoid anyone in Venice is much the same as playing hide-and-seek in a one-room apartment, for there was never a city more compactly composed. It is like a museum with carnivalesque overtones, a vast palace that seems to have no doors, all things connected, one leading into another. Over and over in a day the same faces repeat like prepositions in a long sentence: turn a corner, and there was Lucia, the dollar watch dangling between her breasts. She was so in love with D. But presently she turned on us with that intensity of the wounded; perhaps we deserved it, but it was unendurable: like clouds of gnats her gang would trail us across the piazza spitting invective; if we sat down for a drink they would gather in the dark beyond the table and shout outrageous jokes. Half the time we didn't know what they were saying, though it was apparent that everyone else did. Lucia herself did not overtly contribute to this persecution; she remained aloof, directing her operations at a distance. So at last we decided to leave Venice. Lucia knew this. Her spies were everywhere. The morning we left it was raining; just as our gondola slipped into the water, a little crazy-eyed boy appeared and threw at us a bundle wrapped in newspaper. D. pulled the paper apart. Inside there was a dead yellow cat, and around its throat there was tied the dollar watch. It gave you a feeling of endless falling. And then suddenly we saw her, Lucia; she was standing alone on one of the little canal bridges, and she was so far hunched over the railing it looked as if she were going to fall. *"Perdonami,"* she cried, *"ma t'amo"* (forgive me, but I love you).

In London a young artist said to me, "How wonderful it must be for an American traveling in Europe the first time; you can never be a part of it, so none of the pain is yours, you will never have to endure it—yes, for you there is only the beauty."

Not understanding what he meant, I resented this; but later, after some months in France and Italy, I saw that he was right: I was not a part of Europe, I never would be. Safe, I could leave when I wanted to, and for me there was only the honeyed, hallowed air of beauty. But it was not so wonderful as the young man had imagined; it was desperate to feel that one could never be a part of moments so moving, that always one would be isolated from this landscape and these people; and then gradually I realized I did not have to be a part of it: rather, it could be a part of me. The sudden garden, opera night, wild children snatching flowers and running up a darkening street, a wreath for the dead and nuns in noon light, music from the piazza, a Paris pianola and fireworks on La Grande Nuit, the heart-shaking surprise of mountain visions and water views (lakes like green wine in the chalice of volcanoes, the Mediterranean flickering at the bottoms of cliffs), forsaken far-off towers falling in twilight and candles igniting the jeweled corpse of St. Zeno of Verona—all a part of me, elements for the making of my own perspective.

When we left Sirmione, D. returned to Rome and I went back to Paris. Mine was a curious journey. First off, I'd engaged through a dizzy Italian ticket agent a *wagonlit* aboard the Orient Express, but when I reached Milan, I discovered the arrangement had been entirely spurious and that there were no such accommodations for me; in fact, if I hadn't stepped on a few toes, I doubt that I should have got on the train at all, for everything was holiday-jammed. As it was, I managed to squeeze myself into an airless, August-hot compartment along with six other people. The name of the Orient Express evoked for me the most spine-tingling expectations: think of the extraordinary things that have occurred on that train, at least if one is to believe Miss Agatha Christie or Mr. Graham Greene. But I was not at all prepared for what happened actually.

In the compartment there were a pair of dreary Swiss businessmen, a somewhat more exotic businessman traveling from Istanbul, an American teacher and two elegant snow-headed Italian ladies with haughty eyes and features as delicate as fishbones. They were dressed like twins, these ladies; flowing black and wisps of lace caught at the throat with pearl-studded amethysts. They sat with their gloved hands clasped together and never spoke except when exchanging a box of expensive chocolates. Their only luggage appeared to be a huge bird cage; inside this cage, though it was partially covered by a silk shawl, you could see scuttling around a moldy green parrot. Now and then the parrot would let forth a burst of demented laughter; whenever this happened the two ladies would smile at each other. The American teacher asked them if the parrot could speak, and one of the ladies, with the slightest nod, replied yes, but that the parrot's grammar was very poor. As we neared the Italian-Swiss frontier, customs and passport officials began their tiresome little duties. We thought they were finished with our compartment, but presently they returned, several of them, and stood outside the glass door looking in at the aristocratic ladies. It seemed they were having quite a discussion about them. Everyone in the compartment grew quite still, except the parrot, who laughed in an unearthly way. The old ladies paid no attention whatever. Other men in uniform joined those already in the corridor. Then one of the ladies, plucking at her amethyst brooch, turned to the rest of us and, first in Italian, then German, then English, said, "We have done nothing wrong."

But at that moment the door slid open and two of the officials entered. They did not look at the old ladies but went straight to the bird cage and stripped away its covering shawl. *"Basta, basta [Enough, enough],"* screamed the parrot.

With a lurch the train came to a halt in the mountain darkness. The abruptness of this toppled the cage, and the parrot, suddenly free, flew laughingly from wall to wall of the compartment while the ladies, flurried and flying themselves, grasped for it. The customs men went on taking the cage apart; in the feed tray were a hundred or so papers of heroin wrapped like headache powders, and in the brass ball atop the cage there were still more. The discovery did not seem to irritate the ladies at all; it was the loss of their parrot that upset them. For all at once it had flown out the lowered window, and the desperate ladies stood calling after it, "Tokyo, you will freeze, little Tokyo, come back! Come back!"

He was laughing somewhere in the dark. There was a cold Northern moon, and for an instant we saw him flying flat and dark against its brilliance. They turned then and faced the door; it was crowded now with onlookers. Poised, disdainful, the ladies stepped forward to meet faces they seemed not to see, and voices they certainly never heard.

ISCHIA

(1949)

I forget why we came here: Ischia. It was being very much talked about, though few people seemed actually to have seen it—except, perhaps, as a jagged blue shadow glimpsed across the water from the heights of its celebrated neighbor, Capri. Some people advised against Ischia and, as I remember, they gave rather spooky reasons: You realize that there is an active volcano? And do you know about the plane? A plane, flying a regular flight between Cairo and Rome, crashed on top an Ischian mountain; there were three survivors, but no one ever saw them alive, for they were stoned to death by goatherds intent on looting the wreckage.

Consequently, we watched the chalky façade of Naples fade with mixed anticipation. It was a classic day, a little cold for southern Italy in March, but crisp and lofty as a kite, and the *Princepessa* spanked across the bay like a sassy dolphin. It is a small civilized boat with a tiny bar and a somewhat outré clientele: convicts on their way to the prison island of Procida or, at the opposite extreme, young men about to enter the monastery on Ischia. Of course, there are less dramatic passengers: islanders who have been shopping in Naples; here and there a foreigner—extraordinarily few, however: Capri is the tourist catch-all.

Islands are like ships at permanent anchor. To set foot on one is like starting up a gangplank: one is seized by the same feeling of charmed suspension—it seems nothing unkind or vulgar can happen to you; and as the *Princepessa* eased into the covelike harbor of Porto d'Ischia it seemed, seeing the pale, peeling ice-cream colors of the waterfront, as intimate and satisfying as one's own heartbeat. In the wrangle of disembarking, I dropped and broke my watch—an outrageous bit of symbolism, too pointed: at a glance it was plain that Ischia was no place for the rush of hours, islands never are.

I suppose you might say that Porto is the capital of Ischia; at any rate, it is the largest town and even rather fashionable. Most people who visit the island seldom stray from there, for there are several superior hotels, excellent beaches and, perched in the offing like a giant hawk, the Renaissance castle of Vittoria Colonna. The three other fair-sized towns are more rugged. These are: Lacco Ameno, Cassamiciola and, at the farthest end of the island, Forio. It was in Forio that we planned to settle.

We drove there through a green twilight and under a sky of early stars. The road passed high above the sea, where fishing boats, lighted with torches, crawled below like brilliant water-spiders. Furry little bats skimmed in the dusk; *buena séra, buena séra* [good evening, good evening], dim evening voices called along the way, and herds of goats, jogging up the hills, bleated like rusty flutes; the carriage spun through a village square—there was no electricity, and in the cafés the tricky light of candles and kerosene lamps smoked the faces of masculine company.

Two children chased after us into the darkness beyond the village. They clung panting to the carriage as we began a steep careening climb, and our horse, nearing the crest, breathed back on the chilled air a stream of mist. The driver flecked his whip, the horse swayed, the children pointed: look. It was there, Forio, distant, moon-white, the sea simmering at its edges, a faint sound of vesper bells rising off it like a whirl of birds. *Multo bella?* said the driver. *Multo bella* [very beautiful]? said the children.

When one rereads a journal it is usually the less ambitious jottings, the haphazard, accidental notations that, seen again, plow a furrow through your memory. For example: "Today Gioconda left in the room assorted slips of colored paper. Are they presents? Because I gave her the bottle of cologne? They will make delightful bookmarks." This reverberates. First, Gioconda. She is a beautiful girl, though her beauty depends upon her mood: when she is feeling glum, and this seems too often the case, she looks like a bowl of cold oatmeal; you are likely to forget the richness of her hair and the mildness of her Mediterranean eyes. Heaven knows, she is overworked: here at the *pensione,* where she is both chambermaid and waitress, she gets up before dawn and is kept on the run sometimes until midnight. To be truthful, she is lucky to have the job, for employment is the island's major problem; most girls here would like nothing better than to supplant her. Considering that there is no running water (with all that that implies), Gioconda makes us remarkably comfortable. It is the pleasantest *pensione* in Forio, an interesting bargain, too: we have two huge rooms with great expanses of tiled floor and tall shutter-doors which lead onto little iron balconies overlooking the sea; the food is good, and there is rather too much of it—five courses with wine at lunch and dinner. All included, this costs each of us about one hundred dollars a month. Gioconda speaks no English, and my Italian is—well, never mind. Nevertheless, we are confidantes. With pantomime and extravagant use of a bilingual dictionary we manage to convey an astonishing lot—which is why the cakes are always a flop: on gloomy days when there is nothing else to do we sit in the patio-kitchen experimenting with recipes for American pastries ("Toll House, what is?"), but these are never a success because we are too busy thumbing through the dictionary to give our baking much attention. Gioconda: "Last year, in the room where you are, there was a man from Rome. Is Rome like he said, so wonderful? He said I should come and visit him in Rome, and that it would be all right because he was a veteran of three wars. First World War, Second, and Ethiopia. You can see how old he was. No, I have never seen Rome. I have friends who have been there, and who have sent me postcards. You know the woman who works at the *posta?* Of course you believe in the evil eye? She has one. It is known, yes. That is why my letter never comes from Argentina."

Not receiving this Argentine letter is the real cause of Gioconda's misery. A faithless lover? I have no idea; she refuses to discuss it. So many young Italians have migrated to South America looking for work; there are wives here who have waited five years for their husbands to send them passage. Each day, when I come bringing the mail, Gioconda rushes to meet me.

Collecting the mail is a self-appointed chore. It is the first time during the day that I see the other Americans living here: there are four at the moment and we meet at Maria's café in the piazza (from the journal: "We all know that Maria waters her drinks. But does she water them with water? God, I feel awful!"). With the sun warming you, and Maria's bamboo curtains tinkling in the breeze, there is no nicer place to wait for the postman. Maria is a sawed-off woman with a gypsy face and a shrugging, cynical nature; if there is anything you want around here, from a house to a package of American cigarettes, she can arrange it; some people claim she is the richest person in Forio. There are never any women in her café; I doubt that she would allow it. As noon heightens, the village converges in the piazza: like blackbirds schoolchildren in capes and wooden sandals flock and sing in the alleys, and squadrons of unemployed men lounge under the trees laughing roughly—women passing them lower their eyes. When the mailman comes he gives me the letters for our *pensione;* then I must go down the hill to face Gioconda. Sometimes she looks at me as though it were my fault that the letter never comes, as though the evil eye were mine. One day she warned me not to come home empty-handed; and so I brought her a bottle of cologne.

But the slips of gaudy paper that I found in my room were not, as I had supposed, a present in return. It was intended that we should shower these upon a statue of the Virgin which, newly arrived on the island, was being toured through most of the villages. The day the Virgin was to visit here every balcony was draped with fine laces, finer linens —an old bedspread if the family had nothing better; woven flowers garlanded the cramped streets, old ladies brought out their longest shawls, men combed their mustaches, someone put the town idiot into a clean shirt, and the children, dressed all in white, had angel-wings of golden cardboard strapped to their shoulders. The procession was supposed to enter town and pass below our balcony at about four o'clock.

Alerted by Gioconda, we were at our station on time, ready to throw the pretty papers and shout, as instructed, *"Viva La Vergenie Immocalata."* A drizzling dull rain began; at six it was getting dark, but like the street-tightening crowd that waited below, we remained steadfast. A priest, scowling with annoyance, and his black skirts flapping, roared off on a motorcycle—he'd been sent to hurry along the procession. It was night, then, and a flare-path of kerosene was spilled along the route the procession was to follow. Suddenly, incongruously, the stirring *ratata* of a military band sounded and, with a scary crackle, the flare-path leapt alive as if to salute the arriving Virgin: swaying on a flower-filled litter, Her face shrouded in a black veil, and followed by half the island, she was laden with gold and silver watches, and as she passed, a hush surrounding her immediate presence, there was only the enchanting, surrealistic noise of these offerings, the watches: *tickticktick.* Later, Gioconda was very put out to discover us still clutching the bits of bright paper which in our excitement we'd forgotten to throw.

"April 5. A long, perilous walk. We discovered a new beach." Ischia is stony, a stark island that suggests Greece or the coast of Africa. There are orange trees, lemon trees and, terracing the mountains, silvery-green grape arbors: the wine of Ischia is highly considered, and it is here that they make Lachrimae Christi. When you walk beyond the town you soon come upon the branching paths that climb through the grape fields where bees are like a blizzard and lizards burn greenly on the budding leaves. The peasants are brown and thick as earthenware, and they are horizon-eyed, like sailors. For the sea is always with them. The path by the sea runs along straight-dropping volcanic cliffs; there are junctures when it is best just to close your eyes: it would make a long fall, and the rocks below are like sleeping dinosaurs. One day, walking on the cliffs, we found a poppy, then another; they were growing singly among the somber stones, like Chinese bells strung on a stretching string. Presently the trail of poppies led us down a path to a strange and hidden beach. It was enclosed by the cliffs, and the water was so clear you could observe sea-flowers and the dagger movements of fish; not far from shore, flat, exposed rocks were like swimming rafts, and we paddled from one to another: hauling ourselves into the sun, we could look back above the cliffs and see the green grape terraces and a cloudy mountain. Into one rock the sea had carved a chair, and it was the greatest pleasure to sit there and let the waves rush up and over you.

But it is not hard to find a private beach on Ischia. I know of at least three that no one ever goes to. The town beach in Forio is strewn with fishing nets and overturned boats. It was on this beach that I first encountered the Mussolini family. The late dictator's widow and three of their children live here in what I presume to be a quiet self-imposed exile. Something about them is sad and sympathetic. The daughter is young, blond, lame and apparently witty: the local boys who talk with her on the beach seem always to be laughing. Like any of the island's plain women, Signora Mussolini is often to be seen dressed in shabby black and trudging up a hill with the weight of a shopping bag lopsiding her figure. She is quite expressionless, but once I saw her smile. There was a man passing through town with a parrot who plucked printed fortunes out of a glass jar, and Signora Mussolini, pausing to consult him, read her future with a shadowy, Da Vincian curling of her lips.

"June 5. The afternoon is a white midnight." Now that hot weather is here the afternoons are like white midnights; shutters are drawn, sleep stalks the streets. At five the shops will open again, a crowd will gather in the harbor to welcome the *Princepessa,* and later everyone will promenade in the piazza, where someone will be playing a banjo, a harmonica, a guitar. But now it is siesta, and there is only the blue unbroken sky, the crowing of a cock. There are two idiots in the town, and they are friends. One is always carrying a bouquet of flowers which, when he meets his friend, he divides into equal parts. In the silent shadowless afternoons they alone are seen in the streets. Hand in hand, and holding their flowers, they stroll across the beach and out along the stone wall that juts far into the water. From my balcony I can see them there, sitting among the fishnets and the slowly rocking boats, their shaved heads glinting in the sun, their eyes pale as space. The white midnight is meant for them; it is then that the island is theirs.

We have followed spring. In the four months since we came here the nights have warmed, the sea has grown softer, the green, still wintry water of March has turned in June to blue, and the grape vines, once gray and barren on their twisting stalks, are fat with their first green bunches. There is a hatching of butterflies, and on the mountain there are many sweet things for the bees; in the garden, after a rainfall, you can faintly, yes, hear the breaking of new blooms. And we are waking earlier, a sign of summer, and stay lingering out late in the evening, which is a sign, too. But it is hard to bring yourself indoors these nights: the moon is drawing nearer, it winks on the water with a frightful brightness; and on the parapet of the fishermen's church, which points to sea like the prow of a ship, the young whispering people wander back and forth and through the piazza and into some secret dark. Gioconda says it has been the longest spring she can remember: the longest is the loveliest.

JAN MORRIS
1926–

Formerly James Humphry Morris, Jan Morris was born in Clevedon, Somerset, England, and educated at Christ Church, Oxford. Always adventurous, he became famous at the age of twenty-seven when as a reporter for the London Times *he accompanied the 1953 Mt. Everest Expedition to the 22,000-foot level and set up a communications system there that enabled him to scoop the world with news of Hillary's and Tenzing's achievement.*

During World War II he served as a lieutenant in the Ninth Lancers of the British army, and afterwards he traveled the world reporting on wars and revolutions, wrote many travel books, and became one of Britain's leading journalists and popular historians. Among Jan Morris's books are As I Saw the U.S.A. *(1956),* Islam Inflamed: The Middle East Picture *(1957),* Coronation Everest *(1958),* South African Winter *(1958),* The World of Venice *(1960),* South America *(1961),* The Road to Huddersfield: A Journey to Five Continents *(1963),* Places *(1972),* Travels *(1974),* Journeys *(1984), and an esteemed trilogy constituting a history of British imperialism (1968–1978).*

During the 1960s Morris's friends noticed in him an urge toward cross-dressing and a fondness for feminine gestures and mannerisms. In 1972 James had his gender changed by surgery and became Jan, a transformation she described in her memoir Conundrum *(1972). Although as a travel writer she can be tough when necessary, there seems something feminine (in the old-fashioned sense) in the "niceness" of her vision.*

From PLACES

(1972)

KASHMIR

It was in Kashmir, late in travel and half-way through life, that I first went transcendental. Reality seems distinctly relative in that high and timeless vale, truth bends, distance is imprecise, and even the calendar seems to swing indeterminately by, week blurred into week and Friday arriving unannounced upon the heels of Sunday night.

For my first few days I stuck to the facts, but ever less tenaciously. Nobody else seemed to find it necessary. No decision seemed sacrosanct there, and life was apparently suspended in some limbo between events. I lived myself on a lake of no particular shape or exact location, linked by meandering reedy waterways to a fifteenth-century city down the valley. It took me an hour to get to town, reclining full-length in the cushioned recesses of a boat, while the paddle-man behind me sang high-pitched melodies to himself, took occasional gurgles at a water-pipe, and drank green tea with salt in it. Sometimes I stopped to make an improbable purchase—a jade bangle, a duck for dinner, a chunk of honey off the comb. Sometimes perfect strangers asked me how old my watch was, or told me about their forthcoming examinations in elementary economics. Sometimes, having spent the whole day maundering about the city, I returned to my lake late in the evening with not the slightest recollection of anything specific having happened to me at all.

So in the end I emancipated myself, and soared unimpeded beyond actuality, seldom quite sure where I was, or when, or even sometimes who—answering all questions with abandoned fancy, never seeking a reason or providing a cause. I felt myself disembodied between the green-blue lake and the snow mountains all around, in a gentle Nirvana of my own: nowhere existed, it seemed to me, beyond the celestial vale of Kashmir, and whether the vale existed itself was a matter of individual perception.

I was not the first to enter this airy plane of sensibility. Kashmir has been having such an effect upon its visitors for at least 400 years. The Moghul emperors, who conquered it in the sixteenth century, responded to the vale with a sensual passion, embellishing it with seductive gardens and honouring it with royal dalliances. The British, who became its suzerains in the 1840s, thought it the ultimate retreat from the burdens of empire, and took its magic home with them to the strains of *Pale Hands I Loved, Beside the Shalimar.* Today's wandering hippies find themselves rootlessly at ease there, and Middle Americans who spend a couple of Kashmir days between Treetops and Hong Kong often feel the interlude to have been an insubstantial dream.

Kashmir has always been more than a mere place. It has the quality of an experience, or a state of mind, or perhaps an ideal. The Muslim sectarians called the Ahmadiya believe that Christ did not die upon the Cross, but was spirited away to Kashmir, the last haven of perfection: and the Moghul emperor Jehangir expressed the wish on his deathbed that Kashmir and Paradise would turn out to be, as he had always thought, one and the same place.

In my more lucid moments, I must here interject, I did not *altogether* agree with the Emperor. Looked at hard and realistically, Kashmir falls short of Elysium. Situated as it is high in central Asia, north of Tibet, squeezed between Russia, China and Afghanistan, it can hardly escape the world's contagion. Beside the golf course at Srinagar, Kashmir's capital, one often sees the waiting white cars of the United Nations, chauffeurs patient at the wheel: and there are soldiers about always, and angry politicians, and students with grievances, and unpersuadable men of religion. Kashmir is one of the world's perennial trouble-spots. Though its people are mostly Muslims, it was ruled until 1947, under the aegis of the British, by a Hindu dynasty of Maharajas: since then it has been disputed by India and Pakistan. The whole of the vale of Kashmir falls within Indian territory, but sizeable chunks of the outer state are governed by Pakistan, and legal sovereignty of the whole has never been decided. Kashmir is one of those places, deposited here and there in awkward corners of the earth, that never seem quite settled: a bazaar rumour kind of place, a U.N. resolution place, a place that nags the lesser headlines down the years, like a family argument never finally resolved.

Besides, in my Paradise nobody will be poor: most of the inhabitants of Kashmir are very poor indeed. My Paradise will always be merry: Kashmir is infused with a haunting melancholy. In my Paradise there will be no tourist touts, sharks or hawkers: Kashmir, for more than a century one of the great tourist destinations of the earth, boasts the most charmless touts and indefatigable hagglers in Asia. In my Paradise château-bottled burgundy will flow like water: in Kashmir all but the most extravagant of Moghuls must make do with Indian Golconda, sixteen rupees a half-bottle from the vineyards of Hyderabad.

Where was I? Drifting, that's right, all but motionless across a Kashmiri lake, preferably in a shikara. A shikara is a distant relative of the gondola, canopied, low in the water, looking rather sternheavy and propelled by that boatman with the water-pipe, squatting at the stern.

From *outside* a shikara looks like a fairground novelty, brightly coloured and curtained, and generally full of gregarious Indian youths waving and crying "Hi!," wrongly supposing you to be a research student in comparative ethnology from the University of South Utah. *Inside* the shikara feels a very different vehicle—like a floating capsule or divan, exquisitely cushioned, moving urgently through the water-lilies towards pleasure-gardens and picnics.

Though the vale of Kashmir is 800 miles from the sea, and surrounded on all sides by immense mountains, still its prime and symbolic element is water. The Kashmir thing is essentially a rippling, liquid kind of happening. Geologists say the whole valley was once a lake, and a string of lesser lakes ornaments it still. Srinagar stands in the middle of four, and is criss-crossed too by ancient canals, and intersected by the great river Jhelum. Boats are inescapable in the capital: boats grand or squalid, spanking or derelict; boats thatched, shingled, poled, engined; boats deep with fruit, nuts, timbers, furs, livestock; barges, and punts, and canoes, and skiffs, and elderly motor-boat taxis; above all those floating figures of the Kashmir scene, those vessels of fragrant legend, houseboats.

Kashmiris have always used houseboats of a kind—straw-thatched craft like arks, chock-a-block with cooking-pots, washing-lines and chicken-coops, leaking wood-smoke from their every crack and often ominously clamped together with iron struts. It was the British, though, in the heyday of Empire, who devised the standard Kashmiri houseboat of the love lyrics and the tourist brochures—what one might call the Pale Hands Houseboat. Sensibly denied the right to acquire land in the valley, they took to the water instead, and evolved their own kind of pleasure-craft. I suspect they based it upon the barges which used to form the club-house of Oxford rowing-clubs—themselves developed from the ceremonial guild barges that once conveyed London aldermen up and down the Thames from board meeting to turtle soup.

The Kashmir version has come to be a sort of chalet-boat, or water-villa. It is often gabled, and shingle-roofed. There is a sun-deck on top, with an awning, and the poop is comfortably cushioned, and has steps down to the water. The boat is generally fitted in a Victorian mode: heavy dark furniture, baths with claw feet, antimacassars very likely, hot water bottles for sure. Each houseboat has its own kitchen-boat moored astern, and its attendant shikara alongside, and its staff of resident servants, and its own special smell of cedar-wood, curry, roses and in-grained cigar-smoke: and living upon such a vessel, moored beside the orchard-bank of Nagin Lake, or lying all among the willows of a Srinagar canal, very soon one finds reality fading. The lap of the water takes over, the quacking of the ducks in the dawn, the hazed blue smoke loitering from the cookboat, the soft water-light, the glitter of the dewdrop in the water-lily leaf, the flick of the little fish in the clear blue water, the dim purplish presence of the mountain beyond the lake, fringed with a line of distant snow.

Time expands in such a setting, and loses its compulsion. The hours dawdle by, as the bearer brings you your coffee on the sun-deck, and the shikara man lies on his own cushions awaiting your instructions, and the peripatetic trading boats sidle into your line of vision—"You like to see my jewelry, madam? Any chocolates, cigarettes, shampoo? You want a very nice suede coat, sir, half the price of Savile Row? Flowers, mem-sahib? Haircut? Fur hat? Laundry?" Nothing very particular occurs. A meal comes when you want it. The shikara is always there. The ducks quack. If one considers the matter carefully one finds that the sun rises and sets, and some time between tea and sundowner it does begin to get dark.

Scale, on the other hand, contracts. The focus narrows, within the frame of the Kashmir water-life. The picture gets clearer, more exact, and one finds oneself concentrating upon minutiae, like the number of leaves upon the plucked waterweed, or the twitchy movements of the kingfishers. I took Jane Austen's novels with me to the vale of Kashmir, and perfectly with this delicate awareness of the place did her quill dramas and porcelain comedies correspond.

Sometimes, as I say, I was swishily paddled into town. Then through lily-thick channels we proceeded, willows above us, green fields and apple orchards all around, and as we approached the city the texture of life thickened about us. Barge-loads of cattle glided by to market. Infants sploshed about in half-submerged canoes. Women in trailing kerchiefs, neatly folded about the head, cooked in shanty-boats or washed their clothes at water-steps. Solitary fishermen cast their nets in the shallows: sometimes a man paddled an empty punt along, sitting cross-legged and gnomish in the prow. We passed beneath medieval bridges trembling with traffic, and beside tall houses latticed and mysterious, and past open-fronted waterside stores where merchants sat grandly upon divans, smoking hubble-bubbles and bowing condescendingly in one's direction. We paddled our way, like an admiral's yacht at a review, through flotillas of houseboats—*Young Good Luck, Winston, Kashmir Fun*—all appar-ently De Luxe With Sanitation, some with tourists jolly on the poop, some all dank and deserted, like funeral boats between rituals.

And presently we found ourselves upon the muddy water of the Jhelum itself, with its parade of old bridges (Zero Bridge to Eighth

Bridge) and the brown jumble of Srinagar all around: distractedly I would disembark to loiter through the labyrinth of the bazaars—pursued by suggestions proper and profane, and seldom knowing where I was going. Though Srinagar is only seventy minutes from Delhi by daily jet, yet it is a frontier town of Central Asia. Here since the start of history the caravans from Sinkiang or Kazakhstan rested on their way to India, and these tangled suks are more like Turkestan than Bengal. Here one feels close to the Uzbegs, the Kurds, the Mongols, the merchants of Tashkent or Bokhara: and often one sees exotic figures from the remotest north swinging through the bazaars, in goat-skin cloaks and fur hats, to remind one of the grand mysteries, Pamir and Hindu Kush, which stand at the head of the valley.

Srinagar has its westernized quarters, of course. It has a golf course, and a grand hotel that was once the Maharaja's palace, and a slightly less grand hotel that the British used to frequent, and a bank with a genuine Scottish manager in an Edwardian villa above the river, and a pleasant waterside esplanade called the Bund, and a Club, and heaps of tourist shops, and a Government Emporium of Kashmiri Crafts—carpets, woodwork, paper mâché, jewelry. There are a couple of cinemas in town, and there is a brand-new Anglican church, the old one having been burnt down in 1967 in a fairly obscure protest, it seems to me, against the Six Day War.

But downstream from this enclave, strewn around and within the bends of the Jhelum, medieval Srinagar magnificently survives. No addict of the mouldering picturesque could complain about these bazaars. They possess all the classic prerequisites of oriental allure—spiced smells, impenetrable alleys, veiled women, goldsmiths, mosques, sages, dwarfs. The air of old Srinagar is heavy with suggestion, not too closely to be analyzed; and its lanes are so crowded with shrouded and turbanned personages, so opaque with dust and smoke and vegetable particles, that invariably I lost my bearings in them, and wandering fruitlessly among the temples and the cloth merchants, over the Third Bridge and back past the tomb of Zain-el-Abdin, at last I used to clamber into a tonga, and went clipclop back, to the flick of the whip and the smell of horse-sweat, to my patiently waiting shikara at the Dal Gate. 'Houseboat now?' the shikara man would murmur; and back to the lake I would be unnoticeably propelled, eating walnuts all the way.

Yet it has not been an exhilarating progress. The eye of Kashmir is a brooding, almost a baleful, eye—the eye of the shopkeeper, calculating above his wares, the eye of the military policeman on his trafficstand, the eye of the floating trader, peering ever and again through the houseboat window in search of victims within. The movement of Kashmir is grave and measured, and even the humour of the valley has an enigmatic heaviness, revealingly expressed in shops that call themselves The Worst, or Holy Moses.

The Kashmiris are a hospitable people, but not inspiriting. They seem to be considering always the possibilities of misfortune. In the autumn especially, a lovely season in the valley, the fall of the leaf seems a personal affliction to them, and the passing of the year depresses them like a fading of their own powers. Then in the chill evenings the women disappear to private quarters behind, and the men light their little baskets of charcoal, tuck them under their fustian cloaks and squat morosely in the twilight, their unshaven faces displaying a faint but telling disquiet. "Come in, come in," they murmur, "come and join us, you are welcome, sit down, sit down!"—but for myself I generally evaded their sad hospitality, preferring Miss Austen's gaiety on the poop.

Yet I was half-ashamed as I did so, for their kindness is very real, and all the truer for its reticence—a flick of the head to disclaim gratitude, a discreetly forgotten bill, an unexpected appearance at the airport just when you most need someone to hold the typewriter while you fumble for the porter's tip. There was a touching pathos, I thought, to the Kashmiri style. "How do you like your life?" I asked one new acquaintance there, when we had progressed into intimacy. "Excellent," he replied with a look of inexpressible regret, "I love every minute of it"—and he withdrew a cold hand from the recesses of his cloak, and waved it listlessly in the air to illustrate his enjoyment.

The vale of Kashmir is like a fourth dimension—outside the ordinary shape of things. About 100 miles long by twenty miles wide, it is entirely enclosed by mountains of great height and splendour—a green scoop in the Himalayan massif, hidden away among the snow-ranges, desperately inaccessible until the coming of aircraft, and still magically remote in sensation. The Moghuls, on their holiday progressions to Srinagar, used to climb with convoys of camels and elephants over the southern ridges from Delhi. The British generally came on horseback or in coolie litters over the hill-tracks from the west. Even today, as you fly effortlessly in from the south, the impact of the valley is strangely exciting, as you cross the ramparts of the mountains and see its lakes, its orchards, its great plane trees richly unfolded there below. It is not exactly an escape—one does not escape into an enclave. It is a mood of transference or even apotheosis: a trip without drugs, a pot-less ecstasy.

Kashmir does bear some paradoxical resemblances to other places far away. The country villages with their thatched tall farmsteads, their coveys of plump ducks, geese and chickens, their grain-stores and their woodpiles, look like villages of eastern Europe. The side-valleys of the mountains, down whose lanes cloaked herdsmen drive their sheep, goats and ponies in scrambled majesty to the lowlands, remind me very much of Persia. The waterways of Srinagar suggest to every visitor some less gilded Venice; the evening cry of the muezzin, echoing across the lake at dusk, is an echo of Arabia; for four or five generations every Oxford heart has responded to the willow-meadows of Kashmir, so like the banks of Isis that one can almost hear the cricket-balls and transistor radios of *alma mater.*

But these details of the familiar only intensify the oddity of the whole. There is really nowhere like Kashmir. There are no gardens so voluptuous as the great Moghul gardens around Dal Lake—Shalimar and Nishat, Cashma Shahi and Nazim Bagh—intoxicating blends of the formal and the unassuming, grand with terraces and cool with fountains and sweet with roses, with splendid pavilions at the water's edge, and glorious towering trees. There are no ruins so unexpected as the ancient temples of Kashmir, dotted around the valley in astonishing neo-classical elegance—Greek in their grace, Egyptian in their grandeur, uniquely Kashmiri in their flavour. I know of no crop so startling as the saffron crop of Kashmir—acres of purple crocus-like flowers lavishly splashed like mad paintwork across the valley. I know no holy place more disconcerting than the Hindu shrine of Mattan, where hundreds of thousands of sacred carp thresh their lives away in horribly congested pools, jammed tight together in a seething fishy mass. And I shall never forget the wayside stall, north of Srinagar, where I stopped one day to buy something for my supper: it was piled high with the weirdest variety of game-birds I ever saw—ducks of all colours, huge wild geese, black straggly moorhens, and most authentically Kashmiri of all, I thought, a solitary grey heron all folded inside itself, its neck tucked beneath its belly, its legs crumpled below its rump. (No rooks? I asked. No rooks: the Koran forbade it.)

For the ultimate aloofness of Kashmir the traveller must climb to the rim of the valley, to the high alpine meadows of Gulmarg or Pahalgam. There the separateness of the place achieves a disembodied quality, and the whole valley seems to be resting in some high cradle among the clouds, supported by the snow-peaks all around. You have to walk to attain this mystic detachment—away from the little chalet-hotels and bazaars of the resorts, up through the silent pine woods, along the banks of slate-grey trout streams, up through the last crude huts of the highland shepherds, beyond the tree line, over the granite scree until you stand among the snows themselves, on the rampart ridge.

Often the vale below is half-veiled by cloud, and one sees only a green patch here and there, or a suggestion of water: but all around the white mountains stand, holding Kashmir on their hips—peak after peak, ridge after ridge, with Nangar Parbat supreme on the northern flank to set the scale of them all. Kashmir is, as I say, a place like no other: yet even from such a vantage point, high up there in the snow and the sun, its character is curiously negative. It could not possibly be anywhere else: but it might, so it often seemed to me in the hush of those high places, be nowhere at all.

One can judge it only by itself. The fascination of Kashmir is essentially introspective, a mirror-pleasure in which the visitor may see his own self picturesquely reflected, adrift in his shikara among the blossoms and the kingfishers. It is no place for comparisons. Paradise, here as everywhere, is in the mind.

From JOURNEYS
(1984)

NOT SO FAR

A EUROPEAN JOURNEY

The farm dog leapt from the gate and snapped enthusiastically at my hub caps. Somebody waved goodbye, teacup in hand, from the Parrys' front window. I met the postman in his van halfway up the lane, and through his window he passed me an electricity bill, a notice about next week's bring-and-buy sale at the village hall, and three chances to win £50,000 in a Reader's Digest Prize Draw. There was snow on the high summit of Moel Hebog, the hefty bald mountain in front of me; behind my back the Irish Sea lay silent beneath a cold and western sheen.

I was leaving on a European journey: from this far Welsh corner of the continent, looking across to Ireland, to Montenegro on the other side of it, looking down to Albania. I was about to cross, not just a geographical conglomeration, or a historical expression, but a civilization: between these two extremes some 200 million people, whether they admit it or not, live to a common heritage and a more or less common set of values. This is the ghost of the Roman Empire, still perceptible after so many centuries of exorcism: if the Irish in the West never were subject to the Roman order, and have consequentially lived in tumultuous distemper ever since, the Albanians in the East have long disowned the patrimony, and live in a state of chill and utter isolation, the only people on earth among whom all forms of religion are strictly prohibited.

The rest of us along the route, Welsh, English, French, Italian, Swiss, Yugoslavs, are members really, for all our political styles, of the same spectral commonwealth. The great motorways which now criss-cross all Europe are only late successors to the high roads of the legions. The gradual weakening of nationality in western Europe, the blurring of frontiers, the mixing of languages, even the universal acceptance of bank and credit cards, which means I could really travel from Caernarfon to Cetinje without a solid penny in my pocket—all these phenomena of the 1980s are only returns to the imperial conveniences of Rome.

So I hardly felt I was going abroad, when I hit the main Dolgellau road and headed for England and the southeast: for most Europeans nowadays abroad is somewhere else altogether—east of Suez, say, south of the Equator, Ireland or Albania. "Going far, then?" inquired the garage-man, when I stopped to fill up. "Montenegro," I said, but he was not in the least surprised. "Oh yes," he said. "The wife and I had a nice little holiday at Petrovac a year or two back. Check your oil, shall I?"

It is as though the British Isles are tilted permanently to one corner—the southeast corner, bottom right, where London stands seething upon the Thames. Everything slithers and tumbles down there, all the talent, all the money, and when I got on to the M4 motorway that morning I felt that I was being swept away helter-skelter, willy-nilly across the breadth of England. Around me all the energies of the place seemed to be heading in a single direction—the trucks from Cornwall and South Wales, the tourist buses, the ramshackle No Nuclear estate cars, the stream of expense-account Fords, their salesmen drivers tapping their steering-wheels to the rhythm of Radio One. London! London! shouted the direction signs. London! screamed the blue and white train, streaking eastwards beside the road, and when I turned off to the south and made for Dover, still I felt the presence of the capital tugging away at me, as it tugs the commuters from their mock-Tudor villas day after day from the far reaches of Surrey and pastoral Hampshire.

Mrs. Thatcher's Britain is an uneasy kingdom, a kingdom of anomalies. It is poor but it is rich. It is weak but it is resilient. It is very clever in some ways, thick as mutton in others. It wins more Nobel Prizes per capita than any other nation, yet it can hardly keep its head above bankruptcy. It is socially at loggerheads with itself, but is united in a sentimental passion for the charade of monarchy. Even the sensations of a motorway drive like ours are muddled and puzzling, as we pass out of the poor wild mountains of Wales, where there are far more sheep than humans, so swiftly into the most thickly populated and intensely developed landscape in Europe. The road is bumpy and often interrupted by desultory road works, there being not enough money to maintain it properly: yet beside it the lovely manor houses stand serene as ever in their old walled gardens, the villages cluster cosily around, the cows are plump, the meadowlands green and rich. The mid-day radio news speaks of more education cuts, rising unemployment, falling production, protest marches, civil servants' strikes: but all around us the cars of the indigent British, most of them imported, hasten eastwards at the statutory 70 m.p.h. on gasoline at £1.81 a gallon.

And the queerest anomaly of all is the condition of the southeast, the flatlands in fief to London, for there all the middle-class values, surviving everything that socialism has tried to do to them, complacently flourish through crisis and decline. By afternoon I was entering that cosy never-never land, and it was like entering an imaginary England, in an old movie or a rather dated novel. Glossy and mullion-windowed stood the commuter houses behind their privet hedges and ornamental gates, and there were boats on trailers beside their garages, and horse-boxes often, and girls in jodhpurs trundled about on ponies, talking in such well-enunciated voices that I could hear, or at least vividly imagine, snatches of their conversations through my open roof—"Absolutely super food . . ." "He's an absolute twit . . ." or "God, Jennifer, I do believe this bloody muffle's breaking again. . . ."

Ample dormitory-towns stood all along my route, Haslemere and Guildford, Dorking and Leatherhead: ageless comfortable towns, medieval merged with modern, chain supermarket beside old family grocer, Sew-'n'-Knit or Pots & Things cheek by jowl with Edward H. Rigby, Ironmongers since 1767—smug, fancy little towns with bulging car-parks and gilded municipal clocks, with pleasure-boats lined up for hire on willow-shaded streams, with well-built women wearing headscarves and pushing shopping-baskets on wheels, with Olde Englyshe Tea Rooms and grand half-timbered coaching-inns advertising Real Ales and Scampi-in-the-Basket.

No slums, no rotting factories, no lines of bitter unemployed. This is true Thatcher country. The rotten teeth of Britain are elsewhere—here are only the satisfied digestive juices. You will hear no raw or earthy dialects down here: this is the home of standard English, BBC English, and the accents of the countryside have long since been poshed up or homogenized—even the countryside itself, indeed, for though there are patches of fine green farmland between the towns, it never breaks away altogether from the urban pull, but is like some intermittent park or genteel garden, worked perhaps by business people as a week-end recreation.

It is a pleasant and fortunate country, but it never chills the spine or raises the heart. It is Lotus Land Class Two. But by tea-time anyway I had broken away from it into the open Kentish grasslands, and before it was dark I was running down the cliffside road to Dover beneath its glowering castle, a town all bashed about by wars and history, a town without illusions, not a Lotus-town at all, which inspects my passport with a sneer and shoves me unceremoniously, as if glad to get rid of me, on board a boat for France.

* * *

A boat for France! There is always a boat for France. Night and day for a thousand years or more, if you turn up at Dover you will find a boat for France. The English Channel here is the busiest waterway on earth, and in the high summer season there is a car-ferry out of Dover every ten minutes. Whenever I looked out of the *Free Enterprise*'s windows, as dusk fell over the sea, somewhere out there another ferry was stubbing its bows into the swell: and once I saw, a weird black shape halfhidden by flying spray, the whirring scudding passage of a hovercraft in the grey.

The car was clamped below decks, towered over by the mighty juggernaut trucks, German, Dutch, French, British, Italian, even Bulgarian or Rumanian, which are the colorful familiars of modern Europe. Upstairs the ship had apparently been hijacked by demoniac schoolchildren. They clustered in mobs around the Space Invaders machine. They stormed the souvenir shop. They experimented with foreign currencies in the coffee machine. They tripped up passing stewards. They shouted hilarious insults at each other. They lurched in screaming phalanxes up and down stairs.

Some were British, some French, some Italian, some Finnish for all I know, but physically they were indistinguishable. As we approached the French coast they were marshalled into some sort of discipline by pimply bearded schoolteachers, and I left them standing there waiting for the gangplank to go down in a condition of sullen suppression, interspersed now and then with giggles and belches. Their teachers surveyed them with distaste. A few elderly tourists stood warily around their flanks. The ship docked with a bit of a bump, and faintly above the roar of the starting engines, from far below on the car deck, I heard their eldritch shrieks.

* * *

Years ago the scholar D. W. Brogan warned us that we were about to see a new marvel: a young France, which had not existed since the nineteenth century, before the double decimation of the two World Wars. Well, now we have it, and among all the countries of western Europe, none has changed so fast or so dramatically as France. The French police did not bother to inspect my passport, as I drove ashore at Calais. They are not in the mood for trivia these days. If individually the French are as pesky, as charming, as irreverent, as bloody-minded, as profoundly conservative as ever, corporately they have become forceful and rather flashy. The momentum of Autoroute N_1 towards Paris is twice as powerful as the movement of the M_4 towards London, and this is not only because the speed limit is higher, but because the drivers are more demanding, more exhibitionist and more opportunist, and because Paris is not just the capital of a State but the true hub of the Continent. If the energies of Britain slide down to London as though the country is tilted that way, the traffic from Belgium, Germany, Holland, Sweden even, presses down the Autoroute towards Paris with an eager expectancy.

Everything seems to be brand new on this steely thoroughfare. The road itself is newish, a product of France's "Economic Miracle," the cars are new, the signs are new, and every town we pass is clumped about by brand-new concrete blocks, relentlessly French and functional. When I stop for a cup of coffee, all in the café is automated: the coffee churns from electronic urns, the rolls and croissants are stacked in their identical thousands, all is wink of control light and bleep of computerized till. France is young again. The middle-aged truck-driver standing beside me at the plastic-covered chairless table munches his hamburger with a faraway look, gazing out through the automatic doors as if he sees out there, away beyond the Autoroute, dim visions of soup tureens, checked tablecloths and bombazine.

He is going to have to live, though, with the plastic table and the hamburger. They are the penalties of new youth. Instant food, nuclear power, missile submarines, the anglicization of the French language— all these are part of the ambience of Young France, an ironic factor in that national greatness without which, De Gaulle, the supreme traditionalist once said, France would never truly be France. And yet, and yet. . . .

By nightfall I was in Burgundy, eating snails, drinking Sauvignon de Saint-Bries, and after dinner I walked out through the village to sniff the night air. The long main street was quiet and empty. Only occasionally did a truck roar through to Dijon, or a car spring away with a showy blare of exhausts from the Café des Voyageurs beside the crossroads. Chained dogs barked, one after the other as I passed, from behind high iron gates. Impertinently peering through window-chinks, I caught glimpses of polished brass, ornamental clocks, lace cushion-covers, lines of washing stretched beside fireplaces, all illuminated by the flickering multicolored lights of the TV sets—over which, in every house, dim shawled and coated figures seemed to be silently crouching, very close to the screen. Though as I approached the café I could hear the cheerful sounds of rock, and though there were five or six Yamahas and Suzukis outside it, and a red Renault Turbo, still as I walked up the street beneath the pollarded limes I felt the old France still stirring all around me, embodied above all not in the sights, nor the sounds, nor the texture of the night, but in the smells.

Only slightly intoxicated by the wine, only minimally slowed down by the snails, only occasionally interrupted in my thought—*swoosh!*—by the passing of a truck, as I wandered up the street I identified those old fragrances one by one in my mind. There was the old masonry and woodwork of the village itself, of course. There was hay, and dung to go with it. There was the smell of mossy water, from the old fountain with the lion's head beside the bridge. There was that faint smell of good cooking which, even in the age of convenience foods, still hangs habitually about French homesteads. There was a hint of some evening blossom, lime perhaps, or honeysuckle. There was an emanation of wood fires, and a distinct soupçon of dry rot, and a hint of coffee, and something vinous or brandeine or Chartreusian underlying it all.

At the top of the street I found that the parish church had a large square porch jutting into the street, so I stepped inside, and from its shadows looked back through the trees down the length of the village. Inside that structure, I discovered, all the smells were permanently concentrated, jammed together in a sort of solid essence between the old pillars: food, dog, dung, hay, damp, stone, rot, blossom, fire and lichened water all in one. And so I leant against the wall there for a few minutes, relishing this heady elixir, watching the comings and going from the Café des Voyageurs, whose lights split out across the village street, and whose juke-box beat with a lively thump through the barking of the dogs.

* * *

The frontier between France and Switzerland, in the outskirts of Geneva, is almost indistinguishable among the suburbs, but it is a special kind of frontier all the same. It is the frontier of detachment. It marks the line between a nation repeatedly ravaged, humiliated and ennobled by war, and a nation which has for generations resolutely, almost contemptuously stood aside from the internecine squabbles of Europe— between the grand epitome of the nations, in whose destinies we all seem to share, and a nation which holds itself aloof to the comradeships of pride and suffering. Even today Switzerland is a State apart, an enclave within the Europe of which it forms an essential crossroads, a member of no alliance, an adherent of no bloc, where unemployment scarcely exists, everyone is middle class, and the rich of all nations come to live in bland tax-free alpine villas among the flowers, snows and numbered bank accounts.

Something has gone wrong, though, in this milky paradise. I remember writing, not so long ago, that if ever I felt relieved to cross the border from France into Switzerland, I would know I was getting old—I would have come to prefer serenity to stimulation, calm to excitement. No such denouement threatens now. Switzerland has lost its plush and easy motion, and Geneva, once so sure and dull, now seems above all restless, as though it is unsure of its own identity, and after all these years of complacency, is having second thoughts. It suggests to me one huge airport lounge, sleepless, dissatisfied, inhabited by world-weary duty-free concessionaires and slightly jet-lagged transients, coming and going night and day in a time-zone haze beside the lovely lake.

* * *

The lake is always lovely. At night it is resplendent with its parade of neon signs, red and green and blue and yellow on buildings all around, stacked winking and blinking above the water against the misty background of the mountains. In the daylight it is spectacular with the great plume of its fountain, spouting a couple of hundred feet into the air above the harbor mole, and with the graceful movements of its boats, the veteran launches which potter back and forth from one city quarter to another, the elegant old streamers which, bow-spritted and slant-funnelled, sail swan-like away in the morning mist for their beloved circuits of the lake.

But if the setting is still celestial—if the air is clear and clean—if the clouds sometimes part in the east to reveal the magnificence of Mont Blanc itself, attended by all its pinnacles—nevertheless there is a niggling, prodding sense of unease in the air of Geneva nowadays. "Shall we have a quiet week-end?" asked the *Tribune de Genève* nervously the day I arrived: for though they have not yet had youth riots here (as they have repeatedly in Zurich up the road), still there is an abrasive kind of fizz to the city now, harsh and humorless.

I lunched with a spy of my acquaintance. What kind of a spy he is, who he spies for, or against, I have never been able to discover; but he has all the hallmarks of espionage about him, divides his time between Switzerland and the East, wears raincoats and speaks Greek. We ate little grilled fish at the water's edge, as we generally do when I am passing through Geneva, and discussed the state of the city. Uncomfortable, he thought it, and getting more so. Security getting tougher, I surmised? Banks turning difficult? Opposition hotter? No, no, no, he said testily, nothing like that: only those damned roller-skaters.

Roller-skating is all the rage around the Lake of Geneva. Whole families skate along the promenade. Dogs ride about in rollered baskets, and youths whizz shatteringly here and there, scattering the crowds before them with blasts of the whistles that are held between their teeth. "Dear God, those whistles," said the spy, holding his hands over his ears, and indeed those harsh blasts struck me as a *leit-motif* or perhaps a *cri-de-coeur* of contemporary Geneva, at once aggressive and despairing, cynical and abusive. When after lunch that Sunday afternoon I wandered around the lake to watch the world go by I found that everything I saw, everything I heard down there, was punctuated by the shrill passage of the roller-skaters.

In particular I see their hurtling forms in my mind's eye when I recall a revivalist meeting I found in progress not far from the Pont du Mont Blanc, where the footpath curves around beneath the trees towards the eastern shore of the lake. This was a pathetic spectacle. A young man in a neat grey suit was preaching repentance on the sidewalk, backed by four earnest helpers with guitars, and around them there had assembled a characteristic Geneva Sunday crowd—people of every color, every kind, black people, gowned Arabs, Chinese, a flamboyant covey of Nigerians, three mountain people like Sherpas or Bhutanis, one or two half-hearted local hecklers, half-a-dozen of those middle-aged, middle-class middling sort of men, widowers I expect, to be seen in any park of the Western world wandering aimlessly about on Sunday afternoons.

It was a very subdued brand of fundamentalism that those zealots were offering, there in the city of Calvin himself. The preacher's voice was gentle, the guitars were muted, when they broke into a hymn it was remorseful rather than rousing, and even the hecklers hardly raised their voices. Behind them the lake shone happily, all flags, masts and fountain, and ever and again a dear old Edwardian motor-launch, so overloaded in the stern that her cantonal flag sometimes trailed in the water, cruised from shore to shore like a prop on a circular stage.

The preacher preached, the hecklers mildly scoffed, the guitarists strummed, the motley crowd watched all in silence—and through them in brutal counterpoint hurtled the roller-skaters of Geneva, behind them, before them, between the preacher and his audience, between the guitarists and me, heads down, whistles blowing, on their faces expressions not of fun, humor, fellowship or human sympathy, but of cheerless and unremitting arrogance.

*   *   *

High in the rockface above Chamonix, a huddle of brownish structures, a mesh of steel girdering, a great hole in the mountainside—the Mont Blanc Tunnel. The road winds heavily out of the Chamonix valley to reach it, and the effect is Wagnerian. The white massif looms operatically high above; the great trucks lumber around the horseshoe bends like so many giants; what dread enchantment, you may wonder, dwells within that hole, what fancy of Grimm or Tolkien, what Worm of the Alps?

They tell me that when the tunnel was first opened migrating swallows used it to save themselves a flight over the mountains: and for people of the cold north, like me, it offers an almost symbolic transference to the warm south of our profoundest desires. No birds could fly through it now, for it is a tube heavy always with fumes and chemicals, but still as I climbed up to it that day I felt a bit like a swallow myself, genetically impelled towards the sun. The valley behind me, playing up to the allegory, was thick with grey mist, and the peaks above swirled with cloud: but at the other end of that noxious worm-hole, surely the sparkle awaited me.

And so, magically, it proved. The bare dank rock of the tunnel swept by me in the darkness, the illuminated signs kilometer by kilometer, the little sheltering alcoves with the emergency telephones, and presently far in the distance I saw a tiny circle of bright yellow light, hardly bigger than a pinhead. Like a bird I pursued it, and larger it grew, and brighter, and yellower, and presently it lost its outline, and came flooding into the tunnel to greet me, and dazzled me with its splendor—and it was the sunshine of Italy, on the warm side of the Alps!

I was there where the beakers brimmed. I had crossed the watershed of Europe, and had passed from the grey to the gold. Within the hour I was drifting poetically about on Lake Viverone, drinking martinis and observing the courting displays of the ever-lusty crested grebe.

* * *

There used to be four golden stallions, loot from old Byzantium, gloriously above the great central doorway of the Basilica San Marco in Venice. For 800 years they stood there as the supreme symbol of Venetian independence and stability. When I walked into the Piazza San Marco, though, I found only one beast up there on the gallery, and he was hardly golden, but rather a sort of brown dunnish color, and he had none of the scars and wrinkles of age upon him, none of the dents and roughenings, but seemed to stand there altogether too perfectly, too trim, neat and self-conscious.

What did I expect? demanded the man selling postcards beside the flagpoles below. That horse was a sham. The real ones had been removed to a museum chamber out of sight, and they are to be replaced in the end by four such copies: meticulous copies, lovingly made, exactly proportioned, but inevitably lacking the mysterious fire of genius, antiquity, or divinity. I asked the postcard man what he thought about it, and he said it was progress, that's all, progress, you couldn't stop it. But to my mind the appearance of the first of these poor substitutes upon that belvedere marks a fundamental turning point in the fortunes of Venice. At last pretense has definitively taken over from reality. The ancient metropolis, for more than a thousand years one of the Powers of Europe, has abandoned the long effort to maintain itself as a real working city, and accepted its status as an exhibition place, a holiday town, a conference center, where perfect sham horses make more sense than knocked-about old real ones, and age itself is something to be honored in guide books and scholarly theses, but disguised or circumvented in life.

It is a relief for me. I have been protesting too long, hoping always that Venice would somehow recover its ancient greatness as a great mercantile or financial entrepôt, a channel between East and West, dreading the moment when it would be no more than a museum, petulantly scoffing at its restoration and from time to time declaring the wish that it would sink. Now, quite suddenly, I can scoff and argue no more. Venice has abandoned the old fight, thrown off the nostalgia and the melancholy, and is proceeding with gusto into the ordinary world. It has not been so lively since the fall of the Venetian Republic, nearly 200 years ago.

Often in the evenings I wandered, like everyone else, around the arcades of the Piazza, Napoleon's finest drawing-room in Europe, and wondered at the vivid, boisterous, almost violent new spirit of the place. The café orchestras string away still of course, at "Rose Marie," "Oklahoma," or a contemporary favorite of theirs, "It's Up to You, New York, New York." But they are rivalled nowadays by other sorts of music: transistor music from groups of students huddled upon the steps of the arcades, or crosslegged in circles upon the paving-stones; country music perhaps from a boy with a guitar at the foot of the campanile, with a huge crowd singing and swaying with him in the half-light; snatches of song from hilarious Italian school-children, snatches of trumpet one evening from a man lurching tipsily round the corner of the Doge's Palace wearing a cocked hat and riding-breeches, snatches of cheerful whistle from me, for I rather enjoyed this vigorous new cacophony, and thought if you couldn't have the Four Stallions of St. Mark, you could do worse than turn the Piazza into a kind of disco.

It is not, though, just in the show of it that Venice has changed in the last year or two. More and more it is becoming a city of rich retreat,

where tycoons of Turin or Milan may spend secure and sybaritic week-
ends, where pop stars and millionaires from all Europe may live it up
with wild parties in romantic palaces. The Venetian working people are
being forced out of the city, all too often, by rising prices, to turn
themselves into mainlanders over the causeway in Mestre, where they
may look back to the towers of their ancestral home with mingled relief
and longing. The little neighborhood shops are disappearing one by one.
Carnival has returned to Venice, and for two weeks in Lent the city
bursts into a communal festivity which may well again become, so social
experts assure me, one of the great events of the European calendar.

"Progress, that's all. . . ." Only here and there in the islands of the
Venetian lagoon, still when the weather is right shrouded in a mysterious
suggestiveness, are there pockets of resistance to the Newing of Venice.
Not everybody wants the lagoon jazzed up with casinos, tourist complexes, love-nests or, as is seriously proposed for one island, "Caribbean-
style Beach Complexes." I was told that on the island of Santa Fessola,
for instance, two monks of the Dominican Order had dug themselves
in to resist all change: so I hired a motorboat at once and sailed out there
to meet them.

Until recently Santa Fessola was an isolation hospital, and all its
buildings still stand, slowly crumbling, half-overgrown by prickly creep-
ers and flicked about by lizards. At first when I disembarked upon this
desolate shore I could find no sign of human life: only the dry grass
crackled beneath my feet, and the old doors, sagging upon their rusty
hinges, creaked theatrically when I pushed them. Just when I was about
to give up, though, I heard a shout, and there were the two protestors,
emerging from some hidden recess of the hospital and hastening down
to the water-stage towards me. One was young and plump, the other old
and white-bearded, and a little black dog scampered around them. They
were cheerful men, but implacable. There among the toppling ruins
they would stay, they said, come what may, to ensure that nothing
dreadful happened to the island. Had they any notion what might
happen to it? They raised their hands and eyes to heaven: anything
might happen, they said, as though the Black Angel himself might be
planning to develop the place.

Though the sun shone brightly and the breeze was warm, theirs
seemed a melancholy dedication, so lonely the island, so decrepit those
buildings, so far away the light and life of Venice. When I sailed away
again, and looked back to the ugly white structures among the landing-
stage, their plaster peeling and their roofs beginning to topple, in a
round oriel window on the first floor I saw the weathered, wistful but
still rosy face of the old brother, exactly framed in the window, as in a

Renaissance portrait. He was looking fixedly out at me: when I waved he raised his hand in a tentative way, and from far out in the lagoon I could still discern his presence there, peering motionless through that window.

* * *

In the bare desicated hills above Trieste stands the Yugoslav frontier post. I could see its lights up the road there, but it took me a good hour to reach them. Backed far down the highway to the city were the lines of Yugoslavs waiting to get home after the week-end. They had been to the great street market of Trieste, most of them, to stock up with jeans, radios, coffee or perhaps gold; they had brought their children and mothers-in-law for the ride; now they sat there, engines throbbing, sometimes lurching a few feet forward, sometimes getting out of the car to stretch their arms, waiting helplessly in the gathering darkness to get home again to the Peoples' Republic. The hills were dark and empty all around us: when I looked behind I could see the lights of the waiting cars fender to fender all down the hill towards the sea.

The Yugoslavs were used to it. It is always like this. Halfway up the hill somebody had set up a mobile canteen, and they were selling coffee and hamburgers from the back of a truck. Occasionally some know-all, scudding up beside us on the gravel, plunged on to a dirt track up the side of the mountain, never to be seen again. Once a pair of gigantic trucks, from Mostar, the old Turkish town in Herzogovina, forced their way by sheer bulk and judder yard by yard up the waiting queue, blocking all other movement until, with a hissing of air-brakes and roar of engines, they disappeared triumphantly over the crest of the hill.

At last I reached the frontier post. The lights were dim. An official with a red star on his cap beckoned for my passport without a word and slowly examined every page. Without a smile, without a flicker, with only a gloomy stare he handed it back to me.

"Cheer up," I said.

"Enjoy yourself," he morosely replied, and waved me into the dusk.

* * *

Ah well, Yugoslavia is like that. It hardly offers a laughing welcome to its guests, but there is scarcely a soul in the country who will not respond to a little jollying along, and whose native surliness cannot be softened, given time and practice, into bonhomie. I drove down the grand Adriatic Highway, winding between the high limestone escarpment and the island-speckled sea, in a state of elation, playing Mozart all the way, stopping now and then for grilled fish and prosek, inspecting a church here, a castle there, until I reached the old port of Split, Spalato to the

Italians, and there settled down for a few days doing nothing on the waterfront.

I always feel happy on the Dalmatian coast of Yugoslavia. It suits me. I like its mean between simplicity and sophistication, between communism and capitalism, between the local and the national. I like to go into a supermarket and find it moderately, temperately stocked, without that vulgar profusion of choice which makes the modern Western store seem a little obscene to the traveller, without the boorish austerity of your whole-hog Soviet Grocer No. 4. I like the sense of wry comradeship which, with an almost universal flashing of lights and comical gestures, warns you that there is a speed trap down the road. I like the ships which are always in sight, fishing boats loitering among the green islets, tall white ferry-steamers chugging into port, tankers in dry docks up unexpected creeks, motor torpedo-boats in gray clusters at their moorings, hydrofoils flashing off for Venice—ships always and everywhere along that incomparable coast, pervading every image and crossing every vista.

It is the sexist of coasts, the most virile, the lustiest. Bold are its men, brave its women, doggedly its children hold back their tears; Tito would be proud of them still. I drove out from Split one day to buy a bottle of black wine from a country homestead, and wonderfully earthy and organic was the domestic hierarchy I discovered inside the house: a brawny stubbly farmer-husband, a tough buxom wife, a one-eyed cat, a sprightly terrier, and in a steamy scullery behind the kitchen, the Wine-Mother herself in the fullness of her years, stirring and tasting and stirring again—"Good health, good luck," cried these amiable bucolics as they filled my glass, and bonk, when I returned to the car I tripped on a stick, and went back to town dripping thick black country wine all over the bonnet, as though I had been baptized by gods of revelry.

Not that Split is exactly a frivolous place, any more than Yugoslavia is a frivolous kind of country. The city is built around the old imperial palace of Diocletian, a Split-born Roman Emperor, whose walls still form the outlines of the inner town, and this gives it a mighty imperial stance, with its wide harbor in front, its new concrete suburbs stretching away in heavy clusters to the hills behind. It is a city of terrific innuendo. Its citizens are magnificently stalwart—Split people must be the tallest in Europe, if not in the world—and the place hums with a sort of suppressed dynamism, as if it is always about to break into. . . .

Well, into what? Probably into nothing at all. All Europe is seized with a restlessness these days. It is muffled by prosperity and restrained by the Welfare State in its various guises—as Bismarck once observed, nothing maintains the status quo better than social security for all. In Yugoslavia, though, it is nearer the surface than it is in—well, in Dorking, say. The Yugoslavs are a people accustomed to living dangerously. In war they fought with insatiable savagery, in peace they have walked a political tightrope. They seem to me to be bursting with an energy only just controllable, like steam in a boiler.

Perhaps it is a consequence of their system—not quite tyrannical, not quite free. Perhaps it is a heritage of Balkanism, that fissiparous, conspiratorial instinct which kept this corner of Europe for so many generations in conflict and uncertainty. Or perhaps it is just the natural temperament of the people—Slavs of the Mediterranean, through whose history the warm and the cold winds paradoxically buffet, and in whose spirit the grim and the jolly seem so curiously allied.

Split is a naval base, and when I was driving out of town at the end of my stay I stopped at a traffic light near the fleet headquarters. A very senior Yugoslav naval officer started to cross the road. He was loaded with badges, braid and medal ribbons; but wearing as I was a floppy old canvas hat and a less than spotless blue shirt, just for fun I saluted him. His response was Split all over. First he faltered slightly in his steady tread. Then he brought his hand to the peak of his cap in a guarded and cautious way. And then, as the lights changed, I started forward, and he scuttled with rather less than an admiral's dignity to the safety of the opposite sidewalk, he turned around, all rank and propriety discarded, and shared my childish laughter.

* * *

"Back again," said the magnifico at the café on the road into the Black Mountains, on the last ridge before Cetinje and the heart of Montenegro. We had met before, you see. He is always there, it seems, summer or winter, like a major-domo of these uplands, or a Chief of Protocol. He wears black breeches, and a wide belt like a cummerbund, and he stands about seven feet tall, and speaks in a basso profondo, and tosses slivovic back like lime juice, and is in fact in all respects the very model of a modern Montenegrin.

With this splendid fellow at my side, kneading his moustaches, I sat down on the bench outside the café, and looked back, far down the corkscrew Kotor road, far up the glittering Dalmatian coast, along the way I had come. I had journeyed from one extremity to another, over the shifting and anxious face of western Europe—a continent betwixt and between these days, a continent out of gear perhaps, rickety Britain with its fairy fantasies, young France, half macho, half poet-and-peasant, Switzerland of the fanatic roller-skaters, Italy of the sham horse and the real live monks, Yugoslavia with its lid tippling and clanking, like a kettle on the boil.

"Come far?" inquired the Montenegrin, lighting a short cigar. Not so far, I thought: but over the ridge before us, wrapped in their Godless silence, stood the mountains of Albania.

LAWRENCE DURRELL
1913–

British by birth (although born in India) but wholly Mediterranean by instinct, Durrell has enjoyed a rich career as a novelist, travel writer, and poet. His fiction has been influenced by the work of Henry Miller: "a mildly pornographic fantasia" his novel The Black Book: An Agon *(Paris, 1938) has been called. He is best known for his exotic tetralogy the* Alexandria Quartet, *consisting of the novels* Justine *(1957),* Balthazar *and* Mountolive *(1958), and* Clea *(1960). The style here is lush, the matter cynically political and erotic, and the characters eccentric, some Gothic to the point of freakishness. Anthony Burgess sums up Durrell's fictional milieu thus: "Anything can happen in Alexandria—pederasty, incest, all the convolutions of lust, all the varieties of betrayal. Enter a teashop, and someone will be screaming in terminal meningitis on the floor above, and the cashier will be suffering ravishment behind her cashdesk, while outside a live camel will be slowly cut to pieces." More plausible are Durrell's travel books, which focus largely on the Greek islands. One of the most pleasant is his record of a group bus tour around Sicily—hence "Sicilian Carousel," the advertised name of the tour. It started in Catania and went around the island clockwise to end at Taormina. The tour over, Durrell went on by car to explore some more.*

From Sicilian Carousel
(1977)

Our fellow-travellers! Oh God, what was in store for us? But the hotel to which we repaired was all right in its gloomy way, and at least there was plenty of hot water. So we repaired the damage to our beauty and then held up the bar for a calamitously expensive Scotch, feeling that it might help us to overcome the horrors in store for us. But as time wore on and the pangs of hunger began to twinge at us we moved into the ghastly white light of the long dining-room and took up an emplacement at one of the tables (the group held a strategic corner of the place to itself) marked *Carousello Siciliano*. Indeed wherever we went our reserved seats were thus marked. It was engaging enough, but on this first evening while we waited with impatience for our fellow-travellers to arrive (would it be rude to start?) it sounded ghoulish.

However the Scotch was so expensive we simply couldn't keep on ordering it. We decided therefore to begin, and to hell with the rest of the Carousel. But in that glaring white light with its bevy of indolent waiters everything was indecision. We had taken up positions at the first reserved table and to steady our nerves Deeds tried to be facetious in a reassuring way, telling me that these marked tables had a tang of opera about them, and that he felt he would like to burst into song like a gondolier. But it was heavy stuff and he knew it. Well, boldly we started in on the dinner at last, a disappointing little offering of spaghetti or rice with gravy. It was honest enough fare I suppose but it had clearly been blessed by British Railways. Moreover the waiter who served us was suffering either from a terrible bereavement or a deep Sicilian Slight. He could hardly contain his sobs; his head hung low and waved about; his eyes rolled. He mastered himself for serving, yes, but only just, and when it came to wavering the cheese over the plate his repressed fury almost got the better of him and Deeds mildly took his wrist to help him scatter his Parmesean.

We were well embarked on this introduction to the joys of the island cuisine when there came the noise of a bus and voices of foreign tang— and we knew that our fellows of the Carousel had arrived. They stacked their baggage in the hall and then like ravenous wolves made a bee line for the dining-room where we sat, gazing bravely through our tears at them. "God! They do look ghastly," admitted Deeds, and so they did. And so, I suppose, did we, for when they saw us sitting at a Carousel table their beseeching looks turned heavenward and their lips moved, no doubt in prayer, at the thought of being locked up in a bus with us for two weeks. It was mutual, this first appraising glance. They straggled in in twos and threes until about fifteen to seventeen hungry people were seated around us being served by the sobster waiter and his colleagues. The white light poured down on us turning us all to the colour of tallow. But Deeds had found a very pleasant dry white wine and this helped. In gingerly fashion we started passing the salt and pepper, picking up dropped napkins, and generally showing a leg.

Later of course our companions developed distinct identities but on that first evening in the dismal light it was impossible to distinguish accurately between the Anglican Bishop who had developed Doubts, the timid young archaeologist, the American dentist who had eloped with his most glamorous patient, the French couple of a vaguely diplomatic persuasion and all those others who hung about on the outskirts of our table like unrealised wraiths. Later their characters printed themselves more clearly. Tonight we gathered a few random impressions, that was all. The Bishop was testy and opinionated and had been airsick. He kept sticking his forefinger in his ears and shaking vigorously to clear the canals, as he put it. His wife was both tired and somewhat cowed. We knew nothing then about his nervous breakdown in the pulpit. His name was Arthur. The dentist was shy and hung his head when spoken to in a strong British accent while his partner looked pleasantly saucy. I sympathised with him. The Bishop spoke English as if he had a hot potato in his mouth. The rest of the table was made up by the rather distinguished French couple who could not, I decided, be diplomatic for they spoke no English and were glad to lean on us as translators.

And then Roberto made his relaxed appearance, shaking hands all around and moving smilingly from table to table, slipping from one language to another with smooth skill and checking off our names on the tourist list. He combined charm and kindness; later we discovered that he was efficient as well. He knew Deeds quite well from a previous trip and their greeting was most cordial. My friend explained when he had left us that Don Roberto came of a noble but penniless family and had been a university lecturer in history; but the boredom of academic life with its endless intrigues had sent him in search of something more suitable to a lively nature. He had found it in becoming guide, philosopher and friend to the travellers on the Carousel. His calm friendliness had an immediately reassuring effect; it acted as a catalyst.

We dug deeper into our charmless food and poured out more stoups of wine. It would have been a pity, after spending so much money on the trip, not to enjoy it a little. The French diplomat had a head which came straight off a Roman coin—the benign features of one of the better emperors. His wife was fearfully pale and looked very ill; she was clearly convalescent after some obscure illness and looked all the time as if she were on the point of fainting. The concern of her husband was very evident. The dentist ate his food with a sort of soundtrack; he was clearly a great masticator, and probably a health-food addict. The French Microscopes were far off; they had found another microscope to talk to.

"When I was young," said Deeds, to nobody in particular, "there was a great Victorian moustache-cup among the family heirlooms, out of which my father drank his Christmas punch. On this object the family had had engraved the motto DEEDS NOT WORDS which is perhaps why I am so dashed taciturn."

Though it was relatively late when our dinner was concluded with a pungent *grappa* we were disinclined to turn in straight away. A few of our fellow-travellers took refuge in the lounge where coffee was available and where there was light enough to write postcards, sort papers, count up currency. Roberto was talking to the pretty German girl about archaeology. There were two striking but severe-looking French ladies sending views of the town to their relations. They were very finely turned out and would obviously be destined to match up with the proconsular gentleman and his distinguished but pale wife. We were to be a group speaking three languages—which offered no problems for Roberto. He smiled and waved to us as we passed through the swing doors into the warm and fragrant darkness outside. It was pleasant to stretch one's legs once more, and the hot night was full of flower scents.

* * *

When I woke it was almost seven on a cloudless morning. Time for a dip in the hotel pool before breakfast. And here I found the gallant Bishop performing feats of youthful athleticism while his wife sat in a deck chair holding his towel. His morning boom of greeting proved that he had become acclimatised by now and was ready for anything. He swung about on elastic calves and even was so bold as to go off the top board—at which his wife covered, not her eyes, but her ears. I hoped he would not become too hearty and decide to hold Protestant services in the lounge as is the way of bishops travelling in heathen countries. I returned to pack and dress and then descended to find Deeds eating a slow breakfast and picking his way through the local Italian paper while Roberto guided him with an occasional bit of free translation. The French proconsular couple shared our table and seemed rested and refreshed.

I thought, however, that they eyed me a trifle curiously, as if they too were busy speculating as to what I did in life. The German girl was reading Goethe's enthusiastic account of his own trip round Italy. I hoped to find the text in English or French as I knew no German. The Microscopes were wolfing their food and calling for refills of coffee with the air of people who knew that it was all paid for in advance. They were determined to leave no crumb unturned. Pretty soon, I could see, complaints would start. The British would revolt over the tea and the absence of fish-knives. The French would utter scathing condemnation of the cuisine. Poor Roberto! For the moment, however, all was harmony and peace. The novelty of our situation kept us intrigued and good-tempered. The brilliance of the Sicilian sun was enthralling after the northern variety. And then there was the little red bus which we had not as yet met, and which was at this moment drawing up outside the hotel to await us. It was a beautiful little camionette of a deep crimson-lake colour and apparently quite new. It was richly upholstered and smelt deliciously of fresh leather. It was also painstakingly polished and as clean inside as a new whistle. It gave a low throaty chuckle—the Italians specialise in operatic horns—and at the signal the chasseurs humped our baggage and started to stow.

We were introduced to its driver, a stocky and severe-looking young man, who might have been a prizefighter or a fisherman from his dark scowling countenance. His habitual expression was sombre and depressive, and it took me some time to find out why. Mario was a peasant from the foothills of Etna and understood no language save his own dialect version of Sicilian. He also distrusted nobs who spoke upper class—and of course Roberto spoke upper class and was a nob, being a university man. But from time to time when a word or a phrase became intelligible to Mario the most astonishing change came about in that black scowling face. It was suddenly split (as if with an axe-blow or a sabre-cut) by the most wonderful artless smile of a kindly youth. It was only lack of understanding that cast the shadow; the minute light penetrated he was absolutely transformed. But he was grim about his job, and would not touch a drop of drink throughout the trip; it made Roberto, who was a convivial soul, a trifle plaintive to see such devotion to duty. Well, on the sunny morning we gathered around the little bus and eagerly appraised it, for we would be virtually living in it for a week. It looked pretty good to me—the luxury of not having to drive myself. Mario shook hands darkly with us all, the proconsulars, the Microscopes, ourselves, the German girl, the two smart French ladies and the half dozen or so others who as yet swam in a sort of unidentifiable blur, waiting to develop their pictures, so to speak. Among them, as yet unidentified by science, were the egregious fellow called Beddoes, a Miss Lobb of London, and a rapturous Japanese couple, moon-struck in allure and wearing purple shoes.

Deeds and I settled ourselves modestly in the last two seats in the back row, enjoying therefore a little extra leg-room and a small lunette window of our own. The others took up dispositions no less thoughtful, realising that we would need space to stretch and smoke and doze. Across the aisle from us, however, there was an empty row and this was suddenly occupied by a passenger to whom we hadn't paid attention before. He was a somewhat raffish-looking individual of medium height clad in veteran tweeds with dirty turn-ups; also old-fashioned boots with hooks and eyes and scarlet socks. On his head he wore a beret at a rakish angle from under which effervesced a tangled mop of dirty curls worthy of Dylan Thomas. To everyone's discomfort he smoked shag in a small and noisome French briar. He talked to himself in a low undertone and smiled frequently, exposing very yellow canines. "A rather rum chap," whispered Deeds confidentially, and I could bet that after a pause he would sigh and add resignedly, "O well, it takes all sorts. . . ." The nice thing about Deeds was not only his kindness but his predictability. I felt I already knew him so well by now that I could guess the name of his wife—Phyllis. And so it proved to be. But the chap over the way had started to make conversation—a sort of sharp and knowing line of talk. He said his name was Beddoes and that he was a prep-school master. "Just been hurled out of a prep school near Dungeness for behavior unbecoming to an officer and a hypocrite." He gave a brief cachinnation and sucked on his noisome dottle. Deeds looked thoughtful. Well, I could almost hear him think, if one goes abroad it is to meet new faces in new places.

Yet, at the moment all was harmony, all was beatific calm and indulgence. Even Beddoes seemed all right in his rather sharp-edged way. Later of course we were to ask God plaintively in our prayers what we had done to merit such a travelling companion. But not today, not on this serene and cloudless morning with its smiling promise of hot sunshine and a sea-bathe along the road. The little heartsblood-coloured bus edged off with its cargo into the traffic, feeling its way circumspectly about the town, while Roberto sat down beside the driver and conducted a voice test on the microphone through which he was to keep us intellectually stimulated throughout the Carousel. His own ordeal was just beginning, of course. At breakfast he had bemoaned a guide's fate to Deeds, saying that one was always telling people something they already knew or something they did not wish to know. One could never win. Sometimes, attacked by hysteria, he had tried telling people false facts at breakneck speed just to see if anyone was awake enough to contradict him: but nobody ever did. But today he ran a certain risk with the Bishop as a passenger, for the latter sat forward eagerly, on the *qui vive* like a gundog, all set to ingest Roberto's information. A trifle patronising as well, for it was clear from his manner that he already knew a good deal. Yes, it was as if he were doing a *viva voce* in school catechism. Roberto began somewhat defensively by saying that we would not have time to do everything as there was much which merited our judicious attention. "But we will do the two essential things so that you can tell your friends if they ask that you have seen the Duomo and St. Nicolo." It wasn't too bad as a ration, Deeds told me; but he had spent a delightful hour in the Bellini Museum and the Fish Market, both of which we should be missing on this trip. No matter. Sicily smelt good in a confused sort of way. I was anxious too to get a first glimpse of that curious architectural bastard Sicilian baroque which had so enraptured Martine. "You expect it to be hell, but you find it heavenly—sort of fervently itself like the Sicilians themselves." At that moment our bus passed under a balcony from which apparently Garibaldi had prefaced a famous oration with the words "*O Roma, O morte*".

Beddoes made some opprobrious comment about demagogues which earned him a glare from the sensitive Roberto. At the site of the no longer extant Greek theatre the guide uttered some wise words about Alcibiades, a name which made the Bishop frown. "A dreadful homo," said Beddoes audibly. Deeds looked rather shocked and moved three points east, as if to dissociate himself from this troublesome commentator. I hoped he wasn't going to go on like this throughout the journey. But he was. "Dreadful feller," said Deeds under his breath. Beddoes proved unquenchable and totally snubproof. Moreover he had very irritating conversational mannerisms like laying his forefinger along his nose when he was about to say something which he thought very knowing; or sticking his tongue out briefly before launching what he considered a witticism. Now he stuck it out to say, apropos Aeschylus, that his play *Women of Etna* was based on reality. "The women of Etna," he went on with a winning air of frankness, "were known in antiquity for their enormous arses. The whole play, or rather the chorus, revolves around them, if I may put it like that. The women. . . ." But Roberto was wearing a little thin, at least his superb patience was markedly strained. "The play is lost," he hissed, and repeated the observation in French and German, lest there should be any mistake about it. But this remark of Beddoes was not lost on the German girl who was I later discovered called Renata and came from Heidelberg. She turned hot and cold. Beddoes winked at her and she turned her back.

The parent Microscopes held hands and yawned deeply. I wasn't shocked by this, though Roberto looked downcast. The reaction was at least honest and simple. The proconsulars had the air of having read up the stuff before coming on the trip, as of course anyone with any sense would have done. But I prefer to experience the thing first without trimmings and read it up when I get back home. I know that it is not the right way round, for inevitably one finds that one has missed a great deal; but it gives me the illusion of keeping my first impressions fresh and pristine. Besides, in the case of Sicily, I had my guide in Martine whose tastes, as I knew from long ago, coincided very closely with mine.

Consequently I was not unprepared for the mixture of styles which she found so delightful. The little hint of austerity from the north housed the profuse and exuberant Sicilian mode, which itself glittered with variegated foreign influences—Moorish, Spanish, Roman. . . . But even Catanian baroque managed to convey a kind of dialect version of the Sicilian one, though its elements, fused as they were into several successive bouts of building after natural catastrophes, gave off a touching warmth of line and proportion which argued well for the rest. We paid our respects to Saint Agatha, the patron saint, in the cathedral dedicated to her, which wasn't, however, quite as thrilling as Roberto tried to make it sound—there seemed little about it except the good proportions which we might appreciate. As for Agatha—"I had an aunt called Agatha," said Deeds, "who was all vinegar. Consequently the name gives me a fearfully uneasy feeling."

But St. Nicolo was a different kettle of fish on its queer hill; it had a very strange atmosphere, apparently having been abandoned in the middle of its life to wear out in the sunshine, fronting one of the most elegant and sophisticated piazzas bearing the name of Dante. Apparently they ran out of funds to finish it off in the traditional elated style—and in a way it is all the better for it. The largest church in Sicily according to Roberto, it needs a lot of space-clearance to show off its admirable proportions; just like a large but beautifully proportioned girl might. We draggled dutifully round it, with a vast expenditure of colour film by the German girl and the Microscopes. Beddoes, too, seemed to admire it for he forebore to comment, but walked about and thoughtfully smoked his dreadful shag. Roberto tactfully sat in a stall for a good ten minutes to let us admire, and then launched into a succinct little vignette about the church and the site which, I am ashamed to say, interested nobody. It is not that culture and sunlight are mutually exclusive, far from it; but the day was fine, the voyage was only beginning, and the whole of the undiscovered island lay ahead of us. The little red coach whiffled its horn to mark its position and we climbed aboard with a pleasant sense of familiarity, as if we had been travelling in it for weeks. I was sure that among our party there would be someone who would prove an anthropomorphic soul (like my brother with his animals) and end by christening it Fido the Faithful. I was equally sure that when the time came to part from it Deeds would recite verses from "The Arab's Farewell to His Steed". These sentiments I was rash enough to confide to him, whereupon he looked amused but ever so slightly pained.

But by now we had bisected the town and nosed about the older parts, a journey which involved nothing very spectacular except perhaps a closer look at the little Catanian emblem—the Elephant Fountain with its pretty animal obelisk motif. And now it was time to turn the little bus towards the coastal roads which might bear us away in the direction of Syracuse where we would spend a night and a day in search of the past. But first we had to drag our slow way across the network of dispiriting suburbs which smother Catania as a liana smothers a tree. The sudden appearance of Etna at the end of one vista after another— she seems to provide a backcloth for all the main boulevards—reminded one how often the town had been overwhelmed by the volcano, which made its present size and affluence rather a mystery; for Etna is far from finished yet and Catania lies in its field of fire. But the suburbs—one might have been anywhere; the squalor was not even picturesquely Middle Eastern, just Middle Class. With the same problems as any other urbanised town in the world—devoured like them by the petrol engine, that scourge of our age.

But Roberto was well pleased with us for people had begun to un-limber; the Bishop chatted to the two smart ladies from Paris, who spoke English with the delightful accent of the capital which makes the English heart miss a beat. The proconsul made notes in the margin of his *Guide Bleu*. The Americans became more talkative after a long period of shyness, and the lady remarked loudly, "Yes, Judy is flexible, but not *that* flexible." The rest of her discourse was lost in the whiffle of the horn and the clash of changing gears—Mario was scowling and muttering under his breath at some traffic problem; he was the only one of us who seemed out of sorts. Roberto performed his task dutifully, describing everything through the loudspeaker with elegance. A distinct thaw had set in, however, and our voices rose; we spoke naturally to one another instead of whispering. This is how I came to overhear those tantalising fragments of talk, a phrase here or there, which, divorced from context, were to haunt my sleep. I was to wonder and wonder about the flexibility of Judy, mysterious as a Japanese Koan, until a merciful sleep liberated me from the appalling problem. Then one of the French ladies remarked on a clear note, *"Pour moi les Italiens du nord sont des hommes décaféinés* [For me Northern Italians are decaffeinated peo-ple]", a sentiment which made the Sicilian blood of Roberto throb with joy. But at last the coast road came in sight and we opened throttle and started to hare along upon winding roads above a fine blue sea. Never have I felt safer than when Mario drove; his timing was perfect, his speeds nicely calculated not to awaken his drowsing or even sleeping charges, should they have been snoozing by any chance.

The opening stages of our journey were sensibly enough planned; this first day was an easy one in terms of time and distance. We wove across the vast and verdant Catanian Plain eagerly watching the skyline for the appearance of a stray Laestrygonian—the terrible ogres of the Homeric legend; I had a feeling that Ulysses had a brush with them but wasn't sure and made a note in my little schoolchild's *calpin* [notebook] to look them up in more detail. I did not dare to ask the Bishop or Roberto. The Simeto, a sturdy little river, together with two smaller tributaries waters the plain, and it is celebrated for an occasional piece of choice amber floating in it, which it has quarried somewhere on its journey. But where? Nobody knows.

The old road turns inwards upon itself and slopes away towards Lentini and Carlentini whence a brutally dusty and bumpy road leads us onwards into the hills to draw rein at our first Greek site—a resurrected city not unlike Cameirus in Rhodes, but nowhere near as beautiful; yet a little redeemed by the site and the old necropolis. What landscape-tasters the ancient Greeks were! They chose sites like a soldier chooses cover. The basic elements were always the same, southern exposure, cover from the prevailing wind, height for coolness and to defeat the humidity of the littoral. They had none of our (albeit very recent) passion for sea-bathing; the sea was a mysterious something else pitched between a goddess of luck and a highway. It is not hard to imagine how they were—with their combination of poetry and practicality. There was no barrier, it seems, between the notions of the sacred and the profane either.

After a short briefing we were turned loose among the ruins like a flock of sheep—hardly more intelligent either, you might have thought, to watch us mooching about. The Microscopes had begun to feel hungry, and the pile of box lunches and flasks of Chianti were being unloaded and placed in the shade of a tree against the moment when culture had been paid its due. In the bright sunlight the blonde German girl reminded me a little of Martine, for she had the same thick buttercup hair and white-rose colouring which had made my friend such a striking beauty. But not the slow rather urchin smile with the two swift dimples that greeted the lightest, the briefest jest. Nor the blue eyes which in certain lights reminded one of Parma violets. But I was sure that here she had sat upon a tomb while her children played about among the ruins, smoking and pondering, or perhaps reading a page or two of the very same Goethe—as unconditional an addict of Sicily as she herself had become.

It was, however, a well-calculated shift of accent, of rhythm—I meant to spend the first day in the open air, lively with bees in the dazing heat, and where the shade of the trees rested like a damp cloth on the back of the neck. Little did it matter that the pizzas were a trifle soggy—but I am wrong: for the first faint murmurs of protest came from the French camp about precisely this factor. And the two graceful Parisians added that the paper napkins had been forgotten. Roberto swallowed this with resignation. Far away down the mildly rolling hillocks glittered the sea on rather a sad little bit of sandy littoral, and here we were promised an afternoon swim when we had digested our lunch, a prospect which invigorated me and raised the spirits of my companion. But some of us looked rather discountenanced by the thought, and Beddoes swore roundly that he wasn't going to swim in the sea with all its sharks; he wanted a pool, a hotel pool. He had paid for a pool and he was damn well going to insist on a pool or else. So it went on.

Deeds, on the contrary, declared that things were not so bad after all; that we were all quite decent chaps and that no great calamities or internal battles need be expected. It was true. Even the Bishop, who in my own mind might be the one to inflict deep irritations on us because of his knowledgeability and insularity and patronising air—even he went out of his way to humour Roberto in terms which almost made him a fellow-scholar. I could see that he was a pleasant and conscientious man underneath an evident Pauline-type neurosis which is almost endemic in the Church of England, and usually comes from reading *Lady Chatterley's Lover* in paperback. Deeds had got quite a selection of guides to the island in English and French and these we riffled while we ate. He professed himself extremely dissatisfied by them all.

"It took me some time to analyse why—it's the sheer multiplicity of the subject matter. The damned island overflows with examples of the same type of thing—you have six cathedrals where in other places you would save up your admiration for the one or two prime examples. How can a guide book do justice to them all? It just can't, old man. Here you get six for the price of one, and the very excellence of what it has ends by fatiguing you."

*   *   *

That morning I had some shopping to do, and a suit to get cleaned. At the post office I ran into the two French ladies. They had had a great shock, and they gobbled like turkeys as they told me about it. As usual they had been sending off clutches of postcards to their friends and relations in France—they seemed to have no other occupation or thought in mind. But peering through the grille after posting a batch they distinctly saw the clerk sweep the contents of the box into the lap of his overall and walk into the yard in order to throw all the mail on to a bonfire which was burning merrily on the concrete, apparently fed by all the correspondence of Taormina. They were aghast and shouted out to him—as a matter of fact they could hardly believe their eyes at first. They thought they had to do with a madman—but no, it was only a striker. He was burning mail as fast as it was posted. When they protested he said *"Niente Niente . . .* questo e tourismo . . ."

I transcribe phonetically, and consequently inaccurately—but that is what they said he said; and I took him to be telling them something like "It's nothing at all, my little ladies, just a clutch of tourist junk."

But the links of our friendship had, I observed, begun to weaken already for I had forgotten their names. I racked my brains to recall them. Anyway they were leaving in the morning and were half nostalgic and half irritated by the high price of things and the general slipshodness and insolence of the small shopkeepers. But it is ever thus in tourist centres.

Soon I was to begin my solitary journeys in the little borrowed car, trying, in the days which were left me, to fill in the jigsaw of names and strike up a nodding acquaintance with so many of the places mentioned in the letters of Martine and in the guide. It was rather a breathless performance. I realised then that Sicily is not just an island, it is a sub-continent whose variegated history and variety of landscapes simply overwhelms the traveller who has not set aside at least three months to deal with it and its overlapping cultures and civilisations. But such a certainty rendered me in the event rather irresponsible and light-hearted. I took what I could get so to speak, bit deeply into places like Tyndarus, revisited Segesta, crossed the hairy spine of the island for another look at Syracuse; but this time on different roads, deserted ones. In some obscure quarry I came upon half-carved temple drums which had not yet been extracted from the rock. I had a look at the baby volcanoes in their charred and stenchy lands. Islands whose names I did not know came up out of the mist like dogs to watch me having a solitary bathe among the sea-lavender and squill of deserted estuaries near Agrigento. But everywhere there came the striking experience of the island—not just the impact of the folklorique or the sensational. Impossible to describe the moth-soft little town of Besaquino with its deserted presbytery where once there had been live hermits in residence. Centuripe with its jutting jaw and bronzed limestone—an immense calm necropolis where the rock for hundreds of yards was pitted like a lung with excavated tombs. Pantalica I think it was called.

But time was running out. I had decided, after a chance meeting with Roberto in the tavern of the Three Springs, to keep Etna for my last night—the appropriate send-off. He had promised to escort me to the top to watch the sun come up, and thence down to the airport to catch the plane.

I burnt Martine's letters on a deserted beach near Messina—she had asked me to do so; and I scattered the ashes. I regretted it rather, but people have a right to dispose of their own productions as they wish.

It was the end of a whole epoch; and appropriately enough I spent a dawn in the most beautiful theatre in the world—an act of which Etna itself appeared to approve because once, just to show me that the world was rightside up, she spat out a mouthful of hot coals, and then dribbled a small string of blazing diamonds down her chin. Roberto had been a little wistfully drunk in the tavern; he was recovering from his heart attack over the girl Renata, but he was rather bitter about tourism in general and tourists in particular—there was a new Carousel expected in a few days. I wondered about Deeds, what he was doing with himself; and then I had the queer dissolving feeling that perhaps he had never existed or that I had imagined him. Roberto was saying: "Travelling isn't honest. Everyone is trying to get away from something or else they would stay at home. The old get panicky because they can't make love any more, and they feel death in the air. The others, well, I bet you have your own reasons too. In the case of the officer Deeds you know his young brother is buried in that little cemetery where he told us about the locust-beans—one of the commandos he mentioned. Much younger than him I gather." He went on a while in a desultory fashion, while we drank off a bit of blue-black iron-tasting wine—I wondered if our insides would rust. I had done my packing, I had bought my postcards and guides. I wondered vaguely what Pausanias had been trying to get away from as he trudged around Athens taking notes. A Roman villa on the Black Sea, a nagging wife, the solitary consular life to which he had, as an untalented man, doomed himself?

We walked slowly back to my hotel in the fine afternoon light; and there another surprise awaited me. In my bedroom sat an extraordinary figure which I had, to the best of my knowledge, never seen before. A bald man with a blazing, glazed-looking cranium which was so white that it must have been newly cropped. It was when he removed his dark glasses and grinned that I recognised, with sinking heart, my old travelling companion Beddoes. "Old boy," he said, with a kind of fine elation, "they are on my trail, the carabinieri. Interpol must have lit a beacon. So I had to leave my hotel for a while." I did not know what to say. "But I am sneaking off tonight on the Messina ferry and Roberto has arranged to have me cremated, so to speak."

"Cremated?"

"Tonight, old boy, I jump into Etna like old Empedocles, with a piercing eldrich shriek. And you and Roberto at dawn scatter some of my belongings around the brink, and the Carousel announces my death to the press."

"You take my breath away. Roberto said nothing to me. And I have just left him."

"You can't be too discreet in these matters. Anyway it is just Sicilian courtesy. They often let people disappear like that."

"Beddoes, are you serious?"

It sounded like the sudden intrusion of an *opera bouffe* upon the humdrum existence of innocent tourists. And then that amazing glazed dome, glittering and resplendent. It looked sufficiently new to attract curiosity and I was relieved to see that he covered it up with a dirty ski-cap. Clad thus he looked like a madly determined Swiss Concierge. "Roberto asked me to leave my belongings here with you. When he calls for you at midnight just carry them along; he will know what to do. And it's quite a neat parcel."

"Very well," I said reluctantly, and he beamed and shook my hand as he said goodbye. Then, turning at the door, he said: "By the way, old scout, I forgot to ask you if you could loan me a few quid. I am awfully pushed for lolly. I had to buy a spare pair of boots and an overcoat to complete my disguise. Cost the earth." I obliged with pardonable reluctance and he took himself off, whistling "Giovanezza" under his breath.

His belongings consisted of a sleeping-bag and a mackintosh, plus a pair of shapeless navvy's boots. The suitcase was empty save of a copy of a novel entitled *The Naked Truth*.

Roberto was punctual and accepted full responsibility for the plot concerning Beddoes' disappearance. Apparently the authorities often turned a blind eye to the disappearance of people into Etna. He said: "There's only one other volcano where one can arrange that sort of thing for hopeless lovers or bankrupts or schoolmasters on the run like Beddoes. It's in Japan."

The car drummed and whined its way into the mountains and I began to feel the long sleep of this hectic fortnight creep upon me. I had a drink and pulled myself together for we had to envisage a good walk at the other end, from the last point before the crater, the observatory. It became cooler and cooler. Then lights and mountain air with spaces of warmth, and the smell of acid and sulphur as we walked up the slopes of the crater. Somewhere near the top we lit a bonfire and carefully singed Beddoes' affairs before consigning them to the care of a carabinieri friend who would declare that he had found them on the morrow. The boots burned like an effigy of wax—he must have greased them with something. Poor old Beddoes!

Then the long wait by a strange watery moonlight until an oven lid started to open in the east and the "old shield-bearer" stuck its nose over the silent sea. "There it is," said Roberto, as if he had personally arranged the matter for me. I thanked him. I reflected how lucky I was to have spent so much of my life in the Mediterranean—to have so frequently seen these incomparable dawns, to have so often had sun and moon both in the sky together.

PART V

POST-TOURISM

"There has been, of late, a strange turn in travellers to be displeased." Samuel Johnson's observation, voiced in 1778, applies today, suggesting the tendency in contemporary travel writing toward annoyance, boredom, disillusion, even anger. The emotions, in short, of post-tourism.

Somehow, the bloom is off. Or so one could infer from many current travel books, fit to be subtitled, like John Krich's account of his travels in the Orient, India, and the Near East in 1984, *Around the World in a Bad Mood*. (His depressing title is *Music in Every Room*, a quote from a handbill advertising a horrible hotel in India.) As an epigraph for his book Krich has chosen a passage from Claude Lévi-Strauss's *Tristes Tropiques*, a work which more than any other has helped set the intellectual and emotional style of post-tourism. Published in 1955 (roughly the moment when jet travel began replacing other types), Lévi-Strauss's book opens with a chapter beginning, "I hate travelers and explorers," and goes on to argue the virtual impossibility now of "understanding" anything about other people by "travel" among them in the old sense. As the equally skeptical John Krich says,

> It was a book set in Brazil that told us the most about what we could, or couldn't see in Asia. Claude Lévi-Strauss turned out to be our most articulate ally, whose respect for the savage was tempered by his weariness at ever understanding him, or himself. *Tristes Tropiques* became our true guidebook. . . .

And Krich shares Lévi-Strauss's conviction that modern industrialism has so ruined the world that no place can any longer constitute a refuge from pollution, corruption, and Western-style commercialism. Thus, "trying to escape—at least in ways that travel brochures promise—is like trying to escape death. We know that we can't really do it, but that all the meaning we'll ever find will be in the effort."

It is a rare contemporary traveler who does not pause somewhere in his travel book to deplore the ruin of the environment, a process which seems to have accelerated dramatically since the Second World War.

Observing the atom-bomb test at Bikini Atoll in the late 1940s, David Bradley noticed on the shoreline the "full story of man's coming . . . spread out on the beach: boxes, mattresses, life belts, tires, boots, bottles, . . . rusting machinery and oil drums, all the crud and corruption spread out on the sands, and smeared over with inches of tar and oil." And thirty-four years later Patrick White, traveling in Greece, sounds with similar materials the true note of post-tourism:

> Gythion turned out a somewhat unprepossessing town, with . . . some of the worst plumbing and food. There is a small island, Crainai, where Paris and Helen are said to have enjoyed each other after their elopement. Today the island is linked to the town by a causeway, . . . the Mecca of German hippies with camper vans. It was littered with rubbish and human shit. Still, we enjoyed climbing the terraces of Gythion, asking directions and general information of friendly women, and sipping our ouzo in a cool breeze beside a sea which smelled unavoidably of sewage.

There, the pleasant details—Paris and Helen, the nice women—seem present only to underscore the nastiness. And as Paul Theroux, one of the undoubted masters of the post-touristic vision, walks around the British coast, he does so with a powerful elegiac sense that its former attractiveness is gone forever. "The rock pools of Devon and Cornwall had been violated," he writes, "and Dunwich had sunk into the sea, and Prestatyn was littered, and Sunderland was unemployed. Oddest of all, there were hardly any ships on a coast that had once been crammed with them. 'Once a great port,' the guidebook always said of the seaside towns. And shipbuilding was finished too . . .". (In Theroux there's often a trace, and sometimes more than a trace, of post-touristic masochism. It's hard not to notice how often he enjoys the awfulness he experiences, confirming with pleasure his worst suspicions about the badness of airlines, hotels, guides, and famous places. "You see? I was right!" you can hear him saying. Actually, of course, if the whole operation weren't a form of perverse pleasure, post-touristic travel would never take place and post-touristic travel books would never be written.)

If litter and filth provide one reason for post-touristic dismay, another is the homogenization of the modern world, the spread into even the most unlikely places of the uniform airport and hotel and frozen "international" food and standard "travel agency." Prophesying about the 1960s, Evelyn Waugh observed, in an essay titled "I See Nothing But Boredom Everywhere," that genuine foreign travel would become one of the main casualties. Formerly, he says, "One went abroad to observe other ways of living, to eat unfamiliar foods and see strange buildings."

But soon, he notes prophetically, the world will be divided into "zones of insecurity" dominated by terrorism and, on the other hand, flashy and vulgar tourist sites where one will be conveyed by jet to "chain hotels, hygienic, costly, and second-rate." Although it is now hard to believe, once upon a time, as Paul Bowles recalls, air travel was pleasant. Of a flight in the thirties he recalls, "I had my own cabin with a bed in it, and under sheet and blankets I slept during most of the flight." But forty years later the progress of the tourist industry had brought him to a full post-touristic attitude. "I realized with a shock," he says, "that not only did the world have many more people in it than it had a short time before, but also that the hotels were less good, travel less comfortable, and places in general much less beautiful. . . . I realized to what an extent the world had worsened." His conclusion, mistaken as it may be, will strike some as the only honest one for a person of taste and sensibility: "I no longer wanted to travel."

Standardization, multiplication, and general (if sometimes skillfully concealed) contempt for the customers have evaporated much of the pleasure that used to attend even tourism. The motel-room placard Vladimir Nabokov devises (or perhaps simply transcribes?) in *Lolita* is as good an index of post-touristic disillusion as anything:

We wish you to feel at home while here. *All* equipment was carefully checked upon your arrival. Your licence number is on record here. Use hot water sparingly. We reserve the right to eject without notice any objectionable person. Do not throw waste materials of *any* kind in the toilet bowl. Thank you. Call again. The Management.

P.S. We consider our guests the Finest People of the World.

JOHN CROWE RANSOM
1888–1974

As early as the 1920s some Americans were beginning to sense that respectful pilgrimage to the Old World had perhaps outlived its usefulness for citizens of the New, who would have to create a culture not entirely modelled after European examples. Ransom, the quietly ironic Tennessee man of letters, here offers an early hint of one strain of post-tourism.

PHILOMELA
(1924)

Procne, Philomela, and Itylus,
Your names are liquid, your improbable tale
Is recited in the classic numbers of the nightingale.
Ah, but our numbers are not felicitous,
It goes not liquidly for us.

Perched on a Roman ilex, and duly apostrophized,
The nightingale descanted unto Ovid;
She has even appeared to the Teutons, the swilled and gravid;
At Fontainebleau it may be the bird was gallicized;
Never was she baptized.

To England came Philomela with her pain,
Fleeing the hawk her husband; querulous ghost,
She wanders when he sits heavy on his roost,
Utters herself in the original again,
The untranslatable refrain.

Not to these shores she came! this other Thrace,
Environ barbarous to the royal Attic;
How could her delicate dirge run democratic,
Delivered in a cloudless boundless public place
To an inordinate race?

I pernoctated with the Oxford students once,
And in the quadrangles, in the cloisters, on the Cher,
Precociously knocked at antique doors ajar,
Fatuously touched the hems of the hierophants,
Sick of my dissonance.

I went out to Bagley Wood, I climbed the hill;
Even the moon had slanted off in a twinkling,
I heard the sepulchral owl and a few bells tinkling,
There was no more villainous day to unfulfil,
The diuturnity was still.

Up from the darkest wood where Philomela sat,
Her fairy numbers issued. What then ailed me?
My ears are called capacious but they failed me,
Her classics registered a little flat!
I rose, and venomously spat.

Philomela, Philomela, lover of song,
I am in despair if we may make us worthy,
A bantering breed sophistical and swarthy;
Unto more beautiful, persistently more young,
Thy fabulous provinces belong.

CLAUDE LÉVI-STRAUSS
1908-

This most influential of modern anthropologists was born in Brussels. After studying sociology at the Sorbonne, he took a law degree and taught in a lycée before moving to Brazil in the late 1930s. There he taught at the University of São Paulo and undertook explorations into the interior to observe Indian behavior. When World War II broke out, he managed to get to New York and to find a teaching position at The New School for Social Research. After the war he served the French embassy in Washington as cultural attaché.

In the mid-1940s he began publishing research based largely on his Brazilian field studies, and he later produced the books which helped define and illustrate the new field of Structural Anthropology with which his name is associated. These include Totemism *(1963),* The Savage Mind *(1966),* The Elementary Structures of Kinship *(1969), and* The Raw and the Cooked *(1970). In these works his search was for the deep "structures" underlying all human systems and expectations, the universal contrasts and polarities generating the intellectual, psychological, and social forms common to all peoples. His ability to perceive uniform elements in all human cultures was one result of his sensitivity in inferring the sophistication and complexity of "savage" societies. There are, he found, no such creatures as "primitive peoples."*

Tristes Tropiques *was first published in France in 1955. This translation, by John and Doreen Weightman, appeared in 1973. The author has insisted that the title remain in French. If translated, it would come out something like* The Sadness of the Tropics *or* The Melancholy of the Foreign.

From TRISTES TROPIQUES
(1955)

ON BOARD SHIP

. . . We never suspected that for the next four or five years—with very few exceptions—our little group was destined to provide the total complement of first-class passengers on the cargo-cum-passenger liners of the Compagnie des Transports Maritimes plying between France and South America. We had the choice between second-class berths on the only luxury liner using this route, or first-class berths on less grand boats. Social climbers opted for the first alternative and paid the difference out of their own pockets, in the hope of hobnobbing with ambassadors and thus gaining certain doubtful advantages. The rest of us took the cargo-cum-passenger boats, on which the journey lasted six days longer, with calls at several ports, but where we enjoyed supremacy.

I wish now that I had been able, twenty years ago, to appreciate fully the unheard-of luxury and regal privilege of being among the eight or ten passengers who, on a boat built to accommodate 100 or 150, had the deck, the cabins, the smoking-room and the dining-room all to themselves. During the nineteen days at sea, all this space, which seemed almost limitless through the absence of other people, became our province: it was as if the boat were our appanage, moving with us. After two or three crossings, we felt quite at home on board, and knew beforehand the names of all the excellent Marseilles stewards with heavy moustaches and stoutly soled shoes, who smelt strongly of garlic as they served us with chicken supréme and turbot fillets. The meals, which had been planned along Pantagruelian lines, were made even more copious by the fact that there were so few of us to eat them.

The end of one civilization, the beginning of another, and the sudden discovery by our present-day world that it is perhaps beginning to grow too small for the people inhabiting it—these truisms are brought home to me less tangibly by figures, statistics and revolutions than by the fact that when, a few weeks ago, after a lapse of fifteen years I was toying with the idea of recapturing my youth by revisiting Brazil in the same way, I was told on the telephone that I would have to book a cabin four months in advance.

I had fondly imagined that since the introduction of passenger air services between Europe and South America, only one or two eccentric individuals still travelled by boat. Alas, it is an illusion to suppose that the invasion of one element disencumbers another. The sea has no more regained its tranquillity since the introduction of Constellations than the outskirts of Paris have recovered their rustic charm since mass building developments began along the Riviera.

Between the marvellous crossings of the 'thirties and this latest projected one which I hastily abandoned, there had been another in 1941, which I had not suspected at the time of being so extraordinarily symbolic of the future. After the armistice, thanks to the friendly interest shown by Robert H. Lowie and A. Métraux in my anthropological writings, and to the diligence of relatives living in the United States, I was invited to join the New School of Social Research in New York as part of the Rockefeller Foundation's plan for rescuing scholars endangered by the German occupation. The problem was how to get to America. My first idea had been to say that I was returning to Brazil to carry on with my pre-war researches. In the cramped ground-floor premises in Vichy where the Brazilian embassy had taken up its quarters, a brief, and for me tragic, scene was enacted, when I went to ask about renewing my visa. The ambassador, Luis de Souza-Dantas, with whom I was well acquainted and who would have behaved no differently had I been a stranger, picked up his seal and was about to stamp the passport when one of his counsellors interrupted him with icy politeness and pointed out that new regulations had been introduced depriving him of the power to do so. For a few seconds his arm remained poised in mid-air. With an anxious, almost beseeching, glance, the ambassador tried to persuade his subordinate to look the other way so that the stamp could be brought down, thus allowing me at least to leave France, if not to enter Brazil. But all in vain; the counsellor continued to stare at the hand, which eventually dropped on to the table alongside the document. I was not to have my visa; my passport was handed back to me with a gesture of profound regret.

I went back to my house in the Cévennes, not far from Montpellier where, as it happened, I had been demobilized during the retreat, and from there I set off to explore possibilities in Marseilles. According to port gossip, a boat was about to leave for Martinique. By dint of inquiring from dock to dock and in one grimy office after another, I finally discovered that the boat in question belonged to the same Compagnie des Transports Maritimes for which, during all the preceding years, the French university mission to Brazil had provided such a faithful and exclusive clientele. One day in February 1941, when an icy wind was blowing, in an unheated and practically closed-down office, I came upon an official, whose task it had been in the old days to pay his respects to us on behalf of the company. Yes, the boat did exist and was due to sail, but there was no question of my taking it.—Why?—I could not be expected to understand; it was difficult for him to explain; things would not be as they had been in the past.—What would they be like?—It would be a very long, very distressing voyage and he could not even imagine me on board.

The poor man still saw me as a minor ambassador of French culture, whereas I already felt myself to be potential fodder for the concentration camp. Besides, I had just spent the two previous years, first in the heart of a virgin forest, then moving from one billet to another in the course of a disorderly retreat which had taken me from the Maginot Line to Béziers by way of Sarthe, Corrèze and Aveyron; I had travelled in cattle-trucks and slept in sheep-folds, so that the official's scruples struck me as being rather misplaced. I had a vision of myself resuming my wandering existence on the high seas, sharing the toil and the frugal meals of a handful of sailors who had ventured forth on a clandestine boat, sleeping on deck, and forced during long and empty days into a salutary intimacy with the sea.

Finally I got my ticket for the *Capitaine Paul-Lemerle*, but I did not begin to understand the situation until the day we went on board between two rows of helmeted *gardes mobiles* (militia men] with sten guns in their hands, who cordoned off the quayside, preventing all contact between the passengers and their relatives or friends who had come to say goodbye, and interrupting leave-takings with jostling and insults. Far from being a solitary adventure, it was more like the deportation of convicts. What amazed me even more than the way we were treated was the number of passengers. About 350 people were crammed on to a small steamer which—as I was immediately to discover—boasted only two cabins with, in all, seven bunks. One of the cabins had been allocated to three ladies and the other was to be shared by four men, including myself. For this extraordinary favour I was indebted to M.B. (and I take this opportunity of thanking him), who was unable to tolerate the idea that one of his former first-class passengers should be transported like livestock. The rest of my companions, men, women and children, were herded into the hold, with neither air nor light, and where the ship's carpenters had hastily run up bunk beds with straw mattresses. Of the four privileged males, one was an Austrian metal-dealer, who was no doubt well aware of the price he had paid for the privilege; another was a young 'béké'—a wealthy Creole—whom the war had cut off from his native Martinique and who was felt to be worthy of special treatment since he was the only person on board who could reasonably be presumed to be neither a Jew nor a foreigner nor an anarchist; lastly, there was an extraordinary North African character who maintained that he was going to New York for a few days only (a weird claim, given the fact that we were going to spend three months getting there) and who had a Degas in his suitcase. Although he was no less a Jew than I was, he seemed to be *Persona grata* with all the policemen, detectives, gendarmes and security agents of the various colonies and protectorates—an amazing mystery which I never managed to elucidate.

The riff-raff, as the gendarmes called them, included, among others, André Breton and Victor Serge. André Breton, who was very much out of place *dans cette galère* [in that prison-hulk], strode up and down the few empty spaces left on deck; wrapped in his thick nap overcoat, he looked like a blue bear. A lasting friendship was about to develop between us, through an exchange of letters which lasted for quite some time during that interminable voyage and in which we discussed the relationships between aesthetic beauty and absolute originality.

As for Victor Serge, I was intimidated by his status as a former companion of Lenin, at the same time as I had the greatest difficulty in identifying him with his physical presence, which was rather like that of a prim and elderly spinster. The clean-shaven, delicate-featured face, the clear voice accompanied by a stilted and wary manner, had an almost asexual quality, which I was later to find among Buddhist monks along the Burmese frontier, and which is very far removed from the virile and superabundant vitality commonly associated in France with what are called subversive activities. The explanation is that cultural types which occur in very similar forms in every society, because they are constructed around very simple polarities, are used to fulfil different social functions in different communities. Serge's type had been able to realize itself in a revolutionary career in Russia, but elsewhere it might have played some other part. No doubt relationships between any two societies would be made easier if, through the use of some kind of grid, it were possible to establish a pattern of equivalences between the ways in which each society uses analogous human types to perform different social functions. Instead of simply arranging meetings on a professional basis, doctors with doctors, teachers with teachers and industrialists with industrialists, we might perhaps be led to see that there are more subtle correspondences between individuals and the parts they play.

In addition to its human load, the boat was carrying some kind of clandestine cargo. Both in the Mediterranean and along the west coast of Africa, we spent a fantastic amount of time dodging into various ports, apparently to escape inspection by the English navy. Passengers with French passports were sometimes allowed to land: the others remained parked within the few dozen square centimetres available to each. Because of the heat, which became more intense as we approached the tropics, it was impossible to remain below and the deck was gradually turned into dining-room, bedroom, day-nursery, wash-house and solarium. But the most disagreeable feature was what is referred to in the army as the sanitary arrangements. Against the rail on either side—port for the men, starboard side for the women—the crew had erected two pairs of wooden huts, with neither windows nor ventilation; one contained a few shower sprinklers which only worked in the morning: the other was provided with a long wooden trough crudely lined with zinc and leading directly into the sea, for the obvious reason. Those of us who were averse to crowds and shrank from collective squatting, which was in any case rendered unsteady by the lurching of the ship, had no choice but to get up very early; and throughout the entire trip a kind of race developed between the fastidious passengers, so that towards the end it was only at about three o'clock in the morning that one could hope for relative privacy. Finally, it was no longer possible to go to bed at all. Except for the time difference of two hours, the same was true for the shower-baths, where the idea uppermost in every mind was, if not to protect one's modesty, at least to succeed in finding a place in the crowd under the insufficient supply of water, which seemed to turn to steam through contact with so many clammy bodies, and hardly touched the skin. In either case, there was a general urge to complete the operation quickly and get out, for the unventilated huts were made of planks of unseasoned, resinous pine which, after being impregnated with dirty water, urine and sea air, began to ferment in the sun and give off a warmish, sweet and nauseous odour; this, added to other smells, very soon became intolerable, especially when there was a swell.

When, after a month at sea, we sighted the Fort de France lighthouse in the middle of the night, it was not the prospect of an edible meal, a bed with sheets and a peaceful night's sleep which caused the passengers' hearts to swell with anticipation. All those who, previously, had enjoyed what are called the amenities of civilization, had suffered not so much from hunger, fatigue, sleeplessness, overcrowding and the disrespect in which they had lived for the past four weeks, as from the enforced filth, which was made still worse by the heat. There were young and pretty women on board; flirtations had begun and sympathies had ripened. For them, to appear in a favourable light before the final separation was more than mere coquettishness: it was an account to be settled, a debt to be honoured, a proof they felt they owed of the fact that they were not fundamentally unworthy of the attentions bestowed on them. With a touching delicacy of feeling, they had taken these attentions only, as it were, on credit. So there was not only an element of farce but also a slight hint of pathos in the cry which arose from every pair of lungs. Instead of the call "Land! Land!" as in traditional sea stories, "A bath, at last a bath, a bath tomorrow!" could be heard on every side, while at the same time people embarked on a feverish inventory of the last piece of soap, the unstained towel, or the clean blouse which had been carefully preserved for this great occasion.

This hydrotherapeutic dream implied an exaggeratedly optimistic view of the civilized amenities to be expected after four centuries of colonization (bathrooms are few and far between at Fort de France), but the passengers were soon to learn that their filthy, overcrowded boat was an idyllic refuge, in comparison with the welcome they were to receive almost as soon as the ship docked. We fell into the hands of soldiers suffering from a collective form of mental derangement, which would have repaid anthropological study, had the anthropologist not been obliged to use his entire intellectual resources for the purpose of avoiding its unfortunate consequences.

Most French people had experienced a peculiar war, a *drôle de guerre* [phony war]; but no superlative could do justice to the war as it had been experienced by the officers stationed in Martinique. Their one assignment, which was to guard the gold of the Bank of France, had degenerated into a kind of nightmare, for which the excessive drinking of punch was only partly responsible; other factors, which played a more insidious but no less essential part, were their isolated situation, their remoteness from metropolitan France, and a historical tradition rich in pirates' tales, so that it was easy to replace the old, one-legged, gold-earringed characters by North American spies or German submarines on secret missions. There had thus developed an obsidional excitement which had driven most individuals into a state of panic, although no fighting had as yet occurred—and for the best of reasons, since no enemy had ever been sighted. The conversation of the native inhabitants revealed the same kind of mental processes, only on a more prosaic level: "There's no more salt cod, the island's done for" was a frequently heard comment, while some people explained that Hitler was none other than Jesus Christ, who had come back to earth to punish the white race for having failed to follow his teachings during the previous two thousand years.

At the time of the armistice, the non-commissioned officers, far from joining the Free French, felt themselves in harmony with the Vichy government. They proposed to remain "uninvolved"; their physical and moral state, which had been undermined for months, would have rendered them unfit for active service, supposing they had at any time been up to it; their sick minds found a kind of security in replacing the Germans, their real enemy, but one so far away as to have become invisible and as it were abstract, by an imaginary enemy who had the advantage of being close at hand and tangible—the Americans. Besides, two United States warships cruised continuously outside the harbour. A clever assistant-commander of the French forces used to lunch on board every day, at the same time as his superior officer deliberately stirred up hatred and bitterness against the Anglo-Saxons among his troops.

They needed enemies on whom they could vent their feelings of aggressiveness, which had been accumulating for months; they needed someone to blame for the defeat of France, in which they felt they had no share since they had not taken part in the fighting, but for which, in another sense, they felt obscurely guilty (they themselves, in fact, had provided a consummate example and the most extreme instance of the unconcern, illusions and apathy which had overcome part, at least, of France). In this respect, our boat offered a particularly apposite collection of specimens. It was rather as if the Vichy authorities, in allowing us to leave for Martinique, had sent them a cargo of scapegoats, on whom these gentlemen could relieve their feelings. The soldiers in tropical kit, complete with helmets and guns, who took up their positions in the captain's cabin to interview each one of us individually, seemed to be less concerned with conducting pre-disembarkation interrogations than with giving a display of invective to which we could only listen. The non-French passengers found themselves classed as enemies; those who were French were rudely denied this distinction, at the same time as they were accused of having abandoned their country in a cowardly fashion. The indictment was not only a contradiction in terms; it sounded strange, coming from men who had been living under the protection of the Monroe Doctrine ever since the outbreak of war.

There was no question of baths. It was decided that everybody was to be interned in a camp called Le Lazaret on the far side of the bay. Only three people were allowed to land: the "béké", who was in a category by himself, the mysterious Tunisian, who was able to show some document or other, and myself—as a special favour granted to the ship's captain by the naval authorities; he and I had discovered we were old friends, since he had been chief officer on one of the boats in which I had travelled before the war.

THE WEST INDIES

At two o'clock in the afternoon, Fort de France was a dead town; it was impossible to believe that anyone lived in the ramshackle buildings which bordered the long market-place planted with palm trees and overrun with weeds, and which was more like a stretch of waste-ground with, in its middle, an apparently forgotten statue, green with neglect, of Joséphine Tascher de la Pagerie, later known as Joséphine de Beauharnais. As soon as we had booked into a deserted hotel, the Tunisian and I, still shaken by the morning's events, jumped into a hired car and headed for Le Lazaret. We wanted to comfort our companions, and more especially two young German women who had given us to understand during the crossing that they would be in a great hurry to deceive their husbands, once they were able to wash. In this respect, the business of Le Lazaret increased our disappointment.

While the old Ford was churning its way up steep tracks in bottom gear and I was rediscovering with delight a host of vegetable species that were familiar to me since my stay in Amazonia but that I was to learn here to call by new names—*caïmite* instead of *fruta do condé* (which has the shape of an artichoke and a pear-like flavour), *corrosol* and not *graviola, papaye* for *mammão, sapotille* (sapodilla) for *mangabeira,* etc.—I reflected on the painful scenes which had just taken place and tried to link them with other experiences of a similar kind. For my companions, who had been plunged into an adventurous journey after leading often uneventful existences, the mixture of spitefulness and stupidity they had encountered appeared as an unheard-of, unique and exceptional phenomenon—in fact, as the impact on their private persons and on the persons of their jailors of an international catastrophe such as had never before occurred in history. But I had seen something of the world and during the preceding years had found myself in far from ordinary situations, so that for me this kind of experience was not entirely unfamiliar. I knew that, slowly and gradually, experiences such as these were starting to ooze out like some insidious leakage from contemporary mankind, which had become saturated with its own numbers and with the ever-increasing complexity of its problems, as if its skin had been irritated by the friction of ever-greater material and intellectual exchange brought about by the improvement in communication. In that particular French territory, the sole effect of war and defeat had been to hasten the advance of a universal process, to facilitate the establishment of a lasting form of contamination which would never entirely disappear from the face of the earth but would re-emerge in some new place as it died down elsewhere. This was not the first occasion on which I had encountered those outbreaks of stupidity, hatred and credulousness which social groups secrete like pus when they begin to be short of space.

Only a little while previously, a few months before the outbreak of war, in the course of my return journey to France, I had visited Bahia and had walked through the upper town, going from one church to another; there are said to be 365 of them, one for each day of the year, and they vary in style and interior decoration as the days and seasons differ. I was absorbed in photographing their architectural details, and as I moved from place to place I was followed by a group of half-naked nigger-boys who kept pleading, "Tira o retrato! Tira o retrato!" ("Take a photo of us!"). Finally, touched by such a charming form of begging—they preferred a photo they would never see to a few coppers—I agreed to take a snap to please them. I had barely gone a hundred yards further when a hand descended on my shoulder: two plain-clothes inspectors who had been following me step by step informed me that I had just committed an unfriendly act towards Brazil: the photograph, if used in Europe, might possibly give credence to the legend that there were black-skinned Brazilians and that the urchins of Bahia went barefoot. I was taken into custody, but fortunately was detained only for a short time, because the boat was about to leave.

That boat, as it happened, brought me nothing but bad luck; a few days earlier I had met with a similar experience, just after joining the ship and while it was still at the quayside in the port of Santos. I had hardly gone on board when a commander of the Brazilian navy in full uniform accompanied by two marines with fixed bayonets imprisoned me in my cabin. In this case, it took four to five hours to clear up the mystery. The Franco-Brazilian expedition, of which I had been in charge for the past year, was subject to the official regulations governing the sharing out, between the two countries, of the material collected. The operation had to be carried out under the supervision of the National Museum of Rio de Janeiro, which had immediately notified all the ports in the country that, should I attempt to make a sinister getaway with bows, arrows and feathered head-dresses exceeding the share allotted to France, I must at all costs be taken into custody. However, when the expedition returned, the Rio museum changed its mind and decided to hand over Brazil's share to a scientific institute in São Paulo; I was accordingly informed that the shipment of the French share should take place through Santos and not through Rio, but as it had been forgotten that a different decision had been taken the year before, I was detained as a criminal by virtue of obsolete instructions, which had slipped the minds of their originators but were still remembered by those commissioned to carry them out.

Fortunately, at that time, every Brazilian official still had inside him a concealed anarchist, who was kept alive by the shreds of Voltaire and Anatole France which impregnated the national culture even in the depths of the bush. (Once, in a village in the interior, an old man overcome by emotion had exclaimed, "Ah Monsieur, you are French! Ah, France! Anatole, Anatole!" as he clasped me in his arms; he had never seen a Frenchman before.) So, being sufficiently experienced to know that I should not be sparing in the expression of my feelings of deference towards the Brazilian State in general and the naval authorities in particular, at the same time I took pains to touch on certain sensitive spots; and, to good effect, since, after a few hours spent in a cold sweat (the ethnographical material was packed in the crates along with my personal effects and my books, because I was leaving Brazil for good, and there was a moment of panic when I thought that everything might be scattered on the quayside just when the boat was weighing anchor), I myself dictated to the official a report in which, in scathing terms, he took credit for having allowed me to leave with my luggage, thus saving his country from an international conflict and subsequent humiliation.

But perhaps I would not have behaved so brazenly had I not still been influenced by the memory of an incident which had shown South American policemen in a very comic light. Two months previously, I had been forced to change planes in a large village in Lower Bolivia; I was stranded there for several days in the company of Dr. J. A. Vellard, while waiting for a connection which failed to arrive. In 1938, the air services were very different from what they are today. In remote regions of South America, which had skipped certain stages in civilization, the aeroplane had at once become a kind of local bus for village people who, until then, had had to spend several days trekking to the nearest fair either on foot or on horseback, since there were no roads. Now, a flight which lasted only a few minutes (but which, to be exact, often took place more than a few days late) made the transporting of their hens and ducks quite easy. The passengers, as often as not, were obliged to squat among the fowls, since the tiny planes were crammed with a motley assortment of barefooted peasants, farmyard animals and packing-cases which were either too heavy or too bulky to be carried along the forest tracks.

So, for the lack of anything better to do, we wandered through the streets of Santa Cruz de la Sierra, which had been transformed by the rainy season into muddy torrents. These were forded by means of huge stones placed at regular intervals, like the studs of some pedestrian crossing that no vehicle could ever get past. A patrol spotted our unfamiliar faces, which provided sufficient reason for arresting us and shutting us up, until such time as we could explain our presence, in a room richly furnished in an old-fashioned style. It was in the former palace of the provincial governor, and the panelled walls were interspersed with glass-fronted bookcases, filled with heavy, richly bound volumes. The effect was broken only by a notice-board, also glass-fronted and framed, containing an extraordinary inscription, done in beautiful copperplate, and which I translate literally from the Spanish: "Under pain of severe sanctions, it is strictly forbidden to tear out pages from the archives and to use them for particular or hygienic purposes. Any person infringing this rule will be punished."

Honesty compels me to admit that my situation in Martinique improved thanks to the intervention of a highly placed official belonging to the Ponts et Chaussées who, beneath a rather cool and reserved exterior, concealed feelings very different from those which normally prevailed in official circles. I may have been helped too by my frequent visits to the offices of a religious newspaper, where the Fathers of some Order, the name of which I forget, had stored chests full of archaeological remains dating from the Indian occupation; I devoted my leisure hours to making an inventory of them.

One day, I went into the assize court, which happened to be in session; this was my first, and has to date remained my only, visit to a law court. The person on trial was a peasant who had bitten off a piece of one of his opponent's ears during a quarrel. The accused, the plaintiff and the witnesses expressed themselves volubly in the Creole dialect, the crystalline freshness of which seemed positively uncanny in such surroundings. Their statements were translated for three judges, who were suffering from the heat, since they were wrapped in red, fur-trimmed robes which had lost their crispness in the humid atmosphere. The grotesque garments hung limply round their bodies like bloodstained bandages. It took exactly five minutes to pass a sentence of eight years' imprisonment on the hot-tempered peasant. Justice always has, and always will be, associated in my mind with doubt, scrupulousness and respect. That the fate of a human being could be settled in so short a time and in such an offhand manner filled me with amazement. I could not bring myself to believe that what I had just witnessed had actually happened. Even today, no dream, however fantastic or far-fetched, can inspire me with such a feeling of incredulity.

My fellow-passengers owed their release to a difference of opinion between the naval authorities and the local tradesmen. While the former looked upon them as spies and traitors, the latter considered that their internment at Le Lazaret, even though it was not free of charge, was depriving the town of a source of financial profit. The second view prevailed and, for a fortnight, everyone was free to spend their last French notes, under the close supervision of the police who wove around each individual, and more especially around the women, a web of temptations, provocations, enticements and reprisals. Meanwhile, the Dominican consulate was besieged for visas, and there were any number of false rumors about the arrival of hypothetical boats which were supposed to get us out of our quandary. The situation changed again when the tradespeople in the villages, who were jealous of the big town, argued that they too were entitled to their share of refugees. From one day to the next, everyone was billeted in the inland villages. I was again spared, but being anxious to follow my fair friends to their new abode at the foot of Mont Pelé, I was able—thanks to this final piece of maneuvering on the part of the police—to enjoy some unforgettable walks across the island, which seemed so much more classically exotic than the South American mainland. It was like a deep arborized agate set in a ring of black, silver-flecked beaches, and in the valleys, which were brimful with a milk-white mist, one could only just sense the presence—more perceptible to the ear, through the sound of dripping moisture, than to the eye—of the huge, soft, feathery fronds of the tree-ferns, rising above the living fossils of their trunks.

Although up till then I had fared better than my companions, I was none the less preoccupied by a problem to which I must now refer, since the writing of this book depended on its being solved and this, as will appear, proved to be no easy task. My sole wealth was a trunk full of documents relating to my fieldwork: it included linguistic and technological card-indexes, a travel diary, anthropological notes, maps, diagrams and photographic negatives—in short, thousands of items. The suspicious load had crossed the demarcation line in France only at considerable risk to the professional smuggler who had agreed to transport it. From the reception I had received in Martinique, I concluded that the customs men, the police and the naval intelligence officers must not be allowed even a glimpse of what they would inevitably interpret as instructions in code (the notes on native dialects), or diagrams of fortifications, or invasion plans (the maps, sketches and photos). I therefore resolved to declare that my trunk was in transit, and so it was deposited, still sealed, in the storerooms of the customs house. This meant, as I was later informed, that I would have to leave Martinique on a foreign boat, to which the trunk would be directly transferred (and I had to make a great effort to achieve even this compromise). If I intended to go to New York on the *D'Aumale* (a veritable ghost-ship, which my companions waited for during a whole month before it actually materialized one fine morning, all newly painted like a huge toy from another century), the trunk would have to enter Martinique officially, and then be taken out again. I couldn't have this, and so I boarded an immaculately white Swedish banana boat bound for Puerto Rico. For four days, I enjoyed a quiet and almost solitary crossing, like a throwback to happier times, for there were only eight passengers on board. It was a good thing I made the most of it.

After the French, I had to contend with the American police. On landing in Puerto Rico, I discovered two things: during the two months which had elapsed since we left Marseilles, the immigration laws in the United States had been altered, and the documents I had with me from the New School for Social Research no longer complied with the new regulations; then, what was more important, the suspicions I had supposed would be aroused in the Martinique police by my anthropological documents, and against which I had so wisely protected myself, were entertained to the highest possible degree by the American police. After being accused, at Fort de France, of being a Jewish Freemason in the pay of the Americans, I had the somewhat bitter compensation of discovering that, from the American point of view, there was every likelihood that I was an emissary of the Vichy Government, and perhaps even of the Germans. While waiting for the New School (which I wired immediately) to satisfy the new legal requirements, as well as for the arrival of a F.B.I. specialist capable of reading French (and, knowing that three-quarters of my notes consisted not of French words but of terms belonging to practically unknown dialects of central Brazil, I shuddered at the thought of the time it would take to discover an expert), the immigration authorities decided to intern me, at the shipping company's expense, in an austere, Spanish-type hotel, where I was fed on boiled beef and chick-peas, while two extremely dirty and ill-shaven native policemen took it in turns to guard my door day and night.

I remember that it was in the courtyard of this hotel that, one evening, Bertrand Goldschmidt, who had arrived on the same boat and who was later to become one of the directors of the Atomic Energy Commission, explained the principle of the atomic bomb to me and revealed (this was in May 1941) that the major powers had embarked on a scientific race, the winner of which would be sure of victory.

After a few days, my last travelling companions settled their personal difficulties and set off for New York. I remained alone in San Juan, escorted by my two policemen, who, at my request, accompanied me as often as I wanted to the three places which were not out of bounds—the French consulate, the bank and the immigration offices. To go anywhere else, I had to ask for special permission. One day, I was allowed to go to the university, and my attendant policeman tactfully remained outside and waited for me at the door, so as to avoid humiliating me. And since both he and his companion were bored, they occasionally broke the rules and allowed me, on their own initiative, to take them to the cinema. It was only during the forty-eight hours which elapsed between my release and my boarding the ship that I was able to visit the island, escorted by M. Christian Belle, who was French consul at the time and who turned out to be—rather to my surprise, given the unusual circum-

stances—a fellow-specialist in American Indian matters and full of sto-
ries of the voyages he had made along the South American seaboard.
Shortly before, the morning press had announced the arrival of Jacques
Soustelle, who was touring the West Indies in order to persuade the
French residents to support General de Gaulle; again I had to obtain
special permission in order to meet him.

And so, it was at Puerto Rico that I first made contact with the United
States; for the first time I breathed in the smell of warm car paint and
wintergreen (which, in French, used to be called *thé du Canada* [Cana-
dian tea], those two olfactory poles between which stretches the whole
range of American comfort, from cars to lavatories, by way of radio sets,
sweets and toothpaste; and I tried to guess what the girls in the drugstores with their lilac dresses and mahogany hair were thinking about,
behind their mask-like make-up. It was here, too, but from the rather
special angle of the Greater Antilles, that I first perceived certain features of the typical American town; the flimsiness of the buildings, and
the desire to create an eye-catching effect, made it look like some world
exhibition that had become permanent, except that, in this instance,
one might have imagined oneself to be in the Spanish section.

The accidents of travel often produce ambiguities such as these.
Because I spent my first weeks on United States soil in Puerto Rico, I
was in future to find America in Spain. Just as, several years later,
through visiting my first English university with a campus surrounded
by Neo-Gothic buildings at Dacca in Western Bengal, I now look upon
Oxford as a kind of India that has succeeded in controlling the mud, the
mildew and the ever-encroaching vegetation.

The F.B.I. inspector arrived three weeks after the beginning of my
stay at San Juan. I rushed to the customs office and opened my trunk;
it was a solemn moment. A polite young man came forward and picked
out a card-index entry at random. His gaze narrowed and he turned
fiercely towards me: "It's in German!" As it happened, it was a reference
to the classic work, *Unter den Naturvölkern Zentral-Brasiliens* (Berlin,
1894), written by von den Steinen, my illustrious and distant predecessor
in the central Mato Grosso. My explanation immediately cleared things
up and the expert, for whom we had waited so long, lost interest in the
whole business. Everything was all right, O.K.; I could enter American
territory; I was free.

It is time to stop. Each of these minor adventures recalls other
incidents to mind. Some, like the one I have just related, are connected
with the war, but others, which I recounted earlier, relate to the pre-war
period. And I could add others of more recent date, if I drew on my
travels in Asia of the last few years. But today my nice F.B.I. inspector

would not be so easily satisfied. Everywhere the atmosphere is becoming equally oppressive.

THE QUEST FOR POWER

One trifling incident, which has remained in my memory like an omen, was, for me, the first instance of one of those dubious scents or veering winds which herald some profound disturbance. After deciding not to renew my contract with the University of São Paulo so as to be able to make a long trip into the interior, I had gone on ahead of my colleagues and was travelling back to Brazil a few weeks before they did; so, for the first time for four years, I was the only academic on board; for the first time, too, there were a great many passengers: some foreign business-men, but chiefly a whole French military mission on its way to Paraguay. The familiar crossing was thus made unrecognizable, as was the once serene atmosphere on board ship. The officers and their wives made no distinction between a transatlantic crossing and a colonial expedition, or between their duties as instructors to what was, after all, a very modest army and the occupation of a conquered country. To prepare them-selves, mentally at least, for their task, they turned the deck into a parade-ground, and the civilian passengers were reduced to the status of natives. We did not know where to turn to escape such noisy and high-handed behaviour, which even caused uneasiness among the ship's officers. However, the leader of the mission had a very different attitude from that of his subordinates; he and his wife were both discreet and considerate persons; and they came up to me one day in the secluded corner where I was escaping from the din, and asked about my past work and the object of my mission. Also, they managed indirectly to convey the fact that they were no more than powerless and clear-sighted onlook-ers. The contrast was so glaring that it seemed to hide some mystery or other; three or four years later I remembered the incident, when I came across the officer's name in the newspapers and understood that his personal position was, indeed, paradoxical.

It was perhaps then, for the first time, that I understood something which was later confirmed by equally demoralizing experiences in other parts of the world. Journeys, those magic caskets full of dreamlike pro-mises, will never again yield up their treasures untarnished. A prolifer-ating and overexcited civilization has broken the silence of the seas once and for all. The perfumes of the tropics and the pristine freshness of human beings have been corrupted by a busyness with dubious implica-tions, which mortifies our desires and dooms us to acquire only con-taminated memories.

Now that the Polynesian islands have been smothered in concrete and turned into aircraft carriers solidly anchored in the southern seas, when the whole of Asia is beginning to look like a dingy suburb, when shanty-towns are spreading across Africa, when civil and military aircraft blight the primeval innocence of the American or Melanesian forests even before destroying their virginity, what else can the so-called escapism of travelling do than confront us with the more unfortunate aspects of our history? Our great Western civilization, which has created the marvels we now enjoy, has only succeeded in producing them at the cost of corresponding ills. The order and harmony of the Western world, its most famous achievement, and a laboratory in which structures of a complexity as yet unknown are being fashioned, demand the elimination of a prodigious mass of noxious by-products which now contaminate the globe. The first thing we see as we travel round the world is our own filth, thrown into the face of mankind.

So I can understand the mad passion for travel books and their deceptiveness. They create the illusion of something which no longer exists but still should exist, if we were to have any hope of avoiding the overwhelming conclusion that the history of the past twenty thousand years is irrevocable. There is nothing to be done about it now; civilization has ceased to be that delicate flower which was preserved and painstakingly cultivated in one or two sheltered areas of a soil rich in wild species which may have seemed menacing because of the vigour of their growth, but which nevertheless made it possible to vary and revitalize the cultivated stock. Mankind has opted for monoculture; it is in the process of creating a mass civilization, as beetroot is grown in the mass. Henceforth, man's daily bill of fare will consist only of this one item.

In the old days, people used to risk their lives in India or in the Americas in order to bring back products which now seem to us to have been of comically little worth, such as *brasil* or brazilwood (from which the name Brazil was derived)—a red dye—and also pepper which had such a vogue in the time of Henry IV of France that courtiers used to carry the seeds in sweetmeat boxes and eat them like sweets. The visual or olfactory surprises they provided, since they were cheerfully warm to the eye or exquisitely hot on the tongue, added a new range of sense experience to a civilization which had never suspected its own insipidity. We might say, then, that, through a twofold reversal, from these same lands our modern Marco Polos now bring back the moral spices of which our society feels an increasing need as it is conscious of sinking further into boredom, but that this time they take the form of photographs, books and travellers' tales.

Another parallel seems to me to be even more significant. Intentionally or unintentionally, these modern seasonings are falsified. Not, of course, because they are of a purely psychological nature, but because, however honest the narrator may be, he cannot—since this is no longer possible—supply them in a genuine form. For us to be willing to accept them, memories have to be sorted and sifted; through a degree of manipulation which, in the most sincere writers, takes place below the level of consciousness, actual experience is replaced by stereotypes. When I open one of these travel books, I see, for instance, that such and such a tribe is described as savage and is said still to preserve certain primitive customs, which are described in garbled form in a few superficial chapters; yet I spent weeks as a student reading the books on that tribe written by professional anthropologists either recently or as much as fifty years ago, before contact with the white races and the resulting epidemics reduced it to a handful of pathetic rootless individuals. Another community, whose existence is said to have been discovered by a youthful traveller who completed his study in forty-eight hours, was in fact seen (and this is an important point) outside its habitual territory in a temporary camp, which the writer naïvely assumed to be a permanent village. Moreover, the means of approach to the tribe are carefully glossed over, so as not to reveal the presence of the mission station which has been consistently in touch with the natives for the past twenty years, or of the local motor-boat service reaching into the heart of the territory. But the existence of the latter can be deduced by a practised eye from small details in the illustrations, since the photographer has not always been able to avoid including the rusty petrolcans in which this virgin people does its cooking.

The emptiness of such claims, the naïve credulity with which they are received and which in fact helps to prompt them, and even the element of praiseworthiness which to some extent redeems so much wasted effort (doubly wasted because its only effect is to extend the degeneration that it tries to conceal)—all this implies powerful psychological motives, both in the authors and their public, on which the study of certain native institutions can serve to throw light. Anthropology itself can help to elucidate the vogue which wins it so much harmful collaboration.

Among a great many North American tribes, the social prestige of the individual is determined by the circumstances surrounding the ordeals connected with puberty. Some young men set themselves adrift on solitary rafts without food; others seek solitudé in the mountains where they have to face wild beasts, as well as cold and rain. For days, weeks or months on end, as the case may be, they do not eat properly, but live only on coarse food, or fast for long periods and aggravate their impaired physical condition by the use of emetics. Everything is turned into a means of communication with the beyond. They stay immersed for long periods in icy water, deliberately mutilate one or more of their finger-joints, or lacerate their fasciae by dragging heavy loads attached by ropes to sharpened pegs inserted under their dorsal muscles. When they do not resort to such extremes, they at least exhaust themselves by performing various pointless tasks, such as removing all their body hairs, one at a time, or stripping pine branches until not a single needle remains, or hollowing out blocks of stone.

In the dazed, debilitated and delirious state induced by these ordeals they hope to enter into communication with the supernatural world. They believe that a magic animal, touched by the intensity of their sufferings and their prayers, will be forced to appear to them; that a vision will reveal which one will henceforth be their guardian spirit, so that they can take its name and derive special powers from it, which will determine their privileges and rank within their social group.

Have we to conclude that, in the opinion of these natives, nothing is to be expected from society? Both institutions and customs seem to them like a mechanism the monotonous functioning of which leaves nothing to chance, luck or ability. They may think that the only means of compelling fate is to venture into those hazardous marginal areas where social norms cease to have any meaning, and where the protective laws and demands of the group no longer prevail; to go right to the frontiers of average, ordered living, to the breaking point of bodily strength and to the extremes of physical and moral suffering. In this unstable border area, there is a danger of slipping beyond the pale and never coming back, as well as a possibility of drawing from the vast ocean of unexploited forces surrounding organized society a personal supply of power, thanks to which he who has risked all can hope to modify an otherwise unchangeable social order.

However, this interpretation is probably still too superficial, since among these Indians of the North American plains and plateau, individual beliefs are not at variance with collective doctrine. The dialectic as a whole springs from the customs and philosophy of the group. It is from the group that individuals learn their creed; belief in guardian spirits is a group phenomenon, and it is society as a whole which teaches its members that their only hope, within the framework of the social order, is to make an absurd and desperate attempt to break away from it.

It is obvious that this "quest for power" enjoys a renewed vogue in contemporary French society, in the unsophisticated form of the relationship between the public and "its" explorers. Our adolescents too, from puberty onwards, are free to obey the stimuli which have been acting upon them from all sides since early childhood, and to escape, in some way or other, from the temporary hold their civilization has on them. The escape may take place upwards, through the climbing of a mountain, or downwards, by descending into the bowels of the earth, or horizontally, through travel to remote countries. Or again, the desired extreme may be a mental or moral one, as is the case with those individuals who deliberately put themselves into such difficult situations that, in our present state of knowledge, they leave themselves no possibility of survival.

Society shows complete indifference to what might be called the rational outcome of such adventures. They neither involve new scientific discoveries, nor make any new contribution to poetry and literature, since the accounts are, for the most part, appallingly feeble. What counts is the attempt in itself, not any possible aim. As in the native example just given, a young man who lives outside his social group for a few weeks or months, so as to expose himself (sometimes with conviction and sincerity, sometimes, on the contrary, with caution and craftiness—but such differences are not unknown in native societies) to an extreme situation, comes back endowed with a power which finds expression in the writing of newspaper articles and bestsellers and in lecturing to packed halls. However, its magic character is evidenced by the process of self-delusion operating in the society and which explains the phenomenon in all cases. The fact is that these primitive peoples, the briefest contact with whom can sanctify the traveller, these icy summits, deep caverns and impenetrable forests—all of them august settings for noble and profitable revelations—are all, in their different ways, enemies of our society, which pretends to itself that it is investing them with nobility at the very time when it is completing their destruction, whereas it viewed them with terror and disgust when they were genuine adversaries. The savages of the Amazonian forest are sensitive and powerless victims, pathetic creatures caught in the toils of mechanized civilization, and I can resign myself to understanding the fate which is destroying them; but I refuse to be the dupe of a kind of magic which is still more feeble than their own, and which brandishes before an eager public albums of coloured photographs, instead of the now vanished native masks. Perhaps the public imagines that the charms of the savages can be appropriated through the medium of these photographs. Not content with having eliminated savage life, and unaware even of having done so, it feels the need feverishly to appease the nostalgic cannibalism of history with the shadows of those that history has already destroyed.

Can it be that I, the elderly predecessor of those scourers of the jungle, am the only one to have brought back nothing but a handful of ashes? Is mine the only voice to bear witness to the impossibility of escapism? Like the Indian in the myth, I went as far as the earth allows one to go, and when I arrived at the world's end, I questioned the people, the creatures and things I found there and met with the same disappointment: "He stood still, weeping bitterly, praying and moaning. And yet no mysterious sound reached his hears, nor was he put to sleep in order to be transported, as he slept, to the temple of the magic animals. For him there could no longer be the slightest doubt: no power, from anyone, had been granted him . . ."

Dreams, "the god of the savages," as the old missionaries used to say, have always slipped through my fingers like quicksilver. But a few shining particles may have remained stuck, here and there. At Cuiaba, perhaps, where the gold nuggets used to come from? At Ubatuba, now a deserted port, but where the galleons used to be loaded two hundred years ago? In the air over the Arabian deserts, which were pink and green with the pearly lustre of ear-shells? In America or in Asia? On the Newfoundland sandbanks, the Bolivian plateaux or the hills along the Burmese frontier? I can pick out at random a name still steeped in the magic of legend: Lahore.

An airfield in a featureless suburb; endless avenues planted with trees and lined with villas; an hotel, standing in an enclosure and reminiscent of some Normandy stud farm, being just a row of several identical buildings, the doors of which, all at ground level and juxtaposed like stable-doors, led into identical apartments, each with a sitting-room in the front, a dressing-room with washing facilities at the back, and a bedroom in the middle. Two miles of avenue led to a provincial-looking square, with more avenues branching off, and dotted with occasional shops—a chemist's, a photographer's, a bookseller's or a watchmaker's. Caught in this vast and meaningless expanse, I felt that what I was looking for was already beyond my reach. Where was the old, the real Lahore? In order to get to it, on the far side of these badly laid out and already decrepit suburbs, I still had to go through two miles of bazaar, where, with the help of mechanical saws, cheap jewellery was being manufactured out of gold the thickness of tin-plate, and where there were stalls displaying cosmetics, medicines and imported plastic objects. I wondered if I was at last discovering the real Lahore in dark little streets, where I had to flatten myself against the wall to make way for flocks of sheep with blue-and-pink dyed fleece, and for buffaloes—each as big as three cows—which barged into one in friendly fashion, and, still more often, for lorries. Was it when I was gazing at crumbling woodwork, eaten away with age? I might have got some idea of its delicate fretting and carving had the approach to it not been made impossible by the ramshackle electrical supply system, which spread its festoons of wire from wall to wall, like a spider's web all through the old town. From time to time, for a second or two and over the space of a few yards, an image or an echo would seem to surge up from the past: for instance, the clear, serene tinkling in the little street where the gold and silver beaters worked; as if some genie with a thousand arms were absent-mindedly striking a xylophone. Immediately beyond, I again found myself in a vast network of avenues, which had been driven through the ruins of 500-year-old houses, damaged in recent riots—but they had in any case been so often destroyed and repaired that they were of an ageless and indescribable decrepitude. In exploring all this, I was being true to myself as an archaeologist of space, seeking in vain to recreate a lost local colour with the help of fragments and debris.

Then, insidiously, illusion began to lay its snares. I wished I had lived in the days of *real* journeys, when it was still possible to see the full splendour of a spectacle that had not yet been blighted, polluted and spoilt; I wished I had not trodden that ground as myself, but as Bernier, Tavernier or Manucci did . . . Once embarked upon, this guessing game can continue indefinitely. When was the best time to see India? At what period would the study of the Brazilian savages have afforded the purest satisfaction, and revealed them in their least adulterated state? Would it have been better to arrive in Rio in the eighteenth century with Bougainville, or in the sixteenth with Léry and Thevet? For every five years I move back in time, I am able to save a custom, gain a ceremony or share in another belief. But I know the texts too well not to realize that, by going back a century, I am at the same time forgoing data and lines of inquiry which would offer intellectual enrichment. And so I am caught within a circle from which there is no escape: the less human societies were able to communicate with each other and therefore to corrupt each other through contact, the less their respective emissaries were able to perceive the wealth and significance of their diversity. In short, I have only two possibilities: either I can be like some traveller of the olden days, who was faced with a stupendous spectacle, all, or almost all, of which eluded him, or worse still, filled him with scorn and disgust; or I can be a modern traveller, chasing after the vestiges of a vanished reality. I lose on both counts, and more seriously than may at first appear, for, while I complain of being able to glimpse no more than the shadow of the past, I may be insensitive to reality as it is taking shape at this very moment, since I have not reached the stage of development at which I would be capable of perceiving it. A few hundred years hence, in this same place, another traveller, as despairing as myself, will mourn the disappearance of what I might have seen, but failed to see. I am subject to a double infirmity: all that I perceive offends me, and I constantly reproach myself for not seeing as much as I should.

For a long time I was paralysed by this dilemma, but I have the feeling that the cloudy liquid is now beginning to settle. Evanescent forms are becoming clearer, and confusion is being slowly dispelled. What has happened is that time has passed. Forgetfulness, by rolling my memories along in its tide, has done more than merely wear them down or consign them to oblivion. The profound structure it has created out of the fragments allows me to achieve a more stable equilibrium, and to see a clearer pattern. One order has been replaced by another. Between these two cliffs, which preserve the distance between my gaze and its object, time, the destroyer, has begun to pile up rubble. Sharp edges have been blunted and whole sections have collapsed: periods and places collide, are juxtaposed or are inverted, like strata displaced by the tremors on the crust of an ageing planet. Some insignificant detail belonging to the distant past may now stand out like a peak, while whole layers of my past have disappeared without trace. Events without any apparent connection, and originating from incongruous periods and places, slide one over the other and suddenly crystallize into a sort of edifice which seems to have been conceived by an architect wiser than my personal history. "Every man," wrote Chateaubriand, "carries within him a world which is composed of all that he has seen and loved, and to which he constantly returns, even when he is travelling through, and seems to be living in, some different world." Henceforth, it will be possible to bridge the gap between the two worlds. Time, in an unexpected way, has extended its isthmus between life and myself; twenty years of forgetfulness were required before I could establish communion with my earlier experience, which I had sought the world over without understanding its significance or appreciating its essence.

V. S. NAIPAUL

1932–

A descendent of Hindu immigrants from northern India, V(idiadhar) S(urajprased) Naipaul was born in Trinidad and educated at Queen's Royal College there and later at University College, Oxford. His first work of fiction, The Mystic Masseur, *appeared in 1957, and since then he has produced a steady stream of travel books and novels, of which* A House for Mr. Biswas *(1961)* and A Bend in the River *(1979) are perhaps the most highly esteemed.*

A self-styled wanderer, he has felt estranged from Trinidad because of its cultural poverty, from India because of time and distance, and, although he now lives in London, from Britain because of its cultural complacency and the lingering echoes of imperial color prejudice. It is as a displaced person that he views the world, exploring Africa, India, Iran, and South America only to recoil from their various perversions or simplifications of the Western ideal. His books, usually set in Third World countries, are populated by the now alienated, formerly secure in their identity as colonial charges. Lost souls, Paul Theroux has called them. Naipaul's refusal to represent poverty, squalor, and ignorance as wonderful has led to charges of cynicism, but he insists that his honest exposure of bitter reality is necessary because it may lead to "some sort of action, . . . action not based on self-deception." Departing finally from the India depicted in An Area of Darkness *(1964), he writes: "To be at the airline office at ten, to see the decorative little fountain failed, the wing-shaped counter empty, the tiled turquoise basin of the fountain empty and wetly littered, the lights dim, the glossy magazines disarrayed and disregarded, the Punjabi emigrants sitting disconsolately with their bundles in a corner near the weighing machine; to be at the airport at eleven for an aircraft that leaves at midnight; and then to wait until after three in the morning, intermittently experiencing the horrors of an Indian public lavatory, is to know anxiety, exasperation, and a creeping stupor."*

"The human condition," says Anthony Burgess, "fills him with little optimism." And yet, as this selection indicates, his dark view, post-touristic with a vengeance, is constantly lighted by flashes of comedy, and for all the outrage, you can hear giggles in the background.

From An Area of Darkness
(1964)

TRAVELLER'S PRELUDE:
A LITTLE PAPERWORK

As soon as our quarantine flag came down and the last of the barefooted, blue-uniformed policemen of the Bombay Port Health Authority had left the ship, Coelho the Goan came aboard and, luring me with a long beckoning finger into the saloon, whispered, "You have any cheej?"

Coelho had been sent by the travel agency to help me through the customs. He was tall and thin and shabby and nervous, and I imagined he was speaking of some type of contraband. He was. He required cheese. It was a delicacy in India. Imports were restricted, and the Indians had not yet learned how to make cheese, just as they had not yet learned how to bleach newsprint. But I couldn't help Coelho. The cheese on this Greek freighter was not good. Throughout the three-week journey from Alexandria I had been complaining about it to the impassive chief steward, and I didn't feel I could ask him now for some to take ashore.

"All right, all right," Coelho said, not believing me and not willing to waste time listening to excuses. He left the saloon and began prowling lightfootedly down a corridor, assessing the names above doors.

I went down to my cabin. I opened a new bottle of Scotch and took a sip. Then I opened a bottle of Metaxas and took a sip of that. These were the two bottles of spirits I was hoping to take into prohibition-dry Bombay, and this was the precaution my friend in the Indian Tourist Department had advised: full bottles would be confiscated.

Coelho and I met later in the dining room. He had lost a little of his nervousness. He was carrying a very large Greek doll, its folk costume gaudy against his own shabby trousers and shirt, its rosy cheeks and unblinking blue eyes serene beside the restless melancholy of his long thin face. He saw my opened bottles and nervousness returned to him.

"Open. But why?"

"Isn't that the law?"

"Hide them."

"The Metaxas is too tall to hide."

"Put it flat."

"I don't trust the cork. But don't they allow you to take in two bottles?"

"I don't know, I don't know. Just hold this dolly for me. Carry it in your hand. Say souvenir. You have your Tourist Introduction Card? Good. Very valuable document. With a document like that they wouldn't search you. Why don't you hide the bottles?"

He clapped his hands and at once a barefooted man, stunted and bony, appeared and began to take our suitcases away. He had been waiting, unseen, unheard, ever since Coelho came aboard. Carrying only the doll and the bag containing the bottles, we climbed down into the launch. Coelho's man stowed away the suitcases. Then he squatted on the floor, as though to squeeze himself into the smallest possible space, as though to apologise for his presence, even at the exposed stern, in the launch in which his master was travelling. The master, only occasionally glancing at the doll in my lap, stared ahead, his face full of foreboding.

For me the East had begun weeks before. Even in Greece I had felt Europe falling away. There was the East in the food, the emphasis on sweets, some of which I knew from my childhood; in the posters for Indian films with the actress Nargis, a favourite, I was told, of Greek audiences; in the instantaneous friendships, the invitations to meals and homes. Greece was a preparation for Egypt: Alexandria at sunset, a wide shining arc in the winter sea; beyond the breakwaters, a glimpse through fine rain of the ex-king's white yacht; the ship's engine cut off; then abruptly, as at a signal, a roar from the quay, shouting and quarrelling and jabbering from men in grubby jibbahs who in an instant overran the already crowded ship and kept on running through it. And it was clear that here, and not in Greece, the East began: in this chaos of un-economical movement, the self-stimulated din, the sudden feeling of insecurity, the conviction that all men were not brothers and that luggage was in danger.

Here was to be learned the importance of the guide, the man who knew local customs, the fixer to whom badly printed illiterate forms held no mysteries. "Write here," my guide said in the customs house, aswirl with porters and guides and officials and idlers and policemen and travellers and a Greek refugee whispering in my ear, "Let me warn you. They are stealing tonight." "Write here. One Kodak." He, the guide, indicated the dotted line marked *date*. "And here," pointing to *signature*, "write no gold, ornaments or precious stones." I objected. He said, "Write." He pronounced it like an Arabic word. He was tall, grave, Hollywood-sinister; he wore a fez and lightly tapped his thigh with a cane. I wrote. And it worked. "And now," he said, exchanging the fez marked *Travel Agent* for one marked *Hotel X*, "let us go to the hotel."

Thereafter, feature by feature, the East, known only from books, had continued to reveal itself; and each recognition was a discovery, as much as it had been a revelation to see the jibbah, a garment made almost mythical by countless photographs and descriptions, on the backs of real people. In the faded hotel, full, one felt, of memories of the Raj, there was a foreshadowing of the caste system. The old French waiter only served; he had his runners, sad-eyed silent Negroes in fezzes and cummerbunds, who fetched and cleared away. In the lobby there were innumerable Negro pages, picturesquely attired. And in the streets there was the East one had expected: the children, the dirt, the disease, the undernourishment, the cries of *bakshish* [give me a present], the hawkers, the touts, the glimpses of minarets. There were the reminders of imperialisms that had withdrawn in the dark, glasscased European-style shops, wilting for lack of patronage; in the sad whispering of the French hairdresser that French perfumes could no longer be obtained and that one had to make do with heavy Egyptian scents; in the disparaging references of the Lebanese businessman to 'natives', all of whom he distrusted except for his assistant who, quietly to me, spoke of the day when all the Lebanese and Europeans would be driven out of the country.

Feature by feature, the East one had read about. On the train to Cairo the man across the aisle hawked twice, with an expert tongue rolled the phlegm into a ball, plucked the ball out of his mouth with thumb and forefinger, considered it, and then rubbed it away between his palms. He was wearing a three-piece suit, and his transistor played loudly. Cairo revealed the meaning of the bazaar: narrow streets encrusted with filth, stinking even on this winter's day; tiny shops full of shoddy goods; crowds; the din, already barely supportable, made worse by the steady blaring of motorcar horns; medieval buildings partly collapsed, others rising on old rubble, with here and there sections of tiles, turquoise and royal blue, hinting at a past of order and beauty, crystal fountains and amorous adventures, as perhaps in the no less disordered past they always had done.

And in this bazaar, a cobbler. With white skullcap, lined face, steel-rimmed spectacles and white beard, he might have posed for a photograph in the *National Geographic Magazine*: the skilled and patient Oriental craftsman. My sole was flapping. Could he repair it? Sitting almost flat on the pavement, bowed over his work, he squinted at my shoes, my trousers, my raincoat. "Fifty piastres." I said: "Four." He nodded, pulled the shoe off my foot and with a carpenter's hammer began hammering in a one-inch nail. I grabbed the shoe; he, smiling, hammer raised, held on to it. I pulled; he let go.

The Pyramids, whose function as a public latrine no guide book mentions, were made impossible by guides, "watchmen," camel-drivers and by boys whose donkeys were all called Whisky-and-soda. *Bakshish! Bakshish!* "Come and have a cup of coffee. I don't want you to buy anything. I just want to have a little intelligent conversation. Mr. Nehru is a great man. Let us exchange ideas. I am a graduate of the university." I took the desert bus back to Alexandria and, two days before the appointed time, retreated to the Greek freighter.

Then came the tedium of the African ports. Little clearings, one felt them, at the edge of a vast continent; and here one knew that Egypt, for all its Negroes, was not Africa, and for all its minarets and jibbahs, not the East: it was the last of Europe. At Jeddah the jibbahs were cleaner, the American automobiles new and numerous and driven with great style. We were not permitted to land and could see only the life of the port. Camels and goats were being unloaded by cranes and slings from dingy tramp steamers on to the piers; they were to be slaughtered for the ritual feast that marks the end of Ramadan. Swung aloft, the camels splayed out their suddenly useless legs; touching earth, lightly or with a bump, they crouched; then they ran to their fellows and rubbed against them. A fire broke out in a launch; our freighter sounded the alarm and within minutes the fire engines arrived. "Autocracy has its charms," the young Pakistani student said.

We had touched Africa, and four of the passengers had not been inoculated against yellow fever. A Pakistan-fed smallpox epidemic was raging in Britain and we feared stringency in Karachi. The Pakistani officials came aboard, drank a good deal, and our quarantine was waived. At Bombay, though, the Indian officials refused alcohol and didn't even finish the Coca-Cola they were offered. They were sorry, but the four passengers would have to go to the isolation hospital at Santa Cruz; either that or the ship would have to stay out in the stream. Two of the passengers without inoculations were the captain's parents. We stayed out in the stream.

It has been a slow journey, its impressions varied and superficial. But it had been a preparation for the East. After the bazaar of Cairo the bazaar of Karachi was no surprise; and *bakshish* was the same in both languages. The change from the Mediterranean winter to the sticky high summer of the Red Sea had been swift. But other changes had been slower. From Athens to Bombay another idea of man had defined itself by degrees, a new type of authority and subservience. The physique of Europe had melted away first into that of Africa and then, through Semitic Arabia, into Aryan Asia. Men had been diminished and deformed; they begged and whined. Hysteria had been my reaction, and a brutality dictated by a new awareness of myself as a whole human being and a determination, touched with fear, to remain what I was. It mattered little through whose eyes I was seeing the East; there had as yet been no time for this type of self-assessment.

Superficial impressions, intemperate reactions. But one memory had stayed with me, and I had tried to hold it close during that day out in the stream at Bombay, when I had seen the sun set behind the Taj Mahal Hotel and had wished that Bombay was only another port such as those we had touched on the journey, a port that the freighter passenger might explore or reject.

It was at Alexandria. Here we had been pestered most by horsecabs. The horses were ribby, the coachwork as tattered as the garments of the drivers. The drivers hailed you; they drove their cabs beside you and left you only when another likely fare appeared. It had been good to get away from them, and from the security of the ship to watch them make their assault on others. It was like watching a silent film: the victim sighted, the racing cab, the victim engaged, gesticulations, the cab moving beside the victim and matching his pace, at first brisk, then exaggeratedly slow, then steady.

Then one morning the desert vastness of the dock was quickened with activity, and it was as if the silent film had become a silent epic. Long rows of two-toned taxicabs were drawn up outside the terminal building; scattered all over the dock area, as though awaiting a director's call to action, were black little clusters of horsecabs; and steadily, through the dock gates, far to the right, more taxis and cabs came rolling in. The horses galloped, the drivers' whip hands worked. It was a brief exaltation. Soon enough for each cab came repose, at the edge of a cab-cluster. The cause of the excitement was presently seen: a large white liner, possibly carrying tourists, possibly carrying ten-pound immigrants to Australia. Slowly, silently, she idled in. And more taxis came pelting through the gates, and more cabs, racing in feverishly to an anti-climax of nosebags and grass.

The liner docked early in the morning. It was not until noon that the first passengers came out of the terminal building into the wasteland of the dock area. This was like the director's call. Grass was snatched from the asphalt and thrust into boxes below the drivers' seats; and every passenger became the target of several converging attacks. Pink, inexperienced, timid and vulnerable these passengers appeared to us. They carried baskets and cameras; they wore straw hats and bright cotton shirts for the Egyptian winter (a bitter wind was blowing from the sea). But our sympathies had shifted; we were on the side of the Alexandrians. They had waited all morning; they had arrived with high panache and zeal; we wanted them to engage, conquer and drive away with their victims through the dock gates.

But this was not to be. Just when the passengers had been penned by cabs and taxis, and gestures of remonstrance had given way to stillness, so that it seemed escape was impossible and capture certain, two shiny motorcoaches came through the dock gates. From the ship they looked like expensive toys. They cleared a way through taxis and cabs, which closed in again and then opened out to permit the coaches to make a slow, wide turn; and where before there had been tourists in gay cottons there was now only asphalt. The cabs, as though unwilling to accept the finality of this disappearance, backed and moved forward as if in pursuit. Then without haste they made their way back to their respective stations, where the horses retrieved from the asphalt what grass had escaped the hurried snatch of the drivers.

All through the afternoon the cabs and taxis remained, waiting for passengers who had not gone on the coaches. These passengers were few; they came out in ones and twos; and they appeared to prefer the taxis. But the enthusiasm of the horsecabs did not wane. Still, when a passenger appeared, the drivers jumped on to their seats, lashed their thin horses into action and rattled away to engage, transformed from idlers in old overcoats and scarves into figures of skill and purpose. Sometimes they engaged; often then there were disputes between drivers and the passengers withdrew. Sometimes a cab accompanied a passenger to the very gates. Sometimes at that point we saw the tiny walker halt; and then, with triumph and relief, we saw him climb into the cab. But this was rare.

The light faded. The cabs no longer galloped to engage. They wheeled and went at walking pace. The wind became keener; the dock grew dark; lights appeared. But the cabs remained. It was only later, when the liner blazed with lights, even its smokestack illuminated, and hope had been altogether extinguished, that they went away one by one, leaving behind shreds of grass and horse-droppings where they had stood.

Later that night I went up to the deck. Not far away, below a lamp standard stood a lone cab. It had been there since the late afternoon; it had withdrawn early from the turmoil around the terminal. It had had no fares, and there could be no fares for it now. The cab-lamp burned low; the horse was eating grass from a shallow pile on the road. The driver, wrapped against the wind, was polishing the dully gleaming hood of his cab with a large rag. The polishing over, he dusted; then he gave the horse a brief, brisk rub down. Less than a minute later he was out of his cab again, polishing, dusting, brushing. He went in; he came out. His actions were compulsive. The animal chewed; his coat shone; the cab gleamed. And there were no fares. And next morning the liner had gone, and the dock was desert again.

Now, sitting in the launch about to tie up at the Bombay pier where the names on cranes and buildings were, so oddly, English; feeling unease at the thought of the mute animal crouching on the floor at his master's back, and a similar unease at the sight of figures—not of romance, as the first figures seen on a foreign shore ought to be—on the pier, their frailty and raggedness contrasting with the stone buildings and metal cranes; now I tried to remember that in Bombay, as in

Alexandria, there could be no pride in power, and that to give way to anger and contempt was to know a later self-disgust.

And of course Coelho, guide, fixer, knower of government forms, was right. Bombay was rigorously dry, and my two opened bottles of spirit were seized by the customs officers in white, who summoned a depressed-looking man in blue to seal them "in my presence." The man in blue worked at this manual and therefore degrading labour with slow relish; his manner proclaimed him an established civil servant, however degraded. I was given a receipt and told that I could get the bottles back when I got a liquor permit. Coelho wasn't so sure; these seized bottles, he said, had a habit of breaking. But his own worries were over. There had been no general search; his Greek doll had passed without query. He took it and his fee and disappeared into Bombay; I never saw him again.

To be in Bombay was to be exhausted. The moist heat sapped energy and will, and some days passed before I decided to recover my bottles. I decided in the morning; I started in the afternoon. I stood in the shade of Churchgate Station and debated whether I had it in me to cross the exposed street to the Tourist Office. Debate languished into daydream; it was minutes before I made the crossing. A flight of steps remained. I sat below a fan and rested. A lure greater than a liquor permit roused me: the office upstairs was airconditioned. There India was an ordered, even luxurious country. The design was contemporary; the walls were hung with maps and coloured photographs; and there were little wooden racks of leaflets and booklets. Too soon my turn came; my idleness was over. I filled in my form. The clerk filled in his, three to my one, made entries in various ledgers and presented me with a sheaf of foolscap papers: my liquor permit. He had been prompt and courteous. I thanked him. There was no need, he said; it was only a little paperwork.

One step a day: this was my rule. The following afternoon I took a taxi back to the docks. My wife, who was to be with me for part of my trip, came along. The customs officers in white and the degraded man in blue were surprised to see me.

"Did you leave something here?"

"I left two bottles of liquor."

"You didn't. We seized two bottles from you. They were sealed in your presence."

"That's what I meant. I've come to get them back."

"But we don't keep seized liquor here. Everything we seize and seal is sent off at once to the New Customs House."

My taxi was searched on the way out.

The New Customs House was a large, two-storeyed PWD building, governmentally gloomy, and it was as thronged as a courthouse. There were people in the drive, in the galleries, on the steps, in the corridors. "Liquor, liquor," I said, and was led from office to office, each full of shrunken, bespectacled young men in white shirts sitting at desks shaggily stacked with paper. Someone sent me upstairs. On the landing I came upon a barefooted group seated on the stone floor. At first I thought they were playing cards: it was a popular Bombay pavement pastime. But they were sorting parcels. Their spokesman told me I had been misdirected; I needed the building at the back. This building, from the quantity of ragged clothing seen in one of the lower rooms, appeared to be a tenement; and then, from the number of broken chairs and dusty pieces of useless furniture seen in another room, appeared to be a junkshop. But it was the place for unclaimed baggage and was therefore the place I wanted. Upstairs I stood in a slow queue, at the end of which I discovered only an accountant.

"You don't want me. You want that officer in the white pants. Over there. He is a nice fellow."

I went to him.

"You have your liquor permit?"

I showed him the stamped and signed foolscap sheaf.

"You have your transport permit?"

It was the first I had heard of this permit.

"You must have a transport permit."

I was exhausted, sweating, and when I opened my mouth to speak I found I was on the verge of tears. "But they *told* me."

He was sympathetic. "We have told them many times."

I thrust all the papers I had at him: my liquor permit, my customs receipt, my passport, my receipt for wharfage charges, my Tourist Introduction Card.

Dutifully he looked through what I offered. "No. I would have known at once whether you had a transport permit. By the colour of the paper. A sort of buff."

"But what is a transport permit? Why didn't they give it to me? Why do I need one?"

"I must have it before I can surrender anything."

"Please."

"Sorry."

"I am going to write to the papers about this."

"I wish you would. I keep telling them they must tell people about this transport permit. Not only for you. We had an American here yesterday who said he was going to break the bottle as soon as he got it."

"Help me. Where can I get this transport permit?"

"The people who gave you the receipt should also give you the transport permit."

"But I've just come from them."

"I don't know. We keep on telling them."

"Back to the Old Customs," I said to the taxi-driver.

This time the police at the gates recognised us and didn't search the car. This dock had been my own gateway to India. Only a few days before everything in it had been new: the sticky black asphalt, the money-changers' booths, the stalls, the people in white, khaki or blue: everything had been studied for what it portended of India beyond the gates. Now already I had ceased to see or care. My stupor, though, was tempered by the thought of the small triumph that awaited me: I had trapped those customs officers in white and that degraded man in blue.

They didn't look trapped.

"Transport permit?" one said. "Are you sure?"

"Did you tell them you were leaving Bombay?" asked a second.

"*Transport* permit?" said a third and, walking away to a fourth, asked, "Transport permit, ever hear of *transport* permit?"

He had. "They've been writing us about it."

A transport permit was required to transport liquor from the customs to a hotel or house.

"Please give me a transport permit."

"We don't issue transport permits. You have to go—" He looked up at me and his manner softened. "Here, let me write it down for you. And look, I will also give you your code-number. That will help them out at the New Customs."

The taxi-driver had so far been calm; and it seemed now that my journeys had fallen into a pattern that was familiar to him. I began to read out the address that had been given me. He cut me short and without another word buzzed through the thickening afternoon traffic to a large brick building hung with black-and-white government boards.

"You go," he said sympathetically. "I wait."

Outside every office there was a little crowd.

"Transport permit, transport permit."

Some Sikhs directed me round to the back to a low shed next to a gate marked *Prohibited Area,* out of which workers came, one after the other, raising their hands while armed soldiers frisked them.

"Transport permit, transport permit."

I entered a long corridor and found myself among some Sikhs. They were lorry-drivers.

"Liquor permit, liquor permit."

And at last I reached the office. It was a long low room at ground level, hidden from the scorching sun and as dark as a London basement, but warm and dusty with the smell of old paper, which was everywhere, on shelves rising to the grey ceiling, on desks, on chairs, in the hands of clerks, in the hands of khaki-clad messengers. Folders had grown dog-eared, their colours faded, their spines abraded to transparency, their edges limp with reverential handling; and to many were attached pink slips, equally faded, equally limp, marked URGENT, VERY URGENT, or IMMEDIATE. Between these mounds and columns and buttresses of paper, clerks were scattered about unimportantly, men and women, mild-featured, Indian-pallid, high-shouldered; paper was their perfect camouflage. An elderly bespectacled man sat at a desk in one corner, his face slightly puffy and dyspeptic. Tremulous control of the paper-filled room was his: at his disappearance the clerks might be altogether overwhelmed.

"Transport permit?"

He looked up slowly. He showed no surprise, no displeasure at being disturbed. Papers, pink-slipped, were spread all over his desk. A table fan, nicely poised, blew over them without disturbance.

"Transport permit." He spoke the words mildly, as though they were rare words but words which, after searching for only a second in the files of his mind, he had traced. "Write an application. Only one is necessary."

"Do you have the form?"

"No forms have been issued. Write a letter. Here, have a sheet of paper. Sit down and write. To the Collector, Excise and Prohibition, Bombay. Do you have your passport? Put down the number. Oh, and you have a Tourist Introduction Card. Put down that number too. I will expedite matters."

And while I wrote, noting down the number of my Tourist Introduction Card, TIO (L) 156, he, expediting matters, passed my documents over to a woman clerk, saying, "Miss Desai, could you start making out a transport permit?" I thought I detected an odd pride in his voice. He was like a man still after many years discovering the richness and variety of his work and subduing an excitement which he nevertheless wished to communicate to his subordinates.

I was finding it hard to spell and to frame simple sentences. I crumpled up the sheet of paper.

The head clerk looked up at me in gentle reproof. "Only one application is necessary."

At my back Miss Desai filled in forms with that blunt, indelible, illegible pencil which government offices throughout the former Empire use, less for the sake of what is written than for the sake of the copies required.

I managed to complete my application.

And at this point my wife slumped forward on her chair, hung her head between her knees and fainted.

"Water," I said to Miss Desai.

She barely paused in her writing and pointed to an empty dusty glass on a shelf.

The head clerk, already frowningly preoccupied with other papers, regarded the figure slumped in front of him.

"Not feeling well?" His voice was as mild and even as before. "Let her rest." He turned the table fan away from him.

"Where is the water?"

Giggles came from women clerks, hidden behind paper.

"Water!" I cried to a male clerk.

He rose, saying nothing, walked to the end of the room and vanished.

Miss Desai finished her writing. Giving me a glance as of terror, she brought her tall bloated pad to the head clerk.

"The transport permit is ready," he said. "As soon as you are free you can sign for it."

The male clerk returned, waterless, and sat down at his desk.

"Where is the water?"

His eyes distastefully acknowledged my impatience. He neither shrugged nor spoke; he went on with his papers.

It was worse than impatience. It was ill-breeding and ingratitude. For presently, sporting his uniform as proudly as any officer, a messenger appeared. He carried a tray and on the tray stood a glass of water. I should have known better. A clerk was a clerk; a messenger was a messenger.

The crisis passed.

I signed three times and received my permit.

The head clerk opened another folder.

"Nadkarni," he called softly to a clerk. "I don't understand this memo."

I had been forgotten already.

It was suffocatingly hot in the taxi, the seats scorching. We drove to the flat of a friend and stayed there until it was dark.

A friend of our friend came in.

"What's wrong?"

"We went to get a transport permit and she fainted." I did not wish to sound critical. I added, "Perhaps it's the heat."

"It isn't the heat at all. Always the heat or the water with you people from outside. There's nothing wrong with her. You make up your minds about India before coming to the country. You've been reading the wrong books."

The officer who had sent me on the track of the transport permit was pleased to see me back. But the transport permit wasn't enough. I had to go to Mr Kulkarni to find out about the warehouse charges. When I had settled what the charges were I was to come back to that clerk over there, with the blue shirt; then I had to go to the cashier, to pay the warehouse charges; then I had to go back to Mr Kulkarni to get my bottles.

I couldn't find Mr Kulkarni. My papers were in my hand. Someone tried to take them. I knew he was expressing only his kindness and curiosity. I pulled the papers back. He looked at me; I looked at him. I yielded. He went through my papers and said with authority that I had come to the wrong building.

I screamed: *"Mr Kulkarni!"*

Everyone around me was startled. Someone came up to me, calmed me down and led me to the adjoining room where Mr Kulkarni had been all along. I rushed to the head of the queue and began to shout at Mr Kulkarni, waving my papers at him. He got hold of them as I waved and began to read. Some Sikhs in the queue complained. Mr Kulkarni replied that I was in a hurry, that I was a person of importance, and that in any case I was younger. Curiously, they were pacified.

Mr Kulkarni called for ledgers. They were brought to him. Turning the crisp pages, not looking up, he made a loosewristed gesture of indefinable elegance with his yellow pencil. The Sikhs at once separated into two broken lines. Mr Kulkarni put on his spectacles, studied the calendar on the far wall, counted on his fingers, took off his spectacles and returned to his ledgers. He made another abstracted gesture with his pencil and the Sikhs fell into line again, obscuring the calendar.

Upstairs again. The clerk with the blue shirt stamped on Mr Kulkarni's sheet of paper and made entries in two ledgers. The cashier added his own stamp. I paid him and he made entries in two more ledgers.

"It's all right," the officer said, scanning the twice-stamped and thrice-signed sheet of paper. He added his own signature. "You're safe now. Go down to Mr. Kulkarni. And be quick. They might be closing any minute."

WILLIAM GOLDING
1911–

Born in St. Columb Minor, Cornwall, William Gerald Golding spent a happy, if isolated, childhood closely attended by his father, a noted schoolmaster, and his mother, an early suffragette. After earning his B.A. from Brasenose College, Oxford, he followed family tradition and taught English and philosophy at Bishop Wordsworth's School, Wiltshire. In 1939 he married Ann Brookfield. They have two children.

Two things he credits with significantly influencing his attitude toward life are the sinking of the supposedly unsinkable Titanic *shortly after his birth and his service in the Second World War, when first as a seaman on a cruiser and later the captain of a rocket-firing vessel he witnessed the sinking of the* Bismarck *and the D-Day invasion of Normandy. Already harboring an admiration for antiquity and a fascination with Egyptology and ancient means of expression, his war experiences deepened his distrust of the modern world and sharpened his skepticism about human reasonableness and the idea of progress. His first novel,* Lord of the Flies, *published in 1954 when he was forty-three, is an attempt, as he says, to "trace the defects of society back to the defects of human nature." In the next ten years he produced five more novels, each notably different from the ones before but each exploring in its way the relationship between civilization and the darker elements of human nature.*

In 1983 he was awarded the Nobel Prize for Literature.

From THE HOT GATES AND
OTHER OCCASIONAL PIECES
(1965)

BODY AND SOUL

East Coast blanked out from North Carolina right up to the Canadian border; a half-continent under a pat of fog; nothing visible but the extreme tip of the Empire State Building; planes grounded. Fog, the airman's common cold; all the resources of science are squeaking and gibbering under it; lights blink unseen, radar echoes quiver and ping; the gigantic aircraft lumber round the ramps and aprons like death's-head moths in cold weather; money leaks away. We, the privileged, sit in a sort of underground air-raid shelter, racked by public-address systems and blasts of furious air-conditioning. Evening drags into night. Everything is astonishingly dirty, and time itself is stale. We sit.

Most passengers drift away, to go by train, or try a night's sleep in the airport hotel. But I am going too far to get there any way but by jet. Tomorrow I give the first of three lectures in Los Angeles, on the other side of America. Here it is midnight, or past midnight, or feels like midnight. I am late already, and must go by what flight I can. I cannot telegraph anyone, even though I shall land at the wrong airport.

A loudspeaker honks and burbles. Incredibly, and for the next hour, we have take-off and landing limits. Our plane is getting through; and sure enough, presently it bumbles out of the fog from the runway. I go with our group to Gate Nine, shudder into a freezing night with a dull grey roof. The jet crawls towards us, howling and whistling with rage, perhaps at the fog or perhaps at the human bondage which keeps it only just under control. For a moment or two, it faces us—no, is end-on to us; for here there is no touch of human, or animal, or insect, no face— only four holes that scream like nothing else in creation. Then it huddles round and is still. Doors open and two streams of passengers ooze out. Their faces are haggard. They ignore the night that has caught up with them. They stagger, or walk with the stiff gait of stage sleep-walkers. One or two look stunned, as if they know it is midnight more or less but cannot remember if it is today or tomorrow midnight and why or what. Strange vehicles flashing all over with red lights come out of the darkness, not for the passengers, but to tend the jet. They crouch under the wings and the front end, attach themselves by tubes while all their lights flash, and lights on the jet flash, and the engines sink from a wail to a moan—a note, one might think, of resignation, as if the machine now recognizes that it is caught and will have to do the whole thing over again. But for half an hour they feed it well, while it sucks or they blow, and we stand, imprisoned by the freezing cold and our own need to be somewhere else. Jet travel is a great convenience.

Then we are in, fastening safety belts, and I peer out of the window with a naïveté which seems to increase as I grow older; and a succession of blue lights flick by faster and faster; and there is an eternity of acceleration at an angle of forty-five degrees, while the whistling holes under the wings seem no longer angry but godlike—see what we can do! Look, no hands! The "No Smoking, Fasten Your Safety Belts" notice disappears. Cupping my hands round my face, squinting sideways and down, I can make out that there is a white pat of fog slipping by beneath us, and over it a few stationary stars. An air hostess demonstrates the use of the oxygen masks.

Comfort, warmth flowing back into rigid hands, comparative silence, stillness except for an occasional nudge as the plane pierces a furlong of turbulence; I try to think of what our airspeed means: it remains nothing but arithmetic. The interior of the plane is like a very superior bus. Am thawed and relaxed. They say that this is not the latest mark of jet—do jets come any faster or bigger or plusher?

Glasses tinkle. Air Hostess brings round drinks—not what happens in a bus. Select Bourbon. (Always live off the country as far as possible.) I also secrete the TWA swizzlestick as a memento. Do not cross America often this way. Another Bourbon. That makes the two obligatory drinks before an American dinner. Am cheerful now—but second drink did not contain swizzlestick and wonder if I am detected? Air Hostess approaches for the third time and I cower—but no. She is English and recognizes a fellow-countryman. Speaks Kensingtonian, which sounds odd at this place and altitude. (Note to intending immigrants. Kensingtonian despised in a man. Gets him called a pouf. Do not know exactly what this terms means, but cannot think it complimentary. On the other hand, Kensingtonian in a girl widely approved of, Americans think it cute.)

Peripeteia! English Air Hostess has read my books and seen me on English telly! I instantly acquire overwhelming status. Feel utterly happy and distinguished in a nice, diffident, English sort of way. Neighbour puts away his briefcase—we all have briefcases—then talks to me. Is physicist, naturally. Tells me about jets sucking air in at one end and blowing result of combustion out at the other. Encourage him, from a pure sense of *joie de vivre*. Rash, this, very. Tells me about navigation lights, navigation, fluids, including the sea, acceleration—Bourbon now dying down. Make my way forward to lavatory in diffident but distinguished manner, watched by all the unhappy briefcases who haven't been on telly, or haven't been noticed there by an Air Hostess. Lavatory wonderful, buttons everywhere. Push the lot, just to tell grandchildren. Tiny, ultimate fraction of our airstream is scooped in somewhere and directed to blow a jet vertically up out of the pan. Could balance celluloid balls on it and shoot them down with a rifle, as at fairs.

Return to seat and physicist continues course. American Air Hostess comes and talks. More status. Physicist goes to sleep. English Air Hostess comes and talks about London, Paris, Rome, Athens. American Air Hostess counters with Hawaii and Japan. Slight loss of status. I would like to go to sleep. Body here, can see it sitting in the seat. Soul still leaving Atlantic coast. Time? AHs have got on to books. It's the beard, I think. Beard down there on the deck, just beard. Beard in jet v. distinguished. Bourbon quite dead. Return to lavatory for a bit of peace in less distinguished manner. Jet still playing and cannot be bothered to push all the buttons. Return. Physicist says "Di!" very loudly in his sleep. Die? Diana? Diathermy? AHs wander away. Nod. Have instant vision of Ann with sweeper on carpet. She switches it off, switches off all the sweepers in the world, they fade, whining—am started awake—oh my God, my God! "No Smoking, Fasten Your Safety Belts"—briefcases stirring like sea-life under returning tide.

Am awake, dammit, or rather body is awake; soul two thousand miles behind, passing through Nashville, Tennessee, shall never be whole again, body mouldering in the jet, soul marching on towards Denver. Time? Bump, rumble, rumble, lights, lights! Los Angeles. Time? Enter Belshazzar's Hall. Body finds hall moving slowly, but they can't fool body. Body knows the movement is the world turning to catch up. More halls, enough for whole dynasties of Belshazzars.

Soul will enjoy this when it catches up. More halls, *Mene, mene.* Briefcases have vanished. Tunnels, fountains, lights, music, palms, lights, more halls—they would have to put *Mene, mene* out by roneograph, or use the public-address system. *A message for Mr. Belshazzar!* Am delirious, I think. Find broom supporting man in centre of hundredth hall. Body asks broom politely. "Which way is out, Bud?" Broom answers politely, "Don't arst me, Bud, we just built it." More halls. Movement of earth deposits body in cab which hurls it ten thousand miles through lights to a recommended English-type hotel. Body recognizes bed as English. Has knobs at each corner. Body falls on bed, giggling at thought of soul now plodding through Death Valley. Body undresses so as to get an hour or two of sleep, telephone rings. Bear-leader would like to show body the sights. Body dresses and descends.

Nice bearleader drives body through sunny Los Angeles and up the
Del Monica heights where the fire was. Body sees mountain road
of burnt houses for film stars. Only thing left is row of swimming
pools built on stilts out over the gorge, since there is nowhere else
for them.

Descent to Pacific. Waves coming the wrong way—no, that was the
Atlantic. Sherry in house. Lunch in university. Forty thousand students,
or is it seventy? Own campus police and bus service. After lunch, body
looks at lecture notes, but cannot bring itself to care. Body gives first
lecture and hears its mouth making the appropriate noises. Soul not
really necessary in this game. Has drinks beneath original Beerbohm
cartoons. Has dinner with the Christmas Story lining the road outside,
each tableau the size of a cottage with full-size figures in plaster and
floodlit. Party after dinner. Body is told about the definitive Dickens and
the Boswell factory. Body is nearly frightened to hear itself advise against
the export of American novels. Stick to cars, it says. Soul would be very
angry if it could hear that. Body finds itself getting smaller, or is it larger?
Is led away, and falls on English-type bed with knobs at each corner.

At two o'clock in the morning there seemed to be a second person
present. With the sort of effort one makes to achieve binocular vision,
they united themselves; and soul in body, I was looking at the ceiling
of a hotel bedroom in Los Angeles. The luxury of being whole was such
that I could not sleep, but smoked till I felt like stockfish. The real
trouble was that I had a defect of imagination which would not let me
believe I was where I was, and yet I knew I was in Los Angeles. Being
whole, I was immediately frightened at the vision of tomorrow's lecture
and began to compose it in my sleepless head. That way the day dawned,
and just as I ran out of cigarettes, my nice bearleader telephoned to set
up the morning's sightseeing. We saw the Mormon temple, with a gold
angel on the tower, far larger than any God has in heaven. We saw the
colossal Medical Centre where the corridors run clean out of perspective
to infinity at a point; where the patient is taken in at one end and can
be served up as a complete set of demonstration slides at the other. We
saw the beach—and for a moment I was really where I was—watching
the waves turn over, and stunned by the acute realization that this had
been here all the time, had not been created in Europe and exported
to form part of a set. I lectured again, pleaded for an evening in bed,
but sneaked off on my own—*peccavi*—and had dinner; filet mignon and
a bottle of burgundy-type wine. (Note for wines-men: it was an Almaden
'57; suffered like all California wines from that fatal inferiority complex—but once convinced you were a friend, it would offer you what it
had.) At two in the morning carried my filet mignon and my burgundy-

type wine back to my English-type bed, and lay with my head full of tomorrow's lecture. Dawn.

Nice bearleader came and took me to see the San Gabriel mountains with snow on them and the Chinese Theatre, its pavements with footprints, handprints, graffiti of film stars on them; showed me Hollywood, Gangster's Corner, Mae West's hotel, the William Andrews Clark Memorial Library. For ten ridiculously exciting seconds I held the MS of *The Importance of Being Earnest* in my hands. (You, too, have been awarded an Oscar!) We finished that jaunt in a bowling alley, where the beer was good, the telly in colour and the machines for setting up the pins seemed, in their implacable devotion, to be much more intelligent than anything else in sight.

I lecture, meet students, and pack grip in a flash. Meet faculty. Party. *N*th, I think. Now I am taken to dinner in an English-type restaurant to make me feel at home. Recognize it as English instantly, because the bartender and all the waiters are in full hunting kit. At one moment they gather round a table and sing "Happy Birthday" in close harmony. Los Angeles is the mostest, am utterly happy. What other place et cetera. Am eating abalone, the local must, and talking in six directions at once, but am suddenly seized and rushed away to jet, leaving soul still continuing conversations. Body loses way down to plane and is nearly sucked through engine, ha ha. Acceleration and fifty miles *square* of lights tilts under us. This is the latest mark of jet, they say, can see no difference, that is the Pacific down there, time, eleven o'clock.

American Air Hostess brings round Bourbon. Secrete swizzlestick. Another Bourbon. American Southern Belle-type Air Hostess, v. pretty, guesses I am English and a writer (beard in jet), comes and sits! Immense status SBAH did Creative Writing Course at College. Said to her Prof.: "Ah aim to be a writer." Prof. said: "What do you know about life?" SBAH said: "Ah hev written a critical essay on Thomas Wolfe and a short story which ah would like you to read." Prof. read story, said: "Go and be an Air Hostess"—"So heah ah em!" Delightful girl, there ought to be a lot more of them and there probably are. Supper. Go to lavatory and discover this really *is* the latest mark of jet. Tiny, ultimate fraction of our airstream is scooped in somewhere, led into the pan and merely chases itself round and round and round.

Am tucked up solicitously for the night, but am still able to see out of the window, my goodness me, no sleep with a view like that. America sliding by, 650 miles an hour airspeed with 150 miles an hour tail wind; 800 miles an hour over the ground—no cloud. Cities, gleaming, glowing ravishments slide under us six miles down, lines of phosphorescence scored at right-angles to each other. Moon and snow. Stars, perceptibly wheeling. More molten cities. Body understands that America is crust of earth with fire inside, must break out somewhere, hence these scores, these right-angled lava cracks, these chessboard patterns of luminosity (with here and there a wink of veritable incandescence like the white spark on a red coal), but all soft as the tiny lights of a shock cradle. Garish street lamps, Christmas decorations, traffic signals, window displays, sky signs, now softened, softened. Body lines up jet-hole with city—sees it swallow a whole street six miles long in seconds, how to take the children to school, scoop! three blocks of run-down houses, park, Motel, Motel, Motel, parking lot, cemetery, jump the sparking traffic lights, scoop! Drugstore, Charlies Cheeseburgers, Eats, Frolic Fashion House, Beautician, Physician, Mortician, Realty, News Office Winn Dixie Mount joy Toy-Town Surplus War Stock Crossroads Church of Christ (Airconditioning) Square! Mayoralty Fire Station Police Station Howard Johnson Square! Lights Lights Lights Square! Lights Lights Lights River Square! All sucked in and blown out, scooped up, hurled back, august, imperial, god-like, America, oh from up here and at this power, even unto weeping, America The—

SBAH is tinkling glasses and switching on lights. My God. BREAKFAST! Four hours out from Los Angeles—where soul is still engaged in fierce discussion of freedom, birth control, how to be happy though British, Emblems—four hours out, there is ahead of us the distinction between grey and black that betokens dawn over the curved Atlantic. Sure enough, the sweeper is switched off for a thirty-minutes' descent. Poor soul, no longer the centre of my sinful earth, but setting out just now on that long climb over the Rockies. Fasten your safety belts. And the time is. . . .

PAUL THEROUX
1941–

Novelist, journalist, and travel writer, Paul Theroux was born into a middle-class French-Canadian family living in a drab neighborhood in Medford, Massachusetts. After attending the local high school—"a sink of mediocrity," he has designated it—he went to the University of

Maine and in 1963 graduated from the University of Massachusetts at Amherst. Afterwards he traveled in Africa and wrote some journalism and joined the Peace Corps, which finally expelled him for his very audible and impolite opposition to the Vietnam War.

From 1968 to 1971 he taught English at the University of Singapore, and in 1975 produced the first of his travel books, The Great Railway Bazaar, *a boisterous, unflinching account of a journey through Asia aboard some of the remaining great trains, now, most of them, sadly decayed, if still pretentious. In 1977 he moved to England, where he and his wife and children still live, and continued writing novels, short stories, and travel books, of which the next was* The Old Patagonian Express *(1979), retailing the comedies and horrors of a rail journey from Massachusetts to the southern tip of South America. And in* Kingdom by the Sea *(1983) he wrote of a walking trip around the coast of Britain. His eye for British complacencies and snobberies was so acute that his hosts were not at all pleased.*

Theroux is an honest and thus frequently angry traveler, with no instinctive love of the modern post-colonial world. His nose for the nasty is as sensitive as Jan Morris's for the nice, but his satiric contempt is generally reserved for the contemptible, and even at his angriest he is never uninteresting.

From THE GREAT RAILWAY BAZAAR
(1975)

Peshawar is a pretty town. I would gladly move there, settle down on a verandah, and grow old watching sunsets in the Khyber Pass. Peshawar's widely spaced mansions, all excellent examples of Anglo-Muslim Gothic, are spread along broad sleepy roads under cool trees: just the place to recover from the hideous experience of Kabul. You hail a *tonga* at the station and ride to the hotel, where on the verandah the chairs have swing-out extensions for you to prop up your legs and get the blood circulating. A nimble waiter brings a large bottle of Murree Export Lager. The hotel is empty; the other guests have risked a punishing journey to Swat in hopes of being received by His Highness the Wali. You sleep soundly under a tent of mosquito net and are awakened by the fluting of birds for an English breakfast that begins with porridge and ends with a kidney. Afterwards a *tonga* to the museum.

How was Buddha conceived, you may wonder. There is a Graeco-

Buddhist frieze in the Peshawar Museum showing Buddha's mother lying on her side and being-impregnated through her ribs by what looks like the nozzle of a hot-air balloon suspended over her. In another panel the infant Buddha is leaping from a slit in her side—a birth with all the energy of a broad jump. Farther on is a nativity scene, Buddha lying at the center of attending figures, who kneel at prayer: the usual Christmas card arrangement done delicately in stone with classical faces. The most striking piece is a three-foot stone sculpture of an old man in a lotus posture. The man is fasting: his eyes are sunken, his rib cage is prominent, his knees are knobbly, his belly hollow. He looks near death, but his expression is beatific. It is the most accurate representation in granite of an emaciated body that I've ever seen, and again and again, throughout India and Pakistan, I was to see that same body, in doorways and outside huts and leaning against the pillars of railway stations, starvation lending a special quality of saintliness to the bony face.

A little distance from the museum, when I was buying some matches at a shop, I was offered morphine. I wondered if I heard right and asked to see it. The man took out a matchbox (perhaps "matches" was a code word?) and slipped it open. Inside was a small phial marked *Morphine Sulphate,* ten white tablets. The man said they were to be taken in the arm and told me that I could have the whole lot for twenty dollars. I offered him five dollars and laughed, but he saw he was being mocked. He turned surly and told me to go away.

I would have liked to stay longer in Peshawar. I liked lazing on the verandah, shaking out my newspaper, and watching the *tongas* go by, and I enjoyed hearing Pakistanis discussing the coming war with Afghanistan. They were worried and aggrieved, but I gave them encouragement and said they would find an enthusiastic well-wisher in me if they ever cared to invade that barbarous country. My prompt reassurance surprised them, but they saw I was sincere. "I hope you will help us," one said. I explained that I was not a very able soldier. He said, "Not you in person, but America in general." I said I couldn't promise national support, but that I would be glad to put a word in for them.

Everything is easy in Peshawar except buying a train ticket. This is a morning's work and leaves you exhausted. First you consult the timetable, *Pakistan Western Railways,* and find that the Khyber Mail leaves at four o'clock. Then you go to the Information window and are told it leaves at 9:50 P.M. The Information man sends you to Reservations. The man in Reservations is not there, but a sweeper says he'll be right back. He returns in an hour and helps you decide on a class. He writes your name in a book and gives you a chit. You take the chit to Bookings, where, for 108 rupees (about ten dollars), you are handed two tickets and an initialed chit. You go back to Reservations, and wait for the man to return once again. He returns, initials the tickets, examines the chit, and writes the details in a ledger about six feet square.

Nor was this the only difficulty. The man in Reservations told me no bedding was available on the Khyber Mail. I suspected he was angling for *baksheesh* and gave him six rupees to find bedding. After twenty minutes he said it had all been booked. He was very sorry. I asked for my bribe back. He said, "As you wish."

Later in the day I worked out the perfect solution. I was staying in Dean's Hotel, one in a chain of hotels that includes Faletti's in Lahore. I had to pester the clerk a good deal, but he finally agreed to give me what bedding I needed. I would give him sixty rupees and he would give me a chit. In Lahore I would give the bedding and chit to Faletti's and get my sixty rupees back. This was the chit:

> Please refund this man Rs 60/—(RS. SIXTY ONLY) if he produce you this receipt and One Blanket and One Sheet One Pillow and Credit it in Dean's Hotel Peshawar Account.

Rashid, the conductor on the sleeping car, helped me find my compartment, and after a moment's hesitation he asked me to have a look at his tooth. It was giving him aches, he said. The request was not impertinent. I had told him I was a dentist. I was getting tired of the Asiatic inquisition: Where do you come from? What do you do? Married or single? Any children? This nagging made me evasive, secretive, foolish, an inventor of cock-and-bull stories. Rashid made the bed and then opened up, tugging his lip down to show me a canine gnawed with decay.

"You'd better see a dentist in Karachi," I said. "In the meantime chew your food on the other side."

Satisfied with my advice (and I also gave him two aspirins), he said, "You will be very comfortable here. German carriage, about fifteen years old. Heavy, you see, so no shaking."

It had not taken long to find my compartment. Only three were occupied—the other two by army officers—and my name was on the door, printed large on a label. Now I could tell on entering a train what sort of a journey it would be. The feeling I had on the Khyber Mail was slight disappointment that the trip would be so short—only twelve hours to Lahore. I wished it were longer: I had everything I needed. The compartment was large, well lighted, and comfortable, with a toilet and sink in an adjoining room; I had a drop-leaf table, well-upholstered seat, mirror, ashtray, chrome gin-bottle holder, the works. I was alone. But if I wished to have company I could stroll to the dining car or idle in the passage with the army officers. Nothing is expected of the train passenger. In planes the traveler is condemned to hours in a tight seat; ships require high spirits and sociability; cars and buses are unspeakable. The sleeping car is the most painless form of travel. In *Ordered South*, Robert Louis Stevenson writes,

> Herein, I think, is the chief attraction of railway travel. The speed is so easy, and the train disturbs so little the scenes through which it takes us, that our heart becomes full of the placidity and stillness of the country; and while the body is being borne forward in the flying chain of carriages, the thoughts alight, as the humour moves them, at unfrequented stations.

The romance associated with the sleeping car derives from its extreme privacy, combining the best features of a cupboard with forward movement. Whatever drama is being enacted in this moving bedroom is heightened by the landscape passing the window: a swell of hills, the surprise of mountains, the loud metal bridge, or the melancholy sight of people standing under yellow lamps. And the notion of travel as a continuous vision, a grand tour's succession of memorable images across a curved earth—with none of the distorting emptiness of air or sea—is possible only on a train. A train is a vehicle that allows residence: dinner in the diner, nothing could be finer.

"What time does the Khyber Mail get to Karachi?"

"Timetable says seven-fifteen in the night," said Rashid. "But we will be five and a half hours late."

"Why?" I asked.

"We are always five and a half hours late. It is the case."

I slept well on my Dean's Hotel bedding and was awakened at six the following morning by a Sikh with a steel badge pinned to his turban that read *Pakistan Western Railways*. His right eye was milky with trachoma.

"You wanting breakfast?"

I said yes.

"I coming seven o'clock."

He brought an omelette, tea, and toast, and for the next half-hour I sprawled, reading Chekhov's wonderful story "Ariadne" and finishing my tea. Then I snapped up the shade and flooded the compartment with light. In brilliant sunshine we were passing rice fields and stagnant pools full of white lotuses and standing herons. Farther on, at a small tree, we startled a pair of pistachio green parrots; they flew up, getting greener as they rose. Looking out a train window in Asia is like watching an unedited travelogue without the obnoxious soundtrack: I had to guess at the purpose of activities—people patting pie-shaped turds and slapping them onto the side of a mud hut to dry; men with bullocks and submerged plows, preparing a rice field for planting; and at Badami Bagh, just outside Lahore, a town of grass huts, cardboard shelters, pup tents, and hovels of paper, twigs, and cloth, everyone was in motion— sorting fruit, folding clothes, fanning the fire, shooing a dog away, mending a roof. It is the industry of the poor in the morning, so busy they look hopeful, but it is deceptive. The position of their settlement gives them away; this is the extreme of poverty, the shantytown by the railway tracks.

The shantytown had another witness: a tall thin Indian of about twenty, with long hair, stood at the corridor window. He asked me the time; his London accent was unmistakable. I asked him where he was headed.

"India. I was born in Bombay, but I left when I was three or four. Still, I'm an Indian right the way through."

"But you were brought up in England."

"Yeah. I've got a British passport too. I didn't want to get one, after all they did to me. But an Indian passport is too much trouble. See, I want to go to Germany eventually—they're in the Common Market. It's easy with a British passport."

"Why not stay in London?"

"You can stay in London if you like. They're all racialists. It starts when you're about ten years old, and that's all you hear—wog, nigger, blackie. There's nothing you can do about it. At school it's really terrible—ever hear about Paki-bashing? And I'm not even a Pakistani. They don't know the difference. But they're cowards. When I'm with me mate no one comes up and says nothing, but lots of times about ten blokes would start trouble with me. I hate them. I'm glad to be here."

"This is Pakistan."

"Same thing. Everyone's the same color."

"Not really," I said.

"More or less," he said. "I can relax here—I'm free."

"Won't you feel rather anonymous?"

"The first thing I'm going to do in India is get a haircut; then no one will know."

It seemed a cruel fate. He spoke no Indian language, his parents were dead, and he was not quite sure how to get to Bombay, where he had some distant relatives who seldom replied to letters unless he enclosed money. He was one of those colonial anomalies, more English than he cared to admit, but uneasy in the only country he understood.

"In England they were always staring at me. I hated it."

"I get stared at here," I said.

"How do *you* like it?" I could see he was reproaching me with my color; after all, he was almost home.

I said, "I rather enjoy it."

"Sahib." It was Rashid, with my suitcase. "We are approaching."

"He calls you sahib," said the Indian. He looked disgusted. "He's afraid of you, that's why."

"Sahib," said Rashid. But he was speaking to the Indian. "Now, please show me your ticket."

The Indian was traveling second class. Rashid evicted him from first as the train drew in.

At Lahore Junction I stepped out (Rashid was at my side apologizing for the train's being late) into a city that was familiar: it matched a stereotype in my memory. My image of the Indian city derives from Kipling, and it was in Lahore that Kipling came of age as a writer. Exaggerating the mobs, the vicious bazaar, the color and confusion, the Kipling of the early stories and *Kim* is really describing Lahore today, that side of it beyond the Mall where processions of rickshaws, pony carts, hawkers, and veiled women fill the narrow lanes and sweep you in their direction. The Anarkali Bazaar and the walled city, with its fort and mosques, have retained the distracted exoticism Kipling mentions, though now, with a hundred years of repetition, it is touched with horror.

"Bad girls here," said the *tonga* driver when he dropped me in a seedy district of the old city; but I saw none, and nothing resembling a Lahore house. The absence of women in Pakistan, all those cruising males, had an odd effect on me. I found myself staring, with other similarly idle men, at garish pictures of film stars, and I began to think that the strictures of Islam would quickly make me a fancier of the margins of anatomy, thrilling at especially trim ankles, seeking a wink behind a veil, or watching for a response in the shoulders of one of those shrouded forms. Islam's denials seemed capable of turning the most normal soul into a foot fetishist, and as if to combat this the movie posters lampooned the erotic: fat girls in boots struggling helplessly with hairy, leering men; tormented women clutching their breasts, Anglo-Indians (regarded as "fast") swinging their bums and crooning into microphones. The men in Lahore stroll with their eyes upturned to these cartoon fantasies.

"They invite you out to eat," an American told me. This was at the spectacular fort, and we were both admiring the small marble pavilion, called *Naulakha* (Kipling named his house outside Brattleboro, Vermont, after it, because it was so expensive to build: "naulakha" means

900,000). The American was agitated. He said, "You finish eating and they start eyeballing your chick. It's always your chick they're after. The chick's strung out. 'Gee, Mohammed, why don't you have any pockets in your dhoti?' 'We are not having any pockets, miss'—that kind of crap. One guy—this really pissed me off—he takes me aside and says, *'Five minutes! Five minutes!* That's all I want with her!' But would he let me have *his* chick for five minutes? You've gotta be joking."

The order in Lahore is in the architecture, the moghul and colonial splendor. All around it are crowds of people and vehicles, and their dereliction makes the grandeur emphatic, as the cooking fat and cow-dung make the smells of perfume and joss-sticks keener. To get to the Shalimar Gardens I had to pass through miles of congested streets of jostling people with the starved look of predators. I shouldered my way through the venereal township of Begampura; but inside the gardens it is peaceful, and though it has been stripped of its marble, and the reflecting pools are dark brown, the gardens have the order and shade—a sense of delicious refuge—that could not be very different from that imagined by Shah Jahan, when he laid them out in 1637. The pleasures of Lahore are old, and though one sees attempts everywhere, the Pakistanis have not yet succeeded in turning this beautiful city into a ruin.

Ramadhan continued, and the restaurants were either closed or on emergency rations, eggs and tea. So I was forced into an unwilling fast too, hoping it wouldn't drive me crazy as it manifestly did the Afghan and Pakistani. Instead of somnolence, hunger produced excitable, glassy-eyed individuals, some of whom quick-marched from alleyways to clutch my sleeve.

"Pot—hashish—LSD."

"LSD?" I said. "You sell LSD?"

"Yes, why not? You come to my place. Also nice copper, silver, handicraft."

"I don't want handicraft."

"You want hashish? One kilo twenty dollar."

It was tempting, but I preferred bottled mango juice, which was sweet and thick, and the curry puffs known as *samosas*. The *samosas* were always wrapped in pages from old school copybooks. I sat down, drank my juice, ate my *samosa*, and read the wrapper: ". . . the shearing force at any [grease mark] on the Beam is represented by the Vertical Distance between that Line and the Line CD."

There were forty-seven tables in the dining room of Faletti's Hotel. I found them easy to count because I was the only diner present on the two evenings I ate there. The five waiters stood at various distances from me, and when I cleared my throat two would rush forward. Not wanting to disappoint them I asked them questions about Lahore, and in one of these conversations I learned that the Punjab Club was not far away. I thought it would be a good idea to have a postprandial snooker game, so on the second evening I was given directions by one of the waiters and set off for the club.

I lost my way almost immediately in a district adjacent to the hotel where there were no street lights. My footsteps roused the watchdogs and as I walked these barking hounds leaped at fences and hedges. I have not conquered a childhood fear of strange dogs, and, although the trees smelled sweet and the night was cool, I had no idea where I was going. It was ten minutes before a car approached. I flagged it down.

"You are coming from?"

"Faletti's Hotel."

"I mean your country."

"United States."

"You are most welcome," said the driver. "My name is Anwar. May I give you a lift?"

"I'm trying to find the Punjab Club."

"Get in please," he said, and when I did, he said, "How are you please?" This is precisely the way the posturing Ivan Turkin greets people in Chekhov's story "Ionych."

Mr. Anwar drove for another mile, telling me how fortunate it was that we should meet—there were a lot of thieves around at night, he said—and at the Punjab Club he gave his card and invited me to his daughter's wedding, which was one week away. I said I would be in India then.

"Well, India is another story altogether," he said, and drove off.

The Punjab Club, a bungalow behind a high hedge, was lighted and looked cozy, but it was completely deserted. I had imagined a crowded bar, a lot of cheerful drinkers, a snooker game in progress, a pair in the corner plotting adultery, waiters with trays of drinks, and chits flying back and forth. This could have been a clinic of some kind; there was not a soul in sight, but it had the atmosphere—and even the magazines—of a dentist's waiting room. I saw what I wanted a few doors along a corridor: large red letters on the window read WAIT FOR THE STROKE, and in the shadows were two tables, the balls in position, ready for play under a gleaming rack of cues.

"Yes?" It was an elderly Pakistani, and he had the forlorn abstraction of a man interrupted in his reading. He wore a black bow tie, and the pocket of his shirt sagged with pens. "What can I do for you?"

"I just happened to be passing," I said. "I thought I might stop in. Do you have reciprocal privileges with any clubs in London?"

"No, not that I know of."

"Perhaps the manager would know."

"I am the manager," he said. "We used to have an arrangement with a club in London—many years ago."

"What was the name of it?"

"I'm sorry, I've forgotten, but I know the club is no longer in existence. What was it you wanted?"

"A game of snooker."

"Who would you play with?" He smiled. "There is no one here."

He showed me around, but the lighted empty rooms depressed me. The place was abandoned, like Faletti's dining room with its forty-seven empty tables, like the district where there were only watchdogs. I said I had to go, and at the front door he said, "You might find a taxi over there, on the next road but one. Good night."

It was hopeless. I had walked about a hundred yards from the club and could not find the road, though I was going in the direction he had indicated. I could hear a dog growling behind a nearby hedge. Then I heard a car. It moved swiftly towards me and screeched to a halt. The driver got out and opened the back door for me. He said the manager had sent him to take me back to my hotel; he was afraid I'd get lost.

I set off in search of a drink as soon as I got back to the hotel. It was still early, about ten o'clock, but I had not gone fifty yards when a thin man in striped pajamas stepped from behind a tree. His eyes were prominent and lighted in the dusky triangle of his face.

"What are you looking for?"

"A drink."

"I get you a nice girl. Two hundred rupees. Good fucking." He said this with no more emotion than a man hawking razor blades.

"No thanks."

"Very young. You come with me. Good fucking."

"And good fucking to you," I said. "I'm looking for a drink."

He tagged along behind me, mumbling his refrain, and then at an intersection, by a park, he said, "Come with me—in here."

"In there?"

"Yes, she is waiting."

"In those trees?" It was black, unlighted and humming with crickets.

"It is a park."

"You mean I'm supposed to do it there, under a tree?"

"It is a *good* park, sahib!"

A little farther on I was accosted again, this time by a young man who was smoking nervously. He caught my eye. "Anything you want?"

"No."

"A girl?"

"No."

"Boy?"

"No, go away."

He hesitated, but kept after me. At last he said softly, "*Take me.*"

A twenty-minute walk did not take me any closer to a bar. I turned, and, giving the pimps a wide berth, went back to the hotel. Under a tree in front three old men were hunched around a pressure lamp, playing cards. One saw me pass and called out, "Wait, sahib!" He turned his cards face down and trotted over to me.

"No," I said before he opened his mouth.

"She's very nice," he said.

I kept walking.

"All right, only two hundred and fifty rupees."

"I know where I can get one for two hundred."

"But this is in your own room! I will bring her. She will stay until morning."

"Too much money. Sorry."

"Sahib! There are expenses! Ten rupees for your sweeper, ten also for your *chowkidar,* ten for your bearer, *baksheesh* here and there. If not, they will make trouble. Take her! She will be very nice. My girls are experienced in every way."

"Thin or fat?"

"As you like. I have one, neither thin nor fat, but like this." He sketched a torso in the air with his fingers, suggesting plumpness. "About twenty-two or twenty-three. Speaks very good English. You will like her so much. Sahib, she is a trained nurse!"

He was still calling out to me as I mounted the steps to the hotel's verandah. It turned out that the only bar in Lahore was the Polo Room in my hotel. I had an expensive beer and fell into conversation with a young Englishman. He had been in Lahore for two months. I asked him what he did for amusement. He said there wasn't very much to do, but he was planning to visit Peshawar. I told him Peshawar was quieter than Lahore. He said he was sorry to hear that because he found Lahore intolerable. He was bored, he said, but there was hope. "I've got an application pending at the club," he said. He was a tall plain fellow, who blew his nose at the end of every sentence. "If they let me in I think I'll be all right. I can go there in the evenings—it's a pretty lively place."

"What club are you talking about?"

"The Punjab Club," he said.

.   .   .

Amritsar, two taxi rides from Lahore (the connecting train hasn't run since 1947), is on the Indian side of the frontier. It is to the Sikh what Benares is to the Hindu, a religious capital, a holy city. The object of the Sikh's pilgrimage is the Golden Temple, a copper-gilt gazebo in the center of a tank. The tank's sanctity has not kept it from stagnation. You can smell it a mile away. It is the dearest wish of every Sikh to see this temple before he dies and to bring a souvenir back from Amritsar. One of the favorite souvenirs is a large multicolored poster of a headless man. Blood spurts from the stump of his neck; he wears the uniform of a warrior. In one hand he carries a sword, in the other he holds his dripping head. I asked nine Sikhs what this man's name was. None could tell me, but all knew his story. In one of the Punjab wars he was decapitated. But he was very determined. He picked up his head, and, holding it in his hand so that he could see what he was doing (the eyes of the severed head blaze with resolution), he continued to fight. He did this so that he could get back to Amritsar and have a proper cremation. This story exemplifies the Sikh virtues of piety, ferocity, and strength. But Sikhs are also very kind and friendly, and an enormous number are members of Lions Club International. This is partly a cultural misunderstanding, since all Sikhs bear the surname Singh, which means lion; they feel obliged to join.

Special underpants are required by the Sikh religion, along with uncut hair, a silver bangle, a wooden comb, and an iron dagger. And as shoes are prohibited at the Golden Temple, I hopped down the hot marble causeway, doing a kind of fire-walker's tango, watching these leonine figures stripped to their holy drawers bathing themselves in the tank and gulping the green water, swallowing grace and dysentery in the same mouthful. The Sikhs are great soldiers and throughout the temple enclosure there are marble tablets stating the fact that the Poona Horse Regiment and the Bengal Sappers contributed so many thousand rupees. For the rest of the Indians, Gujaratis in particular, Sikhs are yokels, and jokes are told to illustrate the simplicity of the Sikh mind. There is the one about the Sikh who, on emigrating to Canada, is told that he must prove himself a true Canadian by going into the forest and wrestling a bear and raping a squaw. He sets out and returns a month later, with his turban in tatters and his face covered with scratches, saying, "Now I must wrestle the squaw." Another concerns a Sikh who misses his bus. He chases the bus, trying to board, and soon realizes he has run all the way home. "I've just chased my bus and saved fifty paisas," he tells his wife, who replies, "If you had chased a taxi you could have saved a rupee."

I had a meal at a Sikh restaurant after wandering around the city and then went to the railway station to buy my ticket on the Frontier Mail to Delhi. The man at Reservations put me on the waiting list and told me there was "a ninety-eight percent chance" that I would get a berth, but that I would have to wait until half-past four for a confirmation. Indian railway stations are wonderful places for killing time in, and they are like scale models of Indian society, with its divisions of caste, class, and sex: SECOND-CLASS LADIES' WAITING ROOM, BEAR-ERS' ENTRANCE, THIRD-CLASS EXIT, FIRST-CLASS TOI-LET, VEGETARIAN RESTAURANT, NON-VEGETARIAN RESTAURANT, RETIRING ROOMS, CLOAKROOM, and the whole range of occupations on office signboards, from the tiny one saying SWEEPER, to the neatest of all, STATIONMASTER.

A steam locomotive was belching smoke at one of the platforms. I crossed over and as I snapped a picture a Sikh appeared on the footplate and asked me to send him a print. I said I would. He asked me where I was going, and when I told him I was taking the Frontier Mail he said, "You have so many hours to wait. Come with me. Get in this bogie"— he pointed to the first car—"and at the first station you can come in here and ride with me."

"I'm afraid I'll miss my train."

"You will not," he said. "Without fail." He said this precisely, as if remembering an English lesson.

"I don't have a ticket."

"No one is having a ticket. They are all cheating!"

So I climbed aboard and at the first station joined him in the cab. The train was going to Atari, on the Pakistan border, sixteen miles away. I had always wanted to ride in the engine of a steam locomotive, but this trip was badly timed. We left just at sunset and as I was wearing my prescription sunglasses—my other pair was in my suitcase in the station cloakroom—I could not see a thing. I held on, blind as a bat, sweating in the heat from the firebox. The Sikh shouted explanations of what he was doing, pulling levers, bringing up the pressure, spinning knobs, and dodging the coal shoveler. The noise and the heat prevented me from taking any pleasure in this two-hour jaunt, and I suppose I must have looked dispirited because the Sikh was anxious to amuse me by blowing the whistle. Every time he did it the train seemed to slow down.

My face and arms were flecked with soot from the ride to Atari. On the Frontier Mail this was no problem, and I had the enjoyable experience that humid evening of taking a cold shower, squatting on my heels under the burbling pipe, as the train tore through the Punjab to Delhi. I returned to my compartment to find a young man sitting on my berth. He greeted me in an accent I could not quite place, partly because he lisped and also because his appearance was somewhat bizarre. His hair, parted in the middle, reached below his shoulders; his thin arms were sheathed in tight sleeves and he wore three rings with large orange stones on each hand, bracelets of various kinds, and a necklace of white shells. His face frightened me: it was that corpselike face of lunacy or a fatal illness, with sunken eyes and cheeks, deeply lined, bloodless, narrow, and white. He had a cowering stare, and as he watched me—I was still dripping from my shower—he played with a small leather purse. He said his name was Hermann; he was going to Delhi. He had bribed the conductor so that he could travel with a European. He didn't want to be in a compartment with an Indian—there might be trouble. He hoped I understood.

"Of course," I said. "But do you feel all right?"

"I have been sick—four days in Amritsar I have been in the hospital, and in Quetta also. I was so nervous. The doctors take tests and they give me this medicine, but it does no good. I don't sleep, I don't eat—just maybe glass of milk and piece of bread. I fly to Amritsar from Lahore. I was so sick in Lahore—three days in hospital and in Quetta two days. I cross Baluchistan. Yazd, you know Yazd? It is a terrible place. Two nights I am there and I am on the bus two days from Teheran. I cannot sleep. Every five hours the bus stop and I take some tea and a little melon. I am sick. The people say, 'Why you don't talk—are you angry?' But I say, 'No, not angry, but sick—' "

This was the way he spoke, in long lisped passages, interrupting himself, repeating that he was sick in a voice that was monotonously apologetic. He was German and had been a sailor, a deck hand on a German ship, then a steward on a Finnish one. He had sailed for seven years and had been to the States—"Yes, to every country," he said, "but only for a few hours." He loved ships, but he couldn't sail anymore. I asked why. "Hepatitis," he said, giving it a German pronunciation. He caught it in Indonesia and was in the hospital for weeks. He had never managed to shake it off: he still needed tests. He'd had one in Amritsar. "People say to me, 'Your face is sick.' I know my face is sick, but I cannot eat."

His face was ghastly, and he was trembling. "Are you taking any medicine?"

"No." He shook his head. "I take this." He opened the leather purse he had been smoothing with his scrawny fingers and took out a cellophane envelope. He peeled the cellophane away and showed me a wad of brown sticky stuff, like a flattened plug of English toffee.

"What is it?"

"Opium," he said. "I take it in little balls."

His lisp made "balls" moistly vicious.

"I am a yunk." He broke off a piece of opium and rolled it between his fingers, slowly making it a pellet.

"A junkie?"

"Yes, I take needle. See my arms."

He locked the compartment door and pulled the curtain across the window. He rolled up his left sleeve. His arm appalled me: each vein was clearly defined by dark bruised scars of needle marks, thick welts that made the veins into black cords. He touched his arm shyly, as if it didn't belong to him and said, "I cannot get heroin. In Lahore I am not feeling so well. I stay in hospital but still I am weak and nervous. The people are making noise and it is so hot. I don't know what I can do. So I escape and I walk down the street. A Pakistani says to me he has some morphine. I go with him and he shows me. It is good—German morphine. He asks me for one hundred and fifty rupees. I give him and take an injection. That is how I get to Amritsar. But in Amritsar I get very sick and I cannot get any more of morphine. So I take this—" He patted his right pocket and took out a cake of hashish, roughly the size of the opium blob, but dry and cracked. "Or I smoke this—" He withdrew a little sack of marijuana.

I told him that with his budget of drugs he was lucky to have got into India. At the border post I had seen an Indian customs official ask a boy to drop his jeans.

"Yes," said Hermann. "I am so nervous! The man asks me do I have pot and I say no. Do I smoke it? I say, yes, sometimes, but he doesn't look at my luggages. If I am nervous I can hide it in secret places."

"Then I suppose you don't have anything to worry about."

"No, I am hot and nervous always."

"But you can hide your drugs."

"I can even throw them away and buy more," he said. "But my arms! If they see my arms they know. I have to hide my arms always." He pushed his sleeves up and looked again at the long dark scars.

He told me how it was that he had come to India. In Hanover, he decided to cure himself of his heroin habit. He registered as an addict and entered a rehabilitation center—he called it "The Release"—where he was given 700 Deutsche marks a month and a daily glass of methadone. In return for this he helped clean the center. He never went out; he was afraid that if he did he would meet someone who'd sell him heroin. But an odd thing happened: by staying in he rarely spent his monthly allowance, and he found that at the end of a year he had saved quite a lot of money—enough to live on in India for six months or more.

So he picked up and left, just like that, on a charter flight to Teheran, where his withdrawal symptoms began.

He had carried his dereliction to a derelict land. He was doomed, he stank of death, and his condition was not so different from that of the unfortunates who appeared at the railway stations we passed, gathering for the light and water. There are foreigners who, knowing they are wrecked, go to India to be anonymous in her decrepitude, to age and sicken in the *bustees* [slums] of the East. They are people, V.S. Naipaul wrote recently, "who wish themselves on societies more fragile than their own . . . who in the end do no more than celebrate their own security."

"I take this now." He popped the pellet of opium into his mouth and closed his eyes. "Then I take some water." He drank a glass of water. He had already drunk two, and I realized that the Indian water would kill him if the drugs didn't. "Now I sleep. If I don't sleep I take another opium."

Twice during the night a match flared in the upper berth, lighting the fan on the ceiling. I heard the crackle of cellophane, the snap of the gummy opium in his fingers, and Hermann gulping water.

The signs in Amritsar Station (THIRD-CLASS EXIT, SECOND-CLASS LADIES' WAITING ROOM, FIRST-CLASS TOILET, SWEEPERS ONLY) had given me a formal idea of Indian society. The less formal reality I saw at seven in the morning in the Northern Railways Terminal in Old Delhi. To understand the real India, the Indians say, you must go to the villages. But that is not strictly true, because the Indians have carried their villages to the railway stations. In the daytime it is not apparent—you might mistake any of these people for beggars, ticketless travelers (sign: TICKETLESS TRAVEL IS A SOCIAL EVIL), or unlicensed hawkers. At night and in the early morning the station village is complete, a community so preoccupied that the thousands of passengers arriving and departing leave it undisturbed: they detour around it. The railway dwellers possess the station, but only the new arrival notices this. He feels something is wrong because he has not learned the Indian habit of ignoring the obvious, making a detour to preserve his calm. The newcomer cannot believe he has been plunged into such intimacy so soon. In another country this would all be hidden from him, and not even a trip to a village would reveal with this clarity the pattern of life. The village in rural India tells the visitor very little except that he is required to keep his distance and limit his experience of the place to tea or a meal in a stuffy parlor. The life of the village, its interior, is denied to him.

But the station village is all interior, and the shock of this exposure made me hurry away. I didn't feel I had any right to watch people bathing under a low faucet—naked among the incoming tide of office workers; men sleeping late on their *charpoys* [bedsteads] or tucking up their turbans; women with nose rings and cracked yellow feet cooking stews of begged vegetables over smoky fires, suckling infants, folding bedrolls; children pissing on their toes; little girls, in oversized frocks falling from their shoulders, fetching water in tin cans from the third-class toilet; and, near a newspaper vendor, a man lying on his back, holding a baby up to admire and tickling it. Hard work, poor pleasures, and the scrimmage of appetite. This village has no walls. I distracted myself with the signs, GWALIOR SUITINGS, RASHMI SUPERB COATINGS, and the film poster of plump faces that was never out of view, BOBBY ("A Story of Modern Love"). I was moving so quickly I lost Hermann. He had drugged himself for the arrival: crowds made him nervous. He floated down the platform and then sank from view.

I wondered whether I would find any of this Indian candor familiar enough to ignore. I was told that I should not draw any conclusions from Delhi: Delhi wasn't India—not the real India. Well, I said, I had no intention of staying in Delhi. I wanted to go to Simla, Nagpur, Ceylon—to wherever there was a train.

"There is no train to Ceylon."

"There's one on the map." I unrolled my map and traced the black line from Madras to Colombo.

"*Acha*," said the man. He wore a colorful hand-loomed shirt and he waggled his head from side to side, the Indian gesture—like a man trying to shake water out of his ears—that means he is listening with approval. But the man, of course, was an American. Americans in India practice these affectations to endear themselves to Indians, who seem so embarrassed by these easily parodied mannerisms that (at the American embassy at least) the liaison men say "We're locking you into that program," while the American looking on says "*Acha*" and giggles mirthlessly.

I was being locked into a program: lectures in Jaipur, Bombay, Calcutta, Colombo. Wherever, I said, there was a train.

"There is no train to Colombo."

"We'll see," I said, and then listened to one of those strange conversations I later found so common as to be the mainstay of American small talk in India: The American on His Bowels. After the usual greetings and pauses these people would report on the vagaries of their digestive tracts. Their passion was graceless and they were as hard to silence as whoopee cushions.

"I had a bad night," one embassy man said. "The German ambassador gave a party. Delicious meal—it always is. All kinds of wine, umpteen courses, the works. But, God, I was up at five this morning, sick as a dog. Tummy upset."

"It's a funny thing," said another man. "You have a good meal at some dirty little place and you know you're going to pay for it. I just came back from Madras. I was fine—and I had some pretty risky meals. Then I go to some diplomatic thing and I'm doubled up for days. So there's no telling where you'll get it."

"Tell Paul about Harris."

"Harris! Listen," said the man, "there was a fella here. Harris. Press Section. Went to the doctor. Guess why? He was constipated. *Constipated!* In *India!* It got around the embassy. People used to see him and laugh like hell."

"I've been fine lately," said a junior officer, holding his end up, as it were. "Knock on wood. I've had some severe—I mean, really bad times. But I figured it out. What I usually do is have yogurt. I drink tons of the stuff. I figure the bacteria in yogurt keeps down the bacteria in lousy food. Kind of an equalizing thing."

There was another man. He looked pale, but he said he was bearing up. Kind of a bowel thing. Up all night. Cramps. Delhi belly. Food goes right through you. He said, "I had it in spades. Bacillary. Ever have bacillary? No? It knocked me flat. For six days I couldn't do a thing. Running back and forth, practically living in the john."

Each time the subject came up, I wanted to take the speaker by his hand-loomed shirt, and, shaking him, say, "Now listen to me! There is absolutely nothing wrong with your bowels!"

ACKNOWLEDGMENTS

James Boswell: "The Journal of a Tour of Corsica" from *Boswell on the Grand Tour: Italy, Corsica, and France*, edited by F. A. Pottle and Frank Brady. Reprinted by permission of McGraw-Hill, Inc.

Paul Bowles: "A Man Must Not Be Very Moslem" © 1957, 1963 by Paul Bowles. From *Their Heads Are Green and Their Hands Are Blue* by Paul Bowles, published by the Ecco Press in 1984. Reprinted by permission.

Robert Byron: From *First Russia, Then Tibet*. Reprinted by permission of A. D. Peters & Co. Ltd. From *The Road to Oxiana*. Copyright © 1966 by the Estate of Robert Byron. Reprinted by permission of Literistic, Ltd.

Truman Capote: "To Europe" and "Ischia" from *The Dogs Bark: Public People and Private Places*. Reprinted by permission of Random House, Inc.

Cyril Connolly: Letters to Noel Blakiston, from *A Romantic Friendship: The Letters of Cyril Connolly to Noel Blakiston*. Reprinted by permission of Constable Publishers. "The Unquiet Grave" and "Revisiting Greece" from *Selected Essays*. Reprinted by permission of Persea Books, Inc., 225 Lafayette Street, New York, N.Y., 10012, and Deborah Rogers Ltd.

Bernal Diaz del Castillo: "The True History of the Conquest of New Spain" from *The Discovery and Conquest of Mexico*, translated by A. P. Maudslay. Reprinted by permission of Routledge & Kegan Paul.

Lawrence Durrell: From *Sicilian Carousel*. Reprinted by permission of Curtis Brown Ltd.

Patrick Leigh Fermor: From *A Time of Gifts*. Reprinted by permission of John Murray (Publishers).

William Golding: "Body and Soul" from *Hot Gates and Other Occasional Pieces*. Reprinted by permission of Harcourt Brace Jovanovich, Inc. and Faber & Faber Ltd.

George Gordon, Lord Byron: Letters from *The Selected Letters and Journal*, edited by Leslie Marchand. Reprinted by permission of Harvard University Press and John Murray (Publishers) Ltd.

Ernest Hemingway: From *A Farewell to Arms*. Reprinted by permission of The Scribner Book Companies, Inc.

Herodotus: Excerpted from *History of the Persian Wars*, translated by George Rawlinson, edited by Francis R.B. Godolphin. Courtesy of Random House, Inc.

Christopher Isherwood: "Los Angeles" and "Coming to London" from *Exhumations*. Copyright © 1966 by Christopher Isherwood. Reprinted by permission of Candida Donadio & Associates, Inc.

Samuel Johnson: From *A Journey to the Western Islands of Scotland*, edited by Mary Lascelles. Reprinted by permission of Yale University Press. Letter to John Perkins from *The Letters of Samuel Johnson*, edited by R. W. Chapman. Reprinted by permission of Oxford University Press.

Jack Kerouac: From *On the Road*. Reprinted by permission of Viking Penguin, Inc.

D. H. Lawrence: From *Sea and Sardinia*. Reprinted by permission of Penguin Books Ltd.

Claude Lévi-Strauss: excerpted from *Tristes Tropiques*. Translated from the French *Tristes Tropiques*. Copyright © 1955 by Librairie Plon; English translation copyright © 1973 Jonathan Cape Ltd. Reprinted with the permission of Atheneum Publishers, Inc.

Sir John Mandeville: From *The Travels of Sir John Mandeville*, translated by C. W. R. D. Moseley (Penguin Classics, 1983), copyright © C. W. R. D. Moseley, 1983.

Jan Morris: "Kashmir" from *Places*. Reprinted by permission of A. P. Watt Ltd. "A European Journey" from *Journeys*. Reprinted by permission of Oxford University Press and A. P. Watt Ltd.

V. S. Naipaul: "Traveller's Prelude: A Little Paperwork" from *An Area of Darkness*. Reprinted by permission of Aitken & Stone Ltd.

Eric Newby: "Pera Palace," "The Dying Nomad," and "Airing in a Closet Carriage," from *A Short Walk in the Hindu Kush*. Reprinted by permission of Viking Penguin Inc. and Curtis Brown Ltd.

Pausanius: From *Guide to Greece*, translated by Peter Levi (Penguin Classics, 1983), copyright © Peter Levi, 1971. Reprinted by permission of Penguin Books Ltd.

Marco Polo: From *The Travels of Marco Polo, The Venetian*, edited by Manuel Komroff. Reprinted by permission of Liveright Publishing Company.

John Crowe Ransom: "Philomela" from *Selected Poems*. Reprinted by permission of Alfred A. Knopf, Inc.

Tobias Smollett: From *Travels through France and Italy*, edited by Frank Felsenstein. Reprinted by permission of Oxford University Press.

Freya Stark: From "The Valley of the Assassins" from *The Journey's Echo: Selections from Freya Stark*. Reprinted by permission of John Murray (Publishers) Ltd.

Paul Theroux: From *The Great Railway Bazaar*. Reprinted by permission of Houghton-Mifflin Company.

Pedro Vas de Caminha: Letter to Manuel I, King of Portugal from *Portuguese Voyages*, translated by C. D. Ley (Everyman's Library series). Reprinted by permission of J M Dent & Sons Ltd.

Evelyn Waugh: From *When the Going Was Good*. Copyright 1934, 1946, © 1962 by Evelyn Waugh. Reprinted by permission of Little, Brown and Company, and Harold Matson Company.

William Carlos Williams: *A Voyage to Pagany*. Copyright © 1970 by New Directions Publishing Corporation. Reprinted by permission of New Directions Publishing Corporation.

INDEX